The Free
University
of Berlin

The Free University of Berlin

A POLITICAL HISTORY

James F. Tent

INDIANA UNIVERSITY PRESS

Bloomington and Indianapolis

Manufactured in the United States of America

Library of Congress Cataloging-in-Publication Data

Tent, James F.
    The Free University of Berlin.

    Bibliography: p.
    Includes index.
    1. Freie Universität Berlin—History. I. Title.
LF2405.T46   1988   378.431'55   87-46407
ISBN 0-253-32666-4
1 2 3 4 5 92 91 90 89 88

To Margaret, John, and Virginia

CONTENTS

Preface

When first approached by representatives of the Free University of Berlin to write a history of that major institution, I asked somewhat incredulously: "Why me? Why an American?" However, they had anticipated that question. In essence, the reply was that they dared not choose one of their own number because, although Germany in general and Berlin specifically are not lacking in able historians, they might have difficulty maintaining the objectivity necessary to examine impartially the development of the Free University during its first forty turbulent years. An outsider was needed, and, that being the case, the outsider might as well be an American, since the Americans had had a connection with the university since its founding in 1948. In an earlier study I had already given a brief account of the university's difficult birthing in the midst of the Blockade and Airlift and was presumably already oriented on the subject. Rationalizing to myself, I reasoned that in the land of the blind the one-eyed might be king. Therefore, for better or for worse I put aside my inner doubts and accepted an assignment which I am sure other German historians might have done better—or at least differently.

The Free University has had a fascinating and eventful development. Writing the history of such an institution has proved to be most challenging. Certain problems emerged. First, it was impossible to undertake the research and the writing of this history in just two years and at the same time do proper justice to so complex an institution. Second, faced with the fact that this study had to be confined to one volume, I soon realized that inevitably this would not be the definitive historical treatment of the Free University. I had to make choices for the theme. Given the remarkable political developments at the university and their appeal to the general reader, I chose early in the project to confine this study to the political evolution of the Free University. This is, in consequence, unabashedly a political history. Making this decision meant inevitably that I sacrificed another vital aspect of the university's history: its scholarly and scientific achievements. They are considerable and are worthy of several volumes alone. Therefore, I hope the reader will understand that for practical reasons of space and time I chose to concentrate on the political development of this uniquely political institution of higher learning. Even with that severe limitation, it became apparent that I could not cover all periods of the university's development with equal emphasis. The Free University had experienced a remarkable founding in the late 1940s as the Cold War emerged. It also experienced unique stresses a generation later when the student dissident movement, choosing the Free University as its point of focus, gathered momentum. Therefore, my study concentrated on those two crucial eras in the university's history at the expense of quieter but nevertheless crucial periods such as the two consolidation phases of the 1950s and now the 1980s.

Since a study of so young an institution places it in the realm of contemporary history, I also decided that the perspectives and experiences of those who created and shaped the Free University were an invaluable resource. Therefore, in addition to the usual archival and secondary written resources I applied liberally the results of interviews with as many members of the university community as the time and resources of this project would permit. Although a time-consuming process, the collection of these oral-history sources brought me into close contact with a large number of individuals connected with the Free University and allowed me one generation after the fact to understand better what the mood, the hopes, and the aspirations were of those who founded the university and who were responsible for its subsequent development. This history benefited in many ways from their patience and willingness to impart their knowledge to an outsider. Where possible, I have also tried to put the Free University into its proper setting in a city which has held a unique political and diplomatic position in the world since the end of World War II.

Although written with support from the Free University and on the occasion of its fortieth anniversary, this history is completely my own work. I was free to choose the topics, sources, and emphases, and no censorship, direct or indirect, occurred. That was, in fact, a sacred rule of the project from the start, and it was honored at all times. Given the vast historical resources at my disposal, I had to establish priorities for document collections, and I opted to employ as many resources as I could which a German scholar, for various technical and practical reasons, might find more difficult to obtain. I expect that this study will encourage other historians to produce further research into the period I have investigated and into the activities of the Free University for the same period. Naturally, their studies will employ resources which they can use with greater skill and assurance than I can hope to emulate, so that our works should have a complementary value.

This study benefited from a number of valuable collections which require brief explanation. First, the U.S. National Archives offered resources from several government agencies that yielded priceless information on the early years of the Free University and on the motives of those who founded it and of those who supported them in that effort. These collections include the records of the former Office of Military Government (U.S.) for Germany which cover the occupation period from 1945 to 1949. The Berlin Document Center provided unique information on the ever touchy subject of denazification. The Public Record Office in Kew, London, provided rich documentation on the more skeptical British perspective with respect to Berlin and the founding of the Free University. The files of the U.S. High Commission and the papers of its first high commissioner, John J. McCloy, presented useful information on the Free University from 1949 until the mid-1950s. A long-time supporter of the university, the Ford Foundation, produced excellent materials from 1950 until the 1970s. Finally, the U.S. Mission in West Berlin, and especially the U.S. Information Agency, provided invaluable documents for the 1960s and 1970s. I made liberal use of these materials in hopes that they would provide a worthwhile starting point for future investigations on this subject.

From the German side, this work benefited from the Hochschularchiv, the University Archives of the Free University. The Bundesarchiv in Koblenz produced useful collections of private papers, as did the Landesarchiv in Berlin. Newspaper collections from West Berlin's daily newspaper, the *Tagesspiegel*, were indispensable. Private citizens also donated their papers or copies of them to the cause. Finally, the interviews with eyewitnesses presented a unique source which complemented the collections from the above-mentioned agencies, institutions, and individuals.

Before thanking those who helped in the completion of this project, I wish to stress that I bear full responsibility for what appears. Any errors or omissions are my own.

I am grateful to Professor Dieter Heckelmann, President of the Free University, and Dr. Horst Hartwich, Director of International Affairs at the university, for proposing this project and for giving unstinting support through all phases of its completion. Mr. Peter Th. Walther proved to be a pillar of support, constantly providing me with the perspective and experience of a Berliner. The Free University's archivist, Dr. Armin Spiller, supplied documents and resources at any and all times. The project could not have been completed without their help.

For the use of their private papers and research materials, I wish to thank Robin Hartshorne, Harold Hurwitz, Günther Neuhaus, Gerhard Petermann, David Phillips, Claus Reuber, Horst Rögner-Francke, Ullrich Schneider, Joachim Schwarz, Otto von Simson, Richard W. Sterling, and Wolfgang Wippermann. Those who gave their time for interviews also deserve my heartfelt thanks: Hans Ulrich Bach, Ursula Besser, Helmut Coper, Wolfgang Dumke, Eva Furth née Heilmann, Ewald Harndt, Horst Hartwich, Jurgen Herbst, Otto Hess, Christian and Hannelore Horn, Frank Howley, Howard W. Johnston, Traugott Klose, Rolf Kreibich, Ekkehart Krippendorff, Stanislaw Kubicki, Eberhard Lämmert, Wolfgang Lefèvre, Hans-Joachim Lieber, Gerd Löffler, Gerhard Löwenthal, Richard Löwenthal, Peter Lorenz, Günter Neuhaus, Knut Nevermann, Hermann and Irene Oberländer, Gerhard Petermann, Claus Reuber, Horst Rögner-Francke, Gerda Rösch, Alexander and Gesine Schwan, Joachim Schwarz, Karl Hubert Schwennicke, Ingeborg Sengpiel, Otto von Simson, Werner Skuhr, Dietrich Spangenberg, Werner Stein, Hans N. Tuch, Ingrid Vietig, Paul Wandel, Herman B Wells, Wilhelm Wengler, and Uwe Wesel.

I wish to offer special thanks to Edward Harper and Thomas Homan of the USIA for breaking much bureaucratic red tape in giving access to documents. The same is true for Daniel Simon and his staff at the Berlin Document Center. William Lewis, Sally Marx, Amy Schmidt, and Robert Wolfe of the U.S. National Archives greatly aided me in finding sources. The Ford Foundation provided valuable sources that spanned an entire generation. Dr. Reichart and Dr. Jürgen Wetzel of the Landesarchiv offered sound advice as well as documents. Siegward Lönnendonker opened up his archives on the student movement at the Free University's Zentralinstitut for Social Science Research. Paul Wandel and Rainer Hagen of the GDR's League of People's Friendship provided sources, helpful advice, and contacts from that other Berlin. A number of individuals generously gave of their time and read portions of the manuscript for me: Arnulf Baring, Helmut Coper, Wolfram Fischer, Horst Hartwich, Gerd Heinrich, Georg Kotowski, Wolfgang Mackiewicz, Ernst Nolte, Alexander Schwan , and Richard Sterling. Andreas Timmermann, and his Research Support Group, including Rainer David, Rüdiger Fleisch, and Sylvia Runge, helped greatly with computer technology. Chancellor Detlef Borrmann provided the indispensable computer.

I thank the following contributors for photographs: Aussenamt der Freien Universität; Bildstelle Preussischer Kulturbesitz; Colloquium Redaktion Bildarchiv; Hochschularchiv der Freien Universität; Landesbildstelle Berlin; Gerhard Löwenthal; President of the Free University; Joachim Schwarz; the United States Army; the United States National Archives; and Paul Wandel.

I wish to thank the Volkswagen Foundation, including Dr. Wolfgang Wittwer, for generous support on previous research projects which made this one possible. My thanks also to the University of Alabama at Birmingham for providing support in the publication of this history.

I offer my gratitude to all of those individuals mentioned above, and I offer apologies to any who helped me but whose names I may have omitted.

Berlin and Birmingham, December 1987

Abbreviations

ACA	Allied Control Authority
ADS	*Aktionsbündnis Demokraten und Sozialisten* (Action Coalition of Democrats and Socialists)
AEC	European Advisory Commission
AH	*Aktionsgruppe Hochschullehrer* (Action Group of University Instructors)
AKEC	Allied Kommandatura Education Committee
AL	Alternative List (sister party to the West German Greens)
APO	*Ausserparlamentarische Opposition* (Extraparliamentary Opposition)
AStA	*Allgemeiner Studenten-Ausschuss* (German student government)
BDC	Berlin Document Center
BDM	*Bund deutscher Mädel* (League of German Maidens)
BFW	*Bund Freiheit der Wissenschaft* (League for Scholarly Freedom)
BZ	*Berliner Zeitung* (West Berlin newspaper)
CDU	Christian Democratic Union
COA	Commission on Occupied Areas
CRALOG	Committee of Relief Agencies Licensed to Operate in Germany
CSU	Christian Social Union, sister party to the CDU in Bavaria
DDMG	Deputy Director of Military Government
DFG	*Deutsche Forschungsgemeinschaft* (German Research Council)
DHfP	*Deutsche Hochschule für Politik* (German Institute of Advanced Studies in Politics)
E&CR	Education and Cultural Relations Division
E&RA	Education and Religious Affairs Branch
EAC	European Advisory Commission
FAZ	*Frankfurter Allgemeine Zeitung*
FDGB	*Freier Deutscher Gewerkschaftsbund* (Free German Trade Union)
FDJ	*Freie Deutsche Jugend* (Free German Youth)
FDP	Free Democratic Party
FU	*Freie Universität* (Free University of Berlin)
GDR	German Democratic Republic
HfP	see DHfP
HJ	*Hitler Jugend* (Hitler Youth)
HICOG	Office of the High Commissioner (U.S.), Germany
ICD	Information Control Division
JCS	Joint Chiefs of Staff
JFKI	John F. Kennedy Institute (for North American Studies)
IPS	Institute for Political Science
K-Gruppen	*Kommunistische Gruppen* (Communist groups)

KHG	*Kommunistische Hochschulgruppe* (Communist University Group)
KMK	*Kultusminister Konferenz* (Cultural Ministers Conference of the Federal Republic)
KPD	*Kommunistische Partei Deutschlands* (Communist Party of Germany)
KSV	*Kommunistischer Studentenverband* (League of Communist Students)
KWG	*Kaiser-Wilhelm Gesellschaft* (Kaiser Wilhelm Society)
KWI	Kaiser Wilhelm Institute
LDP	Liberal Democratic Party
NKVD	Soviet Security Police
NOFU	*Notgemeinschaft für eine freie Universität* (Emergency Committee for a Free University)
NSDAP	National Socialist German Workers Party (Nazi)
OMGBD/OMGBS	Office of Military Government, Berlin District/Berlin Sector
OMGUS	Office of Military Government (U.S.) for Germany
OSI	Otto Suhr Institute
OSS	Office of Strategic Services
OT	*Organisation Todt*
PAO	Public Affairs Officer
PH	*Pädagogische Hochschule* (teachers college)
RIAS	Radio in the American Sector
SDS	*Sozialistische Deutsche Studentenbund* (League of Socialist German Students)
SED	Socialist Unity Party (Communist Party in the GDR)
SEW	West Berlin Communist Party
SFB	*Sender Freies Berlin* (Free Berlin Broadcasting)
SHAEF	Supreme Headquarters, Allied Expeditionary Force
SHB	*Sozialistischer Studentenbund Deutschlands* (League of Socialist Students in Germany)
SMA	Soviet Military Administration
SPD	*Sozialdemokratische Partei Deutschlands* (Social Democratic Party of Germany)
TU	Technical University
USIS	United States Information Service
VDS	*Verband deutscher Studentenschaften* (League of German Student Associations)
WRK	*Westdeutsche Rektorenkonferenz* (West German Rectors Conference)
WSC	Working Security Committee
ZI	*Zentralinstitut* (Central Institute)

The Free
University
of Berlin

Origins of the Free University, 1944 to 1948

The Free University of Berlin, now one of the largest universities in Europe, has a unique history. Its very title suggests something special (notwithstanding the assumption of most Americans and others that the word "free" in the title refers to a tuition-free institution for hard-strapped students). The title refers to the desire on the part of a dissident group of students in postwar Berlin, in cooperation with their allies among professors, politicians, publicists, Americans, and other well-wishers, to create a university free of the ideological commitments that were developing at the East Sector's Berlin University, sometimes called University Unter den Linden and finally officially changed to Humboldt University in 1949. The Free University of Berlin began its existence as a corporation under public law with a *Kuratorium* (board of regents) with wide discretion in dispersing the budget provided for it. Although a state institution, the Free University was specifically structured so as not to come directly under the control of a state ministry of education. Thus, it was "free" in the sense that state control was absent or at most indirect. In fact, there had been other free universities in Europe's past, in Amsterdam and Brussels for example, which had been erected with private support to avoid undesirable state interference. Although this effort to erect a "free" university could be easily interpreted as a reaction to ideological considerations—Marxism-Leninism as practiced in the Stalinist era—the institution that emerged was far more complex and ambitious than such an interpretation would permit. The founders aimed to create a university where free inquiry into all fields would thrive. However, the founders also viewed the Free University of Berlin as a reform institution that would abandon the ivory tower and would avoid the failings of the German universities that had silently acquiesced in the Nazis' seizure of power in 1933. Soviet and Socialist Unity Party authorities had undeniably tapped a wellspring of idealism among students in the early postwar years, and certain reform features in the Soviet Zone universities were carried over into the Free University. It would distance itself from the control of the state but not from its society. It would function in a highly democratic fashion with students sharing prominently in the exercise of its self-government. Its admissions procedures would strive harder to attract students from all segments of society.

The thesis that emerges from this investigation is that the conditions that led to the creation of this new institution resulted from decisions of the Allied occupation forces in Berlin, especially Soviet and American. Soviet occupation planning was significantly longer-term and more intricate than that of the Western Allies. American occupation policy in particular was characterized by little preparation followed by intense improvisation and spontaneous decision-making, factors that played a significant role in the emergence of the Free University in 1948. The Soviets imposed unilateral control over Berlin University in 1945, and working with their German Communist allies, who would soon form the Socialist Unity Party (SED), they fashioned a new form of university which would be democratic, as they understood the term. This policy encouraged the first postwar students to form a broad volunteer student association with which to combat fascistic and militaristic thinking. A significant number of the students admitted to Berlin University under Soviet-Zone guidelines were Victims of Fascism *(Opfer des Faschismus)*, and the student body as a whole was older and more mature than normal student populations. Under their influence the volunteer student organization soon assumed a character and independence of its own, and an organized dissident element sprung up which contested the ideological controls that they perceived to be encircling Berlin University. At this point the improvisational nature of American occupation policy became a factor in the development of a new university. In 1945 the Americans had had no higher educational policy to speak of, a situation that reflected uncertainty in American occupation policy toward Germany in general. By 1948, as a result of the pressures of the Cold War, they had adopted a constructionist policy and a vital clarification of American aims. The dissident students were perceptive enough to see that the creation of an alternative university in the western sectors of Berlin would require powerful allies among the citizens of Berlin and support from at least one of the Western Allies. The Americans became that ally, virtually by default, so that by the spring of 1948 the preconditions for the creation of a free university finally fell into place.

BERLIN: A BRIEF HISTORICAL SKETCH

The history of the Free University is intimately tied to the history of Berlin itself. To understand how this unique institution of higher learning came into existence in 1948 requires some understanding of the role of Berlin in the history of the German people and of its division after World War II.

Some historians and political scientists subscribe to the theory that Germany's failure to develop into a democracy on the order of France or Britain stemmed from its failure to urbanize rapidly enough. This was closely connected to the industrialization process and the expansion of an urban proletariat and an urban bourgeoisie. In Paris and London the "sans culottes" mob of the eighteenth century and the new urban classes of the nineteenth century helped force liberal or democratic reforms upon authoritarian regimes. It was Berlin's fate to miss that role in German history by the slimmest of margins. Founded in the thirteenth century during a mostly peaceful German colonization wave that was encouraged by skill-hungry Polish noblemen, Berlin originated as an amalgamation of two small villages. Although the setting, a bleak, featureless plain of sandy soil, noted for its numerous lakes, swamps, and birch forests, seemed unpropitious at first, this initial colonization effort set a precedent for Berlin. Through the centuries Berlin acted as a magnet for various religious or ethnic groups who found the city to be a haven against intolerance in other parts of Europe. For example, Jews escaping from religious tensions in eastern Europe added their skills to the growing population, as did French Protestants from the west. It transpired that the rulers of the surrounding area of Brandenburg, the Hohenzollerns, came to play a leading role in Central Europe following the Thirty Years' War when Frederick William, the Great Elector, raised Prussia to the status of a great power in the affairs of Europe. Even so, Berlin remained small by Western standards. By 1700 the city still had a population of only 20,000 inhabitants, a modest size compared to the half million Parisians or equally numerous Londoners of the same period. Nevertheless, Berlin loomed large compared to the villages and towns that dotted Central Europe. The city became a refuge for such disparate groups as French Huguenots (one of its fine city schools is still called the Französisches Gymnasium), Poles, and other Eastern Europeans at a time when the Prussian government sought skilled labor and productive citizens and was not unduly concerned about their ethnic or religious origins. On the eve of the French Revolution Protestants moved en masse from Salzburg to Berlin after a bigoted bishop ordered them out of Austria. To be sure, Austria's loss was Prussia's gain. Berlin was (and still is) more cosmopolitan than its rivals. To call it a melting pot might be to exaggerate the situation, but Berlin, more than any other German city, witnessed the melding of various cultures and ethnic groups. Periodically, depending upon local economic and political factors, streams of Silesians, Pomeranians, Mecklenburgers, and groups from farther away joined the other religious and ethnic groups in adding to Berlin's development.

In the nineteenth century, when Germany, led by Prussia and Saxony, entered the Industrial Revolution, Berlin proved the maxim that in the accompanying demographic revolution and urbanization process the big cities grew fastest. Partly as a result of state policy but even more because of private initiative, Berlin became a leading Prussian city in industrializing Central Europe. Thus, Berlin added economic growth to its already important role as the capital of a great power. The sociopolitical consequences followed apace. It was the Berliners who forced King Frederick William IV to wear the black, red, and gold Cockade of the 1848 Revolution and to mourn those city dwellers who had fallen in barricade fighting during the heady days of March of that year. The moment seemed to have arrived when Germans would unite peacefully under a democratic banner.

Alas, the new urban classes could not unify their aims, however, and the monarchies recovered their nerve. The Revolution of 1848, the "turning point in German history that failed to turn," produced instead a political reaction that stymied Germany's democratic forces for a generation or more. Nevertheless, Berlin expanded enormously under the ongoing industrialization process, one which had begun in the Prussian capital as early as 1830. By the eve of World War I the "Metropolis on the Spree," as it was now sometimes called, had reached a population of over four million, rivaling London and Paris at last. Presumably, the twentieth century would see Berlin take its place alongside the other great capitals of the West as a political, industrial, and cultural center of the first order. Berlin's development proved to be more complicated than that presumption allowed.

The young capital contained a young university—young by German standards. Opened in 1810 at a time when Berlin was under French military occupation, it was called the Friedrich Wilhelms University after a feckless Prussian monarch. Everyone knew that the guiding spirit was Wilhelm von Humboldt, one of those remarkable Prussian reformers who sought the rebirth of Prussia's institutions after a humiliating defeat by Napoleon and the French. As part of a general educational reform, the new university was supposed to further the self-reliance and the character of its citizens so that they could reach their full potential. Therefore the university was to go beyond mere training or technical education to instill universal knowledge and to encourage its students to think and to create. Universities were to serve *Wissenschaft* (scholarship) as well as to teach the fruits of that wisdom. It was a noble ideal, rarely attained, in part because of the uneasy relationship that evolved between the Prussian state and its universities. Prussia's liberal reform period, inspired by Napoleon's easy victory in 1806, came to a hasty end with his downfall in 1815. Nevertheless, Berlin University, under Humboldt's spiritual tutelage, rapidly became the model university of scholarship and learning in Germany. By the late nineteenth century a "call" to Berlin for a professor meant crowning success, the so-called *Endstation*. German higher education became respected around the world, and Berlin rode the crest of that esteem.[1] If Prussia-dominated Germany produced an effective "marriage" between university, state, and industry following unification in 1871, that model proved to be Berlin.

Even as the university grew in fame, Berlin became the incomparable leader in industrial growth. Already one of the pioneering industrial centers since 1830, the city expanded its lead in the last third of the nineteenth century. New concerns such as AEG, an electrical giant, and the famous Borsig locomotive works headquartered in Berlin. Siemens and Halske, an electro-technical concern, was such an awesome contributor that an entire city district took its name: Siemensstadt. By this time the capital of the Wilhelminian Empire, Berlin continued to expand its lead as an industrial giant. Future prospects seemed bright, until a failure in political leadership blighted German prospects in 1914.

Defeat in the First World War dashed German hopes of becoming a superpower. Even more important, disillusionment and impoverishment in 1918 set in motion a complex train of events that led to a seizure of power in Germany by dangerous right-extremists, only fifteen years after the 1918 Armistice. Berlin, which had experienced an attempted coup by the German Communists (Spartacists) in 1919, seemed destined for a moment to fulfill the capital city's role in spearheading a social revolution, but the radicals were defeated in pitched street battles by paramilitary forces, the much feared *Freikorps*. Fearful of further unrest, Germany's new leaders wrote a democratic constitution in small, safe Weimar instead. Following the disruptions of the immediate postwar period, Berlin seemed to overcome Germany's tribulations and quickly regained its national importance. The Metropolis on the Spree (and it may still regain that appellation one day) became for a time the rival of Paris as the cultural and intellectual capital of the West. To a large extent "Weimar culture" was centered in the national capital, and Berlin became a mecca for those advancing the frontiers in the arts, science, medicine, technology, culture, and academic research. Its famed Friedrich Wilhelms University continued to maintain the world reputation that it had gained in the nineteenth century, and with the return of prosperity in the mid-1920s Berlin as the capital of a new democracy seemed destined to remain an international, urbane center for generations to come. It was characteristic of the university's continuing high reputation that one young Harvard University scholar, Shepard Stone, ignored the advice of some of his seniors to go to Oxford for advanced studies in 1929. His mentor urged him to choose Berlin instead, and Stone, who later was to play a striking role in Berlin's higher education, never regretted that choice. For him the exciting cultural life of Weimar Berlin was as enticing as it was for the fictitious Sally Boles in Bob Fosse's evocative film rendition of *Cabaret* (based on Christopher Isherwood's writings for the same period). Perhaps even more famous than the university were the various scientific research institutes of the Kaiser Wilhelm Gesellschaft, a kind of national society to further science. Largely located in suburban Dahlem, these institutes attracted an astonishing number of famed researchers. Albert Einstein, Max Planck, Otto Hahn, Lise Meitner, Max von Laue, Otto Warburg, and Fritz Haber, to name only a few, made Dahlem a gathering place for Nobel Prize laureates. Seemingly, Weimar Berlin had something to offer everyone. However, because of unprecedented inflation, followed by the Great Depression and mounting political unrest, German democracy suffered an even more devastating defeat in 1933 than it had in 1848. The subsequent seizure of power by irrational elements brought on a second world war within one generation and led to Germany's irreversible decline in 1945. Of all the cities of Central Europe, Berlin felt the effects of this political maelstrom most keenly.

It was ironic that Berlin, a city noted for its large working-class population on the one hand and its sophisticated cultural elite on the other, became the capital of National Socialist Germany. The Nazis never felt fully at ease there. They praised Munich as the *Hauptstadt der Bewegung*, the Capital of the Movement, and Nuremberg as the most German of cities, and it was significant that their most ostentatious pageantry took place in Nuremberg and Munich rather than in the capital. Hitler, Goebbels, and other leaders knew that Berlin was not "their town." Wedding, Lichtenberg, Moabit, Neukölln, Treptow, and other traditional labor districts were old SPD (Social Democratic) and KPD (Communist) centers that endured the Nazis rather than embraced them. The well-to-do districts of Zehlendorf and Wilmersdorf, among others, contained a sophisticated citizenry, leavened with a rich mixture of Germany's leading artists, intellectuals, academics, and even, for their day, "Bohemians" seeking an alternate life-style. Wilmersdorf, especially, had a sizable Jewish population, adding to the cosmopolitan and liberal flavor of Germany's largest city. Even the conservative elements in these prosperous districts, nationalistic though most of them were, looked with suspicion upon the upstart, largely South-German Nazis. To be sure, there were numerous Nazi enthusiasts and "brown" districts, too, but Berlin was never fully a National Socialist city. Berliners had (and still have) the reputation of being fast-talking, quick-thinking, witty, and irreverent. The term *Berliner Schnauze* (Berlin "lip") says much. The Berliners were (and still are) Germany's equivalent to Britain's London Cockneys (with allowances for the more cerebral Berliners) or America's New Yorkers, not exactly the stuff of which regimented Brownshirts were readily made. Neutral observers in the wartime capital were startled to see the indifference with which the Berliners greeted Goebbels's hysterical claims of victory in the first war years.

Nevertheless, Berlin, although hardly representative of all of Germany, was indisputably the national capital, and the Nazis, claiming a national mandate, were firmly in power. To be sure, their policies eventually brought on a national disaster, and the capital suffered the full consequences of Hitler's irrationality and cruelty.

Not surprisingly, the Friedrich Wilhelms University succumbed to Nazi pressure like all other institutions. Nazi purges of Jews, socialists, and free-thinking individuals eliminated entire segments of its fine faculty and cowed the rest into silence. The twelve years of terror that followed eliminated what was left of the Humboldtian ideal. The institution that existed after 1933, although possessed of capable faculty in many instances, was hardly the superb center of learning that it once had been. This scarcely bothered the new leadership. They were concerned with other façades. Even before the Second World War began, the wrecker's ball had been clearing tracts of patrician housing near the Reichstag for some of Hitler and Speer's gargantuan architectural "improvements," aimed at turning Berlin into a kind of imperial city (those areas remain desolate, weed-strewn expanses to this very day). But such self-inflicted damage was a mere curtain raiser for the destruction to come. As the Second World War turned into a total conflict with each combatant's full arsenal being brought to bear, Berlin became the ultimate target of Allied air forces and then, in 1945, of the advancing Allied armies.

The British tried their luck first. Royal Air Force Marshall Sir Arthur Harris ordered his Bomber Command to attack Berlin with no less than nineteen heavy-bomber raids between August 1943 and March 1944. Harris seriously predicted that with American help his "Battle of Berlin" would force the termination of hostilities and end the war. "It will cost between us 400 to 500 aircraft," he stated to Churchill about the Anglo-American offensive. "It will cost Germany the war."[2] Berlin was a tempting target for the Allies. A third of Germany's electrical engineering capacity was situated there, primarily in Siemensstadt. Fully one-tenth of the nation's aircraft engines, machine tools, and precision instruments were Berlin-made. One of every four tanks came from Berlin's giant Alkett factory, as did half of the Wehrmacht's field artillery. The capital was also a vital water artery, connecting the Spree with other rivers, canals, and the sea. Not least, it provided Germany with its most important railway and communication links to the Russian Front.[3]

Despite the importance of the prize, Harris's RAF offensive failed. Berlin was too spread out, too heavily defended, and too stoutly built to suffer the firestorms that mortally wounded Hamburg and Dresden. To be sure, damage was severe, and British saturation bombing turned many of Berlin's fine architectural achievements into rubble in addition to killing thousands of its citizens. On the night of November 22/23, 1943, the Kaiser Wilhelm Memorial Church, today virtually a symbol of West Berlin, took on its now-familiar ruined appearance, an enduring reminder of the heavy cost of total war. Worse was to come. An American daylight offensive got under way in February 1944, and an around-the-clock pounding of Berlin began. Yet, somehow the city continued to function, albeit shakily, as Hitler's capital. This first "aerial" battle altered the city's appearance, but it did not win the war. Only later, in the effort to rebuild, did the total effect of the bomber offensive come to light. It had impoverished Berlin for decades to come. The failure to destroy Berlin from the air in 1943/44 removed any doubt that an invasion of the Continent was the key to winning the war. Allied armies from East and West would have to finish off the Nazis in the conventional way.

BERLIN'S POSTWAR FATE

What was to be done with Germany and its capital after the war? The Allies first addressed that question during a foreign ministers conference in Moscow in October 1943 and then at the first meeting of the Big Three—Roosevelt, Stalin, and Churchill—in Teheran the following month. The wartime leaders agreed to a temporary partitioning of Germany into three zones of occupation until a peace treaty could be agreed upon. As a result of the Teheran decision, a European Advisory Commission (EAC) materialized in London, with high-level representatives from Britain, the United States, and the Soviet Union. A leading member of Britain's Foreign Office, Sir William Strang, the U.S. ambassador to Great Britain, John Winant, and the Soviet ambassador in London, Feodor T. Gusev, conducted the wearisome negotiations for the occupation zones for Germany. They also decided the boundaries and occupation responsibilities of Berlin. The details of those negotiations are ably recorded elsewhere.[4] Suffice it to say here that shortcomings in American planning policy in the wartime Roosevelt administraton had a direct impact upon how the occupation boundaries, including those of Berlin, were decided. President Roosevelt stated openly that he was reluctant to engage in detailed planning for the occupation of an opponent until hostilities had ceased. The British and Russians had no such qualms, and they submitted detailed proposals to the EAC in London for the coming peace. Given his penchant for personal diplomacy, Roosevelt appears to have concluded that he would sit down at the end of the war with Stalin and Churchill and decide the Germans' fate despite any schemes evolved by the European Advisory Commission. That body was, after all, advisory, a fact FDR repeatedly pointed out. However, as the war drew to a close, so did the life of President Roosevelt, and the lack of a forceful American hand in planning the postwar world became painfully obvious. The "advice" of the EAC became the basis for the final settlement of occupation boundaries for the zones and for the special case of Berlin.[5]

    In general, the nation that submitted the first concrete proposal for the division of Germany and of Berlin at the EAC obtained a decided advantage. Although conversations about zonal divisions for Germany as a whole took place at least as early as the wartime summit conferences at Teheran and Cairo, it was a British proposal of June 12, 1944, at the EAC that was ultimately successful. The three zones of occupation that finally emerged were essentially what the British proposed at that early date. The specific proposals for Berlin centered on a Soviet initiative before the EAC on June 29, 1944. The Soviets were proposing that the twenty administrative districts of Greater Berlin, as formalized in a Prussian law of 1920, be divided into three occupation sectors. Furthermore, the Soviets claimed eight of the eastern districts, including the district called *Mitte*, the downtown central district. Despite considerable wrangling and the addition of French representatives in November 1944, the proposals of the British for the German zones and of the Soviets for the Berlin sectors were what finally emerged. The only change was that allowing the French at a later date to carve out a separate zone of occupation and a sector in Berlin from Anglo-American territories.

Several factors in the negotiations proved significant for future developments in Berlin. The inclusion of the Mitte district in the Soviet Sector meant that most German governmental agencies, the university's central administration building, and the bulk of its institutes, including the famed Charité medical center, would come under Soviet control. Of great significance later was the fact that the Americans took almost no initiative at the EAC meetings. Finally, concrete provisions for Western access to Berlin were not concluded in the EAC negotiations.

Ambassador John Winant had no independent authority to conclude negotiations; he depended for instructions upon a cumbersome Washington-based Working Security Committee (WSC) composed of State, War, and Navy Department representatives. Yet, this body had to act unanimously, and there was no unanimity of opinion among the agencies represented on it. The representatives from the War Department's Civil Affairs Division on the WSC were especially suspicious of the Advisory Commission's interference in the military conduct of the war, and they vetoed any initiatives or instructions that might be sent to Winant at the EAC. This intolerable situation continued to exist only because FDR himself was not enthusiastic about the EAC, having reluctantly consented to its founding as a gesture of cooperation with the British. He also conceded—reluctantly—that the Department of State would have to enter negotiations for postwar arrangements at some point. George Kennan was assigned to duty with the EAC for a short time, and he realized quickly that American participation in the EAC was not wholehearted. The President was not alone in his aversion to the EAC. Kennan noted an attitude among the State Department leadership that was "dominated primarily by a lively concern lest the new body should at some point and by some mischance actually do something. . . ."[6] Within the State Department, Robert Murphy remarked later that he had had a long conversation with Winant about Allied rights of access to Berlin, since it was deep in Soviet territory. Murphy had had direct experience with the Soviets in Italy and commented that "they were sharp bargainers who expected other people to be the same." Winant, according to Murphy, was incensed, and stated that an agreement had been reached solely because of his patient efforts to create a close personal relationship with Gusev.[7] Winant was taking a lead from President Roosevelt in expecting that personal diplomacy and charm would win Soviet cooperation after the war. Given FDR's indifference to the negotiations in London, it was ironic that it was precisely the EAC that proved to be the deliberative body from which concrete plans for Germany and Berlin emerged.

Analyses by historians of the protocols on Allied boundaries for Greater Berlin and for Allied control machinery demonstrate that the tough negotiating stance of the Soviets usually prevailed. The discussions were protracted, and although certain interim agreements on boundaries and control machinery were reached in the autumn of 1944, long delays and deadlocks prevented any final agreements until July 1945, when the Big Three met at Potsdam. Part of this tardiness can be ascribed to the inclusion of a French zone of occupation and a French sector in Berlin. Two major omissions occurred in the planning for Berlin. First, the legal position of Berlin within the zones of Germany was not fully resolved on the eve of the occupation. More fateful for the postwar period was the absence of clear-cut Western access routes to Berlin. Only on June 29, 1945, did Generals Zhukov, Clay, and Hill come to an oral agreement about air and surface routes for the Western Allies. The agreements were not followed by formal protocols; they were largely technical and military in nature. These were enlarged upon on November 30, 1945, when the Allied Control Council (ACC) formally concluded an agreement allowing three air corridors to Berlin from the west, from Hamburg, from Hannover, and from Frankfurt. It was these narrow threads to which a Western presence clung when the Blockade began three years later.

Much criticism has been aired about the Allied agreements on Germany and Berlin. Some of it is justified. Certainly the muddle in American postwar planning had unfortunate results for the American negotiators to the European Advisory Commission, at Yalta, and at Potsdam. However, it should not be forgotten that at the time of the negotiations, the Soviets appeared to have all the high cards. They were engaging Hitler's armies most directly and appeared to have an unconquerable lead in the rush toward German frontiers. The Soviets were viewed by their Western allies as a brave and indispensable cobelligerent with whom the Western partners could expect to hammer out any difficulties once the war was completed. And, in fact, despite various irritations, the Western Allies did gain access routes and share in the four-power occupation of Berlin for three years. The occupation zones, it should be remembered, were thought of as strictly provisional—a stopgap that would be succeeded by the terms of a final peace treaty. The difficulties that beset Berlin in 1948 were not the result of inherent weaknesses in the Berlin agreements. Rather, they resulted from dangerous new tensions between East and West that came to be called the Cold War. Only in that climate of mutual suspicion and fear did the shortcomings in the wartime EAC agreements become apparent. In fact, it was only at war's end, during wearisome negotiations with respect to the treatment of Vienna and the occupation zones in Austria, that attention refocused upon potential disagreements in Berlin. One of the key American negotiators, William Franklin, observed that the Soviets were always more flexible with respect to Austrian matters than they were toward German affairs. The contrast soon struck other observers as well.[8]

In May 1945, the fate of Berlin seemed settled by international agreement. The Allies would occupy Berlin jointly, and they would erect control machinery known as a *Kommandatura* to exercise four-power control over the Berliners. But first the city had finally to be won, and given the Nazis' fanatical determination to resist, that meant a gigantic battle. Hitler chose to make his last stand in Berlin. Goebbels's last propaganda blasts were directed at the defense of the Reich capital that it should remain "German." For the Soviets, the last weeks of the war seemed to be a contest to reach Berlin first. However, for SHAEF commander General Dwight D. Eisenhower, who has variously been described as a nonpolitical general or as politically naive, Berlin, by the end of March 1945, was no longer an important military objective. Rather, Eisenhower was concerned about coordinating a nonlethal meeting of the massed American and Soviet armies along the shortest direct route (the Erfurt-Leipzig-Dresden axis) with a secondary thrust from Regensburg to Linz to prevent rumored Nazi efforts at retreating into an "Alpine Redoubt." On March 25, 1945, he sent a message to that effect directly to Josef Stalin with the added information that Anglo-American armies were surrounding and destroying all German forces in the crucial Ruhr District. This decision of first-rate political as well as military importance was a reversal of Eisenhower's strategic thinking of September 1944, when he, Montgomery, Bradley, and other generals of the Western coalition saw German resistance as being on the verge of collapse and a lunge toward Berlin possible. SHAEF even had an airborne division ready for immediate dispatch to a Berlin airfield in the event that a sudden surrender by the Nazis made a Western military presence in the German capital imperative. Stalin knew about these quick-response reserves and, following receipt of Eisenhower's message, it was not long before his inherently suspicious mind concluded that he was the victim of a wily deception. He responded to Eisenhower's message by agreeing to the projected linkup but was noncommittal about his own plans. In fact, he recalled forthwith his top generals, Zhukov and Koniev, to Moscow for an emergency conference. Stalin demanded that they produce plans within 48 hours for the conquest of Berlin, claiming that "the little allies" (Britain and the United States) intended to get there first. In the West reactions to Eisenhower's message were ones of anger and disbelief. Churchill was thunderstruck; Montgomery, whose armies (including the U.S. Ninth Army) stood on the direct line of advance to Berlin, was bitterly disappointed.

Yet, the Supreme Commander would not budge. He was concerned about the (as it turned out, fictitious) Alpine Redoubt, which must count as Goebbels's final propaganda success. He knew that the linkup with Soviet troops beyond Leipzig (toward which German government ministries from Berlin were evacuating) was a logical goal and one which needed careful coordination to avoid casualties from what is today called "friendly fire." Finally, Eisenhower knew perfectly well that the zonal boundaries and those of Berlin had long since been drawn up. He operated on the assumption that they would be honored, and as a cautious general he was not inclined to expend the lives of his troops on an objective that would soon be turned over in large part to the Soviets. Besides, Stalin's massed armies in the East had been on the Oder River for weeks and were seemingly within easy striking distance of the capital.

Thus, in April 1945, as the Allied armies spread across Germany, the startling advance of the Anglo-American forces gave rise to false hopes in millions of hearts that the Western forces might actually take Berlin. In fact, advanced elements of the American forces reached the Elbe River near Magdeburg on April 11, but under orders they halted their offensive. Thus, the final battle for Berlin, when it came, was a German-Soviet contest.

The grim statistics for this last great battle fought on European soil were bad enough. Well over 100,000 Germans died in the final assault on the dying capital. Probably 100,000 Soviet soldiers died storming the city. Despite these gargantuan losses, the bloodletting could have been far worse, had not the general in charge of the eastern defenses, Gotthard Heinrici, deliberately placed his main line of defense on the Oder River rather than directly around the doomed city. Determined not to let Berlin become a Stalingrad, Heinrici held his hard crust defense so long that when it finally broke, few reserves or defenses remained to hinder the Soviet conquest of Berlin. Otherwise, the death toll might have been more staggering than it actually was. Even so, gigantic street battles raged for over a week in the city. The conditions of the final conflict in Berlin are familiar and need no retelling here. It took place because Hitler, buried in his bunker under many feet of concrete and earth, physically deteriorated and mentally unhinged, vowed to continue a fight which any sane observer above ground could see was hopeless. When the last organized Wehrmacht forces in Berlin surrendered on May 2, the role of Berlin in German history changed completely. The capital of the Great German Reich was now a broken, body-strewn hulk, facing an uncertain future under the joint military occupation of four unlikely allies.[9]

THE ESTABLISHMENT OF ALLIED CONTROL IN BERLIN

That the Soviets alone conquered Berlin and then retained exclusive control of it for two months goes far in explaining how postwar Berlin developed politically and economically up to the Blockade. It must be said from the outset that of the four occupying powers, the Soviets were easily the best-prepared victor with plans for occupied Germany. Having supported an appreciable German Communist refugee community since 1933, they placed great importance on planning for new political entities and societies in Eastern and now in Central Europe. Already on April 30, 1945, two Soviet aircraft set down on the outskirts of flaming Berlin with Walter Ulbricht and his staff. They were the advance party of the German Communist Party, the KPD, and they were intent on putting together a provisional government under the watchful eye of the Soviet Military Administration (SMA) in Karlshorst. With their Soviet allies, the KPD organized a Magistrat, or city council, with mayors for each district of the city, including the future British, French, and American sectors. They immediately initiated a drastic policy of denazification at all levels in the public and private sector. To be sure, rough justice was meted out in the wild days following the battle, and so statistics on the numbers of individuals purged under Soviet auspices will always be unclear. No one doubts that the measures were severe— and effective. National Socialism in Berlin died in the ashes of the stricken city.

Supported by their well-informed and energetic German Communist allies, the Soviets created anew the entire administrative machinery for Berlin and placed trusted antifascist and, where possible, politically sympathetic individuals in key administrative posts. Mayors, such as Berlin's first governing mayor, Arthur Werner, were usually not Communists, but their deputies, like Karl Maron, invariably were. Other key posts went to the party faithful. For example, at the local government level police chief appointees were Communists, as were interior ministers at the level of state government. It was characteristic of their high estimation of education that the KPD also placed reliable party members in charge of education departments and ministries. Within a short time they had created a *Volksbildungsamt*, or public education department, subordinate to the Magistrat and responsible, at first, for all educational institutions within Berlin. The leading official at the *Volksbildungsamt* was Otto Winzer, recently returned from exile in the

Soviet Union and destined to become a foreign minister in the future German Democratic Republic. His appointment was characteristic of the KPD's selection of personnel. Noncommunist antifascists helped to create a coalition in the new governments, but key slots, such as those mentioned above, went to members of the KPD.

Moreover, the Soviets ordered the creation of a number of central ministries to oversee all spheres of activity. One of them was the *Zentralverwaltung für Volksbildung* (Ministry of Education), led by an exiled German Communist, Paul Wandel, until recently a valuable assistant to Wilhelm Pieck in all educational and cultural affairs. Wandel was originally from Baden, and as a young man he joined the relatively small Communist Party in the early 1920s, traveling once to the Soviet Union in 1928. In the aftermath of the Nazi victory in 1933, he emigrated with hundreds of others to Moscow, where he ultimately became a secretary to Walter Ulbricht. Wandel performed various wartime duties, foremost of which was the leading of the German section of the Soviet-led Comintern (Communist International) School. There he helped in the training of Communist cadres for the coming peace. Absolutely faithful to the party cause, Wandel was widely regarded by the inner circle as a capable and energetic administrator and a logical promoter of a new Marxist-Leninist society in Germany. He had direct access to Pieck, Ulbricht, and to the responsible leadership in the Soviet Military Administration.[10]

The Soviets put their two months of undisputed control in Berlin to good use. Although the wrecked appearance of the city had scarcely changed when the Americans and British entered Berlin on July 4, 1945 (to be followed by the French on August 8), the control machinery for the city had changed drastically. It took the Americans and the other Western Allies some time to sort themselves out and to begin establishing their respective military government offices in Berlin. The four-power machinery in the form of an Allied Kommandatura, flanked by various subordinate, inter-allied committees, did not begin to function in Berlin until August. It was only then that the thoroughness of Soviet and German Communist reforms became readily apparent. Already on July 11, the Western Allies, in a gesture of goodwill to the Soviets, had initialled an agreement stating that all regulations hitherto adopted by the Soviets in Berlin would remain in force. That agreement, plus the acceptance of a unanimity rule for decisions of the Kommandatura, meant that the Soviets had obtained a veto power in the Allied control machinery in Berlin.[11]

The contrast between Soviet preparations in Berlin with American initiatives is striking. Unlike the Soviets with their proselytizing ideological zeal or the British and French with their colonial experience, the Americans were latecomers to the complex task of managing civil affairs abroad. Such experience as they gained during the post–Civil War reconstruction in the South, in the Philippines from 1898 to 1946, or in the Rhineland from 1919 to 1923 paled by comparison to the vast responsibilites that followed World War II. Already the American government at the highest levels had demonstrated deficiencies in planning for the occupation of Germany during the Roosevelt administration, and little had been accomplished since President Truman's elevation to the presidency on April 12, 1945, to correct the situation.

In fact, a lively debate was still continuing in Washington at war's end as to exactly what overall occupation policy the Americans should apply to the nearly twenty million Germans who had just come under American control. Although Treasury Secretary Henry Morgenthau's "pastoralization" scheme to turn Germany into a land of farmers and shepherds had already been rejected by Roosevelt in the fall of 1944 (under the pressure of American public opinion), the feisty Morgenthau still exercised much influence in the formulation of America's first official occupation policy: Joint Chiefs of Staff (JCS) Directive 1067. This controversial document was a compromise between Morgenthau's punitive approach and a more reconstructionist philosophy favored by the State Department and, to a certain extent, by the War Department. While the wording was harsh and seemed to incorporate much of Morgenthau's discredited plan, State and War Department officials had inserted key loopholes. The chief clause was a so-called "disease and unrest" formula which permitted the U.S. Military Government to extend economic aid to the German population, to ease the threat of hunger riots or serious epidemics. Using such escape clauses to the maximum, the military governor, General Lucius D. Clay, could alleviate the harsher aspects of JCS 1067. Nevertheless, American occupation policy in May 1945 was tentative, and it took two years before a genuinely comprehensive directive that was in any way comparable to Soviet thinking emerged from Washington. The repercussions from America's tardy policy-planning were felt in Berlin immediately.[12]

The Soviets had agreed to the American entry into Berlin only after U.S. forces had withdrawn from the Soviet-designated territories of Thuringia and Saxony (state and province), which the Americans had conquered in the last phase of the war. This movement was completed by July 4, and the Americans entered their sector of Berlin on that day. From the outset there were irritations between the two wartime allies. The Soviets imposed numerous conditions of entry, limiting the size of convoys that could enter the city and evacuating the American Sector only reluctantly. However, despite the prompt arrival of a sizable military government detachment, under Colonel Frank Howley, the Americans inevitably took time settling into their assignment of running the affairs of approximately one quarter of Berlin.

U.S. occupation forces underwent a series of bewildering organizational changes in the spring and summer of 1945. SHAEF, under

General Eisenhower, continued to exist until July, 1945. The U.S. Group Control Council (U.S. Group CC), which had operated under SHAEF, continued to function until the formal organization of the Office of Military Government (U.S.) for Germany (OMGUS) in October 1945. This American military government headquarters, as opposed to the initial Berlin civil-affairs detachment, began entering Berlin on July 11 from Frankfurt. The separate and distinct Office of Military Government, Berlin District (OMGBD) gradually replaced the initial organizational form, the civil affairs detachment that had entered Berlin on July 4. Within a short time the Berlin operation finally dropped the term "district" and became OMG Berlin Sector, or OMGBS. The overall headquarters under General Clay was not fully operational until approximately mid-August. Even then, there were divided OMGUS administrative and operational headquarters in Berlin and in Frankfurt am Main until December 1945, when General Clay unified all military government functions in the Berlin headquarters. The reader will readily understand that the confusion in establishing an overall American occupational headquarters and a separate sector administration in Berlin could not help but delay American and therefore Western Allied initiatives in general. By contrast, the Soviet Military Administration was centered in the Berlin suburb of Karlshorst, conveniently close to the city administration. Directives from the Soviets to their German liaison at the zonal level moved smoothly down to the nearby city administration. The system was already well in place before the Americans arrived.

EDUCATION CONTROLS AND THE
DISPUTE OVER BERLIN UNIVERSITY

Indicative of the Americans' unpreparedness was their educational personnel situation. At first, exactly one officer, Captain Paul F. Shafer, was assigned to oversee all educational activities in the American Sector. A report summarizing his lonely activities was blunt about American preparations in the sphere of education: "American Military Government education officers upon their entry into Berlin arrived with no definite policies." Shafer, who had acquired the function of education officer only through the intercession of a "high-ranking English officer," was responsible for overseeing the administration of fifty city schools and the school administration in the Magistrat, plus coordinating activities in the Allied Kommandatura Education Committee (AKEC). The latter job alone required three days of his time per week, and it became apparent to Shafer immediately that one person could not do the job. Nevertheless, he remained alone in the assignment through February 1946, aided only by occasional help from education officers of the central staff at OMGUS headquarters.[13]

Inadequate planning or staffing did not mean that the Americans failed to administer their occupational duties in their respective zone and sector. Shafer did his best, undertaking a survey of public schools in the American Sector and producing 120,000 emergency school books, which the Americans had reprinted unaltered from Weimar texts. Colonel John J. Maginnis, a senior officer in the Berlin operation, observed in his diary on October 2, 1945, that occupational policy in the U.S. Sector was unfolding smoothly after the inevitable teething problems were solved. "In the matter of education we were far ahead of the American zone proper, where only the Volksschulen . . . had been opened," he claimed. However, Maginnis admitted that this was due to a Soviet policy of rapid reopening. New textbooks, he wrote, had been approved and were now being distributed in the American Sector. In sum, "a fine start had been made in the reeducation of German children."[14] In reality, nothing of the sort had happened. Shafer continued his lonely one-man effort, and even the textbook project soured when the Soviets discovered what they felt were excessively nationalistic passages in the Weimar text reprints and refused to distribute them. Shafer admitted that the incident "did cause some embarrassment and that this interallied squabble had been a source of interest to the Berlin population."[15] Maginnis's observations were characteristic of higher echelon American Military Government thinking of the time. He had taken a pragmatic, short-range view of events—almost inevitable for someone in his position responsible for reviving only the most basic social and logistical needs of the Berliners. He, like nearly all of his countrymen, was as yet unaware of the failure to prepare plans for the long-term development of German society. If the Americans had given little thought to education in general in the summer of 1945, they had given none whatsoever to higher education in Berlin.

It was ironic that Maginnis had noted two weeks earlier in his diary that a controversy had arisen in the Kommandatura concerning control over Berlin University. "The US, UK, and French wanted to establish quadripartite control," Maginnis wrote, but the USSR wanted it to "come within the competence of the Control Commission of the nation occupying the territory in which the institution is located." Maginnis recognized that like the trade unions and political parties, so, too, education had ideological overtones, "and the Russians wanted no divided control in such an important area."[16]

The first German civilian to perceive the growing Soviet control over higher education in Berlin was Eduard Spranger. A world renowned philosopher and educational theorist and a student of the even more famous philosopher Wilhelm Dilthey, he had been associated with Berlin's famed university since 1920. Spranger was a true representative of German idealism, a field which set him apart somewhat from the more empirical Anglo-American world and which may explain why he had difficulty in establishing contact with the Americans after the war. He approached educational theory and educational reform from a Christian-Social perspective and was a pioneer in developing a *geistes-wissenschaftliche Pädagogik*, a uniquely German approach to educational theory that can only be roughly translated as humanities educational theory. For example, in his major works, such as *Lebensformen* (Types of Men) and *Psychologie des Jugendalters* (Psychology of Youth), he examined the effects of culture and history on human ethics and actions. For him education both reflected and could help solve the moral and social problems that confronted youth. He exercised considerable influence upon German education in the 1920s. Not surprisingly, he was diametrically opposed to Social Democratic and Communist educational reformers. Spranger understood Marxism well. It was, after all, a philosophy that had originated in the German-speaking world of ideas, and he was unalterably opposed to it. He also enjoyed a highly successful career in German academia. He became dean of Berlin University's faculty of philosophy and natural sciences (equivalent to a dean of arts and sciences) and counted Albert Einstein among his colleagues. In 1933, Spranger protested the spreading of National Socialist control over the universities and criticized the dismissal of his Jewish colleagues. He also submitted his resignation, which was not accepted, and he somehow quietly made his peace with the Nazis, first by an extended leave of absence in Japan and then in the form of "inner emigration" or quiet resignation from the affairs of the Third Reich. He met Count Stauffenberg in 1944, was subsequently imprisoned by the Gestapo for two months following the failure of the July 20 plot against Hitler, and was finally released when the Japanese ambassador to Germany interceded on his behalf. Spranger survived the storming of Berlin, secluded in his villa in Dahlem, and was in a position to participate at an early stage in the effort to restore public life in Germany and specifically in Berlin.

As an eyewitness to the Soviet victory in Berlin, Spranger understood in the most fundamental way the power of Stalin's legions. The Soviet Army took vengeance for the rapine, murder, and wholesale plundering committed by the German Army, and the population of Berlin, innocent and guilty alike, suffered the consequences. Most of the dazed German survivors in Berlin were convinced that the Soviets would remain in exclusive control of the city. Nor were they alone in that estimation. Colonel Frank Howley, head of the first American detachment into Berlin, was convinced that the occupation would proceed according to the disposition of troops at war's end. Having visited Berlin briefly while preparing for the Potsdam Conference and having experienced exasperating bureaucratic delays from the Soviets already, Howley assembled his detachment upon his return to his main unit near Leipzig. "Gentlemen," he announced, "we are never going to Berlin." The Soviets were hostile, he maintained. "Berlin is a shambles. It's not worth an acre of good land with cattle on it. I think the smart thing is to keep what we've got and let the Russians keep what they've got." To be sure, the repositioning of Allied troops took place anyway, and Berlin passed under four-power control as agreed upon in the wartime deliberations of the European Advisory Commission.

Hinting at the horrors that accompanied defeat in Berlin, Spranger claimed later that he preserved his notes of the first weeks after the truce "in a closely guarded recess within my memory." Like everyone else, he obeyed Soviet orders to clear rubble from the streets, a task made more difficult by the lack of food and drinking water. On May 10, he had to report to a central office to apply for a ration card from the new authorities. This simple move allowed the authorities to check on the past party affiliations of virtually the entire population. Despite his clean record, Spranger discovered a general belief that he as a university professor would as a matter of course have joined the party. The incident was characteristic of what was to come.

On May 21, Otto Winzer, the new *Stadtrat* (city councilman) for education from the *Volksbildungsamt* (Education Office), approached Spranger about becoming an education adviser.[17] Spranger demurred, even when Winzer sought him out again the following day. Shortly after, a group of three professors, Hermann Grapow (Egyptologist), Paul Gieseke (law), and Fritz Rörig (historian), appeared and asked him to take over as the new rector at the Berlin University. Spranger, recalling how the German professoriate had behaved in the crisis of 1933, was not enthusiastic. Still, he felt compelled to accept his share of the burden in building society anew. "For my part, I took on the responsibility out of love for Berlin University with which I have had varying but strong ties for 45 years," he wrote.[18] Spranger's difficulties with the Nazis, his incarceration by the Gestapo, and his international reputation all combined to make him the logical choice to run the university now. He accepted the rectorship, although he was not confirmed by any election. Elections at that chaotic time, without any mail service, phones, or transportation, were simply impossible anyway. Spranger felt the post was temporary and his title on his letterhead listed him as "commissioned to direct the affairs of the university."[19] In early June, the Magistrat confirmed him in his post.

As the first postwar rector, Spranger quickly discovered that his Herculean task included reassembling a cleansed faculty, locating the physical plant, and, not least, dealing with the occupation authorities. Accomplishing even the simplest tasks in Berlin that spring was difficult. Public services and transportation remained at a standstill for many weeks, so he had to walk across the city to deliver messages and to call meetings. Once he even walked to Potsdam for a meeting, a six-hour march that taxed his sixty-three years. Between the end of May and early July, Spranger succeeded in organizing a half-dozen meetings of professors and other educational personnel at the community center in Zehlendorf. The chief subjects of discussion remained personnel, denazification, and finance, plus preparations for a reopening whenever the authorities might allow that. The biggest headache was locating adequate physical facilities, and while he felt a reopening in 1945 was unlikely, Spranger wanted to be ready.

Already on May 20, 1945, about a dozen Berlin notables had heard Spranger expound on his ideas for the reopening. Foremost among his thoughts was the necessity of turning away from the notion that a university should be politicized. Rather, it should be above all an institution of education, an erziehende Universität, he claimed. Furthermore, it should be a university of colleagues, not an institution dominated by a centralized government ministry. Spranger has been described elsewhere as demonstrating the mentality of an older German Ordinarius, whose conception of a reformed university in 1945 was to return to the status of higher education in the days of Weimar or the old Kaiserreich.[20] It was unlikely that the Soviets or their German Communist allies would be much impressed at this conception of higher educational revival, since they viewed the old German universities as bastions of conservatism. Paul Wandel, the president of the Zentralverwaltung für Volksbildung, viewed the overwhelming majority of university professors as being traditionally strongly middle-class in outlook and origins and unlikely to support radical changes in the structure and goals of higher education.[21] Spranger would soon discover this wide discrepancy of opinion for himself. But for the moment, the urgent business of preparation forced everyone to continue to undertake the affairs of rebuilding quickly. On June 11, Spranger was summoned by Winzer, to a meeting of provisional rectors of Berlin higher educational institutions at the City Hall, where he was appointed chairman of a "Committee of Five" responsible for science and university affairs. Simultaneously, the Magistrat confirmed him in his status as provisional rector for Berlin University. Among his colleagues on the committee were a medical scientist, Theodor Brugsch, and a young physicist, Robert Havemann. Exceptions to Wandel's rule of thumb, both proved to be stalwart supporters of a new, Marxist-oriented society. Their appointment to the committee was characteristic of the changes expected by Winzer and the Soviet-appointed Magistrat.

Promptly, Spranger and his colleagues got down to business. They produced denazification questionnaires for faculty and students alike in order to gauge their political activities. They put together a provisional budget for seven faculties in a much reduced university and prepared a catalogue of courses for a possible reopening.[22]

It was not denazification procedures or other seemingly more sensitive political issues that brought control over the university to a head. Rather, it was the matter of where to relocate the university now that most of it lay in ruins. Its central administrative buildings were located in the Mitte, the central district which the Soviets had been at such pains to claim during the discussions on the division of Berlin at the European Advisory Commission. Between Allied bombings and the final ferocious battles that raged in the downtown governmental district at the end of April 1945, the university buildings—along with the entire district—suffered over 90 percent destruction. Since Winzer, Spranger, and the other concerned parties were looking toward a tentative reopening of the university in the autumn of 1945, other accommodations were needed immediately. Given the chaotic conditions of Berlin in that unforgettable summer, it took some time for the aging Spranger to locate an appropriate site. Early on, he considered moving into the former *Luftgaukommando*, a Luftwaffe command center in Dahlem, but the Americans commandeered it on their arrival in early July. Besides, Spranger admitted that its facilities were not appropriate for a university.[23]

Carl Diem, former rector of the Reichssporthochschule (the College of Physical Education), informed Spranger that its buildings and grounds, near the Olympic Stadium, were virtually undamaged. An inspection showed that the facilities, with lecture halls, administrative offices, and accommodations for 2000 students and faculty, were almost ideal. Best of all, according to Spranger, the responsible British education officer, Tom Creighton, in whose zone the sports institute lay, was willing to allow the shift to take place. Pleased that this aspect of his work as provisional rector was showing some progress, Spranger wrote a glowing report of the new facilities to Otto Winzer. They could begin moving university operations immediately, he claimed, and then they could remove the ashes and rubble on Unter den Linden at their leisure.[24] Other observers, such as Spranger's assistant, Hans-Joachim Lieber, were hardly so convinced that the British were prepared to evacuate the sports education complex and claimed afterwards that Diem had overstated his case.[25] Moreover, in his report to the Americans on September 7, 1945, Spranger admitted that a regiment of British hussars was currently quartered at the athletic center. He suggested that if plans to use the athletic center were to fall through, they should consider building emergency structures on the site of the zoological garden.[26] Paul Shafer, the American Military Government officer in charge of education in Berlin, pointed out to his superiors several months later that no move took place because the British authorities had denied permission to turn over the former athletic institute to the university.[27] Considering the Soviet and German Communist decisions that were about to take place, the cooperation of the British had become an academic question in any case.

Unaware of British reluctance to evacuate the former Olympic facilities, Spranger continued to lay great hope on Winzer's approval of a move. Weeks went by without an answer. Spranger then repeated his urgent recommendation for a transfer and reemphasized the need to act with haste before the valuable property went to some other institution in a city where shelter of any kind was at a premium. Only in mid-September did Winzer answer Spranger's suggestion, and even then he did so indirectly. He recommended that the preparatory committee for the university undertake an inspection trip of an alternate site, the diminutive but elegant Kurfürstenschloss, a royal Prussian palace located on the far southeast corner of Berlin in Köpenick in the Soviet Sector. Disconcerted, Spranger nevertheless accompanied the group to the palace. "On that sunny autumn day," he recorded, the palace "utterly charmed us in its decayed state, nestled at the confluence of the Spree and Dahme Rivers." But even in better times it had scarcely sufficed for a modest teacher-training center of the old-fashioned type. Spranger became speechless when several of his colleagues on the preparatory committee expressed great satisfaction at the prospect of moving the university—at least three full faculties—to the rundown palace. "The politics of physical locations found me to be naive at first," he commented wryly, ". . . by that I mean that I thought that once the four occupying powers were established in Berlin and an Allied Kommandatura had begun to function, institutions such as Berlin University and the polytechnical institute in Charlottenburg [soon to be called the Technical University, or TU for short] would not be administered according to the arbitrary fact of where their main administration building happened to be situated." Rather, they would come under four-power control. The university, with its many institutes, was spread throughout the American, British, and Soviet sectors. In fact, some of the institutes were located outside the city limits of Berlin proper. "If I had had any awareness then," continued Spranger, "that the university was supposed to be a purely Soviet-controlled institution, I would hardly have dared to venture as much as I actually did. Despite my residing in the American Sector, I would have feared the prospect of simply disappearing one day."[28]

There had already been storm warnings enough which only the stalwart Spranger would have dared to ignore. In that chaotic summer of 1945, he seemed to run afoul of several bureaucracies. He resided in Dahlem in a handsome villa at Fabeckstrasse 13, and as the American occupation forces settled in, they took an altogether too lively interest in his undamaged house. Subsequently, the Military Government requisitioned it, and, suspicious of his activities, which frequently brought Soviet-licensed vehicles to Spranger's house, they arrested him at the end of July. Thus, Spranger found himself in confinement for the second time in less than a year. Within a week he convinced his captors that he was guiltless, and on August 1 was set free. However, the Americans kept his house, allowing him and his wife to occupy a cellar room.

He immediately attended the next scheduled meeting of the preparatory committee for the university, only to be attacked by one of his colleagues, famed physician Theodor Brugsch, for his apparent inactivity. With the defeat, Brugsch had become a staunch defender of the Soviets and of the new social policies, and he claimed that all had proceeded relatively smoothly when the Soviets alone had occupied Berlin. But now it was becoming more complicated. Brugsch recalled—erroneously—that Spranger had wanted to reopen the university in the American Sector (in fact it was in the British Sector) and Brugsch protested vehemently against any change. "I was opposed," he said, "for the simple reason that the University lay in the Soviet Sector. . . . " Brugsch was inclined to think that the Americans were the most hostile occupying force in Germany and he wanted to prevent the reopening of Berlin University as part of their Morgenthau Plan. He respected Spranger, yet he was motivated by one overriding consideration: ". . . at all costs I wanted to prevent a breakup of the university at the time." For him that meant retaining exclusive control of it by the Soviets.[29] Awareness of the importance of the university was keenest among the Soviets and their German allies.

Still disgruntled over the requisitioning of his house, Spranger nevertheless received a distinguished guest despite his reduced circumstances. Edward Y. Hartshorne, one of Friedrich Meinecke's last students and later a professor of sociology at Harvard University, had written extensively about the Nazi-dominated universities before World War II. After the war, he became, in effect, the senior higher education officer in the U.S. Zone, with his offices in Marburg. Unfortunately for Spranger, Hartshorne had devoted most of his energies to the revival of universities in the American Zone—as distinct from Berlin—and with only a brief stay in the former capital planned, Hartshorne was not acquainted with local conditions. Spranger gave him a written account of his falling out with the Nazis in 1933, and they held a lengthy conversation. The meeting was not a great success. "I was not able to establish any special rapport with him," Spranger recalled. "I had the impression still that the Americans considered me to be the surviving rector from the last year of the Nazi regime."[30] In reality, Hartshorne entertained no such illusions. He recorded his own impressions in his diary: "Spranger looked old and tired. [He] said he had the 'bother' of the University but no power. [He] owed it to the University to do what he could."[31]

Spranger's luck with the other American authorities was scarcely better. John W. Taylor, chief of the Military Government's Education and Religious Affairs Branch (E&RA), tried to call on him one day at his modest office in the *Gertraudenschule* in Zehlendorf. By ill chance, Spranger was out on one of his endless rounds. Taylor then announced to the staff that he had had the pleasure of hearing Spranger lecture in Berlin in the 1920s and would call on the famous pedagogue again. But this was not to be. Bent on locating politically acceptable faculty for the university and constantly interrupted in these efforts by one occupying power or another, Spranger tended to day-to-day affairs instead. Finally, a German contact, Andreas Wachsmuth, after holding discussions with American personnel about democratization efforts, was able to secure for Spranger a meeting with Taylor. When they finally did meet, in late August, Spranger observed that no hint of a previous acquaintanceship remained. Uneasy at this bad start to a crucial meeting, he came immediately to the point. Berlin University was a cultural institution of great importance, he reminded Taylor. It had spread its influence throughout the civilized world. Surely the Americans could not remain indifferent as to who would control it in the future. It must have come to their attention that the university, parts of which were spread throughout the various sectors, should come under the joint control of all occupying powers now that a division of responsibilities in the former capital was rapidly approaching. "I stated this with great emphasis," Spranger recalled, adding that all measures accomplished to date were of a provisional nature and that higher educational issues were still open to settlement. "Especially Mr. Taylor greeted my explanations with icy indifference," Spranger recalled. The Americans seemed incapable of showing even a theoretical interest in the affairs of the university, and Spranger left the Military Government compound with a sense of having accomplished nothing.[32] Afterward, Spranger speculated that Fritz Karsen, a Social Democrat and an educational reformer whom he perceived to be a rival during the time of the Weimar Republic, had caused Taylor's about-face. Karsen was in New York, not Berlin, in the summer of 1945, but the hypothesis maintained that Taylor may have met Karsen during a return visit to the United States. Taylor energetically opposed such conjecture: "As for my having been briefed by Karsen while I was in the U.S. during the summer of 1945, [it is] a figment of Spranger's imagination." A far likelier explanation for the Americans' coolness toward Spranger was an unfortunate misunderstanding of his unavoidable contacts with the Soviets.[33]

Now events moved rapidly to a head. Under pressure from Winzer, Spranger stepped down from the chair of the planning committee on September 4. The transfer of authority over the university from the Magistrat to the *Zentralverwaltung* occurred on October 12. Simultaneously, the Soviets announced that Johannes Stroux, a classicist, was taking over the duties of provisional rector.[34] No one dared criticize the decision officially, although members of the preparatory committee shared their private views with Spranger. "The news that you no longer stand at the forefront of our University moves me greatly," announced fellow member Fritz Rörig. "As rector, as teacher, and as a human being you have embodied German idealism for us, not merely as a tradition but as a working, living force." Rörig felt it was a tragedy that Spranger had served as provisional rector at a time when the major challenges were organizational in nature and before he could offer a spiritual direction for the as yet unopened university. Rörig also hinted broadly that the generally difficult political circumstances as well as internal problems within the university itself were responsible for Spranger's dismissal. "However," Rörig concluded, "I do not wish to talk about that here."[35] Another committee member, philosopher Paul Hofmann, wrote his private regrets to Spranger. He had wanted to offer a public word of gratitude but received a warning from another committee member not to do so. There had been a similar case where a district mayor had sent a thank-you note to someone recently dismissed by an occupation authority. The mayor promptly received his dismissal notice too, "because the occupation authority interpreted this as opposition," Hofmann concluded. "The only thing left to me is to write to you privately what I would like to have stated to you publicly in the name of the Committee."[36]

While still active in trying to revive Berlin's cultural life, Spranger became steadily more disillusioned with his private and public standing in the former capital. His wife had endured the indignity of rape by Soviet troops in the first days of occupation, he had endured imprisonment on no discernible charge by the Americans, and together they had witnessed the confiscation of their home. For them Berlin had become a place of troubling memories and frustrations. In June 1946, the Sprangers left the former capital for Tübingen and a new life. They never returned to Berlin again. Even as he laid down his offices in September 1945, Spranger offered the Americans a gloomy forecast of the plight of higher learning in the former capital. For the university to resume to any degree its former greatness, Spranger prophesied, would require first of all the active support of all four occupying powers. "It will be very difficult to keep Berlin University competitive with others. After all, under present conditions the City provides scarcely any incentives to new faculty or students," he wrote. "Therefore the University must replace its former glories with the richness and scientific/scholarly attainments [of the present]."[37]

ALLIED EFFORTS AT ACHIEVING
QUADRIPARTITE UNIVERSITY CONTROL

Despite their obvious ill-preparedness, the Americans and the British were not as indifferent to the fate of Berlin University as Spranger thought. Without his being aware of it, the Americans and British had immediately raised the issue of four-power control of the university at one of the first meetings of the Allied Kommandatura Education Committee, held on August 20. The British recommended that the AKEC should oversee Berlin University, and the four Allied representatives, including the

Soviet representative, seemed at first to agree to this. The Soviet officer suggested that "a date be set, at which time all information regarding the University be presented and considered by this committee." The date agreed upon was September 3. However, on that day the Soviets did not appear. Nevertheless, one of the American representatives, Captain Paul Shafer, accompanied by Branch Chief John Taylor, immediately raised the issue of control of Berlin University. The chairman of the session (unidentified but probably a British or American representative) produced a paper from the dean of the Berlin University medical faculty ordering his colleagues to prepare curriculum outlines by September 3, which would then be forwarded to Moscow for approval. The letter was clear evidence that the Soviets intended to control directly all functions at Berlin University without regard to the Magistrat or, by implication, the three Western Allies. This was a radical shift in Soviet policy since August 20, when the Allies had first discussed the issue of university control. As the chairman of the September 3 session observed, the Soviets, in consultation with their German Communist allies, had originally decided to reopen only the medical faculty, on the grounds that it carried no political significance. The implication was that other, politically more sensitive faculties would be opened later only after four-power consultation had resolved any inter-allied disagreements. Now, this most recent Soviet action was sending a different and potentially troublesome message.

At the September 3 meeting Paul Shafer immediately submitted a motion based on the assumption of four-power control: "This Committee recommends that Berlin University in all its departments and all technical high schools in Berlin be administered on a quadripartite basis and the *Volksbildungsamt* be required to submit to this Committee a complete statement of past activities, present plans, state of buildings, and all other relevant details." The British, French, and American representatives all agreed to the motion, and to give it concrete form they also supported a proposal to establish a separate subcommittee of the AKEC to deal with Berlin University and the other institutions of higher learning in Berlin. Each nation was to send two representatives. Finally, the chairman of the AKEC recommended that the committee be declared competent to handle the issue of Berlin University and the other higher educational institutions on its own "without reference to Control Council." This, too, was approved by all three Allies.[38]

The minutes of the meeting were clear in describing the institutions in question. Besides Berlin University, the list included the Technical University (in the British Sector), the College of Music, the Academy of Fine Arts, Berlin Conservatory, and the Gauss School of Engineering. There was no doubt that the three Western Allies were concerned by the Soviets' unilateral move in demanding the forwarding of curricula proposals from the Berlin University medical faculty to Moscow.

The broader implications of the Soviet initiative were also not lost upon the Americans. A second portentous move by the Soviets, made simultaneously with the directive for Berlin University, was an order given to the officials of the former Reich Central Office of Education, a section of the former Reich Ministry of Education, to move its offices from the American Sector to Unter den Linden in the Soviet Sector. The individuals affected were informed by the Soviet-appointed mayor of Berlin to make the move or else risk losing their salaries. Paul Shafer noted that the office in question held personnel files for teachers and university instructors for all of Germany, "and if it moved into the Russian Sector, it would then presumably work entirely for the Russians." Shafer made yet another proposal, namely, that all central agencies, organizations, and administrative units concerned with education on a national scale and which were located in Greater Berlin should "be controlled and administered under the Allied Control Authority." Temporarily the AKEC could exercise that function until the ACA was prepared to take responsibility. The British and French readily agreed to Shafer's motion. The meeting adjourned with an agreement to meet again three days later to discuss the issues, hopefully this time with the Soviets present.[39]

The AKEC meeting of September 6, 1945, with the Soviets in attendance, demonstrated the reality of the political situation in Berlin. Undeterred by the pointed moves of the Americans on September 3, the Soviet representative to the AKEC, Colonel Pjartley, in effect rejected all of the Western Allies' assertions out of hand. The minutes of that crucial meeting put the Soviet position bluntly: "Firstly, Berlin University is considered a Prussian University," Pjartley proclaimed. "Secondly, it is not the first University of Germany. The Universities of BONN, HEIDELBERG, and GÖTTINGEN are more important. Thirdly, Berlin University exerts its main influence in the Province of Brandenburg. Fourthly, all matters of administration of Berlin University are the concern of the Soviet Military Administration at Karlshorst and not of the Russian Kommandatura. Fifthly, the only functions of the Russian Kommandatura in regard to Berlin University are ones of political and ideological supervision."[40]

Tom Creighton, the British representative, questioned Pjartley on the matter, looking for inconsistencies in the Soviets' reasoning. They were not long in coming. When asked if the university would be handled differently than the schools, Pjartley rejoined that the schools were in the hands of the Magistrat, while the university, "connected with Brandenburg Province," was in the hands of the Karlshorst (i.e., Soviet) administration. "Does that mean the adminstration of the University is not in the hands of the Germans?" Creighton persisted. "The Magistrat is gradually becoming of less importance and the establishment at Karlshorst is becoming responsible for the whole Russian occupied Zone of Germany," Pjartley continued gamely. The discussion became steadily less elucidating, and, with a deadlock in the offing, the members finally agreed to send the unresolved matter to higher authorities in the Kommandatura since the Soviet member was not empowered to make decisions. The deputy commandants at the Kommandatura grappled with the matter, but the same deadlock ensued. In October the subject advanced to the Allied Control Authority itself, and Paul Shafer recorded what happened next: "The same three-to-one difference of opinion existed even at this level, the highest Allied military-government authority in Germany."[41] The last Allied exchange on the matter occurred on November 16, 1945, when Colonel Frank Howley found an opportunity to raise the subject during a Kommandatura meeting of commandants. His deputy, John Maginnis, recorded the debate: "The Russians wanted to know why we were not supplying tea, since it was on the ration list. Our answer was that we had never agreed to supply it, so we were not going to supply it. We wanted to know when the Russians were going to open the University of Berlin as an all-city university. They said that they had no plans for taking such action. Colonel Howley suggested that we would consider supplying tea if the Soviets would consider opening the University of Berlin." It was a telling moment "that brought a smile all around the table," Maginnis recalled, "but no takers." The Soviets had won the first round.[42]

The Soviet interpretation of control of the Berlin University varied at first, as could be seen by Colonel Pjartley's remarks at the September 6 AKEC meeting. The line that emerged afterwards was that the former Friedrich Wilhelms University had been a Prussian rather than a city university. Since Prussia ceased to exist or at best existed only on paper after 1945, successor states, taking control of the former Prussian provinces, would also exercise responsibility over those institutions which were on their territory. Prussian universities in the Soviet Zone would be controlled by the Soviet Military Administration in Karlshorst. Other former Prussian universities in other zones—Marburg, for example— would come under the control of their American or British military governments or whatever German administrative apparatus the Allied powers designated to exercize that power. The problem with that interpretation, logical though it might appear, was that Berlin was a special case and not part of the Soviet Zone, as had been recognized by all four Allies during their painful months of negotiation on the European Advisory Commission and elsewhere. The university had subsections scattered throughout all four sectors. Had Mitte, Berlin's central district, where the central administration was located, come under four-power administration as had happened in Vienna, the Soviet decision to retain control of the university and several other important Berlin institutions would have been far less likely to occur. This arrangement, combined with the immediate failure of the Allies to make the Allied Control Authority function as the de facto governmental control authority over a re-created central German administration (largely because of French obstruction), resulted in a vacuum which thwarted any smooth functioning of Berlin institutions. Berlin University should logically have come under the control of the Magistrat and thus under four-power Kommandatura control in the summer of 1945. The Technical University, in the British Sector, was administered by the Magistrat until April 1, 1946, when the British, reluctantly following the Soviet lead, assumed a control function over the Technical University. By contrast, the teacher training college, founded in 1946 in the Soviet Sector, remained under Magistrat authority until the division of Berlin city administration in the autumn of 1948.[43]

Equally controversial for the Soviet and later the East German position with respect to the university was the matter of its relationship to its predecessor. Was the university that opened its doors on January 29, 1946, a reopened university, or a new institution with no connection to its predecessor? Even as late as the 150th anniversary of the Friedrich Wilhelms University, in 1960, East German historians were referring to the event as a reopening rather than as a new creation.[44] The *Zentralverwaltung für Volksbildung*, under Paul Wandel, took special care to produce a legal justification for assuming permanent control over the university from the mere provisional control of the Magistrat. This transfer took place in September 1945, following the creation of Wandel's *Zentralverwaltung für Volksbildung*. The justification tendered by Wandel's agency to the Cultural Section of the People's Council was that they had deliberately avoided accepting any continuity between the old Friedrich Wilhelms University and the present university. The institution that opened its doors on January 29, 1946, they claimed, was a new creation, a break with the past. Because no statute existed with which to create a legal entity under public law (i.e., a corporation), a legal standing hitherto enjoyed by all universities in Germany, the *Zentralverwaltung* leadership had decided to regard Berlin University as a subordinate agency of the *Zentralverwaltung*. The *Zentralverwaltung* administered the entire Soviet Zone rather than Berlin. By placing Berlin University under its authority, Wandel was creating a unique administrative link. All other universities in the Soviet Zone were administered by the cultural ministries of their respective provinces or states. If the Soviets and East Germans had consistently followed this interpretation of a newly created institution, then they might have maintained a consistent legal position in not allowing the university to revert to Magistrat control as the opposition students were to demand in 1948.

However, as one West German historian has recently pointed out, the German Communist authorities found it difficult to maintain this interpretation consistently. The *Zentralverwaltung's* report of January 13, 1946, to its superiors was entitled "The Resumption of Instruction at the Universities of Berlin and Halle." The report announced that "in the Berlin University instruction within seven schools will resume once again." The use of the words "resumption" and "resume once again" are significant. Equally significant is the fact that there was no reference at all to the creation of a new university in Berlin under the administration of the *Zentralverwaltung*. Thus, within their own legislation, the legal interpretation offered for exclusive Soviet Zone control had been so stretched that the authors themselves could not consistently abide by that interpretation in the language of their proclamations. The justification for Soviet control of Berlin University had begun with Colonel Pjartley's inconsistent remarks at the AKEC on September 6, 1945, and continued thereafter into the historiography of the German Democratic Republic. To be sure, there were few in Berlin at that difficult time who understood, much less cared about, the legal status of the university. By the autumn of 1945, it was plain that the Soviets would not change their position. However, their decision with respect to control of the university in the summer of 1945 would come back to haunt them three years later.[45]

LINDEN UNIVERSITY OPENS ITS DOORS

Having brought Berlin University under their exclusive control, Soviet Zone authorities wasted no time in preparing it for instruction. Much had already been accomplished in the summer of 1945 in ridding it of Nazis and preparing new faculty lists, budgets, and all the minutiae connected with the administration of a university. Spranger, despite his impending dismissal, had been energetic in directing the first steps and in leading a distinguished preparatory committee, and his successor, Professor Johannes Stroux, worked harmoniously with the same group in preparing for the new semester. The *Zentralverwaltung*, confronted with serious deficiencies everywhere, delayed a reopening repeatedly and finally set the date for January 29, 1946. University authorities, in close cooperation with Wandel's *Zentralverwaltung* and the Soviets, set about creating an institution that would better serve the new society. For example, in September 1945 a *Vorstudienanstalt*, a college-preparatory center, opened in Berlin to prepare young people for the all-important *Abitur* so that they could become university students. Given the dislocations connected with Nazism and total war, there was a tremendous backlog of university-age citizens who lacked the necessary prerequisites to study but who richly deserved the chance and desperately desired it. This special institution, under the aegis of the reorganized university, was a worthy innovation and was unlike anything created in the western zones. The *Vorstudienanstalt* offered approximately one year of instruction to aspiring students. Later, it was replaced by a three-year preparatory program located in a newly created division of the university known as an *Arbeiter-und-Bauern Fakultät*, or working-class school. Wandel's *Zentralverwaltung* created these programs at each university under Soviet control. They were intended, he observed, to bring relief to the legion of young people whose education had been interrupted by the advent of fascism. Just as important was their function in encouraging students of working-class origins to attend universities for the first time.[46]

To be sure, the regular *Gymnasien* of Berlin also helped to take the backlog of would-be students. For example, the former Kaiserin-Augusta-Gymnasium, now the Charlottenburger Gymnasium,[47] offered college-preparatory courses in much the same way as did the university-related *Vorstudienanstalt*.

Simultaneously, university authorities created admissions committees to screen the applicants and to admit the worthiest. In the first semester these committees consisted of faculty members plus representatives from the *Zentralverwaltung für Volksbildung*. Typical of these committee members was Rudolf Böhm, a young ex-soldier who had served as a lieutenant in General Paulus's ill-fated Sixth Army at Stalingrad. Following its surrender, he decided that a continuation of the war was madness and joined the *Nationalkommittee Freies Deutschland* (National Committee for a Free Germany) of German soldiers against the war. Released from captivity in May 1945, Böhm returned to his native Berlin and found employment with the *Zentralverwaltung* as an expert on student affairs. He was young, intelligent, personally engaging, and enthusiastic at the prospect of creating a just, new society. Many of the future founding students of the Free University met Rudi Böhm when applying for admission to Berlin University, and he impressed them. "I am willing to approve your application if you will promise me one thing," Böhm informed one aspiring student, Otto Hess. "You must promise me that you will become politically engaged." Hess readily agreed. He, too, felt that the university had been apolitical and apathetic at best when the Nazis destroyed the Weimar Republic. A new spirit would do it good.[48]

Already in early October 1945, the first public student meeting took place in Berlin. The student representative to the Magistrat and first speaker on that day was Joachim Schwarz, formerly a member of the miniscule White Rose resistance group of Munich students against Hitler, led by Hans and Sophie Scholl. The reportage in the press about this initial student gathering hinted at the ideological clash to come in Berlin. The Western-oriented press, such as the *Tagesspiegel* and the American-licensed *Neue Zeitung*, reported Schwarz as saying that professors and students should not only seek the road to democracy but should strive to achieve a democratic spirit as well. This was not enough for the Communist-oriented *Deutsche Volkszeitung*, which described Schwarz as in no way explaining how the students could achieve a new university. The journalist indicated that everyone by now knew about the heroic exploits of the student resisters and implied that, although Schwarz had been part of that movement, he had later served the Hitler regime. "We cannot demand from people whose first intellectual development consisted of nothing other than Hitlerism . . . and who at most learned opposition to the Hitler regime in their parents' home . . . that they will now know the new way or can point it out to others." For the *Deutsche Volkszeitung*, the clear spokesman for the future on that day was Robert Havemann, self-appointed director of the Kaiser Wilhelm Institutes in Berlin.[49] Proceeding from the premise that Hitler had led the youth astray, he noted that they could achieve a new university only after their conception of history had changed. Denazification by itself was not enough, he urged. The professoriate would have to be rejuvenated with additions from the ranks of this new type of student. In contrast to the other addresses, Havemann's speech "contained a program," the Soviet-Sector paper concluded, "and was an appeal."[50] Robert Havemann, by now a stout supporter of Marxism-Leninism, was determined to create a new society and a new university. Indicative of the ideological split that was about to open, the *Tagesspiegel* observed that in his address Havemann was sharply critical of the students, saying that they would have to earn their academic freedom. He observed that scholarship and science were closely tied to politics, a fact that the Nazis had deliberately hidden. From this point forward the universities would have to provide some basic schooling to the new generation of students. There would now be obligatory lectures on philosophy and the state, he announced. The students (noted the *Tagesspiegel* reporter) stamped their feet in protest at Havemann's assertions.[51]

It would be a mistake to assume that the Soviets' success in retaining control over the university provoked universal shock or dread among university professors and students. Friedrich Glum, a friend of Spranger, reported in mid-October 1945 that, despite doubts by some observers, the majority felt the Russians would fulfill their promise of a rapid reopening. Glum cited the frequent billeting of American forces in private homes as a source of bitterness for some of the professors. He also noted that many professors whom he had interviewed respected the Soviets' interest in scientific and scholarly affairs: "For instance, one Russian officer regularly attended the meetings of the *Kulturbund* . . . whereas no American or British [sic] has as yet been present," he wrote. Glum was scarcely implying that all Berlin academics felt this way. Some with whom he spoke did not believe in Soviet promises and were "extremely worried." This group echoed the words they had heard from a representative of the British Foreign Office with respect to Berlin University: "The fate of the University is the fate of Berlin."[52]

While certain aspects of the reopening, such as the screening of students, were beginning to function, there were other indications that the university was off to a rough start. Paul Shafer had a confidential meeting with Rector Johannes Stroux on December 5, 1945, to discuss university affairs. Stroux, he recalled, was "frank and courageous" and depicted several serious shortcomings to date. "There is considerable confusion as to exactly which governmental authorities or authority are or will be responsible for the University," Shafer recorded. Various components of the university received orders from above but never knew who had issued them. This led to confusion and uncertainty in such crucial areas as the appointment of new faculty. Another potential problem was student enrollments. Stroux informed Shafer that fully 9,000 young people had applied for admission. His own university authorities claimed they could provide for somewhere between 4,000 and 5,000 students. However, the Soviet authorities had issued orders, according to Stroux, limiting the student body to just 2,100 students. (Approximately 2,800 students actually began their studies in the first postwar semester.) Stroux observed that students were organizing themselves spontaneously into political youth organizations as affiliates of the Liberal Democratic Party (LDP) or the Christian Democratic Union (CDU). He was not in favor of such political groupings, claiming that it would divert the students' attention away from studies and toward political activities even before the first semester had begun. Preferable to this was another student organization, recently organized, which was "collaborating with the administration on non-political problems which are characteristic of the . . . traditional university student body organization."[53] This was the *Studentische Arbeitsgemeinschaft*, a generalized organization of student volunteers, deliberately organized to include students from all legally recognized political parties. It was eventually to comprise twenty percent of the student body. Although sounding nondescript in 1945, it assumed increasing importance in student affairs in the months to come. If Stroux was worried about political youth groups forming around the new parties in 1945, he was no doubt amazed afterward at the political role the *Studentische Arbeitsgemeinschaft* took for itself later. One of its first acts was to call upon all would-be students in December 1945 to help clear rubble and to undertake the most immediate repairs in order to accelerate the reopening of the university.[54]

In November 1945, the *Studentische Arbeitsgemeinschaft*, with official support from Wandel's *Zentralverwaltung*, began a modest existence with about two dozen student volunteers. Its stated goal was "the furthering of an anti-fascist, democratic spirit and the elimination of militarism and Nazism among the Berlin students." At first the volunteers held discussions on social and cultural matters, and by the time the uni-

versity opened at the end of January 1946 the organization had grown
to perhaps 150 or 200 students. Besides organizing construction gangs
for emergency repair of buildings, it participated in admissions work
and the distribution of student stipends. Despite its informal, voluntary
nature, it proved so useful that within a few months the *Studentische
Arbeitsgemeinschaft* took on the complexion of a student government.
The *Zentralverwaltung* appointed Georg Wrazidlo as its first head. Wrazidlo, formerly a highly decorated young army officer, had also been im-
plicated in the July 20, 1944, conspiracy against Hitler and was scheduled to be executed at Buchenwald until the Americans freed him in
April 1945. He exemplified the Victims of Fascism whom the Soviet-
Zone authorities wished to enlist in the creation of a new society. To
their credit, the Soviets seemed to have unleashed a spirit of cooperation and goodwill among significant numbers of students in Berlin.[55]

Even as the Soviets and their German subordinates were making
preparations for a reopening, their erstwhile allies in the western sectors were taking stock. There was little doubt that the unilateral decision by the Soviets to reopen Berlin University by themselves caused
more than passing concern for the Americans. The education staff
began to compile lists of university-related institutes and properties in
the American Sector in the winter and spring of 1946. Already in early
November 1945, Paul Shafer had urged the American representatives in
charge of Berlin finances to refuse approval for any further university expenditures.[56] In fact, the Soviets transferred the university budget to the
Zentralverwaltung für Volksbildung on January 1, 1946. Even the American intelligence organizations began to gather information on the university. On January 22 an intelligence officer, E. G. Riedel, serving the
Office of the Naval Adviser at OMGUS, prepared an extensive, if one-
sided report on conditions at the university. He recounted in more drastic form the shortcomings Stroux had observed as preparations for the
opening got under way, and added to the list of problems. Classroom facilities were still not available, wholesale dismissals of former National Socialists no matter how slight their involvement had denuded entire faculties, and replacements were almost impossible to find. The libraries of
Berlin had mostly been dispersed in the war, and returning them at a
time when transportation had largely broken down was almost impossible. Most ominously from Riedel's point of view, the university was
being directed "by two outspoken Communists, Wandel and Nass [*sic!*
probably Dr. Joseph Naas] who have no experience in university work
and financial matters connected therewith."[57] Already the disposition of
the university was beginning to assume political significance to some
Americans who saw it as a pawn in the nascent East-West struggle.

The difficulties encountered by Soviet-Zone authorities in reopening Berlin University were undoubtedly formidable and were similar to
the problems that Germans in all occupation zones faced in reviving a

stricken society and its various institutions. In the American Zone, for example, the universities in large cities such as Frankfurt and Munich were also preparing to reopen at about the same time, in January or February 1946. Their biggest headache was finding even remotely adequate building space among the ruins, a politically unencumbered teaching staff, library facilities, and a system of student admissions that was even approximately adequate to the huge backlog. In the Soviet Zone, where an immediate and radical denazification of teaching staffs had taken place, as against the slower and frequently less draconian efforts in the western zones, there were sharp limits on curriculum offerings and consequently on student enrollments.[58] The critical shortage of politically untainted professors placed sharp limits on all other aspects of university activity. E. Y. Hartshorne, during his brief visit to Berlin in August 1945, had observed denazification at Berlin University at first hand: "Their purge is more extreme than in our Zone," he reported to his fellow American education officers. "Any party member is out, and the result is that only about 200 teachers are left out of approximately 700." Their fate was often less than gentle. "Most of those dismissed have been arrested and interned by the Russians," he recorded in his diary.[59] Those could only have been approximate figures, since the denazification process was hardly complete in the summer of 1945. Moreover, most estimates concluded that there were about 900 teaching faculty at the prewar university. It was a measure of the difficulties involved in the reopening that there were only 120 professors teaching in the first postwar semester. By the winter semester of 1946/47, the number had risen only to 147 and remained at about that level in the autumn of 1948. The small number of full professors was augmented by ranks of aged professors brought out of retirement, from eminent professionals brought in as adjunct professors, and by recruitment from other universities. Even by 1948 the total teaching staff still hovered at 327, only one-third of the prewar total. These figures provide stark answers to why student enrollments were low. The shortage of qualified, politically untainted professors in Berlin was critical.[60]

To the credit of the small university staff, led first by Spranger and then by Stroux, assisted by the Zentralverwaltung under Wandel, and supported by the Soviets under General Pyotr Solotuchin, Berlin University, after repeated postponements, held its inaugural ceremony at the end of January 1946. Inter-allied disagreements softened for a moment on that solemn occasion. On the eve of the reopening, the Soviets invited representatives from the British, French, and American education staffs to attend the ceremony. Tom Creighton, the British member, seeking the right words, expressed regret that there had never been a four-power agreement on the university. Creighton, so the minutes of the meeting read, expressed hope "that the other powers had a contribution to make to the functioning of the University of Berlin, but personally he would like to congratulate the Soviet authorities on having been able to open the University so soon."[61]

The chief speakers on that day were the Soviet representative, General Solotuchin, Paul Wandel from the *Zentralverwaltung*, and the new rector, Johannes Stroux. The ceremony took place in the provisional state opera, the Admiralspalast, and the assembled scholars and students attempted bravely to maintain decorum despite the ruins and general decay around them. A measure of the modest beginning could be gleaned from the fact that ceremonial caps and gowns had to be sent up from Jena for the occasion. All the local academic robes had burned up in the wreck of Berlin. It was also noteworthy that one of the students spoke on that occasion. Georg Wrazidlo echoed the sentiments of renewal and dedication to the building of a new, democratic society. "Years of suffering and of heavy guilt lie behind our people," he exclaimed. "Now at last we can raise ourselves to true freedom and objective work, to the service and blessing of our people and for humanity." Following his presentation, the students loudly applauded one of their own.[62] After the speeches Stroux received his robes of office from Theodor Brugsch, including that symbol of German higher learning, the rector's golden chain of office. This act loosed a storm of applause among the assembled, "because" said Brugsch, "in that moment we recognized that something had not been brought low: learning and the academic tradition." The Humboldtian ideals of teaching and research combined in the person of the scholar would be maintained.[63] To be sure, the freedoms implied in the pursuit of those ideals were not necessarily compatible with the goals of the leaders in East Berlin in constructing a new kind of society. Events soon proved that they were powerfully determined to create that new society and a new university that would serve that society.

THE STUDENTS OF BERLIN

To understand the conflict that soon broke out between important segments of the student population and the Soviet-Zone authorities, it is necessary to examine the background of those lucky few who were admitted to Berlin University in 1946. It is useful to begin by looking at the criteria for admission and nonadmission to the university.

A circular distributed by the *Zentralverwaltung* on December 8, 1945, explained the new admissions criteria for students. An accompanying note also indicated that the authorities claimed to have received threatening letters from disgruntled rejectees, presumably Nazi-oriented elements whose threats showed "how necessary it was to check the 2800 admitted students for Berlin University according to strict political views so that the true democratic students have work possibilities for this first term after the war."[64] The categories of rejectees were comprehensive: All former party members, without regard to their year of birth, were inadmissible. All members of the Nazi youth groups, either in leadership positions or merely as active members, were ineligible. All SA and SS members, all active officers, and all reserve officers in the rank of first lieutenant or above were inadmissible. Moreover, children of formerly active Nazi officials "or those whose parents have been punished by the occupation authorites" were rejected.[65]

Needless to say, such categories, if followed rigidly, would have eliminated the overwhelming majority of aspiring students, most of whom had somehow been caught up in the net of the Nazi mass movement. The admissions authorities were willing to make exceptions for those who could "prove with documents that they fought against fascism during or after the war." The admissions commission also conceded that those born in 1920 or after might gain entrance "if the commission comes to the unanimous conclusion that an anti-fascist development is guaranteed." Admission was also possible for those who had not completed the *Abitur* because of social, political, or racial reasons during the Third Reich. Such applicants would have to submit proof of why they had not been permitted to work toward the *Abitur*. Then they would have to attend special courses to earn the equivalent of the *Abitur*, i.e., they would have to attend the *Vorstudienanstalt*. In essence, there were two major categories of aspirants who could be admitted as opposed to six categories of those who could not: those who had fallen out with the Nazis, and those who could prove by some act after the war that they were now anti-Nazis. As a result of these decisions, those 2,800 students who began attending Berlin University in January 1946 were either victims of Nazi persecution, often the officially recognized Victims of Fascism, or they were the smallest particles in the Nazi apparatus who chose now to throw in their fortunes with the seemingly dominant political movement in postwar Berlin, the Communists. Two unlikely elements were about to meet each other in the lecture halls of the once great Berlin University.

The new regulations of December 8 also directed the universities to establish admissions committees to screen applicants. A committee was to consist of one representative from the school or faculty to which the student was applying, plus "three individuals from public life . . . of whom at least one must carry an academic rank."[66]

The typical student who watched Rector Stroux don the chain of office on January 29, 1946, was lucky to be alive on that momentous day when a cherished institution of Western Civilization was revived after twelve years of Nazi barbarism. He or she had experienced twelve years of Nazi rule, and six years of total war, usually as a lowly cog in the military machine or on the hardly less dangerous home front. Typically, these students had been born during or slightly after the First World War, had begun their elementary-secondary education in the time of the

Weimar Republic, and had seen their education shortened, interrupted, or otherwise altered by the Nazis. They were three or four years older than was normal for student populations. If they were sons or daughters of committed Communist or socialist parents, or were Jewish or half-Jewish, or were connected somehow to resistance to the Nazi regime, then the chance of attending a university after 1933 had virtually disappeared. For all others after 1936, the thirteenth year of college preparatory education at the elite *Gymnasien* had been eliminated in favor of compulsory national labor service and the military. The Nazis had little use for women in higher education and limited their enrollments at universities to ten percent, a rule that was relaxed only in wartime. Most neutral observers had noted a significant decline in academic standards as the 1930s waned.

Georg Wrazidlo, later a central figure among those students who resisted rising Socialist Unity Party influence at Berlin University, or, as it was frequently called, the University Unter den Linden, represented one important segment of those students admitted to studies in 1946. A Silesian from a pious Catholic family, Wrazidlo had at first accepted National Socialism. He became a young officer in a tank regiment on the Eastern Front. By all accounts he was brave and capable, received some of the highest decorations for personal bravery, and seemed the model of loyalty to Germany. Gravely wounded, he convalesced in his native Breslau and simultaneously began medical studies at the university. Then, in the summer of 1944, Wrazidlo became convinced that the Nazis were leading his country into the abyss. He joined a plot of young officers to assassinate Hitler, and when it was uncovered the Gestapo threw him into Buchenwald, where he awaited execution. The Americans liberated him in April 1945, more dead than alive, and he found his way to Berlin. As a rare survivor of the German resistance, Wrazidlo was a logical choice to be one of the first students of postwar Berlin.[67] He was hardly the only resister. Another early student at Linden University was Joachim Schwarz, admitted because he had been in close contact with the White Rose resistance group of students in Munich centered around Hans and Sophie Scholl. One of countless war wounded, Schwarz had convalesced in Berlin and then begun law studies while recovering. His presence seemed to bridge the distance between the students of the Third Reich and the students who would build a new society.[68] Stanislaw Kubicki was from a German-Polish family in Berlin. His parents had suffered under the Nazis. His father, an artist and friend of the anarchist Erich Mühsam, had retained close ties to his Polish relatives in Posen and had been thrown out of Germany in 1934. The father joined the Polish Home Army during the cruel Nazi occupation and, like thousands of others, was ultimately caught by the Gestapo and liquidated. His artist-mother, once a Communist, became politically inactive and survived the war. The son was reluctant to allow his father's harsh fate to be a factor in his admission to studies. However, after two rejections and because knowledge of his parents' social views and experiences reached the admissions committee independently, Kubicki was admitted to study medicine at Linden University.[69]

Otto H. Hess had no reason to be enthusiastic about the Nazis either, but like so many other Germans of his generation, he found himself in uniform after Hitler declared war in 1939. Hess served in the French campaign and seemed destined to remain in uniform as the war steadily widened. However, another fate awaited him. Under the Nazis' racialist Nuremberg Laws, he fell into the category of so-called *Mischlinge ersten Grades*, that is, he was half Jewish. Together with thousands of others who had been conscripted at the beginning of the war and who had been compelled to bear arms for the Third Reich, Hess was summarily dismissed from military service on racialist grounds in 1941. Ultimately, he wound up in a forced labor battalion of the *Organisation Todt* (OT), aiding in the construction of military installations for Germany's armed forces. Such work was frequently dangerous. Another OT survivor and future student, Helmut Coper, recalled leaving Berlin with a group of 256 men of all ages in the autumn of 1944. Because of the brutal conditions, only 106 survived the ordeal. Hess and Coper were among those fortunate enough to return home. Aged thirty-five when the war ended, the former had deferred his studies even longer than most others. For obvious reasons Hess was a logical choice to enter Linden University when it reopened its doors. Given his maturity, natural leadership ability, and anti-Nazi credentials, Hess, like Wrazidlo, became a crucial figure in the events that would unfold at Unter den Linden.[70]

If Hess was one of the oldest students accepted to Berlin University's first semester, Horst Hartwich was, along with Helmut Coper, one of the youngest. Hartwich was the son of a pharmacist, and as an athletic youth who took great pride in his native Prussia and Berlin, he seemed a logical recruit for the Nazi youth movement. However, Hartwich, too, discovered the disadvantages of being half Jewish in the Third Reich. Too young to serve in the military during the war, he found precarious employment as a laborer, was nearly killed in the heavy air raids on Berlin, and was put into one of the dreaded OT work battalions in September 1944. The following April, after months of backbreaking labor on an airfield near Magdeburg, he and his comrades saw an American bombing raid pulverize their efforts in less than five minutes. Freed by the ensuing chaos, Hartwich made his way back to Berlin on foot, just before the onrushing Soviet troops encircled the city. He applied to the *Vorstudienanstalt*, was accepted immediately as a Victim of Fascism, and finished his *Abitur* in time to enter Berlin University in April 1946. It was significant, perhaps, that students Hess and Wrazidlo, who ranked among the oldest and maturest students at Berlin

University, and Hartwich, Coper, and Kubicki, who were among the youngest, all chose to study medicine. They had seen enough inflicting of pain for one lifetime. The time had come to heal instead.[71]

The tale of human tragedy which the first students had to tell seemed endless. One successful applicant, Eva Heilmann, found that the murder of her father, a former Social Democratic Reichstag Deputy at Buchenwald in 1940, had positive repercussions for her in 1946. She could now study chemistry.[72]

Some students did not have the openly anti-Nazi credentials or the proof of persecution demonstrated by students like Wrazidlo or Hess. Like countless others, Horst Rögner-Francke had served as a conscript during the war. Wounded three times, he had been allowed to study part-time at Berlin University while his wounds healed. After the war, Rögner-Francke showed considerable initiative and willingness to aid in the rebuilding of the society and its institutions. In July 1945, he joined Berlin's first student organization, which ultimately became the *Studentische Arbeitsgemeinschaft* at Linden University. Throughout the autumn of 1945, Rögner-Francke labored hard in construction gangs, readying the university for its opening in January 1946. He demonstrated by his good works the qualities needed for building a new society and was one of the 2,800 students who began their studies at Linden University. He wanted to be a dentist.[73] Peter Lorenz had had a similar experience. Like Rögner-Francke, he had no proofs of having been openly antifascist or a victim of Nazism. Like Rögner-Francke, he had finished the war as a soldier. Nevertheless, Lorenz, as a low-status employee in one of the East Zone central ministries, had no Nazi past and seemed a likely young ally in building the new society. He desired to be a lawyer and attended the inaugural ceremony in January 1946.[74]

Herbert Theuerkauf was representative of those first students who decided that the German past had been so horrible that drastic measures were needed to alter the stricken society. Western liberal democracy was for him hardly sufficient to guarantee such fundamental change. The failure of the Weimar Republic had demonstrated that fact. Consequently, he joined the German Communist Party, which, with the forced amalgamation of the Social Democrats of the East Zone under Otto Grotewohl with the German Communists in April 1946, became the Socialist Unity Party (SED). The admissions committee had little difficulty in accepting students like Theuerkauf who promised to create a new society that met with their approval.

Be they officially recognized Victims of Fascism like Hess, or politically unencumbered persons like Lorenz or Rögner-Francke, or converts to communism like Theuerkauf, the first postwar students anticipated a bright future in a new society. Despite the desperately low living standards which confronted all Berliners, the students of Berlin began their studies with renewed hope and a sense that they could overcome the evil of the past twelve years.

CONFRONTATION

The Soviets and their kindred spirits in the SED had recognized and in part been able to channel the idealistic upsurge that many students felt in the first year following the war. However, it became apparent at a surprisingly early moment that unbridgeable ideological differences existed between the Marxist-Leninists and the middle-class elements concerning the role of a university in rebuilding German society. There had been hints of a clash between some students and Soviet-Zone authorities since the autumn of 1945, when committed Communists like Robert Havemann announced the necessity of obligatory lectures for students. There were three main issues which caused the confrontation that developed between students and education officials at Linden University. The trouble centered first upon the admissions procedures that developed at the University Unter den Linden especially in the second postwar semester, which began in the autumn of 1946. Controversy also surrounded the required lectures in social issues and politics, scheduled for the winter semester of 1947/48. Most alarming of all was the arrest and disappearance, starting in March 1947, of students who had disagreed openly with the authorities in East Berlin.

The troubles had not taken long to surface. On May 1, 1946, the first May Day that could be celebrated as an independent labor day in Germany since 1932, the authorities flew the flags of the four Allies over the university as well as a large red flag. Over the entrance to the university hung a large red placard with two clasped hands, the emblem of the newly created Socialist Unity Party. Later, loudspeakers proclaimed the consolidation of the socialist movement. Reactions to this display of SED support at the university were quick to materialize. Twenty-seven students sent a petition to the university rector, Johannes Stroux, protesting the presence of political slogans and symbols on university premises. What made the protest all the more remarkable was that every petitioner was an officially recognized Victim of Fascism. They informed Stroux that they must "protest publicly the exhibiting of flags and symbols of a political party at the university." The university, they added, "serves scholarship and education and is not a party institution. We request that in the future [the University] will refrain from doing this again."[75]

The exhibiting of banners and slogans and the use of loudspeakers may seem relatively innocuous to the present generation in the Western democracies. To the survivors of the generation of 1933–1945, they evoked entirely different associations. It should not be forgotten that the Nazis had pioneered in the use of catchy slogans, which they then broadcast endlessly over public address systems and radios. Countless placards and posters had adorned kiosks and bulletin boards. Bold messages were emblazoned on giant billboards or covered entire sides of buildings, so that the message reached the entire population. The garish flag of the Nazi movement fluttered or hung from every square and street. This, in addition to the terror apparatus, such as the Gestapo, was among the most painful memories associated with totalitarianism, and the evil was compounded by the last great slogans which Goebbels issued as the conflict came to an end: "Total War—Shortest War, Our Walls May Break But Not Our Hearts, Berlin Remains German!" In short, the atmosphere created by this ceaseless propaganda was what later generations would describe as Orwellian. Most Berliners were relieved by the peace that followed defeat not least because they no longer had to endure dunning messages and slogans. However, within the Soviet Sector at least it became apparent that the authorities were determined to use the same media to broadcast their movement's message. Part of the atmosphere of East Berlin that made it so distinctive was the continuation of political sloganeering in a fashion eerily reminiscent of the recent tragic past even if the message was entirely different. If the students, and especially those among them who were Victims of Fascism, reacted strongly against SED placards on university walls, there was a reason for their emotional response.

Although the dispute received brief attention in the press of the western sectors, it seemed an isolated incident, soon to be forgotten. Yet that modest protest proved in retrospect to be the first skirmish in an escalating confrontation. One immediate result was rising tension within the *Studentische Arbeitsgemeinschaft* at Linden University. This all-volunteer group had emerged in November 1945, even before the university had officially reopened, and many students had assumed at first that it was essentially a Communist auxiliary organization. In fact, some of the early discussion leaders were German Communist Party (KPD) members, but the volunteers had emphasized its nonparty status. Its first leader, Wrazidlo, was a member of the Christian Democratic Union (CDU), a fact that did not deter the university authorities from installing him as its chairman. His presence was intended to assure its political neutrality. It soon became apparent that many other volunteers were not Communists either; some of them openly declared their allegiance to the CDU, the Social Democratic Party (SPD), or the Liberal Democratic Party (LDP). Others declared themselves independent of any party. However, the May Day celebration of 1946 and the resulting petition brought the underlying political tensions to a head. The *Zentralverwaltung* removed Georg Wrazidlo from the chairmanship of the student body and replaced him with a provisional chairman, Friedrich Wolf, who was also an SED member. This decision led the noncommunist majority of student volunteers to demand elections to replace the provisional chair. After some delay, the election took place, and Otto Hess, now an SPD member, won handily. The *Studentische Arbeitsgemeinschaft*, which by the fall of 1946 had grown to 850 volunteers, saw the noncommunist membership climb to over eighty percent.[76]

For the moment, at least, calm descended upon the university. The students of Berlin, like their counterparts in all the German universities, pursued their studies with an intensity that astounded many observers who had never before witnessed such steadfastness of purpose among German students. It was not until the beginning of the second semester, in the early autumn of 1946, that another conflict broke out. This time it was more serious, and ultimately it proved to be insoluble.

Who would be admitted to the university to study? That Linden University had had to start small was clear to most observers in the first year after the defeat, even though it was also clear that the demand for higher education was great. Despite a concerted effort to rebuild faculties and physical plant, the number of students admitted to the university for the summer semester in 1946, had been 2,800 and then had risen in the course of that first semester to about 3,200. Still, that was equivalent to only a quarter of the prewar total. By the fall of 1946, the figure had risen to about 4,300 according to official sources.[77] Interestingly, 1,500 students, or half of the student body in the first postwar semester, were women, a much higher percentage than in Western universities. Soviet Military Administration officials were encouraging admissions committees to accept as many women as men whenever possible, according to one source.[78]

Even more alarming than the slow pace of reconstruction was a widespread fear in 1946 among noncommunists in Berlin that the admissions were being skewed in favor of SED adherents. The Americans in Berlin were aware of this problem. They knew because they were reading the Germans' mail. The U.S. Censorship Division of Military Government noted, for example, that a CDU law student, Manfred Klein, had written to a colleague in Munich in late August 1946: "The admission board of the Berlin University consists of 80 per cent SED members; the students, taking an active part in it, were not freely elected, but nominated by the central administration."[79] Another disgruntled Berliner claimed that besides being politically unobjectionable, the successful applicant had to have a father with the exceedingly small monthly income of 600 Reichsmarks or less. At the medical school, he wrote, "48 students out of 800 applicants were accepted."[80]

New admissions regulations had appeared on June 24, 1946, and the screening of the next batch of applicants began in early August. The categories of unacceptable applicants had increased by this time from six to eight. Besides all former party members, active youth group leaders, SA and SS members, former active officers, reserve officers above the rank of first lieutenant, and children of parents arrested by the occupation authorities, the list now encompassed several new groups. These included all leaders within the former *Reichsarbeitsdienst*, or National Labor Service, the *Organisation Todt* (overseers in this forced-labor organization), and the special so-called "Speer Units" which had tried to increase war production in the last months of the war. Futhermore, all former attendees at the *Ordensburgen* (SS-run colleges), *Napolas* (*Nationalpolitische Erziehungsanstalten*, or national political schools), or *Adolf-Hitler-Schulen* were denied admission. Finally, the new list proscribed those "former members of the HJ and BDM [Hitler Youth and League of German Maidens], who have taken an active role in these organizations." Rudi Böhm, writing on behalf of the *Zentralverwaltung für Volksbildung*, admitted that the tough new standards would work hardships on many. "However," he added, "a progressive new generation is not to be had merely through the revision of curricula or the use of new educational methods. Rather, it must be achieved above all through an appropriate selection of student applicants."[81]

Although the sentiment for creating a new "democratic intelligentsia," as the December 8 guideline called it, was widely heralded, almost immediately doubts surfaced concerning the selection process. Associate Professor Else Knake, simultaneously a medical school professor and a medical researcher at one of the Dahlem institutes for biochemistry, was serving as interim dean of the medical faculty in the academic year 1946/47. She expressed concern about the composition of the admissions committees and the criteria used in selecting students. Knake composed a lengthy report on her investigations and circulated it to the medical faculty.

Each applicant had had to submit a *Fragebogen* (questionnaire), a curriculum vitae, a school-leaving certificate, and an essay analyzing a current public issue. Knake observed that she had already seen a *Fragebogen* from Würzburg University in the American Zone, and while *Fragebögen* in the American Zone were notoriously lengthy, they did not ask what the applicant's current political affiliation was. Question 24 of the Berlin *Fragebogen* asked precisely that question. To be sure, the same questionnaire assured the reader that his response was voluntary, but most applicants felt compelled to respond, Knake claimed, feeling that the answer played a role in their chances.[82] Two preliminary examiners processed the written applications. Knake also noted that the same persons served later as primary examiners and that, although they ostensibly came from the *Studentische Arbeitsgemeinschaft*, no one had elected them. Apparently a Berlin University administrator, Frau Dr. Schaumann, had asked for two representatives from the student group, and two SED members had simply appeared one day.

This stage of the application process was vital, according to Knake.

If the written application did not get beyond the preliminary examiners, it was never reviewed again for placement in the pool of applicants who would appear for an oral examination. If the applicant appeared to be caught in one of the eight negative categories, the application process ended then and there. "For example," Knake wrote, "one female student was turned down because her father was an author who, for unexplained reasons, had been arrested." Sometimes the examiners observed that the applicant had had bad grades or simply left "an all-around bad impression" in the vita. Knake did not want to imply that the decision-making by the preliminary examiners was totally arbitrary. For the most part they seemed to be conscientious in abiding by the criteria established by the *Zentralverwaltung.*[83]

Knake met eight examiners personally, at least half of whom were SED members. Knake admitted that most of the examiners tried to be impartial and professional. One exception was a young woman of twenty, a representative from the youth commission and long-time exile who demonstrated a preference for SED candidates "in such a grotesque fashion," wrote Knake, "that I protested against this repeatedly." Knake lodged a protest with Rector Stroux and Theodor Brugsch to have the young woman removed from the admissions process, but, as Knake later pointed out, the young woman came down with diphtheria, and the problem solved itself. The composition of the admissions committee did not always remain consistent. Medical professors were unavoidably absent at times because of tight schedules. Representatives from the public sector and from the professions were not always balanced by university representatives, and the student applicants were not always impressed by the student representatives on the committees, who were appointed rather than elected to the task.

Admittedly the task of screening applicants was arduous. The committees met daily from 9:00 a.m. until 5:30 p.m. with a short midday pause. The oral examination lasted about a half hour, and the committee examined approximately twenty applicants daily, a heavy schedule. Knake was appalled to see that the technical questions in the proposed field of study usually took less time than the political questions. The political questions she overheard included the following: "What do you think about land reform?" "How do you understand democracy?" "When was Bebel born?" "Who was Lassalle?" A crucial question centered around the aspiring young physician's future political deportment: He or she was asked whether or not there would be time away from the medical practice to engage in politics. "Woe to him who replied: No. I only concern myself with my patients. He was irretrievably lost," stated Knake.

Once the applicant had completed the oral examination, the examiners offered their assessments in two broad categories: political and technical. Under the political heading the descending order of desirability consisted of 1) politically valuable, 2) acceptable, 3) not politically compromised. There were three categories in which to rate the applicant's technical expertise: a) very good, b) average, c) unsatisfactory. What happened if an examinee obtained a 3a, Knake wanted to know. The applicant had the technical preparation but was politically inactive. She asked Stroux as rector, Brugsch as a senior university official and deputy to Wandel, and Frau Dr. Schaumann as overall chairman of the admissions commission to respond. Each assured her that in such a case the technical or scholarly preparation of the applicant had priority over political considerations. Schaumann cited examples of acceptances in that very same 3a category whom she had defended despite her concern about possible negative reactions from the Soviets in Karlshorst.

What happened to individuals who did not fall into the obviously desirable 1a category? Would the 2a and 3a categories follow next, or did 1b have priority? Knake emphasized that the political categories under consideration included absolutely no one with a Nazi past. They simply reflected the degree of political interest exhibited by the candidate. The question was a puzzling one, according to Knake, but "before it could be answered from the German side," she recorded, "the Russians intervened."

On September 13, 1946, one of the student examiners called Knake to tell her that the Soviets had just informed the admissions committee of the school of medicine that for the next semester only members of the four recognized political parties or members of the FDGB (Freier Deutscher Gewerkschaftsbund, or Free German Trade Union) or the FDJ (Freie Deutsche Jugend, or Free German Youth, soon to become the main SED youth group) could be admitted. The following day at a meeting of the admissions committee, Knake was present when a Soviet lieutenant colonel arrived unannounced from Karlshorst, examined the 200 successful applications, and declared immediately that in twenty cases the committee had made the wrong decision. He complained about accepting former junior reserve lieutenants, a category specifically accepted in the admissions regulations issued by the Zentralverwaltung with SMA approval. Moreover, he announced that too many women had been rejected. The Soviets, he stated, desired that more women than men should be accepted, or the same number at the very least. He also wanted the admissions personnel to understand clearly that only the politically most active applicants should be accepted. It was a telling moment.[84]

In a noticeable display of courage, Knake visited the Soviet Military Administration's cultural section for universities, where she spoke once again to the unnamed Soviet colonel and to another Soviet official, identified as Frau Dr. Gordon. The result of the tension-filled meeting was that the Soviets actually reduced the number of new openings in medicine at Berlin University from 200 to 140. Added to the 1,160 med ical students admitted the previous semester, the university would now train 1,300 physicians. However, the composition of the group was not what it should have been, according to Knake. She indicated that they were already overcrowded with beginning medical students, whereas there was plenty of space for advanced students needing clinical experience. The Soviets would not hear of it, she claimed. Of the 140 new admissions, 88 were beginning their first semester. "This shows the decided preference for the youngest semester," Knake wrote, "and we can assume that they can shape them politically most readily." This preference for first-semester medical students made no sense in a country where the immediate need for trained physicians was enormous and where the long-term demand for physicians was decidedly limited, she observed.

There was much more in the report that concerned Knake, but in essence her complaints centered on the politicization of the admissions process and the decided preference on the part of Soviet authorities for the youngest possible students. Whereas the German admissions committees had desired to admit larger numbers of young adults in their early to mid-twenties, that is, those whose studies had been interrupted by the war, the Soviets showed a clear preference for eighteen- and nineteen-year-olds. She noticed with concern that the letters of rejection to many aspiring students indicated that they failed to possess the scholarly qualifications, the necessary moral character, or the necessary political qualifications required for admission. The tone of the rejection seemed unnecessarily harsh and vague and seemed to allow no appeal. She was also appalled that a Herr Furkert on the admissions committee, a former locksmith and an SED member, had composed the letter.[85]

Some rejectees received a less harsh notice. Those who had not yet obtained their *Abitur*, having performed national service perhaps as air defense personnel, required an additional half year or a year of school. Those unfortunates were informed that they lacked the scholarly or technical background and should make it up at area *Gymnasien* or at an evening school. "This fact was used as a pretext to reject them," Knake claimed. There was a much surer method of entry, but the applicant had to know it on his or her own: "Children from worker or peasant families with only a basic schooling go for half a year to the *Vorschule* [*Vorstudienanstalt*] of the University," she reported. The attendees learned the basic subject matter and Latin at this school, which the Soviets had specifically ordered into existence. Many of the attendees were Victims of Fascism and ranged in age from 18 to 35. At the end of their intensive studies they received an oral examination partly based on politics and partly based on subject matter and were then admitted to the university. In fact, it had become common practice during the ongoing semester for students at the *Vorschule* to pursue their preuniversity studies and to attend lectures simultaneously. Knake inferred that the aca-

demic preparation for such students was not all that it should be, and
the political factor, already a concern in the regular admissions procedures, assumed even greater importance at the university *Vorschule*.[86]
Knake admitted her sense of frustration over the trend that she saw developing at Berlin University. However, there was little she felt she could
do. She had no regular access to the responsible Soviet authorities at
Karlshorst. During her tense conversation with the Soviet colonel and
with Dr. Gordon, Knake was informed that in the future she should
deal with the *Zentralverwaltung* official responsible for student affairs:
Rudi Böhm.

About the time that Else Knake was compiling her report, Rudi
Böhm was addressing a gathering of the *Studentische Arbeitsgemeinschaft*. Disturbed that the volunteer student organization had not accepted de facto SED student leadership, he made a point of announcing
that recent elections in the Soviet Zone indicated that "the will of the people" had been clearly expressed. He observed further that it was entirely possible for the will of the people to stand in opposition to the
will of the students. "The will of the people has priority!" he emphasized to the largely non-SED audience. The student listeners had had
some experience with such warnings from *Zentralverwaltung* authorities by this time, and one of those students, Otto Stolz, wrote on September 21 to his American contact, a recently arrived higher education officer for the American Military Government, Dr. Fritz Karsen, "We shall
hold our breath waiting to see how the frequently invoked will of the people will come down on the University." In fact, Stolz was worried by a
general political trend in recent weeks. "I can report that at Berlin University and at the other universities of the Zone, we must reckon with a
tougher line," he prophesied to Karsen.[87]

They did not have long to wait. Stolz had indicated to Karsen that
two important meetings were about to take place in the East Sector. The
first was a gathering of student representatives from all universities in
the Soviet Zone held on October 10. This was followed by a Berlin University gathering on October 16 to initiate the university's second semester. The theme of the second gathering was announced as "Where Do
the Students Stand Today?" Paul Wandel, Johannes Stroux, Otto Hess,
and Rudi Böhm were the listed speakers. Hess, as elected chairman of
the *Studentische Arbeitsgemeinschaft*, had to attend both gatherings,
and his experiences at each seemed to confirm Otto Stolz's prediction
of a toughening line in the Soviet Zone. For example, at the gathering
on October 10, the student representatives from the other Soviet-Zone institutions of higher learning were all SED members, and they openly
addressed Rudi Böhm as "Comrade Böhm." Hess, as an SPD loyalist,
pointedly addressed him as "Herr Böhm," and the situation proved
embarrassing for the latter. Until then, Böhm's party affiliation was not
well known. Certainly Professor Knake had been unaware of it. The rea-

son for the lack of information stemmed from the fact that the *Zentralver-*
waltung für Volksbildung and its staff had originally been planned as
part of a central German administration which was supposed to be
above party affiliations. Ostensibly, Rudi Böhm stood aside from party
strife in Berlin. However, Hess scarcely had time to enjoy Böhm's discomfort. A few days later Böhm called on Hess and asked him to pay a visit
to President Wandel. They drove to Karlshorst, where they had lunch
with the director of the *Zentralverwaltung*. It was most unusual for a
mere student to be accorded this honor, especially at a time when the
Berliners' daily ration was still hovering at starvation level. Wandel was
most civil during the meal, and Hess was mystified. The host finally
asked Hess to submit in advance a copy of his address to the Berlin students, set for the following week. They would be sharing the same plat-
form, and Wandel was interested in knowing what Berlin University's
elected student representative had to say. Hess refused outright, and to
his surprise discovered that Wandel accepted his decision without rancor. It was a draw; each would enter the meeting without knowing
what the other had to say.[88]

At the student gathering, held at the same Admiralspalast in the
East Sector where the university had reopened the previous January, the
university leadership addressed the student body on the occasion of
the new semester. It was a time for self-congratulation, since the university was now a going concern despite all the obstacles which devas-
tated Berlin continued to pose. Following a speech by Rector Stroux,
Otto Hess spoke about the activities of the *Studentische Arbeitsgemein-*
schaft. His speech was not notable for anything new, except that he
ended his talk with an appeal to the students to join the volunteer
group in greater numbers. As yet, it encompassed only twenty percent
of the student body, he said, and that was not enough. By contrast it
was Wandel who made news that evening. He announced to the students that the *Zentralverwaltung* was calling for an increase of working-
class representation in the student population.[89]

Wandel left the hall and proceeded immediately to give a press conference at which he made even more significant announcements. He informed the public that the SPD, the CDU, and the LDP had sent him
their objections concerning student admission policies for the impending winter semester. Now he wanted the public to know that he was rejecting those criticisms by the political parties plus similar complaints
in the Western press. There were appeals procedures for those who had
not been accepted, he claimed, and in fact it was the very same
Zentralverwaltung, in cooperation with the university, which was aiding the students in all ways possible. For example, a new student organization was about to be called into existence, he announced, and in the
near future the students would receive their very own news organ, a journal to be called *Forum*. Wandel observed much later that the number of

students of working-class origins admitted to Berlin University in the
first semester had been low, only four percent. As part of his party's determination to open the university to this long-neglected segment of the
population, the *Zentralverwaltung* was working with university authorities to increase the number of working-class acceptees. Despite criticisms from the west-sector press, they were determined to carry
through with this aspect of university reform. Wandel felt he had complete Soviet support for maintaining such a policy.[90]

Within a few days, Rector Stroux responded to widespread criticisms on admissions policy in a letter to the *Tagesspiegel* which attempted to address the charges and counter-charges being leveled.
Stroux, too, admitted that the wording of the rejection notices had been
unfortunate and that the composition of the admissions committees "is
a source of deep concern for us." Yet all the parties were complaining
to him that many of their young adherents had been rejected. The SED,
for example, claimed that 121 members had fallen through. The SPD
lost 45, the CDU 135, the LDP 129, the FDJ (Free German Youth) 66,
and the FDGB (trade unions) 167. While it was possible to assume from
Stroux's words that impartiality had reigned and that students from all
parties had suffered, his letter to the *Tagesspiegel* served only to increase the suspicions so evident in the Berlin press. Simultaneously,
Stroux had sent a similar article to the SED newspaper, *Neues Deutschland*, which imparted much of the same information but did it in
such a way that it appeared to be a sharp attack upon the editors
of the *Tagesspiegel*. The latter accused Stroux of duplicity and a lack
of openness. One of those editors was Edwin Redslob, an anticommunist
of deep conviction and someone who would play a significant role
in university affairs two years later.[91] Stroux, on the other hand, was
one of those well-known luminaries from German academia who, like
Theodor Brugsch, decided to support a new socialist society as envisioned by the SED. A professor of ancient languages, Stroux had proved
to be a far more cooperative rector than Spranger toward the *Zentralverwaltung*. He served simultaneously as rector and as president of the
prestigious Academy of Sciences in Berlin. Wandel was agreeably surprised that despite the rector's undisputed middle-class background
Stroux proved sympathetic to the aims of the SED authorities and
even canceled a visiting professorship at Basel University in 1948
in order to resume his work in Berlin.[92]

However, in the western press, criticism of Stroux and the university administration mounted in the autumn of 1946. The west-sector
media was showing an ever greater confrontational tone in the aftermath of the crucial city elections of October 20, when the west-oriented
political parties dislodged the SED from many of its strongholds in city
government. With respect to higher education, deep suspicions remained in the west-sector press and among large numbers of students

about the admission process which they had witnessed during preparations for the second semester at Berlin University. It was the start of a controversy that continued unabated for over two years.[93] The official SED paper, *Neues Deutschland*, felt compelled to answer the barrage of criticism. It announced that as of November 1946 there were 362 students at the *Vorstudienanstalt* of whom 225 had had no party affiliation. Only 130 were SED members, the paper claimed. However, the western critics pounced on the figures, claiming that virtually all students at the *Vorstudienanstalt*, if not SED members, belonged to an SED-affiliated youth organization.[94] The press war continued.

In reality the hardening of positions that Otto Stolz had professed to see in September 1946 was starting to crystalize. Disappointed by the resistance to SED leadership within the *Studentische Arbeitsgemeinschaft*, Wandel and the *Zentralverwaltung* had come to the conclusion that it was no longer a promising vehicle for progressive (i.e., SED-oriented) student government. Moreover, it was a volunteer organization and not, strictly speaking, a student government. With the election of Hess as the chair and with the SED favorite, Herbert Theuerkauf, running a distant third, the student volunteer group had steadily expanded in numbers and stood at 850 by the autumn of 1946. That it encompassed a fifth of the student body was testament to its vitality at a time when most Germans, including students, exhibited lethargy and wholesale aversion to joining any organization, political or otherwise. But as it grew, the percentage of SED students in its midst steadily dropped. By the autumn of 1946, the Communist contingent had become a small minority of perhaps fifteen percent. Consequently, Wandel's administration had now to accept a permanent SED minority status in the volunteer group or else take their chances with a new student government. This would be no mere association of volunteers. It would be a *Studentenrat*, a student council with officers chosen on the basis of student-wide elections. Its first polling would come in early 1947, and the expectation was that this time the SED would perform much better. Wandel's announcement of the new student journal, *Forum*, seemed a promising step for a student body starved for information and for outlets for self-expression. However, the fact that Rudi Böhm was to be the new editor-in-chief was anything but reassuring to students like Georg Wrazidlo, Otto Stolz, Otto Hess, or Joachim Schwarz.

Even as the press campaign in the western sectors mounted, the opposition parties to the SED sent a joint declaration directly to Wandel about what they felt was unacceptable bias in the admissions procedures:

> The undersigned parties are in receipt of irreproachable evidence that in the fulfillment of admission allotments for study at the Berlin University during the winter semester 1946-47, the choice of applicants was made on the

basis of partisan political considerations. Furthermore, it is now known that decisions by the examining committee for admissions to the University have been altered by members of the *Zentralverwaltung für Volksbildung.*

To correct this situation, the three parties demanded the creation of an examining board whose membership would be drawn up by equal numbers of representatives from the four "antifacist" parties (i.e., the three western parties and the SED). The panel would examine all the evidence and be empowered to redress any shortcomings. "We remain hopeful, Herr President," they concluded, "that you will view this demand as justified and that you will support it in order to secure the democratic character of Berlin University."[95]

Wandel tried gamely to derail the rising tide of protest. He explained at his October press conference that the student admissions policy represented the *Zentralverwaltung's* desire to support working-class representation at the university. As for the offensively worded rejection form, which, among other allegations, suggested that the applicant did not possess the necessary moral qualities for admission, Wandel distanced himself and his administration from it, claiming that they had had no hand in its preparation and admitting that its wording was unfortunate. Although he did not mention it, it was a fact that American Military Government rejection notices being issued at the same time carried a similar wording and had raised identical cries of outrage from students in the American Zone. For better or for worse, the Americans had not distanced themselves from their form. Wandel in doing so admitted to a mistake. The *Zentralverwaltung für Volksbildung* now found itself caught between an inept admissions board announcement on the one hand and the heavy-fisted Soviet colonel at the Soviet Military Administration on the other. Yet, the fact remained that Paul Wandel was the senior German education official present. He became the target of an aroused west-sector press.

"The revelations concerning the admissions committee do not demonstrate mere incompetence," the *Tagesspiegel* thundered, "they demonstrate a deliberate dictatorial act!"[96] In the course of the autumn of 1946, a veritable flood of articles and criticisms appeared in the press of the western sectors, attacking the *Zentralverwaltung* on the issue of admission policies. Wandel and the Soviet-licensed press fought back, defending their efforts to encourage working-class students and denying any wrongdoing. In essence, the two sides spoke past each other, and the conflict simply continued. The *Tagesspiegel*, which spearheaded the press attacks, carried a biting commentary on October 18 under the bold headline "Farewell to Berlin University" and concluded: "It is now a party [affiliated] university. We are striking it off the cultural list for Germany."[97]

Thereafter, a steady drumbeat of criticism emanated from the west-sector press which continued throughout the autumn of 1946. One reason for the stubbornness with which the critics of Wandel and his university policy pursued him was because of the stunning political victory which the SPD, CDU, and LDP had wrested from the SED in the first city-wide elections held after the war, on October 20, 1946. The political composition of the Magistrat changed overnight, and the iron grip which the Soviet-appointed officials had held on so many aspects of city administration was broken.

The implications from this political victory with respect to control of the university dawned quickly on some. Since the summer of 1946 at least, some of the students had been maintaining contact with the Western occupation authorities despite their initial disappointment over seeming Western indifference to university affairs. The American Military Government had achieved greater maturity in 1946, and in June of that year a notable personality arrived in Berlin to work for the Americans. Now an American citizen, Dr. Fritz Karsen returned to his native Berlin to serve as a higher education officer in Military Government's Education and Religious Affairs Branch. Karsen had made a considerable name for himself in the 1920s as an educational reformer among the Social Democrats. He had formed an experimental college-preparatory school for working-class children in Neukölln, the highly regarded Kaiser Wilhelm Gymnasium (which was renamed the Karl Marx Schule for a brief time at the end of the Weimar Republic). It was all for naught. After coming to power, the Nazis seized the school immediately, and Karsen barely escaped abroad on the night the Reichstag burned down, in February 1933. Although American Military Government did not normally employ German emigrants in positions of responsibility, John W. Taylor, the education chief, accepted Karsen's services immediately. He had taught under Karsen for a year at the Kaiser Wilhelm Gymnasium in the early 1930s, and with Karsen now an American citizen, Taylor could sweep the technical difficulties aside.[98]

Immediately Karsen established contacts with Berlin students and sent three of them, Otto Stolz, Herbert Theuerkauf, and Otto Hess, to an international student conference at Marburg in the summer of 1946. Theuerkauf, an SED loyalist, offered strong public criticism of what he felt were renascent militarist and reactionary tendencies among students at the Marburg conference, and Stolz was not above directing Karsen's attention to Theuerkauf's commentary. Stolz also made a point of publicly rebutting Theuerkauf's criticisms to the press. He claimed instead that the Marburg conference had proceeded in a solidly democratic and peace-loving fashion and that Theuerkauf had missed the entire point. Stolz had decided to keep Karsen fully informed on events as they unfolded at Berlin University.[99] Contacts with other Americans quickly followed. One of the striking facts that emerge from the historical record for the fall of 1946 was the tendency of key students like Stolz, Hess, Wrazidlo, and others to turn first toward Karsen and then, in short order, to other Americans in Berlin.[100]

Simultaneously, other students began to unburden themselves to the Americans concerning their experiences while seeking admission to Berlin University. A young law student, Martin Meyer, wrote to the Education Branch at the American headquarters in early November to complain of the prejudice he felt he had encountered. Son of a poor Pomeranian family, he claimed to have received state educational support in the Third Reich only after joining the Hitler Youth, a fact that might now prejudice his entry to the university. Later, he had served in the Wehrmacht in Italy, and as a signal corpsman had had access to Allied broadcasts, the contents of which he promptly forwarded to other anti-Nazis. He even helped conceal the whereabouts of American and English troops caught behind German lines in Italy. Following his release from a British POW camp, where he had taken correspondence courses in law, Meyer came to Berlin and sought entry to the Berlin University law school. His oral examination lasted only twenty minutes, half of which was devoted to politics, he claimed. Meyer had left the fateful Question 24 about party affiliation open and when asked if he had done that on purpose answered: "I belong to no party." He expected a quick decision, but no answer arrived. After repeated enquiries, Meyer finally learned that he had received a 2a for his efforts (politically acceptable with high scholarly attainment) and had been turned down. In the meantime a letter arrived from the Italian Communist Party attesting to his activities during the war. Armed with this proof, Meyer approached the student section of the *Zentralverwaltung*, which immediately took a new interest in his case. His prospects were improving, the officials noted, but he had first to join the SED. After considerable hesitation, Meyer finally joined the party. Thereupon a law expert on the admissions board and Rudi Böhm set the wheels in motion, and within a short time Martin Meyer had become the newest law student at Berlin University. He was also now a member of the SED. On November 2, he wrote to the Americans: "Because I could no longer square my conscience with membership in the SED, I have in the meantime resigned from it despite the consequences that this may have for me." He was writing to the Americans, he said, because he hoped that his case would further the students' demand "to remove their University from the control of the *Zentralverwaltung* . . . and to place it under the Magistrat, i.e. under four-power control."[101]

Others were beginning to voice similar sentiments in public. In a letter to the *Tagesspiegel* the following day, a student, Ingeborg Adam, reiterated an old theme—the demand for a change to four-power control of the university. She felt the newspaper was being premature in striking Berlin University from Germany's list of cultural institutions. "Don't write us off," she pleaded. "Help us instead! Work with us so that the university will come under the new Magistrat. That appears to me to be the better way."[102]

One unsuccessful law student chose an enterprising means of "telegraphing" his and his friends' discontent concerning admissions policies: "We believe the *Telegraf* can forward this proposal to the proper Allied authorities," he wrote to that British-Sector newspaper. The anonymous author claimed that the law faculty was being deliberately choked off and that claims about shortages of seats to the contrary, the *Zentralverwaltung* could easily increase enrollments in the law school. "At this same moment courses are in operation for the training of several hundred peoples' judges," the reader claimed. Like the young woman who wanted Magistrat control for the university, he too had a concrete solution to the problem: "Many other students and I propose that several schools [at Berlin University] be joined to the Technical University."[103]

The editors of the youth journal *Horizont* published a series of student comments concerning admissions policies and posed several courses of action for its largely student readership, based, they claimed, on interviews with large numbers of students and student applicants. The first was the most important: "Placement of Humboldt University under the Magistrat of the City of Berlin; furthermore, the creation of a fifth sector in Berlin which would offer by far the happiest solution to the problem." There were other points, too, such as a call for immediate elections for a fully representative student government, greater freedom to create other scholarly organizations, and an overhaul of the admissions committee to prevent future abuses. However, the unmistakable conclusion that the editors drew was that jurisdiction over the university should revert from the *Zentralverwaltung für Volksbildung* to the newly invigorated Magistrat.[104]

Other students, taking a lead from the *Horizont*, decided on a bold move of their own. Georg Wrazidlo had long shown a willingness to act decisively. Even before Wandel's revelation that the *Zentralverwaltung* was to support the new student journal *Forum*, Wrazidlo and Hess came to the conclusion that the students should create their own independent journal.[105] In postwar Berlin such an enterprise was no easy undertaking. The journal would require licensing by one of the occupation authorities. The Soviets obviously would not approve of it. It turned out that a number of the student leaders, including Wrazidlo, Hess, Stolz, and the former White Rose resister, Joachim Schwarz, were all living in the American Sector of Berlin. Recently, their relations with the American education staff had taken a turn for the better, and they enquired how they might form their own American-licensed journal. The correct authority, as it turned out, was not the education staff but American Military Government's Information Control Division (ICD). The responsible licensing officer at ICD was Frederick Bleistein, a German exile who was now serving the Americans as an expert on the press situation in Berlin. Students Schwarz and Hess approached him in December 1946 and proposed that they publish their journal in the American-licensed publishing house, *Horizont*. Fred Bleistein was sympathetic but he advised the students against such a move. If the as yet inexperienced young publicists should run afoul of the myriad publishing regulations, it might force the American authorities to close down not only their own journal but also the entire *Horizont* concern. It would be much better, the press officer counseled, if they formed their own press for their future student journal.[106]

The chief criteria for obtaining one of the scarce publishing licenses after the war were two: the applicant must demonstrate the proper political credentials, and the applicant should have had considerable publishing experience. Given the tight controls that Goebbels had imposed on all media during the Third Reich, there were surprisingly few Germans after the war who could satisfy both requirements. The first hurdle was most easily solved for the students. Hess and Schwarz, who became the two official applicants, could both demonstrate their Victims of Fascism credentials without difficulty. The question was whether or not they could convince the Americans that they could publish successfully. It was at this point that the talents of students like Otto Hess, Joachim Schwarz, and Otto Stolz bore fruit.[107]

Otto Hess had been an active contributor to newspapers and journals, and even occasionally on radio after the war. He had written early pieces on students and socialism, on Berlin politics under four-power control, and a critical article on the sudden trendiness in studying medicine. Hess had also detailed the evolution of the *Studentische Arbeitsgemeinschaft*, including its difficulties with SED authorities, for the Berlin reading public and in the West German universities. Finally, he was a contributor to the prestigious journal *Das Sozialistische Jahrhundert* (The Socialist Century), so that the American licensing officials had little difficulty concluding that Hess was a worthy candidate.[108]

Joachim Schwarz, too, could exhibit respectable journalistic attainments in the postwar Berlin press. He had written regularly for the *Tagesspiegel*, publishing extensive articles not only on university matters but on world affairs in general. Schwarz was well known to the Berlin public and, just as importantly, to Press Officer Bleistein.[109]

Otto Stolz, although not one of the licensees, was associated with that group and was known already to the Berlin reading public as a familiar journalist. He was fiery, probably the most aggressive opponent of the SED elements at Berlin University among all the Berlin students. By outward appearances, he seemed an unlikely leader of a growing resistance faction in the student body. Polio had crippled him in infancy, but Stolz overcame physical infirmity with his great zeal and determination. From earliest youth a committed Social Democrat until the Nazis disbanded his party in 1933, Stolz immediately found himself permanently at odds with the Third Reich. Forced into silence for twelve years, he was delighted to take up his party's cause once again in 1945. A talented speaker and writer, he immediately found his métier in the world of journalism after the war. As a proved anti-Nazi, Stolz was admitted to the philosophical faculty, where he studied journalism. In reality, he was such an active figure in SPD politics and such a frequent contributor to newspapers and journals that even his friends admitted that Stolz was for long periods a student in name only.[110] He published prolifically in Social Democratic organs, in daily newspapers, and in the youth journal *Horizont*.

After the usual bureaucratic delays, in March 1947 the students Hess and Schwarz received their license to publish, and the first issue of their journal, *Colloquium*, appeared at the beginning of May. Entirely the product of student initiative, *Colloquium* proved popular immediately and sold out its first edition within two days. Even more important was the fact that the growing band of dissident students now had an independent news organ around which they could focus their efforts and through which they could provide information to large numbers of fellow students. Small and decidedly modest in format, it nevertheless gave the appearance of being independent. It took no particular political direction. Co-editor Schwarz was a CDU member, whereas Stolz and . . . Hess were SPD supporters. Besides, students and academics from all the west-sector parties became frequent contributors, adding to its broad appeal. Without the appearance of *Colloquium*, events at Berlin University would, in all probability, have turned out differently than they did. The decision to approach the Americans and found such a journal, made by a handful of students in the autumn of 1946, proved to be of great significance in the months to come.

A second development that later assumed greater importance than seemed apparent at the time was the decision by leading personalities in the *Studentische Arbeitsgemeinschaft* to stand for election in the new *Studentenrat*. In a summary of the *Studentische Arbeitsgemeinschaft's* activities, Otto Hess recounted the considerable accomplishments of that all-volunteer body. It was an institution that had grown out of initial student discussions in the summer and fall of 1945 and had experienced a modest beginning. Originally, subgroups had formed up within each faculty (school) for purposes of political discussion. Its original purpose had been to enlighten students of the dangers of fascism and militarism. But soon the subgroups began to specialize, depending upon the personalities and interests of the group. These smaller units stabilized at a membership of twenty to thirty members each, and the practice quickly developed of electing group leaders. These elected leaders assembled in a kind of informal executive committee. The executive then elected individuals from the student body to serve as experts or consultants in examining various problems. Some concentrated on organizational needs, others on politics, cultural affairs, the press, and so on. The group leaders, experts/consultants, and the chairman, who was elected by secret vote of the entire volunteer body, formed what amounted to the executive council of the *Studentische Arbeitsgemeinschaft*, and it was in this body that the larger issues were weighed and decided by vote. The students of Berlin had performed well in establishing almost spontaneously a highly democratic form of de facto self-government.[111]

They continued their original task of organizing talks and discussions, but the groups quickly added other practical activities as well. They succeeded in erecting a student *Mensa* (dining hall) and a medical and public health service. They formed up construction gangs, procured food and social services for the neediest (they were all needy), provided access to libraries and other learning resources, and even sponsored social balls and other such activities. Given the deprivations of war and the disruptions in their social lives, this last activity assumed importance. Because of their dire poverty and their craving for cultural exposure after so many years of islolation, the student volunteers negotiated with Berlin's cultural institutions to obtain reduced prices for theater, opera, and concerts. They also represented the students to city and occupation authorities on dozens of necessary issues such as ration cards, residence permits, and reduced fares on public conveyances. On their own initiative, the students organized a university-wide lecture series dealing with public and moral issues of the day such as school reform, the state of religion, and, of course, current politics. Academicians, theater directors, philosophers, theologians, and others addressed them. Interesting though such formal presentations might be, the followup discussions often proved even livelier, with everyone joining the fray. For almost all participants such discourses were a powerful tonic after twelve years of Nazi *Führerprinzip*. To their credit, Soviet officials, too, contributed successfully to the lecture series, analyzing current issues and problems in the Soviet Union, portraying principles of Marxism, and presenting materialist philosophy. "Discussions often grew downright stormy," Hess commented, "especially at times when Communist thoughts were uttered, since 95 percent of the student body disagreed with them." Even two generations later, the surviving members of the *Studentische Arbeitsgemeinschaft* still remembered their experiences in their first postwar student organization fondly.[112]

As an experiment in democratic living and democratic decision-making, the *Studentische Arbeitsgemeinschaft* proved to be a huge success. But what was to be its future? The impending *Studentenrat* would presumably take over the functions which the earlier group had arrogated to itself. "Whether or not the *Studentische Arbeitsgemeinschaft* will continue to exist after the elections . . . is uncertain," Hess stated in December 1946. "As far as the SED is concerned, it will be made superfluous." Hess countered by saying that the large noncommunist majority in the volunteer group now felt they had a "political mission" to fulfill, one which could not be met by an unpolitical student government. The large majority of students, having developed a taste for self-government, would accept the demise of their volunteer organization only when they were free to create other political and social organizations of their own. "The most active political forces in the student body have assembled in the *Studentische Arbeitsgemeinschaft*," Hess concluded, "and they will never voluntarily refrain from continuing the work necessary to achieve freedom and democracy."[113]

Forty years later, such words may sound rhetorical to many. In fact, the students were perfectly serious. A large number of the student volunteers and especially their leaders were officially recognized Victims of Fascism, and in organizing their own form of student government they experienced a wave of euphoria after the many years of Nazi regimentation. Confronted by what appeared to them to be a mounting threat to their accomplishments, Otto Hess and the other leaders in the *Studentische Arbeitsgemeinschaft* decided not to let matters drift. If university authorities were going to proceed with the creation of a new student body, then the volunteer students would participate in that forum too. Individual candidates from the *Studentische Arbeitsgemeinschaft* decided to enter the elections despite growing evidence that SED authorities expected a more compliant successor to the volunteer student association. But before the election campaign got under way, several of the student candidates decided to pay a call on the Soviet authorities to exchange points of view.

Signs of growing impatience on the part of the Soviet Military Administration with respect to the non-SED students had begun to mount during the autumn. On December 12, 1946, the leadership of the *Studentische Arbeitsgemeinschaft*, including Georg Wrazidlo, Herbert Theuerkauf, and Otto Hess, visited Professor (serving in the rank of lieutenant general in the occupation army) Pyotr Solotuchin in Karlshorst to discuss recent trends and in the hope of easing hard feelings. However, in the course of the meeting the aroused Soviet official criticized what he felt was unreasonable opposition to the authorities' efforts to create a democratic university. The minutes of the meeting record Solotuchin as saying:

Berlin University must become the best university in Germany in every respect including scholarly achievement and democratization of the University. It must achieve this because it is in Berlin and because Berlin, despite its ruins, was the capital and will remain so. Berlin continues to be the political and spiritual center of Germany because, despite any decentralizing tendencies, Germany will remain united. The leader of our state stated during the war: "The Hitlers come and go, but the German people remain forever." Think about that.

The thrust of Solotuchin's argument was that any attempt to subordinate Berlin University to the Magistrat was to demean it, to turn it into a city institution when in fact it was intended to be a university for all of Germany. The students above all must reject such proposals, Solotuchin maintained. By democratization the Soviets meant the opening of the university's doors to sons and daughters of the working classes in all ways, not just through special preparatory courses. The new student government—as opposed to the *Studentische Arbeitsgemeinschaft*—would have the solemn obligation of continuing that democratization process.

Solotuchin posed a blunt question to the students. Why had they been so passive with regard to attacks upon the university? He hinted broadly that there were dangerous forces behind the many articles appearing in the Berlin press, and Germany had seen quite enough of such worthless elements during the twelve years of Hitler's rule. "I ask myself how it is possible for the students to accept this so calmly?" Solotuchin queried. "I have gone over all of this with Herr Hess last week and do not wish to repeat it now." It would have taken an unusually insensitive student at that moment not to have made the connection between Soviet and SED claims of fascist and militarist elements attacking the university and a strangely lethargic student body that did nothing about it. Solotuchin continued with a long list of what he felt were scurrilous charges by the *Tagesspiegel*, the *Telegraf*, and the *Kurier* against the university and asked once again why the students had remained silent. Their behavior was inexplicable at a time when the British and Americans had seized control of no less than fourteen institutes of the university in their sectors. Yet, no student had protested.

Tentatively several of the students, including Georg Wrazidlo, tried to answer Solotuchin's charges. They claimed that the *Zentralverwaltung für Volksbildung*, rather than the university as such, was the focus of the press attacks. Moreover, many of them, as members of the CDU, the SPD, or the LDP (i.e., as members of officially recognized antifascist parties), would be speaking directly against their own political leadership if they followed Solotuchin's advice. All three parties had declared themselves in open opposition to President Wandel's policies. But Solotuchin was not convinced. "You say you cannot speak against your own parties? But those are unworthy people, and you must always speak out against such elements. They must be exposed. You should support the reputation of your University, which is in the interest of the German People. That goal must become the mission of the student government." With that statement the meeting ended. It seemed doubtful whether any hard feelings had been assuaged on either side. In fact, the Soviet official's charge of renascent fascism and militarism in Berlin was a hint of more drastic measures to come, although the students in attendance that day could not know that.[114]

The elections for the new *Studentenrat* were scheduled for February 6, 1947, but one week earlier Wandel issued an announcement to the students. The elections were proceeding on the basis of a new student statute, he reminded them, as approved by the Soviet authorities. One of the most cherished goals contained therein was the improvement of the social status of the student body as well as an improvement in its technical skills. More pertinent to the impending election was a new restriction placed upon the students. "The student body is not empowered to make decisions of a general nature as, for example, with respect to the administrative jurisdiction of the University or concerning the legitimacy of the statutes. Therefore, discussions concerning such matters expressly exceed the authority of the student body." Furthermore, no candidate who questioned the authority of the university or of the statutes could be found acceptable to hold office, because he would have forgone "any mutually trustworthy cooperation with the leadership of the university or with its administration." To make himself even clearer, Wandel concluded by stating that any member of the university found to be "endangering the fundamental premises and undertakings of the University, must expect to receive disciplinary action."[115] Since the statute which had been negotiated between representatives of the *Studentische Arbeitsgemeinschaft* and Professor Solotuchin had been deliberately phrased as a provisional statute, many students became incensed now that they were not to question it further. The announcement, if enforced, would seriously impair future discussions concerning the running of the university. Another point that rankled was that the new student government would be placed directly under the authority of the rector, and at that moment Rector Johannes Stroux was growing increasingly unpopular with student dissidents because of his refusal to confront the *Zentralverwaltung* on any of the serious issues troubling the university.

Wandel's announcement sent a shock throughout the student body. Soon the west-sector press obtained copies and published it, denouncing Wandel's move as a muzzling ordinance and an attempt at influencing the elections.[116] Just three days before the elections, handbills appeared at several spots around the university accusing the *Zentralverwaltung* of destroying academic freedom at the institution and urging students to boycott the elections.[117] Obviously Wandel's warning had had a galvanizing effect on some. But if its intention had been to warn off potential resisters, it failed. When, for example, Rector Stroux invoked a section of Wandel's order denying two medical students the right to be candidates, two other students came forward at once to take their place.

On the other hand, anonymous calls for a boycott—an ill considered move—failed too. Most students proceeded to vote in the elections for the new *Studentenrat*.[118] When the results were finally tabulated, the nonaligned students had gained a large majority. They promptly chose a political independent, Gerhard Petermann, from among their number as chairman of the new *Studentenrat*. Just as significant was the fact that they decided to raise Otto Hess, former chairman of the *Studentische Arbeitsgemeinschaft*, to became his deputy. In fact, not one of the leading officers in the newly elected body belonged to the SED. Simultaneous elections among the faculty for a comparable representative body had not produced any SED representation either. Most embarrassing of all was the fact that of twenty-eight student council seats being contested, only three went to the Communists, and two of those were from the overwhelmingly SED-oriented school of education.[119] British observers noted that the candidates had stood for elections without declaring formal party affiliations. However, they saw it as "clearly a battle between SED and non-SED factions and consequently very bitter."[120]

The tensions surrounding the February 6 election and the results of that election served to escalate the growing conflict between student dissidents and the *Zentralverwaltung*. One of the "casualties" of the conflict—because soon there would be several—was Else Knake. On the day the elections took place, a lengthy interview with Knake appeared in the *Tagesspiegel*, the very paper that was leading the tide of press criticism. She explained why the students were upset about Wandel's official notice, appearing as it did on the eve of the election. In fact, she had informed the students in a heated discussion about the new governing statute for students (the discussion itself was technically a violation of Wandel's notice) that it was simply a given fact that the student government would serve under the authority of the rector. "Although the students listen to me a great deal," Knake stated, "in this instance I remained isolated in my opinion." It then transpired that Knake had publicly congratulated the medical students for their lively discussions and their determination to think and speak freely. In consequence, Rector Stroux decided to initiate disciplinary proceedings against Knake. The appearance of her interview in the very press organ leading the attack was even further provocation. He dismissed Knake as dean of the medical school.[121] "She showed more courage than all of the men combined," was how one of her former students, Helmut Coper, described her many years later.[122] Knake continued to teach at Berlin University, although her central activities focused at the Dahlem research institutes in the American Sector.

If East-Zone authorities like Solotuchin and Wandel assumed that the university was now the target of a press campaign, they were substantially correct. One of the licensees for the *Tagesspiegel* and a bitter

critic of developments at the university was Edwin Redslob, an art historian and well-known Berlin personality. On the eve of the student elections, he aired his views on the situation privately to another interested
observer, ex-rector Eduard Spranger, who was now living in Tübingen.
"We miss you here greatly," Redslob wrote. "And yet, I think back frequently about how right it was for you to have exposed the leadership
of Berlin University through your departure. Our newspaper is methodi-
cally driving home the point that administration of the University must
revert once again to the Magistrat. At that time [1945] the city representatives reneged on their rights and responsibilities towards the University
in an irresponsible manner. These occurrences are now gradually coming to light and are being subjected to criticism."[123] Pyotr Solotuchin's suspicions of a continuous press attack were well founded. There were indeed powerful critics of Soviet-SED policy in Berlin. To be sure, it was
quite another matter as to whether they were fascist or militarist elements as Solotuchin assumed.

Else Knake's dismissal as dean also marked a new milestone in the
widening conflict over the university. "It is perfectly plain that this matter establishes a precedent," commented the Telegraf, "one which
bodes ill for the right of freedom of expression."[124] An unrelated incident seemed to confirm such suspicions. Prior to the elections, the
Studentische Arbeitsgemeinschaft had organized a series of addresses
to the students by leaders of all four parties in Berlin. The first speaker,
a Dr. Külz of the LDP (liberal party), had already spoken in early February. However, when the second scheduled speaker, Franz Neumann of
the SPD, was about to speak on February 8, Rector Stroux informed him
that an address would not be possible. After some confusion, it transpired that the Studentische Arbeitsgemeinschaft was now expected to
secure permission from the Zentralverwaltung first, a requirement unknown to them until that moment. Neumann was not allowed to speak
to the students.[125] Several weeks later the Zentralverwaltung dissolved
the volunteer organization completely, explaining that the Studentenrat
exercized all the necessary functions that the students required at the university.[126] Otto Hess had been quite right in expressing doubt about the
survival of the Studentische Arbeitsgemeinschaft.

Thus, in numerous ways, the growing antagonisms became manifest. As early as January 1946, Rector Stroux in an interview with the
west-sector press had declared that the students must once again become accustomed to "precise, concentrated, objective work" and indicated that as a consequence, their curriculum would be much more
tightly regulated than heretofore. To avoid the danger of the university's
falling to the level of a technical or trade school, Stroux announced, the
university planned to introduce obligatory lectures of a universal nature.[127] By March 1947, the irritations began to focus upon those obligatory lectures, intended to give the students the kind of broad liberal

arts exposure that strengthened the democratic spirit. Some, but by no means all, of the students felt the obligatory lectures represented an effort at indoctrinating them in the tenets of Marxism-Leninism. The *Zentralverwaltung* denied that intent and refused to give in, claiming that such exposure was necessary to prevent the resurgence of militarism and fascism. Once again, both sides spoke past each other, and the issue remained unresolved. There were wide discrepancies in the students' reactions to such enforced lectures, and individual schools within the university had widely varied experiences with the new program. The medical students, especially, found such lectures onerous. Medical student Stanislaw Kubicki recalled that Robert Havemann was especially well known for his unabashed efforts to present the students with the basics of Marxism-Leninism, a source of much irritation to a majority of the young clinicians.[128] Others took the obligatory lectures more lightly. Eva Heilmann, a young chemistry student, recalled that in the school of natural sciences and mathematics, at least, such required lectures bordered on farce. During lectures following the midday meal, one kindly, aging instructor tried to introduce them to the Russian language, but his proclivity for probing into the Indo-Germanic roots of any given word mystified many and produced a notable torpor among the rest.[129] Other students did their best to evade the lectures. Horst Rögner-Franke, a student of dentistry, had been a discussion leader in the *Studentische Arbeitsgemeinschaft* and remained influential with his fellow students. He found various ingenious ways not to attend the obligatory lectures, one of which was to induce even more plaster to fall into the already dilapidated lecture hall. Then, he or fellow students would raise the alarm about its imminent collapse and cause the lecture to be canceled. Few of the dental students attended the obligatory lectures.[130] However, the noose began to tighten during the winter semester 1947/48, when the authorities announced their intent to enforce attendance more rigidly.[131] In fairness to Wandel and the university authorities, it should be noted that *studium generale* (general studies) had been universally proposed in all zones of occupied Germany after the war. In almost all instances where such programs were erected, they aroused student discontent. (Years later at the Free University, similar efforts to raise political and social consciousness provoked widespread discontent.) In 1947 and 1948 at the University Unter den Linden the issue became ideologically charged and served as one more bone of contention between SED authorities and the rapidly emerging dissident element among the students.

While it was possible for many students to treat the required lectures lightly, they might well have taken more careful notice of an article that appeared at the end of February in the student journal, *Forum*. A law student, identified only by the initials "G. L.," described the recent elections held in the universities of the Soviet Zone, but concentrated on Berlin University. The author explained to the student readership that the *Zentralverwaltung für Volksbildung* had released its announcement just before the election because of the appearance of student candidates, especially in the medical school, who had demonstrated "pro-Nazi and pro-militaristic trains of thought." Furthermore, he claimed that medical students had actually applauded such sentiments during election meetings, a development which the *Zentralverwaltung* simply could not accept. "Given the reactionary behavior of individual students during electoral meetings," the author wrote, "a number of SPD-oriented students, members of all four parties, and progressively oriented students from the medical faculty, signed a resolution and presented it to the Rector [Stroux] . . . . That resolution states that events arising in connection with the election campaign have demonstrated that parts of the student body of Berlin are supporters of fascist, reactionary, and militaristic trends." If earlier Professor Solotuchin had professed to see these dangerous elements as directing press attacks against Berlin University, *Forum*, a semiofficial journal published under the auspices of the *Zentralverwaltung*, was announcing that those elements were now to be found within the university itself.[132] One young medical student, Stanislaw Kubicki, had also heard occasional remarks of a nationalistic nature from individual students. He and a few other students formed a small group to counter such tendencies, but it found few targets and amidst internal bickering soon dissolved itself.[133] No matter how weak or conflicting the evidence, the announcement in *Forum* was an ominous portent of things to come.

Although no one knew specifically what the article signified, in retrospect it proved to be a final warning that Soviet and SED patience with the dissident students, especially those in the medical school, had come to an end. In a kind of calm before the storm, the medical faculty sent a letter on March 4 to Johannes Stroux demanding that he drop his disciplinary proceedings against Else Knake. Stroux did so, but he refused to reinstate her as dean.[134] The faculty appeared to be showing greater independence of action for the first time since the university's reopening. But if their action was intended to send a message to the *Zentralverwaltung* to distance itself from the affairs of the university, it failed.

On March 13, 1947, Georg Wrazidlo took a brief pause from his medical studies and with black bag in hand hurried to meet an acquaintance who had invited him to Berlin's largest coffee house, the Cafe Kranzler, located at that time on Unter den Linden in the Soviet Sector.[135] Their pleasant repast was rudely interrupted when Soviet plainclothesmen suddenly closed in and hustled Wrazidlo off to jail in the East Sector. Wrazidlo's arrest was not an isolated incident. At almost the same time, another student, Gerda Rösch, received an invitation from a fellow student to see a play at the Kammerspiel Theater. She too was seized and carried off to a Soviet prison, leaving her fellow students to ponder the reality that student informers were in their midst. Manfred Klein, a student representative on the newly elected *Studentenrat* and a leading figure in the FDJ (Free German Youth), suffered the same fate. Six students disappeared in this fashion in March 1947. Despite pleas by friends and relatives for their release, or, at the very least, for information about them, Soviet authorities refused for a considerable time even to discuss the arrests. This latter-day Night and Fog was a chilling reminder that totalitarian practices in Germany were not necessarily a thing of the past. Finally, someone found a common thread in the disappearances: all of those arrested had been members of the CDU or its youth affiliate, the *Junge Union*.[136] A secret State Department report on developments in the Soviet Zone theorized that the Soviets were suspicious of students by March 1947: "Most of the students had been attending a young people's congress in the American Zone and thereby apparently incurred the suspicion of the SMA that they were conducting espionage on behalf of the American authorities."[137] Whether motivated by a misunderstanding or by the desire to act decisively, this Soviet move, more than the biased admissions procedures, more than the strife surrounding obligatory lectures, more than the influencing of elections to student government, raised the conflict to crisis proportions and led eventually to a split in the University Unter den Linden.

"I paid a call on Professor Solotuchin in Karlshorst," Otto Hess later recalled, "and pled with him for two hours to release Wrazidlo." Along with Hess, *Studentenrat* Chairman Gerhard Petermann and a deputation of students attended the meeting and added to the heated exchange. The Soviet officials were not to be moved. Besides the blanket charges of militarist and fascist activities, the Soviets accused Wrazidlo of having dangerous drugs in his possession, Hess and Petermann recalled. The Soviets cited as evidence the contents in Wrazidlo's black medical bag. No drug allegations or any other crimes had arisen with respect to Wrazidlo before. Hess reminded the Soviets that medical students carrying medical bags with medical supplies should hardly be considered as perpetrators of sinister activities. It was a brave effort by two medical students to intercede directly with the Soviets on behalf of another. But it did little good. In secret session a Soviet court found Wrazidlo, Rösch, Klein, and several other students guilty of "covert fascist activities" (they quietly dropped the unlikely drug charge), and the students received lengthy prison sentences lasting anywhere from ten to twenty-five years.[138]

For the second time in his young career Georg Wrazidlo, survivor of the horrors of Buchenwald under the Nazis, found himself in a camp. This time it was Sachsenhausen, and he remained there until the authorities erected a new detention center elsewhere. He did not emerge from captivity again until October 1956, at the age of forty. The other arrestees suffered a similar fate.[139] The harsh reality of what happened might well have daunted the rest of the students, because by this time the Soviets and their SED allies had shown that they were deadly serious. In most instances such methods of intimidation would have worked. Yet the remarkable fact was that those students who avoided the arrests and disappearances continued and in fact increased their resistance to what they felt was a new tyranny from the Left. Many years later, in explaining this emotional reaction, one of their number, Helmut Coper, stated: "Many of us had become inured to the brutalizing effects of Nazi rule. After all, when you depart for the work camps [as forced labor with the *Organisation Todt*] with 256 men and only 106 return, then the disappearance of a few students is pretty small change."[140] Put in its proper context, the arrest and disappearance of students in March 1947 was part of a larger Soviet pattern that had developed since the end of the war. Seizures of individual Germans by plainclothesmen in all four sectors had been a common occurrence, and while most knew that Soviet security police, then called the NKVD, were behind such actions, it was almost impossible to pinpoint responsibility. In mid-1946, for example, no fewer than five municipal judges had disappeared, and the remaining judiciary lived in great fear thereafter. There was even an exodus of judges from the Soviet Sector for a time by those seeking to avoid a similar fate.[141] The arrest or disappearance of students could reasonably be expected to bring about the same result: the surviving dissident students would learn their lesson and would either submit to the authorities of the Soviet Zone or depart for a safer existence in the west.

Thus it was more than a little daring, following the arrests, for Otto Stolz to reassert in the *Tagesspiegel*—the very target of Soviet-SED wrath—that Berlin University's problems stemmed from the fact that the university stood directly under the control of the *Zentralverwaltung für Volksbildung*. "It is the one university in the Eastern Zone that comes under the exclusive authority, administration, and 'guidance' of the *Zentralverwaltung für Volksbildung* . . . ," Stolz wrote. Elsewhere cultural ministries, which were controlled, theoretically at least, by some kind of elected provincial assembly, administered the affairs of other universities such as at Jena and Leipzig. "But the *Zentralverwaltung* is a rocher de bronce," Stolz commented. "Immutable, it lets the waves of the otherwise frequently invoked will-of-the-people crash around it." If it had wished to display any democratic tendencies at all, Wandel's administration should have drawn the necessary consequences from the recent elections, he claimed. Yet nothing of the sort had occurred, and the Berlin students lived under the arbitrary rules of the *Zentralverwaltung*. For example, a youth-amnesty law passed by the Berlin City Council apparently did not apply to the students. The *Zentralverwaltung* simply ignored it with respect to the university. "Today, the student in

Berlin is the only German who does not enjoy the possibility of invoking the aid of a parliamentary body in his defense," Stolz continued. "There can be no doubt that he should have this protection and that this No-Man's-Land in Berlin should be put aside."[142] To those familiar with the university conflict, it was becoming increasingly obvious by now that no resolution to the crisis could occur even if the dissident students could enlist Berlin public opinion in their cause. They would need to find more potent allies if any change in their condition were to occur.

Outwardly, a period of calm settled over the university. Press attention subsided for the time being, and the pinpricks administered by students like Otto Stolz had no discernible effect upon the Soviets or on SED authorities. Sporadic arrests or disappearances occurred occasionally, and the students continued to charge that there were informers in their midst. Seen in the larger context, the authorities of the Soviet Zone had, by their standards, shown considerable restraint toward the dissident students up to March 1947. Henceforward, they tended to show their power more openly and to push with greater insistence for changes which they felt the university needed whether those measures incurred student resistance or not.

THE AMERICAN CONNECTION

Against this admittedly local episode in the affairs of Berlin arose the spector of a new kind of international conflict that was, to use Leon Trotsky's phrase, "neither war nor peace." Between the summer of 1946 and the spring of 1947, a sea change in the former Allies' perceptions of each other took place. No exact date marks the onset of the Cold War, but telltale signs had begun to accumulate from mid-1946 onward indicating that the wartime coalition was not destined to survive much longer. It was precisely in Berlin that the irritations and disagreements between the Western Allies and the Soviets always surfaced most boldly. From the outset, the governing of Berlin by the four Allies had proved difficult, and, in retrospect, the enterprise seems to have been doomed from the start. The Soviets and the Americans especially, as the emergent superpowers, proved unable to get along with each other. Their two social and political systems functioned in such utterly different ways that misunderstandings and fundamentally incompatible aims in foreign policy made cooperation impossible. Despite their wartime agreement to share the occupation of Berlin, the Soviets, as bloodied conquerers of the former capital, saw the Westerners as interlopers and unwanted transients in "their" city. Those Americans who dealt directly with the Soviets in Berlin, such as General Lucius Clay or his deputy, the commandant of the American Sector, Colonel Frank Howley, soon learned the difficulties of dealing with representatives from Stalinist Russia. For some, like Howley, the gloves came off almost from the start. In the course of the occupation, he proved to be the supreme "cold warrior" among the Americans in Berlin. Yet, even moderates, such as his deputy, John Maginnis, discovered that working with the Soviets was exasperating: "I found the Russians to be a baffling combination of childishness, hard realism, irresponsibility, churlishness, amiability, slovenliness, and callousness," he wrote. "It became a continuing problem to remind myself that the Russians, who were giving us trouble, were our friends, and the Germans, who were giving us cooperation, were our enemies."[143] And Maginnis was talking about Soviet-American relations in the relatively amicable period in 1945! Strains had developed to a significantly greater extent by the end of 1946. The failure of the various foreign ministers conferences and the subsequent inability of the Allies to establish a peace treaty with Germany were obvious signs of the increasing superpower tension. President Truman's dramatic announcement of a new doctrine to both houses of Congress in March 1947, that he would send aid to Greece and Turkey, brought the conflict clearly into the open.

The ambiguity which John Maginnis had indicated in his statement about American feelings toward Russians and Germans in Berlin was amply borne out by American Military Government's uneven treatment of the students in the first postwar years. Having failed to dislodge the university from Soviet control, Howley undertook several measures that caused deep consternation in the student ranks. In 1945, the Americans seemed to have written off the students of Berlin and were, if anything, a hostile force with which they had to reckon.

Before the ideological lines had hardened, the four Allies had concluded an Allied Control Authority agreement on February 7, 1946, concerning jurisdiction over German institutions of a national character. It stated "that all educational institutions, agencies and organizations, whose former functions were national in scope and all institutions of higher learning will remain for the present under the control and management of the respective zonal authorities." With respect to students attending these institutions there was a significant rider: "Zone commanders will permit the free exchange of students and free access to faculties/courses of instruction."[144] Presumably the Berlin students could reside in any of the four sectors. However, in practice, those who tried to move into the American Sector after the first semester discovered that they could not obtain the indispensable ration cards and residence permits from American authorities. Starting with the second semester in the autumn of 1946, Colonel Howley had issued an oral decree denying residence status for students seeking to attend the university from the American Sector. It was not a written order, but it had the same effect. The only cushion from this strong blow was that it did not affect students who were already residing in the American Sector. The Americans enforced Howley's regulation, much to the annoyance of the Soviets and to the discomfort of the students. Many students who had friends or relatives in the American Sector with whom they might have resided found that it was impossible to do so now because of Howley's order. For example, a law student, Ursula Besser, was the widowed mother of two children, trying to complete her studies in order to begin her career and support a family. She had lived first in Brandenburg in the Soviet Zone but then had the opportunity to join an aunt in Berlin during the semester, a much needed arrangement given her impoverished status. Although well disposed toward the Americans and obviously a hard-luck case, Ursula Besser discovered that the Americans were in fact adhering strictly to Howley's order. She ultimately found less favorable quarters in the Soviet Sector.[145]

Finally, in early January 1947, a Soviet official formally protested this American policy in the Kommandatura, complaining that the Americans were carrying out such an action "to pick at the Soviet authorities." He complained that it was a violation of the ACA agreement of February 7, 1946. "For some reason or other the American authorities make the rule only for the Berlin University, and the Soviet member protests against this decision." The Americans were unmoved and Colonel Howley's order remained in effect.[146] Indeed, Howley repeated the order in a press conference in January 1948. He declared that as long as no agreement existed among the Allies for a unified handling of German affairs, including control of the university, he would deny residence permits and ration cards to the students.[147] In effect, university affairs were becoming embroiled in the Cold War. Fritz Karsen understood Howley's reasoning as follows: "Berlin University is an institution of the Soviet Zone, not of the City of Berlin as a whole. The Russian Zone and the Russian Sector have therefore to take care of the students, but not the City of Berlin as such and particularly not the American Sector." Karsen was aware that the ACA directive referred only to the free exchange of students and was silent on such technicalities as ration cards and residence permits, but he knew perfectly well that the Soviets would continue to argue that such a hard-nosed policy effectively denied newly arrived students free access to the university from the American Sector. In a memorandum to the director of American Military Government's education branch, Richard Thomas Alexander, Karsen described the controversy, and while he felt the Soviets were guilty of precisely the violations they now claimed the Americans were making, he was also somewhat troubled by the harsh effects of Howley's policy. Karsen was in frequent communication with Berlin students and knew the hardships that it worked on them. "It may be questionable whether it was a good idea of the Sector Commandant [Howley] to issue this order at this moment," Karsen noted. "As it has been issued, we should not give in to complaints of the Russians."[148]

Disturbed by the effect the order had on the Berlin students, Alexander decided he would try to get it rescinded, and he asked for advice from Miltary Government's legal section. The chief of the branch, Louis Glaser, was hardly as sympathetic to the students' plight as Alexander and Karsen appeared to be. Glaser admitted that the spirit of the ACA directive of February 7, 1946, called for permission for students to reside in the American Sector. However, it did not specifically guarantee the students the right to live in any sector they chose. He admitted candidly that by denying the students their residence permits the Americans were engaging in "a certain amount of sophistry," but technically they could maintain that position. Glaser felt that this legal issue was part of a larger problem plaguing Berlin University, and he explained it to Alexander.

> The proper zonal authority for a university located in Berlin is the Allied Kommandatura, operating through the Magistrat of Berlin. Since the Soviet authorities have unilaterally decided that the University of Berlin is under the management of the Soviet Zone—a position which has been forced upon the United States authorities but never agreed to by them—then it should be our view that this more fundamental part of the CORC order [the ACA directive of February 7, 1946] needs to be straightened out before minor elements are considered. If the Soviet Command is prepared to agree that the University of Berlin is under quadripartite authority and administered by the Magistrat of Berlin, then it would be possible to re-examine these minor conflicts.

Alexander had not asked for legal advice only. He also sought Glaser's advice on the political aspects of the policy as it affected the students. Glaser harbored strong feelings in that respect, and he represented one pole of opinion in Military Government toward the students. "The University of Berlin has degenerated into nothing more or less than a hotbed of Communist indoctrination," the legal adviser observed. "More than that it is definitely anti–United States." Its staff were instructing students about greedy capitalist manipulations in America, "and the entire University is a breeding ground of hatred of the United States and of U.S. Military Government." There were still several hundred students residing in the American Sector, and a benevolent policy would probably allow in several hundred more, he noted. Glaser could never recommend such a policy. He felt the Americans should not "give any aid or assistance to the University of Berlin whatsoever. On the contrary, I think it should be condemned as an incubator of totalitarian Communism." Glaser felt that Military Government should reserve its space "for people who may not be for us, but are not at least waging a battle against us. In fact I think the United States should go farther and protest against supplying thousands of dollars worth of food to feed Soviet Zone embryo-Communist leaders who wish to fatten themselves in Berlin on American rations while they learn to hate America."[149]

For some in Military Government, like Glaser, the issue was clear-cut. The university and its students were enemies in the Cold War and should receive no help whatsoever. On the other hand there were Americans in Berlin who were not prepared to generalize so easily about the students, and although those who shared Glaser's belief had been in the ascendancy since the autumn of 1946, others who were more intimately concerned with higher education had already begun to find ways to improve the situation. Understandably, the students remained confused about American intentions in Berlin and uncertain as to how to approach the American authorities.

The University Unter den Linden held institutes and properties throughout Greater Berlin, and once the Soviets rejected four-power control over it, a question arose as to how those extensive assets should be handled. In the American Sector this situation was complicated further by the existence of a number of independent research institutions whose sponsor had been the highly respected Kaiser-Wilhelm-Gesellschaft (KWG). Most but not all of these research facilities were located in Dahlem, a pleasant suburb in the fashionable western section of Berlin and part of the American Sector. A measure of the importance of those institutions is reflected in the accomplishments of the Kaiser Wilhelm Institute for Physics. For the first time in history its scientists, led by Otto Hahn, Max von Laue, and Lise Meitner, had succeeded in splitting the atom in 1938. The Dahlem institutes had been among the finest in the world in prewar Berlin, and the question remained: What was to be done with these Kaiser Wilhelm Institutes?[150] And what, for that matter was to become of the university institutes? By one count there were at least seventeen such institutes in the American Sector, and following the Soviets' decision to retain control of the university, the Americans had to decide what to do next. It was a complicated issue because many of the independent Kaiser Wilhelm Institutes also had had university connections. Frequently the scientists who staffed them also held Berlin University professorships. Even the issue of whether Berlin University was a continuation of the defunct Friedrich Wilhelm University or a completely new institution played a role here. If considered a continuing institution, then East-Sector claims on the university-related institutes in the western sectors were stronger. If treated as a new institution, then such claims were correspondingly weaker.

At first the Americans were inclined to move cautiously. Upon their arrival in Berlin in July 1945, their intelligence officers were surprised to learn that German physicists had been quietly holding meetings concerning atomic physics even during that summer. The Americans quickly suppressed such activity.[151] The following October some of the scientists and scholars of the KWG proposed to the Americans that the research foundation be reconstituted, but initial reactions were cool. One of the responsible officers from the education section, Captain Samuel Shulits, contacted F. J. Mann, of Military Government's Office of Political Affairs, and they sent a communication to General Clay's political adviser, Ambassador Robert Murphy, advising him that with public fear about German war potential still high, proposals to organize a central research foundation seemed premature. Murphy had to agree.[152] By the summer of 1946, however, the Americans were willing to allow certain of the research institutes to continue to function on a reduced budget until the occupying power determined long-range plans. The Magistrat approved the budget, a move which surprised the Americans. They had expected a Soviet veto.

The university institutes posed a different problem because of the Soviets' unilateral decision to control the university. The problem grew as the moment for reopening approached. In December 1945, an American officer ordered Otto Winzer to transfer administration of the Botanical Garden from Berlin University to the city's administration for museums, palaces, and gardens. Through the following winter and spring Winzer delayed, hoping to prevent the move, and even Johannes Stroux wrote to the Americans, claiming that the Botanical Garden was vital to the university's teaching needs. Professor Adolf Zucker, on the American education staff, stood firm against Stroux's request, however. "If you will be in a position to change the course assumed by education authorities in the Russian Sector," he replied, "you will very likely find the American group still adhering to their first principle." But by now everyone knew that the Soviets were firmly committed to unilateral control of the university. The Americans stood by their decision, too, and the transfer took place.[153]

Although the Americans were determined not to let the Soviets administer the university institutes in the American Sector, they were not at all sure what to do with them thereafter. Samuel Shulits, a major in the Army Corps of Engineers, inspected several of the university institutes in April 1946. He found after several inspection trips that the Soviets and SED authorities were complying with American regulations. No lectures or instruction were taking place at the institutes, although a few advanced students and possibly some staff were carrying out research for dissertations and the like. Shulits ascertained during his visits that the Soviets were requiring the professors and lecturing staff to conduct all classes in the Soviet Sector. Only an occasional student visitor was now appearing in the institute buildings in the American Sector, to obtain advice or to use the library. The institutes included such fields as meteorology, pharmacy, the Botanical Garden and Museum, and agronomy. Shulits indicated that even the minimal activity occurring at the institutes was too much. "The only way to stop this half-way activity," he wrote to John Taylor at OMGUS headquarters, " . . . would be to close them up completely and compel them to move into the Russian Sector, thus leaving buildings available for educational purposes in the American Sector."[154]

There was little doubt that the ban on activities in the institutes worked hardships on students and staff alike. On July 4, 1946, about thirty pharmacy students sent a petition to the "High American Military Government" saying that the Americans' countermeasures were putting them in an impossible position. They could not effectively carry out their pharmaceutical studies in Berlin as matters now stood. The institute and its director, Professor Thomas Sabalitschka, were uniquely suited to teach them, they claimed, and because of denazification and wartime destruction no substitute for the Berlin institute was available.[155] The Americans asked the British if they could accommodate a transfer of the pharmacy institute to the Technical University, but the British refused, claiming there was no funding available to take on this additional burden at present.[156] If anything was to be done about the hapless institute and other such institutes in the American Sector, the Americans would have to take the initiative themselves.

It was Fritz Karsen who became the earliest and staunchest advocate of a new higher educational institution, an institute for advanced studies in Dahlem. The Americans had identified over forty scientific institutes by the autumn of 1946 in their sector. Karsen convinced his colleagues on the E&RA staff that the creation of a school of advanced studies was entirely feasible, given the number and quality of scientists and scholars available. He held conferences with the directors of the various institutes, starting in September 1946, and soon enlisted their support. One such scientist, Professor Kurt Noack, director of the Botanical Garden, wrote of the promising initiative to Eduard Spranger: "Yesterday the first discussions took place between the directors of the Dahlem institutes of all kinds and the Americans. The attempt will be made to create a postgraduate . . . school without cutting completely the ties with the university in the other sector. It is most encouraging that the Americans want to make Berlin the center of German science once again. Since the Russians have the same intention, we should lack for nothing!"[157]

The American effort to create a school for advanced studies, while not directly connected to developments at Berlin University or the plight of its students, was significant in that for the first time Americans in official positions were taking a more active interest in higher education in Berlin. Plans for the new school made sufficient progress that, in December 1946, the American authorities could make a public announcement of their intentions. The institutes, largely located in Dahlem, were not only to engage in research, but were to help alleviate the shortage of scientists in postwar Germany by taking on a teaching function for gifted advanced students. The announcements specifically avoided calling it a university and denied that it had that capacity or intention. However, it was intended to serve Germans from all the occupation zones, and consequently the *Land* governments in the American Zone were to share jointly with Berlin in the financing of the school. The Magistrat approved funding on a modest scale, much to the surprise of the Americans who had feared that such a move would draw a Soviet veto.[158] Over the long run, however, funding proved to be an almost insurmountable problem for the Dahlem enterprise. For the moment, at least, it was a hint that the Americans' hostility toward the students was coming to an end. To be sure, the problem of the Dahlem institutes was hardly resolved and continued to cause disagreements among the various authorities in Berlin. Wandel recalled hearing a speech by Fritz Karsen to the zonal cultural ministers near Stuttgart on future plans for the institutes. The SED official protested the proposal vigorously, pointing out that several of the institutes belonged to the university and should remain independent of the American initiative. However, the Americans, he said, remained unmoved by his arguments.[159]

At about the time the Berlin public learned that the Americans were prepared to create a higher educational institution in their sector, another German refugee, now an American citizen, came to Berlin. Dr. Fritz Epstein, a specialist in East European studies and diplomacy, had taken on a new assignment for the State Department. The Americans, in cooperation with the British and French, had put together a team of historians to examine official German foreign policy documents related to the Second World War. Epstein had gathered wide experience in the United States, working in the Widener and Hoover libraries, at Harvard and Stanford universities respectively. He had also joined the wartime Office of Strategic Services (OSS) as an expert in Central European affairs and was a logical choice for the war documents project. When their busy schedules permitted, Epstein and his wife, Dr. Herta Epstein, took an interest in the affairs of the Berliners. Herta Epstein became involved in the revival of the churches in Berlin and served as a representative for a consortium of relief organizations known as CRALOG (Council of Relief Agencies Licensed to Operate in Germany) to provide food and other essentials to the impoverished Berliners. Both were interested in seeing what values and interests the students espoused in postwar Germany. Their last contacts with German students in the early 1930s had been harrowing to say the least, and they wondered what changes, if any, had occurred following the defeat.

In the course of 1947, as events unfolded at Berlin University, the dissident students discovered that in addition to Fritz Karsen, they had another American contact in the Epsteins. Otto Hess was one of the first students to meet the Epsteins, and in short order he introduced the other activists and veterans of the *Studentische Arbeitsgemeinschaft*. It became apparent that the students had moved a long way from their reactionary, hypernationalistic ways of 1933, and Epstein felt encouraged to broaden his contacts with the new student generation. Consequently, not long after Soviet arrests of students began to take place, the surviving resisters began to attend fortnightly gatherings at what amounted to a "Salon Epstein" in the American Sector. There the students met each other and American officials in an informal atmosphere free of coercion and far removed from the tense atmosphere at the university. In lively fashion they discussed student problems, tensions with Soviet-SED authorities, and other current issues and became better acquainted with Americans serving in Berlin. The American visitors included personnel from the education branch, officials from Ambassador Murphy's political adviser's staff, such as Richard Sterling, and other officers from Military Government. It was the first time that students could establish meaningful contact with significant numbers of Americans in postwar Berlin. In a certain sense the students transferred their discussions from the defunct *Studentische Arbeitsgemeinschaft* to the west. And at a time when the Berliners were struggling through one of the coldest winters in memory on a near-starvation diet of 1550 calories per day, the warmth of the Epsteins' apartment and the party sausages they supplied were doubly appreciated. "Democratization with wurst," was how one participant, Eva Heilmann, recalled it with a smile, but all agreed that the ability to discuss and to debate freely was the attraction that kept bringing them back to the American Sector.[160]

The students were not the only ones impressed by the experience. Epstein wrote to an American colleague toward the end of 1947 about the family's activities on behalf of the students. "Mrs. Epstein, who is working as a Berlin representative for CRALOG, and I have been active in sponsoring discussion groups of Berlin University students with Americans," he wrote. He had made a point of visiting the old university and had even contacted Friedrich Meinecke, Germany's most venerated historian, who had just attained the age of 85. However, it was the students who impressed Epstein most, with their determination to carry on despite all conceivable difficulties. His experiences dealt most recently with history students but could have applied to any student group. "It is difficult," he wrote, "or should I say, it is impossible to imagine the difficulties under which professors and students have to work in the historical field." Epstein found the university buildings still largely destroyed, few if any rooms heated, and inconceivable shortages of everything. There were no bookshelves, so the students stacked books on the floor according to a crude classification system. Even the possibility of reading was limited, because, as Epstein indicated, "there is no light and no book can be found in the dark winter afternoon."[161] As far as Epstein was concerned, the students of Berlin were a new breed, utterly unlike those he had left behind in 1933.

The growing plans for a school of advanced studies in Dahlem gave rise to a discussion among the E&RA branch chiefs at the beginning of February 1948. The project had hardly been smooth sailing, primarily because there was considerable dissension among the financially strapped Germans as to how the school should be financed and how much influence each contributor would exercise. The Berliners, for example, wished to avoid a constitutional agreement in which a Bavarian finance minister controlled the new enterprise in Berlin. Yet, the *Länder* of the American Zone would be the primary financial backers of the project. Discouraged by the dissension, some Americans, such as R. T. Alexander, considered abandoning the entire scheme. In justifying the project, Fritz Karsen claimed that there was a critical shortage of democratically inclined professors in Germany. Talented students who had finished their regular university studies could undertake advanced scientific or scholarly training in Dahlem in a deliberately created democratic environment. Then, as newly qualified university professors, they could be expected to help build a more democratic spirit in Germany's centers of higher learning.

In this context, the topic of Berlin University arose, and the Americans recounted the failed attempt to bring it under four-power control. As early as 1946, Alexander had proposed the establishment of a new university, the minutes of the meeting recorded. Now, in January 1948, John R. Sala, branch chief for education in the American Sector, announced that he had recently discussed the subject with Colonel Frank Howley. The minutes record Sala as stating that Howley had then ordered Sala "to establish a university in the American Sector of Berlin and has asked him to look around to see what buildings could be used for a university." Sala added to the intriguing information, stating that "it might be that the British would combine efforts on this. If not, we will have one of our own." A major stumbling block, erected two years earlier against the students by Colonel Howley, had just been overcome. Students from the western zones would now be permitted to obtain residence permits in Berlin in order to receive their higher education. The meaning of the language was not entirely clear, although in context it was obvious that the education officers were referring to the school of advanced studies, the newest university project, which Howley had just ordered into existence.[162] Obviously, the openly hostile attitude of some American officials such as legal adviser Louis Glaser, toward Berlin students was growing out of date. And Howley, who had virtually banned students from the American Sector at a press conference on January 7, 1948, had completely reversed himself less than a month later.

John Sala promptly set to work as Howley had ordered, and on March 22, 1948, presented a comprehensive set of plans to his superiors. "Request is made for assistance in establishing a new university in the American Sector of Berlin," he wrote Alexander. "The attached papers indicate preliminary thinking on this subject." Sala indicated that "there are many students and professors in Berlin University who are waging a losing fight for academic freedom and who would be ready to work in a new university." The papers then presented ideas on the general aims of such a university, its organization, the facilities that might be available in the American Sector, financing, and its alignment with Berlin administration. The education staff even prepared a model university constitution. In short, the American education staff, with the blessing of senior officers like Frank Howley, had begun to give serious attention to the need for a new university in Berlin.[163]

By the winter of 1947/48 the dissident students in Berlin had achieved their American connection. They had examined their options realistically, and the most active of them in seeking western support had discovered that only the Americans seemed prepared to give them tangible assistance. The British, noted Otto Hess, had remained icily reserved when he approached them in the spring of 1947 in an effort to secure the release of Georg Wrazidlo from a Soviet jail. Hess recalled that his contact "Mr. Simpson," an adviser to General Sir Brian Robertson, the British commandant, "expressed regret at Wrazidlo's harsh fate but indicated that there was nothing the British could do to help." The students would simply have to accommodate themselves to their conquerors from the east, the aide advised. Hess and his dissident friends concluded early on that if tangible help were to be forthcoming from any Allied source, that source would be American.[164]

CRISIS

Thus, in official and unofficial ways, the Americans and the dissident students in Berlin made their first tentative approaches to each other. To be sure, it had taken time for the new friendship to develop. In the meantime, the dissident movement had remained intact and the university conflict had continued, albeit on a subdued level. While the SED-oriented students had received their journal, *Forum*, in January 1947, the dissidents produced their first edition of *Colloquium* on, of all days, May 1, 1947. The editors, Otto Hess and Joachim Schwarz, promised that it would be a journal that stood above partisan politics. They had a creed to represent and a bold declaration to make:

> Freedom, humanity and the rights of man are for us of inestimable worth, and we shall fight unrelentingly against anyone who attempts to infringe upon them. We shall expose ourselves to much criticism. We know this, and yet we value it. We are even grateful because we know that in the end it shows us that we are on the right path. However, even as we concede the right of criticism to others, as long as it is objective, so too, we demand the same for ourselves. This we wish to state quite openly: In these pages we shall criticise anything that is worthy of criticism. But we reject criticsm for the mere sake of criticism.[165]

For the first half year of its existence, *Colloquium* seemed determined to avoid any controversy with the university authorities. The journal became a popular "conversation" piece as the title implied, offering a variety of articles, commentaries, reviews, and discussions on the state of German universities, student life, and Berlin's cultural revival. Its editors and contributors concentrated on general themes in an apparent effort to avoid exacerbating the ongoing tensions at Berlin University. For example, the Berlin daily press noted that the nonaligned majority in the *Studentenrat* had passed a resolution at the end of April approving the display of the flags of the Allies—including the Red Flag—at the university for the impending May Day celebration of 1947. However, they condemned in advance the display of party emblems and slogans as had happened the previous year.[166] In fact, no such party-oriented displays took place at the university proper, although there were some protests against the SED's use of loudspeakers nearby. The *Colloquium*, which might easily have claimed a moral victory here, studiously ignored the subject.

In comparison to the more handsomely laid out *Forum*, its American-licensed competitor was decidedly the ugly duckling. The large-format *Forum* compared favorably with commercial magazines and journals in size and layout, whereas the pocket-book sized *Colloquium* was restricted to thirty pages per issue because of a chronic paper shortage in the American-occupied areas. Moreover, the same shortage, combined with shaky financing, set a limit of only 10,000 copies per month. The student editors conducted strictly limited business hours around their coursework, and the little press, which had no subsidy at first, led a hand-to-mouth existence throughout the occupation. Despite those painful limitations, the journal achieved genuine popularity with the students and habitually sold out within a matter of days. As an officially licensed journal it could be distributed in all the occupied territories, although it remained largely a Berlin phenomenon. Despite any and all drawbacks, the dissident students looked upon it as their journal, and it helped provide a rallying point and a sense of cohesiveness in the midst of discouraging trends.

If any one mood seemed to prevail among the dissident students at the Berlin University as the year 1947 waned, it was resignation. The Munich-based, American-licensed *Neue Zeitung* prepared a lengthy report about the troubled institution at the end of September 1947, under the headline "University without a Future." The authors claimed that the students, overwhelmingly neutral in their political views if not outright anticommunist, appeared to be tiring of the struggle. "Most members of their self-elected student council . . . declare that in the next elections in November they want to lay down their mandates," the account stated. "They have lost too much time already and are tired of the battle." Besides, it had become apparent that to oppose the various mea-

sures adopted by the *Zentralverwaltung für Volksbildung* was a dangerous game, and the student council had learned that in the long run they
could not successfully resist the policies of the East-Zone authorities.
Even their sharpest weapon—exposure in the Berlin press—seemed to
be of no avail. The professors seemed equally disspirited, the article
claimed, and now in sizable numbers some of the most famous were taking guest professorships and going elsewhere with no guarantee that
they would return. That unloved but respected scholar Rector Johannes
Stroux had taken a guest professorship at Basel University, Switzer-
land, following his harrowing experience with the Berlin press (although he quickly returned to Berlin). A theologian, Professor Fritz
Lieb, moved to Basel permanently. Berlin University lost two able law
professors, Erich Genzmer and Ludwig Raiser, to Hamburg and Göttingen respectively, and a Slavic studies expert, Max Vasmer, accepted a visiting appointment at the University of Stockholm. Hardworking though
the students had proved to be, they could not prevent the decline in quality at Berlin University. "The majority of the student body believes," concluded the *Neue Zeitung*, "that their University will develop further
into the 'SED Institution of Higher Learning' if it continues to be subordinated to the *Zentralverwaltung*. That is why it is a university without a
future."[167] Eduard Spranger had predicted difficulties in attracting talented academics to Berlin and keeping them there, if four-power dissen-
sions continued. The prediction appeared to be coming true.

In September 1947, the editors of *Colloquium* had given a hint of
their willingness to use their journal as an organ of protest. They criticized what they felt was an arbitrary decision by the *Zentralverwaltung*
to dismiss a member of the medical faculty, Dr. Auguste Hoffmann,
whom the authorities accused of failing to disclose a Nazi past. The editors, Hess and Schwarz, who were both officially recognized Victims of
Fascism, reprinted a 1935 letter from an official of the Third Reich
dismissing Hoffmann from all her posts in youth organizations for
lack of conformity to Nazi regulations. They then published a letter
to her by Professor Theodor Brugsch, Wandel's assistant, in August
1947, dismissing Hoffmann on precisely the opposite grounds, namely,
her allegedly intensive involvement in the same Nazi organizations.
Earlier, Rector Stroux had organized a faculty committee to examine
her credentials and the committee had confirmed her complete inno-
cence, according to *Colloquium*. The *Zentralverwaltung* had compounded
the hard feelings by refusing to respond to repeated requests for an
explanation by Hoffmann, by her director, or by the student body.[168]
Other signs of tension mounted. A few weeks later Wolfgang Heubner,
the dean of the medical faculty and successor in that post to Else
Knake, resigned from his position, claiming that political factors were
still playing a dominant role in admissions procedures for medical
students.[169]

In a certain sense the final conflict at Berlin University began in December 1947, when elections for the student council took place once again. The results could hardly have been satisfying to SED-oriented students. Altogether thirty seats had come open, and once again the SED won only three. Candidates with affiliations to the other three parties also garnered a few: the SPD took two, the CDU three, and the LDP one. However, twenty-one of the winners were politically nonaligned. The new chairman, Claus Reuber, was politically independent, and replaced the outgoing Gerhard Petermann, who had also been nonaligned. Reuber, a physics student and a Victim of Fascism, had chosen Berlin University for the continuation of his studies for the eminently practical reason that it opened its doors one semester sooner than did the Technical University in the British Sector. He, too, had been a veteran of the *Studentische Arbeitsgemeinschaft* and was rightly seen by the dissident students as a kindred spirit.[170]

Following their electoral victory, the editors of *Colloquium* did more than just publish the results in the pages of their tiny journal. For the first time they offered a biting commentary, accusing the SED of engaging in tumultuous and blatantly propagandistic electoral tactics. The SED defeat was, they claimed, all the more convincing since its only mandates came once again from that citadel of SED support, the school of education. Another indication of student feeling was that the new student chairmen of the philosophy and law schools, Otto Stolz and Ernst Benda, had won by huge margins even though they held decided political loyalties. They were, respectively, the SPD and CDU youth leaders in Berlin.

What was disturbing to the editors of *Colloquium* was not the election result, which was another stunning defeat for the SED. Rather, they maintained, it was the unprecedented aggressiveness with which the Communist students had conducted their campaign. At a student meeting on December 5, one week before the election, the incumbent council members had delivered summary reports of their activities to a general audience of students. An SED minority appeared at the meeting and proceeded to disrupt it in various ways, repeatedly injecting their views about working-class student admissions in what amounted to a filibuster. When non-SED students protested the disruptions, the young Communists shouted epithets, labeling them as fascists, traitors, or reactionaries. The noncommunist majority left the hall in protest, making the rump session the "overwhelming majority." The SED faction promptly elected representatives to a forthcoming "people's congress." Stolz and Hess condemned such actions as reminiscent of those tactics that had destroyed democracy in Germany once before. Another conclusion which they drew from the incident was equally troubling and echoed the pessimistic reports of the *Neue Zeitung*: It demonstrated "that in Berlin the great majority of students obviously do not have the en-

ergy and courage anymore to represent their views," Hess wrote. "Instead they allow themselves to be terrorized by a tiny minority without
showing any resistance."[171]

The electoral incident of December 1947 proved to be the opening
round in a contest that ended with the splitting of Berlin University. Starting with its January 1948 issue, the group of students around the *Colloquium* began a concerted attack on the abuses which they felt SED
authorities had perpetrated at the university. Otto Hess's serialized commentary, entitled "How Much Longer? The Battle for the University,"
spearheaded the attack in a long, detailed account of the tightening grip
which the SED had imposed on Berlin University and the universities
in the Soviet Zone. The students did not dare criticize Soviet authorities directly. That would have been illegal under the occupation agreements and would have led to the immediate closure of *Colloquium* by
the American authorities. Instead, they criticized the German SED authorities. Hess offered what amounted to a survey of political conditions at
the East-Zone universities and professed to see the same trend at all the
centers of higher learning. His report devoted special detail to the universities at Leipzig and Halle. But he also gave prominent attention to Berlin. Hess claimed that the isolated success of the school of education
was an obvious embarrassment to the SED. Now the representatives of
the *Vorstudienanstalt*, who, he observed, "just happened" to be SED
members, were demanding representation in the student council. This
would bolster the small SED faction of three, a development which
Hess found particularly ominous.[172]

Hess invoked a dictum by Kurt Tucholsky: "Learn to laugh so that
you don't cry," and with that in mind he recommended that his readership glance at a description in *Colloquium* of a recent event: the change
of rectors at Berlin University. Normally the most ceremonial occasion
in the calendar of a German university, the change of high office was accompanied by major speeches from the incoming and departing rectors,
addresses which were expected to crown their careers, especially that
of the new rector. It was simultaneously a cultural event with serious
music, pomp and ceremony, floral displays, and an air of almost medieval solemnity as faculty and students gathered to watch one begowned
"magnificence" (rector) transfer the golden chain of office to his successor.

In a new column to appear in *Colloquium* called "die Glosse" (a
gloss or sneering commentary), an anonymous contributor, who signed
himself "Sisyphus," described Berlin University's recent change of rectors: "There you could see them, a proper president attired in a sweater
but no tie at all, a vice president with a natty Basque beret, a dean in a
loud red tie, and two leading officers of the 'German' *Verwaltung für
Volksbildung*, who were so bored by the speeches of the rectors that
they lit up their cigarettes and pipes." There followed a savage lam-

poon of the entire occasion, a gathering replete with loudspeaker systems so loud that the listeners could not understand the speeches. The audience, including the university officers, huddled in overcoats and attempted to evade the near-freezing water that dripped from the damaged ceiling. The speeches, according to "Sisyphus," were memorable, to be sure, with Theodor Brugsch invoking the name of Humboldt to justify the creation of a "progressive" university, and the new rector, law professor Hermann Dersch, assuring his audience that "With the use of telephone conversations to the *Zentralverwaltung* we shall reduce gigantic boulders to little pebbles." What would this rock-crushing at the university accomplish? "Arm in arm with my deputy rector, I shall lay a path, milestone upon milestone, toward a truly democratic people's university!" he exclaimed. Dersch then broke precedent by announcing that instead of hearing the usual incoming rector's lecture—the crowning statement of his career—the shivering audience should read (by implication they should buy) his forthcoming law book instead! "However, this time it does not deal—as it did in 1934—with a commentary on a 'Law Regulating the National Labor,' noted the venomous columnist in a broad hint at Dersch's less than lily-white past. As the new "Magnificence" rejoined the shuddering deans, who by some strange process had broken all precedent and elected him unanimously, a string quartet raggedly sawed its way into action. "Sisyphus" observed that "they were able to agree on a common tempo after only twenty beats, something the new rector might also want from his new student council."[173]

There was only one pen among the students of Berlin sharp enough to have thrown such barbs: Otto Stolz. Virtually every student knew at a glance who "Sisyphus" really was. Consequently, the transfer of the rectorship, instead of marking another milestone in the rebuilding of Berlin University, became the occasion for a particularly hard poke at the university authorities, at the *Zentralverwaltung*, and at the SED. Probably more than any sober political analysis by Otto Hess, more than open criticisms of SED tactics by other observers, the acid comments of Otto Stolz goaded the leadership of the *Zentralverwaltung* beyond endurance. Wandel knew perfectly well that the dissidents on the board of *Colloquium* had him in their sights. One of them had offered the Berlin University students a seemingly innocent New Year's greeting which was actually a clever play on words using Wandel's own name (In German *Wandel* means "change"):

> First student: "A change must come to Berlin University in 1948."
> Second student: "Wrong! A 'Change' must go."[174]

The pointed criticisms of *Colloquium* did not abate. As winter gave way to spring, Hess's "struggle-for-the-university" column and Stolz's barbed commentaries became regular features in the journal, and, when the opportunity arose, other contributors issued their own selective criticisms. When SED authorities began to deny certain applicants entry into the law school because they had been ten-year-old *Pimpfe* (cubs) in the Hitler Youth, a cartoon appeared, depicting an infant in diapers requesting youth amnesty status.[175] Recalling the practices of the Nazis in demanding genealogical records from all German citizens, Stolz observed that the practice continued in different form under the Communists. He cited a case where a student applicant had burned the proofs of his ancestry with great satisfaction after the war only to learn that he must prove to the admissions committee that his father had been a proletarian assistant fireman rather than a bourgeois engineer on the prewar railway.[176] Then, in a bold move in March 1948, the editors announced the formation of a "Colloquium Club," which was intended to be a "nonpolitical association for furthering the cultural and social life of the students at Berlin's centers of higher learning." Furthermore, it was to operate under license from the American occupation authorities, and those interested in joining were to enquire at the address of Horst Hartwich, a student living in the American Sector.[177] Earlier, the *Zentralverwaltung* had forbidden the formation of student associations at the university other than the *Studentische Arbeitsgemeinschaft* or its successor, the *Studentenrat*. The issue had been a source of irritation to many students, especially the dissidents. Once again they had turned to the Americans for support—and received it.

Beyond the confines of the university, events on a larger scale were also approaching a climax. The communist coup in Czechoslovakia in February 1948 indicated that the Soviets were prepared to consolidate their sphere of influence in Eastern Europe, now that any significant chance for political victories in Western Europe was fading. Josef Stalin's simmering dispute with Marshal Tito over Yugoslavia's separate path to socialism was beginning to flare up, causing the East European Communist parties and especially the SED to adopt superorthodox positions on all subjects. On the Ides of March, 1948, an interested observer of political trends in Berlin, Sir Robert Birley, forwarded his impressions to a colleague in British Military Government, Patrick Dean: "I think there is little doubt that the revolution in Czechoslovakia has had a very great effect in Berlin, causing a general loss of confidence and a fear that similar tactics may be employed there. Students from Berlin University, whom I have seen, are excited by the resistance of the Prague students, but generally depressed by the situation." Birley was worried about future cooperation with students, given the increasing Soviet pressure. "What we have to fear particularly is a movement by Germans in Berlin, who had previously cooperated with us, to insure against future Russian domination, either by ceasing to involve themselves with us or by actually cooperating with the Russians. Once this starts, the rot might spread quickly."[178]

By compensation, other trends were developing that might offset the hardening political position in the East. The pipeline of Marshall Plan aid was beginning to funnel effective support to Western Europe, starting in the spring of 1948. Allied plans for a merger of the western zones of Germany into a new state were receiving wide attention. Locally, at the end of March the Soviets had walked out of a meeting of the Allied Control Council, giving no hint when or if they might return, and General Clay sent a now-famous telegram to his superiors in Washington warning of an ominous trend in his relations with the Soviets. Something was about to happen, he predicted, but he could not be sure as yet what the former ally might try next.[179]

In the context of the miniature war occurring in Berlin higher education, the mounting boldness of *Colloquium*, now a movement and no longer just a student journal, probably forced Wandel's hand. If there was any doubt that a showdown might be avoided, it ended in April 1948 with the appearance of yet another set of attacks on the SED authorities by the students at *Colloquium*. Hess continued to chronicle the demise of democratic institutions at the Soviet-Zone universities. Stolz's fiery pen savaged the *Zentralverwaltung* still, and added such SED luminaries as Wilhelm Pieck and Otto Grotewohl to its list of targets. If the dissident students were expecting some kind of reaction to their continuing criticism, they did not have long to wait.

On April 16, 1948, Wandel sent word through the rector's office that, effective immediately, three students no longer had the right to study at Berlin University. The following day Otto Hess, Joachim Schwarz, and Otto Stolz, the responsible editors and chief commentarist of *Colloquium* respectively, received identical letters from Rector Dersch to the effect that the *Zentralverwaltung* was revoking their right to study "because of publishing activities which act counter to the good manners and dignity of a student."[180] To those intimately acquainted with the longstanding tensions at Berlin University, the move came as no surprise. Dozens of students had already received similar dismissals and had gone elsewhere to study—unless they had had the misfortune to be arrested. The dismissed students and those aspirants who had not been admitted in the first place had gone to swell the ranks of universities elsewhere. One estimate indicated that there were no fewer than seven hundred Berlin students studying at Bavarian universities alone. Given the unyielding stance of Paul Wandel and the *Zentralverwaltung* in the past, Hess, Stolz, and Schwarz should have been packing their bags on April 18 in preparation for a train ride out of Berlin to a west-zone university. The latest dismissals were not ordinary disciplinary cases, however. Stolz was the SPD youth leader in Berlin and a well-known contributor to west-sector daily papers. Hess was also a prominent SPD leader, former chairman of the defunct *Studentische Arbeitsgemeinschaft*, former officer in the *Studentenrat*, and a co-licensee of *Colloquium*. Non-SED observers rated him as the most influential student at Berlin University. Co-editor Schwarz was a leading light in the CDU, a well-known journalist in the Berlin daily press, especially in the *Tagesspiegel*, and, not least, a recognized participant in the student resistance against Hitler. All three students were officially recognized Victims of Fascism. Wandel's decision could hardly have been a casual one. The question was, what would the students do now?

In a convincing display of their recently acquired publishing skills, the ex-students orchestrated a carefully paced publicity campaign in the Berlin press that turned an otherwise obscure academic matter into an event of major political proportions. Hess, Schwarz, and Stolz immediately relayed the dismissal notice to the Berlin newspapers, acquired permission from the American licensing authorities to publish a special issue of *Colloquium*, demanded an extraordinary session of the student council on April 21, and, pending the outcome of that meeting, gave notice of a possible student strike set for Friday, April 23. The showdown had finally come, and a startling new chapter in German higher education was about to begin.

At the same time that critical articles and interviews with the students were appearing in the western press, the three students arrived at the special student council meeting on April 21 to plead their case. A crush of students and university personnel overflowed the senate chamber of the university, and in a tense atmosphere of confrontation, the various parties spoke their case. In a new development, a medical student who was also a part-time reporter for the American-licensed Radio in the American Sector (RIAS), Gerhard Löwenthal, hauled a cable through the portals of the university and, lugging the bulky sound equipment of the 1940s into the meeting itself, proceeded to record the debate live. The antagonists would speak not only to each other. They would speak to all of Berlin.[181]

Long before the meeting took place, the two sides had begun jockeying for position. The dissident students protested loudly that the dismissals had occurred in an arbitrary and irregular way. Led by the new chairman of the student council, Claus Reuber, they claimed that President Wandel and, by implication, Rector Hermann Dersch, had exceeded their authority. Berlin students had traditionally held the right to disciplinary review by a university committee with student representation before any action could take place. This right of Berlin students was sufficiently cherished that even the Nazis had left it in place, and the *Zentralverwaltung* had incorporated it into its disciplinary code for students in December 1947. Yet no committee had considered the present case. Professor Robert Rompe, assistant to Wandel in the *Zentralverwaltung*, claimed that the designated committee had declared the matter outside its jurisdiction, whereupon its student representative, Gerhard Petermann, promptly resigned from the committee in protest. Rompe then confronted Petermann as a member of the student council and warned him and the students not to undertake any "injudicious action" at the April 21 meeting. Otherwise, he warned, "appropriate measures will be taken."[182] Undeterred, the executive of the student council visited Wandel on Tuesday, April 20, to present their case. According to west-sector accounts, he informed them that he was responsible only to the Soviet-Zone authorities and to his own conscience as to who could study at the university and who could not. Under similar circumstances, Wandel declared, he was prepared to take identical action against all those who disturbed law and order at the university.[183]

The following day, in a dramatic exchange with the university and SED authorities, the students challenged the recent action. In a gesture of conciliation, Rector Hermann Dersch suggested that the students, as guilty parties, should admit their wrongs and might then be readmitted. Professor Rompe, who represented Wandel, attempted to defend his boss by claiming that the Zentralverwaltung had not actually expelled the students—only the rector could do that. Rather, he explained, Wandel had revoked their original admission to the university, a right he claimed on the basis of a seldom invoked Soviet-Zone regulation issued in January 1946. According to this reasoning, neither the rector, who was simply passing along the order, nor Wandel, who was following regulations, had exceeded his authority. The majority of students listening to Rompe's explanations openly jeered at what they felt was an attempt to obscure the issue. During the heated debate, a formidable university administrator and SED member, Amanda von Pritzbuer, caused student reporter Gerhard Löwenthal's radio cable to be sliced while she ejected him and his uninvited microphone from the meeting. There was some justification on the part of the students in labeling Pritzbuer—behind her back to be sure—the "Passionara" of the SED. Undaunted, the student council passed by a margin of 18 votes to 3 a resolution by law student Ernst Benda condemning the arbitrary dismissals and calling upon the Zentralverwaltung to reverse its decision.[184] By an even larger margin of 19 to 2 the student council declared that a disciplinary review committee did indeed possess the right to examine the dismissals. By the same margin, the student council voted to issue a letter to Wandel declaring its intent to call a strike if he did not offer an early reply to their demands.[185] The call for a strike was no idle threat. The day before, student groups affiliated with the SPD, the LDP, and the CDU issued a joint strike declaration for Friday, April 23, 1948. It urged the students to forgo classes and to appear at the Hotel Esplanade, located just inside the British Sector in the center of the city, a few hundred feet from the Soviet Sector. The dismissed students planned to address them there.[186]

It was an open question as to who might appear at the Hotel Esplanade on the appointed day. While tensions were running high, the SED-oriented press claimed that the *Studentenrat* had disavowed the strike[187] (which was not true). Moreover, the rigid stance of the *Zentralverwaltung* at the April 21 meeting indicated that Paul Wandel was by no means intimidated by the barrage of critical press reports. On the contrary, he and his deputy, Rompe, had made uncompromising statements that such a strike exceeded the right to free expression, and the abrupt dismissals of April 16 might be followed by others against the striking students. The Soviet-Sector press, such as the *Berliner Zeitung* and *Neues Deutschland*, castigated the dismissed students, especially Stolz, as long-time troublemakers who were against all progressive reforms and who should simply go elsewhere.[188]

At 5:00 p.m. on April 23, a throng of students filled the Hotel Esplanade to listen to what Hess, Stolz, and Schwarz had to say. Members of the student council had posted announcements of the gathering at the university even more quickly than the authorities could tear them down. Later, a dispute arose over how many students actually attended the event. The SED press claimed perhaps 300; the western press suggested over 2,000. In fact, the students spilled out of the hotel into the square outside and the overflow crowd had to listen to the proceedings by loudspeaker. No one could make an accurate headcount in the milling crowd anyway, but the eyewitnesses agreed it was large and voluble. Given the wide publicity that had arisen, including press commentaries throughout western Germany, and complete film coverage, a rarity for that time, Berliners received ample exposure to what in a later time would be called a "media event." As expeditiously as possible, the speakers offered the crowd the salient facts. It was when Otto Hess told them that he and his fellow martyrs had no intention of fleeing to some safe haven in the West that they began to claim the full attention of the crowd. They would stand and fight in Berlin, he announced to accompanying cheers. But it was Otto Stolz who electrified the gathering that afternoon. If the university could not at last come under the control of the Magistrat, he stated, then the time had come to create a new university in the west of Berlin, one at which students could work in a climate free of repression. With a speed remarkable even for those tumultuous times, his words spread through Berlin. The media immediately took up the cry for a "free" university. An experiment unique in European higher education was about to begin.

CONCLUSION

The train of events that led from the division of Berlin at the end of the war toward an East-West crisis in 1948 produced as one admittedly local result the splitting up of Berlin's higher education. The Soviets and their German allies began the occupation with well-laid plans, energetic and bold cadres, and, it must be said, a program that attracted many talented adherents at first. In the case of the university, they intended to transform that institution so that it would further the aims of the new socialist society they envisioned, and their plans were by no means rigid. To be sure, they would not permit a traditionalist academician like Eduard Spranger to lead the effort to rebuild Berlin University along familiar lines. As a result of Soviet and German Communist planning—later with the Socialist Unity Party—several thousand students were brought together and were encouraged to help in the reconstruction of higher education along progressive, democratic lines (as they understood it). The authorities had encouraged them to administer their student affairs largely on their own. Rather than serving one class, the university would serve all classes, thus eliminating the reputation of German universities as elitist and conservative bastions. The implementation of such plans was relatively flexible in the first year after the war, and it appeared that Berlin University would proceed with relative calm toward the new social goals.

The Western Allies, and especially the Americans, entered the occupation without any comparable set of long-range plans and aims for Germany. American inexperience or underestimation of the responsibilities about to be undertaken had unfortunate results immediately. The plans for the division of occupied Germany resulted from British and Soviet initiatives, including the special plans for Berlin. Strategic decisions taken by the American military command ensured that the Soviets would conquer the capital in 1945, so that when the Americans, the British, and the French entered the former capital in July 1945, the Soviets had been in exclusive control for over two months. Acting out of a sense of wartime idealism toward an ally that had endured much, the Americans accepted Soviet initiatives in Berlin and permitted an administrative arrangement that allowed a Soviet veto in the Kommandatura on city affairs. When four-power arrangements at the Allied Control Authority failed to function—largely through French intransigence—the chances for a central German government vanished and the likelihood of four-power cooperation dropped sharply.

American policies toward education and higher education in particular, were ill-defined at first, and nowhere was this truer than in Berlin. Eduard Spranger discovered that fact first. The evidence for a lack of clear goals in this aspect of occupation policy is strong. Although the Americans, in league with the British, attempted energetically to bring Berlin University under four-power control, the Soviet head start in occupying Berlin and their determination from the first to occupy the crucial *Bezirk Mitte* (central district) gave them a commanding lead. American policy continued to drift for a time. The famed research institutes in Dahlem under the Kaiser Wilhelm Gesellschaft received no official support at first, and Berlin University institutes were virtually shut down. The growth of ideological tensions between the Americans and the Soviets saw the students treated with open suspicion by influential officials such as City Commandant Colonel Frank Howley. His refusal in 1946 to allow Berlin University students to reside in the American Sector confused the student population.

Despite these developments, seemingly so positive for the Soviets and their ideological brethren and so negative for those with a Western orientation, a reversal of fortunes took place.

Obviously the advent of the Cold War increased East-West tensions dramatically and forced the Americans especially to establish a clearcut policy in Germany generally. This required strong elements of improvisation in American policy, and local officials began to do just that. Simultaneously, Soviet-SED policy began to encounter resistance on many levels, including that of higher education, and ultimately it lost its flexibility or its ability to win adherents. For the students this resistance surfaced as a result of their efforts to form a democratically functioning self-government at Berlin University. It was a pluralistic body, with representatives from all four political parties and a large number of politically unaligned students. Irregularities in student admissions policies and the enforcement of obligatory lectures, sometimes with overt ideological content, alienated many former supporters. Quite apart from the political issues, those students whom the SED were attempting to control were hardly docile or malleable. They were several years older on average than was normal for student populations. The postwar generation of German students, and especially those admitted to Berlin University, were often officially recognized Victims of Fascism. Others had been unwilling cogs in the vast destructive machine unleashed by the Nazis. All of them had been personally acquainted with the effects of totalitarian terror and most were not inclined to embrace an extreme ideology again. Thus, instead of accepting the controls that the SED authorities had begun to impose upon them with increasing frequency from mid-1946 onward, a significant group of students, now experienced in self-government, began to coalesce into an organized dissident movement. It found its focus in a student journal, *Colloquium*, an American-licensed publication, which was a first indication that American policy might change.

An emotional issue added new impetus to the dissident movement when Soviet authorities began to arrest students in 1947 under the mistaken assumption that they were engaged in acts of espionage, a charge which internal American intelligence reports pointed out was unfounded. Undeterred by such strong-arm methods, the dissident students began to examine their options and decided that in order to achieve any success in establishing a university free of ideological constraints they would need strong allies. Their investigations and experiences demonstrated that among the Western Allies only the Americans appeared able and willing to support them. The improvised nature of

American planning even in 1947 is clear from the fact that the Berlin students' first fruitful American contacts were with private citizens such as Fritz and Herta Epstein or with American officials who had had nothing directly to do with higher education in Berlin.

By the beginning of 1948, Cold-War tensions had reached such a height that the lines of involvement became rigid. The Communist coup in Czechoslovakia, keenly observed by the students of Berlin who watched the resistance offered by the students of Prague, indicated that Stalinist policy was now aimed at consolidating postwar gains in Eastern Europe, an area that included the Soviet Zone and East Berlin. If any doubt lingered, it disappeared altogether when such parties as the SED adopted exceedingly orthodox ideological positions at a time when Stalinism squared off against Titoism. With more influential American Military Government officials beginning to upgrade the importance of higher education policy, the dissident students engaged in a bold strategy of confrontation with SED authorities to force them to relinquish control of Berlin University to a long-proposed four-power arrangement, or, failing that, to call for the establishment of a new university in the western sectors. They could have waited for American or British initiatives in this respect, since both powers were beginning to prepare plans for a possible second university in Berlin. The British, hampered by a lack of resources and the uncertain political climate in Berlin, looked tentatively toward an expansion of the Technical University. The Americans, under Colonel Howley, were eyeing the creation of a university in Dahlem, possibly with close ties to the languishing school of advanced studies. A third possibility was that the dissident students would lose heart, abandon the struggle, and depart like many before them to other universities in the west zone. Instead, they chose a fourth, less likely option: the students, on their own initiative, proposed the creation of a new university in a western sector free of ideological constraints. They had taken care to establish close links with powerful political groups in West Berlin and with the media, so that their appeal to create a new university during a protest meeting over the dismissal of three of their number provoked an immediate public reaction. The preconditions for the Free University of Berlin coalesced in the spring of 1948, two months before currency reform and the ensuing Berlin Blockade and Airlift.

TWO

The Founding of the Free University, 1948

To anyone not acquainted with the events preceding the student protest gathering at the Hotel Esplanade on April 23, 1948, it might have appeared that one of the students, Otto Stolz, had spontaneously come up with an idea which promptly fired the imagination of his listeners: let the students of Berlin who were dissatisfied with the University Unter den Linden found a new institution in the western sectors. This "free" university would then permit the faculty and students alike to research and to learn, unencumbered by ideological constraints. Certainly the immediate media reaction and that of the public in the western sectors were extraordinarily positive. Already on that weekend vital conversations began to take place among students, journalists, city politicians, and American Military Government officials about the dismissed students' audacious proposal. Thus the immediate public reaction to his speech gave the appearance of spontaneity.

The reality was somewhat different. Those dissident students who appeared at the Esplanade on that Friday afternoon were, many of them, veterans of two years of escalating tensions with SED authorities. A healthy measure of idealism, combined with their common adversity, fear, and stubborn courage, had brought many of them together, first in the *Studentische Arbeitsgemeinschaft*, then in the *Studentenrat*, later at the "Salon Epstein," and now at the protest meeting. East-sector and west-sector news accounts differed widely on attendance at that fateful gathering, with the former claiming only three hundred and the latter two thousand attendees. Of greater importance for future developments was the fact that a core of perhaps thirty students had evolved a strategy to end the deadlock at the old university. They had confronted four possible courses of action in that third spring after the war. 1) They could concede defeat, abandon the struggle, and either make their peace with the SED authorities or go somewhere else to complete their studies. 2) It was well known in informed student circles that the British Military Government and a committee of SPD officials had held conversations about expanding the Technical University in Charlottenburg into a full university.[1] 3) With calls for a new university being a feature of the west-sector press since the autumn of 1946, it was conceivable that the other likely Allied power, the United States, might use its vast resources to found a second university. Although the students could not know it at the time, influential American leaders in Berlin like Colonel Frank Howley were already ordering the formulation of plans to do just that. At the end of January 1948, Colonel Howley had commanded his Berlin education chief, John R. Sala, to prepare for the eventuality of a new university in the American Sector. 4) The final possibility was the most daring approach: the students would found a new university which would continue the practice of strong student self-government begun at Linden University. Ideally, such a university would be an experiment in German higher education. There would be a considerable student influence in the administration of the university. The university itself would achieve greater independence from the state, an important consideration for those who had opposed the increasing controls of the SED-oriented *Zentralverwaltung für Volksbildung* over their affairs. This last possibility amounted to a reform institution, one with the potential to revolutionize the entire West German higher educational system.

Of the four possibilities, the first three were the likeliest to occur. Already hundreds of students had left Berlin to study at west-zone universities. Thousands more had made their private accommodation with the SED in Berlin and were busily preparing for their professional careers after long delays imposed by the war and the Nazis. There were precedents for an occupation power opening a new university to suit its own purposes. The French had done so at Mainz in 1946 and were about to do so again at the Saarland in 1948. The British feelers with the SPD to expand the Technical University in Berlin amounted to much the same thing. The Americans had advanced plans for creating a new university in Bremen, and they continued to pressure the *Länder* to aid Berlin in funding a school of advanced studies in Dahlem. John Sala's plans were merely the latest indication that the Americans were preparing to take the initiative in founding a university in the west. But there was absolutely no precedent for establishing a new kind of university, with a different legal basis and a different relationship between students and professors. To put it mildly, the notion of establishing a reform institution seemed farfetched in the anxiety-ridden former capital at a time when East-West tensions had risen to new heights. Given these greater historical likelihoods, it is little less than miraculous that precisely that fourth, improbable possibility was the one that came to pass. How and why this event took place, and the consequences that ensued, form the subject of this chapter.

THE AMERICAN DEBATE

Following the Esplanade meeting on that fateful Friday, events began to move at a bewildering pace. The entire Berlin press commented on the dismissals. The SED papers were predictably critical of the three students, and the west-sector press just as predictably supported them. The significant difference, however, was that the western papers echoed the students' call for a new university while the eastern press concentrated on the narrower issue of the dismissals. Obviously, neither Wandel nor the Berlin University authorities were taking the threat of a new university seriously, and since the entire concept seemed improbable they could hardly be blamed. By far the most crucial developments that occurred that weekend were not being reported in the press. Following the Esplanade meeting, a number of students met with Kendall Foss, a young American reporter on the staff of the American-licensed *Neue Zeitung*, who was in Berlin to cover the breaking story. Impressed with the students' ardor, Foss, who had been reporting about events at Berlin University since the previous year, suggested that they pay a visit to some influential American officials. On the next morning, Saturday, April 24, Foss called on General Clay to inform him what was afoot among the students. A shrewd judge of character, Clay was immediately impressed with Foss and asked him to keep Military Government officials informed on developments. A committee of students, with Foss among them, sought out Clay's cultural adviser, Indiana University President Herman Wells, in his apartment on the same day with their appeal for a new university. On that weekend, the students were also meeting with Mayor Ernst Reuter to seek his support. The answers they received from those high offices would determine what their options really were.[2]

Herman Wells was probably the most vital link in the American chain of officialdom. If he thought that the scheme was practicable, then the chances of garnering American Military Government support would improve markedly. Wells had arrived in Berlin the previous November from Bloomington after Clay had persuaded him to take a six-month leave of absence from the presidency of Indiana University. In a remarkably short time, Wells had reorganized and revitalized the education branch of Military Government. Now, five months later, he was wrapping up his affairs in Germany before returning home. Ever after, Wells never hesitated to credit the idea for the new university to German initiatives: "It would be well to make clear that the idea for a Free University in Berlin was brought to us by disillusioned students from Humboldt University and a young American newspaper man," he recalled. With Foss's help the students described what had gone wrong for them at Berlin University and why they desired to create a new institution. "They proposed the idea most enthusiastically," Wells remembered, and despite some misgivings, he promised that he would speak to General Clay.[3]

Wells had good reason to be cautious about promising the students any aid. In the highest reaches of Military Government, support for educational programs had been uneven at best. Various projects to create new universities in the American-controlled parts of Germany had failed because of a signal lack of support. When, in the spring of 1947, refugee students in Munich had tried to create a new, international university, popularly referred to as the "UNRRA University" or the "DP University," Clay had vetoed the plan. Instead, he ordered existing universities to absorb the mostly Eastern European students.[4] When Military Government education officers in Bremen proposed the creation of another international university, the Bremen authorities took up the cause, until it became apparent that they alone and not the Americans would support it. The scheme became moribund in the spring of 1948. Even Fritz Karsen's pet project, the new School for Advanced Studies in Dahlem, was faring poorly because of disputes among the German *Länder* about financial responsibility. Here, too, the Americans had made no investment, leaving it to the Germans. Thus, Wells had good reason to be noncommittal to the students. He also had to be cautious in approaching General Clay on the subject of yet another university scheme. "I was somewhat skeptical about the feasibility of the whole enterprise," he confessed later, adding that "it would be a very difficult project to initiate but I would take it to Clay."[5]

Already primed by Kendall Foss and aware of the press sensation concerning the three students, General Clay had made a decision of his own. "I was actually somewhat surprised that Clay gave the project enthusiastic support and waved aside the difficulties," Wells wrote. "In fact, he insisted that we attempt to get the institution open by the fall semester."[6] Wells admired Clay's decisiveness, but he knew, too, that the project was extraordinarily demanding. "That took my breath away," Wells later admitted. "I explained that starting a university is a complicated business, that we had to have a faculty, a library, laboratories, and so on. I was sure we would have plenty of eager students, but I was not sure that we could accommodate them in such a short time." Clay was not to be denied, however. "He brushed aside all my doubts, said it could be done," Wells added, "and asked me to put the machinery into motion."[7]

Like Clay, Herman Wells had taken his measure of Kendall Foss, and like his superior, Wells admired what he saw. With the Military Governor's approval, he hired Foss on the spot to serve as his special assistant to aid in the possible creation of a new university in the American Sector. The appointment was most unusual since Foss had had no previous experience with Military Government or with any other official agency. "Foss understood the situation and seemed to have the drive and competence," Wells recalled. "I never really paid much attention to the bureaucratic machinery except when I simply had to," he explained. "If you want to get something done, you get someone who is for it and who has the ability. . . ."[8] Without further ado Wells called together his education staff and set to work. Among those Americans who began studying the issue were Fritz Karsen, in his capacity as higher education officer at OMGUS headquarters, and Howard W. Johnston, a young education officer newly assigned to oversee Berlin-Sector youth activities. "Colonel Howley participated in one of the longest sessions . . . ," Wells added in his report to Clay on April 28, indicating the high priority Military Government had now assigned to the proposal. Indeed, despite his earlier suspicions about Berlin students in general, Howley became one of the strongest proponents of the project once planning had begun. Working at breakneck speed, Wells and his exploratory committee were able to present their preliminary conclusions to Clay only five days after Otto Stolz, Otto Hess, and Joachim Schwarz had announced their call for a new university from the Hotel Esplanade.[9]

The American education officers informed Clay that it was possible to start certain university faculties by the autumn of 1948. However, the Americans would have to act discreetly as well as expeditiously. "The new university should be a German university developed by German leadership," Wells cautioned. The Americans could best help the difficult undertaking by providing certain Military Government support. They could accomplish that objective best by forming "a small staff of three or four men who can give their full time to the project as aides and liaison officers with a German committee and the British." The Americans would also have to be prepared to offer the Germans "dollar funds and emergency purchasing procedures and top priority transportation for certain basic scientific equipment unobtainable here." All divisions of American Military Government would have to cooperate with the Germans, and generally the enterprise would have to be carried out well if it was to be carried out at all. The inevitable competition with Berlin University and wide public interest in the proposal would expose all shortcomings pitilessly. "This is a difficult project," Wells concluded. "It would not be attempted in the States under ideal conditions in less than two years time."[10]

The ad hoc committee justified the creation of a new university on several grounds. First, Berlin University had reopened its doors under exclusive Soviet control in January 1946, "after six months of determined opposition on the part of the Western Allies who wanted to keep it under quadripartite control." The Soviets' unilateral decision to control the university in 1945 over Western protests was by no means forgotten. As far as the Americans were concerned, the issue was very much alive. The report indicated that the Soviet Military Administration through the *Zentralverwaltung für Volksbildung* had created a climate that stifled free expression. Given the increasing pressure, "prominent professors have abandoned their positions for professorships at smaller universities in the French, American, and British Zones," the report stated. Students who criticized the Soviet-led measures either bowed to the pressure and resumed silence, or they departed for the western zones to join hundreds of other Berlin students in a kind of exile. "Great numbers of students have approached Military Government for places in other universities," the committee reported. They claimed that as sons and daughters of bourgeois families they had not had a fair chance to gain admission to Berlin University. Prewar Berlin, with 4.5 million inhabitants, had had 12,000 students attending the university. Postwar Berlin, with a total population of about a million less, found room at the university for only half that number. "The needs of the Berlin population are certainly not met in point of capacity and in the question of freedom by this University," the report concluded. The committee members cited the frequent press reports, student meetings, and personal contacts with influential Berliners as evidence of the need for a new institution. If Military Government were to live up to one of its cherished principles, equal opportunity for all, then it would have to enlist the support of the Berliners.[11]

The Americans saw that the first step to be taken was for prominent Germans from Berlin and the western zones to form a committee to work with Berlin civic leaders, supported where possible by the Americans. They also felt that the committee and its American support "should be coordinated with the British to avoid a duplication of effort." Wells's exploratory committee had discovered that a number of American resources were at hand. They could provide four million Reichsmarks initially, plus two hundred thousand dollars, and perhaps some buildings in Dahlem such as Boltzmannstrasse 4, currently being vacated by Military Government's finance division. They would have to find a new legal and financial basis for the university, since the Kommandatura-dominated Magistrat would surely be stymied by a Russian veto. The Americans thought in terms of resurrecting an old charter, or perhaps establishing the new university as a branch of an existing one, or placing it under the authority of the School for Advanced Studies in Dahlem. The latter had a governing body consisting of representatives from the four Länder of the American Zone plus Berlin, and given the present political atmosphere in Germany, the Americans felt the board would be sympathetic. While the committee recommended affiliation to the Dahlem school, they hastened to add that "the choice should be left to the German committee." Following an appeal to German and American professors to join the staff, the organizers should try to organize schools of social sciences, education, and public administration, since their material support would be less difficult than support for more technically oriented fields such as the natural sciences.[12]

While the exploratory committee established some important principles for the project, especially the primacy of German initiative, it was only a rough estimate that indicated that the project was needed, that it was feasible, and that Military Government should support this German initiative. Thus, with information from Foss and from his own cultural adviser, Clay became fully oriented on the plight of the Berlin students for the first time. Other influential American circles watched the recent events with interest too. "We have been keeping in touch with Ken Foss on this question," John Calhoun wrote to Political Adviser Robert Murphy. "Foss has seen General Clay on two succeeding Saturdays and he came away with the feeling that the General was greatly interested in the problem and in the possibilities of positive American action to assist in creating a university in the Western Sectors. Foss has been appointed chairman of the OMGUS committee which will explore the physical and other problems involved and submit recommendations to General Clay."[13]

The political adviser's office served as a State Department liaison with American Military Government in Germany, and a number of astute observers on its staff looked upon the student initiative with more than casual interest. One of Murphy's staff, Richard Sterling, had been a regular participant in discussions with the students at the Epsteins' "salon" and had kept his colleagues abreast of developments since the end of 1947. They were not altogther surprised that three students had been dismissed, but they were surprised at the resultant public reaction. "The Berlin University crisis has been one of those happenings which by a combination of circumstances has captured the public eye and has come to assume considerable importance to the western-democratic elements in Berlin," wrote another of Murphy's staff, John Calhoun. Given the dynamics of the situation, Calhoun was convinced that the Americans must demonstrate quickly that they backed the German enterprise; otherwise, disillusionment was sure to follow. "I fear that an indefinite delay in supporting German proposals along these lines would tend to make any subsequent action futile," he wrote to Murphy. Knowing that the political adviser was in close touch with Clay, Calhoun urged him to keep the university project on the Military Governor's agenda. "A project of this sort is obviously a gamble," Calhoun admitted, "but I think it is a worthwhile one and it should have considerable significance in underlining our intention to remain in Berlin and to furnish concrete support to the democratic elements here." Murphy was reassuring on the point. "General Clay has this very much in mind," he replied to Calhoun. The Americans understood the importance of the second university in the context of escalating East-West tensions in Berlin. Virtually at the moment of its birthing, the new university had assumed an extraordinary political and international importance. It had become inextricably connected to the Cold War.[14]

While enthusiasm for a new university was beginning to build among influential American circles, it became apparent at an early stage that the British in Berlin had considerable reservations about such

an undertaking. On May 5, 1948, Fritz Karsen paid a call on the educational adviser to British Military Government, Robert Birley, at Birley's
request in order to inform him of American moves to date. Following their lengthy meeting, in which Birley's assistant, Tom Creighton, joined, Karsen came away with the impression that the British
entertained considerable reservations about the entire enterprise. He
described Birley's thinking as follows: "We have to be clear about
the political consequences of such an undertaking, which may be very
grave, and we have a moral obligation to give the professorial staff
physical and financial security."[15] Birley had already given much thought
to the growing split in Berlin higher education that spring. He had
observed to one of his colleagues, in March 1948, that British Military
Government had always protested the Soviets' exclusive control of
Berlin University. "In consequence of their attitude," he wrote, "we
have taken the same line with the Technical University in our Sector."
He knew that the Berlin SPD had proposed transforming the Technical
University into a full university, but Birley was not enthusiastic, at
least at that stage. "I have advised against this for two reasons," he
continued. "(a) It is not a practical proposition in the present conditions
in Berlin to find the necessary buildings and equipment, and (b) There
is not room in Berlin for two full universities. I have consulted the
Political Division and the D.D.M.G. [Deputy Director of Military Government] Berlin, who agree with this view."[16]

The British authorities in Berlin had immediately perceived the protest actions surrounding the student dismissals in the broad context of
the Cold War. With plans for the economic unification of the three western zones in the offing, and a currency reform imminent, the Western Allies faced the blunt fact that Soviet and SED propaganda was pillorying
them as the dividers of Germany and the Soviets as the champion of German unity. In Berlin the student dismissals had contributed substantially to the already charged atmosphere and, according to British thinking, might have induced the Soviets to speed up their timetable. "There
has been a sharpening of the divisions already existing in Berlin which
can only be highly disagreeable to the Soviet authorities," cabled General Robertson's political advisers to the British Foreign Office. The political section of British Military Government felt it was necessary to explain in some detail to Foreign Minister Ernest Bevin the cause of the
dismissals. In doing so, they left no doubt as to who, they felt, bore the
chief responsibility: "The three students undoubtedly occupied themselves chiefly with political activities at the University in opposition to
the SED and had written articles in the University Students Journal [Colloquium], attacking among others the members of the Zentralverwaltung für Volksbildung. . . . They had also been consistently outspokenly
anti-Russian as well as anti-Communist."[17]

The British communication erred in that last respect inasmuch as the students had deliberately omitted any anti-Soviet utterances. Had the students been "outspokenly anti-Russian" in their journal, the Americans would have been obliged immediately to close down *Colloquium*, since criticism of any Allied authorities by Germans was still illegal. The report to Bevin, which undoubtedly had the approval of Robertson and Birley, suggested that while the students had demonstrated an admirable democratic initiative in calling for a new university, and that this reflected a general desire among the students of Berlin, they had not been pushed to the point of revolt as yet. The British, concluded the report, would have to consider the possibility of a new university in Berlin, but it was not a project to be undertaken lightly since it posed, they claimed, "difficulties of a formidable nature."[18] Just a few weeks earlier, Birley had concluded that the British might still exert influence at Berlin University by arranging for British lecturers to join the English faculty, a school popular with the students, and by erecting a British information center with library to attract students and faculty alike.[19] The plan was not a bad one, but it was difficult to implement, in part because of the limited financial means available to British Military Government and also because the authorities in Berlin University were not keen, to put it mildly, on allowing British authorities to place English language and culture staff on the faculty. In fact, the students complained bitterly in the pages of *Colloquium* that university authorities had deliberately refused to fill a much-needed chair in contemporary English literature precisely because of political considerations.[20]

The claim raised by British authorities that the dimissed students had been provocative in their conduct was substantially correct. Following the *Studentenrat* elections of December 1947, and the rough-and-ready SED tactics that accompanied it, it was obvious that a confrontation of some kind was brewing. The students around the journal *Colloquium* were well aware of the growing SED control of universities in the Soviet Zone. Widespread reports in the western press of student arrests in Berlin, Jena, Rostock, and elsewhere were added proof, if any had been needed, that the days of student independence at the Linden University were numbered. Western intelligence reports, both British and American, confirmed that between January and March, 1948, SED authorities were exercising ever greater control at the universities and were resorting to renewed arrests to gain their end.[21] For example, a prominent student at Leipzig University who was active in LDP politics, Wolfgang Natonek, was also arrested in the spring of 1948, an action that was widely reported in the west.

The dissident students in Berlin were undoubtedly aware that their provocative articles in *Colloquium* would produce a response from Paul Wandel and the SED sooner or later. There was also little doubt that following their intense conversations with Americans in official and unofficial capacities, the students had concluded that they were the one Western Ally inclined to offer tangible help. Students like Otto Hess had observed caution and reserve among British authorities when they discussed their difficulties at Linden University. Discussions between British authorities and SPD leaders in Berlin concerning the expansion of the Technical University into a full university might, in the autumn of 1946 when the idea was first broached by students and others, have found a willing response. Now, nearly two years later, one conspicuous fact that emerged was that few students at Berlin University wanted to be party to the British-SPD proposal. "We were prepared to bite on that sour apple if need be," Dieter Spangenberg later admitted, but neither he nor any of the other dissident students was enthusiastic about the prospect. To them the Technical University—which was still heavily damaged—was an unpromising institution in which to create a new democratic university. Their discussions with the Americans encouraged them to hope for much more.[22] Certainly the limited resources of the straitened British placed sharp limits on how much they could invest in higher education in Berlin or elsewhere. A proposal in July 1946 to attach a pharmaceutical institute to the Technical University had failed because of British claims that the resources for support were lacking.[23]

Although the Americans, including their Military Government leadership, had been moving toward support of a new university since the beginning of 1948, they still faced an uncertain situation in May 1948. The dismissal of three students, prominent though they might be, was not by itself sufficient cause to proclaim the existence of another institution. How many more were prepared to take up the uncertain cause besides the obviously committed students connected to *Colloquium*? Where were acceptable faculty and resources to be had? Although the answers to those difficult questions became clear with the passing of time, even the strongest proponents entertained some doubts when the call went out to found a new institution. Several months later, the designated American higher education officer in Berlin, Howard W. Johnston, admitted his early concerns to an officer of World Student Relief, a private relief agency, stating that "there were misgivings on the part of all of us as to the final development of a university in the Western Sectors of Berlin."[24]

The ambivalence of the Americans was perhaps best summarized in the thinking of an early supporter of the students: Fritz Karsen. On April 28 he had signed a memorandum along with Johnston, declaring a new university feasible. However, on May 11 Karsen submitted a different set of views on the proposed university to his superior, Richard Alexander. As before, Karsen was convinced that the students and faculty at Linden University had faced severe limitations on their teaching, learning, and student activities, "and it is to be feared that they will be more restricted in the future." Karsen also saw that the move for a new university was gaining adherents among powerful political circles in Berlin.

The SPD was about to propose a new university at a meeting of the Magistrat. Karsen was confident that the resources to establish a new university were certainly available if the Americans were willing to commit themselves. Finally, he conceded that the idea had gained such momentum already that "it will mean a loss of face for the Western Allies if they do not support this opposition against the Soviets."[25]

Despite these compelling arguments, Karsen saw some urgent reasons why the Americans should keep their distance. Noting that the political situation in Berlin was already tense and that a new university could come into being only if the Americans supported it, Karsen claimed that "it would be considered by the Soviets as a severe attack by the U.S." He feared that the Soviets might even be provoking the confrontation in order to place the blame for the impending split upon the Americans. Karsen was worried about American tenacity as the crisis worsened. "I am not in a position to judge how much risk we are willing and able to take at this moment," he told Alexander. At this stage the Americans had one protest meeting and considerable "political noise" on which to base their calculations. "If only 100 students and some professors had started an exodus in protest against totalitarian oppression," he wrote, "such action would have been much more effective than any protest meeting." Karsen had no doubt that there were "courageous people" at Berlin University, but the blunt fact remained that for the present almost all of them were remaining in place. The Americans could scarcely expect a university worthy of the name to emerge from the ranks of those who had not been admitted to study in the first place. At the moment there were only three dismissals to go on despite earlier rumors that as many as 2,000 more were about to follow. Indeed, Karsen reported that the Berlin University authorities had reopened the case, and it was possible that the three students might now be reinstated. Karsen was convinced that the Americans could not assemble a qualified faculty in time for an opening in the autumn of 1948. "Professors from outside universities will not accept the physical and financial insecurity," he announced. They might be able to attract young assistant professors and the odd foreigner through promises of new titles and financial blandishments, but that would hardly constitute an adequate faculty. His recent conversations with Birley and Creighton had sobered Karsen as much as anything else: "The U.S. will stand alone with that initiative," Karsen warned. "I have the impression that the British are not prepared to support our venture, if we start it." Finally, Karsen left his superior in no doubt as to what would happen if the venture soured. "If our attempt leads to bad consequences for the Germans, they are sure to blame them on us," he warned.

Given the pros and cons, the question was, what should the Americans do? Karsen's conclusion on May 11 was unambiguous: "Much though

I would wish and have wished all along together with you, Dr. Alexander, that a free university should be founded in Berlin, it is my considered opinion that this is a very dangerous moment to start it and that the unjust dismissal of three students is not sufficient justification for doing it now."[26]

Later that month, following a trip to the American Zone, Karsen became even more convinced of the correctness of his decision. Kendall Foss had asked him to canvass support for the new university in the west. Consequently, on May 13, at a meeting of a zonal foundation to regulate the financing of the School for Advanced Studies in Dahlem, Karsen raised the subject only to learn that none of the Länder ministers was prepared to accept a share in supporting a new Berlin university.[27] Immediately thereafter, Karsen had undertaken an ambitious informational trip throughout the American Zone, during which he decided to sample West German reactions to the recent events in Berlin. The results were hardly encouraging. "Answers to cautious questions from students and professors of other universities gave me the impression that there was no enthusiasm, to say the least, for such a foundation," he reported to Alexander.[28] Karsen's pessimistic reaction and his subsequent findings proved to be the basis for a growing conviction among certain education officers that it was not expedient for the Americans to aid in the founding of a new university. The director of the education and cultural relations division, Richard T. Alexander, and his assistant, Sterling W. Brown, accepted Karsen's reasons as valid and toward the end of May submitted a report to General Clay warning against participation in such an adventure. In essence, Clay's senior educational adviser, who had served with Military Government since the summer of 1945, was warning of a disaster if the Americans came to the students' aid.

Another pole of opinion was forming just as rapidly, however. If Alexander was the most senior educationist, Herman Wells stood even higher as Clay's overall cultural adviser, of which the education division was merely one part. With the Military Governor's permission, Wells had hired Kendall Foss as his special assistant and promptly appointed him to chair a "Committee on the Establishment of a German University in the U.S. Sector of Berlin." Its six members represented the chief functions of Military Government, including finance, law, civil administration, information control, and education. The exact brief of the directive was important since otherwise the American group might have been interpreted as the preparatory committee, leaving little room for German participation: "The committee will explore all relevant circumstances and requirements relating to the feasibility of establishing a German University in the U.S. Sector of Berlin and report its findings with appropriate recommendations to the Military Governor, said report to contain an outline plan for the establishment of such a university should the committee deem it feasible." Thus, it had a twofold task: to make a feasibility study, and to submit plans for such an establishment if the committee concluded it would work.

Three weeks later Foss and his committee submitted their findings to Clay. They did not try to diminish the difficulty of the task, but, not unexpectedly, they concluded that a new university could begin functioning in the autumn of 1948, if the Germans and Americans provided solutions to the following six problems: the selection of a sound legal form of organization; immediate and long-term financing, especially in light of an impending currency reform; recruitment of an adequate initial teaching staff; provision of adequate building space; the collecting of sufficient library facilities; and the procurement of laboratory and classroom equipment. Their guiding principle was significant: "The committee believes that the project as it is developing will be (and should be) fundamentally German in its initiation and realization. U.S. participation can properly be confined to moral and material support of a worthy German idea." Foss, who authored the report, informed Clay that German sponsors for a new university were coming forward daily and that already on May 11 the SPD had carried a motion in the Berlin Assembly, by a margin of 83 to 17, calling for a free university in Berlin. Only the SED had opposed it. Now that the Germans were proceeding to organize the project themselves, the Americans were in a unique position to benefit because, Foss observed, "the formula of U.S. support for a German effort avoids the charge of undue U.S. interference in German affairs and relieves the undertaking of a possibly compromising, out-and-out American character. On the contrary quick and generous U.S. support of a German attempt to revive and safeguard the free traditions of learning will be widely taken as appropriate and praiseworthy." He claimed that "the British are stirring around, showing considerably more interest than they did even a month ago," in part because of expressions of support in their own zone. Moreover, Foss noted, "there are also small signs of awakening French interest."[29]

Because the committee posed the impending creation of a university as a German initiative, there were limitations on how much the Americans could do at this stage. Foss reported that his group "found itself unable to develop specific and detailed plans pending the emergence of a German committee whose function it must be to select the course preferred." Yet the Germans faced limits, too. Foss observed that "the German committee hesitates to take the plunge until it learns that its initiative will be supported."[30] Consequently, by the end of May, the Germans and Americans were eyeing each other nervously, debating how far each committee could or should proceed without some assurances from the other. Such tentativeness might strike the observer forty years later as unnecessary. However, the creation of the Free University was a pioneering enterprise in postwar Germany, one in which each side was learning to work with the other. The best Foss could do for the Military Governor was to offer some estimates of the situation.

Echoing Fritz Karsen's worries, Foss laid out a series of risks the Americans incurred in supporting the Germans. First, the Soviets might take the enterprise "particularly hard and react with unusual vigor," he wrote. The Americans could not ignore the dangers here, because they might include such unpleasant repercussions as greater restrictions on German communications with the West, increased kidnappings, the closing off of Berlin University and the State Library to west-sector students, the splitting of the city government, and a vicious press campaign of ridicule "probably featuring cartoons with dollar signs." If the Soviet-Zone authorities were particularly clever they might try "a tactical switch to the utmost freedom at Berlin University," thus taking the wind out of the sails of the promoters of a new university in the west. The Soviets could cause financial troubles for the new enterprise if they undertook a currency reform of their own. However, it was not only the Soviets who posed some risks. The enterprise was complex, and Foss pointed out that overcoming the many hurdles quickly would not be easy. He observed that "the Germans and perhaps our own people may entangle themselves in procedure to the point where action flags and stops." Most ominous of all was a risk the Americans would have to face in the Berlin of 1948: "If it should ever become necessary to withdraw from Berlin," Foss warned, "there would be a somewhat larger group of Germans than already exists with claims on U.S. assistance in leaving the city."[31] In other words, the Americans would have heavy responsibilities if it ever came to a military confrontation in Berlin, a possibility that seemed not so remote in May 1948, at a time when western transportation links were already facing Russian interference.

The American committee under Foss outlined possible solutions to the most immediate problems facing the university. They offered no less than five legal approaches to such a creation. One of the universities in the west could establish a branch institution in Berlin; one of the Länder could provide legislation creating a new university under German public law; private individuals, acting as a board of trustees, could establish a foundation under German private law, although they would have to establish some kind of state status in order to confer degrees; the School for Advanced Studies could take it under its wing; the Technical University might do the same, assuming the British cooperated; or Military Government might create legislation of its own under which the university could operate. The problem was that most of the solutions would take months, even years to enact. Of course Military Government could enact its own legislation expeditiously, Foss claimed, but the German committee might well come up with its own legal solution.

The economic obstacles were major, but according to Clay's financial adviser, Walter Heller (later an adviser to Presidents Kennedy and Johnson), the Americans were in a position to provide interim support from reorientation funds as the need arose.[32] More difficult was the problem of supplying an adequate teaching staff. There was some disagreement on this subject, Foss admitted. However, Howard W. Johnston, Berlin Sector's new university officer, submitted a reassuring letter from a prestigious source: Nobel Prize laureate Otto Warburg. The famed biologist had addressed a letter directly to General Clay, stating that identical doubts about assembling an adequate staff had arisen earlier in the creation of the School for Advanced Studies. To their pleasant surprise, Warburg wrote, "more scholars and teachers from all zones of Germany offered their services than we would ever have been in a position to use." Warburg's opinion was that the situation had not changed since, "so that at the present time there is a surplus of academic teachers available who would be very happy to teach in a university of the U.S. Sector, Berlin."[33] Other German scholars, such as Kurt Landsberg or the art historian and publicist Edwin Redslob, had informed Johnston that they had prepared lists with dozens of names of prospective faculty. Similarly, Professor Walter Braune, an Orientalist, had assured his American contacts that many assistants were available to the proposed university. Guest professors from west-zone universities were a real possibility to fill the short-term gap, and William McCurdy of the legal division had concluded that there were no prohibitions against teaching staff at Berlin University transferring to the western sectors. "They are free to leave one job and take another anywhere in the city," Foss announced.

The legal advisers based their conclusions on ACA Directive 43, which prohibited interzonal moves without approval of the zone commander but did not require that permission from residents moving within the four sectors of Berlin. "Sixty out of 66 professors listed in the Berlin University catalogue already live in the western sectors," Foss informed Clay. To be sure, there were other opinions about faculty to consider, too. Foss admitted that Herman Wells in a recent tour of the American Zone had found as much as twenty percent of university positions unfilled for lack of acceptable candidates. On the other hand, Foss cited a claim from Fritz Karsen, who held strong reservations about the availability of staff but who had, according to Foss, "stated positively that a staff the equal of the present Berlin University could surely be found." However, Karsen's alleged remark was ambiguous as to the quality of the potential staff, and Walter Braune, when pressed, "agreed that there was a paucity of great men." Despite the obvious deficiencies in this vital area, Foss and his committee concluded that the project could garner enough of a staff to make a start "and that this minimum can be gradually exceeded as word of the venture spreads." The Americans might even send some of their visiting professors to Berlin to help out. "The important thing," he concluded, "is for a little band of brave men, modestly housed and shabbily equipped, to stand up and assert their rejection of controlled access to knowledge."[34]

The committee was more sanguine about solving the problems of building space, library resources, and the necessary laboratory and classroom equipment. As a consequence, and despite the risks involved, their conclusions for the project were unequivocal:

1. Politically and morally the project is worthwhile and proper.
2. There are sound and feasible ways of securing the establishment of a university this summer.
3. The project is developing from German initiative.
4. U.S. support is necessary and can be supplied without placing unusual or unbearable burdens upon the regular apparatus of Military Government.

In submitting their report, Foss and the committee had concluded the first phase of their work, he announced. If their recommendations met with Clay's approval, then those whom the Military Governor wished to designate for the task should prepare "to get in touch with the interested Germans and promote positive action."[35]

Had he based his decisions on the report by Kendall Foss alone, General Clay would presumably have had a simple choice. Already one month earlier he had expressed interest in the idea of a new university when Foss and then Wells had first approached him. However, before making a move, Clay, through Wells, submitted Foss's report to Alexander for consideration. This gave the education director an opportunity to gauge the prospects for a new university.

Alexander promptly presented an utterly different set of conclusions to Clay. As one who had helped shoulder the burden of American education programs in Germany for three years, Alexander naturally presumed to understand the situation more intimately than the newcomer, Foss. His higher education officer, Fritz Karsen, had nearly as much experience, and Karsen's thinking, as seen in early reports to Alexander, was clearly evident in this latest report. Alexander and Karsen disputed Foss's claim that an adequate supply of professors was available. "Open-minded and truly democratic professors, as required for a new university, are almost completely lacking, "Alexander wrote. The opinion that a new university "would be enthusiastically welcomed in circles far beyond Berlin . . . is not borne out by statements made to our officers during their recent trips to the Zone," he claimed. In fact, Alexander assured Clay that Karsen had never made any assertion that they could find a staff equal in quality to that of Berlin University. The education regulars flatly denied seeing any British or French interest in the project. They observed that the Germans' sole initiative to date had been to react against Soviet domination of Berlin University, whereas "all the practical steps, such as financing, finding a legal basis, providing space, library and equipment, assembling a professorial staff, and giving it adequate measures of security, would be left to the initiative of Military Government."[36]

Alexander urged Clay to understand that the extraordinary financing of the new university, support not offered to any other institution, "would undoubtedly stamp this foundation as a political act of Military Government." The lack of physical and financial security meant Berlin was unattractive to professors from the west, and Foss's group was deceiving itself if it thought that large numbers of professors might arrive from the Soviet Zone. Alexander offered a blunt rejection of the other committee's assertions. He claimed to have "grave doubts that the project is politically worthwhile." The establishment of a new university by the summer of 1948 was impossible. The initiative lay with the Americans, not with the Germans. Finally, the task would overburden the existing Military Government staff. Alexander had some choice words for the Foss report, too: "The report is sketchy," he informed Clay, "and does not reveal the careful study and analysis that the founding of a university demands. If the committee has done its best, as set forth in the report . . . then it is our opinion that the problem needs to be referred to a more competent and unbiased staff."[37]

The opinion of the education regulars, led by Alexander, could hardly be lightly regarded, and they had some telling arguments about future developments should the university come into existence. "The students trained in this new university will have no chance to work in professions in the Eastern Zone and, by so doing, keeping democracy alive," Alexander wrote. Instead, he predicted that the new institution would "become a training ground for all the democratic-minded young people from the Eastern Zone." These professors and students would have to look for positions in the western zones, "where the established universities are already producing too many professionals." For this and many other reasons, Alexander's staff felt compelled to warn against American involvement. "This office has favored the founding of a university in the U.S. Sector of Berlin for more than two years," Alexander concluded. If the Americans had created a modest university at an early stage when the present tensions were absent, then undoubtedly little political opposition would have arisen. The dismissal of three students hardly justified the current venture. "This office would favor the establishment of a university provided the Germans—students and citizens—in Berlin demand it and demonstrate that students from the Western Sectors are no longer admitted to the University of Berlin and can no longer remain there."[38]

Since Alexander's report represented the thinking of the "old hands" in Military Government, their opinion might have been expected to carry more weight than that of an ad hoc committee formed

under a journalist and outsider, Kendall Foss. The professional education-
ists had, in effect, charged him with being biased and incompetent. Moreover, it was well known that Foss and Karsen had clashed with each
other almost from the moment Wells had appointed the journalist as his
special assistant. When Karsen appeared at the first meeting of Foss's committee, he scanned its composition and announced that the education
and cultural relations division (E&CR) was not represented. Foss replied
that as Wells's assistant he fulfilled that function, whereupon Karsen
went to his immediate superior, a senior military officer, Colonel Emil
Lenzner, and secured permission to remain aloof from the committee's activities. Karsen then informed Foss of his action, thereby infuriating the
younger man, who promptly accused him of being a liar. Even his
friends admitted that Foss could be impetuous, and although he later
apologized to Karsen, the breach never really healed. Alexander's report
was ample evidence of the continuing tensions that existed between
Foss's committee and the education staff.[39]

Although to the casual observer the situation might have appeared
to be at an impasse, there were several reasons why the climate of opinion surrounding Alexander was not as influential as it might have been.
First, Alexander had announced he was leaving Military Government
soon. Fritz Karsen's signature was conspicuous by its absence from Alexander's highly critical report to General Clay on May 29. Instead, a relatively unknown member of the education staff, Sterling Brown, had co-
authored the report. Karsen, as senior higher education officer, should
have been the logical coauthor. Distancing himself from the findings implied his disagreement with Alexander's reasoning. In any case, he, like
Alexander, was leaving Military Government in a matter of weeks. Alexander was respected as a knowledgeable expert on German education,
but his career with Military Government had also been controversial.
Herman Wells assessed him as "a brilliant man from whom we learned
a great deal, but he was not especially gifted as an administrator."[40] Following Alexander's advice, General Clay had steered Military Government into a direct conflict with the Bavarian government over a school reform which Alexander had virtually ordered to be put into operation.
Alexander considered the Germans incapable of meaningful educational reform on their own and was prepared to impose it if need be.
The Bavarians had resisted his reform plans successfully, and Clay, sensing that he had been badly advised, backed off from Alexander's ambitious proposals in the spring of 1948. Understandably, he was less inclined to take Alexander's advice unreservedly now. For his part,
Alexander claimed not to have seen any substantial progress on the
part of the Germans toward democracy in the course of the occupation,
and so he was not inclined to see the dissident students as anything
but an atypical, isolated group in an inherently authoritarian popula-

tion. Despite his admiration for Alexander's knowledge and experience, Wells admitted that the education chief could be difficult: "Not only was he dogmatic," Wells later observed, "he could sometimes be vindictive as well."[41]

Karsen had viewed his mission as one of creating more democratically structured universities in the American Zone, and he had labored hard to get the universities to develop boards of trustees so that those governing boards would establish greater contact with the public, in effect bringing the German university out of its ivory tower. He also wanted greater student participation and power in the university structure and a more egalitarian social composition of the student body. Karsen had urged these reforms at conferences of university rectors, and although they had discussed reforms for several years, few if any changes had actually been made. He had justified his pet project, the creation of the School of Advanced Studies, on the grounds that it would help create a more democratically inclined generation of university professors. However, Karsen left Military Government with a sense of having made little headway in his democratization efforts at the university level. Whoever was inclined to support the creation of a new university in Berlin required large reserves of idealism and faith that the Germans in Berlin could act in a democratic fashion and that American Military Government would follow through on its statements of support. Alexander, especially, lacked that faith in 1948, influenced no doubt by the mixed success of American reeducation programs since the onset of the occupation. Relative newcomers like Kendall Foss and his committee retained the optimism needed for the venture.[42]

Although the Americans had employed relatively few German emigrés in their Military Government, there were some who proved to be particularly influential. Among the most respected in General Clay's entourage was Carl J. Friedrich, on leave from Harvard University and serving as a general adviser to Clay in 1948. Many years later, in retirement, Clay rated Friedrich one of his ablest assistants. Thus, it was perhaps just as well that Friedrich was in a position to see the evolving poles of opinion concerning a new university and, at Clay's request, to comment upon them. Friedrich saw immediately that the proposed university and American support for it had become "intensely political," and he admitted to following it with care. Friedrich announced that he had had several conversations with Herman Wells and with Germans and Americans alike. Writing in mid-June, about three weeks after Alexander's angry report, Friedrich, in a memo to Clay, announced that Alexander's study "appears to be somewhat out of date." In the weeks since the protest meeting at the Hotel Esplanade, publicity and statements of support for the enterprise had snowballed, and Friedrich called into question the validity of the report. "It is evidently written by someone who is unaware of a number of crucial developments, including the interest

of the Lord Mayor of Bremen [Wilhelm Kaisen], and the financial resources which I understand are in sight both from American and German sources."[43]

Friedrich was irritated by the tenor of the critical report, claiming
that it was too academic and failed to explain what further careful
study would do in estimating the feasibility or desirability of the new institution. In essence, Alexander's report "overlooks the importance of timing," Friedrich maintained, and it "fails to point out just what such
study would produce in the way of further information or insight." Alexander's most telling objection, the lack of available staff for the new university, was a point on which Friedrich declared himself satisfied. He
had seen Edwin Redslob's prospective list of faculty and, impressed by
it, had forwarded a copy to Clay. Friedrich had also taken his measure
of the Berliners of 1948, and with respect to their tenacity he entertained no doubts at all. "It is my feeling that there could not be a more determined demand on the part of Germans for the establishment of such
an institution than the strong and explicit statements on the part of the
governmental authorities involved. . . . There is also vigorous and insistent interest of the students." Friedrich urged Clay to consider the enterprise "in light of the international situation." He concluded his remarks
with a ringing endorsement of the Foss report and a rebuke for Alexander. "Since the Germans are demonstrating a determination to have
such a university, it is my opinion that the support of Military Government should be generous and not hampered by an enquiry at every
point as to whether the Germans had done all they could."[44]

Other influential Americans on Clay's staff entertained little doubt
about what should happen. James Pollock, a respected adviser to Clay
on political affairs early in the occupation, returned to Berlin in May
1948, in the midst of the growing crisis. One of Clay's longtime military
staff, General William Babcock, immediately raised the subject of the proposed university. "He wanted to know what I thought of the possibility
of establishing a free university in our sector—could we get a staff and assure them of reasonable tenure? The Soviets," Pollock recorded in his diary, ". . . are utilizing the University of Berlin as a propaganda center,
and it has ceased to be a real university." Pollock, like Friedrich, had
had no immediate connection with educational affairs or with the
E&CR division. Yet, for them, as leading Military Government advisers
where concern with Soviet policy toward Berlin and Germany was of par-
amount interest, there was no doubt that the Americans should support
the new institution in any way they could.[45]

On the same day that Carl J. Friedrich communicated with General
Clay, Saturday, June 19, the main participants in the drama that was
unfolding, the Germans, made a vital move. A small, self-appointed committee of seven had called together a meeting of forty prominent Berlin
citizens to consider plans for the creation of the much-discussed uni-

versity. In a certain sense, this first concrete action by the Germans confirmed the hopes which Americans like Foss, Wells, Clay, and Howley had pinned on German initiative and confounded the critics like Alexander. Friedrich's influential position paper ended whatever reservations still existed in Military Government. In fact, General Clay had already made one crucial move. Taking Financial Adviser Walter Heller's recommendations to heart, the Military Governor had sent Foss to Munich to obtain an account of nearly twenty million Reichsmarks from the income of overt American publications like the *Neue Zeitung*. Foss then transferred the account to a private German trustee just in time for a major event in postwar Germany: currency conversion. Had the sum remained in Military Government accounts on June 19, it would simply have been canceled as part of the effort to keep the quantity of new currency limited and the demand high. Private individuals could, with certain restrictions, convert their Reichsmark holdings as of June 19 to the new, costlier Deutschmark. The rate of exchange was pegged at 1:10. Thus, if the Germans followed through on their intent to found a new university, they would find a nestegg of two million Deutschmarks, a tidy sum, capable of carrying the enterprise through its first year. Clay had deliberately conducted the transaction in secret, preferring to see what the Berliners would do on their own. It was a test which they passed easily. While the Americans had been debating the merits of a new university, the Germans had been anything but idle.

STUDENT INITIATIVES

It did not take long for SED authorities to discern that the student protest meeting at the Hotel Esplanade was more than an isolated incident. Given the attention paid by the western media, the SED-controlled press went on the attack immediately. On the day following the Esplanade gathering, the *Berliner Zeitung* (SED) paraphrased Otto Hess's column in *Colloquium*, "The Struggle for the University," calling the latest development an "Attack upon the University." The "combatants," (the three students) now found themselves cut off from their previous arena, the paper commented, and had to return to their "base," (the American Sector). An SED commentator, "Dr. K.," observed that the Americans were attempting to split higher education in Berlin as part of their overall plan to split all of Germany: "The American imperialists are tearing Germany apart, because they want to dominate the detached western section as their own exclusive colony," he wrote. Thus, even as the Americans were splitting the trade unions, the cultural organizations, and the City of Berlin, so, too, they were now bent on splitting the university. Higher education was a vital target because the German reactionaries and the Western imperialists knew that it trained the coming generation for the leading positions in society. There was no room in the

Western scheme for a socialistically inclined German youth, which explained their bitter attacks on such innovations as the *Vorstudienanstalten* which promised to bring in more students from worker and peasant sectors of society. "The composition of the student body is not an internal concern of the university," the SED commentator stated; "it is a concern of the entire people." Consequently, those who worked for a living had the right to maintain extreme vigilance over Berlin University in order to assure that they did not nurture enemies in their own midst. The *Zentralverwaltung* was exercising precisely that vigilance in dismissing the three students.[46] The rest of the East-Zone press joined the offensive immediately. For example, *Neues Deutschland* charged that the three students were part of the same sinister circles that were "making terrifying progress towards the nazification of the universities of the western zones."[47]

In a lengthy article entitled "Freedom and Dignity," the *Tagesspiegel* countered that the illegal dismissals had forced Paul Wandel and his *Zentralverwaltung* to show their true colors. Wandel had still not drawn the logical consequences from the Berlin elections of October 20, 1946, when the Berlin electorate had voted no to SED control, the paper stated. To be sure, founding a new university now, at the very moment when disruptions of western traffic to Berlin were increasing, would not be easy. "However, democratic self-esteem is growing, too," observed the writer. The students and professors were showing ever more self-awareness in the face of SED intransigence, and a new university would be the consequence.[48] The American-licensed *Neue Zeitung* addressed itself to the practical possibilities of founding a new, free university and speculated on means to fund it and to secure its legal standing. Already on April 27, the press was estimating ways and means to provide library resources, buildings, sources of income, and possible faculty from west-zone and east-zone universities. The press office of the *Zentralverwaltung* had just stated that the creation of a new university in the western sectors was "simply impossible " and "99 percent propaganda." The commentator felt otherwise.[49] In the press, at least, the lines were clearly drawn.

Yet even at this eleventh hour there were still hopes among some that a split could be avoided and the university maintained intact. On April 27, press reports indicated that the *Zentralverwaltung* had backed down from its earlier threat to dismiss any student who had participated in the Hotel Esplanade meeting.[50]

However, the issue was fast becoming a cause célèbre among Berlin students. The chairmen of the student councils of Berlin institutions of higher learning had met on the weekend following the Hotel Esplanade demonstration and called for a meeting of all Berlin students to be held at the Technical University on April 29. The chairman of the Technical University's student government, Hans Ulrich Bach, agreed to support the dissident students in various practical ways, including the provision of temporary office space and equipment.[51] On the same day that the students were gathering at the Technical University, the SPD entered a resolution in the Berlin Assembly proposing that "the Magistrat be empowered to undertake all measures necessary for the creation of a university at which freedom, independence in research and teaching, and the democratic standing of the student body are preserved."[52] After all the press attention and innumerable discussions, this was the first concrete action by Berliners to set the wheels in motion for the creation of a new institution. At the same time that the SPD was entering its motion in the Berlin Assembly, students of all political persuasions began gathering at the Technical University. Even a few brave SED loyalists arrived to defend their party's position.

The students discussed the plight of Hess, Schwarz, and Stolz and in the end agreed to send a letter to Rector Hermann Dersch at Berlin University calling upon him to institute an open proceeding regarding the recent dismissals. The students should have the right to defend themselves, they claimed in their letter. They should also have the right to speak, think, and assemble freely in the type of university espoused by the Western ideals of Karl Jaspers. If Dersch did not respond to the students' demands by May 3, the letter warned, then the student parliament of the Technical University would petition that university's rector to admit Hess, Schwarz, and Stolz to the Technical University in full standing. Thereupon, the student body would issue an appeal to all German universities to aid in the erection of a Berlin university not tied to sector boundaries.

One of the three students, Otto Hess, addressed the students at the Technical University and demonstrated that he was hardly inclined to accept his fate in silence. He accused the leadership of the Zentralverwaltung (i.e., Paul Wandel) of being "totally and unequivocally" committed to an alien ideology. "Such a leadership no longer had the right to call itself German." Such an extreme judgment, which was bound to create further bitterness on the part of the SED authorities, typified the political polarization that presaged the splitting first of Berlin and then of Germany. That Hess, one of the coolest heads among the dissident students, would make such a claim speaks volumes about the strong emotions that had been aroused. He was hardly the only person to use strong language that evening. When, in the ensuing discussion, an unidentified SED student claimed that any German university would have turned out the three students because of their journalistic activities, he drew peals of laughter from the 3,000 students in the audience.[53] As one of those present, Claus Reuber, the current chairman of the Studentenrat at the University Unter den Linden, noted, the meeting on April 29 was the crossing of the Rubicon for those bent on founding a new university. There was no turning back.[54]

At the students' insistence, the student council at Berlin University duly met on May 3 to discuss the dismissals. For those seeking a radical solution, the gathering was a major disappointment. By all accounts it was a stormy debate, following which the council voted 14 to 9 not to strike. More than three hundred viewers were on hand, and this time there was strong SED representation, unlike the gathering at the Technical University a few days earlier. The best that the dissident students could do was to call, by a vote of 16 to 7, for a student referendum on a possible strike. Now, a new danger threatened them at the meeting, when Theodor Brugsch, Paul Wandel's deputy, spoke to the council. He seemed at first to be conciliatory, announcing that in the future the Zentralverwaltung would permit formation of a disciplinary committee with representation from the student council. Despite this tacit admission that a disciplinary committee should review the affair after all, the Zentralverwaltung was hardly about to concede defeat. Brugsch stunned those present when he announced to the student council that the Zentralverwaltung would close down Berlin University completely if the students attempted to strike.[55]

In the midst of the debates, in what by this time had become an annual May Day tug-of-war, the students protested once again about SED celebrations at Berlin University. In 1948, the Communists displayed a huge banner—"More Proletarian Students into the University!"—which neatly summed up their major goal for higher education. The previous year had seen some measure of moderation in that the SED demonstrations had taken place with loudspeakers instead of banners, as a concession to those non-SED protesters who had first raised their voices in 1946. Now, two years later, the banners had returned, a symbol of the militant mood that was so evident to all eyewitnesses of Berlin in the deepening Cold War.[56] The best that the student council could do was to defeat overwhelmingly the final resolution of the day, a Zentralverwaltung-inspired motion condemning the erection of another university in Berlin.

Although that final vote seemed convincing, the student council's unwillingness to declare a strike immediately aroused critical comment in the west-sector press. Some accused the student council of naively giving in to the Zentralverwaltung on the basis of vague promises about reactivating the disciplinary committee. Others observed that the dismissals had involved a matter of principle and that the council had thrown away its chance to show the SED authorities that they were taking a stand on principles. Yet others felt that the students were simply allowing themselves to be cowed by Wandel.[57]

The situation was not so clear-cut as first appeared, however. Paul Wandel had begun to realize that the move to form a new university was gathering momentum. On April 30, the day after the SPD had entered its motion in the City Assembly calling for a free institution of higher learning, Wandel and Rector Dersch received a delegation of forty professors from Berlin University. To their surprise, Wandel immediately conceded a point and agreed to allow the university to review the dismissals. The move preceded Brugsch's statement to the stormy meeting of students on May 3. He was prepared, Wandel said, to entrust the matter to the long-ignored disciplinary committee and the University Senate after all.[58] Fritz Karsen's prediction that moderation on the part of the Zentralverwaltung could kill the incipient university appeared to be happening. For its part, the Berlin University Senate issued a declaration on May 3 condemning any attempt to create another university in Berlin. Such a move would add to the economic and spiritual division of the city, they claimed, and it was bound to fail anyway given Berlin's impoverishment. This was especially true, they concluded, "if the new institution is created on an out-and-out politically combative basis."[59]

Other ominous signs were building, too. If the student council had felt itself under considerable pressure from Theodor Brugsch and the SED contingent of students during its May 3 meeting, it was in part because up to this point the faculty of Berlin University had maintained a resounding silence on the student dismissals. On the other hand, the University Senate, composed of the deans of the various schools, appeared to have taken a strong stand against the proposed second university. Disturbed by an absence of support from their professors, the student council sent letters to each of the university deans. "If we have not turned to you yet concerning the dismissal of the three students," they wrote, "it is not because we are indifferent to your opinion. Rather, we did not wish to anticipate your declaration, one which we had hoped from you." The students felt they had waited long enough and were now asking the faculties through the deans what their silence meant.[60] At almost the same time, Professor Walther Eltester, dean of the school of theology, sent a reply from his faculty suggesting "the participation of all responsible groups" in the writing of a new university constitution. Eltester also proposed that the university conduct its own disciplinary actions in the meantime, "so that any hiatus in the legal existence of the university . . . can be avoided."[61] The effect of such a mild protest seemed uncertain. Although a few individual faculty members—surgeon Arthur Hübner was one—had also raised protests over the dismissals, the central fact that had emerged by mid-May was that no systematic wave of protest had developed among the faculty. Within the university community, at least, the students were apparently on their own.

Reactions among critics of the Zentralverwaltung to the professors' passivity were angry. "It is not only the students who are wondering about the passivity of their instructors," commented the Tagesspiegel. "The workers of Berlin have demonstrated their intentions by showing determination in countering their Communist leadership. This appears to be lacking among the professors."[62] Battles were progressing simultaneously over the trade unions and the university, maintained the commentator, because in both instances the Communists craved those key positions. "Opposition within organized labor has found its leaders," the article continued, "but the student body feels that it has been let down by its professors in its struggle for freedom of scholarship."[63] Disappointment with the professors persisted. Student council media spokesman Ernst Benda, in addressing a CDU group on university affairs at the end of May, declared openly that the continuing silence of the professors had left the students in the lurch and had forced them to take the initiative alone.[64]

Meanwhile, on May 11, 1948, the student council convened again but without the scores of onlookers who had been so much in evidence in earlier meetings. In fact, the student council had begun demanding student identifications or press credentials from those visiting the council sessions after they discovered that some visitors wearing FDJ (Communist youth league) badges were not students.[65] Claus Reuber, the student council chairman, read a letter from the University Senate announcing that that body was convening a disciplinary committee to review the dismissals of Hess, Schwarz, and Stolz. The committee was also to offer a report to the Senate on the legal ramifications of the case and was to conduct a hearing for the three students within a fortnight. On that basis the University Senate would render its decision. In the meantime all parties were to maintain silence on the issue.[66]

If all discussions were to be held in abeyance for two weeks, after which a decision favorable to the three students took place, it was conceivable that despite the noise in the press and the preparatory work by the Americans, moderation by the *Zentralverwaltung* would deflate the entire revolt. However, such a development presupposed that the issue was still confined to the fates of Hess, Schwarz, and Stolz. In reality, their case was proving to be the last straw in a long-simmering conflict over the status of the university, and that became abundantly clear on the same day that Reuber announced the formation of the disciplinary committee. A fiery debate took place in the Berlin City Assembly on May 11, and in the end a noncommunist majority of 83 passed a resolution over 17 SED votes, empowering the Magistrat "to undertake all measures for the creation of a free institution of higher learning in Berlin." The reasoning for the undertaking was clear: "Freedom and independence of scholarship and a democratic attitude of the students must be preserved. The recent actions which led to the dismissal of three students have proved that these conditions do not exist at Berlin University."[67] The resolution resulted from agreement among the SPD, CDU, and LDP caucuses and increased dramatically the likelihood of a new university. Observers at Berlin University understood its import immediately, and, under the guidance of Law Professor Hans Peters (CDU), dean of the law faculty, the Berlin University Senate again declared itself "opposed to any intention to found a second Berlin university."

Peters was an anomaly in the drama surrounding the creation of the Free University. Although a member of the CDU, he broke with his own party on this issue, much to the delight of the SED. Peters's reasoning was straightforward: he did not want university politics to contribute further to the splitting of Germany and Berlin, a position parallel to that espoused by the SED. Consequently, Peters led the opposition in the University Senate. He was also a member of the Berlin City Assembly and had seen to it that five CDU members abstained from the resolution calling for a new university. Using his influential position in the CDU, Peters had tried to amend the SPD motion so as to have the Magistrat "examine" the conditions needed to create a free university rather than actually calling for its creation. The effort failed. Nevertheless, one other non-SED participant voted against the resolution, too. Helmuth Brandt, recently expelled from the CDU and an instructor in law at Berlin University, joined the Communist faction in condemning the SPD resolution. For his part, Peters also penned a lengthy article for one of the Berlin dailies, elaborating his reasons for opposing a new university in Berlin. He maintained that admissions policies were now above reproach, academic freedom existed in fact, and the founding of a "free" university in opposition to Berlin University was a contradiction in terms. "How a Kampf-university, possessed of the barren goal of destroying another one in the same city, can be politically free, is the secret of those who defend the idea," he thundered.[68] Students like Hess were forever after outraged at Peters's public statements in the spring of 1948. Hess had accompanied Peters to a student conference in Hamburg the previous year and maintained that it was Hans Peters who had informed the students of his disgust at what he perceived as flagrant and continuing irregularities in student admission policies by the SED. TU student Hans Ulrich Bach was present during the conversation and recalled the incident similarly. Neither could account for the change in Peters's position.[69]

The Americans followed the debate intently, seeking to gauge the determination of the Berlin political forces on the issue. An observer from Ambassador Murphy's office, Richard Sterling, noted that on May 11 the SPD speakers "stressed the fact that the expulsion of the three students . . . was only an immediate and concrete symbol of the continuing pressure exercised by the SED with the purpose of making Berlin University into a communist training institution." Sterling also had to admit, however, that this latest political action in Berlin was not as clear-cut as it might appear. "The resolution itself was ambiguous in the sense that it did not specifically call for a new university in Berlin but demanded the establishment of a 'free university.' This can be interpreted to mean that the Magistrat would be empowered to explore ways and means of restoring academic freedom to the presently existing Berlin University. Only if the Magistrat were unable to reestablish Berlin University as a free institution would it then propose and support the founding of a new university."[70]

Did the lengthy debate in the City Assembly and the differences of opinion among SPD and CDU delegates presage a split of opinion among the non-SED parties which the SED could then exploit? Sterling did not think it likely: "It is a foregone conclusion on the part of most qualified observers that the SED will not loosen its grip on Berlin University." Therefore, the resolution really implied the second course of action: the establishment of a second university in the western sectors. Sterling, like Alexander, Karsen, and others before him, was worried about another possibility: "However," he wrote, "it is possible that the Sovzone Ministry of Education [Wandel's *Zentralverwaltung*] will make some apparently conciliatory gestures in order to weaken the case for a Western Sector university."[71]

The Americans were well aware that Wandel was now permitting the university to judge the dismissal issue and that the Berlin University Senate had instructed a disciplinary committee composed of two professors and two students to investigate the grounds for the three expulsions. Hess, Schwarz, and Stolz were to receive their "day in court" after all at an official hearing. The implications from Wandel's concession were potentially far-reaching. By outward appearances Wandel's right to dismiss students was being challenged by a suddenly independent-looking University Senate. Nevertheless, there were grounds to be suspicious about the move. Sterling pointed out to his superiors that the Senate, composed of the ten deans, had shown uncharacteristic unity and had voted unanimously to constitute the disciplinary committee. They had done so with the active encouragement of the *Zentralverwaltung*, he observed. Simultaneously, Rector Dersch had imposed a halt to further discussions on the divisive issue, pending the outcome of the review process. "This temporarily silences the Student Council," Sterling noted, "which had been one of the main centers of agitation against the expulsions." Far from showing a change of heart, the American reasoned, Wandel appeared to be seeking a way of making a show of independence and impartiality at Berlin University "no matter how 'packed' the membership of the University Committee may be."[72]

That an effort to defuse the situation was afoot was now well known. The Americans were aware that the three students were engaged in conversations with senior faculty at Berlin University. A confession of sin on their part would likely see their readmission and an end to the crisis. However, that did not appear to be their intention. Despite those mediation attempts, Sterling noted, "Schwarz and Stolz refused and declared the issue was not one centering about their expulsion but

was one of the collapse of academic freedom in Berlin University."[73]
Nevertheless, a question mark lingered. If the disciplinary committee decided in favor of the students and reinstated them, such action might
go far toward proving supporters of Paul Wandel correct: The university
would have shown unequivocal freedom of action.

If the review machinery continued to function as it had in the recent past, then the three students could scarcely expect complete impartiality. In mid-April, when protests first arose that Wandel could not simply dismiss them and that the disciplinary committee should make the
decision, two committee members, Professor Friedrich Möglich (physics
and education) and Dr. Günther Brandt (law), had promptly announced
that the case lay outside their committee's jurisdiction. They had made
the announcement without consulting the third member, student council chairman Claus Reuber, and Reuber had resigned from the committee in protest. Now that the University Senate had turned the issue over
to the disciplinary committee after all, it was significant that Möglich
and Brandt remained as its faculty representatives. Former student council chairman Gerhard Petermann and a fellow student agreed to become
student representatives, and the hearing took place in mid-May.

It was characteristic of the prevailing atmosphere that two of the students, Otto Stolz and Joachim Schwarz, refused to attend the hearing,
claiming that if they entered the Soviet Sector they were in danger of arrest.[74] Their fears were not altogether unjustified. Even as the student
protests were taking place, Soviet authorities had arrested a student, Ingeborg Euler, on May 3, on the pretext that they had found written permission from the French commandant, General Hepp, for Euler to visit
Mainz.[75] With a shudder everyone remembered the wave of student arrests, especially among CDU loyalists, in the spring of 1947. Schwarz,
as a prominent CDU member, felt particularly vulnerable, having been arrested four times by the Soviet authorities already, and Stolz, as the
most prominent gadfly among the dissident students, felt hardly less so.
Thus, it was left to Otto Hess to make his lonely way on May 24 to the
university's disciplinary committee in the Soviet Sector. Not inclined
to become another martyr, Hess took what precautions he could. Professor Robert Rössle (pathology) accompanied him as his faculty advocate,
and fellow medical student Gerhard Löwenthal, still an employee of
RIAS, drove them to the appointment in a prized automobile. Hess and
Rössle entered the hearing while Löwenthal ostentatiously parked their
"getaway" car in front of the building with the motor still idling.[76]

The thrust of the hearing became apparent immediately. Möglich,
as chairman, announced at the outset that the meeting was not a disciplinary hearing, because such a hearing could occur only for members of
the university community. The Zentralverwaltung had revoked the right
of Hess and the others to study, Möglich reasoned, and the disciplinary
committee reaffirmed Wandel's right to take that action. Möglich reite-

rated Wandel's charge that the three students, through their publishing activities, had "injured the manners and dignity of a student." Hess recalled later what the second faculty member had to say: "Herr Brandt participated in the discussions only to the extent of trying through lengthy explanations to demonstrate that the actions of the *Zentralverwaltung* had been justified." After the meeting, Professor Rössle reacted angrily to his colleagues' interpretation, Hess stated, and told him that all expectations of getting a fair hearing were hopeless. Berlin University had fallen to a low state, the older man observed, and his best advice to Hess was to "shake the dust of Berlin from your feet and resume your studies at a West German university."[77]

As Hess and Rössle sped back to the west with their driver, Löwenthal, the two professors on the disciplinary committee composed a report to the University Senate, restating their position that the dismissals were not the committee's province and that the University Senate must make the final decision. Gerhard Petermann and a fellow student representative on the committee, Herr Bornemann, refused to accept that reasoning, withheld their signatures, and submitted a minority report to the Senate, condemning the review process. It was a courageous act, especially for a vulnerable student like Petermann, who was in his final year of medical studies and had yet to undergo the final examinations.[78]

Brave though it was, Petermann and Bornemann's report went by virtually unnoticed. The Berlin University Senate ignored the students' dissenting stance and accepted Möglich and Brandt's findings instead. On May 26, the Senate announced that the disciplinary committee had declared the dismissals beyond its purview. Therefore, the Senate declared that the articles of the three in *Colloquium* had significantly exceeded the bounds of freedom of expression and that they were "highly defamatory attacks upon the various parts of the university and the *Zentralverwaltung.*" The consequences were evil: "This damaged greatly the reputation of the university on the part of the public and weakened discipline among the student body," the Senate continued. "Since one of those involved did not appear at the proceedings at all, another sent a representative, and the third declared that the publications were fully justified . . . the Senate sees no reason to propose any change in the actions taken by the *Zentralverwaltung für Volksbildung.*"[79] The *Colloquium* publications provided the most ammunition for the decision, but it was Otto Stolz's satirical account of the ceremonial changing of rectors which obviously rankled the University Senate most of all.

Although it appeared at that moment that Wandel had won the battle, the victory, such as it was, proved to be Pyrrhic. With the University Senate's announcement on May 26, any uncertainty that hitherto had plagued those Germans and Americans interested in a new university now fell away. Berlin University, and through it the *Zentralverwal-*

tung, was saying in effect that no concessions were possible in the matter. The dissident students could either concede their guilt and shake "Berlin's dust" from their feet as Rössle had suggested to Otto Hess, or they could continue with plans to found a new university. The unyielding stance of the disciplinary committee—with the notable exception of students Petermann and Bornemann—and the obvious distrust the three students displayed toward it and toward the review process in general suggest that chances for a reconciliation had been remote at best. The outcome of the disciplinary proceedings, far from healing the students' grievances, served only to widen the split.

The British, too, were interested observers in these events, if for no other reason than that the only other major Berlin university, the Technical University, lay within their sector, and events at Berlin University were having an impact on their institution. At the end of May, in an assessment of the situation, British Military Goverment's Berlin political adviser, M. Garran, predicted to Foreign Minister Ernest Bevin that "it is possible, and indeed likely, that the disciplinary committee will find the three students guilty of unbecoming conduct and may dismiss them again." A few weeks later Political Adviser Christopher Steel of the same office observed to Bevin that "the disciplinary committee treated the matter very summarily and referred to the University Senate which decided, after brief discussion, to uphold the action of the *Zenteralverwaltung.* . . . The general feeling of the students is that the University authorities showed weakness and that the three students were given no real chance to state their case. The University authorities have undoubtedly lost considerable prestige in consequence."[80]

To be sure, the three students had proceeded on the assumption that there would be no reconciliation. News accounts expressing doubt about the committee's objectivity had appeared even before the disciplinary hearing.[81] Stolz had already accepted an invitation in early May by the SPD, CDU, and FDP student groups at Munich University to give a public address on current conditions for students in Berlin. Billed as a protest meeting, it failed to attract the rector of Munich University, "on the grounds that all the facts pertaining to the expulsion were not available," observed Richard Sterling. Nevertheless, there were signs of growing support elsewhere. The student council at Munich's Technical University joined in the protest as did the chairman of the Bavarian Student Association. Similarly, Erlangen University's student council supported the action and demanded that the expellees be allowed to matriculate at Erlangen. Rector Walter Hallstein offered the same refuge at Frankfurt University, and Stolz claimed that SPD student groups at Kiel and Hamburg had elicited support from their respective rectors. In the western zones, at least, Sterling could report that support appeared to be building for the dissident Berlin students.[82]

The same could not necessarily be said for the ranks of faculty at Berlin University. Historian Fritz Rörig, an old friend of Eduard Spranger, continued to lecture at Berlin University. He was not happy at the drift of recent events and confided his feelings to Spranger: "One specific newspaper is leading a deliberate war against the real Berlin University," he complained. "I hardly presume to defend all of the actions which have occurred here. However, to maintain that there is no more true scholarship at Berlin University is an irresponsible assumption."[83] Nor was Rörig prepared to suffer in silence. He distributed his views in a confidential written statement to his history students on June 8. Rörig felt that the dismissal of three students seemed to have led the rest to conclude that science and scholarship were no longer to be found at Unter den Linden, an assumption he energetically contested. He had just returned from Mainz, in the French Zone, having delivered a lecture which differed not in the slightest from lectures he delivered in Berlin. "Nothing can damage the intellectual bonds between East and West more than propaganda which casts doubt upon the teaching and the professional ethos of the Berlin professors," Rörig wrote. Such irresponsible criticism, he maintained, hindered East-West contacts. If this criticism were justified, then it could not be repressed. "However, if it is not justified," Rörig continued, "then such a criticism which systematically undermines the scholarly reputation of the University can only be designated as irresponsible and damaging to you."[84]

The dissident students perceived matters differently. Despite objections from individual professors like Fritz Rörig, the pace of events quickened following the University Senate's decision to stand by the dismissals. The Senate had ordered the student council to cease any further activity—an unprecedented act in itself—and the student council replied by ordering a special meeting of its members to convene on June 11 at a place "outside the jurisdiction of the University." The west-sector papers reported this news to the public. The SED-oriented *Berliner Zeitung* countered with the announcement that any student found attending the impending meeting would also be subject to dismissal.[85] At about the same time, a meeting of student council representatives from the Soviet Zone (*Studentischer Zonenrat*) was held in Rostock. It resolved that the dismissals of the three students were just and decried what it felt was an attempt to use the affair as a pretext for splitting Berlin University. For good measure the East-Sector press quoted statements, from Uwe Vaagt, a student representative from the British Zone, and from an AStA (*Allgemeiner Studenten-Ausschuss*, the student government) representative from Goethe University in Frankfurt am Main.[86] Shortly afterward, the united student council for the British Zone convened in Hannover and expressly disavowed the position of the British-Zone student at the meeting in Rostock.[87]

On June 8, the same day that the Berlin University Senate issued its warning to the student council, Colonel Frank Howley held a press

conference. When asked by news reporters if the Americans were prepared to help found a new university he replied: "I have never been officially informed of the German intent to create a new, free university in
the western sectors." The Americans were capable of offering building
space in Dahlem and in Lankwitz, Howley stated, but they could do nothing unless a German representative officially approached them.[88]

Now the dissident students began to take matters into their own
hands. At the same time that the Berlin press published Howley's remarks, the students at *Colloquium* announced that in order to prove the
seriousness of their intentions all those interested in founding a new university should sign petitions to that effect at the offices of *Colloquium*
and of the SPD youth group. The press announcements also noted that
those signing the petitions would be guaranteed confidentiality.[89] The
Rubicon had been reached, and it was the students who began crossing it
first.

As scheduled, on June 11, twenty of the student council's twenty-
nine members met at the coffee house of the Taberna Academica in the
Technical University where they had continued to find temporary refuge among the TU students. The Technical University's AStA chairman, Hans Ulrich Bach, had been in close contact with student leaders
at the University Unter den Linden throughout that spring. He and the students of the Technical University provided a safe haven as the crisis developed.[90] Claus Reuber read a common declaration for them all, condemning the "chain of legal infringements" that had taken place at
Berlin University, most prominently Paul Wandel's dismissal of the
three students. Reuber also condemned the passivity of the faculty at Berlin University and announced that the twenty representatives were resigning from their posts immediately. Not only the chairman, but also
the vice-chairman and most of the other officers on the council had
joined the revolt. However, three SED members from the school of education remained on the council, leaving six nonaligned student representatives on the rolls at the old university. The large dissident majority
urged the students of Berlin University not to participate in another
student council election since, they said, that would only lend the appearance of legality at Unter den Linden, a situation that no longer con-
formed to reality. Otto Stolz was also present, "who in his usual polemical way," complained the SED press, "thundered against . . . the Senate
and against the progressive elements in the student body."[91] Stolz was indeed showing his usual combativeness, denouncing the role played by
Professor Friedrich Möglich in the disciplinary review and revealing
that Möglich had been a member of the Nazi Party from 1932 to 1940,
when he was ousted for purely personal reasons (his mistress, Stolz
stated, had been Jewish). Furthermore, Möglich had been a Gau (district) cultural leader and a member of the SA and of the Nazis' academic auxillary, the *N.S. Dozentenbund*, Stolz announced. Worst of all,

Möglich had never been denazified in any court, a fact that had not deterred the current vice-president of the *Zentralverwaltung*, Robert Rompe, from issuing him a document attesting to Möglich's antifascist credentials.[92] The rough-and-tumble of partisan politics in Berlin higher education was becoming ever more obvious as the tensions mounted.

The University Senate responded to the mass resignations by announcing its intent to initiate disciplinary proceedings against the twenty student council representatives.[93] The final student council list at Berlin University before the split showed twenty-nine representatives.[94] It was striking that even at that late stage the three SED representatives were still being elected exclusively from the school of education.[95]

If there had been any lingering doubts about the willingness of students to take a chance on a new university, those doubts were rapidly disspelled in the days that followed. Encouraged by the defection of two-thirds of the student council and by Colonel Howley's signals of potential American cooperation, hundreds of students flocked to the offices of *Colloquium* and to SPD headquarters and entered their names on petitions for the creation of a new university. "With these lists the youth of Berlin and the East Zone clearly raise the demand for an educational institution in which they can be taught in an atmosphere of true freedom," commented the British-licensed *Telegraf*. Some observers, stated the same source, still seemed to believe that the student body, by exerting itself, might yet preserve its necessary freedoms. "But it appears to us," continued the same paper, "that this exertion, commendable though it may be, would permanently condemn the students to sacrificing themselves for an ideal that can never actually be realized at the current Berlin University."[96]

By declaring themselves openly in opposition to the SED authorities and in sympathy with the three dismissed students, a significant portion of the student body, be they the majority of the student council or the hundreds of petitioners, had clearly signaled their intentions. They wanted a new university in the western sectors. No one, themselves included, believed that it was possible for students alone to create such an intricate institution. They needed powerful allies from the most important segments of Berlin life. Political, academic, financial, and mass media leadership would have to help from the German side if anything were to develop from this incipient student revolt.

THE PEOPLE'S UNIVERSITY

Now that hundreds of dissident students had declared their intentions, other voices were soon raised. Encouraged by the students' resolve, seven influential publicists, political leaders, and academicians issued an appeal on June 15, 1948, to approximately sixty prominent citizens to convene at the clubhouse of the Society of Friends of Science and Philosophy in Wannsee on June 19. The seven organizers included some familiar figures in the events that had developed at Berlin University since the war. Else Knake, former dean of the medical faculty, was among the organizers. So was Edwin Redslob, art historian and licensee of the *Tagesspiegel*, who had led the press campaign against SED control of Berlin University since 1946. Crucial to the enterprise was Berlin's SPD leader, Ernst Reuter. An exile in Turkey during Hitler's reign and recently elected Governing Mayor of Berlin (but currently blocked from that post by a Soviet veto), Reuter was a major ally for the supporters of a new university. Two other organizers were prominent academicians, Professors Carlo von Brentano (medicine) and Hermann Muckermann (anthropology). Professor Kurt Landsberg added political weight, since he was serving simultaneously as a city councilman for the CDU. Another councilman, engineer Carl-Hubert Schwennicke, completed the list and represented the LDP. Their appeal went out to prominent Berlin citizens to meet with them for a specific purpose: "Discussion will be held on which possibilities exist for the creation of a new university in West Berlin. From this talk which is expected to be of a purely informational character, the participants undertake no obligations whatsoever. Should a portion of those present come to the conclusion that the founding . . . is necessary and possible, then a committee could form up in an adjoining meeting, which would then undertake the preparatory work.[97]

Four days later the invited guests duly assembled at the clubhouse to consider their options. Kendall Foss described what happened next: "Forty sober and determined Germans met last Saturday afternoon in a German clubhouse in Wannsee to proclaim the need and start the work of founding a free university in Berlin. There were no allied nationals present, no allied statements read, no allied promises made. It was a purely German display of initiative and—in Saturday's tumultuous atmosphere of currency reform, closing frontiers, and Russian threats— courage."[98] The list of guests specifically omitted professors currently teaching at Berlin University, because of the risk to their security. One unfortunate exception was Wilhelm Wengler, a lawyer with a newly completed habilitation at Berlin University, who was shortly to make his presence felt. All but one of the sixty guests invited had agreed to come. However, on the appointed day, June 19, the City Assembly called an extraordinary session to discuss the latest crisis: Currency reform was coming to Berlin, and it was bound to cause grave trouble with the Soviets. Therefore a number of the political figures who had planned to attend the clubhouse meeting, including Reuter, begged off in order to face this new front. The rest of the organizers and their invited guests decided to go ahead with their meeting anyway.

Edwin Redslob explained the reason for assembling the prominent group of public and academic figures on that day. "What we intend here is no conspiracy," he stated. "It is a positively directed plan, serving positive goals." Redslob reminded his listeners that under the recently departed Nazis the search for truth had ceased at the universities and the students had sunk to the level of mere objects. "Wherever this system continues to function—and it can happen in the East as well as in the West—it contradicts the fundamental idea of academic life." Redslob accused SED authorities of steadily reducing the opportunity for free research, the consequence of which was that the students "raised the demand for a new and free university, a demand seconded by the City Assembly by an overwhelming majority." Accordingly, the assembled group, with its collective expertise, had the assignment of determining if a new institution of higher learning was feasible or not. Redslob left no doubt among his listeners that the western sectors, with their many scientific and scholarly institutes and organizations, could carry on a teaching function and be of service to a new university immediately. Like the students, Redslob too felt that the universities had carried some responsibility for the Nazis' seizure of power in 1933. Therefore, he concluded, "we are interested in the question to what extent university operations can be regulated and modernized."[99]

City Councilor Walter May reported to the group that within city government they had done everything possible to remove Berlin University from control of the Zentralverwaltung and to place it under an independent board of trustees, but their efforts had been in vain. "The founding of a second university does not mean that the existing one will be put out of business," he explained. The Germans of the western sectors would have to take the initiative here, but with the help of the occupying powers. May observed that various groups had already been engaged in planning efforts, but now the time had come to coordinate those efforts and to act in liaison with the Allies. Financing for the proposed university would have to come from some source other than the Berlin city government, he announced, "because its budget is dependent upon confirmation of the Kommandatura." Any budget that included support for a new university would unerringly draw a Soviet veto. However, the city could provide other kinds of aid, such as living quarters for students and professors.

The discussions continued for some time, with various participants confirming May's prediction that finances were critical to the proposed enterprise. Professor Richard Thurnwald cited the dearth of financial support as a major reason why the professors had taken a wait-and-see attitude. Another participant, Paul Altenberg, predicted that students receiving a higher education at the proposed university would be denied careers in the Soviet Zone and the western zones were already overcrowded with students. That left only the western sectors of Berlin as a possible outlet. Professor Schiemann was probably the least optimistic, claiming that a "university in the West will mean the final splintering of Berlin. That is the main reason why many professors are against it.

You should not attempt to found something new. Rather you should try to reform that which exists. This idea is being suppressed by the press. The proper course is resistance to the *Zentralverwaltung*." Other pessimistic notes sounded too. Wilhelm Wengler, a specialist in public law, felt that the organizers would have great difficulties in organizing a law faculty. He was of one mind with Schiemann: a chief problem for the students remained unanswered: Where would they make their careers upon completion of their studies?[100]

Such arguments were familiar by then and had given many potential supporters of a new university pause earlier. However, events seemed to be overtaking the hesitant participants rapidly. Thus, Professor Jakobi replied that "we would do well to enter the matter with optimism, because we can hesitate no longer. The conditions are no longer bearable, and the students expect a new university. Finances do not appear to me to be the main question. We all have connections with the outside, and I am convinced that an appeal to outside universities will be heard. What we need is strength and optimism." Although only a student in the august group, Otto Hess felt compelled to speak, especially after Frau Schiemann's statement. He claimed that the students had offered maximum resistance to SED pressure. With few exceptions the professors had left the students "in the lurch from the beginning," he stated. The question of securing a means of existence was a matter which the students themselves could solve. They were studying in the name of science, scholarship, and a broadening education rather than concerning themselves only with bread-and-butter career issues. They (the dissident students) could no longer recommend studying at Linden/Humboldt University, and in any case President Paul Wandel had gone on record as saying that those seeking employment in the east would have to undergo a political test. Thus, the students would have to make their way in Berlin and in the west in any case.

"What we have experienced at Leipzig University shows us what we can expect for Berlin," stated Oswald Bumke. "Therefore I am for the founding." Professor Muckermann was just as emphatic, stating that "we must help the city that has defended itself against the gathering coils. . . . Germany expects this from us." Muckermann wanted the creation of a preparatory committee immediately. Shortly after, Edwin Redslob formally put the question to the forty guests: "Who in this group approves the possibility and the necessity of forming a new, free university?"

In the ensuing count, thirty-eight of the forty persons present voted affirmatively. Only the lawyer, Wengler, and Frau Professor Schiemann dissented. In the end no one actually voted against the question only because Schiemann felt compelled to change her no to an abstention and Wengler walked out of the meeting. Redslob had proceeded directly from the discussion to a vote, and then proceeded to accept nominations for a committee of twelve who would handle the affairs of the future university. Fritz von Bergmann took notes on the proceedings and felt that Redslob handled the duties of chairman well on that first day, adopting a friendly tone that alleviated hard feelings in instances where a minority was outvoted. One notable exception was Redslob's failure to call the first, purely informational meeting to an end in order to allow a graceful exit for those who felt that they could not participate in the risky project. "Thus it came to an unpleasant but scarcely noticeable incident that two participants (Wengler and Henneberg) left the room in protest," von Bergmann recorded.[101] Later, Otto Hess recalled the incident, too: "He [Wengler] claimed to have accepted the invitation to attend under false premises and would never have attended if he had known that the creation of a new university in the west of Berlin was to be discussed. As a faculty member at Linden University, he disapproved the founding of such a university and refused to participate in the gathering any longer."[102]

Those assembled considered issuing a manifesto immediately, but because the political leadership was currently grappling with currency reform and unable to attend the first session, the thinking of the participants was that the manifesto should wait. To be sure, there was such interest among the press and public that they had to issue a communiqué at least. Consequently, they announced that the gathering, consisting of academic leaders, students, and persons from the public sector in Berlin, had decided to create a university in Berlin. Furthermore, they had created a committee of twelve to carry on the necessary preparatory work, to issue a manifesto, and to seek support from the Western Allies.[103] The Preparatory Committee was deliberately designed to appeal to all major segments of the West Berlin sectors. There were several SPD members, led by Ernst Reuter, and a representative each from the CDU and the LDP, Professor Landsberg and Engineer Carl-Hubert Schwennicke respectively. Otto Hess spoke for the students. Several academics, notably Warburg, Knake, and Muckermann, represented the so-called Dahlem Circle, the notable research institutes located in Berlin's most fashionable suburb. To this group were added a medical scientist, Hermann Bermann, and a law specialist, Karl Kleikamp. To its credit, the Technical University added a professor, anthropologist Hermann Muckermann, and a student, Hans Ringmann. Edwin Redslob, as a licensee for the *Tagesspiegel*, rounded off the group, representing the public media.

Kendall Foss, who probably stood closest to the Preparatory Committee among the Americans, reported to Clay his impressions of the Berliners' efforts following the crucial meeting of June 19. To be sure, Foss was not present at the clubhouse. However, he and other Military Government personnel had held innumerable meetings with the interested parties among the Germans. "The students were always the most positive," Foss maintained. "The politicians have been clear and decisive. . . .

They never entirely forgot their party interests, but neither did they ever allow such considerations to hamper them. The academicians have mostly been the hesitant ones. The political aspects mystify them. Working with other and less highly educated groups bothers a good many of them, too. A few have shown themselves [to be] deplorably self-centered and weak; a few magnificently public spirited and courageous."[104] Foss was impressed that the participants at the June 19 meeting acted without express guarantees of aid from the Americans. "They never heard a word of promise about money," Foss assured Clay. "They do not yet know whether their hopes can be fulfilled. But they finally came to see that nothing could possibly happen unless they, as representative Germans, were ready to take the plunge and set about trying to create a haven of free and unfettered access to knowledge and the truth." Foss ended his report with unabashed praise for the Berliners who were now going ahead "undeterred by those besetting fears which arise in every German's mind whenever something occurs to cloud the future of this four-power international city."[105]

The Preparatory Committee convened on the following Tuesday, June 22, to begin the concrete tasks of planning. This time Ernst Reuter served as the chair, a position he could claim as the dominant political presence in the western sectors. All agreed that his was easily the commanding presence in a group not lacking in strong wills. Reuter had unique qualifications and experience in the current crisis that was confronting Berlin in the summer of 1948. A member of the German Communist Party in his younger years, he had been a prisoner of war in Russia in World War I, became a personal acquaintance of Lenin and Trotsky in the Russian Revolution, and remained a Communist until 1922, when disillusionment with the KPD's practices as opposed to its ideals induced him to join the SPD instead. A successful director of public transportation in Berlin in the 1920s, Reuter advanced to Lord Mayor of Magdeburg in 1931 until the Nazis seized power. They immediately threw him into a concentration camp, treated him even more brutally than they did the other hapless inmates, and ruined his health by 1935. Released because of pressure from friends and relatives, Reuter moved eventually to Turkey, where he, along with scores of other notable German exiles, helped Kemal Atatürk in the modernization of that country. When the twelve-year Reich passed out of existence, Reuter did not hesitate to return to his shattered homeland with his family, where they shared fully in the misery that accompanied defeat. Despite his chronic ill health, Reuter became a commanding presence in the ruins, and he worked manfully to rebuild Berlin. It was not long before Ernst Reuter became the political leader of the SPD in the former capital, and his election as governing mayor in the spring of 1948 demonstrated unmistakably his popularity. Only the Soviets, who regarded him as a traitor to their revolution, disagreed, and their veto prevented him from taking office that spring. Soon, with the coming Blockade, Airlift, and splitting of the city, Reuter assumed his rightful place as the elected governing mayor of the western sectors, and he attracted world attention as the courageous leader of an embattled city. Less well known is that in the midst of those awesome events of 1948, Ernst Reuter also became one of the founding figures, in many ways the central figure, in the creation of the Free University of Berlin. He later claimed that the new Free University was, along with West Berlin's new power plant, "my proudest offspring of the Blockade."[106]

It was a rare piece of luck that the leading political figure in Berlin had chosen to interest himself intensively in the affairs of the nascent university. The difficulties to be overcome could only be described as daunting, and the small committee learned quickly what American Cultural Adviser Herman Wells had grasped at the beginning of the crisis. Wells had cautioned Clay that such a project would have required two years under ideal conditions in the United States. Yet, this was Berlin and the conditions were abominable. The Germans were embarking on a most difficult project.[107] Therefore, the enlistment of Berlin's most powerful political and public figures in the foundation process was not only desirable. It was indispensable. The main problems that the committee faced were in trying to locate the necessary faculty for the venture, establishing the legal existence of the institution without incurring a Soviet veto, and securing the minimal material and financial means with which to sustain it in its first precarious semesters. In crisis-ridden Berlin, where the barriers to all surface routes in and out of the city came crashing down on June 24, 1948, those were ambitious goals which might have discouraged less determined individuals.

Although their inclination at the first meeting of June 19 had been to issue a manifesto to the public and to the Western Allies immediately, the committee chose on June 22 to defer that statement for a time. "Repercussions from the incalculable political events now taking place may have to be taken into consideration by the manifesto," was their explanation for the delay. Nevertheless, they formed a subcommittee of three, Muckermann, Redslob, and Hess, to formulate the appeal.[108] They also began work on a letter to the three Allied commandants in the western sectors and formed various subcommittees to begin the arduous work of selecting faculty for the schools of medicine, philosophy, and law. It was significant that the Preparatory Committee adopted a general rule of thumb in organizing the subcommittees: "A student should belong to every committee," the minutes of June 22 revealed. Moreover, the group was not averse to creating the new institution by unorthodox means. Otto Warburg, the one Nobel Prize laureate aiding the founders, suggested that they appoint only young assistant professors (junge Dozenten) initially and invite celebrated German and outside full professors for one and two-week stints. A physics student repre-

sentative from the Technical University, Hans Ringmann, agreed with
the need for a nontraditional approach: "Let us do away with the old university style and create something fundamentally new," he commented.
The students had held out for a new reform institution and were now attempting with some success to realize that goal. Knowing that there
was no time to lose, the subcommittees set about their assignments immediately.[109]

The following evening, Sir Robert Birley had an opportunity to see
for himself how seriously the political leadership of the western sectors
were taking the proposed university. Reuter, his SPD colleagues Franz
Neumann and Otto Suhr, plus the CDU critic of the new university,
Hans Peters, joined the British educational adviser and his assistant,
Tom Creighton, for dinner to discuss the university. Birley recalled urging them to break off the discussions in order to hear an important Soviet radio announcement in response to western currency reform. It
would be a fateful moment for Berlin, he was sure, and he wanted them
to experience it. Birley was more than a little surprised when they told
him that they had already received the written announcement, but, preoccupied with the Free University project, they would defer listening to
the announcement. "They had something more important to consider,"
Birley recalled, and he was impressed by their calm. "From that moment I had no doubt that we in West Berlin would win."[110]

One feature of the Free University was the prominent news coverage which surrounded its founding. Although intended to be an institution where research and learning were to be free of ideological constraints, it was from its inception a university profoundly influenced by
the unique political currents which were dividing the entire city. Press accounts appeared daily of the progress being made, and the founding committee, led by Reuter, concerned itself with placing the new creation constantly before the eyes of the public. The reason for this is not hard to
identify. The dominant political force in Berlin was the SPD, although
all three western parties had largely subordinated their differences to
meet the crisis of the Blockade and Soviet-SED pressure. Universities—
even the Free University—were by nature exclusive or elite institutions,
which educated a select group in society. Traditionally, that group had
been composed largely of middle-class individuals who came from the
ranks of professionals and civil servants. Although the new enterprise
hoped to devote special attention to breaking down this class bias—the
SED policies at Berlin University had earned tacit respect—the average
Berliner who voted SPD would have to feel that the Free University
was to be his or her university. Without overwhelming public support,
the project could even at this stage fail. It was to the credit of Reuter,
an astute politician, and Redslob, an energetic publicist, that precisely
that sense of a "people's university" came to pervade West Berlin in 1948.

Yet, such an approach had its drawbacks, too. The glare of publicity, in the press and on the air waves, was uncongenial to some participants. The Preparatory Committee for the Free University had a unique composition in that unabashed political leaders, publicists, and students were represented in addition to learned professionals. For those individuals used to more traditional academic bodies, operating under the public gaze was unfamiliar and often uncomfortable. Thus, on the day following the first working meeting of the Preparatory Committee, the *Tagesspiegel* not only announced the committee membership, it also announced that Else Knake had written to the authorities at Unter den Linden, informing them of her decision to leave Berlin University.[111] Knake and several members of the Preparatory Committee ultimately chose not to sign the all-important manifesto of July 23 calling for the establishment of the Free University. She had been outspoken on behalf of the students at Berlin University in 1947 and was obviously still committed to establishing an unfettered institution (she had even hosted the Preparatory Committee at her apartment). Nevertheless, she refused to participate in the project any longer: ". . . I believe it is wrong and damaging," she wrote to Chairman Reuter on July 20, "that practical actions are being influenced by political considerations." Knake noted that another announcement in the *Tagesspiegel* after a recent committee meeting had assured the public that the university would open in the coming autumn.[112] Knake assured Reuter that up to the present such an assumption "has not the slightest justification. For this reason I am resigning from the Preparatory Committee."[113]

There were other reasons for Else Knake's refusal to sign the manifesto. Otto Hess, who stood closer to Knake than any other member, had been requested by the committee to ask her to reconsider or at least to help in the difficult task of establishing a medical faculty. Hess knew full well that Knake's reluctance was not connected with the proposed university per se. Rather, it was a problem with the motives of the political leadership. He felt ever after that Knake was imbued with the spirit of a full German professor, an *Ordinarius*, and her perceptions of an institution of higher learning were rather strict. First, the *Zentralverwaltung* had violated them, she felt, by injecting ideological considerations into admissions and curricular policy at Berlin University. Now some of the founding members of the Free University were mixing politics into this venture in equally unwelcome ways. Hess tried to convince her otherwise but to no avail.[114] The declaration of the committee went out without her support. Two other committee members, Professors Kress and Warburg, who were also unhappy with the glare of publicity, withheld their signatures too. Nevertheless, Knake continued to be revered among the students as a person of rare courage.

In a report about the founding efforts for the Free University, Kendall Foss, perhaps because he was unaware of her valor in supporting students earlier, displayed some irritation with Knake. "A faction headed by Frau Dr. Knake . . . began holding out for proof of Allied approval before taking any positive steps," he wrote to Clay. "For three weeks she succeeded in blocking the publication of a proclamation. At the very least, Frau Dr. Knake argued, the committee should wait until it had found some well-known figure who might become the director of the undertaking and shoulder all responsibility." Foss claimed that the rest of the committee finally became exasperated with her desire to have a "father-image" tell them what to do, so "they called for a vote, issued their manifesto [July 24], and waited personally upon the three Sector Commandants to ask for recognition and support."[115]

The manifesto duly went out to the public and explanatory letters were sent to each of the west-sector commandants on July 23, informing them that the Preparatory Committee was now in existence and that it was their intention to found a new university. In describing their actions, the committee tied their decision closely to the fate of West Berlin, itself now a besieged city: "The City of Berlin has proved with its decisive stand against brutal methods that it is not about to place itself a second time under the totalitarian yoke and to surrender the benefits of freedom. In the context of this struggle, it is necessary to preserve academic achievement from influences that otherwise would threaten the objectivity and independence of teaching and research." The proclamation reminded the Berliners that the City Assembly had overwhelmingly approved the concept of a free, independent university on May 11, but the Magistrat, because it stood under four-power control, could do little to help at present because of an inevitable Soviet veto. Therefore a citizens' group had taken the initiative and was now turning to the public in Berlin and elsewhere with its appeal:

> In the same spirit of self assertion with which our City has met the Blockade, a university should take shape and should, as the intellectual center of free Berlin, serve in the healing process for all Germany. We appeal to the people at home and abroad who feel obliged to serve freedom and truth. We appeal to the representatives of the German and Allied authorities and therefore to everyone who respects the rights of the individual. We call upon the youth of all nations and especially to the students at all freely functioning institutions of higher learning. We appeal to the German professors, assistants, and academics abroad to help us with guest professorships or in other ways. We appeal to friends and supporters throughout the world, and ask them for financial and educational support.[116]

Those were brave words, uttered with great conviction by a small, disparate group, and they had the desired effect. The wave of support that immediately welled up from all levels of the Berlin population surprised even the most ardent supporters of the new university and confounded its numerous critics. Whereas in April and May the supporters of a new university were an amorphous, little-known group struggling to achieve even a modicum of credibility and recognition, the dramatic appeal of July 24, coming as it did amidst the roar of airplanes overhead and an eerie silence at the border crossings, had the desired effect. The general appeal that went out to the Berliners the next day asked them to donate money, books, furniture, scientific equipment, volunteer labor, scholarship aid, and even food for the hungry students and teaching staff.

Lucius Clay welcomed the move and after he was assured that the Airlift would work and that West Berlin could be maintained, he replied with words of welcome to Reuter about the creation of a Free University: "I shall watch its growth with keen interest and I should be glad to help in any way possible. The objectives it seeks deserve the sympathetic consideration of all who believe in academic freedom."[117] On the very day following the proclamation, the Preparatory Committee opened a permanent office at Boltzmannstrasse 4 in Dahlem, and with the help of a volunteer staff began receiving a flood of visitors.[118]

PREPARATIONS FOR A NEW UNIVERSITY

Even as material support began to flow in, an important guest arrived from the west to help in the planning. On July 27, August Wilhelm Fehling, who in prewar Germany had been a Rockefeller Foundation representative, was now a *Kurator* (chancellor or chief administrative officer) at Kiel University and was rated by many as perhaps the most knowledgeable administrator in German higher education. By mid-July the Preparatory Committee already considered him as their first choice for curator, but Fehling refused to abandon his post at Kiel. However, he generously donated his vacation time to consult with the Preparatory Committee and to make recommendations. With the cooperation of the British authorities, Fehling arrived in Berlin at the end of July 1948, and immediately examined the situation.

Fehling pointed out that the new university, following German practice, would have to be a creation of the state, a role which the Magistrat, as successor to the Prussian State in Berlin, could fulfill. ". . . [T]his would be the most suitable way," he reported to Reuter and the committee, "provided that the City of Berlin would have the rights of a *Land*." Earlier suggestions of using an existing university to charter a branch were dismissed by Fehling as "artificial and lengthy." Financing was quite another issue and would have to be considered separately.[119]

Fehling had examined the possibility, proposed for some time among SPD members, of expanding the Technical University. "There is no possibility of creating the necessary faculties by expanding the Technical University because consent on the part of the Technical University

cannot be expected," he concluded. Fehling was absolutely convinced
that the venture must proceed in such a way as to make the Free University a separate legal entity.[120]

While the new university could adopt many of the usual forms of self-governance of older universities, including a rector (president), a senate, faculties (schools), and other typical administrative posts, Fehling
suggested the creation of a special governing body, a *Kuratorium* (board
of regents), to make the major decisions. There was a precedent here in
that Frankfurt and Cologne universities (both founded at about the time
of World War I) used the board-of-regents arrangement. The new administrative body would concern itself with larger issues, such as the acquisition and disposal of property, the creation of a budget and payment of
costs, the appointment of administrative personnel, and plans for the
university's future growth. Its composition would have to reflect the special conditions of Berlin and of the situation that had given rise to a
new institution. "The *Kuratorium* must be composed of representatives
of the city, the founders, and the other personalities central to the sponsoring of the university," Fehling stated, although he could not give a precise definition of the composition of the board. However, he could state
unequivocally that the chairman of the board of trustees held the key position. In the beginning at least, such a person would be fulfilling the
role of a chancellor and a minister of education combined. The demands
on such a person would be great, and he would have to make many decisions based on practical necessity.[121] Although Fehling named no
names, the implications from his remarks were clear. The university's all-important board would need someone who could practice politics, i.e.,
the art of the possible: Ernst Reuter.

Like those Germans and Americans who had considered the challenges earlier, Fehling concluded that the hiring of qualified faculty was
probably the most critical factor in making the new university a success. Certainly the problems associated with building space, libraries,
and equipment were daunting in themselves, but the acquisition of a
proper faculty was the sine qua non of the venture. Making the task
even more difficult was the fact that those chosen for the first faculties
would have to represent the major areas of the various disciplines. The
new university could hardly afford to establish offerings in minor fields
at a time when the slender resources rendered each teaching position precious. They must start with a small, able core and then expand later,
and the founders, Fehling stated, would have to develop a thick skin.
They would have to expect strong criticism, not only from the Soviet
side but also from the German universities located in the western
zones. Adjunct professorships, guest professorships, and other part-time
appointments would have to help out in the beginning, and those involved in the founding of the university would have to form small working groups to aid preparatory subcommittees in building each faculty.[122]

Fehling recommended strongly that the founders concentrate on just three faculties at first in order to economize their slender resources. This meant the creation of a *Philosophische Fakultät* (a school of arts and sciences) but without the natural sciences at first. "Conditions allow only the creation of the arts section initially," Fehling wrote. "The creation of a natural sciences component demands significantly more time and resources." Even the resources of the Technical University's natural science sections were inadequate, but Fehling hoped they could still accommodate some of the FU students at first. The law school posed the fewest problems in terms of demand on resources. With adequate large lecture halls and a good library, they could begin operations without undue difficulty. For a time the economists would share facilities with the lawyers in a combined school until resources allowed an expansion and separation of the two disciplines. The problems in opening a school of medicine were not so easily solved. Premedical studies in the basic sciences would place demands which the limited natural science offerings at the Technical University could not begin to meet and the Free University not at all. Therefore, only advanced medical students should receive training initially. Fehling was not sure if the scientific institutes in Dahlem, now being organized into the School for Advanced Studies, could help out, but it seemed a logical possibility. Worrisome for the clinical studies was the fact that the large hospitals in the western sectors were not located near the bulk of the university buildings being planned for Dahlem. Rather, the medical students would have to go to the large clinics in places like Westend and Neukölln.

There was much more detail on administrative and financial regulation in the Fehling report, but in essence he confirmed the initial planning of the Preparatory Committee and the thinking of the Americans under Kendall Foss, who were still providing liaison to the German project. Fehling promptly submitted his findings to the Preparatory Committee, and, exhausted by his intense activity, flew back out of blockaded Berlin to Kiel, where he promptly took to his bed with a bout of rheumatism. His wife reported her husband's findings to an American friend: "He was very much impressed by the display of the air bridge and by the definite attitude of the 'natives'."[123]

Fehling's suggestions reached the Americans quickly, and by August 7 American education expert John Sala could report to City Commandant Frank Howley that the Preparatory Committee was already acting mostly along the lines Fehling had suggested. By this time, the Western Allies had transformed the four-power Kommandatura into a kind of rump tripartite Kommandatura (which still exists) to handle matters in the western sectors. Already on August 6 they discussed the Free University. The Americans gave it unequivocal support at the meeting. The French representative claimed he had too little information and must consult with his commandant first. The British, Sala stated, "could not join us in the project because (1) they feel that the times and conditions are not favorable for launching a project of this size, (2) that they have about all they can finance and handle with the Technical University which costs them seven million Deutschmarks per year." Sala admitted that the British position was disappointing at the moment, but he was not entirely pessimistic either. "Because the British have already help-ed in minor ways," Sala wrote, "it is expected that they will con-tinue to do so and in no way hinder the project." Even the French leader-ship, according to Kendall Foss, "revealed a willingness to cooperate so that the silence of the Berlin representative should not be considered as unfavorable."[124]

Taking the Kiel expert's advice to heart, the Preparatory Committee began immediately the difficult task of locating a teaching staff for the new university. Sala could report by August 7 that various representa-tives had contacted "over 100 prospective professors and Dozenten." No invitations to professors from the western zones had actually been is-sued; yet a few guest professorships appeared to be lining up. There were only a few professors from Berlin University who were willing to make the switch, but, Sala added, "there are indications that more will join later." Since the central office had opened on July 24, no less than 1,100 students had indicated a desire to enter the new university. The Americans estimated that as many as 5,000 would apply, but since the new university could accommodate perhaps only 1,500 initially, the se-lection process would not be easy. Various subcommittees were work-ing on admissions procedures, and acquisition of libraries, laboratories, buildings, and equipment as the project moved into high gear. Sala noted that already German citizens were coming forward with individ-ual contributions, "but contributions can only play a very small part," he added. American Military Government's two million Deutschmark contribution was invaluable, but even it would cover only operating expenses for the first year. "The [Preparatory] Committee estimates that an additional 1.4 million DM will be needed for one-time expendi-tures for the first year."[125]

As the new undertaking gathered momentum, Edwin Redslob paused briefly to update an old friend, Eduard Spranger, on the re-cent events. Claiming that he was working with the same plans and thoughts as in 1945, Redslob asked Spranger to lend his cooperation and trust to the project, even over a great distance. "Many see this new founding as much too much the object of politics," Redslob wrote, "while others view it too much in terms of their teaching positions or laboratories." Redslob admitted that he, too, hoped in coming years to teach his favorite field of art history and to form a Goethe society. Although ambitious to play a leading role in the new university, Redslob confided to Spranger that Ernst Reuter, despite his heavy reponsibilities as governing mayor, was a key figure in all that transpired in the new university: ". . . the manner of his help is so prudent and positive that we can only be very pleased to have him as our chairman." Redslob admitted that not everything had been peaceful, and he revealed that Else Knake had left the Preparatory Committee, but he claimed to have won her continued support in putting together the school of medicine. "In this instance and for other reasons we have put many difficulties and cross purposes behind us," he assured Spranger. "Nevertheless, the founding is making good progress. . . ."[126]

As the Preparatory Committee laid its plans and began to take practical steps, the students, too, continued to respond intensively to the challenge of creating the new institution within an impossibly short deadline. Led by a virtually intact *Studentenrat* that had departed from Berlin University en masse in June, plus a smaller group around the journal *Colloquium*, the students put together their own form of preparatory committee, usually called the Committee of 25. It busied itself with preparing a student component to the university constitution and with coordinating the myriad activities connected with establishing a new university. "The student committee meets weekly to receive a report from the senior Committee of Twelve [the Preparatory Committee] and to discuss the necessary work," commented one reporter, and added: "The deliberateness with which the Committee of Twelve, composed largely of professors, makes its decisions, is frequently a severe test of patience for the youthful idealism with which the students go about their work." Of necessity, the students had had to take on a large share of the work in creating a new higher educational institution from scratch.[127]

In *Colloquium*, in an article of July 1948, about the soon-to-be Free University, Otto Hess summed up the students' expectations for the new institution. In essence he proclaimed that the Free University was envisaged as something different from its older sister institutions. "If a new university is to be more than merely an attempt to preserve honorable but outmoded traditions," he wrote, "then courage must be evident in order to go in new directions." The students would undoubtedly benefit from the experience of their elders, but, as Hess stated, the new generation "has the right nevertheless to find its own way." If the university was to escape from the ivory tower and become more closely integrated into the rest of society, then young instructors would have to form a sense of community with the students and abandon the proclamation of given truths *ex cathedra*. Rather, it was through question and answer, point and counterpoint, that truth emerged. The notion that a university was a kind of reservoir of stored knowledge to be tapped by students for their examinations was simply outmoded. The professors had a greater responsibility than the dispensing of mere knowledge, and the students could not be satisfied with merely attending lectures regularly and finishing their studies at the earliest possible moment. "Authority must be earned daily," Hess wrote, "and is vested in the individual, not in his position. Up to now, the German universities have been run in authoritarian fashion by the [University] Senate and the full professors. The monopoly enjoyed by the *Ordinarien* or full professors in appointing new professors stems from an authoritarian concept which is no longer valid. It must be replaced by self-determination on the part of the entire academic community according to well-regulated levels of influence." In other words, the entire university community, including students, would determine the future composition of the teaching body, a radical departure from earlier practice.[128]

Hess justified this claim because of student initiative in creating a new university in the first place, one free from ideology and state interference. "They thereby proved that they have learned something from the past and that they want to bear the responsibility for their own future. They have earned for themselves the right to contribute to the creation of a new university. However, they also have the duty now to prove that their judgment can work in positive rather than only in negative ways."[129]

Already on July 27, notices appeared in the west-sector press announcing that students could begin the application process by sending a postcard to the new offices at Boltzmannstrasse 4, giving the minimum information needed: name, age, number of semesters completed, and field of study. The students themselves would work out the criteria for selection, and the student committee declared that they anticipated far more applicants than could be accepted. Thus, the selection process would have to be especially severe, "because that is crucial for the spirit and the quality of the new university." The admissions committee, consisting of a faculty member, a representative of the given profession, and a student in the same field, would make the decisions based upon the applicant's scholarly and social attainments. The first announcements promised student applicants that the admissions form would be brief, to the point, and would confine itself strictly to questions relevant to university admissions. Since the students planned to create an institution which deliberately fostered a sense of community, they hoped to find students who would support such ideals.[130] Stanislaw Kubicki, one of the young medical students who helped formulate admissions policies, recalled later what he felt was his most prized contribution to the new university. Suspicious of Soviet-Zone questionnaires that demanded an applicant's political affiliation, and tired of filling in the Americans' 131-question *Fragebogen*, Kubicki was determined to create the briefest document possible. The result was a small form of only seven questions, which brought large sighs of relief from the Free University's first applicants.[131] It was characteristic of the spirit pervading the new university that the students alone handled admissions policy, with virtually no direction from administration or faculty. Such independence was a logical result of their intimate experience with admissions criteria since 1945 at Berlin University, by now a topic of more than passing interest and one upon which they placed great emphasis.

In the first week for accepting preliminary applications, starting on July 24, 1948, no less than 1,200 students crowded into the small, hurriedly opened registrar's office at Boltzmannstrasse 4 in Dahlem to sign their intent to study. Over 3,000 had declared their intent by the beginning of September, and when the official application forms finally appeared on September 11, a rush ensued. One contemporary account claimed that the registrars distributed 2,536 applications in the first three days alone. By the beginning of October, no less than 5,000 applications were awaiting a decision.[132] By the time the first semester began in mid-November, the Free University had processed 5,500 applications but could accommodate only 2,140 students. The review of applicants began in early October and admissions procedures took place along the same lines as had been practiced at Berlin University. To be sure, the political biases that had caused such an uproar at the old university were not repeated—at least in the same fashion. No SED applicants were to be found, nor would they have been accepted had they tried. From the outset a strident anticommunism stamped the entire enterprise, hardly surprising given the political conditions in the divided Berlin of 1948. This militant spirit was to persist until an entirely new generation emerged twenty years later. The Free University, despite its title, was fated never to be free of the tug of countervailing forces.

In the context of the time, however, the innovations in admissions were unusual. Students were prominently represented on the various admissions committees for each faculty, and together with professors and representatives from the professions, they helped select the first student body. It was not an easy task, due in no small measure to the pent-up admissions demand that had existed since 1945 and which had by no means been satisfied by Berlin University or the Technical University. Of the 2,140 acceptees, about thirty percent of those first entering a university came from the East Zone, with most of the rest claiming the western sectors as their home. Of those older students already well along in their studies and now entering the Free University, no less than seventy percent had studied earlier at Unter den Linden. Another twenty percent of the older students came from other Soviet-Zone universities. The rest of the advanced students, or only about nine percent came from West German universities.[133]

Those students who served on admissions committees often had to deal with numerous hardship cases where the applicants claimed to be under physical danger if they remained in the East Sector. Sometimes the admissions committees had to tell applicants to remain in place at Berlin University for the time being because the soon-to-be Free University simply could not prepare them in their field yet. This was often the case for beginning medical students, for whom no instruction or facilities in the basic sciences were as yet available. Some brave students continued to study at Berlin University through the summer semester while helping to prepare the Free University. Often they would pass along information to their fellow students in the East about admissions policies and the chances for admission in various fields.[134]

First indications were that the bulk of those showing interest were disappointed would-be students who, for various reasons, had not yet entered a university. Many had tried at Unter den Linden and had been rejected, or were too discouraged to apply in the first place. The admissions committee of the soon-to-be Free University, like the Soviet-Zone authorities before them, established clear-cut categories of preference for student applicants. Besides high scholarly and moral qualifications, those students who could prove that the Nazis had persecuted them for political, racial, or religious reasons would have preference. Now, several years after the war, the FU students felt another category of would-be students needed help too: Those who emerged from prisoner-of-war camps after October 1, 1947, would also receive special consideration. Those who were enrolled in East-Zone universities but found themselves in political difficulty could expect to receive special consideration, as would those "coming from socially disadvantaged families."[135] Thus, several of the admissions criteria of the Free University approached those of Berlin University in some important ways but differed in others. The dissident students obviously respected certain features of their former university's effort to redress previous social and political ills. Now they had the chance to make some refinements of their own and to eliminate the prejudices they had seen as working unfairly in favor of the SED at the University Unter den Linden which in the autumn of 1948 officially became known as Humboldt University. Of course, in retrospect it became clear that other admissions biases were abundant. No one hung out a sign saying that Communists need not apply at the Free University any more than that noncommunists need not apply at Humboldt University. It was simply an understood fact of life in the divided city.

From the first, the entire enterprise had the unmistakable look of improvisation. This impression began at the gate of the Free University's first and for the moment, only building, the twelve-room Boltzmannstrasse 4, in Dahlem. Visitors recognized it by the small, hand-painted cardboard sign, "Free University of Berlin, Registration," which hung, partially curled upward by moisture, at the garden gate. Inside was a jumble of donated furniture and equipment that had accumulated as the result of private donations. The students, faculty, and administration began with one telephone and a few chairs. They erected the business counter on the ground floor of the former villa and arranged a room apiece for the three faculties upstairs. Fritz von Bergmann carried the duties of the chancellor in the beginning with four student assistants, one of whom dealt with the public, another with faculty affairs, a third with internal university matters, and the last "with things that must be settled outside the office." On the first day alone they received over eighty telephone inquiries and 120 visitors, and mail came pouring in, sometimes with monetary donations ("Even Western currency!" noted one student, Helmut Coper). So much depended upon individual initiative. One student, Christiane Richter, noticed on the first day that the admissions office had no equipment, and she simply appeared the next morning with a prized personal typewriter in her backpack and set to work. Typing paper and ribbons materialized somehow, and the fragile enterprise attained slightly more legitimacy as typed copy replaced the hitherto hand-written communications.[136]

The university administration began under identical conditions. One day shortly after the founders occupied Boltzmannstrasse 4, a young woman, Frau Krüger, appeared and offered her services as a secretary. The embarrassed founders admitted they had no money to pay her, but undaunted she came aboard as an unpaid volunteer until such time as they could create a secretarial position. The Preparatory Committee was leading a Spartan existence too. Somehow, the founders organized chairs for most of the membership, but Fritz von Bergmann had to make do with an upended wooden crate.[137] Besides the students' Committee of 25, other groups of students or would-be students made themselves available to deliver messages, make deliveries, or perform any number of tasks needed to get the enterprise under way. The students were especially pleased that total strangers and people who had never had any connection with higher education were among those donating goods and services to their new experiment in higher education. Kendall Foss reported the spontaneity and enthusiasm of the enterprise to General Clay: "Student volunteers began dragging bits of furniture from every part of the city with which to equip the offices. Firms, individuals, and German municipal officers started making gifts.[138]

A few journalists from the SED newspaper *Vorwärts* journeyed out to Dahlem to see for themselves what was happening and reported back the experiences of several aspiring students to their press bureau in the East Sector: "Behind the counter on the ground floor they [the student registration volunteers] scribbled down their names and addresses on typing paper, asked for their faculty of choice, then announced that the questionnaires might arrive in four weeks or so, and that they would then inform them accordingly." The pair of students left the registration office, supposedly disappointed by the vagueness of the whole operation, according to the reporters, who busily interviewed other applicants with, they claimed, undistinguished or perhaps slightly Nazi-tainted pasts, all of them professing deep pessimism about the entire enterprise.[139] To be sure, no one connected with the undertaking had expected anything but the strongest condemnation in the eastern press anyway. "We are not dealing with universities or ideas. Rather, we are dealing with a shabby political maneuver, of which young people will fall victim," thundered the official Communist daily *Neues Deutschland* at the beginning of August.[140]

In the context of the propaganda war taking place in the public media of Berlin that summer, eastern coverage of the Free University's emergence was, despite such charges, slightly subdued. As the above report indicated, Eastern observers were scornful of the enterprise, and at that stage perhaps understandably so, given its ramshackle physical appearance and strong overtones of improvisation. A few months later that restraint was replaced by condemnations of the Free University that at times matched the vituperation lavished upon the political authorities and institutions in the western sectors. As expected, eastern attacks upon an emergent West Berlin had displayed no moderation whatsoever. "I do not believe that any city in the world has ever experienced such a press and propaganda war as Berlin in these times," wrote a young State Department official, Richard Sterling. "The bitter, repetitive and fantastically lying . . . propaganda blasts of the communist press are met with an inventive energy of the Western press that expresses itself in many ways, sometimes bitter and sometimes very delightful sarcasm, sometimes lies of a subtler nature than those employed by the enemy, sometimes with tremendously moving statements of faith and determination."[141]

BERLIN BLOCKADE

While the founding of the new university received the expected critical treatment in the eastern press, the reader of more than a generation later should not assume that the founding of the new institution was at center-stage in Berlin. Indeed, the major public focus was on other political and economic matters. The flare-up over currency reform had begun with western announcements on June 19, followed by the imposition of Soviet currency regulations a few days later. Soon after, the Western Allies issued orders specifically imposing western currency reform on the western sectors of Berlin on June 24. On that same day the full blockade began, and the mini-airlift that the Allied commanders had organized to provide for their military garrisons had now to be expanded dramatically to provide for an entire city population of over two million people. Nothing like it had ever been attempted before, and if the lessons of World War II were any indicator, the fate of West Berlin was sealed. The population would be starved into submission. The Allies would have to submit to inevitable defeat.[142] Instead, the Western Allies, together with their newly won local allies, the citizens of West Berlin, performed prodigies of improvisation, and the great Airlift began on July 1.

Currency reform was a crucial issue and a major cause of the East-West test of strength in Berlin. General Clay felt its introduction was necessary for economic recovery in the three western zones, and once the Soviets had left the Kommandatura on June 16, he became certain that West Berlin would participate too. His political adviser, Robert Murphy, stated openly that such action "would be particularly embarrassing to the Russians if two currencies circulated in Berlin."[143] The Western Allies negotiated with the Soviets for several days starting on June 20 in an attempt to keep only one currency in the former capital. Clay and the other negotiators became convinced that they would have no control whatsoever over the new Soviet currency being proclaimed, "and that if we accepted it in the western sectors we would henceforth be guests in Berlin."[144] Thus, Berlin received two currencies after all, and a nearly chaotic situation ensued. The Soviets exchanged their new currency for old at a 1:1 ratio. The Western Allies maintained a 1:10 ratio as in the west, making it much scarcer. The Allied authorities were tempted to make the new western currency the only legal means of exchange, but they dared not. "The reason why we did not do this," Richard Sterling reported, "is that there are about three hundred thousand Berliners who live in the west sectors but who work in the Soviet Sector and thus receive Soviet Zone marks as wages."[145] Sterling personally witnessed the chaotic conversion and was dismayed at the hardships and confusion it worked on the Berliners.

Hans Ringmann, the student representative from the Technical University serving on the Preparatory Committee, described its effects on the students to Howard W. Johnston: "Currency reform has hit the students of Berlin particularly hard," he wrote. "Therefore the possibility must be created for a large number of students to continue their studies." Ringmann suggested the creation of a student-loan office (*Darlehenskasse für Studenten*), but the funds for the badly needed project were simply not available at that time.[146] Johnston was no stranger to the students' plight. He requested the most fundamental kind of support for the founders of the Free University from the CRALOG (food relief) organization. "These are the people who are literally risking their lives and sacrificing material advantage in order to take a stand for freedom," he wrote. The students especially were being called upon to perform heavy manual labor in preparing several large buildings for the Free University and would need more food. An anonymous letter also reached Military Government informing them that four members of the Preparatory Committee were living in dire poverty but were too proud to ask for help. Food and some modest financial support would aid them greatly.[147] The Berliners of 1948 were proud and defiant. They were also for the most part gaunt and threadbare as the Blockade worked ever greater hardships.

Eyewitnesses to the dramatic East-West confrontation recorded their thoughts even as the students were carrying on the business of starting their own university. "One of the few happy aspects of this situation—and it is a very important aspect—is that Berlin stands for something free and good today," wrote Richard Sterling to the recently departed Epsteins. "Here is the first authentic German political development where conscience and politics go hand in hand since 1933. At last Germany has meaning again—for Germans and for other peoples. The courage shown here is something for the future to build on."[148]

The Airlift itself worked as an inspiration to Berliners and the Western Allies alike. "In spite of the dismal weather and constant rain accompanied at times by violent thunder storms, American and British planes are at all times overhead, and the air is never silent," wrote Sterling to his family in mid-July.

> The air bridge has been going for two weeks now, and all of us, Americans, Germans, and Russians have been tremendously impressed. Besides bringing vital supplies into the City, this stream of planes has given the policy of the Western Allies a personality and prestige it has not had since the end of the war. Faces in Berlin are always turned up to the sky these days, and one can almost always hear the words "There's another one." The air bridge is the most sensational aspect of a series of events that is unique in every way.[149]

One of those events that fit into the grand series was, to be sure, the Free University, which despite intense poverty, the threat of an uncertain future for the entire city, and nearly unbearable superpower tensions, continued to assume concrete form. Three years earlier Berlin University had arisen literally from the ashes of the former capital. Now, under equally adverse conditions, the dissident students were proving that they could accomplish the impossible once again.

Observers like Sterling were hardly complacent about the crisis. The situation in Berlin was too ominous for anyone to feel pure elation despite the defiant, even heroic attitude of the Berliners. First, there was no guarantee that the Airlift would work or that the Soviets would not undertake further actions that might conceivably start another dreaded conflict so soon after a terrible war. Sterling continued: "First of all, the air-bridge is an operation that requires an enormous effort on our part, and especially upon the part of the British. It is fantastically expensive. . . . Aside from the material and financial factors, the successful continuation of the air lift is dependent upon the continuing crisis atmosphere and its accompanying feeling of exhilaration and determination. This atmosphere and these feelings are almost impossible to maintain over a long period of time." Sterling predicted that criticisms over the Allied handling of the crisis, especially with regard to currency reform, were inevitable. How long could the Berliners and their Western Allies hold out? No one could say, and the young American official, like many another German or American or Briton, ruminated on how affairs had come to such an impasse.

> The combination of generosity, good feelings, naivete, and stupidity, plus the belief on the part of many that evil had been conquered for ever and ever with the fall of Hitler, has led us into a terrible dilemma. We are pledged to hold Berlin and can do so now only by skirting the very edge of war. If we mean to stay, we really are risking war. If we leave, we face a disastrous loss of prestige and leave to the mercy of the Russians thousands of people who have courageously exposed themselves to reprisals by defying the Soviets and bolstering our position. . . . This conflict is weighing heavily upon the minds of many of us here.[150]

Ominous though the situation was, the West Berliners somehow preserved their reputation for wit and irreverence. This spirit was epitomized by the performances of Günter Neumann, Tatjana Sais, and a talented troupe of radio personalities who performed weekly on RIAS under the name *Die Insulaner* (The Islanders). Somehow, the script went, West Berlin had come to be surrounded by water, and now its inhabitants had to make do under these abnormal conditions. Every Sunday afternoon at 5:00 most Berliners crowded around their radios to listen to the cast poke fun at the eastern authorities, sometimes even at the western authorities, and often at themselves. They imitated to perfection such stock characters as Communist bureaucrats and parodied the bland assurances of those in power that all would be well and that solutions were at hand. Thus, a glib announcer solved the coal shortage in December 1948 by assuring his shivering listeners that everyone would be guaranteed a warm room for Christmas; they were shifting the holiday to July 24! The program proved to be such a success that the West Berliners, when referring to the special spirit that bound them together at that time, took to calling themselves *Die Insulaner*.[151] The community of students, professors, and others who were absorbed by the creation of the Free University were a microcosm of the special mood that gripped the Berliners in 1948.

A NEW BEGINNING

Thus, the new university began taking its first concrete organizational steps amidst a deepening international crisis, the solution to which was anything but clear in the summer of 1948. Some observers were still not convinced that the creation of a new institution, even as it took its first tentative steps, was wise or even possible. Displeased over "another example of precipitate American action in Berlin," S. Rolleston of British Military Government felt that the obstacles to success were still "formidable" at the beginning of August, but the situation had developed to the point that the British could no longer stand aloof. "We will shortly be asked by the Germans to assist them in this project," he wrote his superiors in London. "We cannot refuse; however, this may add to our commitments." An assistant in the German Education Department in London, R. D. Thackery, admitted that his section was "still rather chary about this project," partly because they felt "there is no evidence that the many difficulties involved have been fully considered let alone overcome." Echoing Herman Wells's early warning that whatever was done should be done well, the same officer claimed that "in our view unless the new university is an outstanding success and enjoys a good academic reputation from the start, its establishment will do more harm than good."[152]

Sir Robert Birley and August Fehling had already conferred on the subject in early August, and they concluded that the British proposal to expand the Technical University into a full university "has not met with the approval of the Germans themselves or of the Americans even though Dr. Fehling has . . . predicted that shortage of equipment alone will preclude the new university from having any science students." Another high-ranking British observer in Berlin, Christopher Steel, reported to Ernest Bevin at the Foreign Office Fehling's opinion, namely, "that it was most doubtful whether the new university could be started successfully in October; that neither the Americans nor the [Preparatory] Committee seemed to be concerned whether it would have a good academic standard. . . ."[153] Bevin was unhappy that the Germans, with American approval, had announced publicly their intent to start the university in the coming autumn, "since there seems little reason to believe that the formidable material difficulties . . . have been sucessfully overcome." Yet, there was little the British could do about the matter: "I imagine we should find it difficult to refuse help," Bevin informed British Military Governor Sir Brian Robertson at the end of August, and indicated that the Military Governor, in consultation with Robert Birley, should plan to offer what assistance they could to the enterprise.[154]

Certainly British and other Allied help was most welcome to the Germans and the Americans directly connected with the new project, but the participants most intimately concerned were usually not as gloomy about the difficulties as British reports indicated. Even so, little incidents in that tense time could jangle already tense nerves. For example, although the Preparatory Committee had issued its public appeal for aid and for Allied assistance on July 24, they received no official reply from General Clay for several weeks. Then, on August 31, one of its members, Edwin Redslob, chaired a meeting of a subcommittee to create the school of philosophy. By then the committee was concerned at the Military Governor's silence, and they stated that, given the current situation, no university could be founded without Clay's public support. Displaying some tension, they discussed their options once again, claiming that they had moral obligations to the Berliners and to the students coming over from the east. In that context they even dusted off old suggestions about increasing the arts and sciences offerings of the Technical University or seeking ties with a university in the western zone.[155]

Their jitters were for naught. On the very day that they began discussing the horrible possibility of an American pullout, Ernst Reuter received an enthusiastic letter from General Clay offering unequivocal support for the Free University.[156] With the Airlift moving into high gear and the international crisis stabilizing somewhat, Clay could turn to subordinate issues such as higher education once again. Reassured by this knowledge, the Preparatory Committee, in cooperation with the City of Berlin and with the Americans, was about to confound British pessimism on every point.

The Berlin City Assembly announced on July 31, 1948, that it had conducted negotiations with Paul Wandel on the longstanding proposal that the City of Berlin participate in the governing of Berlin University. A board of regents responsible to the City of Berlin, which was in turn responsible to the Allied Kommandatura, was the logical organizational link, they claimed. Wandel, speaking for the *Zentralverwaltung*, rejected the proposal again, stating that he was operating under an order from the Soviets to the effect that the *Zentralverwaltung* alone would continue to govern the university. Wandel had no further maneuvering room in the matter. "With this," summed up the final report, "all efforts on the part of the City of Berlin to share in the administration of Humboldt University must be regarded as having failed."[157]

Since the City Assembly had already charged the Magistrat on May 11, 1948, to undertake all measures to create a university that functioned in a spirit of freedom and independent scholarly activity, the Assembly's announcement of July 31 gave, in effect, the city administration's approval for the creation of a separate university. Consequently, the Preparatory Committee, the students' Committee of 25, and various Berlin citizen volunteers immediately set about writing a constitution for the new institution. City Councilman Walter May was able to render a progress report on September 13, only six weeks after the serious work of organization had begun. May commented that the Preparatory Committee's work was now in high gear, that the founding members were successfully locating physical facilities for the university in Dahlem, that precise plans were materializing for the formation of specific faculties, that a one-time American donation of nearly two million Deutschmarks had solved immediate financing needs, that the creators were recruiting the necessary faculty, and that the students had admissions procedures well in hand. The time had come, he said, for the Magistrat to approve officially the creation of the new university.[158]

With scarcely any hesitation, the Magistrat formally passed a resolution on September 22, 1948, calling for the creation of a "Free University with the legal standing of a corporation under public law." Furthermore, it empowered the city's Office of Public Education to present a new constitution in time for the opening of the Free University in the autumn of 1948.[159] The method of proposing and accepting the new institution had required considerable thought. "The problem," Kendall Foss observed, "had been to find a way to confine the city's approval to an administrative act (which does not require four-power approval) and to avoid a legislative act which would have needed a four-power blessing. Recognition of its existence under public law provided the sought-for answer."[160] Thus, one of the seemingly most complex problems, the university's legal charter, which the Americans had explored in the spring of 1948 and which the Preparatory Committee in consultation with August Fehling had weighed that summer, was solved with dispatch. The new university-to-be had now to complete its constitution and win approval for it in the city administration even as the founding members struggled under great pressure to solve the myriad hurdles in time for an opening in 1948. The reader should not forget that all of this took place at a time when the Blockade wound ever tighter around the city, and disruptions in practically all services and activities mounted accordingly.

Less susceptible to rapid solution was that most intractable challenge for the new university, one which Germans and Americans alike had pondered since the possibility of another university first arose. Where was the faculty to be found? *Tagesspiegel* editor Edwin Redslob, who, next to Reuter, was perhaps the most influential member of the Preparatory Committee, admitted that no easy solution was in sight. "The number of faculty who were prepared to accept the risk of associating with a university in West Berlin was small," he recounted in his memoirs. "General Clay . . . wanted to approve the founding only after I could present a list of fifty names of professors who would accept." With help from researchers, junior and senior academics, even students in Berlin, and with the support of a few key individuals in the universities in the western zones, such as Rector Franz Böhm at Frankfurt University, Redslob put together a list of slightly more than thirty names—not fifty as Clay had desired. "However," Redslob continued, "I remarked to the General that in 1810 Berlin University had had no more teaching faculty at its founding, and so I received the approval of the representative of the United States."[161]

As early as May 6, 1948, Otto Warburg had assured General Clay personally that a new university would be able to obtain the necessary scholars and teachers to begin operation, an assurance he offered on the basis of spirited public response when the School for Advanced Studies had issued an appeal for faculty earlier.[162] Reports from the summer of 1948 indicated that the founders were slowly getting results in their quest to create faculty for the schools of medicine, philosophy, and law/

economics. In the budding school of philosophy, a core of organizers, including Professors Altenberg (comparative literature), Hübner (English), Jakobi (musicology), and Redslob (art history), set about putting together a faculty with the help of a young *Assistent* (roughly equivalent to a lecturer), Hans-Joachim Lieber, and Georg Kennert, a personal assistant to Edwin Redslob. A student, Georg Kotowski, also distinguished himself in locating and approaching potential faculty members. Drawing primarily upon local scholars who qualified as full or associate professors, the organizers could report within a matter of weeks that they had acceptances to teach from fifteen would-be faculty in the school of philosophy and were engaged in serious negotiations with another fourteen. By mid-September, the core of the school's organizers had expanded to include other notables, such as Professors Gerstenberg (musicology), Braune (religion and Near Eastern languages), Dovifat (mass communications), Fels (geography), and Knudsen (theater). The fields of study to date included philosophy, classical philology, German Studies, English Studies, Romance languages, Slavic Studies, history, art history, and musicology. Twelve of the professors being sought were currently lecturing in one capacity or another at Berlin University. Two others were attached to universities in the Soviet Zone.[163] Eventually, thirteen full professors taught for the Free University in the philosophical faculty's first semester. Five associate professors were active, and no less than twenty-nine instructors were offering courses in most recognized fields.[164]

Recruitment for the medical faculty was also making good progress, especially since the Preparatory Committee, including students Otto Hess and Gerhard Petermann, was able to locate facilities and potential teaching faculty at two large hospitals in the British Sector, at Westend in Charlottenburg and at Moabit, and at three sizable hospitals in Neukölln in the American Sector. Redslob, as chairman of the Preparatory Committee, was especially grateful for the organizing efforts of Professor Hans Freiherr von Kress, who established the necessary contacts with the various clinics "and so gave shape to the Medical Faculty."[165] The staff of medical doctors included enough senior personnel capable of university teaching to accept advanced students for clinical studies in most of the accepted fields of medical studies. In the British-Sector facilities, for example, the organizers claimed that existing staff could teach eight out of eleven needed subjects. In the American Sector they claimed to have found "seven highly suitable personalities available for lectures." They had also located provisional lecturers to cover the other necessary subfields in medical studies. The outlook for recruiting experts in the more theoretical fields, such as pharmacology and hygenics, looked promising. The organizers claimed that they could easily fill three professorships in dentistry with qualified scientists, too.[166] Among the names known to the Americans were such medical scientists as Drs. Erwin Gohrbandt and Carlo von Brentano. Eventually, the Free Uni-

versity obtained the services of six full professors in medicine in its
first semester: Hoffmann (ophthalmology), Joppich (pediatrics), Koch
(pathology), von Kress (internal medicine), Lentz (bacteriology), and
Schäfer (gynecology). Four associate professors also began teaching immediately, plus two adjunct professors and fifteen instructors.[167]

They were still experiencing recruitment difficulties in the areas of
law and economics. "There are enough teachers in Berlin who are available and who are prepared to offer the necessary lectures," reported
one panel, "but few of them possess high academic credentials." Similar problems arose with the economists, but the recruiters still held out
hope that enough qualified staff would appear in time for the approaching winter semester. The organizers were looking for further support
from west-zone universities.[168] A confidential American report from the
same period indicated that help of sorts was on the way: ". . . Professor
Carlo Schmid [Attorney General/Minister of Justice of Wurttemberg-
Hohenzollern in the French Zone and simultaneously dean of the
school of law at the University of Tübingen] has indicated a willingness
to provide a visiting professor on rotation. Several professors of the University of Heidelberg, including Professor Alfred Weber, brother of Max
Weber and a sociologist in his own right, have agreed to come as visiting professors. It seems likely that professors at other institutions in the
Trizone will follow this example."[169] It was a measure of the organizers'
desperation that their prospective personnel lists also included Professor Wilhelm Wengler, who had stormed out of the first organizational
meeting for the new university on June 19. The first semester began
with six full professors: Bülow (economics), Drath (public law), Forstmann (economics), von Lübtow (Roman law), Paulsen (economics), and
Tiburtius (commerce). There were only four associate or adjunct professors and no fewer than thirty-two instructors. Wengler transferred to the
Free University in the spring of 1949.[170]

One factor that hampered recruitment of qualified scholars was the
founders' determination not to accept faculty who had been tainted by
close association with the Nazis. This helped exacerbate the difficulties
with the lawyers because, as Georg Kotowski, one of the students helping in the recruitment process pointed out, qualified legal minds in
1948 were usually of an age that they had been forced to join the party
in order to stay in the profession. If they had not done so, they would
have been forced to find another livelihood and would not, in 1948,
have the qualifications to become a law professor.[171] The no-Nazis rule undoubtedly increased the difficulty in securing adequate teaching staff
for the Free University in the beginning, and the founders, most of
whom had little reason to be tolerant of their recent tormentors, found
themselves having to make compromises. (The subject of professors
with Nazi pasts at the Free University will receive further treatment
later.)

Thus, slowly, the founding committees came up with prospective candidates for the faculty of the new university. Many may wonder why this aspect of the Free University's founding proved to be such a nagging problem. The answer lies in the atmosphere affecting Berlin in 1948. First, a climate of fear and oppression was real and pervasive in Berlin, and university faculty were in no way insulated from its effects. At the moment the cry for a new university became tangible, the drama of the Blockade and Airlift had already settled upon the city, which then experienced a rapid split in all of its basic functions. No one was certain that the Allied countermoves would actually work. Two and a half million West Berliners were now on short rations and facing the prospect of another cold and hungry winter. The world was struck by scenes of Berliners hauling deadened streetcars with cables through empty streets after the Soviets had cut off power supplies. Anyone from the outside willing to enter West Berlin to teach at the infant university would not only have to be brave; he would also have to be willing to endure the special discomforts that had become a West Berlin specialty starting on June 24. Currency reform continued to impose a personal financial crisis for most Berlin citizens, too. Those disruptions had not been resolved when the Free University organizers were attempting to hire new faculty. Finally, the new project, even as it began to assume concrete form, was still a fantastic adventure in many ways, and it took a special sense of dedication and a willingness to risk all, to abandon security for an unsure future. With American help, the financing of the enterprise was secure for little more than one semester. The faculty would have to accept positions that were far less secure than the civil service positions offered at Berlin University and elsewhere. In fact, the new Free University had little to offer except the ideals inherent in its title. If the atmosphere of defiance and of exhilaration of the besieged in working for a just cause had not been so prevalent in 1948, the creation of the new institution at such short notice would have been unthinkable. As it was, enough individuals with enough skills were being found who, for ideological reasons and for personal reasons, were willing to take that chance. The recruitment of faculty for the Free University produced no miracles in 1948, but it produced no debacles either. It was a measure of the difficulty of the problem and of the organizers' perseverance that prospective faculty members were being recruited right up to the opening of the university in December, and beyond. The all-important first catalogue of the Free University did not appear until the beginning of 1949, when the first semester was well under way. One of the minor miracles of this unique enterprise was that the founders somehow convinced enough brave men and women with enough skills to make it work. Fortunately, too, they found their human resources largely from indigenous West Berlin sources—a powerful indication of the need for the Free University

in the first place. Moreover, for the good of its future reputation, the
Free University did not arise from the wreck of Berlin University as
some embittered citizens would gladly have wished and as many supporters of Berlin University had feared. It was to begin its existence as
essentially a West Berlin university, meeting a pent-up local demand
for higher education in Berlin and, for the most part, doing it with
a locally recruited teaching body.

A nagging question lingered for a time as the autumn of 1948 approached. Who would lead the new university? At the end of August, during a discussion of faculty recruitment, Edwin Redslob offered the view
that "the Free University must be built up from the top down. Therefore, a celebrated personality should be taken into consideration as rector at the earliest moment." Redslob revealed to his fellow committee
members that negotiations were already under way to find the distinguished new university head.[172] Redslob had been in touch with Eduard
Spranger about the leadership issue a few weeks earlier. "Much of what
we are doing is for me closely related to your plans," he wrote to his colleague in Tübingen. "For this reason I ask you today over a great distance to give us your cooperation and above all your trust."[173] Redslob
was serious in his intent to hire the aged philosopher and educational theorist back to Berlin. He flew out of beleaguered Berlin to urge Spranger
to take the rectorship of the Free University. "However, during my visit
to Tübingen I still could not convince him to return to Berlin," Redslob
confessed, "because he had had to endure many irritations on the part
of the occupation authorities." Redslob also tried his luck with Karl Jaspers at Heidelberg University, but that noted philosopher was in the process of accepting a professorship at the University of Basel and was
about to leave Germany entirely.[174]

By mid-September interest centered on another noted professor of
philosophy, Hans Leisegang, who was presently at the University of
Jena. The minutes of a meeting of the philosophy faculty of September
13, 1948, indicated that he had been under active consideration. Hans-
Joachim Lieber recalled the affair. "On behalf of E. Redslob, I undertook
a trip to Jena and asked Leisegang personally if he were prepared to
take over this position at the new University." Lieber was surprised at
the response: "He informed me at that time [September] that he felt
such a strong obligation to his students that a departure from Jena was
simply out of the question at that time."[175] Despite the rebuff Leisegang
had by no means fully decided on his next course of action and faced
mounting difficulties with government authorities in the Soviet Zone. Although he eventually decided to leave Jena and accept an appointment
at the Free University in time for its first semester, interest had already
turned to an even better-known figure who was already resident in Berlin.

Friedrich Meinecke was rightly called the Nestor of German historians. A venerated scholar and still productive despite his 86 years and chronic ill health, Meinecke had a worldwide reputation which had risen even higher with the recent publication of The German Catastrophe, a study which analyzed the tragic course of German history in the twentieth century. The question was whether or not this great but frail man would be willing to take on the duties of a university rector. Ernst Reuter discussed the idea of recruiting Meinecke with Redslob, indicating that he was hesitant to approach the elderly scholar alone. Consequently, a small committee, consisting of Reuter, Otto Hess, and Professor Paul Altenberg (history of literature), paid a call on Professor Meinecke one day. They found him in his darkened apartment, bespectacled and laboring at yet another writing project amidst a jumble of books and papers. Given his increasing deafness, it took considerable effort even to communicate with Meinecke, much less to get him to consider the idea of becoming rector. However, Reuter, a resolute and charming advocate, sweetened the pill by offering to create a post of deputy rector (Geschäftsführender Rektor) to relieve Meinecke of responsibility for day-to-day affairs. Somewhat mollified, Meinecke found the offer more to his liking and decided there and then to accept. Reuter spotted the changed mood and in gratitude for the aged man's willingness to serve asked if there was not something else he could do to help Meinecke perform his duties. The eminent historian had remained an avid reader despite his failing eyesight, and now he jumped at the offer. He announced that he would dearly love to have an increased power allotment for his apartment to run a prized 100-watt light bulb and so illuminate his library during those precious hours when the power was running in West Berlin. Reuter is reported to have blinked at this modest demand, but the Governing Mayor recovered quickly. Since he was still formally in charge of Berlin's Office of Transportation and Utilities, he promised Meinecke he would do his best, and the bargain was sealed. The Free University had recruited its first rector.[176] Soon after, the Preparatory Committee met to receive the glad news. They then asked Edwin Redslob to leave the proceedings for a few minutes, and while he nervously paced an outer office they promptly elected him to be the deputy rector. The higher administration, too, was beginning to take shape.

Despite obvious progress, those who had taken up the Free University as their cause had had to overcome continuing skepticism in influential circles as the summer waned and autumn approached. Ernst Reuter devoted increasing attention to the enterprise and hired an assistant to advise him in higher educational matters and to provide day-to-day support for the Free University. Ingeborg Sengpiel, recently a lecturer in economics at Linden University, and previously a student of one of the great names in economics in Germany, Professor Konrad Mellerowicz, had also become disillusioned at political developments at Unter den Linden. She had been impressed at first with the SED's commitment to provide equality of opportunity in all professions to women, but ultimately she could not accept its stern ideology and left Berlin University in the summer of 1948. Sengpiel seriously considered leaving Berlin entirely, but through family connections she met an eminent social scientist and political force in Berlin's SPD, Otto Suhr. Suhr felt that Berlin badly needed young professionals like Sengpiel. Knowing of Reuter's growing commitment to the new university, Suhr sent Sengpiel's vita to the Governing Mayor, and Reuter, who had an eye for talent, invited her to his provisional offices at *Bahnhof Zoo* for an interview. Their meeting went well, and Sengpiel promptly received the position. Her distinguished mentor, Professor Mellerowicz, got wind of the negotiations, however, and hurried over from Linden University to warn the Sengpiel family to keep their daughter away from so shaky an enterprise as the Free University. It would never materialize, he assured them.[177]

Mellerowicz was hardly alone in his well-meaning but pessimistic advice. When the Preparatory Committee issued its public appeal at the end of July for support for the new university, it had directed it to the western zones of Germany and across international borders. A few days after the appeal was issued, a meeting of the West German Rectors Conference took place on July 27 in Braunschweig. The assembled presidents of the West German universities considered how to respond to the appeal. Their reactions demonstrated that for those not immediately caught up in the multidimensional drama unfolding in Berlin the notion of creating a new university was as dubious as it had appeared to Professor Mellerowicz. Rector Ludwig Raiser of Göttingen University announced to the assembled presidents that his own university senate had urged a discussion of future support for the new enterprise. Raiser, the minutes recorded, told his listeners that the "Berlin founders are directing sharp criticisms against the West because hitherto it has reacted lethargically to calls for help."[178]

Walter Hallstein, dean of law at Frankfurt University and one of the most influential figures in West German higher education, left the assembled educational leaders in no doubt where he stood with respect to the Free University. He declared himself openly opposed to the project, partly because material conditions for the enterprise were so negative. "Much more important is the following reservation," Hallstein declared. "If a Free University for the western sectors is erected, then the university at Unter den Linden will subseqently become purely a university of the East and is lost to us or it will suffer irreparable damage." The western rectors had up to that time made a strong effort not to undertake measures that would split off the universities of the Soviet Zone from the west. "This has actually provided an outstanding intellectual and moral boost for those elements who want to maintain contacts with the West," Hallstein announced. "If we give up on the university at

Unter den Linden, that will have symbolic meaning." Hallstein predicted that the *Zentralverwaltung*, which, he claimed, had up to then attempted to retain the appearance of Berlin University as an all-German university, would simply abandon those efforts. "Little more than a political demonstration will have been achieved," Hallstein predicted. "The universities are thereby damaged and the price paid is too high." The minutes record that none of the other university presidents in attendance offered a dissenting opinion.[179] For the present, the Free University could expect little help from the universities in the west. Their leadership, at least, had adopted a position similar to that of Hans Peters of the CDU and were judging events in terms of preserving those fragile links to German unity that still remained. It was a noble thought, but it also demonstrated that an almost unbridgeable gulf existed between those who lived in beleaguered Berlin and those who lived outside of it. To be sure, as far as the founding members of the Free University were concerned, Hallstein's pronouncement produced little effect. They continued with their plans at top speed.

BIBLIOMANIA

One ticklish technical problem that outweighed most others in importance was the creation of a library for the new university. With the Americans providing financial support and making available building space in Dahlem, those potentially worrisome obstacles were, for the moment, surmountable. However, adequate library resources were another matter and required an enormous effort on the part of faculty, administration, and students to solve. The founders quickly organized a library committee to survey the needs for the new university as well as the resources that might be available to them. The Americans associated with the project, such as University Officer Howard Johnston, worked closely with the German founders in locating the much-needed resources.

The library committee, with the aid of student volunteers, began canvassing Berlin for materials at the end of August, and exhibited considerable ingenuity in locating valuable collections. One of the choicer finds was a 40,000-volume library on international law. American Military Government's Adjutant General's Office had, during its three years in Berlin, put together a reference library of over 100,000 volumes, and Johnston contacted its staff in early September with a request for help. When General Clay first put together a support committee at OMGUS, he had urged all divisions of Military Government to support the new university in any way possible. His suggestion produced tangible results: "The Reference Library will be happy to assist students and faculty of the Free University in every way possible," replied Librarian Henry Dunlap to a request for support.[180]

The American education section also observed that there was a sociology collection of 5,000 volumes available in Berlin, "and in addition scores of other libraries in the 137 scientific projects in the American Sector." John Thompson, head of the education section in Military Government in Berlin, pointed out that a mouth-watering prize for the library collection also loomed just out of reach: "The heart of the library, however, will have to come from Marburg where a million well selected volumes belonging to the State Library in the Russian Sector of Berlin are now stored." Tempting as that prize was, it was to remain out of reach because of the Blockade and because of the legal problems inextricably bound up with ownership of the former Prussian book collection. The Marburg collection remained out of reach for the rest of the occupation. In fact, it was fated to arrive in West Berlin only in the 1970s, more than a generation later. But for the founders of the Free University in 1948, new sources were imperative. The Americans were well aware that the Soviets had banned all students associated with the forthcoming Free University from libraries of the Soviet Zone and East Berlin. In a meeting of September 14, Johnston informed Herr Freygang, the librarian of the new university's future library, that Military Government's Information Control Division was already preparing "a survey of all books in big and small libraries belonging to public and private owners." The idea of issuing a public appeal for book donations or loans arose, but Freygang pointed out that the result would likely be "quantity rather than quality," and he demurred.[181]

Freygang also pointed out that their efforts to date had demonstrated weaknesses in the arts, philosophy, and languages. Fortunately, the expected holdings in economics, law, and medicine were much more comprehensive, thus compensating somewhat for the scarcity of faculty in the first two areas. The Americans decided to conduct as comprehensive a survey as limited time and means allowed. Johnston noted that there were extensive collections of books in some of the housing requisitioned by Military Government officers, and an inventory should include those collections "to protect the (German) owner and also to furnish a basis for bargaining." Johnston observed that it would be unwise simply to requistion such resources, "because of the injustice to the German owners and because the books collected would probably contain at least fifty per cent of non-usable books."[182]

One large collection that was particularly welcome was the 6,000-volume library of deceased historian Hermann Oncken, presently stored at the Museum for Ethnology in Dahlem. At first the FU authorities hoped only to gain access to the Oncken collection and were delighted to learn that the museum authorities were equally eager to be rid of it. By late October, an army of volunteers were dragging books and shelves to a nearby university building and creating the core of a promising historical library. The library committee of the budding university quickly located other valuable collections. Walter Gerstenberg, director of the soon-to-be institute of musicology, wrote to Johnston excitedly in November 1948 to say that they had located a history-of-music collection of great value but that there was no money available to pay the modest price being demanded. Johnston was interested and an American specialist soon inspected the collection. He reported to his own Military Government authorities that American support "would at once make the music section of the Free University one of the most outstanding in Germany." The Americans provided additional sums of expensive Deutschmarks, and the Free University took possession of the valuable collection.[183]

The library committee for the nascent university was at pains to husband its limited resources, and because the new Deutschmark was considerably more valuable than the Soviet occupation marks (Eastmarks), the book purchasers usually obtained their collections with varying quantities of each. Usually the agreed-upon purchase price would be paid half-and-half in each currency with the Deutschmark providing considerably greater purchasing power. The founders of the new library discovered that there was a considerable number of private collections in Berlin of deceased professors, and frequently the hard-pressed relatives of the deceased scholars were pleased to sell them. The public response to the Free University, it should be remembered, was extremely positive in Berlin, and civic pride in the new institution was intense. Moreover, in those financially straitened times, when almost no one had sizable quantities of the newly introduced Deutschmark, the income from sales of books was more than welcome. Usually the purchase prices were reasonable, and in many cases the Free University became the beneficiary of handsome book donations by citizens who somehow could afford the luxury of being philanthropists.

Despite the Blockade, the West Berliners continued to go back and forth with only moderate interference to the Soviet Sector and to the Soviet Zone. Today, a generation after the building of the Wall, this freedom of movement seems odd, especially since the Blockade was intended to force the withdrawal of the Western Allies. The Blockade was directed primarily at the shipment of goods, however, not at the movement of people. Taking advantage of this situation, many student volunteers began locating private book collections in the east as well. "It was noteworthy," stated one purchaser, Hans-Joachim Lieber, "that many bookshops in the Soviet Zone held large collections of scholarly and scientific works despite the effects of war, bombardment, and a poor book supply thereafter. They were willing to supply them for western currency." Other student volunteers discovered another interesting phenomenon when obtaining supplies of books in the east for their new university. "Naturally, many book dealers in the vicinity of Berlin as well as at, for example, Leipzig had heard of the intention to found a Free University," recounted Georg Kotowski. "In purchasing books we determined that the dealers would only offer their carefully hoarded supplies when they realized that we were purchasing on behalf of the Free University."[184]

Not everyone was as kindly disposed as the booksellers of Leipzig and East Berlin. Customs agents seized one volunteer's entire supply of western currency that had been intended for further acquisitions for the Free University. Then, one morning a truck rolled up to one of the newly acquired university buildings, and the driver and his assistant rapidly unloaded 600 medical books for the school of medicine. They then departed immediately, without saying anything to the students who gathered to look at the valuable collection. Gratitude soon changed to alarm as the would-be recipients became suspicious about the origins of the collection. As a precaution, Howard Johnston asked Military Government's Public Safety Branch to investigate while the books were put into storage for safekeeping. That proved to be a wise precaution since the investigators learned that the collection was originally Polish and that until recently it had been in the possession of Soviet authorities. Despite the heavy temptation to use the medical collection, the founders returned them to the Soviets rather than endure the potentially embarrassing charge that the Free University was starting its existence with doubtfully acquired books. The incident, though minor, was one index of the ill feeling that existed at the official level between East and West with respect to the new university.[185]

The library collection that burgeoned for the new university in the autumn of 1948 was hardly centered in one place. German universities traditionally spread their library collections among the various institutes and departments. The Oncken collection, for example, was centered at the history department at Boltzmannstrasse 3. In fact, it would be years before the Free University would have a central library building. A separate library facility was an unthinkable luxury in 1948. Nevertheless, the collection grew quickly as the hardworking student volunteers combed the city, obtaining the best bargains they could find. The results were impressive. By early December 1948, when the new university opened its doors, Howard Johnston could claim that no fewer than 350,000 volumes were available to the students and professors, a remarkable feat considering that the founders had started from scratch in building a library collection just three months earlier.[186]

A NEW CONSTITUTION

The conditions that gave rise to the Free University of Berlin were unique in the annals of German higher education with students providing the major impetus in the early stages of the project. Given the control exercised by the *Zentralverwaltung* over Berlin University, the relationship between the state and the university formed a major concern for the founders of the Free University, be they students, professors, or participants from Berlin's public life. Therefore, the constitution which they composed in the summer and autumn of 1948 differed from the charters of other German universities in several important ways. The innovations can be divided into two categories. First, the students were to secure unusually prominent representation in the operations of the university. They conducted most of their own student affairs and served on most committees and boards, usually with full voting rights. This included the very highest body, the Board of Regents. The second remarkable feature was the unusual link that was developed between the new university and the state, in this case the City of Berlin. Whereas most German universities were controlled by a ministry of education within a state government and received a budget from the state as regulated by the state ministry of education, the Free University was to establish its link through the Board of Trustees with the Governing Mayor (in this case Ernst Reuter) serving as the chairman. The budget for the university would be established by the board, which, of course, would have strong university representation, thus eliminating an intermediary link such as a ministry of education or Berlin's Office of Public Education. These reforms were the core of what came to be known in German academic circles as the *Berliner Modell* and reflected the founders' desire to establish a kind of reform university and a possible model for other German universities. In later years, under utterly different circumstances, this Berlin Model became controversial and the subject of much debate before it was finally abandoned in 1969. However, in 1948 it reflected faithfully the unique political and social conditions of the West Berlin academic community and was for its own time a highly successful experiment.

The constitution provided that the new institution would be known as "die Freie Universität Berlin," the Free University of Berlin, and was entitled to carry its own seal, govern its own affairs, and administer its own budget. The new constitution explicitly stated the university's goals: "The university has the responsibility to serve scholarly research and teaching through freedom and independence to the community of scholars and teachers. It is to prepare students for those professions for which scholarly and scientific education is necessary and proper."[187]

The Free University was by no means a radically constituted university in most respects. Like its sister institutions, it maintained its own academic self-administration. The constitution established the usual positions for a rector (annually elected president), a senate (deans, the rector and his deputy, representatives from the associate professors and instructors, and, significantly, two student representatives), and the faculties (schools consisting of all of the full professors, three annually elected representatives for the associate professors, and one annually elected representative each for the lecturers and for the students). The deans were elected annually from the ranks of the full professors in each school. The senate would appoint full professors on the recommendations of the various schools, and these appointments required confirmation by the Magistrat of Berlin. With two student representatives in the senate, the student body had, in effect, a say in the appointment of full professors, an unprecedented innovation. It caused some nonstudents, such as Friedrich Kruspi, West Berlin's university administrative official for the Magistrat, to be ill at ease.

The powerful *Kuratorium* (Board of Trustees), which controlled the purse strings and which was a key feature of the Free University, consisted of the mayor of Berlin or his designated representative, the director of finances for the Berlin Magistrat (later Berlin Senate), the director of education for the Berlin Magistrat, three representatives from the City Assembly, the rector and prorector (deputy) of the Free University, and, last and by no means least, a student from the Free University. These members would elect to the board annually three prominent persons from Berlin public life. The board would also choose a curator (chancellor or chief adminstrative official) for the Free University to oversee its financial operations in line with directives of the board.

The new constitution explicitly recognized the student body as an official component of the university. That body consisted of all officially matriculated students and was empowered to produce its own student constitution providing for a large measure of student self-government. The students were to have a prominent role in establishing admissions policy, in creating disciplinary procedures, and in making the technical arrangements for instruction, such as classroom and lecture scheduling and the like. The students were proud of the rights and responsibilities which the new constitution specifically granted them. One of their number, Eva Heilmann, who would within a few semesters be elected chairwoman of the first student assembly, summed up their feelings about the Free University's constitution: "And when the constitution of the new university was written, the part that students had played in establishing it was recognized by assigning to them more responsibilties and rights than the students of any other German university had ever had. It was granted to them to manage their own affairs and to cooperate actively in the administration of the university."[188]

While the students had unusual rights of representation on such important committees as the Board of Trustees, the University Senate, and the faculties, the prevailing spirit caused the participants to look at the unusual arrangement in a different way than might be the case forty years later. While proud of their accomplishments in helping to create the new institution, the students did not think of their new status as a springboard from which to challenge the authority of the professoriate or the administration. On the contrary, the participants viewed student representation as carrying a heavy responsibility. The students were taking on part of the heavy burden of making the fledgling university function. Those one or two students elected to represent the student body on the key committees were painfully aware that they would have to immerse themselves in the specific issues of that committee, knowing that they represented the entire student body. "None of us ever expected in our wildest imaginings to have parity in representation with the faculty," commented one early student, Wolfgang Kalischer, many years later. The workload was often heavy in those first semesters when the creation of a new university required major decisions. Sometimes the duty could be unpleasant, "as when a student representative might be called upon to break a tie among opposing factions of the faculty," Kalischer added.[189] What made the Berlin Model work, following the founding of the Free University in 1948, was a sense of shared purpose by all of the founders, students and faculty alike, a spirit made sharper by the awesome obstacles that they had to overcome together in impoverished, blockaded Berlin.

The new constitution had admirers outside the founding members as well. Ambassador Robert Murphy in the Political Adviser's Office examined the Free University's constitution and waxed enthusiastic over it to Secretary of State George C. Marshall: "The Free University is among the most democratically organized higher institutions in Europe, and certain of its principles may well serve as a guide to other universities in Germany. Of particular interest is the fact that it incorporates a concept heretofore generally rejected by German academicians, namely student membership in the Senate (governing body) of the institution."[190] Murphy was sufficiently impressed with the new university and its founders that even before it officially opened its doors he recommended that the State Department "familiarize interested university and educational associations in the United States with the history of this development particularly with a view to arousing interest and support for . . . the university in America's academic circles."[191] The Americans at least were well pleased with what the German founding members had accomplished since that moment in April 1948 when the students had called for a new university from the Hotel Esplanade.

To be sure, the writing of the new constitution was not without its problems. Already at the end of August, the Preparatory Committee's secretary and the Free University's future chancellor, Fritz von Bergmann, had been charged with producing preliminary drafts of the constitution in cooperation with the Magistrat's higher educational expert, Friedrich Kruspi. Kruspi was not at all enthusiastic about seeing the creation of a new university with a radically different connection to the local government, (the proposed Board of Trustees). Such an arrangement would leave the Office of Education effectively removed from financial control of the Free University. The link was also at variance with other higher educational institutions in Berlin, such as the Technical University. Student tempers flared, however, when a journalist claimed to overhear Kruspi stating that "the student is the object, not the subject of a university constitution." Kruspi emphatically denied the remark.[192]

By early September, von Bergmann reported to the Preparatory Committee some difficulties in preparing the constitution, and a district mayor, Karl Kleikamp, joined the discussions. City Councilmen Walter May, Kiellinger, and Holthöfer joined in the work, which received input from members of the Preparatory Committee and from the students through their Committee of 25. By early October, Kleikamp was able to present a first draft to the Preparatory Committee, which then polished and amended it. The founders felt that the new constitution had to receive official approval quickly so that the university could legally send letters of appointment to the professors. The technical and legal problems were often complex and not easily solved. For example, the appointments for the professors were presumably for life even though appointees were not officially civil servants (Beamte), as was the case at other universities. (This civil-service status finally materialized for professors at the Free University in 1952.) Then, too, there was some hesitation on the part of the City Assembly in accepting Paragraph 24 of the constitution, which recognized the existence of the Preparatory Committee as a transitional body during the young university's first year of existence. Some members of the City Assembly were astonished to see two students represented on the University Senate, a hitherto unheard-of procedure. Nevertheless, the Magistrat rendered its approval of the constitution on October 14, and the City Assembly granted its assent on November 4. To be sure, the enterprise had not been without disagreements, yet on the whole the founders were pleased. "Despite a few objections, the Preparatory Committee is grateful to the Magistrat and to the City Assembly for their quick passage of the constitution," commented the founders on November 9. A week later, using the controversial Paragraph 24, the founders forwarded to the director of the Office of Education the names of Friedrich Meinecke as rector, Edwin Redslob as his deputy, and three deans for the faculties of philosophy, medicine, and law/economics. Thirty nominations for the teaching faculty followed. It was characteristic of East-West tensions at that time that the founders also forwarded a second, confidential communication nominating two professors "whose names must be kept secret because of political reasons."[193]

FIRST COMMENCEMENT

There were little time and few resources to spare for any lavish ceremony for Germany's newest university. By the end of October the Preparatory Committee was sufficiently confident of its accomplishments to schedule the onset of the first semester for November 15. In a few special instances preliminary courses began as early as November 8. With generous cooperation from the Technical University, Edwin Redslob held a public address there at the end of October in which he gave a progress report and declared to the delighted audience the opening dates for the Free University. Redslob thanked all of the students for their support and indicated that, after initial hesitations, support for the new university was also arriving from the other Western Allies, the British and French military governments, as well as from West German universities. Redslob was cautious in his remarks about any difficulties that had arisen in the creation of the new university, but one student, Fischer-Bothof, speaking for the students, expressed outright displeasure with Friedrich Kruspi's delaying tactics. Angered at his continuing opposition to the new constitution, a majority of students voted a resolution to the Magistrat calling for Kruspi's dismissal. Fortunately, another university representative, Professor Paul Altenberg, calmed the situation, indicating that the slight differences had been resolved and predicting that the constitution would sail through the city government without delay. It did so.[194]

It was a measure of the scarcity of resources and the refusal to stand on ceremony that some lectures actually began taking place in movie theaters and other public or commercial buildings until such time as other physical accommodations became available. On November 15, exactly on schedule, Edwin Redslob held one of the first lectures (on "Basic Principles of Painting") and he never once referred to the events surrounding the creation of the Free University to the 130 students who crowded around on stools and folding chairs. His unspoken message was clear: the time had come for the learning process to resume.[195] On the same day, Walter Hübner opened his lecture on English literature with these ringing words: "A university has meaning—and this is especially the mission of the Free University—when through spiritual togetherness, it takes up the struggle for truth every day."[196] It was characteristic of the haste with which the enterprise began that the teaching faculty continued to arrive even as the semester was already under way. For example, Professor Hans Leisegang, famed philosopher and briefly a possible choice as rector of the Free University, had left Jena after all because of political differences with the East-Zone authorities. After a few weeks of hesitation and in great secrecy he arrived in Berlin, and without further ado started lecturing on November 25 to enthusiastic crowds of students.[197]

Howard Johnston, accompanied by the British University Officer in Berlin, Peter Whitley, dropped by the newly functioning Free University on a weekend shortly after classes had begun, and reported to his superiors that

German initiative has made this great community undertaking possible . . . we were both amazed at the intense activity everywhere. Saturday afternoon was not a time for classes, but we ran into at least 600 students, professors, and political leaders meeting in committees, moving furniture, typing lists, sorting books, or taking notes from the bulletin boards. Being with them for two hours gave us quite a lift; their high spirits and determination in spite of the Blockade and Soviet threats are truly remarkable.[198]

Peter Whitley was scarcely less excited and spoke with pride of the event long after: "I was also involved, peripherally, in the founding of the Freie Universität," he reminded other veteran university officers, "but because of official British policy, this was (to my regret) entirely on a personal/informal basis." Because he was closest to the situation, Whitley had judged it differently than had many of his countrymen.[199]

The meaningful work of the Free University really began in mid-November, just under seven months after the fateful dismissal of the three students, and the founders decided to prepare a commencement exercise to celebrate their new creation. Lacking any facility even remotely adequate for the task, they chose to hold it in the Titania Palast, a large public hall in nearby Steglitz that could hold 2,000 spectators. The hall would be free for the lavish occasion only on December 4, the owners said, and so for reasons dictated by the straitened circumstances of the time, the Free University officially opened its doors on December 4, 1948.

It was a ceremony long remembered by the newly forged academic community and its supporters. Terrible weather and sickness in hungry, shivering Berlin took their toll on the guest list. Friedrich Meinecke reported less than an hour beforehand that a bad cold had confined him to his bed. Various rectors and academic personnel from the West German universities called frantically to say that the weather had canceled the Airlift flights into Berlin arranged for them by the British and American authorities. Only the French had had better luck, and a professor and a student arrived from Tübingen to represent the sister universities of the west. Despite the less than ideal conditions, the speakers on that day rose to the solemn occasion.

Ernst Reuter had influenced the creation of the new institution from the start, and he proved once again to be the central figure at the moment the Free University was officially born. He led the ceremony with a moving speech in which he recounted the painful steps that they had taken since the previous summer which brought them together for the commencement exercise. "The lectures have already begun," he stated, "and I am proud to say today in my capacity as chairman of the Preparatory Committee: THE FREE UNIVERSITY OF BERLIN IS FOUNDED!" Reuter thanked all of those who had made the new institution possible, and it was significant that the first group he recognized was the student body. "As a man who is already in his eighty-fourth semester," Reuter said amidst general merriment, "I must offer the first word of thanks to you, my young students. This university was born from the spirit of the youth. . . ." Reuter also recognized the invaluable support of the Western Allies, of the ranks of professors who had risked so much to support an impossible cause, and of the hard-working members of the founding committees, who had worked full time, often with little prospect of reward, to make the institution possible. Reuter made it unmistakably clear why the new university was necessary and why he had supported it. Describing the ideology of the East Zone as one which enslaved minds and controlled thoughts, he stated that a university as the West understood it could not exist there. "Universities should be centers of free activity, free creativity, and free thinking, not centers where politics in the narrow sense of the word are perpetrated. . . . In a world of slavery a free university, i.e., a Universitas Litterarum, is impossible. Therefore it was the students first of all—the pressure fell upon them most—and after them other responsible men who recognized that they could not remain where the flag of freedom no longer waves." Reuter ended with the hope that Germany's newest university would "remain in the years to come a living expression of the urge to be free in this proud city."[200]

With the help of a novel radio link from his sickbed, Friedrich Meinecke made his voice count on that day, too. "With joy I hear the voice of youth," he began, "and welcome its call for a new university for a truly free center of scholarship and learning." For Meinecke, freedom was defined as "the innermost sense, the moral and spritual self-determination [heard] through the voice of one's conscience." The personality emerged in an individual's life only in the presence of freedom. Yet, freedom, Meinecke maintained, led directly to self-denial, to self-discipline rather than to egoism. Freedom, he repeated, came through "self-discipline rather than disciplining and conditioning through outside force according to some mass model of an authoritarian, totalitarian nature. These ideas of freedom and personality are, when seen from a universal and historical perspective, the wellspring of the European ideal and of Western, Christian culture. It is these ideals which are being contested in the world today." Meinecke viewed the Free University as one isolated skirmish in a great contest of spiritual and temporal power. The aged historian asked if it was necessary for this conflict to be fought out between the old and new universities of Berlin. "The great majority of my colleagues who remain there would apparently say no," he answered. "However, I know what soul-searching and what turmoil and anguish exist there." Some regarded it a "useful error" to remain in place, but for Meinecke there could be no such rationalization. He did not mean to say that those who were still in the east were now hopelessly compromised. "We know that there, too, despite misconceptions of the present situation in which they are caught, the striving toward truth and freedom has by no means been halted." Rising above the resentments and emotion that understandably gripped the Berliners in their divided city, Meinecke ended his speech with hope for reconciliation in the future. "May the thought of initiating a conflict between the two universities remain distant," he told the 2,000 listeners. "Not conflict, rather competitive zeal should be our motto! May the day come when we can reunite. It would be the same day longed for by all peoples of the world, the day when the poet's line is fulfilled: Peace, peace on earth!"[201]

The speeches of the day were not the only memorable aspect of the opening. Edwin Redslob fulfilled the traditional role of a German rector on such an occasion by offering a thoroughly scholarly treatise on a subject in which he was expert. However, he did it in such a way as to draw upon an art-history theme which was tied closely to the spirit of the present enterprise. Redslob offered an analysis of the sculptures of Naumburg Cathedral in his native Thuringia which represented three virtues: Veritas, Justitia, and Libertas (truth, justice, and freedom), the concepts that had been central to the establishment of the Free University. Formerly the official artist of the Weimar Republic and experienced in the designing of official emblems, Redslob had personally produced the official seal of the Free University after exhaustive trial and error. An imposing replica now hung above the speaker's podium for all to admire.[202]

The students heard a worthy representative from their number, too, as dental student Horst Rögner-Francke reminded them that nearly three years earlier they had attended a similar ceremony and experienced a similar outpouring of idealism, which had then gradually withered. Now the prospects appeared different, and Rögner-Francke begged his young colleagues to maintain their momentum. "Take care that this effort has not been in vain, that the spirit at the creation will not be diluted, and that future generations will hold to it."[203] It remained to be seen what future generations remembered of the founding spirit of the Free University.

The organizers of the commencement exercise had felt it was important to demonstrate at once that the new venture was not emerging in isolation, despite the desperate circumstances affecting Berlin. Therefore, among those on the podium and who spoke that day was Professor Ebeling of Tübingen University, who took it upon himself to represent the west-zone universities now that the fragile air link was temporarily cut. The provisional mayor of Berlin, Louise Schroeder, spoke for the city, as did Professor Apel, who, on behalf of the Technical University, welcomed the arrival of another university to West Berlin. A student, Albrecht von Brunn, from the French Zone, praised the students' accomplishments and brought words of encouragement from his fellow students in the west. There were also two Americans present that day to round off the celebration.

The founders of the Free University had, despite a frosty beginning, come to respect Colonel Frank Howley, the U.S. Commandant in the American Sector. Once they had won him to their cause, they found that his influence and decisiveness helped them solve endless problems. At the beginning of the ceremony Ernst Reuter specifically singled him out for praise before the large German audience. Howley, who gave the appearance of a professional soldier and whose aggressive ways had earned him unending hostility from the Soviets as well as admiration from the west, surprised his listeners with his lucid remarks on December 4. Echoing the refrain of earlier addresses that a university worthy of the name required an atmosphere of freedom, he suggested that by no means were all the problems the students had to overcome physical. "I am glad that it was the students who stood in the front ranks of this conflict," he announced, but Howley had some advice for the young people who would soon be studying the thinkers and writers in their professions. He wanted them to give balance and proportion to their studies. "If you examine Nietzsche's pessimism and dark nihilism, I would propose that you interest yourself in Kant's internationalism," he suggested. "If you immerse yourselves in the works of Marx with his emphasis on material conditions for the existence of humanity, I would suggest that you not forget that there was a Francis of Assisi who described things which simply are not to be explained by materialism. And I would hope that if you concern yourself with the discoveries of Röntgen, that you would remember that the most important realm of humanity cannot be conveyed through mere x-rays."[204]

The last speaker that day was in some ways an unusual guest to have at the opening ceremony of the Free University. He was not a German and had had nothing whatsoever to do with the founding of the Free University. Yet, his mere presence rather than any words he offered on that day warmed the hundreds of onlookers. Playwright Thornton Wilder was perhaps the most admired guest on that day, even though it was something of a coincidence that he happened to be in Berlin at all. Invited to give a lecture on his plays at the Free University, he was hugely popular with the students, who convinced him to prolong his stay long enough to contribute to the opening ceremony. Wilder simply offered the greetings and well wishes of Yale and Princeton universities, with which he was closely associated, plus the greetings of American universities in general. Genuinely impressed with the exemplary spirit that pervaded this bold experiment in higher education, Wilder hoped "that the coming generation of students will recall with pride the times in which this university was born."[205] In reality, Thornton Wilder stood at the podium because his plays, such as *Our Town* and *The Skin of Our Teeth*, had struck a deep, responsive chord with German audiences. Frequently, he had created for his theatergoers an atmosphere of traditional, what the Americans called small-town, values that did not seem oppressive or farfetched. His message was an optimistic one which many desperately wanted to believe: There has been much anguish, catastrophe, and grief in this world, but there is something in human nature that allows us—sometimes by the slimmest of margins—to overcome all adversity. Wilder's works gave the founders of the Free University hope for a better future. Speaking another language and coming from another land, he had no ties to any occupation force or to any official policy. His very presence was a promising sign that the Free University would be international in its outlook and that it would face the future with growing confidence.

REACTIONS

On the eve of the Free University's founding, a sometime educational adviser to British Military Government, Lord Lindsay, pronounced his verdict on the entire undertaking: "I heard a lot about it in Berlin," he wrote to a German emigré friend, economist Adolph Lowe, who had moved to New York. "I think it is a great mistake and is almost certain to be a flop." Lindsay also claimed that even some American experts were still opposed to it, as was Britain's expert, Sir Robert Birley. "Birley . . . consulted the universities of the British Zone," Lindsay added, "who were all against it."[206] However, Lindsay was not permanently stationed in Berlin. Neither was he current on the subject anymore. Other outside observers had been equally suspicious of the entire undertaking. Herbert Marcuse remained highly critical of the enterprise, describing Edwin Redslob as "a questionable asset" in a letter to Fritz Epstein. Yet he had to admit he was wrong in his prediction that the university would never come into existence. "I have to correct my report on the Freie Universität in Berlin," he admitted to Epstein; "it has now started functioning."[207]

Other British observers in Berlin and London, who were hardly inclined to put as rosy a view on the subject as were the heavily committed Americans, also watched the growth of the Free University carefully. British Military Government representatives, as well as the French, were in attendance at the memorable commencement in the Titania Palast. Within ten days of the Free University's official opening, they began making a new assessment of the situation. In a confidential dispatch to Ernest Bevin at the Foreign Office in London, Michael Garran, a political adviser to British Military Governor Sir Brian Robertson, reported on recent developments at the Free University, particularly the first commencement exercise. "The German Organizing Committee [Preparatory Committee] has pursued its plans with more success than had been commonly anticipated . . . ," Garran admitted. He recounted the painful absences of Meinecke and west-zone university representatives from the ceremonies, but he felt that the willingness on the part of French authorities to send scholars from the University of Tübingen was significant. Garran then listed the various accomplishments of the founders in finding physical facilities and in overcoming the legal, personnel, financial, admissions, and other hurdles in order to permit the Free University to open its doors. To his surprise, the Soviet-Zone press had only offered one major propaganda blast by reprinting (yet again) an article by the Free University's reliable nemesis, Hans Peters. "Apart from that," Garran reported, "comments in the Soviet-licensed Press have mostly been confined to short, scathing references, and there have been surprisingly few serious attacks."[208]

"The 86-year-old national liberal professor Friedrich Meinecke has taken on the role of 'savior' just like 'good old Hindenburg,' a fateful precedent. It is a dubious political society which has assembled here." The *Neues Deutschland* went on to name names of faculty members who allegedly had a National Socialist past: Redslob, Dovifat, Hübner, and Knudsen were, the newspaper claimed, former Nazis, be they card-carrying members or not. Other doubtful figures included the former leading Nazi legal theorist Carl Schmitt, who until 1945 had been a member of the law faculty of the old Berlin University. The paper assured its readership that Schmitt was about to join the Free University.[209]

The British saw the entire project as being feasible only because the Americans were supporting it heavily, and Garran pointed out the continued divided counsels in the American ranks with respect to the Free University. He claimed that the cultural adviser to General Clay, Alonzo G. Grace, had offered the opinion as late as September 11 that the Americans should dissociate themselves from the project and support British efforts to expand the Technical University. Several Anglo-American meetings to discuss that possibility had failed to make progress, "largely, it appeared, through the opposition of Mr. Kendall Foss, General Clay's representative, to any proposals which might endanger his own project." Garran noted that Foss had now left Berlin and that cooperation between the two universities seemed much likelier. He pointed out several possibilities of sharing staff and facilities and predicted that "it seems probable that the two universities will regard themselves as partners rather than competitors." He even thought a merger might still occur in the future if the Free University found itself in difficulties.[210]

The Foreign Office staff in London conceded that despite widespread adverse publicity from Lord Lindsay and from leading articles in the London *Times*, the critics seemed not to have judged the situation accurately. "The new university has been established by German initiative," wrote P. G. B. Giles of the Foreign Office's German Education Department. He hoped for cooperation with the Technical University as Garran had predicted and was generally upbeat in his assessment. "If the new University maintains the interest and support of Germans, it

may yet establish itself in the academic life of Berlin, despite the prestige of the Humboldt University." Moreover, Giles was prepared to
admit something which the British advisers had not been willing to recognize: "It seems certain from the present despatch," he conceded, "that
the project has turned out better than might have been expected." Another staffer, Harold Worsfold, of Bevin's General Economic Department, had recently interviewed a German medical doctor in the British
Sector and then had done some observing of local conditions himself.
The German physician, identified only as Dr. Bender, was reported as
being "keen on the new University because it offered a means of continuing the medical training of students resident in our [the British] Sector,
who would not attend the old University in the Russian Sector."
Worsfold's views were similar to that of the German: "I note that the medical faculty seems well staffed," he observed, "and it seems that it may
meet a real if temporary demand, as [does] indeed the whole University."[211] Thus, the British, who had long been cool to the entire enterprise, had finally to admit that they had miscalculated the worth of the
new university and had underestimated the steadfastness of its founders.

To be sure, the American and German participants were hardly so re-
strained. Kendall Foss, in his final report to General Clay before leaving
Military Government, was exultant. "Perhaps it is fair to say at this
stage that a baby has been born. It is somewhat scrawny, and it will
need careful feeding, but it is alive and it plainly means to stay alive unless the whole daring venture of maintaining a free Berlin collapses."
For Foss the existence of the Free University was "proof that there are elements in Germany capable of responding effectively to a constructive
challenge." [212]

The German founders were impressed too. In inviting General Clay
to the opening exercise (Clay could not accept and sent Colonel Howley
instead), Friedrich Meinecke and Edwin Redslob took the opportunity
to express their gratitude to the key Americans who had aided them.
"We know how valuable the interest was, Herr General, which you exhibited starting last spring for the Free University. We are especially grateful to you that at your bidding Professor [Carl Joachim] Friedrich and
Mr. Kendall Foss stood by us in word and deed during the founding of
the University."[213]

While the students and faculty of the Free University went about
the business of scholarship and learning, simultaneously continuing
the complex process of making the university function, news reports
of Germany's newest university spread throughout the divided nation.
In the western zones, coverage was predictably positive, and in the
east predictably negative. For the moment the sense of accomplishment
in Berlin was strong, but much remained to be done if the Free University
was to find an accepted place in the German academic world. Danger

signals abounded amidst the jubilation. The rectors of the West German universities had convened in Würzburg in November 1948, and, as the result of an initiative by Tübingen University's Rector Erbe, once again they grappled with the issue of the Free University. In the discussion that followed, the assembled university leaders decided that the political situation in Berlin was still unclear, and they remained reluctant to take a stand on the Free University for fear of hastening the division of the German academic world. The assembled leaders decided to avoid making any official pronouncement with respect to the Free University.[214] The new university had a difficult mission now: It must prove itself among its older peers, a severe test that would require another decade at least. The Free University would have to consolidate its gains.

CONCLUSION

In December 1973, when the Free University celebrated its twenty-fifth year, the *Kommunistische Studentenverband* (KSV) at the Free University recognized the occasion by organizing a large gathering at the university's spacious Auditorium Maximum. They listened to an address by Tilman Fichter, a young academician charged with the responsibility of producing a historical documents series for the Free University. From the documentation he had assembled, Fichter informed his audience of 900 listeners about the founding of the Free University, but in the ensuing discussion the KSV-dominated audience concluded that the Free University had in no way resulted from the work of students. Rather, it was a creature of the American Military Government, which sought to use it to divide and destroy Humboldt University and to recruit its faculty to the new institution.[215]

The historical evidence from German, American, and British sources paints a very different picture than the radicals' assessment on the occasion of the Free University's twenty-fifth anniversary. Exactly one generation earlier, other dissident students, who had reached an impasse with the Soviet-Zone authorities in the spring of 1948, had begun to canvass the Western Allies, especially the Americans and British, for support as early as December 1947. They concluded from those efforts that the Americans alone were in a position to support their lofty—if not foolhardy—scheme of erecting a new kind of university that would allow scope for the functioning of a strong student government much on the scale of the old *Studentische Arbeitsgemeinschaft* at Berlin University. A group of students centered around the student journal *Colloquium* became the nucleus of a significant, dissident group, led by such key figures as Hess, Schwarz, and Stolz. Subsequently, sufficient numbers of students reacted strongly enough to the dismissal of three of their number that German political circles and members of the journalistic world began to take them seriously. The impasse at Berlin University remained unresolved with the result that the great majority of the duly elected student council resigned from Berlin University en masse and called for other students to sign petitions indicating their desire to study at a future university in the western sectors. Berlin University students responded by the hundreds to this appeal. It was then that other German elements entered the affair and gave substance to what had hitherto been a student revolt. Key political figures such as Ernst Reuter, representatives from the media such as *Tagesspiegel* licensee Edwin Redslob, and scientists/scholars such as Else Knake or Hermann Muckermann issued a call for other prominent Berlin citizens to convene for the purpose of creating a new university. It was then that the students' isolation ended, and the possibility of creating a new university dramatically increased.

Up to this point, the Americans had been sympathetic but largely passive. It was only after influential groups of Berliners joined with the students on June 19, 1948, and then openly declared their intentions on July 24 that the Americans took overt action.

Did the Americans direct the affairs of the founding members of the Free University for the purpose of diminishing or destroying Humboldt University? Once again the historical evidence demonstrates otherwise. American policies in the occupation with respect to education in general and higher education in particular were stamped by strong improvisation. Much depended upon the initiative of local Military Government officials, most of whom lacked the professional background to take a lead in influencing German policies and institutions. At best they could exercise a controlling function or provide some kind of support. They were seldom initiators. The case of the founding of the Free University bears this out. Berlin students such as Otto Hess or Otto Stolz established links with Americans like Fritz Karsen, Fritz Epstein, or Richard Sterling in hopes of enlisting future support. The contacts were unofficial, and the individuals contacted were not senior enough to rate as decision-makers. In fact, Epstein, who may have provided the initial key link, had no official connection with Military Goverment whatsoever. Later, as the founding process began, American Military Government assigned people like Kendall Foss and Howard W. Johnston to the task of supporting the organizational efforts of the German founders. Foss was a journalist with a knack for organization who caught General Clay's eye. Johnston was a social work officer originally assigned to Berlin to work in youth programs, a relatively low-priority assignment, and then hastily transferred to the newly erected post of university officer. It was true that Herman Wells informed Clay that a new university was feasible—just barely—but then he departed from Berlin immediately. After the American officials in Military Government hotly debated the feasibility of a new university, it took the weight of Carl Joachim Friedrich, perhaps the only individual in American Military Government who understood the German university, to convince General Clay to support the project. These were hardly the actions of a Military Government with a set plan and bent upon destroying Berlin University as yet another front in the rapidly escalating Cold War. Frank Howley was probably the one officer who viewed the founding unemotionally in its Cold-War context, but as a professional soldier who had played a confrontational role vis-à-vis the Soviets since 1945, his actions were hardly surprising. Howley's policies toward higher education in Berlin gave every appearance of taking East-West tensions into account, as when he banned the movement of students into the American Sector—much to the dismay of his own education officers. Then, reversing himself, in January 1948 Howley had ordered his education staff to make plans for a new university, a project that ignored the importance of German initiative and that had almost no prospect of success. He quickly abandoned it in favor of the Free University, once the dismissal of the three students set another, more spontaneous plan in motion. Howley might have been confrontational, and he might have been opportunistic. That hardly made him the creator of the Free University.

By contrast, developments in the summer and autumn of 1948 suggest strongly that the organizational work and conception of the Free University were entirely German. The students around *Colloquium* and on the *Studentenrat*, most of them veterans of the *Studentische Arbeitsgemeinschaft* and the "Salon Epstein," had developed their own plans, found their potential allies, and then confronted Paul Wandel and the *Zentralverwaltung für Volksbildung*. Later, it was individuals like August Fehling, Ernst Reuter, Paul Altenberg, and Otto Hess, to name only a few, who produced the detailed plans that resulted in the Free University. They developed their own unique "Berlin Model," a factor that, far from attracting outside faculty, tended to make many potential professors, including those at Berlin University, suspicious of this experiment in German higher education. Though they might not have admitted it to themselves, the founders of the Free University, especially the students, had adopted certain features from East-Zone higher education, such as a continuing admissions priority for socially disadvantaged students. Still, the institution that emerged was unmistakably German in nature. Americans like Foss, Johnston, and Howley simply did not have the professional training or the experience to influence the shaping of the Free University. The reform university that emerged was the product of the experience and the thinking of German students, politicans, academicians, and civil servants. It resulted from the unique conditions of postwar Berlin and of a postwar generation of students who had disavowed totalitarian movements. The Americans could and finally did provide indispensable material and moral support. After all, the Berliners who founded the Free University had to believe that they had an ally behind them because even the brave and the disciplined could not remain defiant in a vacuum of resources, both material and spiritual.

The new university that emerged in divided Berlin was, despite its unique founding, scarcely in an enviable position as 1949 approached. It could hardly expect to maintain ties with any of the universities in the Soviet Zone. The response of the West German universities reflected a wait-and-see attitude, so that the Free University at the moment of its creation existed in a kind of limbo. Despite prodigies of saving, it had only enough financial support from the Americans' one-time donation to function for approximately one semester, and then the City of Berlin would have to take over the responsibility for support. But Berlin in the midst of the Blockade was a city wracked by high unemployment, the exodus of business and industry to the western zones, currency woes unknown in the West, and a continuing crisis atmosphere that frightened many. The coming years would test West Berlin's new university nearly as sternly as did its difficult birthing. It remained to be seen how the Free University would meet the challenges of consolidation and growth.

Berlin, Central District, May, 1945.

Berlin University Reopens, January 29, 1946. Despite western protests the Soviets and German Communists reopened the ruined university under their exclusive control. Rector Johannes Stroux (r. center) appeared in traditional academic robes borrowed from Jena.

Georg Wrazidlo

Otto Hess

Otto Stolz

Joachim Schwarz

Arguably the most influential students at Berlin University, these former persecutees under Hitler's Germany played a central role in developing a student dissident movement.

General Lucius D. Clay

Herman B Wells

Colonel Frank Howley

Fritz Epstein

Friends of the Free University. Fritz and Herta Epstein established
the first meaningful contacts between students and American officials. Herman Wells determined that a new university was feasible.
Lucius Clay and Frank Howley offered crucial support once the
students proved their determination.

Helmut Coper   Horst Hartwich

Gerda Rösch   Georg Kotowski

Each of these postwar students contributed significantly to the creation of the Free University, either as organizers of the student government at Berlin University, as martyrs during the wave of student arrests, or as individuals who exposed authoritarian methods at the university to the public.

Stanislaw Kubicki

Dietrich Spangenberg

Peter Lorenz

Gerhard Löwenthal

Eva Heilmann

Gerhard Petermann

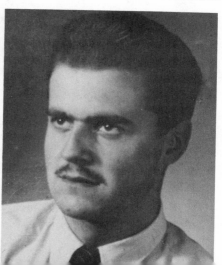

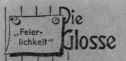

„Feierlichkeit" **Die Glosse**

„Ich bring' es im Leben sicher nicht weit, mir fehlt der Sinn für Feierlichkeit", so klagte Fontane. Hätte er aber die „feierliche" Rektoratsübergabe an der Universität Berlin miterlebt, dann würde er sicher konstatiert haben, daß wir uns des Sinnes für Feierlichkeit entschieden entschlagen haben, was daraus hervorgeht, daß die Teilnehmer an der „Feierstunde" es am weitesten im Leben gebracht haben, die in ihrem Exterieur am unfeierlichsten wirkten.

So waren zu sehen: ein richtiger Präsident mit Pullover ohne Schlips, ein Vizepräsident mit Baskenmütze, ein Dekan mit rotem Schlips und zwei führende Beamte der „Deutschen" Verwaltung für Volksbildung, denen die ganze „Feier" so langweilig war, daß sie während der Festrede der neuen Magnifizenz ihre Pfeifen, beziehungsweise Zigaretten, in Brand setzten.

Die Lautsprecher-Anlage brummte so laut, daß die Worte der Redner nur schwer verständlich waren. Vielleicht brummte sie aber auch deshalb, weil der Vizepräsident Brugsch sehr überzeugend nachwies, daß Humboldt den Ansprüchen der Zentralverwaltung in bezug auf Fortschrittlichkeit doch nicht ganz gerecht geworden sei. Nach diesem verheißungsvollen Auftakt ergriff Seine Magnifizenz, der jetzige Prorektor, das Wort, um der jetzigen Magnifizenz, dem ehemaligen Prorektor, Amt, Würde, Bürde und die Rektorenkette zu übergeben.

Auf dem Podium saßen, frierend in ihre Mäntel gehüllt, die zehn Dekane und dachten darüber nach, wie es gekommen, daß sie den neuen Rektor einstimmig gewählt. Die Herren der Zentralverwaltung, die dazu einiges hätten sagen können, enthielten sich jeglicher Äußerung, weil sie ebenfalls froren und darauf bedacht sein mußten, dem unablässig von der Decke tropfenden Naß auszuweichen.

Den Höhepunkt der Feier bildete — wie sich das auch gehört — die Rede der neuen Magnifizenz. „Durch Telefongespräche mit der Zentralverwaltung würden unüberwindliche Felsblöcke zu kleinen Kieselsteinen." (Telefon ist eben besser und hat noch den Vorteil, daß man's im Fall der Fälle abstreiten kann.) „Arm in Arm mit dem Prorektor werde er von Kilometerstein zu Kilometerstein den Weg zur ‚echten demokratischen Volksuniversität' zurücklegen!"

Die Herren der frierenden und von immer heftiger werdendem Tropfenfall bedrohten Festversammlung gewann sich Seine Magnifizenz dadurch, daß er auf die zum geheiligten Brauchtum gehörende Antrittsvorlesung verzichtete und dafür, im Leben stehender Jurist, der er ist, auf ein von ihm verfaßtes, demnächst erscheinendes Buch verwies. (Diesmal handelt es sich nicht — wie 1934 — um einen Kommentar zum „Gesetz zur Ordnung der nationalen Arbeit".)

Ein Streichquartett kämpfte entschlossen gegen Nässe und Kälte an und konnte sich schon nach den ersten zwanzig Takten auf ein gemeinsames Tempo einigen, was sich der neue Rektor auch von dem neuen Studentenrat wünschte. SISYPHUS

"A Commentary." This savage glossover by "Sisyphus" (Otto Stolz) on the changing of rectors at Berlin University stung SED officials and helped precipitate a crisis.

Changing of the Guard at Humboldt University. In May 1948, the youth magazine *Horizont* depicted the Communist takeover by showing a deposed Humboldt glancing at a new figure (Paul Wandel) on the university's pedestal.

Paul Wandel. First president of the Soviet Zone's *Zentralverwaltung für Volksbildung*, Wandel attempted a gradual transformation of Berlin University into a Marxist institution.

Letter of Dismissal. On April 16, 1948, under Wandel's orders, Rector Dersch dismissed the three leading student dissidents from the university.

Berlin University's Student Council Meets, April 21, 1948. Angered by Wandel's action, the *Studentenrat* protested the dismissals. In the foreground (l. to r.) were Hans-Joachim Gaebler, student council chairman Claus Reuber, and Horst Rögner-Francke.

Student Admissions Office in Dahlem. Determined to avoid ideological biases in admissions, Free University students handled applications themselves. Given the Cold War atmosphere, only noncommunist students applied.

Friedrich Meinecke. Despite his advanced age, famed historian
Friedrich Meinecke served as the Free University's first rector. He
urged the founders to create an institution with its own positive
goals rather than attempt to split the old university.

Founding Day. On December 4, 1948, the founding members
gathered at the Titania Palast for the formal opening of the Free
University. In the presence of high German and American officials
the founders declared the creation of a democratic institution with
strong student representation and minimal state interference.

Governing Mayor Ernst Reuter (l.) and Deputy
Rector Edwin Redslob (r.) Confer. Reuter gave
crucial early support to the Free University.
Publicist Redslob focused media criticism at Communist control of the old university and supported
student efforts to create a new one. Both helped
attract much-needed funding for the new
university.

Help for the Free University. On
October 12, 1949, U.S. High Commissioner John J. McCloy first visited
Dahlem. Initially inclined to merge
the Free University with the Technical because of high costs, he soon
thought otherwise. (Front l. to r.:
Ernst Reuter, John J. McCloy, and
Howard W. Johnston. At extreme left
is Fritz von Bergmann.)

Franz L. Neumann. A political scientist at Columbia University and Ford Foundation consultant,
Neumann was one of several emigré academics
who helped the Free University. He suggested that
it emphasize the social sciences.

Friends in High Places. Shepard
Stone was well acquainted with
Berlin higher education, having
earned his doctorate there in 1933.
Like McCloy, he aided the Free Uni-
versity, first as an official in the High
Commission and later as an official
of the Ford Foundation.

The First Mensa. The university's hastily erected cafeteria served as a focal point for its first students. Group identity was central to the functioning of the university's Berlin Model.

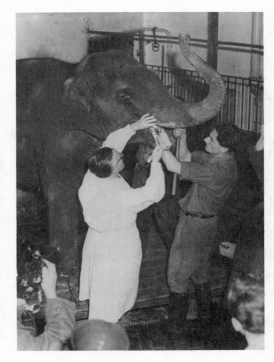

Catsandratsandelephants. Student veterinarians help treat an unusual patient. Because of irreconcilable political differences with authorities in the newly constituted GDR, the veterinarians moved west in 1951.

High Commissioner James Conant (c.) presents a donation to Rector Ernst Hirsch (r.) in 1955. Conant continued strong American financial support. Former exile Hirsch garnered generous German funding, including civil-service status for Berlin professors.

The Free University. Its campus-like setting included the philosophy faculty in an older structure at Boltzmannstrasse 3 (rear center) and next to it the 1950s-style Henry-Ford Bau and University Library. The economics and social sciences faculty (left center), law faculty (right center), and Mensa (left front) faced each other across a meadow. Modern structures in the extreme background housed the Osteuropa and Otto-Suhr Instituts.

President Kennedy Becomes an Honorary Member of the Free University in June 1963. This occasion marked the high-point of American involvement in the affairs of the Free University. Behind Kennedy (l. center) is the FU Director of International Affairs, Horst Hartwich.

A Generation of Dissidence Begins. By 1965, student protesters demanded restoration of those prerogatives envisaged in the Berlin Model. Here, AStA chairman Knut Nevermann (l. center) and Rector Hans-Joachim Lieber (r. center) address protesters. Despite his liberal credentials, Lieber soon fell out with the dissidents, many of whom were his former students.

New Methods of Demonstration. Rejecting violence at first, student protesters experimented with sit-down strikes.

An Incident. In June 1967, the autocratic Shah of Iran visited West Berlin. When his advance-men, the so-called *Jubelperser*, began striking protesters, an ugly mood developed. Student Benno Ohnesorg was killed the next day.

Funeral Cortege for Benno Ohnesorg. Outraged at Ohnesorg's death, thousands of West Berlin students joined the procession. His martyrdom galvanized a student generation.

Rudi Dutschke (third from l.). Arguably the most influential dissident of his generation, Dutschke attended an anit-Vietnam War rally in February 1968. His attempted assassination soon after by a confused young person escalated student violence.

Student protest climaxed in the occupation of the FU rector's office in May 1968. Founded under the premise that the Red Flag would never fly over it, the Free University witnessed red flags aplenty by 1968.

Anarchy reigns. Wearing the rector's robes, a student protester symbolically proclaims the arrival of a new era.

Werner Stein

Gerd Löffler

Dismayed at the FU community's inability to solve its differences, political leaders from the SPD assumed a major role in instituting changes. West Berlin's senator for science and art, Stein, and his successor, Löffler, led the reform effort.

Graffiti. Some groups were determined to replace pluralistic learning with what they called "socialistic studies." The attempt provoked strong reactions from moderates and conservatives, who gradually gained the upper hand as the 1970s waned.

Mammoth Buildings for a Mammoth University. This structure is the "Rostlaube," in Dahlem, a rust-colored giant whose many departments and institutes are situated along labyrinthine corridors and "streets." In the left rear is the "Silberlaube," the university's newest cafeteria.

Rolf Kreibich

Eberhard Lämmert

Dieter Heckelmann

Presidents of the free University. The creation of a stronger chief executive eased some problems and exacerbated others. Kreibich (1969–1976), a former assistant, attempted the role of intermediary, but extreme polarization negated his efforts. Lämmert (1976–1983), a full professor, had the support of moderate and left-leaning factions but the polarization continued. Heckelmann (1983 to present), a law professor, ushered in a consolidation phase. He was the first president to be reelected.

THREE

The Consolidation of the Free University, 1949 to 1961

In the period between the Blockade and the building of the Wall, the Free University succeeded in establishing itself among the institutions of higher learning in Germany. That accomplishment alone was proof of its need in the first place. It also confirmed the acumen of its founders and testified to the continuing high quality of its leaders who guided it through its difficult transition from scarcely more than a statement of intent in 1948 to a respected university one decade later. However, its development was hardly so straightforward or predictable as its founders might have assumed as they departed the Titania Palast on opening day, December 4, 1948. By 1961 several of its frankly experimental characteristics such as the Berlin Model, including student codetermination, and the Free University's hope to serve as a bridge with the East were either showing signs of wear or had atrophied to a large extent. Moreover, this frankly experimental university proved not to be the beginning of a reform movement as its student founders had so fondly hoped. Rather, the Free University proved to be a unique model that emerged from an unusual set of social and political circumstances. Far from influencing its sister universities to the west, it discovered in turn that ultimately it must accommodate them instead.

In the course of its first twelve years, the Free University had to solve numerous problems in order to take its place among the West German universities. It had to attract—and in fact ultimately did attract—a competent faculty in all the accepted fields, the sine qua non of any good university. To accomplish that basic goal, the new university had to solve a host of problems, including grave financial woes. It had to locate the resources to establish the physical plant, libraries, laboratories, and other such facilities which any good university must possess. It had to test the intricacies of its own unique form of self-administration as well as establish acceptable administrative links with the people and City of Berlin. Committed to forging international ties, it had to establish itself in the confidences of the academic world of the Federal Republic and then in the international arena. While meeting these ambitious goals, the Free University also took on the de facto function of a university for East German students who, for various reasons, could not attend universities in the newly established German Democratic Republic. For the duration of this second phase in the Free University's development, one-third of its student body came across the GDR and city frontiers from the east to the university, a little-recognized fact for which it deserved much credit. All of this was accomplished in a city that endured slow growth and painful restrictions on its way to economic recovery. West Berlin did not participate in the "economic miracle" to the degree that the more favorably located cities of the Federal Republic participated. A measure of its disadvantage was the fact that in 1949 industrial production in the western sectors fell to less than half of its pre-Blockade level despite the best efforts of the Airlift. Thereafter massive aid from the Allies, combined with growing support from the Federal Republic, allowed West Berlin gradually to rebuild.[1]

In more orthodox ways, the Free University ultimately justified the hopes and ideals set forth for it in its first decade. By the early 1960s it had become a major center of research and learning in the German-speaking world, where its unorthodox style was balanced by undoubted excellence in many scientific and scholarly fields. To cite just one outstanding example, it helped lead the way in bringing German scholarship in social and political research back into the mainstream after a twelve-year hiatus under the Nazis.

If the expansion and consolidation of the Free University could be listed as great successes, there were other developments in the decade of the 1950s that foreshadowed significant problems for the university's future. The much lauded Berlin Model did not evolve as its creators had intended. Gradually, the student body changed in its values and outlook—inevitably so—after the immediate postwar student generation entered the professions and made way for later student cohorts who knew little or nothing of the events that had led to the creation of the Free University in the first place. The harmonious working relationship between students and faculty, which had been the driving force behind the Berlin Model, did not survive the first decade in several important respects. In fact, ten years after its founding the Free University found itself in the midst of a student-faculty clash concerning freedom of expression, a clash that foreshadowed the awesome confrontation that would loom up twenty years after its founding. Intended to be an institution free of ideological constraints and political factionalism, the new university discovered from the outset that, noble as that goal might be, the Free University never came anywhere near achieving so blissful a state in Dahlem. On the contrary, the atmosphere that emerged at the Free University proved from the first to be intensely political, one that swung violently from implacable anticommunism in the period after 1948, to growing student protest by about 1955 over such issues as continuing East-West tensions, West German rearmament, and the nuclear arms race. Finally, as the second Berlin crisis developed, instigated by Nikita

Khrushchev in November 1958 and culminating in the building of the Wall in 1961, distinct echoes of the old Cold-War mentality reemerged.

Relative to its founding period, or to the great upheavals that were to come in the 1960s, the Free University appeared to have entered a period of calm and of steady growth in its first decade. But beneath the outward calm, social and political forces were evolving that would bring the Free University to the attention of the world again, and not in a way which many would have predicted.

PROBLEM SOLVING AND GROWING PAINS

Even as the first semester got under way, numerous subcommittees, erected under the Preparatory Committee, began to tackle masses of detail in what was still a hastily improvised undertaking. With only three faculties (schools) functioning—medicine, philosophy and mathematics, and law and economics—and the law/economics faculty an imperfect hybrid at best, the founders would have to show rapid progress in organization and faculty expansion if the new University were to achieve legitimacy in the public eye and in the academic world. They showed themselves equal to the challenge, although no one claimed that the solution was elegant or quick.

The status of the philosophy faculty was hardly enviable, and its rapid expansion to include a genuine natural sciences and mathematics division was an absolute necessity. Fortunately, a stopgap solution of sorts was available. There were about twenty research institutes in Dahlem that were still formally attached to Humboldt University and two that were directly funded by the *Zentralverwaltung für Volksbildung*, although those eastern connections were becoming tenuous, given the Blockade. The buildings, equipment, and, above all, the educational potential of those scientific institutes for the struggling new university were highly desirable. By late January 1949, the philosophy faculty (at this stage equivalent to a college of arts and sciences because it contained a chair in mathematics) created a math and sciences subcommittee under Professor Walter Behrmann to prepare for the creation of a division for natural sciences and mathematics. Their intention was eventually to become a separate faculty. Besides contributing to the growth of its various scientific fields, the future faculty would also train secondary-school science teachers and, most important at this stage, instruct beginning medical students in the basic sciences.

"As long as the division still does not have at its disposal sufficient institutes," explained Behrmann, "it must remain satisfied with the hospitality offered by the Technical University."[2] Yet the Technical University could scarcely meet that need, as the Preparatory Committee well knew. Understandably, the Free University quickly developed a more than casual interest in the still independent scientific institutes of Dahlem. Public curiosity was heightened when in January 1949 the *Tagesspiegel* published a lengthy article concerning the scientific institutes and indicating that they were in danger of being plundered by Soviet authorities.[3] While claiming that the article was substantially correct, Redslob communicated with Reuter on the subject and indicated that the article exaggerated the facts in some ways and contained inaccuracies. Some of the institutes were already under Magistrat control, he claimed, and two others, for pharmacology and psychology, which the Free University desperately needed, were not even mentioned in the article.[4]

Subsequently, Free University authorities discussed the problem with the Americans, and in mid-March 1949, Fritz von Bergmann, now the Kurator, received permission to inspect those scientific institutes with links to the older university. Von Bergmann found no less than eighteen institutes of value and promptly reported his findings to the Preparatory Committee. Chairman Reuter as promptly referred the matter to the Magistrat (over which he also presided), and on April 6 that body concluded that a transfer of authority over the institutes to the Free University was necessary. Accordingly, the Magistrat sought support from General (formerly Colonel) Frank Howley, and on April 25 the latter issued authority "for the immediate administrative transfer to the Magistrat of Greater Berlin of all the scientific institutes. . . ." The move did not imply transfer of legal title, and in fact the German authorities set up a separate financial account for the institutes into which they would pay rent until the complex legal issues with Humboldt University were finally resolved. Thus, within a matter of weeks the new university had acquired the potential to teach biology, including both zoology and botany. They had also obtained institutes for pharmacology, plant physiology, meteorology and geophysics, and pharmaceuticals, plus a central biology institute, among others. The new university was rapidly acquiring emergency means with which to offer premedical studies, a vital link on its way to becoming an accepted institution of higher learning. The transaction was a good measure of the cooperation that had grown up between the Germans and the Americans since the previous year, and it also showed the enormous advantage to the Free University in having Ernst Reuter chair the Preparatory Committee while serving simultaneously as Governing Mayor of Berlin.[5]

No one considered the absorbing of the former Humboldt University institutes as anything but an expedient. Ever since the summer of 1948, when August Fehling and other experts examined the Free University's options, they knew that the creation of a complete faculty of natural sciences and mathematics would be expensive. Institutes for organic and inorganic chemistry, to name only two, were urgently needed if the Free University was to offer genuine premedical training. Artificially delayed by the effects of the Blockade and severe financial shortages, the faculty of natural sciences and mathematics finally split off from the philosophy faculty in the summer of 1951. It did so with the approval of the Berlin Magistrat and in aniticipation of sizable American funding scheduled for the near future.[6] The acquisition of this newest and perhaps most expensive faculty was vital to the scientific development of the new university. Its realization was a powerful tonic not only for the hard sciences but also for medicine and other disciplines. It enabled preclinical (premedical) students to matriculate at the Free University and it encouraged the growth of other sciences. In that same summer of 1951 the entire veterinary medicine faculty of Humboldt University transferred to the Free University, a sign not only of continuing political tensions in the east but also a tangible measure of the medical profession's growing confidence that the new university could offer its students a solid preparation in the natural sciences.

THE LAW SCHOOL

Fate dictated that there would be no quick cures for the Free University's law faculty. Some referred to it as the "Sorgenkind" or ailing child (or, less charitably, the "runt") of the new University, and its problems were representative of the serious obstacles to growth for the university as a whole in its early development. The reader may recall that few recognized legal scholars were available to join the faculty in 1948, and the law faculty had started life as a combined faculty with economics, and with a large number of junior instructors. Part of the reason for this shortage is that there was in all of Berlin a dearth of law professors. Humboldt University, too, had had few enough to begin with. It should also be remembered that the Free University was founded as a corporation under public law, not as a state institution. Those who threw in their lot with the Free University had had to forgo their status as civil servants and the accompanying pension, insurance, and other rights accorded professors elsewhere. Then, too, the young lawyers in postwar Germany were plagued by an almost inevitable involvement with the Nazis who had demanded their entry into the party at the time they entered their profession. West German universities had bridged the gap by hiring older, politically unencumbered professors near or at retirement age, but the Free University, chronically strapped for funds, could hardly afford that luxury and followed a self-imposed rule of hiring no professor over the age of 60. In retrospect the rule appears harsh, but the struggling university felt it could hardly afford to offer full pension rights to individuals with only a few more years of service in the offing.

Thus, the law component of the new faculty started out with only two full professors, von Lübtow and Drath, both of whom were absent from Berlin during large parts of the first semester as they severed previous ties with other universities and made their way over the borders into Berlin. Even that simple feat was not really so simple. Von Lübtow had moved from the university in Rostock, and the disgruntled GDR authorities had confiscated his personal library for a time; most of the first semester had passed before he could settle into his duties.[7] A further mark of the university's great need was the appointing of Wilhelm Wengler to the law faculty in the spring of 1949. He had just been accorded his final law degree (habilitation) at Humboldt University in the summer of 1948 and was entitled to the title of law professor. Wengler's skills were too desperately needed for the appointments committee to worry unduly about his abstention on a crucial vote for the creation of a free university on June 19, 1948, at the clubhouse.

Four full professors, rounded out by Professor Lange, were teaching law by the spring of 1949, while the bulk of the instruction was handled by practicing lawyers in West Berlin. By the summer of 1949, the situation had stabilized to the point that, with four full law professors available, the first major division of faculties at the Free University took place. Following lengthy and sometimes fractious discussions, the law faculty became a separate entity on August 1, 1949, matched by the creation of a faculty of economics and social science on the same day. The tender tree that was the Free University had begun to grow.

Thus, in various ways the original three faculties consolidated themselves during the first hectic semester and began to extend branches to cover the most vital educational needs. It was hardly an orderly or elegant process. Lectures and meetings were still taking place in public buildings, such as a movie theater, the Onkel Tom Kino, in Dahlem. The student body was, for the most part, shabbily clad and living on a diet rated at only a few calories above the starvation level (a situation that had existed for the most part since 1945). The Blockade blockaded still, until Josef Stalin, aware that he had made a major propaganda error, called it off in May 1949. For the founders of the Free University, as for the citizens of West Berlin in general, there was renewed hope for the future.

SELF-ADMINISTRATION

One of the hallmarks of the new university, which was evident from the moment that students and administrators entered the little building at Boltzmannstrasse 4 on July 24, 1948, was the willingness of students and faculty to take responsibility for arranging their own affairs. The students especially showed great initiative in establishing the necessary offices and bureaus to make the university function. The students' "Committee of 25," a provisional merging of the majority of the old *Studentenrat* at Humboldt University with the smaller but still influential group around the journal *Colloquium*, had immediately set about the business of erecting the Free University in cooperation with Ernst Reuter's central Preparatory Committee. Having arrogated to themselves the role of a founding committee, this student leadership recognized that its legitimacy as a student government was really de facto and that it must be replaced by a more regular procedure. Consequently, once the first semester got under way, the students held elections on February 17, 1949, for a student government, which carried the orthodox German title of Konvent (student parliament), and its executive committee, the AStA (*Allgemeiner Studenten-Ausschuss*). Democratic procedures were now functioning, and with the creation of the Konvent and AStA, an important milestone in the development of the Free University had been reached.

In the summer of 1948 one of the first moves of the Preparatory Committee and the Committee of 25 had been to establish an admissions board and admissions criteria for incoming students in cooperation with faculty. A medical researcher, Freiherr von Kress, headed up the admissions bureau; Helmut Coper became the student consultant to this influential body, and students like Stanislaw Kubicki helped prepare admissions criteria and the deliberately brief, seven-question application form. It was a measure of the efficiency and conscientiousness of the new board that it had processed 5,000 applications, interviewed 3,500 applicants, and finally admitted 2,140 students within a matter of weeks. The participants had had to juggle professional qualifications, humanitarian needs, and political considerations in equal measure, and yet despite the undoubted disappointment for the majority who could not be accepted initially, no scandal ever arose over the admissions procedures at the Free University in those trying first semesters. In its second semester the new university counted 3,850 students, nearly double the first semester figure. One year after its opening, nearly 5,000 students were admitted.[8] The admissions system evolved by the students also included an appeals mechanism. University Officer Howard W. Johnston in an internal report expressed admiration for the students' accomplishments: "The entrance machinery has been praised for dispensing with the endless questionnaires required in the east zone, and so far this office has been able to determine the process of selection has been honestly and efficiently run." Of the 2,140 students enrolled in the first semester, only 590 had come from Humboldt University: 40 from the medical faculty, 200 from the law/economics faculty, and 350 from the philosophical faculty.[9]

Another example of student initiative was the creation in September 1948 of a *Studentenwerk* (Student Welfare Office) to help alleviate somehow the human misery that still struck the student population with full force. The several hundred of the successful applicants who were transferring from Humboldt University or from Soviet-Zone universities had no reserves of western currency and needed help immediately. The Student Welfare Office, under a student, Werner Günter Grimke, and Herr von Brunn, immediately issued appeals to industry, to the press and through personal letters to thousands of private individuals for donations. The ensuing response netted several thousand Deutschmarks and Eastmarks. The same office, after protracted negotiations with the Allied Kommandatura (minus the Soviets), obtained improved ration cards for Free University students. A public appeal for student lodgings netted five hundred private rooms throughout the western sectors although eight hundred needy students, mostly from the East, desperately needed shelter. The same group sought part-time work for impoverished students, but this effort, like all others, was hampered by prevailing conditions. "Work solicitation became very difficult," observed the authors of the Student Welfare Office, "because the stagnant Berlin economy could hardly place work opportunities at our disposal." (Students also volunteered to unload the aircraft which were steadily landing at Tempelhof Airport, but no funds were available to employ them.)[10] The same group oversaw the construction of a crude wooden dining hall, which it outfitted with the most crucial cooking equipment. With admirable thoroughness, they also established a tailoring shop and a shoe repair shop to administer to student needs "at reasonable prices."[11] The Magistrat waived even the modest student fees for over five hundred of the neediest students.

In cooperation with the students some of the American supporters had been busy too, soliciting aid, clothing, and books for the FU students, as had Fritz and Herta Epstein. Success was hardly automatic. The Americans received unsettling news from the Geneva-based World Student Relief about one innovative effort to help the Free University. The National Student Association in the United States had planned an intercollegiate fashion show in cooperation with the fashion magazine *Mademoiselle*, the proceeds to benefit the Free University. The project fell through when the magazine's editors received word from their Berlin correspondent that the Free University "was nothing more than an anti-Soviet propaganda machine where little or nothing of an academic nature was taught." Johnston was furious and informed the Swiss-based relief agency that *Mademoiselle*'s Berlin correspondent was either "oriented towards the East or does not know what he is writing about." He also asked that World Student Relief consider donating money and especially overcoats to west-sector students for the harsh winter ahead.[12] In many ways, large and small, the Americans helped out in the consolidation process. Thus, at the end of January 1949, Johnston informed Edwin Redslob that the American authorities would earmark for the university a ton per month of the most urgently needed supplies over the Airlift "with a minimum of red tape." The Free University would choose the items.[13]

Fortunately, Fritz and Herta Epstein, two early friends of the FU students, enjoyed smoother progress in seeking aid. Upon returning to Stanford University in August 1948, they inspired the students there to organize an aid drive that accumulated several tons of clothing, shoes, and books. These supplies arrived in the early spring of 1949, the first tangible evidence for the students of the Free University that American students were supporting them.[14]

One of the busiest new establishments with prominent student involvement was the Free University's *Aussenkommission*, or Committee on International Affairs. As soon as the first administrative offices were established in the summer of 1948, the students' Committee of 25 was busily canvassing support from West German student governments. The group around *Colloquium* prepared a memorandum describing the events that had led to the creation of the Free University and circulated it through the committee to student groups throughout the western zones. Disturbed by the apathy of the West German rectors at the Braunschweig Conference, they determined to achieve a high visibility, at least among other students. The student leaders of the International Affairs Office, Friedrich Wilhelm von Sell and Horst Hartwich, made a point of contacting outside student groups whenever possible—not always an easy prospect in divided Berlin. Thus, when the Marlowe Society, a group of Cambridge University students, appeared in the city, Hartwich arranged a tour of the Free University for them and meetings with the students. The gatherings were sufficiently successful that the Cambridge students returned to England with high praise of the enterprise, and a favorable article about the Free University appeared in the London *Times* in September 1948.[15] The same largely student-run office saw to it that thirty foreign students (mostly Chinese and Americans) were admitted to the Free University in the first semester, thus continuing a German university tradition of maintaining international connections. However, the new university was embarking upon an international program on a scale that was without precedent. Von Sell visited the West German universities to spread word of the enterprise in Dahlem and succeeded in gaining admittance of the Free University to the new *Verband Deutscher Studentenschaften* (VDS), or the League of German Student Associations, which became the dominant student organization in western Germany. However, von Sell left the International Affairs Office in December 1948, so that by the following January, student Horst Hartwich alone was running it. The *Aussenkommission* was composed of professors and students who worked jointly to guide the office's activities. It, along with the Student Welfare Office, was seeking ties with American and other universities for aid, exchange programs, and other linkages. (Years later, the title *Aussenkommission* was dropped in favor of *Aussenamt*, which translates as Office of International Affairs. Hartwich became its permanent director and as of this writing runs the *Aussenamt* still.)

By the spring of 1949, the Student Welfare Office was already able to demonstrate tangible results. The students at Freiburg im Breisgau forwarded DM 661.75 of aid to the Free University, the first German student group to do so. Student associations at Erlangen and Hamburg had also launched appeals to help the students at the new university, and student exchanges were already beginning. For example, several FU students would be traveling to American universities later that year, and the University of Lund in Sweden had also accepted an exchange student for 1949. During that same spring, the Office of International Affairs developed plans to invite a student from each West German university to spend a semester at the new university and to experience life in the divided city. It was the first modest step in the Free University's long-term effort to attract students from the West to Berlin.[16] There were a host of other smaller offices which provided for student cultural activities, business affairs, press relations, student health, and even sports activities. In other words, the students continued to do what they had been doing with considerable success since the end of the war: they ran their own affairs.

Once the emergency period was over, the Free University's *Aussenamt* began more systematically to build international ties. It began to invite outside scholars to Berlin to offer guest lectures and to conduct research. It continued to invite foreign students to study in Berlin, and that group expanded considerably as the initially small budget expanded. The Free University developed linkages to foreign universities, at first in Western Europe and the United States (such as at Columbia and Stanford universities), later to Third-World institutions, and later still, when the Cold War ebbed, even to East European universities such as Leningrad University. It actively encouraged members of the university community to research and study abroad, and strongly promoted joint research and publication efforts with outside scholars. The reasons for this unusual emphasis upon international contacts was straightforward: the Free University was situated on a political island. International programs were, as Hartwich later stated, "an appropriate way to overcome the isolated position of Berlin by building and maintaining contacts to the outside scholarly and scientific world."[17] Moreover, it was in the Free University's own interest to establish national and international contacts quickly. It had to prove that it was a serious institution of higher learning in order to quell any lingering doubts that it was merely a political phenomenon. The Free University, partly from desire and partly of necessity, led all German universities with its vigorous international programs.

The record of accomplishment by students and faculty of the Free University during the first semester was by any standard impressive and was doubly so given the siege conditions under which they operated in Berlin. However, it was also obvious that despite their best efforts the founders of the Free University, together with the city's two and a half million inhabitants, were leading a hand-to-mouth existence.

Thrift, idealism, industriousness, and isolated appeals for help were not enough by themselves to bring the Free University through its infancy.

MONEY MAKES THE WORLD GO 'ROUND

The founders and contributors to the Free University discovered that if they had a "scrawny infant" on their hands, to use Kendall Foss's phrase, it was an infant that demanded expensive nourishment. When General Clay had ordered the apportioning of nearly two million Deutschmarks in profits accumulated from the *Neue Zeitung* and other American-licensed publications to the Free University's needs, it had sustained the university for the first semester of operations. American Military Government continued that practice for the next year, so that between August 1948 and July 1949 another DM 400,000 flowed into the university's accounts. While the Americans accumulated and administered these sums, the Germans could rightly claim that these funds represented capital from German sources since they accrued from subscriptions and advertisement earnings drawn from the German public. True, the education branch of American Military Government in the Berlin Sector had contributed another DM 28,140 from various reorientation funds for book purchases, the only sum that actually flowed from indisputably American coffers. In the spring of 1949, Ernst Reuter had secured Magistrat approval for almost DM 450,000 from Berlin for the Free University, so that it ended its first academic year with a slight surplus. Welcome though that development was, it was also clear that the university could not endure another year on so slender and unusual a budget.[18]

In conversations between the Free University's leaders, including von Bergmann, Redslob, and Reuter, and General Clay's cultural adviser, Alonzo Grace, they arrived at a plan whereby the City of Berlin would appropriate what it felt was needed for another year of somewhat expanded operations at the Free University. Then the Americans would pay half that budget. With some slight juggling of figures, Grace committed his education and cultural relations division to expending DM 2,602,800 for the Free University. A higher umbrella group in Military Government known as the Interdivisional Reorientation Committee received the proposed plan next, but it delayed a decision until General Clay's successor, General George Hays, took over as Military Governor in May 1949. It was at this moment that an old malaise in American Military Government recurred. Reorientation programs in Military Government had been neglected until mid-1947, when influential voices had convinced its highest leadership that reorientation programs to encourage democratic practices in Germany needed significantly greater support. Later, General Clay had been impressed by what he saw at the

Free University and had offered unusual financial backing during its crucial founding phase. But now, in May 1949, Clay's immediate successor, General Hays, had no such personal attachment. Subsequent discussions within Military Government saw the American appropriation reduced from the expected DM 2.6 million to DM 1 million instead. The experience was a rude awakening for the Free University's creators to the vagaries of bureaucracies and budgets in American Military Government. In some embarrassment, the senior American education officer in Berlin, John C. Thompson, described what befell the Free University's hapless chancellor, Fritz von Bergmann: "During August, 1949, Dr. von Bergmann . . . has spent most of his time and energy in fighting off creditors and in granting partial payment of bills that are most urgent. Salaries for August have not been paid in full. Neither is the Free University able to pay for current premiums on the insurance." Worse still, no relief to the crisis appeared to be in sight. The City of Berlin was still staggering under a budgetary crisis resulting from the economic repercussions of the Blockade. Thompson could only urge his American superiors in Germany and in Washington to do more to help the new university out of its severe budgetary crisis.[19]

The crisis was sufficiently severe that General Maxwell Taylor, the U.S. commander in Berlin, sent a strong memorandum to the senior American official in Germany, John J. McCloy, in mid-September warning him that the Free University had not even received the reduced million-mark donation and would be bankrupt by the end of the month. He pointed out that the university, in taking over the responsibility for various Dahlem research institutes, a responsibility it could scarcely avoid, had inevitably increased its operating expenses. The Berlin commander warned McCloy that the crisis was reacting unfavorably upon the university, "the maintenance of which is important to us both on educational and political grounds." He asked High Commissioner McCloy to provide the promised million Deutschmarks immediately. McCloy was taken aback. "Where do I get one million Deutschmarks for such a purpose?" he asked his financial adviser.[20]

There then followed a strange series of events which indicated that even in high places in the American Government long-term commitments to and goals for the Free University were not yet fully understood. McCloy had assumed his duties as head of the American High Commission in Germany (HICOG) on September 1, 1949. He had none of General Clay's direct experiences of Berlin and had to feel his way into the novel situation produced by the four-power arrangement and further complicated by the East-West split. It was characteristic of the new American presence in Germany that his headquarters, unlike those of Clay, were now located in Frankfurt am Main, far removed from troubled Berlin. And now McCloy was forced to grapple with the Free University's financial woes.

At a meeting on October 11, 1949, McCloy and his staff discussed their priorities. "Will you please include that Free University," McCloy's assistant William Babcock requested, ". . . because they are going to close up." McCloy had a radical solution to that problem, however, as the minutes to the meeting revealed: "That university has gotten some more money," McCloy replied, "but [it] can't stand by itself, and I think it had better join up with the technical university of the British to give it a little body. . . . Now, they will resist that. They won't want to do it, but I want to use that money as leverage to bring that together, so you have got something there. It is uneconomic."

Babcock indicated that American Military Government had already tried once to achieve the union of the Technical University and the Free University and had even found support among some Germans, "but the British were opposed to it," he added. McCloy was not deterred. "The British say they are willing now," he retorted, "but if there is any opposition on the part of the Germans, we ought to use that money for leverage. This education business is disturbing to me."[21]

McCloy followed up his words with actions. A day after the HICOG staff conference, he flew to Berlin to meet with Mayor Reuter and to see the Free University in person. It was obviously a moving experience for him, and his subsequent actions indicated a new ambivalence as to what should happen to the troubled institution. McCloy's first action was to telegraph Secretary of State Dean Acheson in Washington requesting that the stalled payment for the Free University be forwarded immediately through emergency channels to alleviate the worst effects of the budget crunch. After some grumbling by Acheson and further prodding by McCloy, the unusual request was honored.[22] Von Bergmann was able to keep the creditors from the door for a while longer.

Plans for the forced merger were by no means abandoned, however. Once set in motion, the bureaucratic forces continued to work toward the consolidation of higher educational institutions in West Berlin.

Not long after McCloy's visit, OMGUS education chief John Riedl flew into Berlin for several days of talks with Britain's chief education officer in the city, L. E. Ditchfield, and their two staffs. By now plans included the merger not only of the Technical University and the Free University but also, among others, of the Pädagogische Hochschule (Teachers College), which had recently transferred from the Soviet Sector. Berlin education officer John C. Thompson recorded the Allies' reasons for so radical a move: By means of a merger, they would consolidate administrative offices, combine physical facilities, and eliminate duplication in curricular offerings. However, Thompson was not convinced that the responsible German authorities, especially Reuter and City Councilman Walter May, would support the Anglo-American proposal, and he suggested they sweeten the pill by offering considerable financial backing to cover the initial high costs of consolidation.[23] The British prediction in December 1948 that a merger of universities might yet be necessary seemed to be coming true, and sooner than most would have predicted.

Yet, as quickly as the crisis developed, it promptly dissipated. The reasons were twofold. First, the German authorities, led by Councilman May, let it be known loudly and clearly that they were not in favor of the merger. May cited technical reasons, such as the dislocation caused by such a move, and the difficulty of administering so large a body of students (8,000) in one place. He was also at pains to explain to the Anglo-Americans that they should not confuse the disparate goals of the Free University and the Technical University. The two institutions of higher learning served different purposes, "the function of the Free University being the teaching of the traditional subjects of law, medicine, philosophy, and pure science, whereas the function of the Technical University is the imparting of knowledge in the field of applied or technological science." In other words, the proposed merger would violate German academic tradition. May did not give an outright no. He simply agreed to study the proposal further.[24]

The Germans also took the initiative in ending the financial crunch. Fritz von Bergmann had taken to phoning Reuter's office frequently about the Free University's financial headaches. Reuter's university consultant, Ingeborg Sengpiel, fielded the calls until finally the exasperated mayor replied: "He should leave me in peace. He will get his money."[25] His commitment to the Free University as strong as ever, Reuter fulfilled his promise. At his urging, the Magistrat made up for the shortfall in funding by appropriating DM 4.1 million for the fiscal year 1949/1950 to keep the creditors of the Free University at bay. No one was happy about the situation, but the city government and its executive, the Magistrat, were demonstrating their loyalty to their new creation in the most fundamental way: They were paying the bulk of its basic operational costs. Ernst Reuter proved to be a stout friend of the Free University during its first five years, and with his good offices the Magistrat and the new Federal Republic contributed enough funding to maintain the university's basic operations. Edwin Redslob, too, was energetic in seeking support wherever he could. He could report to Reuter in May 1950: "I discovered the greatest understanding at the Ministry for All-German Affairs, that the Free University must be helped financially by the Federal Republic. They not only donated the sum of DM 2.5 million, but have interceded already with the Finance Ministry and with other offices."[26]

Thus, German institutions were combining their resources to keep the Free University alive. Moreover, at this crucial early stage they were joined by an influential group of American political and educational leaders who were in a strong position to support the Free University and who began to show greater resolve. McCloy, for example, even while he was setting plans for a merger in motion, had also agreed to release an additional DM 500,000 to the Free University following a meeting with its leaders and with Magistrat officials on October 18, 1949. There were strings attached. The Americans urged the university's leadership to limit student enrollments to 5,000 for the time being and not to engage in new construction projects. Enrollments for that semester were held to 4,946 and grew only slowly thereafter. The student body did not significantly exceed the 5,000-ceiling until the spring of 1954.[27]

McCloy's ambivalence about the university quickly ended. He, too, demonstrated his support in the most fundamental way. For a period of three years, starting in 1950, the Free University began receiving DM 2 million annually from McCloy's High Commission, a sum that exceeded donations to all other German institutions and which sometimes caused tensions within the ranks of the High Commission's public affairs officers. HICOG aid officer David Maynard reported in December 1953 to James Conant, McCloy's successor, that in the current year grants to the Free University had been made "at the expense of a large number of other projects . . . which has made cultural officers throughout Germany feel that they are being slighted in favor of the Free University."[28] There was little doubt that official American support for the Free University, starting with General Clay and continuing under John J. McCloy and later James Conant, was timely and significant.

Subordinate to McCloy but still highly influential in winning support for the university was Shepard Stone, who had served as a special counselor to McCloy in 1949-1950 and then became his director of public affairs for two years. Thereafter, Stone transferred to the Ford Foundation in 1953 and eventually became one of its leading officials. With a doctorate from the old Friedrich Wilhelms University and with a consuming interest in Berlin affairs, Stone also proved to be a well-placed friend of the Free University and of Berlin.

Other influential Americans were also offering timely support. Ambassador Robert Murphy had moved from Berlin as Clay's political adviser back to Washington in early 1949 for a short stint as director of the State Department's Office of German and Austrian Affairs. Thus he could follow the advice of his own Berlin memorandum of November 20, 1948, calling for support for the Free University from among American universities. In that capacity he had cooperated in releasing a joint statement of American intent by the State Department and by a private American educational group, the Commission on Occupied Areas (COA), which was in turn an offshoot of the American Council on Education. The latter was a leading lobby for American institutions of higher learning. One of the two leading figures in the COA was none other than Herman B Wells, who had informed General Clay in April 1948 that the creation of the Free University was feasible. The joint declaration of the Commission and the State Department addressed the question of whether or not the United States should adopt a less ambitious cultural program with the new Federal Republic of Germany in line with cultural programs in other sovereign nations or whether it would continue along the more intensive reorientation lines as executed by the recently defunct Military Government. The statement was unequivocal. Its proponents held that the Americans had a commitment to encourage democratic and peaceful practices in Germany and that those goals could hardly be viewed as being already accomplished simply because a central government now existed in Bonn. Rather, those lofty ideals remained "the hardest and the longest of all our responsibilities in Germany and, for the long run, the most decisive."[29] Part of that long-term commitment was support for the Free University.

Already in the summer of 1949, when the financial crisis was brewing, several American scholars with close ties to the State Department had traveled to Germany to act as expert consultants concerning American reorientation programs and to assess needs in aiding the recovery of German higher education. Typically, one of their stops was Berlin, and invariably the visiting experts were impressed with what they saw. Historian Eugene N. Anderson had performed part of his graduate work under Friedrich Meinecke in the time of the Weimar Republic before completing his doctorate at the University of Chicago. Later he served with the wartime Office of Strategic Services as a German expert, then transferred to the State Department after the war to help develop reorientation programs for Germany. Anderson took his first glance at the Free University in July 1949. "There is more chance of making a modern, progressive university of the Free University than of any other university in the Western Zone," he informed John C. Thompson, "but there will be much help needed from America." By that Anderson meant moral and financial help. The Americans must be willing to send capable educators to the Free University and to open up their purse strings as well.[30]

Just as influential was a brilliant political scientist and German emigré, Sigmund Neumann, who was on leave from Wesleyan University to examine the state of the social sciences in Germany for the State Department. After touring the western zones and Berlin, he concluded: "There is an enthusiasm in the Free University not found in any other German university in the three Western Zones." Neumann observed that the Free University had come into existence as a protest against the infringement of human rights and was following a different path than the western-zone universities. He observed that as a new institution "it has broken with many German university traditions, and hence is fertile soil for modern progressive democratic ideas."[31] Given these experts' enthusiastic endorsements of the new university, it is not surprising that McCloy threw off his early reservations and quickly became an ardent supporter of the Free University.

It was not merely a case of American experts visiting Berlin that helped the university. Mayor Reuter visited the United States in the spring of 1949 to seek help for his ailing city, and as a senior State Department officer, James Riddleberger, pointed out, Reuter hoped also in his capacity as chairman of the university's board of trustees "to have the opportunity of stimulating American interest in the Free University. . . ." Riddleberger reminded his subordinates of Robert Murphy's early proposal to acquaint American universities with the Free University, and indicated that Reuter's presence would help.[32]

As a follow-up that November, Edwin Redslob undertook a similar tour to promote the Free University, the first German rector to do so after the war. His visit included a trip to Columbia University, which had a number of influential personnel who had been keenly interested in recent German developments, including Dean William Russell, Professor Franz L. Neumann, and retired General Dwight David Eisenhower. The latter was currently serving as Columbia's new president. Plans had already been going forward for Columbia University to act as a kind of sponsor for the Free University, as the State Department had hoped. Neumann wrote to the State Department's expert in charge of American cultural relations with Germany, Henry Kellermann, to say that at his university they were friendly to the idea of sponsoring the new German university and to suggest that he, Neumann, should pay a visit to Berlin in turn. Kellermann approved the idea at once, with the result that Redslob visited Columbia in December 1949 to meet Eisenhower, while Franz L. Neumann investigated conditions at the Free University. Both initiatives brought happy results.[33]

Redslob, as one of the first German officials to visit America in an official capacity, was naturally apprehensive about how he would be received so soon after the war. He need hardly have worried, he confessed later, and described his whirlwind tour as "three weeks of goodwill" in which he acquainted or reacquainted himself with American academicians and with German emigré scholars. Carl J. Friedrich summed up the rector's accomplishments at Harvard University: "Redslob made a splendid impression upon all who heard him," he wrote to a colleague at the State Department and indicated he, Friedrich, was helping to organize the shipment of much-needed books to the Free University.[34]

However, the most crucial meetings took place in New York and Philadelphia with Eisenhower and with potential financial backers such as the Carl Schurz, Rockefeller, and Ford foundations. Frank Howley had already contacted those and other major foundations in early 1949, and although their representatives had expressed admiration for the new university, they had generally been pessimistic in their replies, claiming that their institutional charters generally raised technical difficulties which hindered donations to the Free University. For example, their oper-

ating rules often prohibited making contributions of a general nature especially outside the United States or outside the English-speaking world.[35]
It was going to take personal diplomacy and convincing arguments to
arouse interest among major philanthropic organizations. Redslob carried a heavy responsibility.

At Columbia University, after a shaky start with Eisenhower during
which the former general observed that there were too many reactionaries at German universities, Redslob described the special conditions at
the Free University and succeeded in establishing a good rapport. In
the end, recounted Redslob, Eisenhower turned to his German guest
and said: "We shall go to the limit of our means in order to help you!"[36]

In retrospect, the early efforts of key Germans and Americans in establishing links between the Free University and potential benefactors
in the United States marked the beginning of a special relationship that
was to have long-lasting and far-reaching consequences. Now, both public and private financial sources were beginning to materialize to sustain the Free University in its growth and to allow it to develop along
lines different from other German universities. The generous resources
of West Berlin and of the Federal Republic were, of course, the primary
vital source. Yet, undeniably, American public and private resources
were the second major fount.

REFORM UNIVERSITY: FRANZ L. NEUMANN REPORTS

In December 1949, while Redslob was in the United States, Franz L.
Neumann arrived in Berlin to examine the state of higher education
there, and at the conclusion of his trip he submitted a report of his
findings to his State Department hosts. Portions of his report dealt also
with the newly revived Hochschule für Politik (College of Political Science), also founded in December 1948, but the bulk of his remarks centered on what he felt was a unique institution in the world of German
higher learning: the Free University of Berlin. Neumann urged that official government and private American resources be marshaled in its support precisely because the Free University showed the potential to be a reform university and was not immediately casting itself in the role of
simply another German university—although he claimed to see definite
trends in that direction. Its progressive tendencies were what made it
an attractive target for American aid. Besides, the Americans had by
now undertaken a serious obligation: "U.S. Government support for the
FU is necessary because the institution was created largely by the U.S.
Government," wrote Neumann, "which has the moral duty to see the experiment through."[37]

The Free University seemed to be a natural leader in the rebuilding
of political science in Germany, and exposure of students in this field
was vital. "The FU trains the students for public life," Neumann ob-

served to the University Senate. "We desire in public life, especially in the civil service, reliable democrats." Therefore, it was his advice that they should create eventually a complete faculty of political science at the Free University. He also called for the creation of a division for evening school offerings for those who did not yet possess the indispensable *Abitur*.

Yet, there were several major problems afflicting the young institution. "The foremost problem is the lack of truly outstanding scholars," Neumann stated. The entire Berlin situation was still too tense to make it appealing for many, and the new university held few attractions for professors employed in the west. "In addition, the Western universities consider the FU as a predominantly political rather than academic institution and are thus inclined to look down upon it as second-rate," Neumann stated. It was precisely this assessment that compelled some professors at the Free University to want to develop it into an orthodox German university as rapidly as possible. Neumann worried too about the relationship between city and university. Ernst Reuter, although a powerful friend of the Free University considered it "too much his own child. . . ." Another powerful political figure, Councilman Walter May, criticized the university as being too aloof from political life and from the population of Berlin, Neumann stated. "This is a justified criticism," claimed Neumann. However, he felt May was behind an effort to consolidate all West Berlin higher educational institutions, which May, as an SPD functionary, could then control as a political "boss." The various faculties were even more at odds with each other than at other universities because of the intense competition to obtain the slender resources available.[38]

Finally, although he found much to admire in the students of the Free University, Neumann concluded that they, too, posed something of a problem. "On the whole, the students are probably the greatest single asset of the FU," he wrote. "They are intelligent, politically alert, hard working, and likeable." Their self-government was proving to be well-run and successful, but Neumann, himself a product of German higher education, was uneasy about their unique right to have a say in faculty appointments, a right guaranteed them by their representation in the University Senate. He was uneasy, too, that so many students coming over from the east were concentrating at the Free University. Many were not harried democrats, he claimed. On the contrary, he felt some were fascists who "should be carefully watched." The FU students were already fighting reactionary tendencies found at other Western universities, he noted. Neumann had high praise for their "bitter and intelligent fight" against student *Korporationen* (fraternities) and *Altherrenbünde*, or Old Boys organizations. Thus partly because of its potential as a reform university, partly because of the Americans' moral commitment, and also because the university itself faced urgent problems that demanded massive support, the Americans should come to its aid.[39] Although some of his predictions and anxieties were ultimately not borne out by subsequent developments, Neumann's assessment was for the most part shrewd and accurate. He had identified the core problems and challenges confronting the Free University. He saw the university's potential as a progressive institution, and he made it clear to his American hosts that they had a special obligation to further an experiment which they had helped to begin.

FU STUDENTS CONTRA KORPORATIONEN

A few months before Franz L. Neumann had arrived in Berlin, *Colloquium*, the student journal closely identified with the Free University student founders, published a lead article entitled "Akademischer Mummenschanz" (academic masquerade). The article featured a horrifying photograph of a gaping young man who wore heavy steel and leatherlined goggles with oversized straps that pinned his ears close to his head. He was also sporting a rounded metal nose guard that extended grotesquely over his upper lip, and a heavy leather neck protector that emerged from a stoutly padded leather jacket. Obviously designed as physical protection, these safeguards served only to confine rather than eliminate the slashing wounds that were inextricably a part of this violent sport. The student's face in the photograph was a mask of blood with deep gashes about the forehead, mouth, and left cheek. He was a member of a *Schlagende Verbindung* (student dueling fraternity) or *Korporation*, and influential students of the Free University were indicating by word and picture that such activities had no place at their new institution. The grisly photo carried the ironic subtitle "In memory of a Matter of Honor."[40] The student parliament at the new university went so far as to secure a pledge from incoming students that they would not join the *Korporationen*, dueling or otherwise.[41]

The reason for this self-imposed student restriction at the Free University against membership in such organizations was peculiarly rooted in modern German history and scarcely had any Anglo-American equivalent. *Korporationen* in some form or another had existed for hundreds of years as social organizations based loosely upon the student's geographic origins or religious preferences. Starting with a new, nationalistic form of student organization, the *Burschenschaft*, at Jena in 1814, a decidedly political dimension appeared. For example, student veterans, returning from the Napoleonic wars, pledged to unite all the German states under one government. The student group had a father protector, the first *Alter Herr* (Old Boy), so to speak, in Turnvater Jahn, a nationalist and an organizer of paramilitary athletic organizations for youth, the *Turnvereine*. From the first, most student organizations professed an almost romantic allegiance to Christianity, defined in religious or "racial" terms—thus barring non-Christians, i.e., Jews, from entry. Vater Jahn, for example, had been openly antisemitic.

In the Restoration Period (1815–1848), these student organizations became closely identified with German nationalism, were liberal (in the nineteenth-century meaning of the word), and were opposed to the reactionary policies of Metternich. Their revolutionary role was short-lived, however; in an official crackdown following a nationalistically inspired assassination of the dramatist Kotzebue by student Karl Sand in 1819, Metternich quickly suppressed any further revolutionary tendencies among the *Burschenschaften* and *Korporationen*. While the same student groups played at times an important role in the revolutions of 1848 in Germany, their more progressive or democratic features were completely submerged following Bismarck's unification of the German states in 1871. Thereafter, the German student fraternities became largely centers of hypernationalism, arch-conservatism, and social elitism. Given the influential role of their patrons in society, they were also widely regarded as organizations that promoted a student's subsequent career.

The fraternities often bore latinized German names such as "Germania" or "Alemania" or "Borussia," and they remained fundamentally unchanged in their outlook following the national defeat in 1918. In fact, the Nazis made rapid headway among most university students in the years of the Weimar Republic, and Hitler's youth leader, Baldur von Schirach, had obtained outright control of most student government associations, the AStAs, by 1931, two years before Hitler and his minions seized power in Germany. The *Korporationen* lingered on a few years longer until Nazi *Gleichschaltung* (leveling) absorbed them into its national student apparatus starting in 1935. To be sure, there were certain differences among the *Korporationen*. Some were Protestant; others were Catholic. Some were more socially discriminatory than others. Many still engaged in dueling and most wore distinctive sashes or ribbons bearing two or three colors. To the Nazis, who were uncomfortable with independent organizations, even conservative, nationalistic ones, the differences among the *Korporationen* counted for little. They had forced them all out of existence and into the party apparatus by 1938. Some, protected by their patrons, the *Alte Herren*, claimed to have carried on a furtive unofficial existence after 1938.

After the war, the occupation authorities were suspicious of such organizations and forbade them in all four zones for a time. The Soviets and Paul Wandel's *Zentralverwaltung* banned them permanently, so that not a trace remained at Berlin University or in the Soviet Zone. The Americans were highly suspicious as well and had immediately placed fencing on their list of proscribed militaristic or nationalistic activities. The chief education officer in Hessen sent a strongly worded re-

minder of that ban to the rectors of his *Land*.⁴² The British and French
had done the same for a time, but starting in 1947 the British Military Government had conceded that the *Korporationen*, some of the Catholic
ones, for example, had not carried the responsibility for Hitler's early successes, and they were granted legal recognition once again. Given this toe-
hold in the legal system, the *Korporationen* rebounded with remarkable
speed. They and their patrons, the *Alte Herren*, re-formed at Göttingen
and Bonn, and elsewhere, and as the control functions of the American
and French military governments relaxed, the student fraternities became an open and growing phenomenon at other universities of the western zones by 1949. American university officers in Bavaria voiced disapproval of such groups, but they were largely ineffective in their
criticisms, especially when Military Government authority ended in September 1949. The *Korporationen* and their *Alte Herren* quickly re-
claimed their property, seized first by the Nazis and then by the
occupation authorities.

It was in Berlin and specifically at the Free University that the battle lines hardened concerning the *Korporationen* and their right to re-
group. In November 1949, the *Konvent* (student parliament), paced by
its AStA, proclaimed that formally matriculated students and personnel
at the Free University could not belong to dueling fraternities or ribbon-
carrying fraternities. In that same November, Dr. Albert Vock, a representative of the League of Catholic Students wrote to the university's AStA,
criticizing press attacks on the *Korporationen* and accusing the university of discriminatory actions in forbidding FU students the right to join
such organizations while attending the university. Vock was also at
pains to point out that not all of the *Korporationen* engaged in duels.
His accusation unleashed a forceful reply from an AStA representative,
Georg Kotowski, who systematically rebutted Vock's arguments, claiming that the *Korporationen* had accommodated themselves altogether
too well with the Nazis and that in essence they had no place in the
Free University. For his part, Vock fired off an angry rebuttal to Kotowski, reminding him that *Korporation* veterans had been prominent
in the attempt to assassinate Hitler. Neither side was in the least convinced by the other, and the dispute developed into a longstanding
contest.⁴³ There was no doubt that the students meant business. An
American report on educational developments for November 1949 announced that "an instructor of the Free University was dismissed for organizing an *Altherren* group." The Americans were pleased that only fourteen students had been involved in the group, and even they had
apparently been coerced into joining. Pleasing too was the fact that it
was the Free University which took action, without any prompting from
the outside. "The energy with which the Free University students and
professors are attempting to eliminate the *Altherrenschaften* is in con-

trast to the ineffectiveness of most of the Western German universities in those matters."[44]

The timing of this emotional dispute was indicative of a phenomenon scarcely noticed at the moment. The controversy had flared up in the winter of 1949/50, during the third semester of the new university's operations and about the time that the Free University was beginning to assume a more orderly if not fully ordered existence. Its student population was approaching 5,000, more than double the number at the beginning, and a much higher percentage of beginning students, aged eighteen to twenty, were entering the university at this time than had been the case in the immediate postwar semesters. For the most part these new students had been too young to serve in the armed forces during the Hitler years, although most had gone through the Nazis' youth organizations. Those who were old enough to have served in the Second World War found that their enthusiasm for feats of physical derring-do had rapidly diminished after the first experience of combat. For most of them the activities of a dueling fraternity seemed either trivial or pointless after experiencing real danger. "The primary reason for a young man to engage in a duel is to prove his courage," stated ex-soldier Horst Rögner-Francke. "Our generation, many of whom suffered multiple wounds in combat, scarcely needed to demonstrate that kind of courage any longer."[45] Other founding students at the Free University, who had been officially recognized as Victims of Fascism after the war, had equally strong views. "They had proved to be reactionary organizations during the time of the Weimar Republic," observed Eva Heilmann, "and they were almost uniformly antisemitic." Otto Hess echoed the same sentiments strongly.[46] For many of the founding students, opposition to the Korporationen was an emotional issue, and they took up their cause with genuine fervor. Their fear was that the banned organizations and the Alte Herren, would make rapid progress in recruiting young beginning students through such blandishments as inexpensive housing, the attraction of belonging to a group, and the prospects of enhanced career advancement in later years. While potentially attractive features at any time, they were particularly so in dreary, partially destroyed Berlin, where everyone's future seemed less than certain.

Franz L. Neumann had visited the Free University at the time the controversy over the Korporationen had first arisen. He was of one mind with the student critics. "The students are fighting a bitter and intelligent fight against the revival of the corporations and the Altherrenschaften," Neumann reported. "They are, so far, successful whereas in all other German universities this fight has been lost. The students must receive our support here." He recommended to the American authorities that financial support be given to AStA to enable them to obtain such badly needed items as better material facilities, including a student club. "They need more such facilities if they are to compete successfully with the financial power of the *Altherrenschaften*," he concluded.[47]

The longstanding impasse ultimately found a curious end. University regulations banning student participation in the *Korporationen* were legally challenged in the courts in the 1950s. Simultaneously, innumerable debates over acceptance of *Korporationen* raged at the Free University, but they had come to nothing when, in October 1958, a decision by the highest court of appeals in the Federal Republic finally caused the Free University to do away with its ban on participation in *Korporationen*. While the ban was then formally abolished, the great majority of the university's students continued to view membership in them with suspicion. A Free University AStA chairman, Eberhard Diepgen, whose status as a Korp-Student was about to cause a scandal, commented in the early 1960s that the *Korporationen* had increased their popularity because of the coming of the "mass university." Students simply needed to find a social niche, and the *Korporationen* were fulfilling that need.[48] In later years, a number of founding students softened their views on the fraternities somewhat, claiming that their blanket condemnation of all *Korporationen* might have gone too far, and admitting that individuals who had been members of the student organizations were not necessarily biased or racist.[49] At the time, however, in the early 1950s, the specter of the renascent *Korporationen* was undoubtedly anathema to many and induced large numbers of students in the founding generation to seek ways and means to counter their influence. It is scarcely an exaggeration to say that the campaign against the *Korporationen* influenced for a time the social development of the Free University. It was significant that an appeal for tolerance of the *Korporationen* by Diepgen in an official FU publication in 1963 had been accompanied by yet another strong criticism of the same organizations by a fellow student, Dietrich Schmidt-Hackenberg.[50] In fact, Diepgen's status as both ASTA chairman and Korp-Student simultaneously proved to be too much of a contradiction. Other students called for a referendum, and in mid-1963 they voted him out of office. However, it was hardly the last that Berliners and the university community were to hear from the resilient student leader. He is now the governing mayor of West Berlin and undoubtedly a force to reckon with in city politics for many years to come.

A COMMON PURPOSE

During their bitter contest with the *Korporationen*, the Free University's founding generation tried to obtain better housing facilities and fringe benefits for the students. They hoped also to increase the students' sense of belonging to a community. They would try to improve the students' chances of completing their university training and therefore of making a career later, independently of the support of the *Alte Herren* or similar patronage infrastructures.

The size of the early FU community should always be kept in mind in understanding the atmosphere and the group dynamics that occurred there in the first five or six years of its existence. While enrollments climbed quickly from a bit over 2,000 in 1948 to 5,000 a year later, they then reached a plateau that still had not significantly exceeded 6,000 until the summer semester of 1954. Growth thereafter was steady but not exorbitant, and the Free University doubled in size again to about 13,000 students only in 1961. In the early years, therefore, the student community was of a sufficiently finite size that its student government representatives could grapple with issues concerning the entire student body and could demonstrate effectiveness in resolving them.

Hans-Joachim Lieber, a student of Eduard Spranger, and one of the first assistants at the Free University (and fated to become its penultimate rector), was intimately concerned with student affairs in the early years. He admired the students' contest with the *Korporationen* and recalled the possibilities at their disposal in combating the urge to become members. As an assistant at the philosophy faculty, he was concerned for the welfare and success of the students, many of whom, despite normalization trends in higher education by the early 1950s, still lacked some of the academic qualifications normally associated with the recipient of an *Abitur*. Between one-third and two-fifths of the FU students in the 1950s came from the GDR, and generally they had to reckon with another year of coursework to gain the equivalent of the West German *Abitur*. Therefore, under the leadership of Professors Wilhelm Berges and Hans Herzfeld, Lieber, along with students and other assistants, organized an office for common student affairs. Their goal was to found a comprehensive tutorial system for the Free University, the first of its kind in West Germany.

The main task of the tutorial service was to offer practical advice and moral support for incoming students who might otherwise have difficulties in adjusting to academic life. The project began in the philosophy faculty in the winter semester of 1951/52 with the creation of eight study groups in the history section, the Friedrich Meinecke Institute, and spread quickly to the other faculties once its effectiveness became known. The organization of the *Tutoren-Gruppen* (tutorial groups) was kept deliberately simple. An advanced student, equivalent perhaps to an American graduate student, would meet weekly with his or her group of five or more beginning students. The older student helped orient the new students to their studies, the fields and personalities available in their common field, and possible course offerings. He or she might introduce them to the library system, answer myriad questions about living and studying at the university, and even help organize the newcomers' social life. Many of the tutorial groups took on a life of their own and began to enter seminars together to study some commonly evolved theme. Within a year, in 1952, the university's Board of Trustees, in recognition of the worth of the tutorial services, began to provide some financial support to make the worthwhile undertaking a university-wide program. After a time, the Ford Foundation, in one of its early grants to the Free University, supported the experiment, too. It should also be remembered that the Free University started with a remarkably small teaching staff, so that the student-to-professor ratio was not favorable. Thus, tutorial services were a welcome complement. Rather than shrinking with time, the need for such programs actually increased as the number of partially prepared students from the GDR rose. Yet, the creation of a tutorial system, today a commonplace at many universities, had few counterparts in the German academic world of the early 1950s. The inspiration derived partly from the effort to involve students in the affairs of their fellow students and to develop a sense of student kinship in that finite body of about 5,000 young people.[51]

George N. Shuster, then president of Hunter College in New York City and an acknowledged expert on German higher education, examined the Free University in the mid-1950s and was suitably impressed by the tutorial scheme. "It seems to me an innovation of which the University may be justly proud," he reported to Rector Paulsen. "Many of the tutorial groups achieve a measure of comradeship which transforms the members from complete strangers to each other into friendly associates who begin to sense the fact that a modern university student should not think merely of himself but should take an interest in the whole community of mankind." Shuster's only criticism of the project was that it was seriously underfunded and needed more support to be effective. It proved to be a prophetic observation.[52] The Ford Foundation would eventually contribute to the program, but demand seemed always to outrun supply.

Similarly, the FU students, with administrative support, obtained at an early stage a clubhouse for students in the rustic Frohnau district of northern Berlin in order to provide some physical amenities. Later, this same impulse gave rise to the concept of a *Studentendorf* (student village) in which hundreds of students would reside in low-cost housing, thus obviating the temptation to seek *Korporation* lodgings. In October 1951, HICOG education officer G. R. Koopman, advised Shepard Stone to warn the ministers president of the various Länder about the continuing growth of the *Korporationen*. Koopman felt that one effective way to combat the *Korporationen* was to provide alternative living arrangements: "Social living together is a normal desire and can be utilized for democratic ends."[53] The *Studentendorf* was intended to put this idea into practice.

In the Free University's early years, the students ate their meals in common. A hastily constructed wooden structure in the center of the classroom area, homely though it was, became a central gathering place for students and faculty where at least once a day they dined in common, conversed and disputed in common, and perhaps solved various problems in common. The meals, supported from various public sources, from the city or from American free lunch programs, were an important supplement to the diet of the students and academicians of Germany's most impoverished city. Most members of the FU community, including its medical students, gathered there consistently, first to ease their hunger and then to interact with each other. The students of the Free University had helped contribute to a special spirit at the new institution, but someone who knew them well, Fritz Epstein, was still appalled at their poverty when he returned to Berlin in 1950, two years after currency reform and at a time when observers were already beginning to talk about an economic miracle in West Germany. In August 1950, Epstein listed a number of ways in which the Americans could help the university and its students. One of his suggestions hinted at the stark conditions under which the students still lived: "Another extremely important point," he reminded John Riedl at HICOG's education branch, "would be the improvement of material conditions for the bulk of the students who have to live on the verge of the existence minimum."[54]

Most former Free University students who remembered the late 1940s and early 1950s recalled that political partisanship was largely absent among the student adherents of the three western parties. To be sure, an almost rabid dislike of the SED existed, but, not suprisingly, contacts between FU students and their ideological nemesis across the city were minimal after the division of Berlin. They might have been and in a sense were worlds apart. Thus, there was a relative political consensus among the students who attended the Free University, and their elections in the early days hovered around seventy percent participation, extremely high by today's standards but still not enough to prevent grumbling by the student editors of *Colloquium*. Nevertheless, such significant participation by students indicated confidence in their self-government system. Eva Heilmann, the first woman to be elected to chair the Konvent (student parliament) in 1951, described some of the activities of student government representatives. Students complained about waiting overly long for meals at the modest Mensa because of a lack of spoons and forks, which had constantly to be recycled. "One of the members of parliament was sent to investigate," Heilmann explained, "and he found the complaints justified." Thereupon, they organized an oversight committee of three students and a professor to monitor service, quality of food, and prices. Heilmann also recalled that flooding of walks on the still shabby dining premises was still a prob-

lem, and so one "rainy day we invited members of the building department for lunch; after that they saw the reasons of our complaints on
this score and gave priority to the repairing of the path." For Heilmann
such actions were indicative of a new spirit. "One must judge these actions against the background of most German universities where students can do very little about their common problems."[55]

With little aid available to help with medical care and insurance,
the *Studentenwerk* (Student Welfare) negotiated for a low-cost group insurance for the mostly poor students. It should be recalled that it was a
student group and not an administrative arm of the Free University that
took that initiative. The students also opened a health clinic, staffed by
advanced medical students and supervised by a medical doctor.[56]

Between students and faculty there was an unspoken agreement
that student involvement in university governance, including student
government, was a serious responsibility. Students and faculty alike
were expected to fulfill their roles in it conscientiously. Thus, Wolfgang
Kalischer, an elected representative of the eight-member student executive, the AStA, found that he was required to attend a Wednesday evening gathering of the philosophy faculty in his capacity as an AStA officer. This duty conflicted with a seminar meeting convened by one of
the more formidable personalities of the early Free University, Professor
Hans Leisegang. The latter was a stern and demanding teacher, and a
scholar of high enough reputation to have been considered seriously for
a time as the first rector of the new university. Student Kalischer had to
approach this representative of the German *Ordinarius* to ask his permission to skip a class! Kalischer recalled that Leisegang accepted the unusual request manfully, and as the relieved student turned to depart,
Liesegang suggested that Kalischer appear in his office on the day following the seminar. Leisegang had an important point to make to his students and since Kalischer would be absent during the class, he should receive follow-up instruction on the same point. Needless to say, tutorials
for individual students by full professors were an exceeding rarity in
the German university—or any university for that matter. To be sure,
the incident was minor, but it also reflected the essence of the relationship that made the Free University's Berlin Model function with notable success for at least a decade.[57]

THE POOR BLOODY ASSISTANTS

Although the Free University succeeded in creating a successful community of teachers and learners and in creating a constitution which regulated its affairs well, there were gaps and potential weaknesses too. It
could hardly be otherwise in what everyone realized was an open experiment in higher education. Specifically, the Free University failed to establish a firm position for the *Assistenten*, the untenured teaching assis-

tants, lecturers, and other junior faculty who were roughly equivalent to untenured lecturers in American universities. Much later, this group came to be called the *Mittelbau* or mid-level faculty who occupied a position in the university somewhere between the full professors and the students. Nowhere in its new constitution did the *Assistenten* even appear, whereas the standing of the full professors and the students received careful attention.

Dissatisfaction with their lot surfaced early among the assistants. Already in January 1949, three young members of the *Philosophische Fakultät* sent a memorandum to Rector Redslob seeking formal recognition of their status. "For over five months the assistants of the Free University have worked for the establishment of its seminars and institutes, but without any legal recognition or the regulation of salaries," they wrote.[58] Within a short time they and assistants from the other faculties reminded the university leadership that they still had no recognition in the constitution and no representation on the university's committees. Given their middle position between the students and the professors, and the fact that they were the designated succeeding generation of scholars, the assistants claimed that they should have formal representation in the Academic Senate and on the councils of the individual faculties. "The fact that the assistants of the Free University, in cooperation with the students, played an essential part in erecting it," they claimed, "justifies giving them the opportunity to work toward those goals established for the university at its outset."[59]

The Academic Senate was sufficiently moved by this challenge that it asked the assistants' leadership to send more detailed information, and in March they complied. They cited a recent statement made by Otto Hess at a student government congress in Hamburg that they felt also echoed their sentiments nicely. Hess had been at pains to point out that the new university represented a major departure from old norms. "Given the general stagnation of German university life," he had remarked, "the eyes of students far beyond those who gave rise to the FU look with hope upon this new undertaking." The assistants claimed that in that spirit they hoped for three structural changes at the Free University. They should try "to overcome the unhealthy encapsulation of the university away from social and political life." Further, they should try "to build up the the sense of solidarity of teachers and learners above and beyond the level of a purely educational institution into long-term relationships." The third point was perhaps the most important: "The FU should make an effort to provide its academic self-administration the broadest possible basis in fulfillment of democratic principle by giving the largest possible number of university membership a codetermining function in shaping their University."[60]

That spring the faculty formed a committee of five with Hans Leisegang as its chairman to explore the issue further and to address the assistants' memorandum. Then all of the assistants met with the committee on May 28, 1949, for a joint discussion. Leisegang reported on the meeting, stating that "in principle" at least the faculty could support the idea of representation of assistants in the Academic Senate and in the various faculties. However, it quickly became evident that Leisegang, with the support of the committee, was not at all in favor of such a move. Furthermore, he took sharp issue with several points in the assistants' memorandum of the previous January. Leisegang refused to accept the claim that general stagnation had set in at the German universities, and while he might accept some form of representation for assistants, it became obvious that large differences of opinion on the subject existed. "To be a university assistant is not to be in a profession, and the assistantship is no corporate entity," Leisegang stated flatly. "It is a transitional phase which serves above all to educate succeeding scholarly generations." Leisegang observed further that assistants were examined biennially in any case, and those who had proved unfit for the academic world were simply weeded out. For this reason alone, he reasoned, it did not appear to be necessary or appropriate for them to have formal representation as a recognized entity at the Free University. The committee had come to the conclusion also that the assistant's ties were to be made directly with the professor rather than with the institute in which he or she worked. "He who becomes an assistant," Leisegang continued, "places himself in a position of trust and in a relationship of trust, and as long as that lasts he receives the best representation, that of his professor." Leisegang also added that assistants should be protected from "unwarranted exploitation by the professor." But even here he felt that formal organizational ties such as trade unions were inappropriate in the academic world. They would destroy the relationship of trust between professor and assistant which he felt was so important. Leisegang recommended instead that assistants and professors should reach informal agreements so that, for example, the former would by mutual agreement work only six hours per day for the latter.[61]

For the time being at least, little was done. Eventually, in March 1951, the assistants received recognition through a set of university regulations. However, the latter specifically stated that an assistantship was not to be considered an occupation, and the rest of the regulations dealt with details concerning the proper qualifications for assistantships and other technical details. It said nothing about representation in the Academic Senate or the faculties. Thus, the assistants, unlike the professors and the students, remained in a kind of limbo, unrecognized in the Free University's constitution.[62] One reason for this state of affairs was their small numbers. Exact figures are not available, since assistants were not even mentioned in the university catalogue in the early years, but there were at best only a few dozen assistants at the university in its first years of existence.

Signs of dissatisfaction appeared periodically, as in 1957 when representatives of the FU assistants sent an 11-page memo to the faculty complaining about difficult working conditions at the university. They were too few to teach effectively, they claimed, and the activities they were supposed to undertake to improve teaching and learning were in fact now simply bureaucratic routines, little more than time-consuming clerical details, the report claimed. Moreover, the vacuum in which they existed meant that the assistants had no legal right to make complaints or issue reports. They were fully dependent upon the willingness of the faculty to hear their complaints. They uttered the hope that their request for recognition would not continue to be ignored.[63] It proved to be a forlorn hope. The report had no discernible effect, and no further discussion emerged concerning their uncertain status. However, the obvious and continuous dissatisfaction of at least some of the assistants was a hint of trouble to come. In the next generation at least, the status of the assistant would become a major issue confronting the Free University.

HENRY FORD II COMES TO TOWN

In June 1950, two years after the Preparatory Committee first met, Edwin Redslob, now serving as rector in his own right, prepared for a crucial meeting with the commandant of the American Sector, General Maxwell D. Taylor. Redslob was preoccupied with the Free University's chronic problem: poverty. "The economic status of the Free University is not favorable," he stated forthrightly. "Despite its extensive growth and the expansion of the student body, it will have no more funding for the next fiscal year than it did in the past year." Berlin's budget would not allow any more funding than already allotted. The Free University was in a chronic monetary crisis. Official American aid had amounted to DM 1 million in the fiscal year just ending. The new university appeared to be on the verge of becoming a refuge for an entire faculty of veterinary medicine that was planning to move en bloc from Humboldt University to the Free University—the only time such a mass exodus was to happen. Yet, the financial burden would be heavy. The Free University had expanded its teaching body—an absolute necessity if it were to retain credibility—and its budget for faculty had increased by more than a third in the same year and was approaching DM 1 million alone. The City of West Berlin had come up with DM 4,150,860 in the economically difficult fiscal year 1949/1950 and increased it to DM 5,276,000 for 1950/1951. Still, it was not enough. The question was, what could they do to relieve the chronic budgetary crisis? Redslob was hoping that the Americans would be willing to double their contribution for the coming year.[64]

Another veteran observer added his voice to the chorus of support for the Free University. Fritz Epstein was in Berlin for the summer semester of 1950 as one of the early guest professors. Even he, who had been intensely involved in the founding students' first plans to create a new university in 1947/1948, was not prepared for what he encountered in 1950. "I am truly amazed what in only two years time with our strong moral and material backing has been achieved," he wrote to HICOG education director John Riedl. "Never before in the history of German universities in modern times had educators and administrators alike been confronted with a similar formidable task, where the fulfillment of urgent present-day tasks had to be linked with long-range planning for the future." Epstein saw the Free University as a worthy object of continuing American support: "As a long-range project, I consider the Free University one of the best investments made in Germany, actively promoting German-American cooperation in the academic as well as the political sphere." Consequently, he recommended greater all-around support for the Free University: "A firmer financial fundament will have to be worked out by re-defining and assuring the future annual contributions to be made by HICOG, the West Berlin Magistrat, and possibly the Bundesregierung," Epstein counseled.[65]

Fortunately, American public commitment to the Free University remained strong and continuing. Epstein's pleas had some effect. Howard W. Johnston, who was about to return home to the United States after two years as a university officer, was still in a position to intercede directly. He made frantic last-minute appeals to his superiors at the High Commission to grant the university's request for greater HICOG support. The miracle happened—much to the disgruntlement of other German and American officials whose own programs were unbalanced by the sudden doubling of aid to the Free University in the amount of DM 2 million. Redslob and von Bergmann, who had hurriedly produced the university's projected budget needs at Johnston's request literally overnight, expressed great gratitude to the young university officer for his efforts. In appreciation of his accomplishments, the Free University bestowed upon him the status of an honarary citizen of the FU community.[66] It was a mark of the new university's great need that it received part of its increased installment in advance from the Americans even before the new fiscal year actually began, to pay for the creation of an urgently needed Institute for Political Science, which opened in the summer of 1950. The large American public donations, starting in 1948, were designated as general funds, contributing to the overall development of the Free University. Other specialized donations arrived periodically, earmarked for special purposes, such as the accumulation of libraries or improvement of medical facilities. For example, in the autumn of 1950 the medical faculty received nearly DM 317,000 from the "McCloy Funds" for medical equipment and books. The Rockefeller Foundation added another DM 20,000 for books for the humanities and social sciences. The students received x-ray apparatus for their student-run clinic to check for one of postwar Berlin's scourges, tuberculosis. A relatively modest sum of DM 5,000 arrived from the Americans in the autumn of 1950 to pay an architect's fees, so recorded Fritz von Bergmann, "for plans for new construction should financing from the American side possibly materialize in the future." It was a tantalizing hint of things to come.[67] The total budget for the Free University for the fiscal year 1951/1952 approached nearly DM 9.3 million of which DM 6.8 million came from sums approved by the Berlin Senate and DM 2.5 million from the Americans, much of it organized by HICOG's able new university officer, Carl G. Anthon. Significantly, only DM 200,000 of the total was earmarked for building construction, a miniscule sum, given the university's urgent need of more physical plant.[68]

With an increased American contribution available to keep the university's creditors from the door once again, a number of its leaders and supporters made immediate plans to seek support for a more orderly growth. "Hitherto, the university has found accommodations in existing research institutes, and it suffers from a lack of space," wrote Edwin Redslob to Howard Johnston's replacement, Carl Anthon, in the autumn of 1950. "The lack of a large auditorium is especially unfortunate," he added and then informed Anthon that a Berlin architect, Hermann Fehling, had already drawn up plans for an innovative structure that would combine the much-needed auditorium with large lecture halls as had recently been done at the university in Tübingen. In fact, an FU building commission was already in place, drawing up designs for a future "campus" in Dahlem, and the indefatigable Fehling was already putting plans on the drawing board for a large student dwelling complex. Other Americans, such as HICOG education adviser John Riedl, were also interested in the expansion of the Free University. Riedl felt that the university needed a central library and urged that it take priority over other urgently needed structures such as an institute of chemistry.[69] The question was, where would the capital come from for such ambitious undertakings? The answer proved not to be the public purse of the Americans or the already strained resources of the Berliners. Even they had their limitations, and no one could deny that the Free University was already a recipient of handsome sums, given the general impoverishment of the times. Instead, the source turned out to be a private benefactor of considerable renown. No less a philanthropist than Henry Ford II, grandson of the great automotive pioneer, had taken a personal interest in the financially ailing new university and was making plans to come to Berlin.

As early as January 1949, Frank Howley had contacted the Ford Foundation, among others, asking for support for the new university, but the initial reaction had not been encouraging. Hitherto, the Ford Foundation, founded in 1936, had invested in philanthropic projects primarily within Michigan. However, following the death of Henry Ford in 1947, the settling of the wills of the pioneering automobile manufacturer and his son Edsel meant that the modest foundation would soon oversee nearly $500,000,000. In one stroke it had become the largest foundation in the world. Its board of trustees established several broad areas of activities, including support of contributions to world peace, to freedom and democracy, and to the advancement of economic well-being which would support democracy. One category, especially, gave hope to the economically ailing Free University: The Ford trustees also proposed to support "activities to strengthen, expand, and improve educational facilities and methods to enable individuals more fully to realize their intellectual, civic, and spiritual potentialities; to promote greater equality of educational opportunity; and to conserve and increase knowledge and enrich our culture."[70] Already in 1948 the Ford Foundation was beginning to gear up for larger operations, and those with a nose for fundraising began lining up with their requests.

Thus, it was fortunate that Edwin Redslob's visit to the United States came when it did, in December 1949, as a follow-up to Frank Howley's initial appeal to the newly expanded foundation. These tentative contacts were also followed up in 1950 by Franz L. Neumann and Carl Anthon, who apprised the Ford Foundation leadership further, especially foundation president Paul G. Hoffman, of the university's activities and needs. Probably the most influential contact at the early stage between the Ford Foundation and the Free University came through John J. McCloy. Paul Hoffman had already spent some time in Europe after the war, as an official at the U.S. Economic Cooperation Administration, and had met with the HICOG director several times. The future Ford Foundation president had traveled to Berlin in 1950 to attend an industrial fair, and the two had discussed the university's problems together. McCloy, who knew his way around the world of high finance, was well aware of the vast resources of the new philanthropic foundation. Moreover, he was a supreme fund-raiser himself, and he followed up the meeting with a detailed memorandum to Hoffman on the Free University's needs. "I know that you understand," he wrote to Hoffman, "that the prospect of a democratic, international university in Berlin is exciting to us here, and vitally related to our aims in this country."[71]

McCloy's trusted director of the Public Affairs Division at HICOG, Shepard Stone, had prepared the memo on the Free University. It laid out the hopes and expectations of the Americans with respect to the university. Stone observed that European universities in general, but particularly in Germany, had become too tradition-bound, a weakness exacerbated by two world wars. As Stone saw it, they were "not organized to meet the political, social and economic challenges posed by communism or totalitarian attacks from the right." Stone also claimed that "Europe needs a new international university that can train the men and women required to meet these challenges." For him Berlin was the logical site because it had adapted to meet the political stresses of the times. "In the ideological test Berlin has given proof of courage, of devotion to freedom," he wrote. "A vigorous, new university in Berlin would serve all the peoples of the Continent in the years and decades ahead." Stone outlined the new university's most immediate needs, including physical facilities, room for expansion, a library, plus funds for visiting lecturers and new, interdisciplinary programs. "The Free University of Berlin offers a unique opportunity to build international understanding," he concluded, "to strengthen democratic conviction and cooperation and to develop democratic leaders in Europe."[72]

Stone's information and McCloy's communication with Hoffman obviously had some effect upon the Ford Foundation. Hoffman's assistant, Joseph McDaniel, assured McCloy that the foundation officers were holding discussions "in which the Free University of Berlin has been the main topic, and I can assure you there is deep interest in this institution on the part of the Foundation."[73] Shortly after, Franz L. Neumann opened discussions directly with Hoffman about the new university, reiterating its difficult financial situation. Before long, other prominently placed individuals were doing the same thing. Henry Kellermann, the State Department's senior expert on German cultural affairs wrote to Hoffman about the importance of supporting the growth of the Free University, as did the senior American officer in Berlin, the successor to Frank Howley, General Lemuel Mathewson.[74] It must have been obvious to the Ford Foundation officials that Americans in high positions placed as great importance to the growth of the Free University as did the Germans themselves.

In April 1951, after months of conversations with HICOG officials, the Free University's new rector, medical scientist Professor Hans von Kress, wrote directly to Paul Hoffman, explaining the current situation. Enrollment at the university had increased to nearly 5,700 students by now, nearly 2,000 of whom came from the east. The faculty, including all ranks, numbered about 225, offering the relatively high instructor-to-student ratio of 1:24 (the ratio of full professors to students was, of course, far worse, exceeding 1:100).

The university was carrying on its operations in an odd assortment of 35 buildings, most of them located in the American Sector. Redslob, for example, had to conduct his art history lectures in a commercial movie theater. Because of a lack of resources, the Free University had not been able to make much progress in a number of important areas where it hoped to function as a reform university. Those included the following five areas: an increased awareness of the importance of political science for research and teaching within all disciplines; the enhancement of research and teaching in East European studies; the encouragement of interdisciplinary work among the various faculties; the creation of an evening or adult division of the Free University; and the expansion of exchanges with foreign professors.

"The chief demand in expanding the Free University in general and specifically in furthering the above-mentioned goals," von Kress noted, "is the creation of adequate new buildings. Above all there is great need for lecture halls." Von Kress then elaborated on the specific space needs, already estimated in detail by architects, including a large auditorium and lecture complex, a central library, and a new Mensa or student cafeteria. The total building cost was estimated to be an eye-popping DM 4.25 million, twice the sum with which the Free University had made its start two years previously.[75] The estimated costs for supporting the reform goals of the university were expected to add another ten percent to the grant. In other words, the Free University was asking for a monumental sum from a private foundation, even so large an institution as the Ford Foundation.

The proposal met with a warm response in New York. Three months later, in June 1951, Henry Ford II, accompanied by Paul Hoffman, flew into Berlin to examine the situation personally. On hand to greet them were Ernst Reuter, Otto Suhr, Rector Hans von Kress, and several HICOG officials, including John McCloy. Ford, like so many visitors before him, was impressed with what he saw at the Free University. At a crucial meeting between Ford and West Berlin's political leadership, including Reuter, the American guest asked his hosts bluntly if they considered the Free University to be a temporary expedient or a permanent institution that could count on continuing Berlin support. Was the city prepared to provide land in Dahlem for the projected buildings? Ernst Reuter promptly assured Ford of Berlin's commitment to its new university and von Kress was prepared to give written assurances.[76]

At first, the Ford Foundation representatives made no decision, claiming that the Foundation's board of trustees would decide the matter later that summer. A HICOG officer recorded that the Free University's request posed problems for the private foundation. "In conclusion, Mr. Hoffman stated that the Free University's application would ordinarily have been declined by the Foundation, since the latter does not finance building projects of American universities. However, the enthusiastic recommendations of Mr. McCloy, Mr. Stone, and his staff in Frankfurt and Berlin convinced him and Mr. Ford of the vital importance of the Free University in educating and reorienting German youth."[77]

A few weeks later, Alvin C. Eurich, who oversaw the Ford Foundation's education branch, made a follow-up visit to Berlin to talk to responsible officials. "In these discussions," noted a HICOG observer, "stress was laid upon the development of work in political and social sciences and especially upon the question of the relationship of the Hochschule für Politik and the Free University. Dr Suhr . . . expressed his willingness for the Hochschule für Politik to be merged with the Free University in accordance with the plan drafted by Professor Franz Neumann in the summer of 1950." The Ford Foundation representative let it be known that while the bulk of the large grant would be consumed for construction purposes, the justification for the grant really lay elsewhere.[78]

The Free University's innovative programs counted for more in the long run. Eurich returned to the Ford Foundation, assured by what he saw and heard. On July 16, 1951, the Free University received welcome news from Hoffman. The Ford Foundation had approved $1,309,500 for the university, an enormous sum for the day and an unprecedented private donation in postwar Germany. Most was to be devoted to construction of physical facilities, an exception to Ford's rule. A total of $119,000 was earmarked for innovative programs.

In combination with the sums from the City of Berlin and from the U.S. High Commission, the Ford Foundation grant helped the Free University to consolidate and to put its innovative plans into operation. The event marked the beginning of more than a decade of massive Ford Foundation grants for the Free University. The most visible reminder of the Ford grants remain the large buildings in the central university district. Yet, the deeper impact of those donations, intended also to make the Free University an innovative educational institution, lingers on in the minds of a generation of students who attended the Free University in its and their youth. Shepard Stone was ecstatic and wrote to a friend shortly after the donation proclaiming a triumph: "I want you to know . . . that we took our promise seriously. Fred Burckhardt [of the American Council of Learned Societies] and a group of Americans who were determined that, if possible, the Free University would be a great international modern university, are now at work with officials of the university and the City of Berlin. . . . the Ford Grant will some day be responsible not only for the firm establishment of a democratic university behind the Iron Curtain, but also for a great and liberal institution."[79] Hopes were running high at Germany's newest—and poorest—university.

THE LAW FACULTY, THE "BRANDT AFFAIR," AND DENAZIFICATION

In 1951, even as momentum was gathering for the infusion of significant new aid to the Free University, its law faculty composed a lengthy memorandum concerning its development during the first three years of operation. It was hardly a tale of unremitting success. "The position of the law faculty within the Free University of Berlin was unfortunate from the start," stated its composers, headed by Wilhelm Wengler. "The law faculty of Linden University [now Humboldt University] provided no reservoir from which the law faculty of the Free University could draw."[80] At first only two law professors, Drath and von Lübtow, accepted appointments. They were augmented in the spring of 1949 by two more, Lange and Wengler. In that same spring the combined faculty of law and economics split into their respective components after sometimes stormy discussions. The few law professors available felt that their needs were scarcely recognized by the founders of the new university, and morale in the first years was anything but strong. There were several reasons for the unhappy state of affairs. The law professors felt that, in line with German academic tradition, they should control political science at the Free University, a desire that collided directly with the wishes of such eminent political scientists as Franz L. Neumann and Sigmund Neumann (no relation) and Otto Suhr. But perhaps the single most important cause of this distress was a personnel decision: the appointment of law professor Günther Brandt to the law faculty. The appointment of Brandt assumed far greater importance than did other faculty appointments because it enmeshed the law faculty in a conflict with the new university's influential student body and went to the core of the Berlin Model. Did students really have the right to help judge faculty appointments? The Brandt affair tested that right and gave rise to the first serious clash of opinion at the Free University.

Brandt had been one of two professors assigned to the disciplinary committee at Berlin University and charged with reviewing the dismissals of the three students Hess, Schwarz, and Stolz. He, along with Möglich, had upheld Paul Wandel's right to withdraw the students' right to study and had therefore refused to recognize the proceedings as a disciplinary review. The three offenders were no longer part of the university community, so held Brandt, and Wandel had been within his rights to dismiss them. "The right of free expression should in my opinion be open to every student," stated Brandt in a reply to the Studentenrat in April 1948, after the dismissals. "But at the same time it is limited by the fact that Germany at present is occupied territory and that the occupying powers have forbidden oral and written attacks upon them."[81] If the students wished to appeal the dismissals, Brandt's advice had been to communicate with Wandel directly. However, public reaction to the decision was strongly negative, and the upholding of the dismissals had gone far toward galvanizing public opinion in the West in favor of creating the Free University in 1948.

Now, almost two years after the incident, Günter Brandt wanted to join the law faculty at the Free University and was receiving strong support from the law faculty. At first, the appointment proceedings seemed to go smoothly. The two student representatives at the University Senate, Horst Hartwich and Horst Rögner-Francke, raised no objections since they were unaware of Brandt's role in upholding the dismissals in 1948. Later, during a review process, however, the students learned about the imminent appointment of Brandt, realized who he was, and raised an immediate protest. If the law faculty had not been so badly understaffed, the matter might have been settled more amicably. There had been other instances where students and faculty had disagreed on potential candidates, usually arising out of discussions over an individual's degree of involvement with the Nazis. Now, however, the issue was far more emotional and immediate than that, and it concerned a faculty that was admittedly the "*Sorgenkind*" (ailing offspring) of the Free University. The result was a bitter dispute from which neither side retreated, and it caused some faculty members to call into question for the first time student involvement in the administration of the Free University. The protagonists viewed it even then as a test of the relationships of the various parts of the university, especially that between students and professors. Franz L. Neumann, who was visiting the new university at that time, saw fit to comment on the matter and to question the wisdom of allowing students to help decide faculty appointments.

Following a two-day conference on the subject in February 1950, the student parliament declared that it stood by its decision to oppose Brandt's confirmation to a full professorship. Furthermore, it declared that to its regret "a fruitful cooperation with Herrn Professor Dr. Dr. Wengler is no longer possible," a statement that reflected the tensions that had arisen during the dispute. Wengler, for his part, felt the students were acting irresponsibly, attempting to make judgments of an academic nature, and he wondered openly why the students examined every minute detail of Brandt's appointment while allowing applicants with former connections to the Nazis to enter with little or no difficulty. If Wengler had desired to nettle the students, he could scarcely have found a better way. "This charge is without any foundation," declared the students in a written rebuttal. "We can prove the opposite instead." The problem, they noted, lay in the complicated rules surrounding denazification. "If a professor was a member of the NSDAP and has then denazified in the proper fashion, then we see no reason to go after him so long as he unreservedly makes the ideals of the Free University his own. By doing so, he is making a personal compensation and is contributing to his own rehabilitation." The matter hardly remained an internal dispute either. The students received public support from the SPD through its university section, an indication of how seriously they took the disagreement. Calling the student body one of the pillars of the Free University, the group declared itself "opposed to all attempts to weaken the influence of the elected student representatives or to defame them."[82] The disgruntled law professors claimed that the students' actions were further hindering their largely frustrating task of trying to entice other law professors to West Berlin.

Wengler's reasoning in calling for the appointment of Brandt was straightforward. The Free University desperately needed competent law professors, and Brandt was competent. Furthermore, Brandt was no Communist; rather, he was a longtime SPD member, a fact that carried weight with Wengler, who himself had suffered under the Nazis and who had left Humboldt University for the Free University in 1949. Finally, the judgment issued by the disciplinary committee in May 1948 was neither known to him nor, he felt, pertinent to Brandt's appointment. More important was the establishment of a competent law faculty, no easy task in postwar Berlin.[83] Neumann admired Wengler's ability but was ambivalent about him. As consultant to the Ford Foundation, he wrote afterwards: "Wengler (international law) is an outstanding scholar but an exceedingly difficult person who dislikes his students and is disliked by them."[84] Certainly the Brandt affair had raised tempers on both sides.

It would go too far to say that the appointment of Brandt spelled the end of the Berlin Model, although for the moment it certainly put strains on the special student-professor relationship that was so characteristic of the Free University during its first years. Certain too was the fact that this first serious dispute at the university was a warning that if in the future significant differences, lasting over a considerable time, were to arise between students and faculty, the basic premises underlying the Free University could be strained to the breaking point. In 1950, the affair was brief, albeit bitter, and was resolved in a significant way. Brandt was appointed in the status of adjunct (honorary) professor and proved to be an effective law instructor in succeeding years. In other words, students and faculty reached a compromise with which each side could live, although rancor was hardly absent. It remained to be seen what would happen if the clash recurred. Certainly Franz L. Neumann, who visited the Free University during the Brandt affair, was worried about that vital student-faculty relationship when he made his assessment in early 1950, and he was still concerned in succeeding years. The student right to vote on faculty appointments in the law faculty ceased at about this time. It is fair to say that the law faculty acquired the reputation as perhaps the most conservative faculty at the Free University. The issue of student rights was a fateful one and was by no means resolved in 1950. It would come back to haunt the Free University in the future.

The charges and countercharges about denazification that arose over the Brandt affair pointed up a problem which the Free University, like every other German university, had to face. Where should it draw the line in making faculty appointments? The issue had confronted the founders of the new university with ethical problems from the start. The students, some of whom were Victims of Fascism, had little reason or desire to be soft on ex-Nazis. However, they and the newly formed faculty also had to recognize that their young institution faced a critical shortage of skilled academicians. For example, in creating the philosophy faculty, the founders originally settled upon an economist, Albrecht Forstmann, as the first dean. He was capable, and he seemed to have the necessary political credentials, having been incarcerated in Sachsenhausen Concentration Camp from the end of 1936 to 1940 for criticizing the Nazi regime. Yet, he was not all that he seemed at first glance. Further investigation showed that he had joined the NSDAP in 1932, before the Nazis seized power, and had apparently been an enthusiastic supporter at first. However, he was an impulsive man whose incautious remarks at a party had finally betrayed him, and the Gestapo had arrested him. Upon release from Sachsenhausen, he was also dimissed from the party. After the war, Forstmann's fortunes revived, and he received a professorship at the University Unter den Linden before he presented himself to the Free University. His publications looked good, the primary reason he received the nomination to become the first dean. However, his luck did not last. Further evidence indicated that Forstmann had written tracts which were imbued with National Socialist aims and which approved of the Nazis' plundering of the French economy. When French Military Government in Berlin heard of Forstmann's selection as dean in 1948, their chief official, General Ganeval, protested the decision personally with Ernst Reuter. When the students got wind of his background, they too protested his appointment as dean. Forstmann was subsequently excluded from the Free University.[85]

This is not to say that the neighboring university in East Berlin was faultless with respect to denazification. Friedrich Möglich, a physicist and educationist, had served on the disciplinary committee which dismissed Hess, Stolz, and Schwarz in 1948. Like Forstmann, Möglich had joined the NSDAP in 1932. Like Forstmann, he had fallen out of favor with his party. In his case it was because he had had a long-term affair with a Jewish woman, a violation of the Nazis' racialist laws. Subsequently, he was dismissed from the NSDAP in 1940. That might have worked in his favor after 1945. However, the records clearly indicated that Möglich had disavowed the woman and in fact had justified his actions with the claim that his paramour did not look Jewish. She gave the appearance of the quintessential German "Gretchen," he claimed. Möglich in his appeals for reinstatement into the party stated repeatedly that he had remained an ardent antisemite. The Nazis rejected his appeals and reduced him in rank at the Friedrich-Wilhelms-University. After the war, Möglich became a full professor at Berlin University and joined the SED.[86]

These examples were atypical in that the individuals had been old party members who had run afoul of the system they once had embraced. More typical of those with a Nazi past who joined or rejoined the faculties of a German university after the war, were middle-aged academics and professionals. As medical doctors, lawyers, civil servants, and the like, they frequently joined or felt compelled to join such Nazi auxiliary organizations as the N.S. *Studentenbund* (students' league), *Dozentenbund* (lecturers' league), *Ärztebund* (physicians' league), and so on. With time, the Nazis consolidated their grip on society. They required those in the professions to join the party itself if they were to remain in their field. Typically, the date of entry for such persons was May 1, 1937. Usually such individuals had held no position of rank or responsibility in the NSDAP. They were taking the path of least resistance, and the Nazis were satisfied with their outward conformity to their movement. To be sure, there were exceptions among these professionals, some of whom were genuinely committed to Nazism or were notorious opportunists. After the war when the Allied powers were establishing denazification procedures and determining relative degrees of guilt or involvement, these professionals were usually categorized as *Mitläufer*, or followers, and they were considered to be significantly less compromised than the leaders. In 1946, American and German legal experts in the American Zone had established five denazification categories: Major Offender, Offender, Lesser Offender, Follower, and Exonerated. The first three categories snared several thousand individuals in the American Zone. By contrast, those ranked in the Follower category numbered in the hundreds of thousands, a fact that goes far in explaining why denazification under American auspices bogged down under a sheer weight of numbers. National Socialism had, after all, been a mass movement.[87]

By the time the Free University was founded in the autumn of 1948, the significant period of denazification had already waned. The Soviets had announced at the beginning of that year that they were putting an end to the political purge altogether, and the Americans hastened to follow suit. By that time, after more than three years of general impoverishment, society as a whole longed for reconstruction and normalization, and increasingly it saw denazification as an obstacle to that end. Indignation over the Nazis' many crimes had already begun to ebb and was being replaced by a desire to rebuild. With Military Government approval, university authorities in the American Zone were already reinstating qualified academics who had earlier been dismissed as having a Nazi past. The Free University began taking on its faculty at precisely that phase in the admittedly disorderly denazification process.

Of the approximately thirty individuals of professorial (associate or above) rank listed in the Free University's first catalogue for the winter semester 1948/49, seven had formerly been members of the NSDAP. Of these, two had joined in 1933 (the so-called *März-Gefallenen*, or little opportunists who jumped onto the Nazi bandwagon once they had seized power). The other five had joined in 1937. A further five individuals had been members of the N.S. *Lehrerbund* (teachers' league) or the *Dozentenbund*. (The author compiled this information from the records of the Berlin Document Center, which produced party membership cards, membership files for auxiliary organizations, evidence of professional activity requiring state funding, and sometimes internal party assessments of an individual's political reliability. The BDC also informed the author that their lists are not complete, and therefore there is no guarantee that the above figures are absolutely correct.) It is important to remember that except for the Forstmann episode, none of the seven appointments mentioned above took the students or the rest of the FU community by surprise. Student representatives in the faculties or in the Academic Senate were aware of an individual's political past, and many of these student representatives, as recognized Victims of Fascism, voted for appointments with their eyes open. They were forced to weigh the needs of their institution in comparison to the desire to remove the last vestiges of National Socialism. They made compromises. Each of those first-semester appointees with a Nazi past was, by the standards of the day, a Follower.

Contemporary American authorities were not alarmed or surprised at the presence of "Followers" at the Free University or in West Berlin. In October 1949, Eric Wendelin, a political adviser in the newly established U.S. High Commission, reported on the state of denazification to the senior American military officer in the West Sectors, General Maxwell Taylor. There had been claims recently that a resurgence of Nazism threatened in West Berlin. Wendelin stated that to offer precise information would require months of investigation of about 40,000 cases on appeal, a wearisome project. However, he felt he could issue an unequivocal statement to the American commander immediately: "Resurgence of Nazism in the Western Sectors of Berlin on the basis of present information is practically non-existent." Wendelin commented briefly on denazification and allegations of a "brown resurgence" in the Soviet Sector too. There was little doubt that the Soviets and the SED were trying to win German nationalists to their side. They had also attacked the issue of denazification in a decidedly pragmatic way. "The Soviets have never hesitated to employ individual Nazis in top positions," he informed Taylor, "when it has been to their advantage to do so." He mentioned the specific example of Paul Markgraf, former Nazi and now a police president in East Berlin. Wendelin summarized the eastern authorities' approach. "If they are useful, forget their past; if they are not useful, make propaganda capital out of their elimination."[88]

It became popular in the late 1960s and early 1970s for student groups to "expose" the political past of FU instructors who had joined the National Socialist movement.[89] They were hardly revealing anything new to the founding members of the university, many of whom had far greater justification in condemning any lingering Nazi influence in society and in their university. The spirit which permeated the Free University in its first dozen years was utterly devoid of sentiment for a return to right-wing totalitarianism. Postwar exposure of the move-

ment's monstrous crimes, combined with Germany's crushing defeat
and subsequent impoverishment, had served to discredit Nazism thoroughly. The record of the Free University with respect to the appointment
of former National Socialists did not differ markedly from that of
the West German universities or, for that matter, from the east with
respect to the reinstatement of Nazi small-fry.

PIONEERING INSTITUTES

With funding from the City of Berlin beginning to rise and with independent support arriving in quantity from HICOG, the Ford Foundation,
and other sources, the Free University could begin to embark upon innovative programs and concepts in the early 1950s. Outside observers
such as Franz L. Neumann and Sigmund Neumann had good reason to
be impressed with the new spirit afoot at the Free University, a center
of learning where they felt that research and learning in fields ignored
or neglected by other German universities could be more readily furthered. Among those programs upon which the Free University built a
reputation in the course of its formative years were the social and political sciences, East European studies, American studies, and international comparative studies in law. The two emigré German scholars had
examined such programs in Western, especially American, universities
and they were at pains during their postwar visits to German universities to point out deficiencies in offerings based on their comparative experience. Sigmund Neumann, for example, felt that German university
students in general tended toward overspecialization because they concentrated strictly on professional career training. Furthermore, German
practice tended toward "the exclusively theoretical and philosophical approach to the social sciences with complete neglect of the concrete field
study and analysis." Political science was, he felt, not treated as a genuine, separate discipline. Despite the recent cataclysmic war, nationalism and a parochial view of the world were still present at the German
university. Combined and concerted research efforts were still a rarity.
Sigmund Neumann concluded by saying that higher education still
showed a "complete neglect of an education for social living."[90] Yet, he
was hopeful that prospects could improve in the teaching of the social sciences at the Free University. He was encouraged that Otto Suhr had succeeded in reestablishing the Hochschule für Politik in Berlin after a
fifteen-year hiatus. He noted too that "it has found a fortunate working relationship with the Freie Universität . . . ," and Neumann strongly urged
the Americans to support it.[91]

Franz L. Neumann, in reporting on events at the Free University a
few months later, had much the same advice, rating Suhr's Hochschule
as a vital institution. "It caters to everyone who is interested in political
science . . . ," he observed, and he desired to coordinate the affairs of

Suhr's institution with the needs of the Free University. "The ideal solution," Franz Neumann concluded, "would be the merger of the FU and the HfP," although he knew that such a merger could hardly happen instantaneously. Neumann had met with the senate of the Free University and had touched on the necessity of reintroducing political science into German higher education, i.e. of reviving a German academic tradition rather than importing an American discipline as some critics in the University Senate claimed. His arguments appeared cogent. Political science would, he claimed, "train students for public life and . . . assist in the reform of the FU." It would help "break down the aloofness of the FU from the population of Berlin," and would lower the barriers that existed among the various disciplines, he added. Neumann's practical advice was to create jointly with the Hochschule für Politik a research institute at the Free University specializing in political science. Ideally it should have separate funding, probably American backing, and ultimately a separate faculty for the same discipline should be created.[92] Edwin Redslob had begun conversations on the subject of such an institute for political science as early as December 1949 during his trip to the United States, and he could announce the following June that the Rockefeller Foundation had approved a three-year $50,000 grant to help see the new foundation through its first semesters.[93]

Accordingly, on July 28, 1950, the pioneering Institut für Politische Wissenschaften (Institute for Political Sciences, IPS) emerged under the signatures of Edwin Redlsob for the Free University and Otto Suhr for the Hochschule für Politik, plus several professors on their respective faculties. Its first director was Professor O. H. von der Gablentz, who was succeeded in 1951 by Professor A. R. Gurland, and he, in turn, by Professor Otto Stammer in 1954. The institute's function was to promote "research into public life, particularly through historical investigations and representative inquiries." The staff expected to engage in research, keeping two considerations in mind: the altered status of Germany after 1945, and the special status of Berlin between East and West. They wished to conduct research on Western democracies and how they functioned, on the effects of totalitarian rule in modern states, including its political structure, its social and ideological bases, and its effects upon culture. A third and immediately relevant goal was to be an inquiry into Germany's recent past and its present situation.[94] The IPS was doubly necessary at this stage since the Free University was barred by the Berlin City Assembly from duplicating the activities of other institutions of higher learning such as the Hochschule für Politik.[95]

Shortly after the IPS began functioning as an institutional link between the Free University and Otto Suhr's political scientists, Fritz von Bergmann described his expectations for it. "It reflects the desire of the Free University to cause political science, which hitherto has been treated as purely a research activity, to be drawn increasingly into teach-

ing. It should enable a broader education than previously possible of lawyers, economists, historians, educators, etc." To be sure, such expectations demanded more instructional staff who were expert in political
science, and naturally the costs to meet this educational goal would
rise. Thus, one of the requests made to the Ford Foundation by the leadership of the Free University was the inclusion of some funding for the
IPS and for several other ambitious undertakings, such as the Osteuropa
Institut and the Evening University projects. The Osteuropa Institut
proved to be a particularly successful undertaking and served later as a
model for other institutes specializing in area studies.[96]

The reader will recall that the Ford grant of July 1951 had provided
that ten percent of its funding be devoted to those projects while the
bulk went to the construction of urgently needed buildings.[97] Similarly,
American public support through HICOG funding was earmarked for support of the same goals. Thus, High Commissioner James Conant, Mc-
Cloy's successor, informed the FU leadership two years later in June
1953 that one of the goals which the American funding expected to further was to "develop the political and social sciences, both in teaching
and research."[98]

In essence, the senior researchers at the Hochschule für Politik (the
HfP) took on a second hat as professors of political science at the Free University. Those students who studied political science at the HfP could
earn the equivalent of the master's degree starting in 1955. Soon, they
had the right to transfer to the Free University to continue under their
same professor or professors on work toward a doctorate. Their distinguished first director, Otto Suhr, also continued to play a highly active
role in Berlin politics, so much so that in 1955 he became the third Governing Mayor of Berlin, succeeding Ernst Reuter and Walter Schreiber.
Upon Suhr's death in 1957, the city lost a capable mayor, the HfP its
founding director, and the Free University a distinguished political scientist. However, the way was also cleared for the logical move that many observers like Franz L. Neumann had predicted from the beginning. For
Neumann the "extreme shortage of specialists in political and social science in Germany . . . makes it inadvisable to permit the development of
political and social science in two competing institutions."[99] Thus, a
merger was highly desirable.

With the consent of both higher educational institutions, the Berlin
Assembly passed legislation in July 1958 which fully incorporated the
HfP into the Free University. It became known, and rightly so, as the
Otto Suhr Institute, and retains the name to this day. To be sure, the ini-
tials "OSI" tempted its members to find a contraction. It has been re-
ferred to popularly as the "OSI" (pronounced oh'zee) ever since.

James Conant, in approving yet another sizable HICOG grant to the
Free University in 1953, had listed the purposes for American funding
in the field of the social and political sciences. They closely mirrored

the goals of the university's leadership itself. Besides improving teaching and research, the aid was intended to allow the Free University to "a) play a more active and responsible role in the community; b) achieve a more thorough-going internationalism at all levels of teaching, research, and student life; c) effect a more democratic relationship between professors and students; d) develop the political and social sciences, both in teaching and research; and e) assure students a responsible voice in university affairs."[100] Thus, the Free University's undoubted commitment to furthering the political and social sciences made it one of the leading institutions in Central Europe in reviving the Germans' once respectable contributions in those fields. By striving to obtain the five goals listed by Conant, the Free University took a pioneering role in educating its students for participation in a western-style democracy. The net effect of the two institutes, the IPS and later the HfP, upon the Free University was to help to impart a singular awareness of the importance of political science to succeeding generations of students in a broad range of disciplines. This effort, plus other programs unique to the Free University, encouraged large numbers of its students to become engaged in the political process. They did so, and to a degree unusual for a time when most student bodies were characterized by political docility and a single-minded concentration upon studies and career preparation. The emphasis which the founding members of the Free University placed upon building political awareness into German higher education goes far in explaining the new consciousness of the student body.

INSTITUTE FOR EAST EUROPEAN STUDIES

The Free University considered itself from the outset to be an institution caught on the dividing line between East and West. Therefore, one of its early emphases was to encourage the development of scholarly research in the field of Eastern European or Slavic Studies. The field of inquiry was hardly new to German higher education. Before World War II the universities at Breslau and Königsberg had specialized in this field, but after the war they ceased to be German universities, the first-named coming under Soviet jurisdiction and the second reopening as a Polish university. Of all the West German universities, the Free University lay farthest to the east. Moreover, no university had greater motivation to want to understand the Eastern European states. In short, the Free University was a logical site to become a center of Slavic Studies. The desire to establish such a center surfaced virtually at the moment the Free University was founded. An instrumental founding figure was Fritz Epstein, himself a Slavicist by training, and in the philosophy faculty one of the earliest appointments was Professor Max Vasmer. Fritz Epstein was one of the first exchange professors at the Free University, arriving in the summer semester 1950 to teach Slavic history. Epstein outlined a number of problems and challenges for HICOG's education chief, John Riedl, one of which was to offer a proper balance of courses in East European history, law, economics, and religious development. "This would sharpen the profile of the [Free] University in a cultural-political sense," Epstein claimed, "and increase its influence as a medium of honest analysis and undistorted knowledge about the European East."[101]

To be sure, a chair or two in Slavic languages or history or a guest professor in the field hardly sufficed to create a center of Slavic studies. It would take resources and determination to assemble enough experts in enough areas to create such a center. Once again it was funding from skillful HICOG officials like Shepard Stone and Carl Anthon and later from the Ford Foundation which, in combination with German sources, made the Osteuropa Institut possible. The institute opened its doors on November 24, 1951, paced by two capable experts, Max Vasmer for languages and literature and Werner Philipp for East European history. Vasmer had taught at Berlin University, then left ostensibly for a guest professorship at the University of Lund in Sweden, where he seriously considered remaining. In the meantime, the Free University came into existence, and Vasmer joined in the enterprise. Philipp was at the newly opened University of Mainz in the French Zone, but the temptation to create a genuine center of Slavic studies was too great. He transferred to Berlin in 1951 in time for the opening of the Osteuropa Institut. A financial grant from the Rockefeller Foundation gave the institute its initial underpinning.[102]

To be sure, there were problems associated with the new undertaking. Some HICOG officials were unhappy with Vasmer as director of the Institut because of his continued membership in the Academy of Sciences located in East Berlin. Like a number of other notable scholars who had been members of the prewar Academy, Vasmer had vowed to remain in an all-German institution. He reasoned that "he survived Nazi domination of the Academy, and that he will survive the Soviet domination of the Academy." Franz Neumann was relieved to hear that HICOG opposition had ceased, if only because it was apparent that the position of chairman was a rotating one, and Vasmer would be replaced anyway.[103] The Cold War was never far from Berlin or the Free University.

Professors Walter Meder and Karl Thalheim provided expertise in East European law and economics respectively. The major thrust of research and teaching was to be the Soviet Union, with secondary interest in Poland and Czechoslovakia, and finally in the rest of the East Bloc. The new institute rapidly acquired other fields of expertise, such as art history, geography, and sociology. Specialists in East European medicine and in education also emerged. The Osteuropa Institut began publishing the results of its first researches in 1953, a remarkably short lead-time, and by approximately 1957 it had acquired a solid reputation in the German academic world as a leading center of research and teaching. Its library on opening day in 1951 amounted to approximately 8,500 volumes, modest by any standard, but had risen to over 100,000 plus extensive newspaper collections within about ten years. Similarly, only fifty students were enrolled in the institute's programs in 1951. By the winter semester of 1964/65, over five hundred FU students were majoring or minoring in East European Studies. The feat of creating such an institute and turning it into a major center of research and education within approximately one decade spoke highly of the personnel who pioneered the creation and who justified the outlay of German and American resources for doing so.[104] Already in 1956, an American evaluator, George Shuster, described the Osteuropa Institut as "a scholarly establishment of a very high order of competence, integrity, and diligence. It is excellently directed and planned, and the esprit de corps so far achieved is most heartening."[105]

INTERNATIONAL PROGRAMS

As has been noted earlier, the creation of the *Aussenkomission*, later the *Aussenamt* or Office of International Affairs, was one of the earliest actions taken by the founders of the Free University, a sign of the very real sense of isolation that threatened those living in West Berlin. Its programs continued to grow in importance in the 1950s. Franz L. Neumann was particularly enthusiastic about this aspect of the Free University, stating that it was "the only German university which receives foreign and particularly American scholars with open arms."[106] In the summer semester of 1952, for example, no fewer than twenty-six visiting professors were lecturing at the Free University, nearly ten percent of the teaching body. The Ford Foundation paid the grants for four of them, the Oberlander Trust for another, and HICOG for yet another. The Free University paid for the rest, a concrete demonstration of its determination to establish international ties. Neumann was impressed with the close relationship that usually emerged between the visiting professors and the students and commented somewhat acidly that "the relationship between the Exchange professors and the students is on the whole infinitely closer than that between the Free University professors and the German students."[107]

One of those visiting professors sponsored from HICOG funds was Ernst Fraenkel, famed German-American political scientist, who returned to help reintroduce German higher education to the very fields in which it had held a prominent position prior to 1933. Eventually, Fraenkel would become a full-time faculty member at the Free University where he finished his distinguished career at the FU's center for American studies, which eventually came to be called the John F. Kennedy Institute. There were other prominent American scholars at the Free University at the same time Franz Neumann was reporting and lecturing, many of whom were German emigrés: Paul Tillich, from the Union Theological Seminary; Robert Uhlich, from Harvard University; and Eric Barnes, from Dickinson College, who was to become the pioneering head of the Institute of American Studies. In succeeding semesters other American luminaries joined the ranks of those teaching at the Free University: historians Theodore Von Laue and Hans Rosenberg, sociologist Seymour Lipset, neurologist Paul Hoefer, mathematician E. J. Gumbel, classical philologist Kurt von Fritz, law professors Arthur Schiller and Paul Hays, Near East specialist Karl Menges, and Italian literature expert Enrico de Negri, all from Columbia University. It was a stellar group, funded in large part by a separate Ford Foundation grant to Columbia in the early 1950s which now paid direct benefits to the Free University.[108] As the 1950s came to an end, Horst Hartwich, the university's long-serving director of the Office of International Affairs, reported unequivocally that it was the Ford grants that had enabled the university "to establish and improve international relations to a degree far beyond the former possibilities." Two years later, Frederick Burckhardt of the American Council of Learned Societies could report a satisfactory result to the Ford Foundation. As the Free University entered the 1960s with a much improved budget, its commitment to international contacts had not lessened. "The University has greatly expanded its own budget for guest lectureships, and therefore new funds for this purpose would not be requested from Ford."[109] The Free University was permanently committed to building and maintaining international ties, a logical priority considering its isolated location.

EXPERIMENTAL HIGHER EDUCATION

GENERAL STUDIES

To accentuate the general educational content of its university studies, the Free University created an interfaculty committee to coordinate efforts to encourage the students to become better informed through general lectures and presentations on such topics as society and politics, economics, and cultural developments. In other words, the aim was to create a plan for general studies in order to eliminate the perceived danger of educating students too narrowly. "These efforts should make a practical beginning for a reform of academic life in Germany that has been attempted for thirty years, one which has not found anywhere a concrete solution." The proposal intended to raise the scholar's sense of social responsibility. "The Free University feels it can come closer to this goal if it strengthens its ranks of professors and assistants, and thereby reduces the size of classes and seminars." The proposers used experience at American universities as the promising model for this effort. They noted that for economic reasons, German students were concentrating almost exclusively on those studies which prepared them for careers, so that the tendency was to finish their university careers with only a narrow professional or technical education. If the committee could help the various faculties develop contacts with each other, then the offerings of the various faculties could be broadened in content to alleviate so narrow an approach.[110]

University Officer Carl Anthon reported positively in 1952 on the Free University's efforts to impart a general education. He noted that the university had instituted a program of "University Weeks which precede the regular academic semester. The present semester was introduced," he added, "by a special series of French lectures, given by three eminent visiting French scholars."[111]

TUTORIAL SYSTEM

In an effort to combat the influence of the *Korporationen* among the students, the historians of the Friedrich Meinecke Institute had developed a unique system of student advisement and self-support. This pioneering tutorial system began to spread throughout the Free University and continued to expand through the 1950s. "Tutorial groups," commented one American observer in 1953, "limited largely to the history department last year, have now been introduced not only in the other fields of liberal arts, but also in the natural sciences and economics and social sciences departments. More professors have realized the value and effectiveness of these groups, and it appears that they are now soundly established."[112] Sometimes the new program had to proceed despite opposition. Franz L. Neumann reported: "The Law Faculty under its past dean had discouraged all these experiments, but happily enough the students did not care about the hostile attitude of the dean and organized a tutorial system with their own resources."[113]

Later, starting in 1958, the tutorial system was to experience a dramatic expansion when the Ford Foundation donated a million dollars expressly for the purpose of supporting this innovation in German higher education. The historians of the Friedrich Meinecke Institute were once again in the vanguard. They inititiated a series of ambitious field trips to historical sites in Europe, where teams of students and historians would examine intensively the historical remains and the historical record of a given area. This had the advantage of breaking out of the isolation of West Berlin, but it served an even more important purpose. As one participant put it: "The determining factor was the realization that the only way students can be afforded satisfactorily comprehensive training in the approach to the study of history is by means of intensive faculty team-work and a lively exchange of ideas here and with scholars at other German universities and abroad."[114] Such cooperation was the essence of the Berlin Model, and the successes at the Meinecke Institute, where most of the professors participated wholeheartedly, demonstrated that as the 1950s ended, the community of teachers and learners was functioning well.

EXTENSION COURSES

The Free University demonstrated consistently in the years following its founding that it was prepared to try unorthodox programs and experiments in order to break out of the traditional higher educational molds. Even as the new university was being formed up in the summer of 1948, some of its creators were looking for ways to provide educational services to portions of the population who were not normally considered university material. In August 1948, for example, a committee of university instructors, led by a medical scientist, Dr. Thomas Eckert, put together a proposal to create a *Funk-Universität*, a university of the airwaves and circulated it to American and British military governments, to RIAS (Radio in the American Sector), and to the Preparatory Committee of the Free University. Eckert noted that admission to any institution of higher learning was decidedly limited in postwar Berlin, and that presently no means for continuing education existed. A university of the airwaves was a logical and much needed service.[115] It was characteristic of the enterprising spirit at the Free University that the idea gained acceptance, and one year later, in the summer of 1949, the experiment began in earnest, providing Berliners in all sectors with a variety of courses in basic academic subjects. The Free University was the first institution to try this new approach in Germany.

Another convincing piece of evidence that the Free University was willing to try pioneering educational methods was its decision to create an evening division in the early 1950s to cope with the continuing education needs of adults. "It happens frequently that people who are qualified to attend universities must reject higher studies because of economic reasons and must find employment immediately, perhaps in a bank or in the business world. As they progress in their careers, the lack of a scholarly background becomes increasingly disruptive. For such people it would be very useful if they could attend evening classes in law or economics and receive a systematic scholarly education." Other possibilities included the use of evening courses for those who for various reasons had not yet obtained the *Abitur* and who could, through the evening division, prepare for the examinations leading to the *Abitur*. The Free University in proposing such a program realized that it was embarking on an uncharted course: "We should not fail to mention," the authors of the proposal stated, "that such an evening university represents a novelty in German academic life. Experience in this respect is simply lacking."[116]

The idea of an "evening university" had arisen early among the founding members, alongside plans for a general studies program. It had also found eager reception in the education committee of the Berlin Assembly. Thus, the idea had an incubation period of several years while the Free University was consolidating itself and seeking the necessary funds to put this experimental concept and others into practice. Adult education and continuing education were hardly new concepts in Germany. Ever since the end of World War I, if not before, Germans had developed *Volkshochschulen*, adult education centers, through the width and breadth of the country. The Free University's "evening university" was not intended to compete with those traditional programs. Instead, it was supposed to maintain the high standards of the daytime offerings and enable intellectually capable citizens to complete a university degree or at least qualify for acceptance to the university. It should be remembered that in the West Germany of the early 1950s the universities stood out as small, elite institutions. The mass institutions of today were not even remotely considered possible then. Indicative of the scale of operations of the Evening University was that it opened its doors in the spring of 1952 to an enrollment of only 104 students. The majority were under age thirty, although a quarter more ranged in age between thirty and forty. Nearly half were women. A quarter of them were business employees, with the next largest group coming from social welfare agencies. The small group represented a cross-section of Berlin. Thirteen of them even represented the unemployed![117] The venture was admittedly experimental and for that reason alone encountered strong obstacles from the beginning.

Carl Anthon, the HICOG university officer at the Free University in the early 1950s, applauded the university's effort to create the equivalent of an American extension division. "Owing to the special difficulties existing in Berlin," he reported to his superiors, "the Free University was forced to set up a rather modest, limited program, which would not compete with existing institutions of higher education. At the present time most of the students of the thirty-six evening courses listed in the catalog are normal day students; only some 75 others are employed professional persons who wish to improve their training."[118] Obviously, Germany's strong tradition of adult education courses for laboring people in the *Volkshochschulen* was having a negative impact upon the Free University's experiment. Franz L. Neumann was rather harsher in his criticisms, but they were directed elsewhere. "This is not so much the fault of the Free University," he wrote to his colleagues at the Ford Foundation, "as that of Senator Tiburtius who is weak and unreliable." Neumann had discussed the evening courses repeatedly with Tiburtius, who concurred that it must be a joint enterprise of all Berlin institutions of higher learning. "But although Tiburtius talks about this a great deal," Neumann added, "he has done nothing. Not even a single preparatory step has been taken to put his promises into operation. It is due to the default of Tiburtius that the Free University has entered single-handedly into this experiment."[119] The evening extension was a bold innovation, and the university deserved credit for making the attempt.

This was hardly the first or the last time that the Free University encountered stubborn resistance to change. Traditions counted for much at German universities, and those who attempted change had to reckon with resistance. Yet, the founders of the new university were willing to try the experiment anyway. This new, flexible approach in higher education was due in part to the pent-up educational needs of large numbers of the population. Although the worst backlogs in German higher education had occurred in approximately the first five postwar years, the passage of a few years hardly settled the problem. Moreover, the West Berliners of the early 1950s were still poor by everyone's standards—except for the even poorer East Berliners. The number of lives that might have taken a different direction under better conditions was legion, and the FU leadership was trying to come to grips with that altered educational demand.

Such conceptions as the Funk-Universität or the Abend-Universität were a healthy sign that the Free University was seeking to build bridges to the many elements in Berlin society that had stood behind its founding in 1948. Its popularity remained high in all segments of the West Berlin population in the years following the Blockade, and especially its second rector, Hans von Kress, sought assiduously to build ties between the city and the university. It was no accident that these experiments in higher education came to pass under his leadership. Von Kress was a happy choice as the second rector of the Free University. A specialist in internal medicine, he had sat out the Nazi years in political obscurity. Yet, as a scion of an aristocratic family, Kress von Kressenstein (related to the founders of the K-Mart chain!), he was not exactly a favorite of the SED authorities after the war. Von Kress became a member of the Preparatory Committee and the first dean of the medical faculty. Elected to replace Edwin Redslob as rector in 1950, he brought talents and qualities to the job which the university desperately needed at that stage in its development. The Free University represented a major investment for the struggling City of West Berlin. Ernst Reuter was obviously well-disposed toward the new university, but Reuter hardly represented all of his own party, the SPD. To a much greater extent than in the 1960s or today, the postwar SPD represented the blue-collar vote and blue-collar needs. Franz Neumann (not to be confused with Franz L. Neumann from Columbia University) represented that powerful wing of the SPD. Other influential personalities in city government, such as Friedrich Kruspi or Walter May, also needed convincing in order to accept the admittedly heavy financial demands the Free University placed on West Berlin. Edwin Redslob, while undoubtedly effective in publicizing the university before the Berlin public, was, as an art historian and Goethe expert, not temperamentally well-suited to the rough-and-tumble of Berlin politics. Ironically, von Kress, despite his aristocratic origins, was able to build effective ties to the Berlin political leadership. "Through tact and diplomacy," commented a HICOG official, "he has greatly improved the relations between the University and the City Government and political leaders."[120] Von Kress also worked closely with the Ford Foundation to obtain funding for construction and for the experimental programs cited above. As experiments in higher education aimed at breaking down the ivory-tower image of the university, the Free University's efforts under his leadership to build programs for nontraditional students deserved high praise. Certainly no other West German university was attempting the same goals.

It would be misleading to say that all of these experimental programs blossomed and multiplied. After a few years the RIAS-operated Funk-Universität scaled down its operations as the number of listeners declined and more of the university-age population attended the steadily expanding universities. The Abend-Universität continued to suffer from a low enrollment. Its courses were sometimes esoteric, which added to the enrollment problem, and its clientele was also limited since the program was deliberately elevated so as not to compete with the traditional Volkshochschule. Its advocates admitted that they had failed to publicize the program well. This, plus the high costs and the reluctance of a few of the professors to teach at nontraditional evening hours, placed definite limits on it. Yet, an appreciable number of FU professors made their rounds of an evening, presenting classes to nonacademic and working-class Berliners in the 1950s. It was a rare phenomenon for the German academic world. Probably its biggest problem was that as a pioneering program the Abend-Universität was years ahead of its time, and the necessary work of preparing the public for the idea had yet to come.

CATSANDRATSANDELEPHANTS

One of the more curious episodes in the early years was the creation of a school of veterinary medicine at the Free University. Since West Berlin was effectively cut off from its hinterland, such a school might cater to the needs of Berlin's many house pets and perhaps even occasionally to the zoo's odd saurian or pachyderm. Astonishingly, West Berlin still had several thousand head of cattle and horses in 1950, a little-known fact but hardly one that significantly buttressed arguments for the creation of an entire school of veterinary medicine. In reality, the deciding factor in this case was not practical demand; it was Cold War politics.

From its postwar beginnings, the veterinary school at the University Unter den Linden proved to be staunchly anticommunist. Its representatives on faculty councils and student councils were always politically independent and never members of the SED. In fact, reports indicated that among the two hundred students and faculty perhaps only six or seven students and none of the faculty were SED loyalists. When in the summer of 1948 the majority of the university-wide student council resigned to cross over to the western sectors, the student representatives among the veterinarians started to follow suit. However, the then dean, Martin Lerche, urged them to resume their duties at what had now became Humboldt University. In 1948, at least, it was a physical impossibility for those trying to build a new university in West Berlin to assemble the necessary resources to create a school of veterinary medicine. Moreover, in that time of great want and threatening blockade, most observers, for obvious reasons, did not see this specialized discipline as having the same priority as the larger, more traditional fields, such as philosophy, law, medicine, and the social sciences.[121]

By 1950, however, the situation had changed. First, the notable lack of enthusiasm among the great majority of the veterinarians and their students toward the SED had become ever more obvious. As the SED consolidated its control, the time finally came when the veterinarians had to declare their loyalties. Thus, in December 1949, Herr Fritsche, an official from the *Zentralverwaltung für Volksbildung* and university consultant from the SED, appeared at a meeting of the veterinary students and called upon them to help celebrate Stalin's birthday. The majority of students were so bold as to reject the plea. In fact, their chairman demanded that Fritsche and the other nonveterinarians, who had suddenly appeared, leave the meeting. They did so, but immediately a sharp campaign developed against the school in the eastern press. The SED was suspicious anyway since in 1948 the veterinarians had made perfectly clear their intentions to secede. Pressure in other ways built up for the veterinarians to conform to the new social and political realities in the GDR. The university administration altered the school's constitution so as to ensure a strong SED voice in the school council, and it organized new elections at the end of 1949. The majority of students replied with a kind of passive resistance in that eighty percent of them turned in invalid ballots. By March 1950, rumors were rife that the entire school would be transferred away from Berlin to Greifswald or perhaps Leipzig where state control would be stronger. It was at that time that various professors and students, led by veterinarian Paul Koch, again approached the Free University authorities for help.

Following these renewed contacts, Professor M. H. Fischer, director of the Free University's Physiological Institute, wrote to his medical dean, who in turn contacted Rector Redslob to say that a unique opportunity to attract an entire faculty was at hand. Within a matter of days, Redslob was in touch with Mayor Reuter and shortly after that with the

Federal Republic's first minister for Inner German Affairs, Jakob Kaiser. Redslob was determined to scoop up the entire faculty if he could. "The Free University has long made it clear that it wanted a veterinary division of the Medical Faculty," he stated. "The matter did not appear urgent, and the difficult financial situation for the City and therefore for the University hindered its realization." Redslob referred to the recent internal elections at the veterinary school in the east and to the possible transfer of the entire school away from Berlin. "Since one of the professors . . . is already being watched and some of the students are being threatened," he added in a separate note, "it is necessary to handle this matter in the strictest confidence."[122]

There was little doubt that politics was a central motive for both sides in this matter. The dissatisfied students and faculty who were planning to make the transfer informed their contacts at the Free University that the timing of the event for the spring of 1950 could prove embarrassing to the SED. "They mention," Redslob noted, "not without reason, that this secession, which would occur before the eyes of the world, would be the best answer to the planned provocation during the gathering at Whitsuntide [an FDJ-led world youth congress to be held in East Berlin in June 1950]."[123] Paul Koch, the unofficial leader of the secessionist group, and about thirty students felt sufficiently threatened that they had already moved to the west sectors and refused to return to the east.

However, matters hardly proceeded as quickly as the secessionists or Redslob had hoped. As it turned out, the area of greatest controversy lay in the financing of veterinary medicine at the Free University. Redslob, von Bergmann, and the veterinarians, led by Koch, devised various schemes of temporary, emergency financing with the expectation that the Bonn government would be willing to help too. However, realists like Reuter, his university consultant Friedrich Kruspi, and City Commissioner Walter May were not to be deceived easily. They estimated that such a faculty would cost at least DM 1.2 million or more, a sum that was well beyond the current means of West Berlin or the Free University. There followed considerable wrangling about finances. Given the desperate situation in which the more prominent secessionist veterinarians found themselves, it was not long before tempers flared. Horst Rögner-Francke, one of the Free University's student representatives in the *Kuratorium*, felt it necessary to emphasize the human factor in this case to the students' old adversary and budgetary hawk, Kruspi. "When I pointed out that the students of the school of veterinary medicine are now caught in exactly the same situation that we faced two years ago," Rögner-Francke stated, ". . . Herr Kruspi remarked that of course he would help the 28 students who can no longer study there."[124] Kruspi was prepared to ignore the fate of the individuals who had not yet sought refuge in the west sectors, an action Rögner-Francke found unacceptable.

Finally, at a meeting of the university's Board of Trustees in August 1950, Reuter and the city officials approved of the new veterinary school in principle. Yet, the financing would have to come from such diverse sources as the Bonn government, from the U.S. High Commission, city funding, and the already hard-pressed Free University. Each held back until the other would commit its resources, and so a frustrating waiting game ensued. Those destitute students and faculty who had already fled to the west formed an emergency committee and eked out a precarious existence with private donations until such time as funding came through.[125]

Finally, on May 26, 1951, more than a year after the discussions for a transfer began, the Free University opened a division of veterinary medicine within the school of medicine with seven professors, approximately thirty assistants, and two hundred students, all of whom had transferred from the east. The Americans had originally been willing to match a city contribution of DM 300,000 for the first year, but the negotiations had been so protracted that the U.S. Commander in Berlin, General Lemuel Mathewson, had to inform Redslob that the promised sums from the previous fiscal year were simply no longer available. As compensation, he announced that the Americans were releasing several buildings in the rural Berlin district of Düppel for the veterinarians, a worthwhile contribution to the Free University if not exactly what it had originally sought.[126] The site at Düppel grew to be one of the vital centers for the veterinarians where they could work with large farm animals. They also obtained accommodations in Dahlem near the university center. The bulk of the funding came from German sources.

With the approval of the Berlin Senate, the veterinarian division finally became a separate school or faculty in its own right on April 1, 1952. Thus, the unique transfer of a sizable portion of a university body including students and faculty from the Humboldt University to the Free University took place in an unexpected field and at an unexpected time. As it turned out, the divided City of Berlin provided more than enough animals, large and small, to satisfy the two schools of veterinary medicine at the two universities. It was also just as well that the protracted birth of the Free University's veterinarian school precluded needless propagandistic blasts by those who were eager to continue their Cold War skirmishing. Like the rest of the Free University's faculties, the veterinarians joined in the process of consolidating their newly established school amidst perennially tight budgets and limited resources. The Free University's school of veterinary medicine continues to provide valuable training and service despite and perhaps because of the city's strict boundaries. True, the herds of cattle and horses in West Berlin have diminished somewhat, but the "catsandratsandelephants"—not to mention the many citizens' beloved dogs—continue to flourish to this day with the help of the Free University's veterinarians.

ERNST HIRSCH AND THE CONSOLIDATION PROCESS

Ernst Hirsch served as rector of the Free University from 1953 to 1955. He was as important for the university's development as was Hans von Kress or Edwin Redslob. If von Kress built bridges to the City of West Berlin, the latter built equally important bridges to the West German academic community. Hirsch represented an important minority in the university community. He was a former German emigré, returned from a twelve-year exile in Turkey to help the straitened law faculty as a guest professor in 1951. Eventually, he was able to effect his permanent transfer and devoted his considerable talents to leading the Free University during an important part of its consolidation process. It was well that he entered his duties as rector when he did, because no sooner had the university gained a talented leader than it lost a trusted and valuable friend. Ernst Reuter had never fully regained his health after two years in a Nazi concentration camp, and his burdens upon returning to Germany after the war had been heavy by any standard. He died suddenly on September 30, 1953, honored and mourned by all West Berliners but nowhere more so than at the Free University. Ernst Hirsch, who had known him in their exile in Turkey, was gripped by the loss like everyone else.

Hirsch had now to deal with an altered political situation in West Berlin. The new Governing Mayor, Walter Schreiber (CDU), while hardly disinterested in the well-being of the Free University, did not have the personal commitment to it that Reuter had exhibited. There had long been a body of opinion among some Berlin political and administrative figures that the Free University had enjoyed too great an independence from the state, and they contrasted its unique status to West German universities. This group included Joachim Tiburtius (CDU), himself an adjunct professor at the university and simultaneously Senator for Public Education in Berlin, along with Friedrich Kruspi (FDP), a civil servant who headed the *Amt für Hochschulen* (Office of University Affairs). The latter had incurred the wrath of FU students in 1948 when he delayed official approval of the university's constitution in the Berlin Assembly and in 1950 when he was lukewarm about taking in the veterinarians. As early as 1952, Tiburtius and Kruspi had begun preparing a new university law for Berlin that would have altered considerably the status of the Free University and the Technical University. In essence, they would have resorted to the system of administration applied to West German universities, i.e., they would have come more directly under the control of the senior cultural affairs official of the state government. In the West it would have been the Kultusminister (Minister for Cultural Affairs). In Berlin it would have been the Senator for Public Education, Senator Tiburtius, assisted by Friedrich Kruspi. The proposed legislation would have ensured that the senator gave final approval to all new statutes in the Free University constitution, regulated enrollment levels and fees, and approved all new faculty appointments. To sweeten the pill, the law also called for the upgrading of the professors at the Free University and the other institutions of higher learning in Berlin to civil servant status. They would become *Beamter*.

Reactions to the proposal were strong. Opinion among SPD supporters was uniformly hostile, and it raised a furor within the higher educational circles. Joseph Polarek, of HICOG's Public Affairs Division, commented on the situation in January 1953. "The Free University, which is the most autonomous and progressive institution of its kind in West Berlin or the German Federal Republic, would be hardest hit. Its relations with the Ford Foundation, which gave it a grant of $1,309,000 early this year for the very reason that it was an independent rather than a city institution, would be seriously damaged." Polarek predicted that any change in the status of higher education in West Berlin would be protracted, and he predicted a difficult time ahead for the hapless Tiburtius. Even the CDU was divided on the issue and would in all likelihood return the bill to Tiburtius for modification. "In the latter event," Polarek wrote to his superiors in the State Department, "Senator Tiburtius, a member of the CDU and even now a member of the . . . Free University, would be caught in a squeeze between his chief subordinate for university affairs, Dr. Kruspi, and his associates in the Free University. Since Senator Tiburtius is not a man of strong personality, it appears that a long and bitter battle may rage over his head on the principle of city control of educational institutions."[127]

The issue continued to stir controversy for the next year. Hirsch, as a representative of the law faculty, represented the university before Berlin officials. His argument was, briefly, that the Free University was a unique institution, created under unique circumstances. It emerged because of a consensus that emerged among the SPD, CDU, and FDP to support it in 1948. It had also enlisted the support of almost the entire West Berlin public opinion. Finally, it had created an unusual community between faculty and student body, both recognized in the constitution as making up the FU community. The students especially had taken the initiative in creating a new institution once what he called the Sovietization of higher education in the Soviet-controlled territories began, a primary fact that explained their unusual status in the new university's constitution. Hirsch was unequivocal in stating that the Free University should remain a corporation under public law with its Berlin Model rather than allowing itself to become just another state-run institution. To drive home the point, he prepared a major address celebrating the Free University's fifth anniversary on December 4, 1953. In it, Hirsch repeated his arguments before the faculty and students. The press was there in force too, since Tiburtius and his deputy, Kruspi, were also invited. Hirsch rendered his speech amidst warm applause, a fact that the two city officials could hardly overlook since they "were in the first row of the audience where they were in a position to appreciate the Rector's emphatic remarks." Numerous other city officials, including representatives from the Berlin Senate and House of Deputies, heard him as well. "It is not likely, therefore," observed Polarek, "that the university's draft law, although heavily modified in the intervening twelve months, will be brought up in the near future."[128] There had been some question earlier as to whether the Free University's own law faculty really supported their university's unusual status. Ernst Hirsch dispelled any doubts for many years to come.

However, it was important that the Free University retain the support of the West Berlin city government, now that it was dominated by the CDU. Polarek was relieved to see that Hirsch had that goal in mind: ". . . it is the new Rector's intention—and he is already at work on it—to try to strengthen the relations of the Free University with the Senate and the House of Deputies and with the press."[129] Half the members of the *Kuratorium* were city officials whom the Free University could hardly afford to alienate. Thus, Hirsch became a familiar figure within the corridors of city hall during 1954. At stake was the status of the university's professors, an issue which would undoubtedly affect its future development. The immediate issue was a decision by the Berlin Assembly to institute a new retirement law in 1954, which, had it been confirmed, would have required all professors to retire at age 65. While it certainly was not true that the professors of the Free University were a gerontocracy, the older professors had certainly been prominently represented in the first semesters of operation, which had also been the case at most other German universities. Enforcement of such a law would have decimated the Free University's teaching ranks. Hirsch appeared before his own university senate and then before city officials, such as Mayor Schreiber and Senator Tiburtius, to plead his case. The matter threatened to grow serious, and Hirsch even tendered his resignation at one point, but ultimately he got his way by ensuring the passage of a more flexible law that allowed for later retirement.

The problem was intimately connected to a larger issue, namely, the legal standing of professors at the Free University. Normally, a professor was simultaneously a *Beamter* (a civil servant), since universities in Germany traditionally had been state institutions. The Free University had come into existence as a corporation under public law, in part to allow the Magistrat to create it through executive decree rather than requiring a vote which would unerringly have drawn a Soviet veto. Thus, the Free University was not, strictly speaking, a state institution, and its professors did not enjoy the status of state officials. This, in addition to lower pay scales and the scarcity of teaching and research resources,

had contributed to the slowed growth of the faculty and had denied potential faculty talent to the new university. "As long as Berlin was a capital, Berlin University had had an incomparable position," Hirsch stated
in a report on the subject. An appointment to the old university had
meant the crowning of a career. "Since Berlin leads an island-like existence, and the Iron curtain . . . cuts through it, the thought of living
here or accepting a lengthy stay is now unattractive to many Germans
in the Federal Republic." Hirsch recognized that there was a special
spirit afoot in the university and in West Berlin, but the only way to get
outsiders to understand it was for them physically to be present and to experience the situation directly, perhaps as a guest professor. To attract
quality faculty, the Free University would have to offer more than a special spirit, attractive though that was. It would have to increase salaries
to make them competitive to the rest of the Federal Republic and it
would have to offer the same secure civil-service status that professors enjoyed in the *Länder* of the Federal Republic.

In long, arduous negotiations with city officials, Hirsch by dint of
his personality and undoubted legal skills, convinced the city administration that a first-class university would require ample incentives. By the
time he retired from his post in 1955, exhausted and in ill health, Ernst
Hirsch had succeeded in raising the salaries of the FU professors and secured for them the rank of civil servants with all of the usual fringe benefits that befitted a state official. For the first time in its existence, the
Free University possessed the framework from which to build a faculty
on competing terms with universities in the Federal Republic. It is
scarcely an exaggeration to say that in terms of academic potential the
Free University came of age with the completion of Ernst Hirsch's duties as rector. He was to remain at the university for the rest of a long
and distinguished career as a law professor but, aware of the heavy demands of the office, he never served as rector again.[130]

Hirsch's crusade to secure the independence of the Free University
from state control while at the same time enlisting the most generous possible state support pointed up a potential problem area for the Free
University. It existed in a kind of uneasy relationship to the state.
Partly because the university was functioning smoothly under his rectorship, partly because West Berlin's social and political system was still
marked by an overall consensus, and partly because of Hirsch's diplomacy, outstanding issues such as the professors' status were resolved
relatively amicably. That was not to be the case a decade later when
different conditions prevailed.

"STATE UNIVERSITY OF THE GDR"
THE FREE UNIVERSITY AS A SOCIAL SAFETY VALVE

While it was true that some students and founding members of the

Free University were disappointed at the small number of professors and the modest number of students who transferred from Berlin University to the new one in 1948, the Free University's ties to the citizens of East Berlin and to the Soviet Zone—soon to become the German Democratic Republic—proved to be long-lasting and, until the building of the Wall, mutually, if unintentionally, beneficial. To be sure, few spoke of this special function in such terms at the time. Almost thirty percent of the students came from the east to the Free University in its first semester in 1948. Berlin University officially changed its name to Humboldt University on January 26, 1949, finally ending the confusion in terminology which had arisen concerning the successor institution to the Friedrich-Wilhelms-University. Slightly more than a quarter—590 to be exact—of the founding FU students had transferred from the older university that autumn.

As has been observed already, the ability of the Free University to absorb new students was strictly limited in its first semesters. The Americans, for example, had urged the German founders to limit the student body to approximately 5,000 students, a condition of their HICOG aid program which had the effect of being a numerus clausus. The university's leadership largely succeeded in remaining within this limit for the first several years. Yet, the makeup of that student population is instructive concerning its multifaceted function during its first decade. The majority of FU students were, during its first decade, West Berliners. That figure varied from 54 to 59 percent until the late 1950s. Then it began to fall as the number of students from West Germany began to increase. Largely unrecognized but of equal significance was the fact that up to 1955, the percentage of students from the east was also strong and actually rose for a time, reaching a high of 41.5 percent in the winter semester of 1949/50. Then it tapered off to 33.3 percent by the summer semester, 1955. In other words, at any one time during the early 1950s at least one-third of the FU students came from the GDR, including East Berlin. In the summer of 1950, Fritz Epstein was taken somewhat by surprise by the growing numbers of FU students who had entered from the GDR. "From the fact that the number of applications for admission to the Free University goes far beyond its physical capacity, it can be seen that the institution has gained wide publicity and recognition in the Soviet Zone," he reported to the HICOG education authorities.[131] Epstein was pleased at the phenomenon, seeing in it ample justification for the founding of the Free University in the first place.

As the university's enrollment expanded significantly, starting in 1955 after relatively moderate growth during its first seven years, the percentage of GDR students at the Free University began to drop. However, the absolute numbers of such students remained constant or even rose slightly until 1961, when the Wall, for obvious reasons, disrupted this pattern. Just before the building of the Wall about 6 percent of the FU stu-

dents came from East Berlin, and roughly another 30 percent came from
the rest of the GDR. On the other hand, the percentage of students arriving from the Länder of the Federal Republic to study at the Free University amounted to only a few percent in its first years of operation. In
1955, with the added incentive of study grants from the Federal Republic, that portion reached double figures for the first time, hitting 11.5 percent, and it continued to mount thereafter. Thus, one-third of the FU student body was entering from the Federal Republic by 1962. With the
large absolute increase in student enrollments after 1955 and the increasing percentage of students from the west, the relative representation of
GDR students at the Free University declined gradually until the Wall
caused a precipitate fall in their numbers. Thereafter, the GDR had of necessity to absorb its students into its own higher educational system.
Yet, the fact remained that from 1948 until 1961, the Free University provided higher education for hundreds, even thousands of students from
the GDR annually. What explains this surprisingly constant stream of students from the east to the Free University despite the division of Berlin
and despite continuing East-West tensions?

First, the founders of the Free University felt a special obligation to
help fellow students who had concluded that they could not function
in the newly emerging Marxist-Leninist society of the GDR. It should be
remembered that one of the categories of student applicants who were expressly favored in the Free University's admission requirements from
the first were East-Zone students claiming to suffer from pressure by
SED authorities. By itself, such a policy might have accounted for such
a flow during the first few semesters when the two nascent German
states were sorting themselves out. However, the strong GDR attendance
pattern held true until that watershed year of 1961. Therefore, a further
explanation is in order.

Without actually saying so, the GDR authorities acquiesced in the existence of the Free University as a learning center for some of their own
student-age population. They were serious in seeking to raise the percentage of working-class students (*Arbeiter-und-Bauer Kinder*) at their universities, including Humboldt University, and it was their rough-and-ready
methods in attaining that goal which had caused much of the discontent at Berlin University from 1946 on. Not only Berlin University (now
Humboldt University) built up its pre-university training facilities.
Every GDR university did so. The eight-month *Vorstudienanstalten* were
replaced by the three-year *Arbeiter-und-Bauern-Fakultäten* (worker and
peasant divisions) in the late 1940s to bring youth from those classes up
to the academic standards needed to attend a university. Gradually, the
percentage of students of working-class origins rose in the GDR to more
than fifteen percent, three times as high as was typically the case at the
West German universities. However, there was a price attached to this significant effort at social direction by the SED authorities. The numbers

of university students in those early years were severely limited because of sharply reduced resources. After all, the GDR was an extremely poor country and had no outside economic support such as the Marshall Plan. In encouraging working-class admissions, the SED authorities inevitably encountered the blunt fact that they would have to cut back elsewhere. For them, the decision reached was to limit the number of student admissions from middle-class or bourgeois families until such time as the society had achieved a proper balance, according to SED precepts, and the backlog of working-class students was absorbed. That process could and, in fact, did take many years. The question was, what would happen in the meantime to those sons and daughters of middle-class families resident in the GDR?

Aware that they faced a potentially explosive social issue and a high likelihood of frustration of aspirations among an articulate portion of the population, the GDR authorities, without actually saying so, turned a blind eye toward students of middle-class families whose sons and daughters applied to the Free University for university studies. Those less fortunate or more desperate simply voted with their feet. Singly or as families, they left the GDR for the west to make a new start. But for those who remained, the Free University proved to be a less drastic solution. Examples of how the process worked abound.

Werner Skuhr was one of the generation that had the good fortune to come of age in the immediate postwar period rather than during hostilities. He completed his *Abitur* in Leipzig in 1947 and wished to study law at the nearby university. However, Skuhr had already joined the Soviet Zone's miniscule liberal party, the LDP, as a kind of personal protest against the dominant SED, and he knew that, in consequence, admission to legal studies was virtually impossible. He opted for modern languages instead and was duly accepted. Several semesters later, in mid-1948, it became apparent that the general climate was worsening rapidly. A political crackdown ensued, resulting in the arrest of a prominent LDP student leader at Leipzig University, Wolfgang Natonek. This act sent a shock through the ranks of the liberal students. By his own admission somewhat naive about politics at that time, Skuhr went about his studies until a few days after the crackdown when he chanced upon an acquaintance who promptly posed an ominous question: "What, haven't they arrested you yet?" Shortly after, Werner Skuhr decided to pay a visit to West Berlin.

He was amazed upon his arrival to see that the Blockade had started and that the Airlift was in full swing. The Leipzigers had heard nothing about it yet! Undeterred, he applied to the newly founded Free University and, after a waiting period, was accepted in its second semester in foreign languages. Eventually he shifted to political science instead and achieved his *Diplom* or master's degree in that field under Ernst Fraenkel and Otto Suhr. This meant that he had to enroll later in the latter's Hochschule für Politik.[132] Werner Skuhr was one of many who had had to face a difficult decision in those days when the frontiers of the two Germanies were forming an ever harder crust.

Hermann Oberländer was a bright 1949 graduate with excellent grades from his Oberschule (high school) in a small town near Karl-Marx-Stadt. The son of a physician, he hoped to enter the same field. After completing his Abitur, he had begun to work as a volunteer in a city hospital in order to get practical experience while awaiting the results for his application to medical school. However, the father's social station worked against the son in this instance. Young Oberländer was turned down for medical studies. Naturally he was disappointed, and, coming from a family of pious religious beliefs, he told the hospital chaplain of his sad news. The latter was sympathetic and asked if the young aspiring student might consider studying theology instead of medicine. Certainly, was the reply. One of his greatest heroes was Albert Schweitzer. Without saying anything more, the chaplain then sent word to authorities at the Evangelical Seminary in Zehlendorf in West Berlin about the disappointed student applicant. Shortly after, he received a telegram from them asking him to appear for an interview. Astonished, Oberländer despaired of making the lengthy trip until a generous relative donated the fare. He arrived in West Berlin in November 1949 for his interview. It went well. He returned home as a full-fledged student of theology, and a week later returned to take up his studies in West Berlin. Oberländer refused to give up his dream of studying medicine, and within a few semesters transferred to medical school at the Free University. To be sure, his financial situation was perilous, but he, a GDR citizen, had become a student at the Free University.

Oberländer's future spouse, Irene, finished school near Dresden in 1950 and longed to study musicology. Two years and many rejections later, she had to admit that her family's bourgeois status and strong religious views were working against her. She might have overcome that deficit by joining the SED's youth movement, the FDJ. She had refused to do so, however, and her rejection notices said with wearisome uniformity that she might reapply once she had shown the necessary social progress—i.e., she should join the FDJ. Still she refused, and in desperation applied to the Free University. Beckoned to Dahlem, Oberländer arrived in Berlin two hours late for her interview, unnerved by travel delays, bewildered by the vast metropolis, and plagued by hunger and thirst which her empty purse could not still. Fearful that her interview would not go well, she finally met the admissions committee for musicology and learned with growing dismay that only two openings were available. However, cheered by the kindness and sympathy displayed by the admissions committee, including its student member, she did her best at an accompanying piano recital and, to her astonishment, received one of the two prized slots. Glad of the chance to study after years of waiting, Irene Oberländer threw herself into her studies, taking course overloads that might have daunted others who had not awaited such an opportunity for so long.[133]

Sometimes the political past of the older generation directly affected the new. Christian Horn completed his *Abitur* at the Lessing Oberschule in Döbeln near Freiberg in 1949 but knew that he would never study at a GDR university. He was lucky to have arrived even that far in the educational system, because his father, formerly a lawyer, had been tried by a Soviet military court and incarcerated in the former Sachsenhausen Concentration Camp after the war, where he died in 1947. The father had lost a leg in action early in the war, but instead of mustering out of the army had chosen to stay on as an intelligence officer. That decision proved ultimately to be his undoing. At one point he worked in the *Abwehr*, a position which soon counted against him under the Nazis after Admiral Canaris's downfall in 1943. Tried but not convicted of conspiracy against Hitler, he was nevertheless ordered back into the field as punishment despite his grave physical handicap. He somehow survived that ordeal, and although he reached a political accommodation with the Soviet Zone authorities at first, his *Abwehr* activities eventually surfaced. He might have survived the war; he did not survive its aftermath. Now, faced with the blunt reality that the sins of the father would have repercussions, the son immediately began to look for alternatives.

It was widely known that the Free University tended to give preferential treatment to GDR applicants. Christian Horn arrived in West Berlin in March 1950, hoping to study law. The timing was not favorable, however, so he gained acceptance at the Hochschule für Politik, studied there for a semester, and then transferred to the Free University law school. There was room for only a hundred law entrants for the winter semester of 1950/51, and GDR students accounted for forty of them. The rumors Horn had heard at home had been true. He took to his studies with a will, completed all of his degree requirements promptly, established himself in the profession, and ultimately became a judge. There was little doubt that the Free University proved to be his salvation in achieving a higher education and subsquently a career that matched his abilities. Horn was not alone. One by one his three brothers and sisters made their way to the west as well. One brother, ten years his junior, could not even attend the *Oberschule* because of his father's past. Desperate, he fled the GDR in 1955 to West Berlin at age fourteen, attended an orphan's school, and ultimately studied medicine at the Free University.

The GDR did not discriminate on its exclusions on the basis of sex. While applying at the DHfP, Christian Horn met another new arrival from the GDR, Hannelore Wille, the daughter of a well-to-do farmer from Havelberg in Saxon-Anhalt. Disappointed that her father's "Kulak" status prevented her from studying veterinary medicine in the GDR, Wille, along with no fewer than six of the nine members of her class of 1949, had decided to try for admission in West Berlin. However, the Free University had no veterinary school as yet. Undaunted, she, like Horn, began at the DHfP, and ultimately, because of her success in studying political science and the realization that women veterinarians would never gain acceptance among the male-oriented farmers of Germany, she continued her political science studies under the direction of the formidable Otto Suhr and added a specialization in East European Studies at the Free University. Eventually she became a political science professor at the Free University, a career made possible because of the willingness of West Berlin higher educational institutions to take in GDR students.[134]

The phenomenon was hardly confined to the immediate postwar period. In the later 1950s, Ingrid Vietig, the daughter of an optician and a housewife, grew to maturity in Potsdam just outside (Greater) Berlin. Like the Oberländers and the Horns before her, she had performed well at her *Oberschule*, receiving her GDR *Abitur* in 1958. A good student, she hoped to attend Humboldt University to complete a degree in pharmacy. Under other circumstances, her high grades and general competence would have made her a prime candidate for studies, but two problems stood in the way. First, there was still a sharp ceiling on the number of openings to universities in the GDR at that time. Moreover, she, too, came from a middle-class family, and even in the late 1950s the GDR was still emphasizing the advanced education of children from worker and peasant households. Vietig was turned down at Humboldt University without any official reason being given. The same applied to half of those in her class who had sought admission to Humboldt University. Of the sixteen *Abitur* recipients in the Potsdam Oberschule that year only three were accepted for university studies. It had continued to be a German custom that those who earned the *Abitur* could expect to attend a university. This was obviously no longer the case in the impoverished GDR of the 1950s with its political and social goals. She could have accepted that decision and gone on to learn a trade. Several of the young men in her class joined the army. Others entered technical or vocational schools. However, Vietig and her family decided that she should try to fulfill her academic potential, and they considered their options. Applying to another GDR university seemed pointless since it was likely that the family's social origins would similiarly prejudice her chances. Besides, the family were not well-to-do, and the costs of sending their daughter to live in another town, like Leipzig or Jena, were simply too high. The Free University in nearby Dahlem thus seemed a logical possibility. Without further prompting, Vietig applied to the Free University. So did several of her classmates.

To her pleasure and surprise, Ingrid Vietig learned within a short time that she had been accepted for a pharmacy apprenticeship, which, if she was industrious, would lead to a degree-earning program at the Free University. Several other young people from her school had a similar experience. Indeed, as many of her classmates began preparing for studies at the Free University as were accepted at Humboldt University, which was several miles and, politically speaking, several light-years away from Dahlem. Thus, for the next few semesters she traveled daily with several former schoolmates and hundreds of other students via the S-Bahn (S for Schnellbahn or rapid transit rail line) from Potsdam to West Berlin, a distance of only a few miles, attended her classes, and returned in the evening to her parents. In other words, she was a commuter student to the Free University from the GDR. To be sure, the police and customs officials made periodic checks of the students' books and learning materials, trying to prevent the importation of Western literature. Generally, however, it was a live-and-let-live situation. Typically the commuters experienced a seven-minute wait at the border crossing at the modest station at Griebnitzsee, during which the border guards made a preemptory search or glanced at identity cards. Occasionally security tightened, but it was obvious that GDR authorities tolerated if they did not explicitly endorse the existence of these commuter students.

To be sure, Vietig's life as a student was little easier than it had been for the first generation of students who arrived from the GDR in the late 1940s. She had first to add another year of general education to her GDR *Abitur* to satisfy West German educational requirements. Whereas the GDR *Abitur* had received equivalent recognition to a West German *Abitur* in 1949, that parity had disappeared by approximately 1952. Vietig's practical work in a pharmacy had required two years before she could formally make application. Only then could she be admitted to studies at the Free University in her chosen field. Yet, despite the difficulties involved, it was a path chosen by hundreds of young GDR people living within commuting distance of West Berlin. The Free University, it should be remembered, had at any given time several thousand GDR students prior to the building of the Wall.[135]

Although East and West Berlin enjoyed relatively easy access to each other before the building of the Wall, starting in 1952 West Berliners were not allowed to enter GDR territory, only East Berlin. Still, S-bahn lines went both east and west and north and south across West Berlin into GDR territory. The East and West Berlin subway systems, part of the same system in the recent past, still functioned largely as one despite two separate administrations. Another factor, not to be sneezed at, was the skill with which the puckish Berliners learned to avoid police security checks and roadblocks. For thirteen years the Berliners and the GDR police played a cat-and-mouse game, one in which the adept mice usually won.

Obviously only a favored few of the GDR attendees at the Free University could be student commuters. As Saxons studying in Prussian Berlin, students like Skuhr or the Oberländers enjoyed returning to their respective families and friends during semester breaks, which typically lasted seven or eight weeks. Students like Horn or Skuhr felt politically too vulnerable to undertake such a journey often, but others regularly visited their families. However, gradually the ready access disappeared. Thus, after several years of this routine, Hermann Oberländer returned home in the summer of 1952 to find his mother somewhat distraught. The police had paid her a call, she said, and they told her to send her son to them when he returned home. Perplexed, he went to the police station, whereupon one of the officials asked what he was doing in his time away from home. Oberländer answered truthfully: he was studying at the Free University. The policeman then demanded to see the student's GDR passport, and when it was produced he promptly cancelled it, informing Oberländer that he must leave the country within a fortnight. He did so, and for several years renewed his resident permit in West Berlin, a kind of stateless person until eventually he worked out the details of becoming a Berliner officially as well as de facto. One by one, the ties between the two Germanies were coming undone.

Law student Horn had fewer illusions. During a visit to his mother at Christmas in 1950, she told her eldest son that for his own good he should not return to Saxony again. He never did. His future wife had better luck for a time. She returned regularly to Havelberg to visit her parents and to imbibe the rural atmosphere where she had hoped to become a veterinarian. Once she embarked on advanced studies at the Free University's Osteuropa Institut, however, Horn decided to accept stark political reality. The latter institution was looked upon with considerable suspicion by GDR authorities in those days of the continuing Cold War, and she did not wish to push her luck too far. She replaced her GDR passport with one from West Berlin in 1954. Nevertheless, for years after the Blockade and the splitting of the two Germanies, Berlin witnessed an interesting spectacle at the end of each semester. Saxons and Thuringians, Pomeranians and Mecklenburgers, and others, students from all parts of the GDR, would assemble at the various railway stations of the divided city to find their way back home. Speaking with their distinctive regional dialects, they met each other, swapped tales and experiences, and headed back to their families from a Berlin university even as generations had done before them. It was as if there had never been two Germanies.[136] And, given their straitened circumstances plus the frequent shortages in the hard-pressed GDR, they engaged, it must be said, in small-scale smuggling. This usually entailed the secreting of such scarcities as North-Sea herring, possibly chocolate, or some other cherished item which was habitually in short supply. Relatives and friends of the returning sons and daughters flocked around and purchased modest quantities of the precious items. The students received a small profit, and the grateful purchasers obtained a long unobtainable item. The net result was that everyone was content. Most students were convinced that the GDR customs officials knew perfectly well what was happening, and as long as they remained discreet, all went well. They were, after all, be they West Germans or East Germans, caught in a situation not of their own choosing.

Finances were always a problem for those who arrived from the east. Those students who succeeded in attending the Free University from the GDR also received a small monthly stipend in Deutschmarks from the university to enable them to cover the attendant costs of studying in the west. The early arrivals began receiving city assistance indirectly, in the form of favorable exchange rates. They would take 80 Eastmarks to a special bank, the Lohnausgleichskasse, or exchange bank, at the end of a month and receive 80 Deutschmarks in return. Since the actual exchange rate was 4:1, this practice amounted to a healthy subvention. A year later, as West Berlin became economically sounder, city authorities turned the 80 DM into an outright stipend and eventually raised it, by stages, to 100 DM. No one claimed that the 80 to 100 Deutschmarks were princely sums, but they enabled the students to buy the minimum learning materials they required. Without these funds they could not hope to obtain such necessities. After all, their Eastmarks counted for little in the west. The students estimated that after paying for rent and other basic costs, they had at most one mark per day to meet expenses for the rest of the month. Most worked at some kind of part-time job. To pay 20 pfennigs for the subway or the S-Bahn was for many an unaffordable luxury.

However, their newly adopted city was not rich either and the West Berlin authorities expected concrete results from those students who were receiving scarce state resources. Each of them had to produce two Fleißscheine (performance sheets) within a given semester, demonstrating that he or she was mastering a particular subject or subjects. Usually the sheets were based upon completion of a Fleißprüfung, or midterm examination. Moreover, it was understood by all that they must complete their studies within a specified set of semesters or else forfeit further aid. Trust was a good thing, but Fleißscheine were better. Fleiß means diligence or industry in German, and the GDR contingent were known for their industriousness even among a general student body recognized for its willingness to study hard. In a certain sense they were a preselected group, possessed of high intelligence and strong motivation to succeed. Frequently, they formed study groups according to their major subjects and divided responsibility for absorbing knowledge from the formidable reading lists.[137]

Some of the GDR students at the Free University were not so favored as Vietig, coming as they did from remote parts of East Germany. They had to have minimal living quarters in West Berlin and a modest living allowance as well. The Oberländers, for example, helped other Protestant students in building a student dormitory near the Free University, at Rudeloff Weg 27, where they could find affordable lodging. In essence, support from the West German authorities for such students began with their entry into West Berlin and continued through to the conclusion of their studies. Of necessity, the GDR students at the Free University learned to stretch their pennies to the limit, and they found ingenious ways to do so in a divided Berlin with two competing currencies. Bargain hunters learned that groceries and meat were to be had at student-affordable prices in Kleinmachnow, just a few station stops on the S-Bahn south of Dahlem, and, not accidentally, in the GDR. The students knew of a particularly good shoe repair shop in Babelsberg and frequented its expert cobbler for many years. A barber on the lower level of the S-Bahn station at Griebnitzsee cut many a male student's hair at prices which they could afford. Alas, after 1961, weeds began to grow over the abandoned stretches of track which once had carried those thousands of impoverished GDR students of the Free University to their favorite haunts.

Once their studies were complete, the new GDR degree recipients, hundreds of them each year, went on to make their careers in West Berlin or in West Germany. There were occasional exceptions. For example, one FU graduate from the GDR with a specialization in church music went back to a highly successful career in his native Dresden. A young product of the Free University's recently established veterinarian school returned to his village in Thuringia to carry on his aged father's practice—much to the relief of the local citizens. However, most GDR citizens attending the Free University had made a clear choice. Whether willingly or not, the GDR students at the Free University had accepted their departure for careers in the west. It was the price they were willing to pay to obtain a new lease on life. Their departures also created a new social mix at the universities of their former homeland.

The west absorbed the higher educational costs for the GDR contingent, a fitting responsibility since the overwhelming majority would build their careers in the west anyway. The system worked because both sides stood to gain from it. The east benefited in the short run in that the Free University acted as a social safety valve for middle-class students and their families who could not study in the GDR. The west benefited in the long run because of the young talent it absorbed into its society. The indirect consequences resulting from a sizable contingent of GDR students at the Free University were far-reaching, and since they applied to the universities of the Federal Republic in general, they constituted a gigantic plus to West Germany as a whole. GDR students at the Free University added their own special dimension to West Berlin's frankly experimental institution of higher learning in Dahlem. Given their elementary and secondary education in the GDR, the recent products of East European socialism saw matters in a different light. Vietig, for example, while grateful for the chance to read literature from the Enlightenment and the tradition of individual rights and freedoms, was, nevertheless, appalled at having to read the works of those in the conservative, German nationalist tradition such as Binding.[138] Hannelore Horn was amazed to find that her western classmates knew nothing about *Arbeiterliteratur*, i.e., blue-collar literature. In some ways this created a gulf in their perception of events with their newfound friends from the west.

To be sure, the GDR students were hardly monolithic in their educational, social, and political leanings. Some were embittered by their experiences in the east and were appalled at the discrepancies between SED ideals and realities in the new Communist state. Then, too, many of them felt painfully the effects of a form of reverse discrimination, given the GDR's prejudice against, and suspicion of, citizens of middle-class origin. In 1950, Franz L. Neumann had worried about so many GDR students congregating at the Free University and had suggested openly that they posed a kind of neo-fascist menace to the fledgling university. After all, they stemmed from the social recruiting grounds that had nourished the National Socialist movement one generation earlier. That threat never materialized, however, after the world's most terrible war. To be sure, the social and political developments of the post-1945 period could not be assessed until more time had passed.

Given the tenor of the times, it is not surprising that the sentiments expressed by a significant portion of the FU student body in its early years was strongly, even shrilly anticommunist. That was hardly a phenomenon confined to the Free University. The West German universities were entering—or rather continuing—a long period of staunch anticommunism and political conservatism closely attuned to what came to be called the Adenauer Era. The period is one usually characterized as a restoration, as far as higher education was concerned. Within that context, the Free University emerged as a relatively moderate university with a tendency toward social and educational experimentation and political moderation. GDR students contributed perhaps a disproportionate share to that international and cosmopolitan atmosphere which set the Free University apart from its sister universities in the west.

An American student, Doris Esch, an exchange student at the Free University from the University of Michigan in the late 1950s, recorded her experiences in studying in Dahlem. She was impressed that the students whom she contacted felt obliged to form an opinion on theses presented by their professors. By her own admission, she learned to think critically for the first time in her life. Discussions and seminar sessions were for her "demonstrations that students could enter into a community of learning . . . with such widely known and respected professors as Gollwitzer, Weischedel, Stammer, Lieber, and Hofer." Just as impressive to her was the fact that the process of discussion and "*Auseinandersetzung*" or critical analysis took place informally and frequently among the students themselves. The students were intensely interested in their nation's past, she claimed, and were of course absorbed with the problem of German disunity. Yet, perhaps the most memorable of her experiences at the Free University were Esch's contacts with students from the GDR.

Most dramatic of such meetings occurred when periodically several hundred students from Humboldt University arrived at the Free University to dispute with its students. "I could scarcely maneuver through the maze of East and West German students who stood in small huddles and shouted and gestured at one another with excitement and frustration. The remarkable thing about this situation was that no real discussions seemed to be taking place; the students from the East and the West were talking *at* one another, rather than *with* one another. Each side seemed absolutely convinced of its rightness and refused to listen seriously to the arguments presented by the other side."[139] Each side used the word "democratic" differently, the western students referring to constitutional government, the secret ballot, and civil liberties, whereas the eastern students spoke of equalizing career opportunities by favoring children of workers and peasants at the university. It was impressive to watch the discussions unfold, not only because of semantic problems but because the FU students joined in mass while the Humboldt students, especially the younger and more provincial of them, tended to leave that to certain spokesmen. "They were surprised to meet with such spontaneous and genuine opposition," she recorded, "and somewhat overawed by their first contact with the Free University of Berlin."[140]

Esch experienced more meaningful contacts with GDR students who, like Ingrid Vietig, were studying at the Free University. From them she learned "something of what it means to live in East Germany and what motivates young people to leave their homes and families to come to the West." Most were not so fortunate that they could commute from their homes, and she witnessed intensely emotional family reunions in the dormitories. "I have also heard refugee students express anxiety for the welfare of relatives back home, loneliness in being separated from them. . . . I have been impressed by the serious attitude with which these students approach their studies and by the keenly critical way in which they try to evaluate what they see and hear in the West as they search for something that they can really believe."

Perhaps her most rewarding encounters with GDR students were with young theologians studying at Humboldt University. They were able to meet in one another's rooms, she said, and they became close friends. "My East Berlin friends made it quite clear to me that to be a Christian in East Germany means to be forced to make clearcut decisions about whether one will serve God or mammon. . . ." Those who preferred their religion had to reckon with being barred from higher education and personal advancement in the professions. To be sure, this was nothing new. Early GDR arrivals in West Berlin from pious households such as the Oberländers had also had to make clear-cut decisions. Now, nearly a decade later, Esch expressed admiration for the idealism of her young East German contacts and was awed by their sense of working for a greater good. "Their attitudes challenge us in the West!" she exclaimed. "They view their studies as a preparation, not merely for their own futures, but as a trust to the society in which they live." They constantly had to make the choice in deciding when to comply and when to resist their political and social system, she observed. "They feel a great responsibility to think clearly and to communicate truthfully with all—even at tremendous personal risk."[141]

Thus, the GDR students who for various reasons studied at the Free University were a special challenge. They had not been able to integrate into their own society, and there were problems for many of them to integrate into western society, which obviously carried its share of weaknesses too. That a number of the student leaders in the dissident movement at the Free University in the mid-1960s came from the GDR at the end of the 1950s or in the early 1960s—Rudi Dutschke is the most prominent example—added special significance to the Free University's role as a "state university of the GDR."

THE SHUSTER REPORT

A few months after Ernst Hirsch retired as rector, a distinguished American guest visited the Free University to evaluate its progress. George Shuster, president of Hunter College, an extremely well-versed expert on German higher education and, for a few years, a cultural relations adviser to the High Commission in Bavaria, came to Berlin and examined the Free University after eight years of operations. Like so many before him, Shuster was impressed by what he saw and impressed by the special spirit which contributed so wholesomely to the way in which students and professors intereacted. He was impressed, too, with the large and newly built Henry-Ford-Bau, the cental building of the Free University with its great halls, such as the "Audi Max," and its new library. The first genuine *Mensa* or commons was now in operation, a vast improvement over the primitive wooden barracks that had fed the founding members of the Free University for years. At last the physical plant was growing beyond the old and often decrepit buildings which the university had taken over from the Americans and from previous institutes in Dahlem.

There were problems too. Shuster admired the effort of the many professors to persevere in research and teaching despite the chronic lack of resources. He was well aware of the many contributions the university had received to build itself up from nothing, but there had been a price, too. The FU professors had to compete hotly with each other for the chronically limited resources, and the institution hardly offered an atmosphere of physical well-being. "Judged by American standards," Shuster reported, "it is cramped and often so out at the elbows that these rub irritatingly against each other." He did not mean to say that it was a free-for-all; they still retained a healthy sense of community. ". . . the system tugs and strains towards its appointed goal with a unity which is quite manifest although the several parts never appear to be wholly synchronized." Shuster found numerous examples of professors working with dogged persistence, such as an antiquities expert who painstakingly patched together fragments of papyrus and shards into a usable collection. "This is a symbol of the dogged, often magnificent determination with which learning is served," he stated.[142]

One feature of the university that bothered Shuster was the office of the rector. "The life of a Rektor is harassed to an extent which even an American university or college president might well find incredible," he told the new FU rector, Andreas Paulsen. "He carries a full complement of lectures . . . plans and carries out discussions with the Kuratorium, and represents the institution at an almost endless number of functions." Shuster observed that he had to deliver numerous carefully prepared public speeches, "and yet he is pestered with trivial matters day in and day out." If someone lost a key, the matter found its way to the rector. His reward was a mere pittance above his salary as a professor and nowhere near covered the obligations of public office. Shuster noted that the rectorship passed around to the various faculties on a kind of rotational basis, but he criticized it as offering few rewards, and it was so demanding that it could break the officeholder's health. "An American observer cannot but admire this readiness to expend oneself to the breaking point for rewards which are non-material," he opined. Still, he had to admit that hitherto the Free University had been served by public servants of undoubted quality and he cited Ernst Hirsch and the current rector, Andreas Paulsen, as examples. Even so, the term of office and the demands it placed on the individual were too great. Shuster was pragmatic enough to know that no institutional change would come anytime soon. The tradition of the one-year or two-year rectorship was simply too great to expect change.[143]

Shuster also had a high regard for the Free University's hardworking chancellor, Fritz von Bergmann, who had the often tense responsibility of parceling out the chronically short resources. The American praised him for his ability "to steer a straight and narrow path between the inevitable competing imperialisms which characterize academic life in Germany and elsewhere. The annual budgets of the University are marvels of very detailed presentation, resembling advanced audits." Together, the rector and the chancellor thrashed out the FU budget with the Berlin Assembly, Shuster reported, and "with these bodies the Rektor and the Curator wage their annual campaigns." Shuster observed, too, that John J. McCloy was "a zealous fosterer of the University, and Ambassador Conant has shown it a warm personal friendship," so that the still-young institution was fortunate in having influential friends. It was planning for its own growth well and had the good fortune to have continuing high-quality leadership. In terms of future growth Shuster was cautiously optimistic: "One may conclude that while the problems to be solved are many and the means with which to do so are very limited, the plan of development which has been sketched out by University leaders is entirely adequate and that if it can slowly be carried out, the Free University will become a very great institution, provided that the quality of the faculty and of the student body keeps pace with its growth."[144] Shuster admitted to some apprehensions about the future well-being of West Berlin, which he felt was no longer the center of celebrated artists and writers, leading newspapers, or since the death of Ernst Reuter, renowned statesmen. It was his hope that the Free University could become the cultural center of West Berlin, and he cited the many excellent public lectures and events taking place at the Aula and elsewhere to justify that claim.

Shuster had much more to add about specific programs and institutes of the Free University. He obviously ranged over the complete institution to make his findings, offering high praise to the faculty of veterinary medicine in rural Düppel near an American military installation: "This is, perhaps strangely enough, one of the most impressive parts of the University, not merely because of the quality of the work done there, but also because of the excellent rapport which exists between the Faculty, the workmen and the students."[145] The chemistry professors had worked wonders to secure the necessary equipment for their students, "about as good an illustration of 'never say die' as I have witnessed in my time."[146] He singled out Dr. Peter Goeldel, the director of the Institut für Leibesübungen (Institute of Physical Fitness), as an outstanding example of what capable faculty could do. In imparting respect for a sound body and a sound mind, Goeldel showed himself to be a man "with ideas, democratic convictions, zeal and good humor—in short, an excellent exemplification of what leadership in this area ought desirably to be."[147]

To be sure, Shuster was especially concerned with those more orthodox programs and academic concerns upon which the Free University would achieve more widespread recognition, such as its Institut für Internationales und ausländisches Recht (Institute for International and Comparative Law), led by the brilliant Wilhelm Wengler. He felt the Amerika Institut had made a good start in introducing American Studies to Berlin students. He had high praise for the Free University's desire and ability to educate so many students from the GDR, and he was pleased to see that the new university was not paying mere lip service to international programs. Nearly two hundred guest professors had come to the Free University since its opening, helping to create a genuinely international atmosphere.[148] The historians, led by Hans Herzfeld had developed their Friedrich Meinecke Institute "into a distinguished center of scholarly activity and good teaching."[149]

In short, Shuster found the Free University to be an extraordinary university for students and faculty alike eight years after its founding. "This University is certainly no revolutionary academic establishment," he stated, "but it does have a very appreciable spirit of experiment and innovation, a sense of special corporate political and spiritual dedication, and a notable openness of mind toward students."[150] To him the faculty and students of the mid-1950s were trying earnestly "to keep alive the noble ideal of the universitas—that is, of a community of scholars and students which is concerned with the whole of knowledge. . . ." He admitted that given the university's physical setting and limitations not all of its faculty were the best. There were in fact substandard instructors too. "But I was impressed," he hastened to add, "by the overall quality of the men and by the earnestness with which learning is being fostered." Even the general poverty of the students had its positive side, since it largely eliminated those class differences which had injured student bodies earlier. "The Studentenwerk, the tutorial system, the participation by students in the work of major committees, the relative freedom of give-and-take which characterizes not a few lecture rooms and seminars—these are signs of a new era which I trust the University will continue to foster."[151] The Free University was, in his estimation, worthy of the generous support it was getting from Berlin, from the Federal Republic, and elsewhere. "I am profoundly convinced," Shuster concluded, "that our solidarity with the Free University will pay larger dividends in terms of mutual good will and cooperation than could in all probability be earned anywhere else in the world."[152]

It was a cheering evaluation in many ways, and obviously Shuster held out great hope for the Free University. His greatest qualifications and concerns were for the setting of the Free University. West Berlin, despite the hardiness and industry of its inhabitants, had to be subsidized like a "sick grandmother or an impecunious uncle." Everything in it existed "in a sort of miniature" although it still carried the character of a large city. Shuster was not sure that the Federal Republic, even despite its economic miracle, could do more for Berlin, "though its industrial prosperity is real and its tax revenues both very considerable and efficiently collected. . . ." On the negative side, it also had to shoulder heavy social and military burdens now that it was part of NATO and had just agreed to rearm. "We shall have to be grateful if this part of the Western World manages to keep its head above water as effectively as it has in the past," he wrote.[153] Another potential concern was also one of the university's strongest assets to date: "The greatest single challenge to the Free University is its student body," Shuster observed. They were beset by many current problems, including general poverty and the desire to enter career training immediately upon entry into the university without concerning themselves with general studies. Their *Abitur* was, he felt, not what it once had been. The students from the east were an expensive burden to carry. They had to earn their extra thirteenth school year practically as grantees of the state, and received monthly student stipends thereafter. Many of those from the east could hardly be called idealists, having never reflected on such totalitarian movements as Nazism or thought about trying to create a better Germany as the students of the immediate postwar period had done. Moreover, the university authorities found that students from the east frequently maintained a strong reserve with respect to all authority. "It is difficult to establish communication with them," Shuster noted. "They are accustomed to keeping silent lest some ill-considered word get them into trouble, and they normally look on older people, especially those tainted with officialdom, as potential sources of difficulty."[154] Moreover, their academic preparation was even more uneven than in the west, and advising them on future careers was correspondingly more difficult. Shuster even worried about their moral health, young as they were, scattered about the city, and forced to find part-time work to make ends meet. He was worried that some of the institutional features that had worked up to the present might not continue to do so much longer. The German university in general had expected a measure of student self-help that was greater than in America, but he feared it could not stand up to the current demands, especially in Berlin. Student government was not what it had been in 1948: "Although student representatives have been accorded a most unusual amount of recognition," Shuster commented, "it is no longer true that they confer as partners or equals. In the first place, any onlooker will see clearly that although the student leaders exercise their functions, they do not quite know what to make of these. In the second place, the dignity and time consciousness of the professors makes itself quite manifest."[155] Shuster held out hope for the tutorial system that had been operating for several years, and he looked forward to the construction of a *Studentendorf*, a student village in which students, especially those from the east, could live in a healthy community spirit and perhaps produce a variation of a college system as practiced at some British or American universities. Nevertheless, for him, the ongoing poverty of West Berlin and the challenge of what to do with with the students of the Free University remained the major questions for the future.

TOWARD THE WALL

In one respect, George Shuster proved to be wrong. West Berlin and the Federal Republic continued through the rest of the decade to grow economically. This was especially important for Berlin because it had entered the era of economic growth tardily and more sluggishly than any of the ten Länder of the Federal Republic. Nevertheless, the West Berlin of the mid-to-late 1950s became a boom town. As the Blockade receded in memory, industry and various private enterprises took heart; the economy began to grow, and then to accelerate, as confidence soared. While the giant prewar concerns, such as Siemens and AEG, did not return their corporate headquarters to Berlin, the major corporate giants maintained large divisions there once again, and profitable fields, such as that traditional Berlin breadwinner the electro-technical industry, blossomed once more. The city reeked of paint brushes, wet plaster, and the smells of construction materials, while forests of cranes and construction ladders dotted the sky. Scaffolding dappled the walls of buildings that either arose anew or were at last casting off the rubble and ruin that had blighted Berlin since 1943. West Berlin became the brash and naughty city of nightclubs, teeming restaurants, neon-lit bars, cafes, and shops. The Kurfürstendamm and seemingly every other street echoed to the din of air hammers and the rumble of cement mixers. The story is too familiar to bear retelling here, but what applied to Berlin applied doubly so for the Federal Republic, and state revenues expanded accordingly. So, too, did the budget of the Free University. In 1948, its entire budget came to about DM 2 million, admittedly an emergency situation. In 1949, the budget from all sources did not exceed DM 6 million. By 1958 the budget was approaching DM 30 million, with most of it coming from Berlin and the Federal Republic.[156] That was to double again by the early 1960s, and such sums did not include extra one-time allotments for special purposes. From 1948 to 1963, official American grants to the Free University reached DM 22.8 million and the Ford Foundation presented another DM 12.7 million, with the amounts in each case roughly balanced between construction projects and the financing of ongoing innovative programs. Special American aid for the construction of medical clinics and the America Institute in the 1960s were nearly to double again, astonishing sums for just one institution.[157] Such figures explain how Ernst Hirsch succeeded in getting the Berlin Senate to raise the salaries of the professors to competitive levels and to expand the teaching ranks of the Free University. It was well on its way to becoming the major western institution that leaders like Ernst Reuter, John J. McCloy, George Shuster, and a host of other visitors and well-wishers—to say nothing of two million West Berliners—ardently desired.

Yet, in other respects Shuster's concerns about the students proved justified. The very success of the Free University in rising from its five-year plateau after about 1955 began to produce strains on the university community. Whereas it had started out as an academic community of about 2,200, within six years it went over 6,000. Steadily thereafter it grew, until it was 12,000 by 1961 and about 15,000 by 1964. Although modest growth in comparison to the expansion the Free University would undergo from 1969 to the mid-1980s, it seemed frightening enough to those who experienced it at the time. Moreover, such growth was sufficient to burden dangerously the social services and infrastructure which the university had painfully evolved from the first. The *Studentendorf* about which George Shuster had held high hopes in 1956 opened its doors in November 1959. But the long anticipated tutorial arrangements that were supposed to turn it into a German Oxford or Cambridge foundered within a few years on a lack of expertise among personnel, a chronic lack of funds for ongoing social services, and probably on a lack of tradition in the German-speaking world for such concepts.[158]

Although some of the students who succeeded to the offices and dignities in student government proved as capable as the highly conscientious founding students of the Free University, their age sank steadily toward the norm for student populations as society recovered from the trauma of World War II. The signs of this change in attitude began appearing in various small ways. Student participation in Konvent and AStA elections had run as high as 80 percent in the immediate postwar semesters. By 1951 it started to sag, rose momentarily after the 1953 worker uprising in the GDR, and then plummeted to less than 50 percent thereafter.[159]

Isolated lapses in performance by student officers surfaced. In March 1954, a U.S. Information Agency officer recorded an unsettling event: "The president of the student body [AStA chairman] resigned in February after considerable pressure from dissatisfied students who thought him unrepresentative of the students and an inadequate administrator. Few candidates were available to succeed him, and the vote in favor of Klaus-Dietrich Gotthardt was very narrow."[160] Apathy in student politics was becoming a fact of life at the Free University. Other telltale signs appeared. Thus, in 1955, at a regular session of the student parliament, one officer openly criticized what he called gross incompetence in the conducting of admissions procedures by a student in the law faculty. One of the cherished prerogatives of the students, the right to help select future students, was obviously no longer so cherished. The young offender of 1955 had not the slightest familiarity with the admissions procedures that had caused such tensions in 1945-1946 and helped considerably in bringing the Free University into existence.[161] By 1958, isolated voices were being raised, reminding the students that they were not part of the founding generation and should look to their own concerns and interests. The university must live in the present and not in the past.[162] The revelation was as sad as it was true; it was also inevitable.

Another phenomenon that surfaced as the 1950s waned was a growing contest between students and faculty over the right of student government to conduct referenda and take official positions with regard to major political and social issues of the day. This reached its high point in 1958 and 1959. Such issues as West German rearmament, the spiraling nuclear arms race of the superpowers, the winding up of European involvement in the Third World, such as the bloody French disengagement from Algeria, and other major issues produced a serious debate within the various bodies of the Free University. The matter had even gone so far that the faculty organized a special committee to examine the right of academic groups (such as the student government) to take political stands. The academic community which had so impressed natives and visitors alike with its common resolve and mutual respect was experiencing unaccustomed strains.[163] To be sure, in the late 1950s such disputes appeared as mere pinpricks in an otherwise exciting and smoothly functioning university.

Then, on Thanksgiving Day, November 24, 1958, Soviet Premier Nikita Khrushchev announced that he was resolving the Berlin impasse once and for all. The Americans, British, and French had just six months to leave Berlin, he proclaimed. Although the squabbles in the FU community did not immediately cease, the grave international crisis—Berlin's second in little more than a decade—had a sobering effect on everyone. Gradually, the faculty-student confrontation took a back seat to the drama that overtook Berlin. Thus, on August 13, 1961, when the Wall went up, the political issues of rearmament and nuclear-arms considerations that had seemed so immediate in 1958 paled to insignificance. Overnight nearly one-third of their fellow students no longer had the opportunity to study at the Free University, and the students who remained to study in Dahlem turned their talents and energies for a time to trying to help their luckless comrades across the Wall. August 13, 1961, was a watershed date in the fortunes of the Free University. It marked the end of its first consolidation phase, a phase marked by striking successes in a great number of ways. Nevertheless, the young university was proving to be a turbulent institution, and there were no guarantees what direction it would take next. The decade of the 1960s had begun in dramatic fashion. Its end would prove to be hardly less dramatic.

FOUR

The Free University in Crisis, 1961 to 1968

In 1948, the Free University came into existence in the midst of a major crisis in East-West relations. It resulted from the ideological tensions we associate with the Cold War. Yet, the foundation principles that underlay the Free University at the outset of the Cold War crumbled one generation later. For convenience' sake we refer to that turning point as the 1968 Revolution, although the events of the 1960s crowded one upon another from the middle of the decade until at least 1972. What emerged thereafter was a heavily transformed institution that had little to do with the brave little enterprise that had emerged in Dahlem during the Blockade and Airlift. From a modest university of perhaps 14,000 students in 1962, it grew into a giant educational institution of nearly 40,000 students in 1976. Its organizational structure had changed entirely. Its reputation was in decline. The Free University's "Berlin Model" was so heavily transformed as to be unrecognizable, and the aspirations of its creators and many friends to build a university of national stature, even preeminence, had faded—at least for the time being.

To an observer standing in the middle of Dahlem in the spring of 1961, surrounded by the gleaming new structures of the Free University, the future must have appeared clear and bright. The university had made remarkable progress in its brief thirteen-year history. Since the mid-1950s it had expanded modestly but steadily and was now educating 12,000 students, about the same number as the old Friedrich Wilhelms University had educated before World War II, and this for a smaller West Berlin population of about two million citizens. The number of students attracted to Berlin from the Federal Republic had risen steadily since 1955, prompted in part by stipends, in part by the Free University's growing reputation as a worthwhile center of learning, and for young males in part because they were not obliged to perform military service while obtaining a higher education in Berlin. Perhaps just as attractive was the Free University's reputation as an unconventional university, one that was somehow more open and innovative than its sister institutions in the west.

The university and its host city had benefited from the rise in prosperity which had finally come to Berlin in the late 1950s, although Berlin had lagged behind the Federal Republic during the first phase of the "economic miracle." From its threadbare origins and dependence upon handouts from the Americans and any other source it could find, the Free University was now asking for and receiving ever larger budgets with which to expand in quality and in quantity. The city itself was now a bustling metropolis once again. By 1961, Berlin had achieved the reputation of being the liveliest town in Central Europe, especially for young people. It offered neon-lighted streets with cafes, bars, dance halls, and nightclubs, one of which even featured telephones at each table so that the guests could converse with each other anonymously. West Berlin was culturally alive again if not quite at the level of Berlin during the days of the Weimar Republic. It boasted superb museums, an excellent philharmonic orchestra, vibrant opera, rich and varied theater, many fine art galleries, and much more. Its restaurants were many and sumptuous. Berlin also played another important role in Europe. It was also known, informally, as "Treffpunkt Berlin," as the meeting place between East and West. Its special status, unique geographic location deep within the GDR, and the personal freedoms and relatively high prosperity of its citizens made West Berlin a magic attraction for people from all points of the compass.

Within the cultural sphere, the Free University was an attraction in its own right, and future students from the various *Länder* of the Federal Republic began to arrive in ever greater numbers. They were attracted by the Free University's emergent reputation in a number of disciplines. The Free University had become an exciting center for students of political science and sociology. Physics and related sciences were once again a going concern, thus carrying on a tradition in the very city where the atom had first been split. The Free University was also gaining a reputation among *Germanisten* (German Studies specialists). Its efforts to create institutes with an interdisciplinary approach were continuing evidence of the Free University's commitment to innovation in higher education and research.

The likelihood was, in that summer of 1961, that the various factors that had coalesced in earlier times to produce a great city and a great university might come together yet again to restore Berlin to something like its former station despite its painful political split. True, there were distress signals just beneath the surface. Tensions between student government leaders and professors had flared up for a brief time in the late 1950s and led to an unpleasant row. On a wider stage, the current diplomatic crisis that was brewing reminded everyone that West Berlin's status was not as clearly regulated on the diplomatic front as was desirable. Nevertheless, far worse crises had come and gone before. Despite all, the Berliners had kept their nerve.

THE WALL

Outward appearances in that summer of 1961 were deceptive. Two major events were taking shape that were to affect profoundly the status of Berlin and of the Free University. They were the building of the Wall in 1961, and the arrival of a genuine youth movement in Germany in the mid-1960s, the first of its kind in several generations. The two events, while largely unconnected, were not entirely separated from each other, as will be seen below.

The coming of the Wall, on August 13, 1961, sent a shock across Berlin, through Germany, and throughout the world. It was the culmination of a crisis that had begun in November 1958, when Soviet Premier Nikita Khrushchev demanded the withdrawal of Western forces from Berlin. In a broader sense it was the culmination of the East-West deadlock that had existed since 1945. The invisible barriers that had been erected since the East-West falling-out in 1948 were now replaced by a highly tangible one. To general relief, the Soviet ultimatum did not lead to war. Instead, it led to the Wall, a blunt instrument of East German political policy designed to eliminate the loss of many thousands of its most productive citizens by closing the hole in the dike. Walled cities are not exactly a new phenomenon in Germany or in Europe. The Berlin Wall was simply the first one to work the way it did, to stop the voluntary flow of population in the surrounding area rather than to repel invading armies. The Wall has been effective in accomplishing its objective. East German society experienced an economic recovery in part by stanching the flow of its young lifeblood abroad. To be sure, the negative effect of the Wall upon West Berlin was immediate.

Most of all, the Wall powerfully reinforced the impression of West Berlin as a kind of island at odds with the ideological sea around it. Large, cosmopolitan cities can scarcely afford to carry the image of insularity, and the Wall produced exactly that effect. Overnight, West Berlin became less attractive to people who entertained anxieties about living in the midst of East Germany. Probably just as important was the subtle, low-grade tendency of the Wall to discourage heavy industrial, technological, and other long-range investment in West Berlin. This psychological disadvantage held sway until the Quadripartite Agreement of September 1971, which regularized West Berlin's standing and access to the West in most ways, thus diminishing to a great degree the chronic uncertainty over the city's status. However, the 1971 agreement also signaled the end of an era of confrontation for West Berlin. The drama that attached to the city as a bastion of freedom in a totalitarian sea slowly ebbed and world interest shifted elsewhere. The large press corps of old disappeared and West Berliners went on about their business.

Numerous incentives by the city and massive subventions by the Federal Republic have shored up West Berlin businesses and enterprises over the years, and it appears to have shared in the economic expansion— and reversals—of the Federal Republic. Still, its population, already significantly older than urban populations in the West, began to shrink. Nearly 2.5 million Germans lived in the western sectors in postwar Berlin. The population now hovers around 1.8 million and is expected to be about 1.7 million by the year 2000. Each year 20,000 more citizens die than are born in West Berlin, a statistic that is not wholly made up from migrations from the Federal Republic. Only 15 percent of the population is under the age of fifteen, whereas 22 percent is over the age of sixty-five. This is virtually the reverse of such statistics for the Federal Republic. The higher fertility of the foreign, largely Turkish population offsets the decline somewhat. Subsidies from the Federal Republic, amounting to DM 10 billion per year, have stabilized the economy and have sustained living standards at levels comparable to those in the west. However, the Berliners, traditionally known for their local pride, are not happy at receiving such huge largess any more than the citizens of the Federal Republic are enthusiastic about dispensing it. It is a national burden from which no one really benefits except, in a negative sense, the East Germans and the Soviets. By most standards the amount of support seems huge, but it still represents only one-half of one percent of the Federal Republic's gross national product. It is a burden that can be, has been, and will continue to be borne. An odd consequence of the Wall has been a steady stream of tourism to West Berlin to see it, a sojourn enhanced by the graffiti that have sprouted on the West Berlin side. Wall art has become a part of the city's cultural scene.[1]

Viewed as another kind of West Berlin business or long-range investment, the Free University shared to the same degree the rest of the city's burden after 1961 in trying to attract to Germany's largest walled city the necessary components of successful higher education: talented faculty, resources for research and instruction, and capable students.

One immediate result of the sudden split of Berlin was the loss of hundreds of students from the GDR. Stripped of its unique role as an unofficial state university for the GDR, the Free University had to look elsewhere to make up the painful loss. The result was a decision by the university's leadership and city education officials to seek more openly and aggressively students from the various Länder of the Federal Republic. This was part of a stated desire that all citizens of the Federal Republic should visit West Berlin at least once. This trend had begun before 1961 but was now powerfully reinforced by the Wall. It also reinforced the Free University's goal of rising to the status of a national university, one which could attract students from all parts of the land. Far from shrinking in student population after 1961, the Free University continued to expand steadily. Prior to the Wall it had a student population of 12,000. In the immediate aftermath, attendance hovered at about the same level. By 1962 it had climbed to 14,000, and it exceeded 15,000 in 1964. The percentage of students from the Federal Republic (as opposed to West Berlin) exceeded one-third of the total student body for the first time in 1962. The Free University had demonstrated moderate but consistent growth since its founding and was now attracting significant numbers of students from the Federal Republic despite the Wall.

For a brief time the repercussions of the Wall upon student opinion reinforced the anticommunist tendency that was so prevalent in the late 1940s. Students helped other students dig tunnels under the Wall and otherwise found ingenious ways to circumvent the barrier, which steadily rose higher and broader. Cold War rhetoric reached new heights in the aftermath of August 13, 1961.

Perhaps this pro-Western fervor culminated when President John F. Kennedy came to West Berlin in June 1963. His visit was punctuated by an almost hysterical outpouring of hospitality and gratitude by the West Berliners when he spoke to a public gathering and then later received honorary membership at the Free University before an enthusiastic crowd. The crowds were so massive and dense that public media specialists, unprepared for the response, could not get word through to their studios of the public spectacle that was unfolding around the American president. Although much repeated since—often with disillusionment—his ringing words of the day, "Ich bin ein Berliner," sent a thrill through the crowd which no one among the hundreds of thousands present ever forgot. Kennedy won the hearts of the West Berliners on that day, and his visit, as reflected in the enthusiastic crowd response, symbolized the high point of American prestige among the citizens of the Federal Republic after the Second World War.

GREAT EXPECTATIONS AND MODEST REALITIES

Various outside observers had looked upon the Free University in its unique setting in West Berlin as potentially one of the great universities of the Western World. Within a year of the building of the Wall, discussions were going forward in Washington to aid the sealed-off city and to ensure that morale would not decline. For example, American public funding went to the construction of a huge medical center for the Free University, the Klinikum Steglitz, which was designed to be an innovation for the German medical profession, putting many clinics and specialties under one roof so that the many experts could benefit mutually from their combined knowledge and experience. The U.S. State Department allocated $60 million for the new medical center alone, a sum that dwarfed the already huge public and private American outlays to date. Even private foundations decided to contribute in various ways to help West Berlin out of its post-Wall blues.

At the Ford Foundation in the spring of 1962 a discussion took

place among its influential trustees as to what the future would bring to
Berlin. They viewed the situation openly as having major political ramifications: "Among the points in the world where the United States and
the Soviet Union are engaged none is more significant than Berlin," the report stated at the outset. "For obvious reasons, the maintenance and development of Berlin as a vigorous free city are essential." They viewed
the Western commitment to remaining in Berlin as unshakable and predicted that it was possible that within a decade decreased tensions
might produce a Central Europe in which "a flourishing, democratic Berlin will have a challenging role to play." Political and military guarantees, although basic, were not enough by themselves to help. Berlin
needed a reinvigoration of its economic, cultural, and artistic life. The
Federal Republic was already directing large sums to Berlin through a system of tax incentives and subsidies. The American government had
also contributed generously through such projects as the Memorial Library and the university's medical center. The Ford trustees made mention of their own Foundation's support one decade earlier "for brains,
bricks and mortar," as they put it, to help consolidate the Free University. Now, following the crisis of August 13, 1961, General Lucius D.
Clay, in consultation with authorities in West Berlin and in Bonn, had invited the Ford Foundation to consider making further major outlays
in Berlin. Subsequently, a long-time Ford official, Shepard Stone,
and a Ford consultant, Frederick Burckhardt of the American Council of
Learned Societies, visited Berlin in May 1962.

Berlin was a city of great cosmopolitan quality, the two officials
stressed. What was needed now, over and above military and economic
assurance, was for Berlin to attract "the type of people who are the carri-
ers and leaders of culture and of enterprise and who arouse hope in the
future." They suggested, for example, that Berlin's major industries
should rotate capable young managerial talent into the city as a leavening. Other dimensions of Berlin cultural life were still flourishing and
were capable of attracting performing artists from all over the world.
The Ford Foundation could help that promising trend with scholarships
and other aid. Novelists and poets seemed to find Berlin congenial and
should be encouraged. The Foundation might encourage the growth of
an urban planning center, a center of political science and sociological research in a town gripped by ideological tension, or a Princeton-style institute of advanced studies. Yet, assistance to the two universities, the Technical University and the Free University, remained central to this effort
to invigorate Berlin's cultural life. "In the universities Berlin needs
more outstanding talent for the faculties," they observed. The Ford officials recommended that in addition to ongoing programs, the Ford Foundation should support the expansion of the Free University's currently
modest American Studies program into a major center "to cover all
phases of American studies. This will require funds for outstanding pro-

fessors and for more opportunities for postgraduate and graduate students to study in the U.S.A." This program, in conjunction with others which Ford and other public and private agencies might support, would enable the island that was now West Berlin to become "a more vigorous part of the mainland of Europe and the world."[2]

Obviously, those who had already supported the Free University in the past entertained high hopes and expectations for the university in the 1960s. Sigmund Neumann, another consultant to the Ford Foundation and long-time friend of the Free University, reminded the Foundation leadership in the summer of 1962 why so much American public and private aid had gone into the young institution. "It was a tacit assumption of ours," he wrote, "that the Free University was to serve as a pilot enterprise not only for a revival of German academic life, but also to a considerable extent as a laboratory for the necessary transformation of the German system of higher education in line with the pressing needs for leadership recruitment in a democratic society." Neumann was on the whole pleased with the university's development since 1948, which, he assured the Ford trustees, had "gone far beyond the expectations ever hoped for by any of us who were involved in its creation during our tour of duty in the OMGUS." Neumann had to admit that the character of the university had changed, however. "Its coming of age means at the same time that the pioneer days are gone—probably forever," he opined, and added, "This goes for students and faculty alike." For example, at the recent opening of the Otto Suhr Institute on May 7, 1962, the student representative had regretted the passing of the special spirit of the old days and had called urgently for its renewal, a task he assigned to the "more awakened and alert political science students." Neumann wished them success, noting the "refreshing difference among the Free University students compared with their confreres in other German universities . . . but it is now only a difference in degree not in kind."[3]

Two years earlier Neumann had expressed the fear "that reactionary tendencies which have made themselves increasingly felt in all other universities will reassert themselves in Berlin."[4] Even as early as 1958, outside observers were fretting over the future development of the Free University. Joseph E. Slater, a professor of American literature and history at Rutgers University and then consultant to the Ford Foundation, spoke with individuals in the U.S. Embassy, in the Bonn government, and within educational circles in Germany about the Free University. All agreed that the university was now "an excellent institution . . . but there is a concern that it will turn out to be just another classical German educational medium rather than a source of new ideas and reform, unless new ideas are constantly pumped into it."[5] Stone, too, was worried by the potential development and asked rhetorically: "What have we been trying to do during the last ten years? Make the Free Univer-

sity a reactionary center of scholars?"[6] If the student body had changed
in character since the founding years, it was hardly alone. "The changing atmosphere is even more evident among faculty and administration," Sigmund Neumann observed in 1962 as the trend became more noticeable. "The majority of the staff members being by now of a later
vintage is eager to revamp the image of the university in accordance
with traditional patterns." Neumann was not surprised at the trend and
reminded his readers that the Free University still smarted under the accusation by the older West German universities that it was "merely a
political enterprise, obviously supported by outside groups who do not
appreciate the genuine and independent character of the German academic world." This long-standing reproach tended to make matters
more difficult for defenders of the Free University's reformist role.
Neumann continued: "While this widespread attitude often reflects a dangerous and downright reactionary attitude, it puts those on guard who
are really interested in the lasting impact of the Free University on the
whole academic life in Germany to be aware of the deep-seated resistance against any change, and to merge therefore the efforts of necessary reforms with vital traditions of a respectable and in many way[s] admirable past."[7]

Neumann was by no means pessimistic about the future of the Free
University, claiming that in "responsible circles" he had found "a very
positive and even enthusiastic attitude toward the Free University
which is often held up as the exemplary institution of higher education
in Germany." However, the institutional features that set the Free University apart from other universities and which excited admiration were
"almost exclusively projects piloted by the Ford Grant, i.e., interdepart-
mental institutes, tutorial plans, Studentendorf, the study of political
science and current history [Zeitgeschichte]." Neumann also felt that
even those innovative programs brought accolades to the university
"which it may not deserve yet in view of the shortcomings all too
familiar to those of us who have labored with them." The special
community spirit which had been such a notable feature of the Free
University in the early days was, in comparison to West German universities, still commendable. "Just the same," Neumann continued, "it is
especially in this area that the Free University is falling short of its
aims and increasingly so with the tremendous growth of the institution."
Despite these and other criticisms, Neumann was more pleased than
concerned with developments at the Free University and he professed
to see that the university's "pilot enterprises have, by and large, succeeded and have been taken up by the university in a multiplying
fashion."[8]

Sigmund Neumann's evaluation of the Free University in 1962
proved to be his last effort. Already gravely ill with cancer, he succumbed only a few weeks after he submitted his findings to the Ford Foun-

dation's Shepard Stone. Stone had also had a long involvement with the Free University, and he continued to observe developments at the university and to confer with other knowledgeable observers. Like Neumann, Stone, too, saw both promising and troubling developments at the Free University. Writing to a colleague, James Killian of the Massachusetts Institute of Technology, just as the student protest movement of the 1960s was getting under way shortly after the Kuby and Krippendorff incidents (which will be described below) had taken place, Stone observed that it was "difficult to come to an objective judgment of the Free University." On the one hand it had become a major institution of higher learning despite its unfavorable geographic position. Its expansion since 1948 was without parallel, and Stone could claim in 1965 that the Free University was "one of Germany's leading universities." Seen from another perspective, the university faced some potential problems. Despite various innovative features, he wrote, the university "chose generally to follow the regular German organizational pattern rather than to start with new educational concepts which would have been more closely related to the requirements of German and Atlantic needs of the 1960s." Stone continued: "The system of institutes, professors, etc., follows, I believe, the regular German pattern."[9]

Stone was pointing out a crucial dilemma for the Free University that came into even sharper focus a few years later. The Free University was being pulled in at least two directions at once. One tendency toward reform and innovation had been present since the university's birth. The conscious desire to bring about changes in German higher education had been apparent. However, the West German universities had scarcely been affected by innovations at the Free University. Even more influential reformist pressures had failed. For example, in 1949 a commission of university scholars and prominent Germans had produced under British patronage a Gutachten zur Hochschulreform, a Memorial for University Reform, sometimes known as the Blue Book. This report, which received wide distribution, concluded that the German universities of the postwar era should attempt to change their structure so as to function more democratically, minimize the authoritarian relationship that traditionally existed between student and professor, and generally depart from the pattern of the old pre-1933 university. Probably the Free University came closest to matching the tenets of the Blue Book, although the university derived its reform impulse from local conditions rather than from the British report. In fact, the Free University had come into existence before the Blue Book was even published. In essence, the leadership of the West German universities simply ignored the British-sponsored reform proposals after 1949. No major discussions took place within or among the universities as to their nature or what reforms were worthwhile. The report was met with a deafening silence that persisted down to the mid-1960s, when the student movement began.[10] In essence, the Free University, when confronted with the realities of its situation with respect to the more established universities, had had to face the blunt fact that it must accommodate itself to a higher education system. It could not exist in limbo. The only system to which it could turn—for obvious ideological reasons—was that of the Federal Republic. This unspoken but compelling reason explained the Free University's second major tendency, the tendency to conform to the more conservative higher education system extant in West Germany. The Free University was in the unfortunate position of being a reform-oriented university in a system in which the keynote was restoration. The eruption of disagreements between students and senior officials at the university mirrored that underlying tension. As Hans Simons, yet another consultant to the Ford Foundation, stated in January 1967, a year after the first student disagreement: "The heated discussions about student prerogatives, university reform and revised study programs cannot conceal the fact that the underlying issue is a deep disagreement between professors and students in their response to these effects of the restorative period." In other words, a generational conflict of major proportions was now under way and its focus was centered squarely at the Free University.[11] The conflict developed on several plains. It concerned German foreign policy, especially as it involved the "other Germany" (the German Democratic Republic); it involved domestic West German social and political development; finally it involved internal higher education policy, issues which directly concerned the functioning of the Free University.

THE EVOLUTION OF YOUTH ATTITUDES IN THE FEDERAL REPUBLIC AND BERLIN

Unexpected as the outpouring of sentiment toward Kennedy was on that sunny day in June 1963, the mood of disillusionment that spread among the West Germans toward America, presidents notwithstanding, also developed with astonishing speed. The trend began among the youth, and especially the students, before it affected broader segments of the population. Anti-Americanism became a salient feature of the German youth movement of the 1960s, and it has often been seen ever since as a combination of a reaction to the excessive pro-America image of the 1950s and the profound disappointment with America that emerged in the course of the long Vietnam War. In reality, the impunity with which the East Germans built the Wall had already initiated a process of disillusionment in some circles of German society. Among Social Democrats, the liberal Free Democrats, and numerous journalists there was profound disappointment that the Soviets and the GDR got away with building the Wall without a strong countermove from the West. The Americans could with equal validity point out that the Wall, built on GDR–East Berlin territory, could only be removed at the risk of war. Such blunt realities were hardly consoling to the German critics, however. They saw the massive new barrier as concrete evidence of a splitting up of Germany, and some began to reconsider the basic premises of German foreign policy that had existed since the young Federal Republic was born. Inevitably, that criticism had to include the United States as the senior partner in the Western Alliance.

To understand the youth movement of the 1960s, it is necessary to examine the basic attitudes of German youth since 1945. Other investigators have described the German generation that came of age during World War II and in the immediate postwar years as the skeptical and conformist generation.[12] It lasted perhaps twenty years or a bit less, and was succeeded by a protest generation in the mid-1960s that disavowed most of the values and motives of the previous generation. The skeptical generation had grown up under the Nazis and served as the many cogs in Hitler's war machine. Those young people had helped to build Germany into a superpower and were everywhere triumphant in the early war years. Political and ethical considerations aside, it was an exciting time to be young and German, and hundreds of thousands had felt the exhilaration of assuming responsibilities and power in the most literal sense, as officers and leaders in the innumerable Nazi and military organizations. The gathering coalition that ultimately defeated them gave many youth secret pause to consider the movement and its founder which led them to disaster, but such considerations came too late. Disillusioned by total defeat in 1945, thwarted of any carefree youth as previous or later generations knew it, the young people of occupied Germany refrained in their great majority from joining any political organization or movement. The postwar revelations of the atrocities of the Nazi era effectively confirmed the brutalities of the Third Reich to most Germans, and they sought identity either as individuals or perhaps as good Europeans but not as Germans. Instead, they turned inward, determined to make up for lost time by advancing personal careers as rapidly as possible. Students wished to complete their studies promptly and then enter the professions in order to provide themselves with some measure of physical and material security as quickly as possible. It was, in the west at least, a strongly anticommunist generation, and the Adenauer era (1949-1963), with a conservative, colorless leadership, satisfied its minimal political interests and needs. Participation in political parties, to say nothing of political movements, was the preserve of a small minority. While conservative, it was not truly a reactionary era. The pluralistic party system functioned, and the extreme class antagonisms of the Weimar era were largely absent. The reassertion of traditional authority in such areas as the bureaucracies, the judiciary, education, the two churches, and in family life were what gave it its conservative stamp. There was considerable pride in producing the *Wirtschaftswunder*, the Economic Miracle, which seems to be the most meaningful accomplishment to emerge from the bland years of Chancellor Adenauer.

It was characteristic of the times that people looked back upon the early years of the Federal Republic in terms of consumer waves or trends. There was the so-called *Ess-Welle*, or gluttony trend, where stomachs, long empty, were sated—with disastrous results for the national waistline! This was followed by fads for ever better transportation, starting with bicycles and escalating to motorcycles and automobiles. Clothing, appliances and foreign travel all had their day too. With time, the young of 1945 raised families, became middle-aged, and the poverty of the postwar years gradually faded from view.

The sons and daughters of the skeptical generation came of age in an utterly different world. Those who entered their majority in 1965 had scarcely experienced the war, and postwar privations were but a dim childhood memory. They had grown up accepting de facto the split of Germany into two parts, and generally their knowledge of recent German history was sparse. They looked to the West, toward European integration and toward America as the image to follow. American slang, jeans, music, and the "American Way of Life" appeared as desirable goals. This basically youthful popular culture emerged as a powerful delineator between the older generation and the new in the mid-1960s. Their internal values were still basically those of their conformist parents at first, but several trends that flowed together at about this time were about to produce a sea change in attitudes among West Germany's young people. Nowhere was this trend more apparent than in West Berlin.

Other observers have noted that there had been youth movements in Germany before: in the eighteenth century, when the Romantics banished the Enlightenment, or at the end of the nineteenth century, when the first youth groups as we understand them emerged to criticize the hypocrisy and stuffiness of their Victorian elders. In a certain sense the growing popularity of Nazism in the Weimar era was also a youth phenomenon, of protest by young people, many of them war veterans, against what they perceived as a bland, ineffective government.

The youth movement of the 1960s coalesced from a combination of factors—a coming of age of young people who for the first time confronted their nation's recent past, a growing frustration over the divided status of Germany, which the Wall had just demonstrated in the most fundamental way, and a youthful desire to shake their society out of its complacency and its materialism. This meant that the youthful generation of the mid-1960s questioned the most fundamental premises of their society: its methods of production and distribution, its ideology, and its social institutions, including the family, religion, schools and universities, and the State in general. It should come as no surprise, then, that the new generation was inclined to question all authority. In fact, it became fiercely antiauthoritarian. With respect to the State, some and then many young people disputed the Federal Republic's foreign policy of refusing to recognize the GDR. With the coming of the Vietnam War, they also called into doubt the special relationship existing between the United States and the Federal Republic. In effect, this meant that they also called into doubt the Western orientation in German foreign policy. All of this took on added significance in West Berlin, where ideological tensions and the practical effects of foreign policy were always more apparent than elsewhere. Moreover, Berlin had proved to be an irresistible headline-grabber. Events that occurred there caught the public attention more readily than did events in other German cities, a result of its divided status and the dramatic crises that had occurred there periodically since World War II. Therefore, when the youth movement began to take shape, it did so in Berlin first. And because the students formed the most articulate element in that emerging dissident generation, it should not come as a surprise that the point of focus for so much that happened in the turbulent decade of the 1960s occurred at the Free University of Berlin.

For a time, when the skeptical and conformist generation was moving through the higher education system, the views of students had largely paralleled those of the major political parties. That consensus began to break down in the late 1950s over such issues as the Suez Canal conflict and the Algerian war. However, it was the volatile issue of rearmament in West Germany that aroused the greatest discussion, especially when rearmament was also tied to the possibility of atomic weaponry for the newly created *Bundeswehr*. Whereas the Social Democrats had opposed such measures but had loyally stood behind Chancellor Adenauer when he produced the votes for a new army, certain student groups refused to accept the verdict. Over 5,000 students from the Free University and the Technical University organized a protest demonstration in April 1958. It was the first significant development in a series of political tensions that led ultimately to the creation of a genuine student movement. At about the same time, a journalist, Erich Kuby, speaking at the Henry Ford Bau, uttered a highly controversial statement to the effect that the Free University was anything but free and had been formed in reaction to Humboldt University in East Berlin. To be sure, most of the FU community bitterly resented Kuby's claim.

In January 1959, a student congress met in Berlin at the Free University to protest atomic weaponry. The statements that issued from the student representatives laid the blame for the second Berlin crisis at the feet of the Adenauer government, which, they claimed, had led to a hardening of the division of Germany with no hope of improvement. Rearmament was a cul-de-sac. The student group that proved to be the pace-setter in the divergence from Adenauer policies was the *Sozialistische Deutsche Studentenbund*, the SDS (no relation to the SDS in the United States). Contacts arose between students in the SDS and in an intellectuals' club, Das Argument, with members of the East German youth organization *Freie Deutsche Jugend* (FDJ) and with the tiny Communist party in West Berlin, the SEW.[13] Most of the left-leaning members of the western organizations had little sympathy for the Communists, but they could agree on some issues and a dialogue with the east was essential if any kind of pan-German initiative were to occur. Thus, SDS representatives attended an FDJ congress in East Berlin in 1964, the first time that any western student group had done so. To be sure, large segments of the West Berlin press, two-thirds of which was controlled by the conservative newspaper magnate Axel Caesar Springer, were more than displeased by the budding student dissident movement. Springer's newspapers, most of which appealed to working-class readers, bitterly opposed the dissidents and accused them of being in league with Moscow. In the early 1960s the student dissidents were a tiny minority which sought to attract attention and notice by means of demonstrations and strong statements. The tactic succeeded beyond all expectation. The movement grew to the point that the left-leaning dissidents attracted probably a majority of politically engaged students to their ranks by about mid-decade. To be sure, this was a student phenomemon that scarcely carried over into other important elements in society such as working-class youth.

ERICH KUBY

Within these broader social and political developments among the youth, the Free University became a focal point for the left-leaning groups because of its dramatic past as the focal point of East-West tensions. Yet, the student movement began at the Free University in a curious way. Erich Kuby was a journalist for the large-circulation Munich daily paper, the *Süddeutsche Zeitung*, and a sometime visitor to the institutions of higher learning in Berlin since the autumn of 1949. His first article on the subject (November 26, 1949) showed an unusual detachment toward both the Free University and Humboldt University, and he devoted most of his space to describing conditions at Humboldt University. Kuby was above all saddened by the split of higher education in Berlin. He had words of criticism and praise for both universities: "The AStA in Dahlem, an elected body, is the focal point of energy at the University. Appointed by rector and senate, the Student Council at Unter den Linden is decidedly not." Yet Kuby found other praiseworthy features at Humboldt University. It continued to receive strong Soviet support and encouragement. Its "worker and peasant faculty" seemed to be functioning efficiently in readying young working-class Germans for university careers. His visit to both institutions led him to conclude that "The Humboldt University reacts in a far less polemical way toward the Free University than the other way round. If one is a bulwark of Marxism-Leninism . . . then the Free one is a 'Kampfuniversität.'" Kuby's message evoked angry responses among early FU students such as Liselotta Berger who dismissed his attempts to steer a way between the superpowers as long as people like Georg Wrazidlo were incarcerated in concentration camps.[14] Kuby had a talent for arousing controversy, admittedly a useful talent for journalists. However, the relatively mild criticism which he evoked in 1949 was nothing compared to the reaction which resulted from some comments he made at the Free University nearly ten years later in 1958. Disillusioned with the stolidly anticommunist politics of the Adenauer era, which he blamed for the ever-hardening split in Germany, Kuby returned to the Free University. One of his pronouncements produced an immediate sensation: "Only the basically polemical situation in Berlin is able to hide the fact that in the title 'Free University' there is an antithetical connection to the other one. It is fixated upon the unfree university on the other side of the Brandenburg Gate. In my opinion this is a connection which . . . is scarcely reconcilable with the scholarly and educational goals of a university." He offered a parallel, stating that the founders of the Federal Republic of Germany produced a title that in no way reacted to the German Democratic Republic. To have adoped a name that was antithetical to the east would have been to perform a great disservice.[15] Today such remarks would probably go largely unheeded, primarily because the Federal Republic and the Free University have consolidated themselves and have achieved firm identities. The emotional reactions which followed Kuby's remarks in 1958 demonstrated forcefully that such national and institutional self-assurance was hardly so firmly established. The rector at the Free University declared Erich Kuby persona non grata at the Free University, and subsequent rectors did the same. In 1960 and again in 1963 he was forbidden to speak at the Free University.

Then, in the spring of 1965, the outgoing AStA chairman, Wolfgang Roth, had, in cooperation with the sociology faculty, under the leadership of Ludwig von Friedeburg, issued invitations to Kuby, to a conservatively oriented journalist, Krämer-Badoni, and to a Marburg economic history professor and Marxist, Wolfgang Abendroth, to discuss the development of the Federal Republic. The debate was to take place on May 8, 1965, twenty years after the defeat of the Nazis. For students like Wolfgang Lefèvre, the newly elected AStA chairman, May 8 was an important day in the calendar of democratic development in Germany. It marked the defeat of fascism and made possible the creation of a new society. Lefèvre, and other students who would soon lead the dissident student movement, consciously chose May 8 as a day of remembrance in preference to January 30, which many in the Federal Republic selected as the day of remembrance for when the Nazis had seized power in 1933.[16] Following the precedent of his predecessors in office, Rector Herbert Lüers refused to allow Kuby to speak on the property of the Free University. What happened next was startling. It was nothing less than the beginning of the student movement at the Free University—and in the Federal Republic too, for that matter.

Instead of accepting the rector's decision as previous student bodies had done, AStA chairman Lefèvre, criticized Lüers's actions openly to the public, claiming that Kuby's remarks in 1958 were "well-considered" and that he should not be banned from the Free University because of them. Besides Lefèvre, eight former AStA chairmen wrote to the rector urging him not to ban Kuby's presence at the university. Herbert Lüers did not see it that way at all. He refused to relent, and Kuby had to speak at the Technical University instead. Over 400 students protested Lüers's decision on the same day, an indication of things to come, and Erich Kuby rapidly became a cause célèbre among the Free University students. The 400 students demanded to speak to the rector, and since Lüers was absent from Berlin, it fell to his deputy, Ernst Heinitz, to answer the protesters. Heinitz refused to speak to the group. On that same day when Kuby was to speak, the AStA leadership distributed a leaflet to students protesting the ban and at the same time raising a larger issue. Echoing the students at the University of California at Berkeley, the Free University students demanded the right "to hear any person speak in any open area on campus at any time on any subject." In other words, the Berkeley Free Speech Movement, which had been the beginning of the student movement in the United States, became the rallying cry of students unhappy with the highest leadership of the Free University. In making their announcement, the AStA leadership even left the free speech principle in its original English. They were self-consciously following Berkeley's lead.[17]

Sensing that the issue of free speech was potentially explosive, some of the university's administrators had counseled Rector Lüers to allow Kuby to speak at the Free University. Their view was that Kuby speaking at the Free University was far less sensational than Kuby not speaking at the Free University.[18] However, Lüers had followed different advice and the issue continued to fester. Kuby spoke at the Technical University and achieved another garland of notoriety not only by indicting the Free University but also by referring to the Germans as "the dumbest people in Europe," i.e., they had allowed the Federal Republic to develop along, as he saw them, reactionary lines. Erich Kuby enjoyed being a gadfly.[19] In a fit of journalistic solidarity Günter Grass, who openly despised Kuby, announced nevertheless that he would refuse to speak at the Free University. He promptly turned down a long-standing invitation to speak there.

The issue mushroomed. Major newspapers and magazines began to sense a dramatic conflict shaping up at the Free University, and most carried accounts of the student-administration split. The demonstration of 400 students who protested on May 7 when Kuby was to have spoken at the Free University, had grown to 3,000 students within a matter of days. An equal number of students signed petitions to the rector, urging him to allow Kuby to speak at the Free University. The protesting students were demonstrating against what they felt were Lüers's muzzling efforts. On May 15, the Free University Konvent, the full session of the student parliament, convened and unanimously condemned Rector Lüers's decision to ban Kuby. Lüers held firmly to his position, stating that he was within his rights, under the university's constitution, to ban Kuby even as previous rectors had banned him from the Free University. Two days later, students at the Otto Suhr Institute, formerly the Hochschule für Politik, called for a strike, which effectively ended classes on that day. Already on May 11 they had established picket lines at the OSI and outside the nearby rector's office, manning them continuously day and night for a week. Some students hoisted slogans on boards; others, following the lead of the advertising world, hastily constructed "sandwich man" boards, parading up and down as if advertising foodstuffs. Ekkehart Krippendorff, who was to figure prominently in the student movement as the 1960s progressed, observed that until then no one in Germany had demonstrated in such a fashion before. Drawing upon his three years in American universities from 1960 to 1963 during the civil-rights marches, and having read Gene Sharp's influential pamphlet "How to Organize a Peaceful Demonstration," he updated the Berlin students on this unfamiliar form of protest. The momentum was beginning to build.[20]

Lüers, with the unanimous backing of the deans, formally responded to the students' protest actions with an angry reply on May 20. Total freedom of speech as advocated in the Berkeley formula was an unreasonable demand by the student body, which itself was only one part of the university community. "The rector of the University," he added, "is responsible for ensuring that it does not become a site for public gatherings which are incompatible with the goals and the dignity of a university." Lüers then ended his reply with the warning that the student body was obliged to adhere to the principles on which the Free University had been founded. Lüers repeated that the demands of the Konvent and various other student organizations were illegal and could not be granted. The students would have to conform to limitations of the law like everyone else.[21]

Press attention mounted further. The world of yellow journalism, known in Germany as the "boulevard press" and consisting primarily of such mass-circulation dailies as the *Bild Zeitung* and the *"BZ"* (*Berliner Zeitung*), began to comment as well. The West-German press king, Axel Springer, who largely controlled the boulevard press in Berlin, was making his displeasure with the student protesters clear. Such coverage was often openly demagogic. For example, the *BZ* asked rhetorically if the Free University students were demanding that Nazis and Communists be guests of the Free University as well, and to make its point doubly clear it published a cartoon depicting a dissident student being led between a grinning storm trooper and an equally delighted Communist goon.[22] The Free University was demonstrating once again its ability to attract the attention of the mass media and in a way which its founders could scarcely have foreseen in 1948. Even the GDR press saw fit to comment on the disturbances at what they had come to call the "Dahlem University," and it must be said that they did so factually and, at this stage at least, with comparatively little gloating.[23] Far more polemical in their coverage of the events at the Free University were the *Spandauer Volksblatt*, a left-leaning paper, and the tiny *Wahrheit* (Truth), a West Berlin Communist newspaper. The more conservative and highly respected *Frankfurter Allgemeine Zeitung*, or *FAZ*, attempted to maintain neutrality at this stage, waiting to see how the affair would end. Nevertheless the *FAZ* also saw fit to publish a letter by an irate Berliner, Peter Gramatzky, who claimed that the strike at the Otto Suhr Institute had been directed by a small group exceeding its mandate. Furthermore, he claimed, it had galvanized support by "borrowing" students, including attractive female students, from other schools to spread the false word that the entire student body was striking. The inference was that a group of conspirators, rather than popular pressure, were directing the strike action.[24] Unabashedly conservative papers, such as *Die Welt* and the Springer-owned *Berliner Morgenpost*, had already taken up the cudgels early on against the student protests and especially against their strike action.[25] Already the public media were squaring off against FU groups and against each other. The well-known *Tagesspiegel*, which had figured so prominently in the events leading to the creation of the Free University in 1948, remained neutral, siding with neither the rector nor the students.

The Free University's Academic Senate, including two student representatives, entered the picture by the end of May, backing Lüers and rejecting the protests of the students. Lefèvre, speaking for the AStA, declared himself "deeply disappointed" with the result, and the impasse continued. In fact, it sharpened. On May 28, during commencement exercises for the impending summer semester, 1965, Lefèvre, in his capacity as head of the student government executive (AStA), proclaimed that the community of learners and scholars at the Free University was threatened by Rector Lüers's precedent in banning Erich Kuby. Lefèvre's action provoked fierce protests from some of the professoriate and from some of the newly admitted students. Others warmly applauded him. Enraged by Lefèvre's speech, law professor Karl-August Bettermann finally stood up and announced in stentorian tones that Lefèvre was offering a political speech on that solemn occasion, and that he and other professors would walk out of the commencement if the rector, Lüers, allowed Lefèvre to continue his polemical address. Lüers scarcely needed urging. He interrupted Lefèvre's address and led him away from the podium. Feelings had run so high that Lefèvre could not continue his speech anyway, and he left the Auditorium Maximum amidst great tumult. "It was pretty depressing," he recalled afterwards. "The incoming students were not oriented on the issues and saw my address as inappropriate to the occasion."[26] Once again the press reported the incident widely, and the success Lefèvre achieved in drawing attention to his cause was not lost upon him or his supporters. The politics of confrontation was proving effective in drawing attention to their cause.

Far from being intimidated by his recent ejection, Lefèvre and his supporters called for a special session of the student parliament, the Konvent, a few days later. By all accounts it was the stormiest meeting of students in West Berlin in many years. Not only the seventy-five parliamentarians, but also five hundred curious students and a few professors attended, filling the hall. One of the two speakers of the Konvent, Rudolf Gantz, announced that he was resigning his position in protest over the actions of Rector Lüers and because of the support offered the rector by the University Senate. Professor Werner Philipp, dean of the school of philosophy, declared that a crisis atmosphere was developing between students and professors and that a better way had to be found to settle differences and misunderstandings among them. That was sound advice, but passions were running high that evening, and it was doubtful whether many students were prepared to accept Philipp's voice of moderation.

Lefèvre, for example, played back a tape recording of his commencement speech and then read the portion he had not been able to complete. The students who were present fiercely contested Lefèvre's actions, with conservative and left-oriented factions alternately attacking or applauding him. Some labeled his actions deliberately provocative and called upon him to resign. Equally passionately, others defended Lefèvre and centered their arguments on the principle of free speech. Lefèvre entertained no doubts on the matter. He felt that as the duly elected chairman of the AStA, he represented the student body of the Free University. Were the students a fully recognized entity within the university, or were they merely a dependency of the rector with no say in the deciding issues? Lefèvre assured his listeners that he had no intention of accepting a compromise or of apologizing to the rector as some were suggesting that evening.[27]

The newspapers also reported an ominous new development. Both the far left and the right agreed that they were prepared to terminate the Berlin Model because, they claimed, the student body was not being treated as an equal partner in the FU community. Nevertheless, a majority of Konvent representatives declared themselves still in favor of the Berlin Model. At 2:00 the following morning, the sleepy delegates also voted approval of Lefèvre and the AStA's actions by a majority of 36 to 18. Stormy late-night meetings were to become a common feature at the Free University in the years to come.

By early June, the outlines of the conflict were becoming clearer. Journalists began probing the motives of the various parties more deeply, and the results of their investigation showed that the "Kuby Affair," far from being an isolated incident, was the flashpoint that revealed longstanding grievances among several parties, especially among the students. Although the much-vaunted Berlin Model had been in existence for nearly eighteen years, dissatisfactions with its performance were now surfacing frequently. Among some student groups, such as the Ring Christlich-Demokratischer Studenten (Fellowship of Christian-Democratic Students), and within the Korporationen, or student fraternities, voices were rising again for a claim initiated by one of the oldest student organizations, the Verband deutscher Studentenschaften, VDS (League of German Student Governments), to resign from all university committees —the heart of the Berlin Model—and to gain recognition of the student body as a separate legal entity. Instead of professing a harmony of interests among the parties at the university, the students should simply accept an adversarial relationship not unlike that between unions and management.[28]

Even Lefèvre found that too much. He claimed that such a move would be a step backward for the students. The left-oriented students were quoted as saying: "Thanks to the Berlin Model we have our place at the university, but our place is decidedly that of the outsider. We are constantly being outvoted in the various academic committees, and we have no influence in practice. We should simply put an end to this charade." The prorector, Ernst Heinitz, claimed that the university administration had long had an excellent relationship with previous AStA chairmen, thus intimating that Wolfgang Lefèvre was the great exception. He also denied that students were simply outvoted or overruled in university matters. Lefèvre countered by saying that despite their protests the students saw their grants being changed in part into loans, that the university was removing students whom it felt had not shown enough academic progress over many semsters, and that students had not been able to participate in discussions concerning reform of the core curriculum in the school of arts and sciences. Finally, a committee to reform the university's constitution included five full professors. There were no students on that committee.

Professor Heinitz, speaking for the rector's office, observed that the Kuby Affair had been a regrettable incident, one which they should try to avoid in the future through better communication between rector and AStA leadership. However, he also added that the power of the rector remained "decisive." Lefèvre, on the other hand, had drawn different conclusions. He envisaged in future a "parliamentary university" with a rector operating under the direction of a stronger legislative branch. That branch would produce a parliament composed of the recognized categories or interests—the full professors, the assistant professors and lecturers, and the students. Moreover, its sessions would be completely open, rather than secret as was the case now in the Academic Senate. Lefèvre also felt that the student body, as represented by its AStA and its Konvent, had the right to "take a stand on all issues."

Heinitz, on the other hand, disputed that claim, saying that the AStA and Konvent should confine themselves to university issues and should allow existing political organizations, such as the SPD, the CDU or the FDP student organizations, to take stands on issues of a general political nature.[29]

The results of several weeks of steadily increasing tension were hard to gauge at first. A greater regard for student desires and needs was one healthy development. The Academic Senate met in mid-June and decided that a student representative should belong to the newly constituted committee to consider changes in the university's constitution.[30] Professor Lüers was in any case approaching the end of his duties, and his successor, Professor Hans-Joachim Lieber, intimated that instead of upholding traditions rigidly he would be looking for reasonableness as the fundamental element in future affairs.[31] However, as the summer of 1965 progressed, lengthy wrap-up articles appeared in major papers, such as the *Süddeutsche Zeitung* and *Die Welt*, which indicated uncertainty about the future of the Free University. For example, the liberally inclined *Süddeutsche Zeitung* observed that the main actors in the confrontation, the AStA students and Rector Lüers, were so impassioned "that on all sides they fear that an end is coming to that experiment which had begun in 1948 with such élan and goodwill. They fear, not without reason, that Germany's 'community of teachers and learners' at the Free University will sooner or later disintegrate." The South German paper expressed the almost pious hope that despite inflamed passions somehow reasonableness would ultimately prevail "not only among the students," a not-so-subtle slap at Professor Lüers's unsubtle handling of the affair.[32]

In the more conservative camp, *Die Welt* pointedly referred to the leftist students on the AStA, whom they identified primarily as SDS adherents, as too far left to belong to any of the major political parties. They were *"Frondeurs"* or leaders of a fight against central authority who eschewed any moderate goals or demands. Furthermore, they consisted of only 100 to 150 highly committed individuals whose persistence and demagogic tactics enabled them to influence far larger numbers of less involved students. In other words, there was a conspiracy afoot. In any case it appeared to observers in the conservative camp that the Free University was in for a long period of convulsion and troubled times. That prediction was entirely justified.[33] A curiously mild denouement to the Kuby Affair occurred when Lüers and Kuby communicated directly with each other, composed their differences, and the latter spoke at the Auditorium Maximum in the autumn of 1965, to a Protestant student organization. Considering the inflamed opinions that had ensued from enforcing the ban, it seems in retrospect a pity that Lüers and Kuby could not have produced an amicable accord several months earlier. Nevertheless, the Kuby Affair was hardly the cause of the dissident student movement. Rather, it was symptomatic of a deeper malaise that was soon to make itself widely felt.[34]

THE FRATERNITIES' LAST HURRAH

If there had been provocations on the left, there were also provocations to be seen on the right. One reason why Rector Lüers had acquired notoriety in the eyes of the left-leaning students was his attendance at a banquet in June 1965 celebrating a century and a half of the *Burschenschaften*, the student fraternities. By the early 1960s the student fraternities had grown to 50,000 members, a respectable showing considering that there were less than 300,000 students attending German universities in toto. Matters had reached a head at the Free University in 1963 when the Konvent, temporarily dominated by conservative-inclined students, had elected a fraternity member, Eberhard Diepgen, as chairman of the AStA. Although the Free University had been forced by the laws of the Federal Republic to repeal its ban on fraternity membership, a majority of the FU community, students and faculty alike, still distrusted and disapproved of them. This fundamental fact was amply borne out once Diepgen's fraternity connection became known. Opponents of Diepgen's elevation to such high student office forced a referendum, in which no less than 72 percent of the student body voted. Diepgen was voted out of office, and the Konvent which had elected him was dissolved. The seeming victory of the fraternities at the Free University had been short-lived. Scarcely two years later, the fraternities held their national banquet in Berlin, and among those attending that gala event were Rector Lüers and conservative law professor Karl-August Bettermann, who had found Lefèvre's commencement address so unpalatable. The widely reported speeches appeared provocative to many students, especially those arrayed on the left. Bettermann referred to the controversy over Kuby and declared: "As long as you have had the words honor, freedom, and Fatherland emblazoned on your banners, you cannot expect that all students or the majority of the population will praise those words." Bettermann referred specifically to the recent demonstrations at the Free University and challenged his student listeners: "I call upon you in this hour to help us create the proper working climate at this University once again and to prevent the honor of this University from being endangered. . . . Prepare a new beginning; bring our University back to order. In this sense of the word I call upon you: Turn out lads!"[35] Those were strong words, and in Germany the associations between the fraternities of old and excessive nationalism were still strong. Many on the left felt that Bettermann's remarks were tantamount to the calling out of storm troopers into the street. It need hardly be said that no such event occurred. Nevertheless, the suspicion of the student left was aroused by such provocative remarks. Former student representatives in the FU Academic Senate also wrote to Rector Lüers to protest his presence at the fraternity banquet.³⁶ Divisions and suspicions within the student body deepened.

EKKEHART KRIPPENDORFF

As the conflict over Erich Kuby was still simmering and worries about the fraternities were acute, another incident occurred which led to ever greater tensions at the Free University. In mid-May, 1965, when students were demonstrating at the Otto Suhr Institute, a young assistant for political science at the OSI, Ekkehart Krippendorff, fired off a broadside in one of Berlin's left-leaning newspapers, the *Spandauer Volksblatt*. Krippendorff had returned from a three-year sojourn to Harvard, Yale, and Columbia universities, where he had discovered that some leading personalities in his field, such as Max Lerner, contributed regular columns in local newspapers. Impressed by this practical experience and dismayed at the conservative influence of the powerful Springer papers in Berlin, he now wrote his own column for the tiny liberal daily in Spandau.³⁷ On this occasion he appealed to the public to help maintain freedom of expression, rather than leaving that task solely to the students at the Free University. He saw that basic democratic principle as being threatened by Rector Lüers's actions. "From what we have heard, even the prominent scholar Karl Jaspers could not speak at this Free University or rather he could not be invited because the Rector did not agree with his viewpoint on the German Question."³⁸ Krippendorff had received that information from an assistant who worked under Professor Sontheimer. The occasion was to have been the same twentieth anniversary of the end of the war in Europe. Krippendorff's action was unprecedented. A young, untenured lecturer was publicly criticizing the highest official at his university.

This extraordinary act drew an extraordinary response. First, Krippendorff, who in the meantime had received further information about the affair, amended his statement about Lüers five days later in a five-line retraction notice. "This information was, as I have learned in the meantime, false," he stated to his readership. "Professor Jaspers was unable to accept this invitation because of health reasons."³⁹ Lüers was hardly mollified. A few days later he sent a stinging reply to the same paper, explaining that the invitation to Jaspers had originated with Professor Kurt Sontheimer in his capacity as an official of the FU Senate. Lüers then quoted Jaspers's reply in which the famed philosopher had cited his delicate health as the reason for turning down the invitation. The rector concluded his letter with a heavy rebuke to Krippendorff: "Such accusations, made without journalistic thoroughness, rob a reporter of his credibility."

Nor was Lüers content to let matters rest there. In a letter to the young assistant he demanded a written explanation, indicating that this would help the rector decide the fate of Krippendorff's contract with the Free University which would soon be up for renewal. Obviously shaken, Krippendorff replied with a stout apology, indicating that he had erred badly in publishing unsubstantiated information and indicating that Professor Sontheimer too had rebuked him for his rash pronouncement. Krippendorff begged for forgiveness.[40] Lüers was not moved and called instead for nonrenewal of Krippendorff's contract. Krippendorff, a budding scholar, had the obligation to get the facts right, Lüers maintained, and had to be properly informed before penning so public a criticism rather than afterward when the harm had already been done. Lüers concluded: ". . . your conduct is incompatible with your contractual duties. In consequence a working relationship is sufficiently impaired that trust and cooperation cannot be expected and cannot be assumed on the part of the Free University."[41]

Coming hard on the heels of the Kuby Affair, this new "Krippendorff Affair" brought renewed tensions just as the dust had begun to settle on the earlier incident. This time the reactions were quicker and, if anything, even more intense. Several professors, including Krippendorff's immediate superior, Gilbert Ziebura, publicly criticized the harshness of Krippendorff's fate. Another faculty member at the OSI, Professor Otto Heinrich von der Gablentz, went even farther. He addressed the Konvent in mid-July and accused Lüers of taking too legalistic a view in such cases and of ignoring the spirit that was supposed to bind all members of the Free University into the much desired "community of teachers and learners." Krippendorff observed much later that von der Gablentz had held no sympathy with his own views whatsoever, being, in his opinion, an old-fashioned Prussian conservative. But in this instance his sense of propriety was outraged, since Rector Lüers had bypassed him, the OSI's director, in his haste to punish Krippendorff.[42] For good measure, von der Gablentz also stated that even more professors might have protested Rector Lüers's actions had it not been for his imminent departure from the rectorship. "The relation of trust toward the present rector," he added, "has been tested to the limits by this and other instances." He also claimed that the incidents were embarrassing to the Free University and were hurting its credibility among the public.[43] His pronouncements produced a strong reaction among faculty supporters of Lüers, and feelings ran so high that von der Gablentz actually initiated disciplinary proceedings against himself in order to push matters to a head. Several weeks later he retracted his strongest statements on the matter, and the disciplinary action was quietly dropped.[44] Nevertheless, the affair demonstrated that the troubles brewing at the Free Univeristy were not drawn purely along generational lines.

The conflict was further complicated by the fact that tensions now existed between Sontheimer and Lüers, with the latter dissatisfied that Sontheimer had invited Jaspers to speak without consulting the Academic Senate beforehand. If the strains crossed generational lines, they also existed within the ranks of the faculty. Lüers's position was weakened somewhat by Sontheimer's revelation to the press of a letter the rector had sent him the previous March condemning Sontheimer's invitation to Jaspers. "The Academic Senate takes special offense," he wrote Sontheimer, "that you had already begun correspondence with prominent individuals in order to invite them without the approval or even the knowledge of the appropriate authorities, namely the Rector and the Academic Senate." Lüers noted that Jaspers had forestalled further embarrassment by rejecting the invitation. Besides, the Academic Senate in debating the issue of commemorating Germany's defeat maintained that January 30 (the day the Nazis seized power in 1933) might be the more appropriate date for reflection upon Germany's unhappy past. Consequently, the Academic Senate decided that the Free University was not celebrating May 8 at all. Lüers continued: "The Academic Senate announced too that in the instance where an acceptance had occurred, it would have resolved the impasse by empowering me to rescind the invitation with all due circumspection."[45]

It remained for the reader to interpret the evidence as to whether Rector Lüers was objecting to Sontheimer's headstrong actions or to the desirability of having Jaspers speak at all. And indeed, the various political groups squared off, each choosing to interpret the letter in its own way. A student, Knut Nevermann, spoke directly with Jaspers by phone and asked him bluntly if anyone at the Free University had disinvited him. The aged Jaspers would not answer the question, Nevermann recalled.[46] The confrontation continued. Krippendorff, not unexpectedly, felt that the tardy publication of Lüers's letter to Sontheimer confirmed his original suspicions about the conservative rector, and he was privately furious with Sontheimer for not publishing it sooner.[47]

For his part, Sontheimer suggested publicly that the case hardly provided a precedent for the principle of freedom of speech in the Federal Republic. A cultural commentator for the prestigious weekly Die Zeit differed. For him the Krippendorff Affair was a "test case of what we in this country consider to be democracy: the right to say yes or the right to criticize," and he hinted strongly that Lüers had sought to prevent an appearance by Jaspers because of political motives.[48] Sontheimer, unwilling to let that judgment rest, replied several weeks later that "there is not the slightest reason to assume that Rector and Senate would have cancelled Jaspers's invitation because of the stated motive."[49] Thus, no clear decision emerged.

Yet, in this second confrontation in as many months, a recognizable pattern emerged. Students began to organize protest actions once again, and at a meeting of the student body as a whole in mid-July they boldly called for Rector Lüers's resignation, an unheard-of action at the Free University up to that time. Lüers simply ingnored the suggestion.[50] A large majority of the Academic Senate, contrary to von der Gablentz's claims, backed Rector Lüers once again. However, six professors declared in an open letter to the entire FU community their disapproval of the way the university's leadership had handled the crisis, thus reinforcing the impression that the faculty were by no means solidly joined on the handling of the issue. Student groups such as SDS renewed their picketing and made preparations for a possible strike. One eyewitness to these events, Uwe Schlicht, a *Tagesspiegel* reporter and former FU student, reported that leaflets and flyers distributed by the student groups were significantly increasing tensions. Another, older member of the university community, Wilhelm Wengler, commented angrily that student actions of this type were beginning to be a permanent feature at the Free University. He claimed that the current trouble stemmed from a chronic woe among the students. They wanted to take positions on all manner of social and political issues which they could not possibly influence.[51] Wengler had retained his suspicion of student involvement in university governance. Even as they had done earlier, some individuals, such as student government representative Peter Müller, proclaimed the death of the Berlin Model because of the imbalance between the powerful professoriate and the palpable weakness of the students.

One reporter cited Müller as claiming that after the experiences of that semester, the goal of the Berlin students must be to push for a change in the university's constitution because the Berlin Model no longer functioned.[52] The students then marched a short distance to the rector's office and held a half-hour silent protest.

By this time the atmosphere had become sufficiently charged that an ominous new development emerged. On July 22, 1965, Professor Rudolf Schilcher, an economist and dean of the Free University's school of economics and social sciences, announced that he was transferring to the brand new university at Bochum in the Ruhr. "I cannot continue to work at the FU under the present conditions," he explained. "The possibility of accomplishing scholarly work does not exist any more given the actions of the AStA, Konvent, several student groups, and some professors. The atmosphere is too poisoned." He also predicted that professor-candidates from elsewhere would be unlikely to take positions at the Free University for the same reason.[53] Schilcher became the first of a long line of professors who in the coming years would abandon the Free University for greener—or at least calmer—pastures.

Otto Hess, director of the Colloquium Verlag (Colloquium Press) in Berlin and still a close observer of the Free University, publicly expressed his views too. The student body at the Free University and elsewhere had become so apolitical, Hess claimed, that it was possible for a group of 150 determined people to succeed easily in gaining the upper hand. "Those of us who founded this University are disappointed with its subsequent development," Hess stated. "The indivisible community of teachers and learners, of university and life, this great opportunity which existed at the beginning has been played out."[54]

Berlin's Senator for Higher Education and the Arts, Werner Stein, felt compelled to examine the controversies wracking the Free University and after speaking to Lüers, to the professors, and to student government leaders sent letters both to the Academic Senate and to the AStA urging them to resolve their differences in order to save their common institution from further harm. They should do so, he wrote, because "a continuation of the disturbances could as a consequence make the intercession of the State necessary."[55] Seen in retrospect, this was a development of considerable importance because it marked the first instance in which political leaders from the City of Berlin felt compelled publicly to intervene in the internal affairs of the Free University. Senator Stein began quietly working out a new university law for the Free University, which, because of the unpopularity of such a move and because his boss, Mayor Willy Brandt, wanted to avoid undue controversy at a time when the SPD might be able to enter the Bonn government for the first time, remained strictly unofficial. Two years later, in the summer of 1967, Stein unveiled his draft university law, but under radically different conditions to be described shortly.[56]

Even before Stein's intercession, Lüers had pulled his punch to the extent that he had allowed Krippendorff to receive a study grant for his habilitation, his next research project after the Ph.D. and leading possibly to a professorship. In explaining his justification for recommending Krippendorff for such a generous fellowship, Lüers remarked that "the generosity of the stipend should be extended to the point that he (Krippendorff) will not feel compelled to take up other part-time jobs as has been the case so far."[57] Presumably that category included part-time journalism! It was a sensible compromise matched by a refreshing expression of humor. Alas, by the summer of 1965, compromise and the light touch had come too little and too late to stem the growing crisis.

Following its experiences with Erich Kuby and Ekkehart Krippendorff, the Free University had developed within weeks from an apparently normally functioning urban university into a crisis-ridden institution whose very basis was being questioned. It had happened in so short a time because the two incidents were symptomatic of longstanding strains, growing differences of opinion in politics and social issues, and sharply differing perceptions on the functioning of a university. These strains had surfaced periodically in the past. The Brandt-Wengler controversy of 1949 and more recently the antinuclear stance of the student body in 1958 had broken the outward calm. However, those differences had been overcome somehow, with one party or another giving way or a compromise being effected. By the summer of 1965, however, it became obvious that the fundamental social and political position of influential groups of students had changed. Some of the university's ablest students, who were simultaneously its student body leaders, had demonstrated that they were not prepared to accept decisions made by the rector or by the Academic Senate. The generation gap that was in the process of gripping most of the Western world had now struck the Free University with a vengeance. Until 1965 the university had been recognizably the same institution as the one founded seventeen years earlier. After 1965 it entered a prolonged crisis which was to affect profoundly its organization, its nature, its size, and its reputation. The Free University had been born in crisis and had then settled into a relatively quiet consolidation stage; now it had come full circle to another crisis and, as in 1948, it emerged from that trauma an utterly transformed institution.

By coincidence, the Free University was about to go to press with a book summarizing its development since 1948. The contribution by a student, Wolfgang Juche, on student government at the Free University caused considerable discomfort among the representatives on the University Senate. In essence, Juche's point was that "student government has been stripped of a number of its functions." Student representatives were in office too short a time to maintain any continuity and were significantly less informed on developments than was the university administration, according to Juche. "The attitude of a number of professors, who are for a separation of the so-called student matters from the university affairs, helps to restrict the responsibility of the students."[58] Perhaps even more controversial was the student's claim that the student body, through its representatives on the AStA and Konvent, was entitled to exercise a general political mandate. "Whoever contests the right of the student adminstration to take a stand on political issues destroys its basis," Juche announced. He also proclaimed that an important function of the FU AStA was to "promote a sense of civic responsibility" among the students by exposing them to current political issues. "Prominent politicians and scholars from throughout the political spectrum are invited to discuss current issues with the students," he added.[59]

Even so, the events of 1965 demonstrated clearly that the dissident students belonged to a small minority at first—Otto Hess had suggested that they amounted to only 150 young people. Many of the newspapers covering the events printed readers' letters, including, significantly, contributions by fellow students, condemning the confrontational tone of the AStA leadership and calling for moderation. At the same time that controversy centered upon Kuby and Krippendorff, other, lesser disagreements arose which indicated a growing political rift between old and young, left and right. For example, when word reached the press that some students were organizing a series of lectures by academicians from East Berlin's Humboldt University, to be held at the Free University's Student Village, a howl went up in the West Berlin press. Even Giesela May, a gifted East Berlin chanteuse and singer of Brecht/Weill songs in the Lotte Lenya tradition, stirred controversy with her public appearances in Dahlem. The conservative-oriented press was also quick to note that leading dissident voices, such as Wolfgang Lefèvre, Peter Müller, and others, were simultaneously members of political organizations almost exclusively grouped on what came to be called the New Left. Foremost among these youth political organizations was the *Sozialistische Deutsche Studentenbund* (SDS). There were other left-wing student groups as well, such as the *Sozialistische Deutsche Hochschulbund* (German Socialist University League, or SHB), the *Liberale Studentenbund Deutschlands* (League of Liberal German Students), and the *Evangelische Studentengemeinde*, a Protestant student organization. However, SDS was the bellwether of the dissident movement, and its members were prominently represented in the Free University's AStA and Konvent. One observer of the Kuby and Krippendorff affairs noted that major changes in the FU student population had occurred in the brief years between the building of the Wall and 1965. Whereas in 1961 thirty percent of the FU population were GDR-based students, the number of those originally from the GDR and still studying at the Free University had fallen to less than five percent by 1965. During the same period those students officially residing in the Federal Republic had risen to forty percent. "Many are concerned," the reporter continued, "that the Free University could be deliberately turned into a battleground by groups that have established themselves to the left of the political parties." These included precisely the youth groups mentioned above, and the consequences could be far-reaching. "These groups in combination with the Argument Club (another Berlin-based group) and a few 'humanitarian' groupings have taken over the official student offices," the *Tagesspiegel* reporter observed. With student participation in university elections regularly falling below fifty percent, and where the rights of Berlin students under the Berlin Model were greater than elsewhere, the reporter openly asked if the much-acclaimed Berlin Model could long survive.[60]

It should be stressed that while most observers noted that the dissident leadership at the Free University was small, it was also influential. Even the *New York Times* rated the left-leaning FU students as "the articulate and intellectual leadership of the university movement in West Berlin as in many other universities."[61] It was with a sense of relief that most of the university community completed the summer semester of

1965. Many departed for summer holidays with a sense of uncertainty about what the future held. Were the recent disagreements and confrontations a fluke, or did they reflect deeper problems?

POLITICS AND THE UNIVERSITY

Even as the first major political crisis at the Free University was brewing in 1965, the seeds had been planted for further trouble in the years ahead. By the mid-1960s it became apparent that the universities of the Federal Republic were turning into ever larger institutions with soaring enrollments. Despite the founding of several new universities at about this time and despite attempts to expand the rest, serious overcrowding took place. The large numbers of new students—virtually all of them recipients of the coveted Abitur—overwhelmed exisiting physical plant and facilities to an alarming degree. The Free University shared in that unsettling experience. From 291,000 students in all universities of the Federal Republic and West Berlin in 1960, the number had leaped to over 400,000 by 1966 and continued to expand rapidly thereafter. In an effort to alleviate the problem somewhat, both the West German Rectors Conference (WRK) and the Cultural Ministers Conference of the Federal Republic (KMK) recommended that the universities set definite time limits on the number of semesters a student could attend a university. In conformity with those guidelines, the medical school and the law school of the Free University decided upon specific measures to limit the number of semesters which their students could attend the university.

The timing of these changes, coming as they did hard upon the recent tensions, was unfortunate to say the least. This time they were to lead to a broader coalition of dissatisfied students who felt that their rights were being ignored by the faculty and administration of the Free University. Any hopes that the Kuby and Krippendorff affairs might remain isolated incidents faded as the academic year 1965/66 progressed. Just as ominous as student dissatisfaction with university governance was their growing preoccupation with international affairs, specifically the war in Southeast Asia.

By a twist of fate, the first significant event in the new academic year was the holding of a student election in the autumn of 1965. AStA Chairman Wolfgang Lefèvre and his vice chairman, Peter Damerow, were voted out of office and replaced by Niels Kadritzke and Gerd Börnsen, members of the rival SHB. The reason for this unexpected upset was that Lefèvre and Damerow had signed a petition the previous summer calling for peace in Vietnam. Because the petition stemmed from an organization close to the East German Communist Party (SED), it was not long before critics claimed that the AStA leaders were fellow travelers of the Communists at best, and an uproar ensued. Berlin's senior education official, Senator Werner Stein, issued a public statement on the matter, stating that anyone who signed such a petition "must . . . know that he is putting himself in close proximity to SED policies." Stein left little doubt as to what should follow next. "When the conduct of the AStA chairman does not satisfy the student body," he concluded, "then it is up to them to draw the necessary consequences." The Konvent's main committee also took issue with Lefèvre and Damerow, and in October 1965 the full Konvent voted both Lefèvre and Damerow out of office.[62]

Even as Heinrich Lüers's time in office approached its end in the fall of 1965, interest focused upon his successor, Hans-Joachim Lieber. Lieber had been an assistant under Eduard Spranger in the last days of World War II. He later helped in the founding of the Free University and became one of its first assistants. Later still, he was one of the first to finish his habilitation at the Free University and rose through the ranks to full-professor status. He had shown a long and continuing interest in student affairs, helping to create and implement the student tutorial system. He was an active scholar, publishing widely and richly deserving his status as a full professor. He was a competent administrator as well as scholar. By June 1961, at the age of 38, he had risen to the status of dean, one of the youngest in West Germany. For two years he successfully directed the affairs of the Free University's large and amorphous Philosophische Fakultät (school of liberal arts), where he kept relative harmony among the tension-prone teaching body. At the same time he retained respect and popularity among students with his seminars on Marx and Marxism. A sociologist, Lieber was interested in Marxism primarily as a sociological phenomenon. He was not himself a Marxist as such. In the late 1950s and early 1960s his students acquainted themselves with Marxism, and it was acknowledged that an FU student could gain an introduction to Marxism through studying it under Hans-Joachim Lieber. Otherwise, the opportunity scarcely existed in a city which felt the chill winds of the Cold War daily.

It is hardly an exaggeration to call Lieber an academic success story at the moment he was elected to the position of Rector of the Free University in the summer of 1965. At the time, the honor seemed to be the capstone to a productive, successful career. And to those who were alarmed by the sudden confrontation between students and faculty at the Free University, he seemed to be the logical candidate to bridge the generation gap and to heal recently opened wounds.[63]

Given the arrival of moderate student leaders and a liberal rector, it might have appeared that the Free University was once again set on a course leading away from confrontation and extreme politicization. However, appearances were deceiving. First, on the broad political horizon, the reservoirs of goodwill among growing numbers of students toward the Americans were beginning to recede. Daily television coverage of the Vietnam War began invading everyone's living room in the autumn of 1965. In line with this growing national concern, the triumphant SHB leaders proved to be as disturbed by American involvement in Vietnam as their predecessors had been. "My successor, Niels Kadritzke, followed exactly the same policies as mine," Lefèvre later observed.[64] Meanwhile, the SDS demanded room at the university's central building to erect a Vietnam exhibit to draw attention to the war in Southeast Asia. The university leadership, under Rector Lieber, turned down the request with the by now familiar explanation that a political demonstration should not occur within the university. Not to be outdone, the SDS leadership pressed its demand again, and the university leadership as firmly repeated its decision to forbid the exhibition. Rector Lieber was discovering that his job was to be no easy one. He stated afterward that he had no intention of playing the role of censor or majordomo but that he was trapped by the house rules of the Free University. He tried, for example, to interpret the internal regulations in such a way as to allow the AStA to use university lecture halls that were somewhat removed from the center of campus. "The intentions behind these efforts were misunderstood," Lieber claimed, "and were denounced as the institutionalizing of censorship and as intended to lame the student body politically. And in the end they were not legally acceptable."[65] Lieber even went so far as to ban on-campus demonstrations by pro-American student groups in order to preserve an evenhanded policy and in hopes of preventing an incident in which violence might flare up. The Free University's Academic Senate approved Lieber's actions. Lieber later related that bomb threats had begun to plague him and other university officials, and although repeated searches of buildings had turned up nothing as yet, the danger still existed that extremists from one side or another might target one of the political groupings at the designated spot chosen for its demonstation at the university.[66]

In February 1966, the fragile calm finally broke. A crowd of 2,000 demonstrators, most of them students, assembled at the Maison de France in Berlin's downtown shopping street, the Kurfürstendamm, to protest the war in Vietnam. Within a short time five hundred of them marched to the nearby Amerika Haus, pulled down the American flag, and set it at half-mast. Someone threw eggs at the building while most of the demonstrators staged a sit-down strike. Soon the police arrived and forcibly removed those demonstrators who had ignored the order to disperse. To those who experienced the explosive events of the late 1960s and 1970s, the demonstration of February 5, 1966, seems in retrospect unexceptional. However, it was the first event of its kind in postwar West Berlin, and it caused an immediate sensation. The demonstrators were gratified to see that it attracted instantaneous media attention. The low-brow press attacked the students vehemently, in part because until then no one had dared to attack American policy and American symbols so boldly. After all, the Americans were still remembered by the great majority of Berliners for standing with them during the dark days of the Blockade and Airlift. True, Rector Lieber wrote to the senior American official in Berlin the following day to apologize for the violent actions at the Amerika Haus—thus infuriating the dissident students—but the trend was strongly in the other direction. It may be said that on February 5, 1966, the honeymoon between Berliners united behind an *Insulaner* mentality (the sense of solidarity during the Blockade of 1948) and the Americans began to crumble.

Those who organized the demonstration had not done so as a mere spontaneous gesture. Two chroniclers of the student movement, Tilman Fichter and Siegward Lönnendonker, explained the motives of the leading political group for the events of February 1966.

> The SDS was convinced that Berlin was the last place on earth in which the population identified with the policies of the United States, almost without exception. Precisely for that reason Berlin became a kind of nerve ending of American domestic politics because if the intelligentsia in Berlin went into the streets against the American war in Vietnam, then conservative circles in the United States would feel abandoned by their last friends. By means of a calculated escalation of the campaign in West Berlin against the American prosecution of the war, the anti-war movement in the USA was to receive massive support. That was the internal concept of the Berlin SDS.[67]

To be sure, it was by no means certain how much notice the Americans at home would in fact take of student demonstrations in far-off West Berlin. Nevertheless, the dissident students hoped to exercise some influence in stopping the war.

What applied to West Berlin applied to an even greater extent to the very institution which the Americans had supported over a generation: the Free University. Although confirmed socialists (more in a pure Marxist sense than anything espoused by the SPD in West Germany or the SED in East Germany), the members of the SDS admitted that they represented the bourgeois intelligentsia rather than any traditional blue-collar group in society. They claimed that their presence at the Free University caused consternation among conservative circles in society. "By means of their prompt reaction, the reactionaries demonstrated that they understood already that at the Free University the '*Insulaner* Consensus' had been seriously brought into doubt."[68] In other words, both the left and the right were beginning to see the Free University as an institution possessing symbolic importance far beyond that attached to any other university in Europe.

The air of impending confrontation and the growing awareness among various political groups that events at the Free University produced front-page news made it unlikely that a political moderate could ease tensions. Given the issues that focused at the Free University—the

question of German unity (with particular reference to Adenauer's policies), international affairs (most notably growing concern and criticism
about American involvement in Vietnam), and internal pressures and
problems in German higher education—the position of university rector
was inevitably bound to be a difficult one. This is obvious in retrospect. It was hardly so obvious in the autumn of 1965 when Lieber took
up his duties.

No sooner had the first major political demonstration taken place
in downtown Berlin than yet another confrontation took place at the
Free University. Angered by Rector Lieber's refusal to allow political demonstrations, students began to organize protests once again. While Lieber
was temporarily away from Berlin, one of the Free University's stalwart
legal minds, law professor Ernst Hirsch, attempted to regulate what
kinds of student gatherings were permissible and what were not. The
task was probably a hopeless one, and one better left unattempted.
However, the Academic Senate, nervously aware of rising tensions,
had hurriedly approved Hirsch's proposal on February 16, 1966. Henceforth, FU facilities could not be used by students for political gatherings.
The only exception allowed by the Academic Senate was placing the
student *Mensa* (cafeteria) at their disposal.

Angered by what they perceived as a fait accompli by the Academic Senate, which they felt was deliberately excluding any student participation, the AStA leadership penned a letter of protest and resigned
en masse. For good measure they also prepared a statement to the press explaining their actions. Once again a confrontation loomed. The AStA students wanted to know why, if the Free University was banning political
demonstrations of any sort, the university had a professor specifically responsible for increasing political awareness (Sontheimer). Furthermore,
why did the AStA regularly elect a student representative to handle issues concerning the two Germanies and political issues in general?
That student expert had never been censored for engaging in politics,
the students claimed. As long as students demonstrated a properly anticommunist attitude, their actions were not merely tolerated, they were
supported. Those evincing left-leaning policies immediately encountered difficulties.

Two days later Rector Lieber held a press conference in an attempt
to defuse the situation, but the event had just the opposite effect. Besides the journalists, many students attended the gathering and pointedly raised the above questions and many others besides. Lieber looked
to Kurt Sontheimer, who was still smarting from the Krippendorff Affair, for support. However, the latter was disillusioned with recent developments in university politics and was involved in an internal dispute
of his own with the Academic Senate. A few days earlier, he had presented Lieber with a prepared statement criticizing the Academic Senate's recent actions. Despite Lieber's plea to confine the issue to inter-

nal discussion, Sontheimer went public with his criticisms at a press conference. The Academic Senate promptly denounced the action and called for Sontheimer's resignation from his position as political adviser to students. Sontheimer's thoughts had been moving in the same direction. Without warning, he announced on the spot his resignation from his post as the Academic Senate's political affairs expert. Disagreements within the faculty itself were occurring at an ever-increasing rate. It appeared that the new rector's headaches were just beginning.

At this point Berlin's Senator Stein entered the picture again. He urged Lieber on February 23, 1966, to "reconsider the recommendations of the Academic Senate." Stein pointed out that given the unique origins of the Free University and the traditional broad rights enjoyed by its students it was not a wise policy to deny them the use of lecture halls and other university facilities for political meetings. Lieber understood Stein's message clearly and did his best to create an acceptable arrangement. He proposed that students be permitted to use university facilities if the gathering served a serious educational purpose and did not interfere with the normal academic functioning of the university.[69] Following that sensible proposal the Academic Senate decided in the summer of 1966 to drop its ban on political gatherings at the Free University by students. However, more damage had been done, and once again Berlin's political leadership had intervened in an internal matter at the Free University. The Free University was presenting the appearance of an institution unable to resolve its own affairs. A precedent was now established that was to lead to far more intense intervention by Berlin Senate authorities. The days of the Berlin Model, with its maximum insulation from state influence, were numbered.

Now events began to pile one upon the other. At a second press conference, on February 17, 1966, the rector announced his displeasure with a new policy instituted by the editors of the Free University's informational bulletin, the *FU Spiegel* (FU Mirror). The students had begun to publish anonymous ratings of professors' courses, an unusual if not unknown practice in German universities.[70] Lieber took up the cudgels on behalf of the faculty, many of whom were distinctly unhappy with the practice, claiming that their anonymous reviewers could act arbitrarily and without accountability. Seven of them threatened to leave the Free University for other academic posts, Lieber claimed. However, the students of the AStA discounted that statement, claiming they had not found any professor who would admit to being one of the seven. Whether the undisclosed seven were serious about moving or not, one central fact stood out: Distrust and confrontation had continued to develop between influential groups of students in the AStA and the professorial ranks of the Free University. Far from soothing the various factions, Rector Lieber found himself caught in the midst of increasingly bitter strife. One of his colleagues, Professor Richard Löwenthal at the

Otto Suhr Institute, summed up Lieber's predicament to a longtime associate of the Free University, Shepard Stone:

> While the present Rector, Professor Lieber, is much more liberal, he has been insecure in reacting to the opposing pressures of the radical students, some of whom were his own pupils, and the more authoritarian-minded members of the faculty, and has committed some mistakes, such as the attempt to impose a ban on political meetings within university buildings. The result has been a willingness not only of the extremists but also of basically reasonable leaders of the student self-government to distrust the University authorities and misinterpret their actions.[71]

However, even at this stage it should be recalled that the number of dissident students was not particularly large. Those who were actively engaged in confrontational politics up to this point still probably amounted to only a few hundred students. The great majority of the 15,000 were still going about the business of learning and preparing for careers even as the previous generation of FU students had done. The SDS, for example, had perhaps 125 members, of whom only about a fifth were truly active. In the summer of 1966, however, the situation changed dramatically.

ZWANGSEXMATRIKULATION (FORCED DEREGISTRATION)

The growing student population in the Federal Republic and West Berlin had brought on a crisis as the existing universities attempted to accommodate the increasing human flow into West Germany's already overburdened institutions of higher learning. Following recommendations by the Cultural Ministers Conference and the West German Rectors Conference, the law and medical faculties of the Free University produced guidelines intended to limit the number of students admitted to study and also to weed out students who were not making sufficient progress in their studies. Thus, the FU Medical School established enrollment limits. They also established the rule that students must pass their first examination (Vorphysikum) within three semesters of entering the university and their second examination (Physikum) within seven semesters. Medical students were to have completed all work within fourteen semesters. The law faculty expected its students to have completed their work within nine semesters.

There were certain longstanding arguments to support such guidelines. A responsible higher education system was not supposed to train students for positions that did not exist. Given the German university system's tradition of posing few examinations and therefore few grades, it was not easy to evaluate a student's progress or performance until he or she had attempted one of the major examinations. Human nature being what it is, some students tended not to perform as intensively as they might have done under the lash of an impending test or other such measurement. The life of a German student was, by many standards, a congenial one in that individuals allotted their own time to their studies as they saw fit. The student of song and fable who led an easy existence had his real-life equivalent in that some students whiled away weeks and months in pursuit of pleasure or, more profitably, in seeking broader knowledge. Awakening at last to the realities of study, they then spent a few terror-filled weeks cramming for the fearful examination. The phenomenon was as old as the German universities themselves.

Many thrived in this atmosphere of great personal freedom, one which expected the individual to be self-disciplined and self-motivated. However, some students were either too immature (many began the equivalent of American graduate school at age 19 or 20) or too undisciplined to hold to a demanding curriculum, and the Free University like all German universities, had its share of "ewige Studenten," or perpetual students. It was this minority which the law and medical schools were attempting to eliminate, or better yet to prevent from materializing, when they established their new guidelines in the spring of 1966. The students hardly saw it in that light.

At another time and under different circumstances, the new measures might have caused little excitement. However, enrollment limitations and the up-or-out policy created by the respective schools without student participation proved to be a red flag and a serious miscalculation of the students' mood. To those students who by the spring of 1966 had already been at loggerheads with the FU administration for over a year, the new practice was, in their words an "administrative procedure," i.e., an arbitrary administrative measure imposed upon them without their consent. "Limited admissions and [compulsory dismissals] are an attempt to cover up longstanding neglect in the realm of university reform," the students declared. "They are making the students responsible for this situation."[72]

The students complained that they were the victims of obsolete courses of study which should have been overhauled long ago. Moreover, the crowded condition at the universities was a contributing factor in the lengthening stay at the universities for many young people. If the universities were prepared to adopt the concept of "Zwangsexmatrikulation," they claimed, then they had better be prepared to adopt urgently needed reforms first. Merely applying pressure upon those who were accepted to study would hardly by itself solve the basic problems confronting the Free University or any other German university.

What happened next was a mushrooming of student dissatisfaction far beyond the few hundred students who had confronted the Free University administration or professors on previous issues. It was at this time that the students' monthly bulletin, the *FU Spiegel*, came into its own as a mouthpiece for the rapidly growing dissident movement. It would be an exaggeration to state that this voice of dissidence functioned like the *Colloquium* of the late 1940s, but undeniably it mirrored the discontent of many students with "the Establishment." The *FU Spiegel*, in its June 1966 issue, featured a large meat grinder on its cover and discussed the issue of student admissions and dismissals. It quoted the spokesmen for the law and medical schools. The law professor representative, Karl-August Bettermann, was already a familiar face to those who had observed the Kuby Affair and especially the flap concerning fraternities. The editors of the *FU Spiegel* quoted him on the current issue, and his latest statement proved to be fully as controversial as his earlier, widely quoted address to the fraternities. Bettermann declared that with respect to the admissions measures being contemplated, "it is not a matter of curricular reform; rather it is a matter of reforming students."[73] This was precisely the line of reasoning that some students had suspected of Bettermann and other like-minded conservative professors. According to this reasoning the existing curricula and conditions for study at the Free University were adequate. It was the students who were at fault. The student leaders took Bettermann's pronouncement as a clarion call to action. On June 15, the Konvent decided to call for a strike vote.

What Bettermann sowed, Lieber proceeded to reap. The call for a strike became an issue in itself and bogged down in legal wrangling. The liberal rector refused to permit the strike vote by refusing to allow university property for the balloting, claiming it was against the Free University's constitution. The issue actually landed in a court of law, with AStA students disputing Lieber's decision and Law Professor Bettermann, as Lieber's representative, defending it. The legal battle was inconclusive and soon became irrelevant anyway. A measure of the hard feelings that ensued was to be seen in the way the commencement exercises were celebrated at the Free University in the summer of 1966. Following the precedent of Wolfgang Lefèvre, the new AStA chairman, Knut Nevermann, proposed to address the political issues hanging over the university, and he submitted his address to Rector Lieber beforehand. Lieber described Nevermann's statements as "untruths and half-truths," but at least he attended the ceremony in his capacity as rector. The Academic Senate refused even to go that far. In an unprecedented action, it boycotted the commencement entirely! It was left to a lonely Rector Lieber to step before an aroused student assembly.

What followed had all the dramatic markings of the stage. Lieber addressed the incoming students with the usual words of welcome and advice. True to his word the AStA chairman presented his critical address to the new students concerning the outstanding issues at the Free University and criticized the professoriate for boycotting the function. Lieber, true to his earlier statement, criticized the "untruths and half-truths" in Nevermann's address, whereupon the entire AStA and Konvent leadership walked out of the auditorium amidst the cheers of the newly admitted students. This time the students stood behind their student leaders, in contrast to the cool reception Lefèvre had experienced exactly one year earlier. Hardly had the student government departed when Bettermann and two like-minded professors entered the auditorium and took their seats among the few professors who had chosen to attend. With that, the commencement ceremony of June 1966 reached a climactic end and the dramatis personae finally completed their dramatic entrances and exits.[74] Unfortunately the various characters were not play-acting, and little sign of humor or goodwill was to be found.

After the commencement the two student representatives to the Academic Senate resigned in protest, claiming that Rector Lieber and the other professors on the Senate made their real decisions elsewhere. Their charge was not altogether unfounded.

A group of perhaps nine senior professors, including former rectors von Kress and Heinitz and Kurator von Bergmann, had met regularly with the current rector to discuss the major issues confronting the university. The group was very much alive and functioning under Rector Lieber. "Naturally, this was no official committee," commented Günter Neuhaus, a professor of internal medicine and influential participant in university affairs. "However, it played an extraordinarily important role within the framework of university politics." Lieber explained later that it was this influential group, consisting of moderate SPD and a few liberally inclined CDU-oriented professors, that had prevailed upon him to become a candidate for the rectorship. Their reasoning had been that although the unwritten rules indicated that the next rector should be from the medical faculty, the times were not normal. It would be better to choose a rector not on the basis of an informal rotation system among the faculties but rather on the basis of who could best solve the current crisis.[75]

Within days a call went out for a convening of the entire student body, and on June 21 no less than 2,000 students gathered at the Free University to discuss recent events. An overwhelming majority voted for a resolution calling upon Professor Bettermann to resign as admissions director for the law school. The student body also criticized Rector Lieber for his attack upon the AStA chairman and for vetoing a strike vote. At the same meeting students began circulating a petition to protest the new admissions and dismissals standards, and within a matter of days over 7,000 students had affixed their signatures to it. For good measure the students criticized the "cabinet politics" of the Academic Senate and demanded more democratic decision-making.

The Academic Senate was to meet the following day, and accordingly the students called for a demonstration in its immediate vicinity, another indication of their increasing boldness in the ever-widening conflict. The cleft between students and professors became obvious to all as on the appointed afternoon the Academic Senate met in one large hall while more than 3,000 students convened one floor below it to pass their own resolutions in a decidedly boisterous fashion. The fact that a law student, Franz Kirchberger, a representative of a conservative Catholic student organization, could meet the previous evening with the SDS-oriented Wolfgang Lefèvre to work out a joint protest action was indicative of the students' new militancy. The students demanded not only redress on the admissions and dismissals issue. They raised all the other prior grievances as well. For example they wanted a retraction of Lieber's recent public rebuke of Nevermann, removal of restrictions on student use of university facilities for political meetings, and Krippendorff's reinstatement as an assistant. Even more significant, they demanded a restructuring of the university's major decision-making committees to include one-third professors, one-third assistants, and one-third students. This marked the first time that triple parity, soon to become a major issue, was openly raised. Just as significant was their open appeal to Senator Werner Stein to use his political influence to ensure that similarly constituted committees could be organized to undertake educational reforms.[76]

Following the announcement of their demands, a delegation of students ascended the impressive stairway of the Henry Ford Bau to present their grievances personally to Rector Lieber and the Academic Senate. In effect, the Senate turned the student demands down, and as a result the 3,000 students milling about the ground floor staged Germany's first "sit-in." The two separate meetings, of professors upstairs and students downstairs, continued into the evening hours. The professors finally gave up at 10:00 p.m. The students continued to debate until the early hours of the following morning before they finally passed a resolution. Lieber had shuttled between the two groups attempting to prevent further confrontation. He even sought out the service personnel to keep the entrances to the large building open so that the students could continue to meet. Finally at 2:00 a.m. the students issued a statement. The assembled announced that they were not fighting merely for the right to attend the university for a longer period. "It is of far greater concern," they stated, "that decisions which concern the students should be arrived at democratically and with student participation." The students also proclaimed that their fight to seek democracy should hardly be confined within the context of the university. Rather, they would have to work with all "democratic organizations" to democratize society in general. Moreover, they wanted to put an end to "oligarchic domination," by which they meant the overweening influence of the full professors. Finally, the students declared: "We turn against all those who violate the constitution in any fashion even though they claim to be working within the framework of the constitution."[77] The demand for democratic decision-making in university affairs was undoubtedly the most important development as far as the Free University's future development was concerned.

Yet, as the winter semester 1966/67 approached, the discussion of reform began to be affected by the way in which discussions were held and by the behavior of the discussants. The political atmosphere at the Free University sharpened and tempers were raised. This became clear when Rector Lieber held a public address on November 19, 1966, at the registration ceremonies for incoming students. He spoke about educational reform, and at the students' request agreed to meet with a group of them to discuss the matter at length on November 26. At first, the discussion went well, the participants remaining calm. However, some students began passing around a flyer—now a common phenomenon at the university—which stated "We Can Expect Nothing from This Discussion." That was rude enough, but worse followed. The unknown authors claimed that an unbearable situation reigned at the Free University, a result of the university's "specialized idiots" (namely, the professors), who were merely training more specialized idiots. The Academic Senate and the FU administration were marked by "narrow-minded arrogance," according to the same flyer, and it implied that Lieber might listen to their complaints with a certain personal sympathy but that in reality he was merely a bureaucrat. There then followed an unprecedented act. One of the students wrested the microphone from Lieber and began shouting out the text of the sharply worded flyer to all of the assembled. Angered by this "battle of the microphone," Lieber turned on his heels and strode out of the room. Yet another threshold had been crossed, and the seeming inviolability of the professor and of his classroom had come to an end. A period of turmoil was at hand which would fill the lecture halls with frequent confrontations, disruptions, and partisan ideological disputes.[78]

Obviously, some of the newly emergent radical students enjoyed provoking the university authorities. It transpired that it was one of the first of the FU commune members, Eike Hemmer, who had grabbed the microphone from an astonished Lieber. Afterward, Lieber demanded to know who the impertinent student was, but neither the AStA chairman, Nevermann, nor the SDS representatives would betray his name. However, at this stage such behavior was too much for many of the students, who voiced their disapproval along with the outraged rector.[79]

THE BERLIN MODEL IN TROUBLE

Seen in retrospect, the commencement exercise of June 1966 with its accompanying sit-in and Lieber's unsettling "battle of the microphone"
that autumn pointed up one unalterable fact. There was no longer a
shared sense of teachers and learners at the Free University. The admissions and dismissals issue had served to forge a broad coalition of students from both left and right, with conservative religiously oriented fraternities making common cause with students from the SDS and other
left-leaning student organizations. By this time there was little middle
ground left among the older and younger generations at the Free University, and it is safe to say that the spirit of the ailing Berlin Model
breathed its last in the summer semester of 1966. The students had
found in the admissions controversy a "bread-and-butter" issue which
awakened far more immediate interest than more abstract concerns
about freedom of speech or the morality of American war-making in Vietnam. No one wrote an epitaph for the Berlin Model at the time, although some observers were astute enough to note its passing. Proof of
this unwelcome breakdown of the FU community was everywhere painfully evident, from angry outbursts by students against professors and administrators, and vice versa, to walk-outs, sit-ins, teach-ins, and the
like. Of interest was the striking reassertion of student power and student initiative in reshaping the institutional structure and nature of the
Free University in the turbulent years that followed.

From this point forward two phenomena became noticeable. First,
the group dynamics of protest over broad political issues led rapidly to
the building of a broad student movement, first in Berlin and then
throughout the higher educational system of the Federal Republic. Second, the growing disturbances led ineluctably to the conclusion by
many at the Free University that their institution needed a major overhaul. The SDS remained the banner organization of the protest movement for some time, although various other dissident groups emerged, acting at times as rivals and at other times as allies. This new generation
rapidly pushed its own leaders to the fore as spokesmen for "The Movement," and several took on the attributes of charisma—Rudi Dutschke
is the outstanding example.

Offshoots of "The Movement" included the founding of communal
living groups which deliberately turned their collective backs upon
middle-class or "bourgeois" morality and life-styles. In Berlin the first
of these experimental social groups, founded in January 1967, became
known as Kommune 1, another shortly after as Kommune 2. Within
these diverse groups protest, especially against perceived threats from
the State, became a way of life, and their members became the vanguard in demonstrations that took place ever more frequently in West Berlin in the late 1960s. Photographs of the early dissidents of 1965, for exam-

ple, show earnest young men and women clad in conventional suits, ties, and other "bourgeois" dress. "I used to keep a suit and tie in my office," former AStA chairman Knut Nevermann recalled, "and when I went over to see Rektor Lieber, I would throw them on because it was expected of students addressing the rector in those days."[80]

Within a year or two they were adopting new styles of dress, a different sexual code, their own jargon—in other words, a life-style that set them apart from their elders. Typically, such actions were directed against American involvement in Vietnam and against economic and political repression throughout the so-called Third World. The commune movement deeply shocked the majority of Berliners, who, despite the naughty reputation of their city, still maintained a strong puritanical streak, especially among the working class. The commune members, on the other hand, claimed they were throwing off the hypocrisies and double standards of bourgeois society by dispensing with nuclear families and by changing sexual partners frequently. They explained their motives openly, declaring that they sought the emancipation of women, especially from traditional and subordinate roles. The citizens of Berlin even learned of the problems that some members of the communes experienced in achieving orgasm. For many citizens, these social experiments were not only shocking; they were lurid, and the popular press had a field day with them. Chroniclers of these groups, the SDS, and left-wing organizations noted that communard leaders like Fritz Teufel and Rainer Langhans became ardent readers of the low-brow BZ and Bild and were satisfied only when they could read sensational stories about themselves. "If there were neat photos of them to be seen, then the Revolution was on the march," wrote the chroniclers of the SDS movement. In other words, the young radicals revelled in their newfound notoriety.[81]

It was about this time that the dissidents, arrayed in various groups, began referring to themselves as the Ausserparlamentarische Opposition—APO for short—or extraparliamentary opposition. The members of this shifting, amorphous group considered the Social Democratic Party's decision to enter a "Great Coalition" with the Christian Democrats a betrayal of the SPD's political and social principles. On the left, at least, the CDU/CSU was anathema, and Willy Brandt's decision to join them was disillusioning to say the least. It robbed society of an effective opposition. The various dissident groups therefore arrogated to themselves the title and the function, as they saw it, of APO.

The APO, drawing support from SDS, SHB, and the communal movement, was hardly a unified body. Although most of the commune members were students or former students, their influence upon the subsequent development of the Free University was sporadic at best. More disciplined left-leaning students, such as the soon-to-be-famous Rudi Dutschke, openly broke with the communes, claiming that they were ill-disciplined and too flighty to undertake a major role in reshaping society and its institutions such as the Free University. The stage was set for the splitting of the left-oriented student movement into various factions, a process that accelerated in the late 1960s and finally led to the voluntary dissolution of the SDS itself in 1970.

The events of 1966 also demonstrated that on the level of higher education the Free University especially was in need of a major organizational overhaul. Now that the much lauded FU community consensus had broken down, the students were demanding, in one sense, to be treated as a union with the right of Mitbestimmung, or codetermination. This concept, peculiarly German, was an offshoot of postwar efforts to end Germany's decades of labor unrest, a factor many had seen as helping to weaken the social fabric of the Weimar Republic and thus leading to the subsequent take-over by the Nazis. Starting in the late 1940s, larger unions, such as the autoworkers at the newly founded Volkswagen auto concern, had demanded the right along with management to make decisions in formulating company policy. In that difficult time, when class lines had been blurred by general poverty and when leaders from all classes of society were attempting to heal old social wounds, the concept seemed worth trying. In essence, labor and management would make peace in order to rebuild Germany's sadly run-down economy. Mitbestimmung proved successful since both management and labor actively sought cooperation, and its image was enhanced as West Germany entered two decades of unparalleled economic growth.

Thus, the concept of Mitbestimmung became the goal of various student groups, paced by the SDS, in achieving a more democratic Free University. According to this reasoning, the university would become a vehicle for the further democratization of society. The student body would function as a bloc and would work with other components to make policy and decisions. Thus, professors might form one bloc, assistants and other junior faculty were lumped together in what came to be called the Mittelbau or middle group, and students formed the third bloc. The constellation was called Drittelparität, or triple parity. Later, when university employees formed a fourth group, the subsequent variation was known as Viertelparität, or quadruple parity. It took three years for this concept to move from the initial discussion phase to reality. By German university standards, the pace was extraordinarily quick. However, it should not be forgotten that the period from 1966 to 1969 also formed one of the most turbulent eras ever witnessed in German higher education.[82]

GATHERING STORM

Before major structural changes could take place at the Free University, a "revolution" took place. The confrontations and conflicts at the Free

University and in West Berlin had not yet reached their apex by 1966. Much more was to follow in the waning years of the decade, and in the end there would even be martyrs to the student movement. At first, it did not appear that matters would go that far. Richard Löwenthal, one of the more influential personalities at the Otto Suhr Institute, felt assured in reporting to Shepard Stone as late as the spring of 1967 that despite various protest actions the Free University was still functioning reasonably well: "On the other hand," he told Stone, "the damage so far has remained much more limited than, for instance, in Berkeley. There has been no single disturbance during lectures or seminars and generally no interference with the actual work of the University. The same leaders of the student self-government who have proclaimed highly critical general views of the projected reform of studies . . . have cooperated in the commissions dealing with the reform of studies . . . in a constructive way to the satisfaction of the academic authorities."[83]

Löwenthal's assessment was more accurate with respect to events taking place within the confines of the Free University up to that point than within the larger context of West Berlin. Starting in December 1966, several student groups at the Free University, including the SDS, organized anti-Vietnam protest marches in the center of the city. Thus, on December 10 marchers gathered in a downtown area designated for a protest march. However, the protesters quickly departed from the agreed-upon march route. Instead, they broke up into small units, only to be called together again by student leaders at a given signal, whereupon they held protest chants and otherwise demonstrated amidst bustling Christmas shoppers on the Kurfürstendamm. The novel tactics of this "demonstration stroll" confused the police at first, but then they waded in and cleared entire sections of the broad boulevard of pedestrians. The police made 74 arrests that day, a few of whom were bystanders caught up in the melee. Immediately, charges of police brutality were raised, and the AStA leadership at the Free University sent a letter of protest to Berlin's Mayor Heinrich Albertz, who just as promptly rejected it. The *FU Spiegel* carried an eyewitness account by a student who, as a nondemonstrator, happened to be at the busy Kurfürstendamm. The latter had witnessed a policeman clubbing a demonstrator, and, after demanding the policeman's name, was himself promptly arrested.[84]

The SDS then called another protest action against police brutality for the following week, and a similar demonstration materialized—with identical results. The police arrested a further 86 demonstrators, including two journalists, and the cycle of violence continued. The following January saw police searching the offices of the SDS for evidence of illegal activity. When they confiscated membership files, students and professors protested a breach of civil liberties in the affair, and ultimately the files were returned to the SDS. The event demonstrated that on both sides an ever more hostile attitude was building. A miscalculation or an irrational act might see police and students involved in even more dangerous clashes, with a corresponding increase in violence.

Evidence for this mounting suspicion and hostility in the spring of 1967 was plentiful. For example, on April 5, 1967, the police arrested eleven members of Kommune 1 and accused them of plotting to assassinate U.S. Vice President Humphrey during his visit to Berlin. The police found crude smoke bombs and bags of flour, pudding, and coloring, suitable items for a rowdy demonstration but not the evidence needed to convict anyone of an assassination plot. No weapons turned up. Nevertheless, it was clear that preparations were under way for violent demonstrations. It was also obvious that the police were becoming ever more wary at a time when foreign dignitaries were visiting West Berlin. For their part, the AStA leadership urged the students to demonstrate vociferously against the American presence in Vietnam. Thus, when Vice President Humphrey appeared on April 6, over 2,000 students demonstrated against him and in front of the offices of newspaper magnate Axel Springer. The police made further arrests, and Rector Lieber uttered a strong statement against the methods of students of Kommune 1. Berlin's Mayor Albertz turned over a list of seven students involved in the Kommune 1 "plot" to Lieber during a meeting of the Kuratorium. The rector began disciplinary proceedings against them.

Finally, on April 19, the mounting disturbances grew to include the Free University as well. Rector Lieber had recently received a request by AStA chairman Hartmut Häussermann to use a room at the Henry Ford Bau in which he could report to the students on the events of recent weeks. Lieber hesitated at first. The Academic Senate was meeting on the same evening, and he feared that an identical situation to that of June 22, 1966, could arise where the Senate met on one floor and protesting students on the other. Nevertheless, it was now clear that students should not be prevented from having university facilities available for political meetings, and so Lieber reluctantly agreed to the student gathering. The evening of April 19 proved to be a memorable event. After an excited student meeting, an AStA representative appeared unbidden at the Academic Senate with the demand that disciplinary proceedings against the seven Kommune 1 students be dropped. Outraged by this action, the members of the Senate unceremoniously ejected him from the room. Thereupon AStA chairman Häussermann called the official meeting to an end and declared himself the leader of a "spontaneous protest gathering." In effect, the Senate once again came under siege as the students staged a second major sit-in within a year. Repeated demands for the students to disperse had no effect. Lieber and the Senate representatives then conferred, and for the first time in its history the Free University witnessed the arrival of police on campus, called there by its rector. Former AStA chairman Knut Nevermann advised the students to offer no violence but merely to remain sitting where they were, and the police began carting out inert students. After they had carried out no fewer than three hundred protesters, the police began to tire, and Berlin's police president informed Lieber that they would discontinue the fruitless action. The students were simply slipping around the building, entering through a side door, and rejoining the crowd of students and perspiring police. Lieber admitted later that the students' nonviolent tactics were rendering the use of police ineffective, and he was loath to call them in again thereafter. The crowd of students finally dissolved of its own volition in the wee hours of the following morning.[85] The action was instructive about the limits in resorting to the use of city police in a campus environment. However, Lieber made his anger at the students' actions abundantly clear. He initiated disciplinary proceedings against the four AStA leaders and against Rudi Dutschke. The confrontation of April 19 demonstrated that the lines were blurring between university politics and general social and international issues.

Then, a few weeks later an incident occurred reminiscent of the kinds of incidents in Europe's turbulent past that had preceded revolutions, as in 1830 or 1848. The spiritual crossroads for the German student movement was reached on June 2, 1967, when an FU student, Benno Ohnesorg, died from a policeman's bullet during a protest demonstration in front of the German Opera. On the evening of that day the Shah of Iran, on a state visit to West Berlin, had decided to attend a performance. Generally viewed by the Western public, including the Germans, as a curiosity, this fabulously wealthy ruler of an exotic kingdom aroused only antipathy among many student groups because of his despotic rule at home. An overflow crowd of 2,000 students had gathered at the Free University's Auditorium Maximum on the evening of June 1 to listen to an exiled Iranian, Bahman Nirumand, speak about cruelty and injustice under the Shah. The crowd decided to demonstrate. On the afternoon of June 2, they learned firsthand some of the oriental potentate's less lovely methods when they clashed with several busloads of the Shah's so-called *Jubelperser*, or professional boosters. Thereupon the Berlin police waded in and dispersed the students, a move that caused much bitterness and may have explained what happened next. That evening a larger crowd, composed largely of students, gathered outside the opera to protest the Shah's presence. By this time, political demonstrations had been going on for two years in West Berlin, and this one seemed little different from the others. The outcome this time, however was hardly normal. Police lines had already been established, and emotions on both sides were beginning to rise. A few students even began throwing eggs, tomatoes, and smoke bombs at the police, who as promptly threw them back. The arrival of the *Jubelperser* raised tensions even more, and many eyewitnesses recalled an ugly mood building up between police and demonstrators as the Shah arrived. Later in the evening the baton-wielding police had without warning pushed the crowd across the street into a confined area where, in essence, it became trapped. In the milling, confusion, and clashes that ensued, the violence reached new heights. Police claimed that unidentified demonstrators began throwing rocks at them. Enraged, they charged the confined crowd, and in the resulting melee Ohnesorg was shot through the head by a plainclothes police inspector. Subsequent hearings absolved the policeman of deliberate wrongdoing. He claimed to have pulled his revolver in self-defense, only to have it jolted and discharged in the scuffle that followed. The student participants strongly disagreed. Sharp disagreement in the public eye arose, and an unmistakable dark cloud hung over the event thereafter. One observer, an SPD functionary, Gerd Löffler, was present at the demonstration and, while not a witness to Ohnesorg's death, was appalled at the violence shown by students and police alike. As a political leader, he later headed an investigative commission that faulted both sides for the needless violence that led up to the shooting.[86]

As a result of Ohnesorg's death, the trend toward confrontation quickened perceptibly. The dissident student movement now had its first victim, and his perceived martyrdom went a long way toward creating a climate of hatred and fear among young people against centers of authority, i.e., toward the State. Ohnesorg's fate brought the generational conflict into sharper focus. Fellow students transported his body from Berlin across East Germany to his native Hannover for burial. In an unprecedented move the GDR border guards let the mourner/demonstrators through without fees or the usual stringent security checks. Even dissident leaders such as Knut Nevermann were surprised at the gesture. "We never found out who arranged this free passage," he recalled. "However, upon our return to Berlin everything was back to normal." Ohnesorg's burial attracted thousands of students and some professors from around the Federal Republic. Memorial services occurred at the Free University as well, with an estimated 15,000 people in attendance. Faculty members, too, were shocked at the act, and one, Professor Loos, dean of the philosophy faculty who had once instructed Ohnesorg, uttered a moving eulogy for him at the Free University. Ohnesorg's student friends received the dean's words cooly. It was, after all, the generation that was beginning to proclaim its mistrust of anyone beyond the age of thirty.

It was at about this time that students and other young people, loosely grouped together in their *Ausserparlamentarische Opposition*, spread throughout the Federal Republic.[87] West Berlin and its Free University were proving to be the pace-setter for an entire student movement. National and international attention focused ever more regularly on the increasingly controversial Free University. Earlier that year, Hans Simons, a knowledgeable German-American consultant to the Ford Foundation, had urged the university's longtime financial supporter to make a survey of the Free University in order to assess its needs and the direction it should take. The aftermath of Ohnesorg's death produced a radically different climate. "Dr. Simons and I agreed . . . that this is not the time to make a survey of the F.U.," Shepard Stone wrote to a colleague. "This is now in abeyance."[88] Better times would have to come before any objective assessment of the Free University could occur.

Within a short time it became clear that the Ohnesorg tragedy had had a polarizing effect on everyone. Allegations of police brutality arose immediately, and following a lengthy investigation, West Berlin's mayor Albertz and his police commissioner ultimately resigned from office. There was little doubt that they had reacted with unremitting hostility to the student protest movement. Yet, within the dominant political party in Berlin, the SPD, there was a strong feeling that student protesters were also at fault. "The turning point in the student movement may not have come with Ohnesorg's death," SPD Education Senator Löffler stated. "The turning point may have come an hour earlier when someone started throwing rocks at police."[89] Verbal and physical violence were becoming a way of life to some of the Free University's students.

Students held lengthy discussions about the shooting and its ramifications. For much of the public the event was caused by demonstrators bent on making trouble, and the popular press, especially the Springer press, heaped blame upon the students. Richard Löwenthal's predictions of a milder political climate in the offing in 1967 were now confounded by events. Others in a position to gauge the students' mood in Berlin also noted that June 2, 1967, was a turning point. "After Ohnesorg's death," commented FU art history professor Otto von Simson, "student protest became significantly more active."[90] Aroused student activists, such as Wolfgang Lefèvre and Knut Nevermann, agreed that June 2, 1967, was a watershed in the dissident movement, as did Berlin's left-leaning Senator for Education, Werner Stein.[91] Within days of the shooting, Stein unveiled a draft university law aimed at altering the Free University's constitution so as to create what he felt was a more democratic institution. It would include greater student influence in decision-making. Some of Berlin's SPD leadership like Stein wanted to prevent a further deterioration of relations between their party and students, and a new university law appeared to be one way to demonstrate that intention. Moreover, it was becoming obvious by now that a fundamental premise behind the Free University was no longer valid. It had ceased to be a community of teachers and learners.[92] Stein's action signaled the beginning of a prolonged, often acrimonious debate on university reform. Major structural changes were about to take place at the Free University at a time of great turbulence and inflamed political opinion. An aroused dissident movement, encompassing thousands of young people, was now on the march, and it showed every indication of enlisting the majority of students to its cause.

DAYS OF RAGE

Students from SDS and other left-leaning groups began to organize ever larger demonstrations and actions against the Vietnam War and to criticize more openly the shortcomings in their own society. Ever since the forging of an SPD-CDU "Great Coalition" in 1966 to run the Federal Republic's affairs, student disillusionment with the SPD had reached new heights. The "System" was working against them, or so they thought. In the autumn of 1967 students from the Free University, from the Technical University, and from other West Berlin higher educational institutions gathered together at the Auditorium Maximum to form what they rather grandly called the *Kritische Universität* (Critical University). The latter was hardly the imposing alternative institution to the Free University which its title suggested. Instead of becoming a break-away university of dissident students—much like the Free University in its early days—the Kritische Universität served as a kind of forum for some thirty-odd working groups. The participants, including students and even a few faculty from the Free University and from other higher educational institutions in Berlin, announced their intent to explore various ills in the current bourgeoisie-dominated society. Some groups consciously offered critical viewpoints in opposition to courses currently being taught at the Free University. Others discussed newly popular themes such as sexuality and power, and technology and society. Still others examined the affairs of the much-despised (by the left, at least) Springer newspaper empire, and structural problems associated with German universities, economic and social problems in West Berlin, architecture, art, society, etc. The results were modest at best. The founders had hoped to build bridges, using the Critical University, between students and working-class elements, but that remained a hopeless illusion. West Berlin's blue-collar world remained steadfast in its aversion toward the largely bourgeois students. Nevertheless, the experiment provided an intellectual leavening for future developments. The architectural group began a series of citizens' initiatives aimed at preventing massive urban renewal projects in Kreuzberg, a departure point for greater sensitivity in shaping the urban environment which continues today. Other groups began a systematic campaign to educate the public about the horrors of the Vietnam War. Still others, led by the SDS faction, began pushing more energetically for reform of the universities that was to have a direct impact upon the Free University within a short time. Pretentious though it was, the Critical University managed during its fleeting existence to have an impact upon several social and political issues of the day.[93]

The student movement at the Free University managed also at this time to find an ideological leader who also showed signs of charisma. Rudolf "Rudi" Dutschke, originally from Brandenburg in the GDR, was one of those visionaries who had problems adjusting to any political system. He had refused to perform military service in the east, partly because of pacifist principles rooted in his strong religious beliefs. He was barred from higher education in the GDR as a result. He started studying at the Free University even before the Wall was erected and chose to remain in the west after August 13, 1961. A student of sociology and political science at the Otto Suhr Institute, Dutschke came to know Professor Lieber well and was one of the latter's star "pupils" until he broke decisively with the rector during the clashes at the Free University. Possessing a mane of straight black hair, flashing eyes, and an arresting oratorical style, Dutschke stood out in any crowd. He had a quick mind, absorbed theory well, and became a kind of chief ideologue for the oft-fractious SDS. Because he was an accomplished public speaker, and because the public media were focusing increasingly upon student activities at the Free University, Dutschke became the subject of intense media attention. However, he never served in the AStA or in the student parliament, preferring instead to work within the SDS.

Dutschke acknowledged Herbert Marcuse as one of his ideological godfathers, and he made no secret of his contempt for bourgeois society. No lover of GDR-style Marxism-Leninism either, Dutschke hoped with other SDS members to begin a movement that would transform Western society in a true Marxist sense while at the same time avoiding the pitfalls of what he and they called *Vulgärmarxismus* or vulgarized Marxism in Eastern Europe. Reflecting Marcuse's eclectic interests, he and other left-oriented students were also interested in Freudian theory and the implications it held for bourgeois society. Dutschke was also intrigued with Mao Tse-Tung and, echoing the Chinese leader, he uttered the prophecy that the newly politicized students of 1968 would begin their "Long March through the Institutions." That is, armed with their new ideology, they would have an increasing effect upon society as they pursued their careers in education, the civil service and the other professions. This was no idle boast, and it caused much trouble later when a *Berufsverbot* (lock-out decree) was attempted by executive order by civil authorities in order to single out radicals and thus prevent the very phenomenon which Dutschke had proclaimed.

Marxism provided a theoretical and historical framework for a systematic attack upon bourgeois society, and there followed a kind of Marx Renaissance at the Free University and elsewhere in the late 1960s, paced by the SDS leadership. One of the other attractions of Marxism to the students of this time was the *Bürgerschreck* or horror it evoked from their largely middle-class parents. Especially in West Germany Marxism carried negative associations because of Germany's ideological split after 1945. "It also had a provocative significance," one Berlin SDS member observed, "especially in a country such as Germany where Marx had been thoroughly banished, where you could terrorize the middle class just by carrying around a copy of *Capital.*"[94]

After Ohnesorg's death, Dutschke achieved ever greater prominence in the student movement. He was one of those who led the campaign against the impending *Notstandsgesetze* (national emergency laws) in West Germany, which the left-leaning elements felt were endangering democracy. Dutschke and his like-minded dissident friends, who had once been closely associated with Lieber, turned against the liberal rector with an intensity they reserved for no one else, especially after the episode with the police at the first sit-in at the Free University. After one demonstration during which he was temporarily held by police, Dutschke discussed politics with the young policemen who had detained him. Earlier, several of them had attended a seminar led by Lieber, during which they had imbibed some Marxist theory along with other political theory. But SDS ideologue Dutschke was not impressed. "Those poor police comrades," he commented, "what a lot of crap that Lieber fed them!"[95] There was an element of patricide in the radicals' extreme dislike for their former *Doktorvater*. Knut Nevermann recalled that he and his friends took to calling the rector "H-J" Lieber, a not-so-subtle play on his initials, which were the same as those of the Hitler Youth.[96] Liberals were no longer popular with the left in 1967.

Dutschke was a passionate opponent of American involvement in the Vietnam War, so much so that he disrupted two church services in Berlin on Christmas Eve, 1967, with an appeal to the public to combat the violence in East Asia. Somewhat surprisingly, Dutschke still retained his strong religious convictions despite his radical and somewhat eclectic political views. However, he made his church visits that Christmas primarily in fulfillment of his slogan: "We cannot arouse them without provoking them." He succeeded on both counts. Some enraged parishoners, despite their advanced years, fell upon him and beat him bloody. Worse was to follow. After a busy winter of leading demonstrations, organizing an anti-Vietnam-War congress at the Free University with Herbert Marcuse in attendance, and becoming a well-known figure in the mass media, Dutschke received the unwelcome attentions of a young unemployed worker named Josef Bachmann.

On Maundy Thursday, 1968, the chief editor of the German magazine *Stern* interviewed the now famous Dutschke and asked him if he felt personally threatened by the impassioned political climate in West Berlin. Dutschke replied in the negative. His friends were looking out for him, he stated. Besides, he no longer went about alone. A few hours later, Bachmann, a disturbed twenty-two-year-old drifter from West Germany, stood waiting outside an apartment on the Kurfürstendamm, directed there by some of Dutschke's unsuspecting friends. When Dutschke emerged with his bicycle, Bachmann shot him three times, critically wounding him. Bachmann fled, only to be wounded in turn by police a short time later in a gun battle.[97]

The ensuing uproar hastened the politicization of many thousands of students in West Berlin and in the Federal Republic. Although not dead, the disabled Dutschke was never again able to play as active a role in student politics, and for all practical purposes he became another martyr to the movement. (Dutschke ultimately died in 1979 of a complication resulting from his injuries. Young Bachmann had already taken his own life in prison in 1970.) It was a measure of the polarization process that anti-Dutschke sentiment was nearly as unrestrained as pro-Dutschke sentiment following the assassination attempt. A Berliner wrote to Der Spiegel afterward, stating: "It was the most beautiful Easter gift imaginable to hear that Dutschke had been put out of action." Another asked, "When will this communist pig Dutschke finally croak?"[98] Others wrote directly to Dutschke and were equally unrestrained. "It's a pity that you didn't croak, you filthy spy. You have reaped that which you sowed. Someday someone will kill you, you rat . . . ." Passions were on the rise in the Germany of the late 1960s. Fortunately there were voices of moderation too. The president of the Federal Republic, Gustav Heinemann and his wife conveyed their sympathies, and a reserve army officer from Hamburg offered condolences of which democrats of any nation could be proud: "I learned of the attack upon you with anger and bitterness," he wrote. "I can support perhaps only 20 percent of your political goals, but I value your character 100 percent."[99]

The cycle of hatred and violence in Berlin spiraled ever downward, and the stage was set for ever more radical groups of young people to emerge. This was the time when charges of conspiracy and counter-conspiracy became rife, and for some young people, "The State" came to be associated with dangerous repression and the advent of a second stage of fascism. Some of these dissident students became convinced that they were victims of a vast conspiracy, and they announced to sympathetic listeners like FU sociologist Harold Hurwitz that they considered themselves in all seriousness to be the latter-day Jews of Germany.[100]

It was in that fateful year of 1968 that the violence and demonstrations and the semblance of a revolutionary upsurge in Europe and America reached a kind of climax. For example, in May the French students and trade unionists combined in a powerful coalition centered on Paris that came close to toppling the government of Charles de Gaulle. In Czechoslovakia, the "Prague Spring" led by Alexander Dubcek was in full flower and seemed about to offer "socialism with a human face" in the East Bloc. The war in Vietnam was going badly for the

Americans following the Tet Offensive of the previous February. Decisive parliamentary debates in the Bundestag in Bonn that May concerning the *Notstandgesetze* or national emergency legislation had brought into the street no fewer than 50,000 protesters who felt the laws would restrict personal freedoms. The laws were intended to give greater authority to the executive branch of government in the event of a sudden war or some unexpected catastrophe. Memories of a similar Article 48 of the Weimar constitution, whereby President Hindenburg had held extraordinary power, were still fresh and suspicions were easily aroused. Opposition to those impending laws was a driving force for many on the left in 1968 and helps to explain their near frenzy during the seemingly endless numbers of demonstrations that took place in that year. They felt that successful passage of those laws by the CDU/SPD Great Coalition had provided a concrete example of political collusion among the major parties. In their opinion it endangered the very basis of democracy in West Germany. Thus, there was a sense of dangerous frustration by the various elements that made up the APO. Despite their best efforts, the emergency laws had been enacted anyway. A sense of crisis permeated the dissident left in 1968.

It was in this context of seeming revolutionary change that the AStAs of the various Berlin universities, including the Free University, announced that they were willing to sanction the use of violence against the property of oppressors such as the State if not against indviduals in order to advance their revolutionary ideals. In fact, a split arose between those willing to sanction violence against persons as opposed to those who opted for the milder use of violence solely against property in pursuit of their aims.[101]

Following the passage of those emergency laws in Bonn on May 30, 1968, demonstrations broke out at no fewer than twenty-five universities across West Germany and West Berlin. This was the time when student protesters began entering university halls on a large scale for the first time, interrupting lectures and seminars and demanding mass participation in protests. It was also at this time that take-overs of entire institutes occurred. The students at the Free University spoke not only of sit-ins and teach-ins (leaving such terms in their original English), they added another variation of their own: a "go-in." This consisted of entering the class or seminar of an instructor, disrupting the ongoing subject, and urging the assembled students to support some cause or to debate an issue of immediate concern. Often the students would hang out banners on the walls of the occupied buildings announcing that such-and-such a site was being renamed after a revolutionary hero. Thus, the Otto-Suhr-Institut fleetingly—if one believed the banners—became known as the Karl-Liebknecht-Institut. Similarly, on the outer walls of the Seminar for German Studies hung a huge banner proclaiming it, somewhat incongruously, to be the Rosa-Luxemburg-Institut. The same was true elsewhere. For a few days students in Frankfurt even called their institution the Karl-Marx-Universität.

The irony for the Free University was now complete. A university whose founders had proclaimed it to be free from ideological constraints, especially Marxism-Leninism, now saw its buildings almost uniformly covered with banners, slogans, and graffiti proclaiming the victory of this or that radical left cause. The Free University reached its twentieth anniversary on December 4, 1968, and it was indicative of the times that no thought was given to celebrating it. Fritz von Bergmann, still serving as the Free University's kurator or chancellor, noted the aggravated feelings of the entire FU community and added: "Thus there is not the slightest reason to celebrate this regrettable development."[102]

In Berlin the demonstrations that summer became larger and more violent. They finally culminated in a bloody clash with the police in front of a court of justice at Tegeler Weg in November 1968. A radical lawyer, Horst Mahler, was in the process of being disbarred because he had participated in a particularly destructive demonstration against the Springer newspaper chain the previous spring. Estimates of the damage had run into hundreds of thousands of Deutschmarks, and the authorities had decided Mahler had helped incite the disturbances. For his part, Mahler was highly popular with the students because he had pressed vigorously for full disclosure of the events that led to the death of Benno Ohnesorg in June 1967. A thousand supporters turned out on that fateful November 4, and this time the violence-against-persons faction had their day. In an outpouring of rage, the students hurled paving stones at the surprised police. When it was over, 21 students and no fewer than 130 policemen were in hospitals being treated for wounds. The "Battle of Tegeler Weg" was a turning point for many. It was a sobering lesson about the limits of violence in pursuit of political goals. "For me it was the moment when I had to take stock of where we were going," recalled Knut Nevermann. He decided that he would withdraw from politics and concentrate on his law studies instead.[103] Others drew different conclusions and set themselves upon a course that led them into ever more serious confrontations with police and with the authority of the State. For a few, it led down the slippery road toward irregular war against their own society. The recruits for terrorism got their start in the violent demonstrations in that year of political confrontation: 1968.

The distinction between violence toward property and violence toward persons was in many ways artificial, because the two blurred in the real world of emotionally charged demonstrators. The discussion on the use of force had been going on since before the death of Ohnesorg, and the tendency toward violence had been rising steadily for more than a year. The old maxim that violence begets violence was being proved once more on the streets of West Berlin and at its Free University. The "days of rage" that erupted so frequently in 1968 gave special meaning to that year. It was characteristic that the generation of dissidents was also known as the '68 generation thereafter. Some appeared to be permanently alienated from their society.

It made little difference that meaningful numbers of citizens of the Federal Republic had now begun painfully coming to grips with the German past. A polarization process had begun by mid-1967 that actually led some—fortunately only a few—young people down the path ultimately to terrorism. Ulrike Meinhof, later a leading figure in the notorious Baader-Meinhof Gang in the 1970s, began her politicization process in the late 1960s in the demonstrations, sit-ins, and teach-ins at the Free University. She and like-minded students-turned-revolutionaries, such as Andreas Baader, ultimately formed urban terrorist groups, not unlike the Uruguayan Tupamaros, bent upon a hopeless armed struggle against the State. They had convinced themselves that they were living in a fascist society. Less dangerous but pertinent to the development of the Free University was the disintegration of the SDS into quarreling factions that ultimately saw its demise in 1970. In its place, so-called *Rote Zellen* (Red Cells) and *K-Gruppen* (Communist Groups) rose up to pursue their ideological ends in the various departments and faculties of the Free University. They proved to be a significant and often worrisome factor in the subsequent development of the Free University in the years ahead.

THE END OF AN ERA

Those who worked, taught, and learned at the Free University in the waning years of the 1960s frequently refer to their troubled institution of the time as a dinosaur, dragging its leathery tail into the modern era. The metaphor crops up again and again. The Free University's various faculties were overly large and cumbersome. Its *Kuratorium*, which coordinated the university's budget between the City of Berlin and the university's Kurator, the long-serving Fritz von Bergmann, received constant criticism as meeting too infrequently to regulate the institution's basic needs. The various research institutes, into which were funneled the crucial funding for the professors' projects, were also experiencing difficulty in achieving long-term support, and inevitably the fierce competition among them for support led to rivalries and irritations among the professors. This was a longstanding problem at the Free University and was recognized as one of the occupational hazards borne by all German professors. Theoretically, the rector and his administration, supported by the permanently seated Kurator, were to regulate such problems and keep them within manageable limits.

Theoretically too, the rector was expected to play a leading role in settling outstanding differences among the recognized components of the FU community, including those arising between students and professors.

One outside observer at this time was Hans Simons, professor of political science at Yale University, a German-American with intimate knowledge of German universities, of which he was a product. He analyzed the current state of the Free University in early 1967. Far from despairing over a supposed decline in standards at the university, he looked elsewhere for the root causes of discontent. In essence the Free University had ceased to be a pioneering institution, he maintained. Simons felt that "the academic authorities have failed to realize the need for further innovations and reforms." He added: "this omission too is understandable; after all, the FU hardly excludes itself from the thorough restoration which brought zest to West Germany's economy but malaise to its politics—both with U.S. support." Thus, a general disagreement over West German political and social development had arisen between the older and the younger generations. Simons continued:

> The heated discussions about student prerogatives, university reform, and revised study programs cannot conceal the fact that the underlying issue is a deep disagreement betweeen professors and students in their response to these effects of the restorative period. The line is neither firmly nor finally drawn. Many people are unaware of it. . . . But on the whole the professors quite naturally enjoy the large benefits which they derive from prosperity, and they do not mind, or even welcome, its political concomitants. The students, however, regard their share in the material well-being of West Germany as offensively small, and they resent the state of politics which they hold responsible for their "deprivation."[104]

Given these fundamental differences between the two sides, there was little likelihood of an early solution to the current crisis. The students, Simons noted, tended to couch their politics and agitation "in the terminology of syndicalism and class struggle as if it were applicable to the relations between them and their teachers." Inevitably, this was irritating to the professors, who reacted vigorously if not aptly. "The ensuing quarrel becomes self-perpetuating." It was a situation which was hardly peculiar to the Free University alone. However, Simons's observations occurred at a time when the thinking of the dissident students and radicals was undergoing rapid transformation. Some, like Knut Nevermann, reflected afterward that the pace of change in ideology and what was permissible in the way of protest actions was astonishing and advanced sometimes from day to day.[105]

Certainly there were problems associated with the Free University which did not arise elsewhere. After all, it had arisen amidst unique political conditions and was inevitably influenced by its geographical setting. Its founders had been idealistic, and the everyday realities were disappointing. "The enthusiasm and dedication of its founders . . . has given way to cynicism and self-seeking," Simons observed. For many, the fight against communism had now "been replaced by an urge to know it better and condone as much of its methods as possible." Disenchantment had come with the normalization of society. "For most of the faculty, joining the FU was a venture," Simons observed. "Now it has become routine, and its reward has to be tangible. The old generation of those who returned or remigrated to Berlin is in retirement. The younger people have a stake in their career, not in the place to which it carries them. All this is normal—but it is precisely what the FU was not supposed to be."[106]

Although founded as an institution at which scholarship and teaching were to be free of ideological considerations, the Free University had never been able to achieve that goal. Unstated but nevertheless implicit in the Free University's founding was its desire to fulfill a political function through academic means. With the passage of time and because of major political and social changes in both West and East Germany, that unstated role had had to be abandoned or at least heavily modified. The Free University had sought to become academically respectable, and its implicit political mission became controversial. Erich Kuby's taunts had demonstrated that fact clearly. Faculty and students and all manner of observers from the outside began to disagree on the meaning of the Free University. The faculty, longing for academic respectability, were seeking to keep the university out of politics. The current generation of students sought by contrast to reintroduce the broader political issues into the university forum and to establish links to all manner of potential sympathizers, be they the student movement of West Germany or other nations, trade unionists, or even their once-feared neighbors across the city in East Berlin.

It was little wonder that the Berlin Model, the "community of teachers and those taught," a community that was supposed to regulate its own affairs, no longer worked. The students and faculty no longer formed a government capable of working out compromises or establishing a consensus. A victim of major outside forces, the Berlin Model could no longer be brought back to life by changes in internal university policy. For a time, the antagonists had railed at each other, each side claiming that the other was responsible for the decline. Each had yearned nostalgically for a return of the old spirit, and, sadly, nothing had come of that forlorn hope. The senior faculty and their chosen leader, the rector, wanted to restore the traditional respect for academic authority in Germany. However, the hierarchical society that had underpinned such respect—one might almost say deference—had disappeared. The students and dissatisfied elements among young assistants and university employees hoped to increase their standing in the university's self-government. However, their conception was of an adversarial relationship, a syndicalist standpoint that rejected the notion of the university as functioning as a unit. Yet, the latter was the only way in which, in the long run, student influence could maintain a significant voice. Each side sought its own advantage, often for personal reasons but cloaked those motives behind strong moral arguments. Each side saw sinister designs by the other. The professors' dignity was outraged; the students' desire for equality admitted no possibility that the professors' knowledge and experience counted for anything. Thus positions hardened. The antagonists no longer talked with each other, Simons noted. Rather, they shouted at each other.[107]

That the setting for this irreconcilable conflict was West Berlin ensured that the conflict would take place in the glare of public scrutiny. The American presence in Berlin as de facto protector, combined with the Americans' controversial war in Vietnam, simply added fuel to the flames of internal disagreements that had already surfaced at the Free University. Those who had opposed Germany's rearmament in the first place and who continued to disapprove the existence of a conscript army, found that the protests at the Free University grabbed headlines. Those young men who were liable to the draft and who were determined not to serve—draft dodgers in the eyes of the conservatives—also found studying at the Free University convenient. The Wall in the late 1960s had long ceased to be a rallying point of opposition to the Communists. In fact, the situation had normalized to the point that many students hoped that an even better rapprochement could be reached with the East.

LIGHT RAYS AMONG THE CLOUDS

Although the general political climate at the Free University continued to worsen in the late 1960s, it should not be forgotten that the majority of classes continued to meet. Teaching and scholarship in most fields proceeded apace, and the Free University continued to grow and to consolidate in numerous ways. To be sure, this was hardly the kind of news that appealed to journalists and media specialists, who focused instead on the demonstrations and confrontations that were so highly visible. One of the ironies of the late 1960s was that two American-supported projects at the Free University were coming into reality after a lengthy gestation period. The Klinikum Steglitz, one of Europe's largest medical centers, opened its doors in the autumn of 1968 after ten years of preparation. A gift to the Berliners from the American people of DM 67 million had initiated the novel project, and in later years a newly prosperous Germany had added literally hundreds of millions more. It was intended to bring most medical specializations under one roof where they could interact better with each other, a bold concept in the medical world. It was characteristic of the times that the dedication ceremonies, which included high German and American officials, such as the Bundesminister for Health Affairs Käte Strobel and American Ambassador Henry Cabot Lodge, witnessed angry student disruptions. After the usual dedication speeches were heard, several students rushed forward and the usual battle of the microphone began. One student protester, more agile than the rest, reached his goal and decried the presence of an American "war criminal," i.e., Lodge, at the ceremony before being yanked away.[108] The thrust of the student protest was that American humanitarian gestures in Berlin were more than offset by the brutal prosecution of the war in Southeast Asia.

At about the same time, the Ford Foundation was engaged in its final great philanthropic undertaking for the Free University: the opening of the new facilities for the John F. Kennedy Institute for North American Studies, in January 1967. It was a project that cost $650,000 to initiate and which was intended to carry on with German resources. The Kennedy Institute opened with the largest library of Americana on the European Continent and was expected to become the major center for American Studies in Central Europe. Planning for the new institute had begun five years earlier in quieter times, and the irony that it became operational in the midst of a wave of anti-Americanism among the students was hardly lost upon contemporary observers. Klinikum Steglitz and the John F. Kennedy Institute proved to be the last major American philanthropic undertakings on behalf of the Free University.[109]

Another irony of a pleasant sort was also taking place at the Free University at the very moment the student protest movement was crystallizing. In January 1968, the Free University, which had long had an international affairs program without peer in the German-speaking world, formalized a pioneering direct exchange program with the second-largest Soviet institution of higher learning, Leningrad University. This unique link required a healthy gestation period before it was forged, but in the end it proved enduring and a model of mutual international cooperation. In November 1965, Rector Lieber attended a reception at the Czechoslovakian Military Mission in West Berlin. The Mission, an institutional legacy from the postwar years, served unofficially as a kind of meeting ground between East and West in *Treffpunkt* Berlin. For example, Lieber could not have attended such a function in East Berlin so soon after the building of the Wall. It appeared at first to be an uneventful evening, but then a Soviet ambassadorial official to the GDR, Minister Boronin, appeared at the reception and entered into a conversation with Lieber about faculty exchanges and institutional ties. Intrigued by this approach, Lieber expressed immediate interest in an exchange. A few weeks later Boronin and other Soviet officials appeared in Dahlem to discuss the subject further.

At first it seemed wildly improbable. At almost every turn there were serious technical problems and bottlenecks, much of it connected to Berlin's complicated four-power status. Were Western exchangees to obtain their visas in the Soviet Embassy in East Berlin (where West Berliners still could not travel since 1961)? Or were they to obtain them from the Soviet Embassy in Bonn? The latter recourse implied that West Berlin was an integral part of the Federal Republic and this choice was bound to cause international friction. These and dozens of other seemingly minor points needed clarification, especially since the Quadripartite Agreement on Berlin was still years in the future, and Willy Brandt's *Ostpolitik* was as yet only a dream.

Yet, the Soviets were extending feelers in Germany and elsewhere in Europe and the West. Détente in the post-Khrushchev era appeared likelier than at any time since World War II, and the Soviets seemed genuinely interested in ties to the Free University. Horst Hartwich, the university's director of international affairs, played a central role in the negotiations because of his long experience in establishing the Free University's links with universities from all parts of the globe. His minutes for a meeting with Boronin and the latter's assistant on January 20, 1966, recorded the Soviets' motives. "Both gentlemen emphasized," Hartwich recorded, "that for over fifteen years no contacts have existed between Soviet and West-Berlin scientists and scholars. These ties should be resumed once again. We agreed with them."[110]

Hartwich was as good as his word. The Soviets also meant business. However, years of hard negotiation lay ahead. In the end the two universities reached an agreement, and a long-term faculty exchange began which continues to this day. It was the first direct exchange of its kind between Soviet and West German universities and awakened considerable interest in the Federal Republic. Hartwich, as the central negotiator, made it clear who had made the first move. "The initiative for the negotiations, which finally led to the conclusion of an agreement in the spring of 1968, started with Leningrad University," he wrote to an inquirer from Hamburg University. "Since we too were interested in creating long-term scholarly contacts with a Soviet university, we went to great lengths to bring the proposals to a successful conclusion."[111]

Thus, it was an eventful day when in January 1968, the leaders of the two universities met in Dahlem. Leningrad University's senior vice president, N. P. Penkin, and other officials met with Rector Harndt, Hartwich, and the FU leadership two years after the complex discussions had begun. The Soviets toured various FU institutes and departments to meet with FU faculty. Obviously satisfied, they suddenly told their hosts that they were ready to do business. It had not been known when Penkin arrived that the Soviets wanted an accord immediately, and something close to panic ensued when the Soviets' intentions became clear. Afterward, representatives of the Deutsche Forschungsgemeinschaft (DFG), West Germany's national science foundation, were somewhat miffed that the Free University was handling the negotiations so independently, but the negotiators, who had coordinated with the DFG as best they could up to that point, had been forced to act quickly. "At the urgent request of the Soviet guests during their stay in Berlin, an agreement was codified and signed," Rector Harndt wrote in explanation.[112] The accord proved to be a singular achievement in establishing closer Soviet–West German cultural ties and was a harbinger of the new mood of détente which ultimately culminated in the Berlin Quadrapartite Agreements of 1971. Even the Federal Republic's Foreign Office took an interest in the new institutional ties between the Free University and Leningrad University and asked to be informed about the general political mood of the Soviets as the two sides began sending delegations to their respective cities.

Periodically thereafter Free University officials and Leningrad University officials have fine-tuned their accord, and annually groups of faculty from virtually every academic discipline arrive in Leningrad and West Berlin to teach and to research. One of the first Soviet academicians to participate in the exchange was none other than Sergei Tulpanov, formerly a senior cultural affairs officer in postwar Berlin and an influential official with respect to the old University Unter den Linden. He, Hartwich, and other long-serving educators at the Free University met with each other after a twenty-year hiatus, and while the main theme of their conversations was the achievement of greater rapprochement, there were obviously bitter-sweet memories on both sides about the events that had led to the creation of the Free University and to the splitting of Berlin higher education in 1948. To be sure, not everyone was enthusiastic about this pioneering exchange. Gerhard Löwenthal, formerly a RIAS reporter and now a well-known conservative television commentarist, harshly criticized Tulpanov's presence at the very university which had emerged as a result of the Cold War. However, by 1969, at a time when détente and the student protest movement were in full bloom, the Blockade and the brave little educational enterprise in Dahlem appeared ever more remote.[113] A new era was at hand.

A FAREWELL TO THE OLD FU

Unfortunately, success in the foreign-policy sphere and in the opening of major new institutes had scant impact upon the Free University's mounting internal woes. One undeniable fact that emerged from the extended period of student protests was that the Free University was no longer a unique institution in German higher education. Similar trends could be seen elsewhere, and the political usefulness—to put the matter bluntly—of the Free University to the United States was fast disappearing. Already by 1967 the protest movement had caught on in other university centers, such as Frankfurt, Bremen, Hamburg, and elsewhere. The protest movement at the Free University was also merging rapidly with the movement in the Federal Republic. Yet, the period of turmoil was by no means over when Rector Lieber completed his term of office in the autumn of 1967. It was just beginning.

Even in the best of times the position of rector at the Free University as elsewhere was a trying one. At the end of his one- or two-year term, this leading academic official was frequently exhausted from the intense work schedule and had to be sent away for one of Germany's traditional rest cures. Ernst Hirsch had had exactly that experience. A decade later Hans-Joachim Lieber was even more severely tested during his rectorship, a term of office marked by two years of continuous conflict by the time he handed over the reins of office to his successor, Ewald Harndt, in October 1967. To be sure, the times were no longer normal.

Harndt, a professor of dentistry, had become rector through the traditional process of selection at the Free University. The medical faculty knew that their turn to nominate a rector was next. They had already waited an extra term for Rector Lieber in hopes that he could end the rising conflict. Now, in October 1967, they had their way, and Harndt, who knew the job was a perilous one but who reasoned that he was approaching the end of his professional career anyway, donned the traditional academic robes and chain of office associated with the rectorship. To all outward appearances the lovely ceremony appeared normal, with the outgoing rector, Lieber, offering words of farewell and of encouragement for his successor. The incoming rector offered a scholarly presentation in the traditional style. Beneath the ceremonial ritual, however, the smoldering tensions at the Free University were just as potent as ever, as the hapless Harndt was about to discover.[114]

A frail, scholarly man, Harndt fitted nicely the image of a kindly and learned German professor. His private hobby was that of an amateur philologist, tracing the origin of French words that were part of the dialect of Berliners. As the longtime director of a medical clinic, Harndt was accustomed to authority, had long had amiable relations with his staff, and was unprepared for the disturbances to come. In better times he would undoubtedly have been treated with deference, as befitted his status as FU rector, a demanding office that would require much of him before he departed at the end of his term to the near-obligatory rest cure. However, it was his fate to take on the rector's duties when the institutional form, still clearly recognizable from its roots in 1948, was breathing its last. He was no crisis rector, and that was the tragedy of his election. A crisis was at hand.

Moreover, Harndt had a skeleton in his closet. He, like so many professional people of his age, had joined the National Socialists on May 1, 1937, in order to remain in the medical profession. A so-called *Mitläufer*, or follower, he never held any party office or function. He simply accepted the line of least resistance, like millions of other Germans.[115] Harndt's past was known to the now-aroused students at the AStA and to other dissident student groups, and they were hardly in a forgiving mood in that symbolic year 1968. Indicative of the mood of the times was the greeting offered to Rector Harndt by the new AStA chairwoman, Sigrid Fronius, when Harndt was formally re-elected that year. The FU Spiegel, the monthly magazine of FU students and object of considerable wrath from the FU administration at least since the time of Rector Lieber, published a collage on the outside back cover. On one side stood the bespectacled, elderly Harndt, looking almost perplexed. On the other side stood Fronius in a state of dishabille, exposing her ample bum in Harndt's direction and signaling her unmistakable contempt for the rector. Unfortunately, she forgot to smile. This was no lighthearted student prank, and no one was laughing.

Even more distasteful was the appearance some months earlier of a letter to the editors in the FU Spiegel from members of Kommune 1. In it they made fun of Mayor Klaus Schütz's war wounds and belittled his marriage and family in a highly provocative fashion. Various members of the FU faculty, many of whom were by no means unfriendly to the student dissidents, wrote to the editors, informing them that they would not receive or read the FU Spiegel again so long as it saw fit to publish such scurrilous personal attacks. Rector Harndt issued a harsh denunciation of the affair, comparing it to the methods of Goebbels and the Nazis.[116] Aware that they had gone too far, the student editors wrote a letter of apology to Schütz. It wasn't until almost a year later that they published an apology in their magazine, but by then irreparable damage had already been done.[117]

The Fronius-Harndt collage proved to be the final straw for university authorities, who had borne the costs of the offical student magazine, which by then was in its fourteenth year of operation. University funding ceased forthwith. Despite private student contributions, which allowed it to carry on for a time, the FU Spiegel's days were numbered.[118] So, too, were the days of the AStA. Each of its chairmen had fallen into a confrontational role with the university's authorities since 1965. AStA was not to survive another year.

Harndt was more retiring than his predecessor Lieber had been, and he seemed for a brief time to avoid the controversy which had plagued the rectorate since 1965. His luck ran out, however, in June 1968. The AStA had called together a meeting of student representatives from all faculties in order to air complaints about the alleged misconduct of a professor at the FU's Department of East Asian Studies. The Academic Senate had heard the charges but refused to consider disciplinary proceedings, and so the student representatives called upon Rector Harndt to appear at their meeting. Harndt did not appear at the meeting, and so the students marched the short distance from the Auditorium

Maximum to the rector's office and simply occupied the building. Harndt appeared but refused to speak under duress. The police were called out and surrounded the modest rectorate, which by this time had nearly a hundred students jammed inside. The situation looked tense, and considering the fates of Ohnesorg and Dutschke, the potential for disaster was clearly present. However, both sides were beginning to cope with disorder and protest. Berlin's education senator, Gerd Löffler, heard about the encounter at the rector's office and hurried to the occupied building to soothe tempers and to avoid a clash. The police kept watch but used no force. The students, with locked arms in the occupied rooms, began to relax. Someone tuned in a radio, an impromptu dance ensued, and an air of frivolity overcame the protesters. Some of the younger policemen, so claimed the newspaper accounts, looked as if they wanted to join in the "happening." A colorful Kommune 1 personality, Fritz Teufel, announced grandly that he was the new rector, and in that self-proclaimed capacity he sent letters of dismissal on official university stationery to various professors who had incurred the wrath of the protest movement. The practical joke ruffled some feathers, but at least no one was hurt this time.[119]

However, the occupation of the rectorate in June, 1968, had a symbolic meaning. The Free University, at least in the institutional form that its founders had made it, expired in that year. The Free University of 1948 had lasted two decades, and the society and city in which it existed had changed mightily. Now this notable institution of higher learning would have to change too. Already social experiments were being organized in various parts of the Free University, most notably at its Otto Suhr Institute, in an effort to overhaul the troubled institution and to make it function in a new age. However, the process of change would not be neat or orderly, as the next chapter amply attests. In fact, the last eighteen months of Harndt's rectorate were marked by rising violence. Student occupation of various buildings and institutes because of internal university conflicts or because of general political issues resulted in the rector's ever-more-frequent resort to the West Berlin police to restore order. The potential for an incident similar to the Ohnesorg tragedy was clearly present, and even moderate voices began to be critical of Harndt's actions as rector. Senator Stein publicly expressed the fear that police on campus might sooner or later produce an explosion. Harndt caused further dismay when he refused to instate an assistant at the Free University, Bernd Rabehl, because the latter, admittedly a left-radical, refused to swear allegiance to the West German constitution. The dean of the philosophy faculty, Professor Wolfram Fischer, no friend of the dissidents, found that too much, and Harndt eventually gave in to general pressure. Ewald Harndt proved to be the last rector to serve the Free University.[120]

Evidence that time had run out on the old university was amply attested to by the near anarchy that reigned in many of the faculties and institutes of the Free University in the second half of 1968 and in 1969. The merriment, or at least the avoidance of violence, that characterized the student occupation of the rector's office in 1968 did not last. Hans Simons, consultant to the Ford Foundation, visited the Free University several months after the end of the summer semester of 1969 and was shocked by the conditions prevailing in Dahlem. "According to latest reports, last summer was the worst yet," he informed his colleagues in New York. "After a series of attacks on faculty members, including jostling and kicking, throwing 'colored eggs,' slashing of tires, vandalizing offices, and in a few instances damage to private homes, including attempts at arson, the city police were kept on campus in strength. This probably prevented some violence. Anyway, most lectures and seminars met as scheduled, often under direct police protection. But the whole atmosphere precluded meaningful work beyond a minimum routine."[121]

It remained to be seen how the members of the Free University would solve the chronic confrontations that were wracking it by the end of the decade. It would take unusual courage, wisdom, and patience to end the endless conflict, and in 1969 there was no guarantee that such qualities were present. In retrospect it is easy to find fault with the various parties involved. The student leaders were by turns innovative and unreasonably provocative in their efforts to address major issues of the day. Officials of the Free University and of West Berlin reacted too frequently to the young dissidents with undisguised hostility. Their official actions could at times be described as clumsy at best. Worse still, their inflexible responses reinforced the frequently outrageous behavior of those militants who favored pushing the confrontations to extremes. Undeniably, some radicals openly embraced the call for revolution by 1968. One incontrovertible fact arising from the confrontational tactics of the radicals was to enlist on the side of the dissidents thousands of students and even some faculty members who might not completely share their political views but who did share their distaste for the unimaginative response by those in official positions. A wiser and more flexible official reaction, starting with the Kuby Affair, would hardly have precluded a student protest movement. However, it would have mitigated the magnitude and the seriousness of that movement. By 1969, after four years of crisis, the polarization of views was so extreme that even the prospect of major reforms at the Free University was not enough to alleviate the problem. Years of crisis still lay ahead.

FIVE

The Free University and Reform, 1968 to 1983

Developments at the Free University in the decade of the 1960s had held surprises for everyone. Prior to 1965, no one had predicted the emergence of a student protest movement or that, as a consequence, it would be necessary to restructure the Free University extensively. Yet that is what transpired. On the other hand, a casual observer, looking at events in the City of West Berlin as a whole from approximately 1969 to the mid-1970s, might have concluded that the violent demonstrations and confrontations with police lessened considerably and that a normalization trend was underway. Such an observation would have been deceptive. What had happened was that the various dissident groups had shifted their activities to a considerable extent away from the Kurfürstendamm and from other downtown areas to the university's campuslike enivronment in Dahlem—a development welcomed by the political leadership of West Berlin. Governing Mayor Klaus Schütz had more or less openly declared his hope that the protesters would leave the downtown area for the more secluded lecture halls and institutes of the universities. That meant, without his especially saying so, the Free University. Thereafter, something approaching an academic civil war raged almost unchecked for the next three years, during which the polarization process, which had been building since 1965, worsened. It is fair to say that this period witnessed the nadir in the Free University's fortunes until by mid-decade a gradual amelioration process set in, a trend which continues today, more than a dozen years later.

The decade of the 1970s saw West Berliners coming to grips with other problems besides the dissident student movement. They had to adjust to what is now conveniently called a "postindustrial" society where the manufacturing sector of the economy steadily slipped in importance as compared to the service sector. West Berlin began seeking the establishment of "high-tech" industries instead, hoping to become a kind of Central European "Silicon Valley," or "Route 128, Boston."[1]

West Berliners also had to recognize finally that the old *Insulaner* or islander mentality of 1948, whereby the overwhelming majority had held common political and social values, no longer held sway by 1980.

343

Small but vocal dissident groups had emerged from the student movement of the 1960s which continued to exist in various, shifting groups
and coalitions thereafter. West Berliners had to accept the fact that diverse groups, often arrayed along generational lines, would have to
exist alongside each other, each espousing different social and political
values. Not least, West Berlin had to struggle with striking demographic
problems, including the continuing phenomenon of a high percentage
of aged citizens, a continuing stagnation of its German-born population,
and, for a time, a significant increase in asylum-seekers from the Third
World. However, the picture was hardly one of unrelieved doom. A Western diplomatic accommodation with the Soviets in September 1971 produced significant improvement in West Berlin's status with the conclusion of a Quadripartite Agreement between the three Western Allies
and the Soviets concerning the Divided City and access through the
GDR. This complicated document saw as its main achievment the easing and regularization of western access to West Berlin and of West Berlin to the outside world, including the GDR. A consequence of this normalization process was that the lot of those who taught and who learned
at the Free University was eased. After many years of a kind of subtle
throttling, they could expect to enter and leave the city without excessive difficulty. The special supplements to professors' salaries—known
unofficially as Zittergeld, a mild form of hazardous-duty pay that had existed since 1961—came to an end. That was all to the good, but it
meant, too, that another special feature of living in West Berlin and teaching at the Free University had ceased to exist. In this respect the normalization of the Free University along the lines of West German universities continued.

A NEW UNIVERSITY LAW

In other vital ways, however, life at the Free University was for a time
anything but normal. The seemingly ceaseless teach-ins, sit-ins, occupations of buildings, "go-ins," and other disruptions of classes had been a
prominent feature on the FU campus since mid-1968. With the West Berlin police constantly entering university property to quell disturbances
or to provide protection, the atmosphere was for many students and faculty hardly conducive to effective learning, teaching, or research. Even before the crisis had become acute, efforts had begun by a few to restructure the Free University in such a way as to create what they called a
democratic university in which the members could once again believe
that they shared equally in and were identified with the activities of
their university. That, at least, was the ideal. It was an effort in many
ways to recover the tight-knit sense of identity that had been a hallmark of the old Berlin Model. If, under the old system, the FU students
had had a right to be heard on all major university committees—the cen-

tral feature of the university's Berlin Model—that right had sufficed for nearly a generation to make students identify with the academic community. For various reasons enumerated in the last chapter, that consensus had come to an end in the mid-1960s when a genuine student dissident movement emerged, resulting in a sharp generational conflict. If a new university law could be achieved in which the students' rights were clear and recognizable, then their sense of shared purpose would be heightened, the endless conflicts and disruptions would come to an end, and a healthier institution would emerge.

That, at least, was the hope of the reformers. It also justified the principle of *Drittelparität* (triple parity) at the Free University whereby the new law would recognize the existence of three groups at the university: the *Hochschullehrer*, or professors; a second group, which was designated the *Mittelbau*; and finally the students. It was not, as the name implied, strictly speaking a parity scheme whereby the groups enjoyed complete equality of voting. Instead, it was weighted in a 7:4:3 ratio, with the professors still possessing the dominant position. Nevertheless, the term used to describe this new voting relationship remained ever after *Drittelparität*.

Just as important as the formal creation of these three groups was the restructuring of their internal composition, at least for the professors and the *Mittelbau*. Under the old system the *Ordinarien* were the full professors, followed by associate ranks such as the *Extraordinarien*, and the *ausserplanmässigen Professoren*, who were similar to adjunct professors. There was no doubt that prior to 1969 the *Ordinarien* had been the most influential group. Under the new system their influence was considerably reduced by the ranks of new grades of associate professors which were raised from what until then had been called unofficially the *Mittelbau*. These were the *Assistenten* and *Oberassistenten*, who had completed a doctorate and were working on a habilitation, a kind of second, extended dissertation which would give them the *venia legendi*, the right to become full professors. These were for the most part untenured positions roughly equivalent to an instructor in the United States. Another important component in the pre-1968 *Mittelbau* had been the *akademische Räte* and *Oberräte*, who were also Ph.D. recipients but who held tenured positions and who generally did not intend to complete the habilitation or move on to the professorial rank. They were content to remain in such a subordinate but secure status at the university. Both groups in this unoffical *Mittelbau* formed the core of junior instructors at the Free University and elsewhere who taught the *Grundstudien*, the basic courses for students in their first year or two at the university. A Berlin law, the *Fachhochschulgesetz* of 1971, created new categories of professorships for those *Assistenten* and *akademische Räte* who wanted to apply for them. The *Ordinarius* or full professor now received the civil service status of a "C-4." Those *Assistenten* and *akademische Räte* who could demonstrate that, in addition to producing a dissertation with some kind of distinction, they had also produced some additional publications might apply for two levels of professorship, the newly created "C-3" and "C-2" associate professorships. Human nature being what it is and given the more exalted status of a professorship, hundreds of younger academicians, meeting those qualifications in the early 1970s, applied to become professors. The bureaucratic wheels began grinding, and in an ironic sense of timing as many as 500 of the former *Mittelbau* became tenured associate professors on April 1 (Fools' Day), 1972. They have been referred to as the *April-Professoren* ever since. With one stroke, the Berlin Senate had diluted to a large extent the rank and status of the professor. Simply stated, on that day the *Ordinarienuniversität* was finished. This helps to explain why the ranks of professors after 1969 and especially after passage of the *Fachhochschulgesetz* of 1971 were not only enlarged but began to take on a much more heterogeneous political outlook than had been the case before 1969.

The second group, the new *Mittelbau*, drew its members from individuals somewhat more junior on the academic scale than those who had just moved into the new professorships. Most of these individuals held untenured positions. These included junior academicians who before the reforms had been known as *Lektoren* (instructors) and *Lehrbeauftragte* (part-time instructors). It also included dissertation holders who could not qualify for or had decided not to qualify for the new professor categories. With passage of the 1971 law a new *Mittelbau* category of instructors, the *Assistenzprofessoren*, or untenured assistant professors, came into being. As might be expected, they instructed in the basic courses, ostensibly under the direct supervision of one of the tenured professors, and were presumably working on the habilitation in order to rise up into the tenured ranks. In addition, there were now the *wissenschaftliche Assistenten*, who held degrees equivalent to a master's degree. They may have passed a *Staatsexamen* (state examination) in a particular field. Several salient facts pertained to the new *Mittelbau*. First, they were almost uniformly untenured and inclined to feel insecure in their positions. Second, they were much closer in age, outlook, and academic qualifications to the students, especially to the older ones, and the outlook of this new *Mittelbau* generally inclined more toward the outlook of the students in the troubled years ahead. Finally, the supervision ostensibly exercised over them by the tenured professors was, in many disciplines, mostly honored in the breach.

The *Mittelbau*, which until 1969 had often been referred to informally as the *Assistenten*, had not received any recognition under the old Free University constitution. Yet it had grown considerably in size since the university's founding, and it had conducted a large amount of the day-to-day instruction that took place at the university. Depending upon the faculty to which they were attached, the members of the *Mittel-*

bau had formed one of the least contented groups at the university prior to the mid-1960s, and periodically they had demonstrated that discontent in decades past. Many but by no means all of the junior faculty complained of the vulnerability of their position vis-à-vis the full professors, upon whom they were fully dependent. They had had little recourse in cases of arbitrary behavior by a senior faculty member. This was, it must be stressed, in no way a universal phenomenon. Depending upon the field and the personality of the full professor, many *Assistenten* had received invaluable encouragement, direction, and material support for their own work. When the system worked correctly, the junior faculty member completed his or her habilitation and with the aid of the full professor entered the ranks of the senior faculty. Nevertheless, the question remained. What happened if one party or the other became dissatisfied? Those who labored to produce a new law hoped to regulate the position of the *Mittelbau* at the Free University. Later, this concern was extended to service personnel as well.

Ever since a conflict had broken out at the Free University in 1965, Berlin's Senator for Arts and Sciences, Werner Stein, a physicist, SPD member, and a Willy Brandt appointee to that senatorial post, had begun work on a draft law for the university. By then a physics professor, Stein had come up through the ranks at the Free University as one of its earliest assistants. He knew the university well and was concerned at the polarization that had taken place. Stein was willing to consider a new constitution for the university. However, he had had to delay his hopes of proposing a new bill for a time since university reform was obviously highly controversial, and his party, the SPD, wanted to avoid as much controversy as possible in 1966 at a time when it appeared that its leader, Willy Brandt, had a chance at last to share power in Bonn with the CDU's Georg Kiesinger. Thus, Stein shelved the bill for the time being—only to pull it out of his drawer again a few days after the death of Benno Ohnesorg. Within the Free University itself, various groups of students and professors began to discuss a future reform. However, the main planning was not to be held at the university where interminable discussions on such reforms brought no results. Instead, Stein's initiative produced the immediate result that within the Berlin SPD-dominated House of Deputies various groups came together to work on such a law. From mid-1967 until August 1969, a group of SPD officials, along with FU students and some FU professors, hammered out drafts for a new law. They included Senator Stein, and another influential figure in Berlin education, the SPD's Senator for Schools, Gerd Löffler. From the academic side Professors Alexander Schwan, and Werner Skuhr from the Otto Suhr Institute, plus students Knut Nevermann, Wolfgang Lefèvre, and Ulf and Niels Kadritzke were frequent contributors. Some assistants, such as Ekkehart Krippendorff, participated too. Generally speaking, the issue attracted primarily the attention and energy of the left wing of the SPD, which is not to say that all of the above-named were SPD loyalists. On the contrary, some individuals like Lefèvre and Krippendorff stood considerably to the left of the SPD and were openly hostile to it. It was widely known that higher education and cultural affairs were generally the field of interest reserved for the SPD's left-wing intellectuals. Certainly, there were CDU and the liberal Free Democratic Party (FDP) members on this academic affairs committee of the Berlin House of Deputies, but the SPD-oriented group, with the help of their junior partner, the FDP, generally prevailed. The CDU eventually condemned the resultant bill in the harshest terms but could not defeat its passage.

Using Stein's original draft and an old SDS tract, Hochschule in der Demokratie, from 1961 as a guide, the committee settled upon Drittelparität as one of the central features in the bill. Other features included the restructuring of the schools or faculties at the Free University and their relationship to the various research institutes. One loud complaint had been that many of the faculties were too large and unwieldy. The creation of a Fachbereich, roughly equivalent to an oversized American university department, would make the academic discipline more manageable. Finally, a major feature was the creation of a long-term presidency with greater executive rights to replace the discredited rectorship. This would result in a more unified administrative structure with an enhanced staff working under the president. The quasi-independent status of the old curator was to be ended, and the new chancellor, in charge of finances, would work within the enhanced and unified executive dominated by the president.

Much of this innovation was completely untried in German higher education, and the discussions were long and involved. Even before such a law could be finalized, and because the Free University was in the midst of ongoing crises, a small group of reformers at the university's Otto Suhr Institute had begun working on a constitution which would try out in miniature what Stein's and Löffler's group was attempting to assemble on paper for the university as a whole. The experiences which the OSI reformers encountered in seeking to alter their institute's constitution proved to be a portent of the passions which a future university law would elicit. Later events confirmed the view held by the SPD and by Willy Brandt that such legislation would have controversial results.

Led by Professors Schwan and Skuhr, the left-oriented members of the strife-ridden OSI produced a new constitution by the spring of 1968. It was a measure of the urgency that surrounded the reform effort that some professors who later became identified as strong opponents of the OSI constitution and the 1969 University Law were supporters of change at first. The list of contributors to the new constitution also included Professors Baring, Löwenthal, von Eynern, Jäckel, and Sontheimer. Indicative of the coolness with which the full professors from the rest of the Free University greeted this reform, was the decision by the university's Academic Senate to turn the constitution down completely. Equally indicative of the tenor of the times, the Berlin Senate immediately approved the creation of a model constitution at the OSI, proof that the two senates were completely at odds with each other over the issue of university reform. Encouraged by this outside political support, the reformers at the OSI promptly returned the controversial constitution to the Academic Senate for reconsideration. Not to be outdone, the university senators rejected the constitution for the second time within a week. The academics were at pains to point out that they viewed the proposed OSI constitution as unwanted state interference in the affairs of the Free University.

Now matters came to a head. As noted earlier, one of the striking developments in university affairs was the tendency of the city officials to enter into internal disputes within the Free University with ever-greater frequency after 1965. It had become obvious that FU committees were not capable of uniting to produce any future legislation to deal with the university's reform. In an unprecedented act, Stein as Senator for Arts and Sciences, along with his SPD colleague Löffler, galvanized their party's support, and the SPD-dominated House of Deputies passed the necessary legislation. The new OSI constitution would be permitted on the basis of a piece of enabling legislation, a Vorschaltgesetz, or interim law, that went into effect in 1968. The professors could rail as much as they liked. The reform would go through. The OSI's new constitution began functioning in October 1968, with the meeting of its Institutsrat (institutional council), the first academic unit in Germany to try a new system of power-sharing. It was not truly triple parity, because the full professors, while no longer in possession of an absolute majority, nevertheless still formed the most influential minority group. Even so, there were many in the Free University who found this experiment intolerable. If the reactions of the Academic Senate, the rectorate, and individual professors were any measure, then the enactment of a full-scale university law, scheduled for the following year, would be bound to cause even greater discord. Slowly, the stage was being set for a confrontation that would take years to overcome.

THE UNIVERSITY LAW OF 1969

The victory of Stein and Löffler set an obvious precedent for the future. The law which emerged was hardly confined to one segment of one committee. It was an issue which generated wide interest in the public, and various parties added their opinions. Hans Simons, a longtime observer of FU developments, was in Berlin while the experimental law was being discussed. "I attended meetings of the city assembly where it was debated," he wrote to his colleagues at the Ford Foundation, "as well as faculty and student meetings when its features were discussed. At the last reading of the draft, some of its features were added or drastically changed through motions from the floor. It is surprising that relatively consistent and reasonable regulations emanated from cross-purposes and confusion." However, Simons could not be sure how it would unfold. Only the future could tell if it would succeed in its purpose, namely, to create a university capable of carrying out effective teaching, learning, and research on the basis of a more democratic constitution.[2]

Only the most salient features of the 1969 University Law can be mentioned here. It stated clearly at the outset that the universities (in this instance both the Free University and the Technical University) "have the right to their own academic administration. Within the framework of the law they regulate their own autonomous constitutions." They would also regulate their own financial administration as well as the status of their civil servants. This appeared not to be a radical departure from the older Berlin Model which had guaranteed an unusual independence to the Free University in 1948. In practice, however, the State (as represented by Berlin's Senator for Arts and Sciences, Stein, and his successors) would intervene frequently in the years ahead, and the Free University would become the subject of much inquiry and investigation by various members of the Berlin Senate and the House of Deputies.

It was a law that reflected the political and social concerns of the 1960s. The universities, it noted in its preamble, were expected to serve the same cause of freedom as guaranteed in the West German constitution by furthering the cause of scientific research, teaching, and studies and by encouraging cooperation of teachers and learners. "Among the responsibilities of the universities," the preamble continued, "is the preparation of students for their professions and for their responsibilities in a free, democratic society in the same sense as the Basic Law [the Constitution of the Federal Republic of Germany]."[3] In other words, the university was no longer an institution concerned solely with the promotion of science and scholarship. It was expected to help educate citizens with respect to the social and political values of the society. In short, the university was expected to abandon its ivory tower image.

The new law made this point abundantly clear in other ways. For example, the universities were expected to provide a continuing education function, including adult education. They were expected to help promote international scientific and scholarly cooperation. The law stated that university reform was a continuing, evolving process, and it proclaimed that it was the responsibility of the State and of the universities "to develop and test new structures, organizational forms, and methods of training. . . ." In other words, the university was to show greater flexibility in establishing its methods of structure, its forms of governance, and its academic programs than it had shown in the past.[4]

While the explicit establishment of social and political goals was a new feature of the 1969 law, perhaps its most important departure was in the radical restructuring of the university administration. The new law eliminated the position of rector and replaced it with a much stronger executive: a presidency. This new chief official was to be elected for a term of seven years. The president would be freed from all research and teaching duties in order to perform the duties of his office better. He or she was to fulfill the function of a manager, not unlike the director of a large, efficient corporation. Thus, the law specifically permitted candidates for the high office who were not university professors. Not specifically mentioned in the law but implicitly permissible was the creation of a presidential staff to help this new executive with university administration.

Traditionally, the faculties of the Free University had rotated the role of rector among themselves in an unwritten gentlemen's agreement, and the Academic Senate, the highest functioning representative body within the university, then formally elected the candidate put up by the faculty whose turn it was to have the honor of choosing the next officer. That was why the unfortunate Ewald Harndt, virtually the only candidate in the medical faculty who could forgo a clinical directorship, had ascended to the rectorship in a time of crisis. The election of the president was to be an entirely new procedure. The law created a new elective body, the Konzil, which was to have representatives from all parts of the university community. Each Fachbereich (department) would elect two professors, two junior faculty, and two students to the Konzil, which in turn would elect the president. This Drittelparität was a key feature of the new law. It meant that with one blow the power of the full professors in university politics was drastically reduced. Whereas earlier they had dominated the Academic Senate and the students had had a small voice with only two representatives, now the students had fully one-third of the votes, and the junior, untenured faculty had the remaining third. Theoretically, the professors could be outvoted by the other two blocs, and in some of the more polarized departments and institutes precisely that kind of bloc voting proceeded to take place once the new law was in operation.

The Academic Senate continued to exist. However, its composition was altered as well. This smaller body of twenty-four elected representatives included eleven professors, six junior faculty, five students, and two service personnel. This was Viertelparität, or quadruple parity, where once again it was possible for the various blocs, if they acted in unison, to outvote the full professors. The justification for this arrangement was straightforward: the representatives in each of the bodies were expected to act as responsible, rational citizens. This assumption underlay the expectations of the lawmakers that a university could function as a democratic institution.

This sharing of decision-making was also carried down to the level of the department. Each had its own *Fachbereichsrat* or departmental council composed of seven professors, four junior faculty, three students, and one service personnel (almost invariably described in the popular press as "the cleaning lady" although that individual might be a nurse, librarian, or other specialist personnel in a given department). Once again, it was possible for the professors to be outvoted at this level.

A notable feature of the new law was the dissolving of the nine *Fakultäten* and their replacement with twenty-four (later twenty-one) smaller *Fachbereiche* or departments. The intent here was to create more manageable subdivisions. Under the old system the faculties or schools had grown too large and unwieldy. The philosophy faculty, for example, had numbered nearly eighty full professors and had proved in the end to be difficult to govern. The *Fachbereiche* were directly responsible for the teaching and learning process and were the basic functioning unit in the university. Parallel to them were created the *Zentralinstitute* (ZI), or central research units, composed of interdisciplinary working groups, or other research groups that might be needed to carry out the professors' second major goal, namely, research. The *Zentralinstitute* were organized as interdisciplinary institutes of research and learning like the Osteuropa Institut, the Institute for Social Science Research, the John F. Kennedy Institute for North American Studies (JFKI), the Institute for Pedagogical Studies and Curricular Development, or the Latin America Institute. Professors at a *Zentralinstitut* were also members of the *Fachbereich* in their field; thus the historians at the JFKI were simultaneously members of the *Fachbereich Geschichtswissenschaft*, the department of history. The same arrangement worked for the political scientists at the OSI. This double membership worked well in some cases but was also capable of producing friction between the ZI-members and the "pure" *Fachbereich*-faculty. There was also a third type of academic unit, a *Zentraleinrichtung*. It included service centers such as the university's language laboratory, its physical education center, or its audiovisual center, to name just a few. Funding for the research institutes was to be regulated through the office of a university chancellor, the successor to Curator Fritz von Bergmann, who, after twenty-one years of distinguished service, was going into a well-deserved retirement. Besides, it was widely known that von Bergmann was sharply critical of the new law, including the significant change in the status of his office.[5] The new chancellor served within the office of the president, and the intention was to create a more unified executive where financing was more closely joined to the central administration rather than kept apart under the old rector-kurator system.

Finally, the new law demonstrated the chief lawmakers' general discontent with student leadership during the preceding years of crisis. It failed to include either an AStA or a Konvent. Because students were prominently represented at all levels of the university, the justification was that these traditional student bodies were no longer needed. In reality, one of the prime architects of the new law, Senator Stein, had no intention of renewing a center of controversy and trouble. Stein felt that attempts by earlier AStA chairmen to exercise a general political mandate had been merely provocative. By broadcasting stands on general political and social issues which it could not possibly influence, the AStA had alienated the general public to a high degree.[6]

Outside observers from the U.S. Mission in Berlin secretly agreed with Stein's decision although he did not know that fact. "It appears that the abolition of the *Allgemeiner Studentenausschuss* (AStA) was a wise move," stated Mission Director Brewster Morris to his colleagues at the State Department, "since it has deprived the radical students of a rallying point for University-wide actions. They have also lost the subsidy which they had used to print pamphlets publicizing their activities. Furthermore, and perhaps most importantly, the radicals have lost their asserted "right" to speak for the student body as a whole and to pass political resolutions on their behalf.'"[7]

On August 1, 1969, the law went into effect and overnight the Free University became a different institution. The changeover was hardly as smooth and orderly as the lawmakers had hoped, and there were surprises in store for everyone. The SPD, with some FDP support, was the undisputed political force behind the new experiment. The CDU, which had offered alternative bills, remained highly critical, but as a minority party could not affect the outcome. The 1969 University Law was from the moment of its passage highly controversial. The more radical student groups were just as violently opposed to it as was the CDU but for entirely different reasons. One group, speaking for the large school of economic and social sciences, issued a manifesto claiming that the law must provide such features as an AStA and Konvent, various additional reform clauses, *Viertelparität* at all levels of administration, and explicit recognition of the *Konzil* as the highest decision-making body at the Free University. "The Student body will instigate active resistance against any university law which does not contain these essentials," the broadside proclaimed.[8] Trouble already lay on the horizon.

FINDING A PRESIDENT

The assumption of central preparers of the new law like Werner Stein and Gerd Löffler of the SPD was that a person with the qualifications of a corporate director would take over as president of the Free University. With a budget that expanded by roughly one third from year to year, the Free University was a large university and getting larger and more complex with each passing year. That fact alone helped to explain many of its administrative problems in recent years. However, by the summer of 1969, after four years in the political limelight as an institution wracked by dissension, no discernible rush of presidential candidates was to be seen. Throughout the Western world the lot of a university president had come to be viewed as unenviable, and in the United States, simply to use one example, the public was struck by the appointment or election of a rash of young university presidents in their twenties and thirties to those high positions. It was an obvious effort to close the generation gap and infuse new blood into institutions traditionally run by old men.

In West Berlin, SPD leaders Stein and Löffler were thinking in different terms. Their ideal was a university president with administrative experience who shared their general political views and who was prepared to execute the new law faithfully and with energy. Such a person, they hoped, would retain the respect of the senior faculty and at the same time would, as a result of his or her progressive (i.e., left-of-center, SPD-oriented) political beliefs, be able to draw large segments of the *Mittelbau* and of the student body to his side. The controversies and violence would die down, and the Free University would function smoothly once again. They seemed to find their ideal candidate in an acknowledged German Studies expert, Professor Eberhard Lämmert. However, Lämmert was engaged in negotiations for a position at Heidelberg University and would not allow himself to be drafted as a candidate. Still only in early middle age, he also felt that his scholarly projects still held first priority and that a demanding administrative post would inevitably retard his standing as a *Germanist*.[9] Disappointed, the SPD leaders cast their nets again. Some in the Berlin House of Deputies looked longingly at a successful industrialist like Herr Beitz, who had restored the sagging fortunes of the giant Krupp Concern. Such a figure should be able to bring order to the Free University, they hoped. However, no candidate from the corporate world ever seriously considered taking the controversial post. Some professors in the philosophy faculty nominated a law professor from Frankfurt, Rudolf Wiethölter, but within a week he withdrew his candidacy altogether. Finally, former Rector Hans-Joachim Lieber announced that he would be willing to stand for the position. Despite his tension-filled years in the rectorship from 1965 to 1967, Lieber felt he could act as the bridge between students and faculty. He was still young and vigorous and had more experience at the job than anyone else. Consequently, Lieber, with the backing of key SPD officials like Löffler, became one of the prime candidates for the office of Free University president.

During that same summer of 1969 another member of the FU community announced his candidacy. Rolf Kreibich, then an unknown thirty-year-old assistant at the university's Institute for Sociology, threw his hat into the ring. An SPD activist in local Berlin-Charlottenburg politics, Kreibich was by his own admission arrayed on the SPD's left wing.

Originally from the GDR, he had completed a master's degree in physics at the Technical University in Dresden and then had transferred to the Academy of Sciences in East Berlin. Disillusioned with the orthodox Stalinism that dominated the SED in the late 1950s and early 1960s, Kreibich left the GDR in 1961 and settled permanently in West Berlin, where he changed his field of study from the natural sciences to sociology. Like many other FU students, such as future astronaut Reinhard Furrer, Kreibich participated in student initiatives in helping fellow students to escape over the Wall. Kreibich had no use for Marxism-Leninism as practiced in the other Germany and could prove it by his actions. However, he was not averse to trying some social experimentation with the society in his second German homeland. If the first had proved not to his liking, the second proved not to be his ideal either. The difference was that he had a greater opportunity to help initiate social reforms in the West. And it was precisely the Free University which in 1969 provided an unusual opportunity to make a democratically reconstituted social institution function. In later years, critics repeatedly claimed that Kreibich was a kind of closet Communist, a charge he denies vigorously. "That was simple nonsense," Kreibich said in reply. "Given my experiences and political difficulties in the GDR, I was in no way close to the communists or Marxists."[10] Kreibich had gained considerable experience at working with *Drittelparität*, that triple-parity power-sharing scheme at the Free University's sociological institute following the promulgation of the *Vorschaltgesetz* of 1968, and he had proved to be a popular figure among the junior faculty and students there. Therefore, when the 1969 University Law went into effect and an election was called to choose the first president, Kreibich was a logical candidate.

If the two candidates were judged in terms of experience and professional attainment, obviously Lieber, a full professor and former rector, had the edge. However, political tensions at the university in the summer and autumn of 1969 were sufficiently great that in reality the dark horse had the better chance. For his part, Kreibich proved to be an energetic campaigner, making the rounds of the various faculties and spreading the message, especially to the students and to the *Mittelbau*, that if elected he would observe the spirit as well as the letter of the 1969 law. His administration would not be calling the police onto campus, and it would make a serious effort to implement the democratic provisions of the new law.

As the election drew near, political leaders such as Gerd Löffler, Berlin's Senator for Schools, could see that Kreibich's prospects for victory were rising fast, and Löffler was worried about what effect the election of so young and inexperienced a candidate would have on the traditional sources of power at a German university, the full professors. Löffler even paid a call on Kreibich on the evening before the vote to urge him to withdraw from the race in order to let Lieber, who also had SPD backing, take the presidency by default.[11] Kreibich refused, and the following day won handily.

The event turned the German academic world on its ear, and the surprise result was anything but pleasing to the more conservative Berlin and FU circles. The new FU president had to be confirmed by the Berlin Senate, and given CDU and to some extent FDP opposition to the 1969 University Law, there was certainly sentiment within the Berlin Senate to refuse confirmation. However, Senator Stein, the central figure in the passage of the University Law, would not hear of such a move. Under the rules of the new law, Kreibich had won fairly and squarely, and Stein left his fellow senators in no doubt that they were obliged to confirm Kreibich in office. Although even a few individuals within his own SPD were apprehensive about Kreibich's election, Stein had the votes to carry the day. At age thirty-one, Kreibich had become the youngest university president in Germany, a decidedly controversial development, as the coming months would amply confirm.[12]

POLARIZATION

The long chain of events that had led to the election of Rolf Kreibich as president clearly demonstrated that the Free University had entered a prolonged period of crisis, one which required unusual measures to overcome. If for the majority of students and junior faculty Kreibich and his staff appeared to be a solution to the chronic woes, other powerful elements at the Free University drew utterly different conclusions. Kreibich admitted immediately that only a small minority of the full professors had voted for him. His electoral base was obviously the *Mittelbau* and the students; he was not likely to make much headway in directing the affairs of senior academicians, many of whom were twice his age. Consequently, he had to reckon with a powerful and articulate opposition to his policies. Kreibich later admitted to having reservations about entering the contest at all. "At that time the FU was an ants' nest," he observed. "It was an institution in deep conflict." Nevertheless, the challenge to reconstitute the university was sufficiently attractive to him that Kreibich pressed on anyway.[13]

He was not wrong about the dangers of an aroused and powerful opposition. At the same time that he became the university's first president, Kreibich was confronted with the formation of a new opposition organization known as the *Notgemeinschaft für eine freie Universität* (NOFU), the Emergency Committee for a Free University. It instantly became known as NOFU to its friends and foes alike and was referred to by that acronym ever after. Within a few months, the NOFU, which was concerned primarily with affairs at the Free University and the Technical University but especially the former, was joined by a larger umbrella organization concerned about academic freedom and standards at all West German universities. The latter took the name of *Bund Freiheit der Wissenschaft* (BFW), or League for Scholarly Freedom. This BFW held similar views to NOFU, and it attracted a galaxy of professors, publicists, and other prominent personalities who were voicing their concern about the politicization of the universities. Not surprisingly, NOFU, and shortly afterward the BFW, became bitter critics of Kreibich's administration, and a long-term battle of politics, of publicity, and of nerves ensued. It became in essence a battle for hearts and minds. "And in the *Bund Freiheit der Wissenschaft*," commented a Ford Foundation official, William Bader, following an investigative visit to German universities in 1971, "we have a fair symbol of the breakdown of the political isolation of the German universities. In their effort to take the German university into contemporary German life, the reformers have brought contemporary German political life into the German university." Bader spoke about the BFW to Vice President Uwe Wesel, who described it as "an *ad hoc* organization of German scholars largely of the senior and conservative variety who are organizing a campaign against the *Reformuniversität* movement. . . ." Bader quoted Wesel as stating that the group was "financed secretly by large industrial combines operating out of Frankfurt," and the Ford Foundation official admitted to his colleagues in New York that Wesel might have had a point there. It was "a statement, by the way, which might be true."[14]

This is not to say that Rolf Kreibich formed the opposite pole to NOFU in the polarization that had occurred. Kreibich had expressed the desire to be the *Vermittler* or middleman among the diverse groups that formerly had been known as the FU community. The dubious distinction of forming the opposite political pole went to the various left-wing student splinter groups that had emerged from the now defunct SDS and other radical-left causes. Within the faculties, which would soon break down into the smaller *Fachbereiche*, militant left-wing students had formed up so-called *Rote Zellen*, or red cells. Frequently their demands far exceeded any of the calls for redress of old grievances such as freedom of speech and assembly or curricular reform which had marked the demonstrations of 1965. Following the "Marx Renaissance" of the late 1960s and the subsidence of major demonstrations on the streets of Berlin, these groups, having been rebuffed in their efforts to exert influence among working-class groups in Berlin, had retreated back to the Free University, and some were openly hoping to create Marxist centers at the Free University, at the Technical University, at the Teachers College, and at the other higher educational institutions. There they combined their extreme ideological goals with more practical demands such as curricular reform in a crazy blend of extremist politics and legitimate student concerns. They took on odd-sounding names according to the department to which they had attached themselves. Thus, the economists' *Rote Zelle Ökonomie* advanced their cause under the banner of *Rotzök*, a sound that was fully as discordant as NOFU. To be sure there were other variations. The German Studies radicals who composed the *Rote Zelle Germanistik* proclaimed themselves to be *Rotzeg*, while the radical English majors chose the equally ominous sounding title of *Rotzang*. There were more than a half dozen of these red cells at any given time.

By 1971 the first of the so-called *K-Gruppen*, or Communist groups, had emerged. It called itself the *Kommunistische Studenten Verband* (KSV), the Communist Student Association. Later still, it was transformed into the *Kommunistische Hochschulgruppe* (KHG), or Communist University Group and was usually viewed as a Maoist organization. There was even an orthodox Communist group that emerged, the *Aktionsbündnis Demokraten und Sozialisten* (ADS), which tended to draw ever closer to the political line of the miniscule West Berlin Communist party, the SEW. The latter was, in turn, a handmaiden of the East German SED, and, as might be expected, had an extremely limited appeal to West Berliners. These left-wing organizations were often unstable and usually of short duration, so that various other splinter organizations of the K-groups emerged and submerged from one year to the next. The K-groups tended to be even more militant than the red cells and often included elements who were not connected with the Free University. They tended to resort more openly to intimidation and strong-arm tactics than the red cells. Some were self-proclaimed Maoists; others were Stalinists; yet others were Trotskyists; and they all engaged in interminable bickering on the finer points of ideology.

Although the names of these shifting groups sounded utterly fierce, the reality was often rather different. *Rotzang*, for example, with its militant name and manifestos, sounded as if it was at least as threatening and disciplined as, say, the Red Guards during Mao Tse Tung's Cultural Revolution. In fact, *Rotzang* was composed of little more than half a dozen chaotic individuals whose personal characteristics were sufficiently unstable that they usually posed more of a threat to themselves than to the Free University or to society in general. Observers from the U.S. Mission in Berlin were not entirely displeased at the advent of these radical groups, since it was a sign of growing disunity on the left. "As a result of the AStA's demise," cabled U.S. Mission officials to the State Department, "and also as a result of less inspiring leadership and internal bickering within the 'movement,' the radicals have been split into smaller, much less effective 'red cells' at the faculty and departmental level. By their failure to mount an effective protest to the AStA abolition, the radicals also displayed their impotence. This cannot have failed to have some effect on the attitudes of the moderate majority of students."[15]

However, there was also no doubt that these extreme left groups were capable of causing considerable disruptions and mischief in various departments at the Free University, and they became a source of great anxiety to moderates and conservatives alike. To be sure, among those who belonged to NOFU they were anathema. Yet Kreibich, too, saw them as a major headache. "The K-groups were a big problem for us," he observed later, adding that "some of the red cells were also dangerous."[16]

Suffice it say that the German press had a field day with the formation of such exotic-sounding groups, and, depending upon the political leaning of the reporting media, they recorded in detail the antics of one group or another. The more outrageous the behavior and demands of a splinter group or the more sensational the revelations made by NOFU, the more intense the coverage became. Within a short time each side grew more adept at playing to the mass media while at the same time trying to influence opinion at the Free University. NOFU, especially, became expert in appealing to the media. Each side came to view the other as the archenemy. For the left-wing groups NOFU assumed monstrous proportions. Among those radical circles the very word became an epithet, inducing a fear not unlike that of, for example, the ton-ton macoutes among the Haitians. Because the members of NOFU largely remained anonymous, the left played a game of trying to identify who the members really were. The NOFU members fully reciprocated this fear and loathing when referring to the KSV and to other such groups. Needless to say, such implacable hostility could only add to the woes of anyone brave enough or naive enough to want to take over the reins of the troubled Free University.

William Bader continued his investigations for the Ford Foundation and reported on the reform wave sweeping over the German universities and particularly the Free University. He commented upon the way the German press was handling this new phenomenon. "As the university situation and the politics in Germany become tightly interwoven, one must be prepared for a high order of partisanship in the reporting of German newspapers. For example, it is clear that a newspaper as well known in Germany as Die Welt and another even more prestigious— the Frankfurter Allgemeine Zeitung—are now clearly identified with the conservative side of the educational issue. The Bund Freiheit der Wissenschaft will be feeding this kind of press campaign against the reform university concept." If there was prejudicial reporting on the right, there was also slanted coverage on the left. "On the other hand," Bader continued, "the newspaper Die Zeit is less partisan in its presentation, and there are a few newspapers, such as the Süddeutsche Zeitung, that actively support the university reform concept."[17] Among the latter was the Frankfurter Rundschau, a daily that at that time stood to the left of the SPD.

THE GREAT FEAR

There was a world of difference between Kreibich and his followers
and the NOFU group as to how to tackle the problem of dealing with
the more disruptive elements at the Free University. This explains in
good part why for a time the FU administration and a significant portion of the senior faculty became locked in a lengthy duel. When
Kreibich was elected to the presidency in the autumn of 1969, something approaching panic ran through the ranks of the full professors. A climate of suspicion, anxiety, and outright hostility reigned on all sides,
not unlike the shudder that went through the French provinces in 1789
after the storming of the Bastille—albeit on a smaller scale. For a time
the polarization that was so palpable at the Free University at the end
of the decade worsened in the first years of the new decade.

"West German Leftist, 30, to Head Free University," ran a headline
in the New York Times in November 1969, and a kind of mobilization
process began to take place among the various political groupings at the
Free University.[18] Within days NOFU had proclaimed its existence, various groups of professors and students were issuing manifestos praising
or damning the unexpected election outcome, and a general air of expectation hung over the Free University. Senator Stein felt compelled to
issue a public statement in support of Kreibich, saying in essence that although he had not estimated the strength of the various groupings in
the Konzil accurately, nevertheless he felt he would be able to work in relative harmony with Kreibich. It was not exactly an overwhelming endorsement. However, Stein meant what he said, and he demanded
Kreibich's confirmation from the Berlin Senate.[19] The Senate confirmed
the young president.

It was a measure of the temper of the times that the first meeting of
the Konzil, in November 1969, could not even take place in the
university's Auditorium Maximum because that imposing hall was presently occupied by 500 students, mostly red cell members who were protesting the continued existence of a disciplinary committee at the Free
University. The Konzil organizers moved their meeting to the quieter
John F. Kennedy Institute instead, but even then the first meeting had
to take place in the midst of police-student clashes as the protests continued.[20]

For his part, Kreibich had given a press conference soon after the Konzil meeting on the eve of the presidential election to explain his goals
for the next seven years. He stated at the outset that he intended to create a more democratic institution. Students and even service personnel
would have more rights. He and his staff would make frequent use of
the frankly experimental clauses in the new constitution. "The conventional university has become a travesty of its spiritual claims," Kreibich
declared in justifying the extensive changes and experiments he pro-

posed to undertake. Universities as presently constituted were not meet-ing the needs of a modern, industrialized society, he felt. The univer-sity should be an emancipatory institution.[21] Less than a week later he was the new president.

Given the existing tensions, it can hardly be said that Kreibich was al-lowed a honeymoon period in which to adjust to the needs of his new of-fice. Within days, one of the more influential deans, Wolfram Fischer of the large social sciences faculty, paid a call on Kreibich to urge him to combat the attempts on the part of Rotzök to destroy "bourgeois" econom-ics in favor of a Marxist curriculum. Kreibich refused to take a position on the dispute, and the more conservative elements at the Free Univer-sity took that as a lesson of what to expect in the future. Within days NOFU was in existence, and in an extraordinary move the deans of the still-existent faculties met with Berlin Mayor Klaus Schütz—a meeting to which Kreibich specifically was not invited. The deans, including Otto von Simson, of the philosophy faculty and an avowed NOFU leader, aired their grievances to Schütz, the chief of which was that the new president was not willing to combat energetically the disruptive ac-tivities of the red cells who were now targeting the classes of certain pro-fessors. Kreibich, they claimed, was unwilling to use police to enforce calm and was thereby abetting the student radicals. Disciplinary commit-tees might exist on paper but had obviously become a dead letter under the new Kreibich administration. Schütz expressed sympathy; however, he was not about to undertake any action of his own.[22]

Within a short time Kreibich replied to the sharp charges by some of his most senior faculty. Obviously miffed at the attack, he declared that von Simson was leading a campaign to discredit him. It was his hope, he said, to act as a middleman between professors and students, adding that a reform of the university without professorial cooperation would be illusory. Kreibich even promised that he was prepared to use the protective powers of the State (namely, the police) to assure the safety of persons and property if they were threatened. However, as if to confound any possible amelioration in the midst of this faculty-administration imbroglio, the villain in the piece, the red cells, de-clared a "battle week" ahead, and the disruptions of selected classes con-tinued. A convincing demonstration of continuing distrust by the senior professors toward the new administration occurred when the Kon-zil, using triple-parity voting, installed Kreibich's first vice president, law professor Uwe Wesel. At age thirty-six, Wesel became the "old man" in the new administration. With a law degree from Munich Univer-sity, Wesel had only been in Berlin for one year but was already ad-mired by many of the dissidents for his support of student causes. This hardly ensured his standing among the other professors. No fewer than twenty of the thirty-one professors left the Konzil meeting in protest over Wesel's elevation. Wesel admitted long afterward that he had embraced a more radical political course after coming to Berlin in 1968, due in part to the highly charged atmosphere. He recalled emerging with other law professors from a university building which was in the process of being occupied by students. One of his colleagues, Karl-August Bettermann, spotted one of his assistants in the crowd and, angered at her participation in the sit-in, he announced his intention, as Wesel recalled, to dismiss her from her position. Shaken by the experience, Wesel felt he had come to a crossroads where he must turn left or right. He moved steadily to the left, and, given his charm and his genuine talent for public communication, he quickly became the darling of the student left. It was a source of pride for Wesel that he alone in the Kreibich administration was still able to carry on a dialogue even with the truly radical elements on the FU campus.[23] His vice presidency also proved to be fully as controversial as the presidency of his even more youthful president.

Given the flurry of rumors and the near panic that reigned following the election of Kreibich, it was hardly surprising that outside observers were worried about what direction the new administration would take. A public affairs officer of the U.S. Information Agency in Berlin, Hans N. Tuch, had been watching events unfold at the Free University since 1967. He decided to pay a call directly upon Kreibich in December 1969, and hear him out. "He makes a positive impression," Tuch reported to his boss, U.S. Mission Director Brewster Morris. Kreibich's basic motives in becoming president of the university were, as the new president related to Tuch, "to make the Free University as pertinent to contemporary society as it was when it was founded in 1948, and to carry out university reform on the basis of the new Berlin law. . . ."[24] Kreibich was also willing to discuss his general political and social views. Tuch recorded Kreibich's observation that "political realities as he knew them in the early 1950s and even in the late 1950s when he moved to West Berlin from East Germany had changed, and one should no longer consider East-West relationships in the same stereotypes of friend versus enemy (Freund-Feind) which had been pertinent then. He considers himself as within the legitimate political framework of the German democracy and said that he had been in local (Charlottenburg) SPD politics, albeit on a relatively low level and on the left wing."[25]

Kreibich also ventured some opinions concerning the gulf existing between the university and the public in society. Tuch understood him to say "that it was a university's obligation—or rather it was a professor's obligation—to bridge the gap between the highly complicated, sophisticated concepts of contemporary science (and politics) and the capacity to understand them among average people. He felt that outstanding scientists like Einstein could do that by also being humanists; most of today's university professors cannot."[26]

There was no doubt that the new president was fully committed to the recent reforms embodied in the 1969 University Law. "Kreibich alleges that reform contemplated for the university will strengthen the democratic system," Tuch recorded, "since by broadening the base of democratic decision-making in the university, even the professors, who must give up some of their past prerogatives, will gain in the long run in their ability to contribute to scientific and intellectual developments by communicating with the students as more equal partners." Kreibich acknowledged, too, that many students would undoubtedly fail to recognize that the professors had not only a store of knowledge but also sheer experience of life as yet unavailable to younger people. Yet he remained optimistic that the new egalitarian thrust would succeed. "Kreibich did not think that the academic level would necessarily drop through this democratization process," Tuch stated.[27] On the whole, the senior American officials in Berlin, although cautious in their initial assessment of Kreibich, were agreeably surprised by the positive impression that he made.

URSULA BESSER CONTRA ULRIKE MEINHOF

It is doubtful that Kreibich would have been so optimistic had he been able to foresee some of the crises already looming over the Free University. As if to highlight the radical atmosphere at the moment the new president took office, an incident began building which was to have tragic consequences for West German society and for the Free University as well. A mass-communications course was currently being held at the university entitled "Radio Laboratory: Possibilities for Agitation and Enlightenment on Radio." The person offering it was a part-time instructor of the name Ulrike Meinhof. One of the CDU's specialists in university affairs and a member of the Berlin House of Deputies, Ursula Besser, decided to ask some probing questions about the propriety and even the legality of permitting such courses to be offered for credit. She directed a blunt question publicly to SPD Mayor Schütz, wanting to know why the president of the Free University would allow Meinhof to offer a course for credit where the intent was to transform an academic course into a training program for political agitation. The class participants were mostly members of extremist splinter groups, such as the "Red Guards" and the "Red Spartacus League," she said. Schütz answered that Berlin officials were already investigating the matter and were in touch with the director of the university's Mass Communications Institute, Professor Harry Pross. Several weeks later, after more prodding by Besser, the SPD leadership, paced by Schütz and Senator Stein, replied that Meinhof had not actually violated the constitution of the Federal Republic. Furthermore, the mayor rejected suggestions that Meinhof simply be dismissed. After all, it was the right of the FU faculty to decide on her further employment rather than outside political offices.[28] It was a stinging rebuke to Besser.

Outwardly, it appeared that the city administration was backing the university administration in trying to ward off outside interference in curriculum offerings at the Free University. In fact, it was part of an ongoing CDU-SPD dispute concerning university reform and the limits of political dissent. Ultimately, the issue proved highly embarrassing to Schütz, to his party, and to the university. A few months later, in May 1970, the same Ulrike Meinhof planned and executed the daring escape of her ideological compatriot, Andreas Baader, from the library of West Berlin's Institute for Social Issues (independent of the Free University). Baader, who had been convicted of arson two years earlier in the burning down of a warehouse in Frankfurt, was accompanied by two police wardens on a visit to the institute to obtain reading matter. This was an unusual liberty arranged for him by his legal adviser, Horst Mahler. The latter, it will be recalled, had been involved in the Easter demonstrations of 1968, and his disbarment had occasioned violent riots at Berlin's Tegeler Weg later that year. In this case the trust was not repaid. Meinhof and other accomplices had laid an ambush, and in the ensuing shoot-out the two policemen were seriously wounded and an innocent bystander was fatally shot. Baader and Meinhof escaped to form their soon-to-be-famous gang, and a new chapter in German terrorism began. Besser's sharp questioning about the Meinhof course several months before this incident made it all the more embarrassing to those who had attempted to gloss over the problem of a glaringly radical curriculum offering at the Free University.[29]

WALTER PABST AND THE "PEOPLE'S COURT"

In the meantime, the newly organized NOFU began to issue regular reports under the title of "Free University under Hammer and Sickle," in which they attacked the various left-wing student groups, claiming that they were attempting no less than an ideological takeover of the entire university. An atmosphere of confrontation now reigned at the Free University, and it was hardly NOFU alone that began firing salvos. For example, the red cell group for Romance languages, Rotzrom, had begun systematically to disrupt the lectures of Professor Walter Pabst because of his publications during the Hitler era, which they found to be fascistic. President Kreibich made a point of being present during one of those "go-ins," and it was at his suggestion that Pabst and his accusers agreed to meet in a few days to debate the charges publicly. On the appointed day no fewer than four hundred students and twenty professors appeared at a large hall of the university to hear the debate. It proved to be a momentous gathering. Among those present were Professors Richard

Löwenthal and Ernst Heinitz, both of whom had been forced into emigration at the advent of the Nazis.

Löwenthal was a legendary figure on the German left who, in his youth in the time of the Weimar Republic, had joined the Communists only to split with them when he saw that the SPD was fighting National Socialism more effectively. After the Nazis' seizure of power, he spent much time in Prague aiding the German resistance to Hitler before barely escaping to England on the eve of World War II. During the war he became a radio journalist and perhaps the most widely known German emigré voice in the battle of the airwaves. Having become a British subject during the conflict, he continued in journalism in the postwar period, wrote a distinguished tract in 1947 entitled *Beyond Capitalism*, then took a degree in political science at Harvard University before arriving at the Otto Suhr Institute in 1960. Thus, it was an authoritative voice on that December day in 1969 which urged the students of *Rotzrom* to realize that Pabst, also a journalist during the war, could scarcely have survived under National Socialism without making outward compromises with that violent regime. Löwenthal carried the battle to the younger generation that day, and none could reproach him of all people for being soft on or ignorant about the Nazi past.[30] He could even afford to be provocative as well. He told the most radical students gathered there that their chanting of slogans in unison, their incessant interruption of speakers with whom they disagreed, and their intolerance of other viewpoints reminded him of nothing so much as the actions of German students under National Socialism.[31] The dissidents did not like his remarks on that day.

Ernst Heinitz was scarcely less authoritative a participant at that fateful gathering. Being Jewish, he had also had to emigrate after the Nazi takeover, and went to Italy, whither eventually the Holocaust also came. Despite the ever-present danger of capture and certain death, he had survived. Heinitz, an SPD member, was by now an elderly man, who, in his retirement, had been providing legal counsel gratis to dozens of young people caught up in litigation stemming from the many demonstrations and arrests of recent years. He was, therefore, hardly an arch-conservative and like Löwenthal had no reason to want to excuse the crimes of the Nazis. Heinitz stood up and issued the stunning announcement that Pabst as a staff member of the German consulate in wartime Florence had personally aided in the saving of hundreds of lives of Jews in Italy. Had he been uncovered, the penalty would have been death.

Under normal circumstances, such powerful evidence would have been enough to have freed the accused from further charges or harassment. However, the atmosphere that reigned at the Free University was not normal. Löwenthal might point out basic facts of life under the Nazis. Heinitz might reveal the actions of a brave man. It made little difference to the radicals. Undeterred, the Rotzrom leaders entered a resolution that Pabst should be removed from the Department of Romance Languages and that two junior faculty, to be chosen by the students, should be approved. This move proved to be a miscalculation. The same young radicals had agreed beforehand with Kreibich not to propose such a provocative resolution. Now they had blandly broken that oral agreement. No sooner had they done so than all of the professors rose as one and angrily left the auditorium. Fortunately, the majority of the remaining students refused to approve the resolution, and Kreibich admonished the most radical students not to hinder the path to further reform by provocative behavior. Psychic and physical violence would have to yield to enlightenment, he claimed.[32] It was an admonition that was to be observed largely in the breach in the months ahead.

The Pabst Affair was indicative of the unforgiving and militant mood that so often marred relations between left-wing students and some professors in those troubled times. The radicals produced a kind of witch-hunt atmosphere that the professors and other faculty of the older generation found to have disturbing parallels with the charged atmosphere of Nazi times. Moreover, the Rotzrom resolution had obviously had the intent not only of discrediting Pabst but also of installing two junior faculty who would presumably share the same political views as Rotzrom. The Pabst Affair made more of an impression within the FU community than it did before the public, and while the valiant efforts of two distinguished former German exiles had exonerated Pabst in most eyes, it was an issue that quickly faded from public view.

Kreibich in proposing a public airing of the Pabst controversy was trying to enter into his role as *Vermittler*, or middleman. Yet it was obvious that neither the angry professors who walked out of the meeting nor the student radicals who went ahead with their militant resolution had displayed any appreciation for his intervention. After the meeting he had explained his dilemma to American officials at the U.S. Mission. They recorded that the new president felt he was caught between two mutually hostile, unforgiving camps.

Kreibich stated frankly that it was on one hand, the opposition to him by the conservative elements at the FU as represented primarily by the faculty (the professors); and on the other hand, the destructive activities of the left radicals (the so-called Red Cells). In regard to the latter, he argued that it was necessary to engage the radicals on their own terms, something that most professors are incapable of doing, by not letting them get away unchallenged with their irrational phraseology and demands. He engages them and tries to make them look ridiculous in the eyes of the other students, thereby to cause them to lose their effectiveness with their Nazi-like terror methods. He does not know whether he will succeed in this.[33]

Already, a few short weeks after Kreibich's election, it appeared to outside observers from the Mission that the new president and his university were in a difficult position. One American, Hans Tuch, was pleasantly surprised at the results of the interview. "He was willing to explain his views and did so intelligently, convincingly, and lucidly." Like so many others, Tuch had been unsure what to expect because of the sensationalism surrounding the young assistant's sudden elevation to high office. Following the talk, Tuch related to his superiors that Kreibich had succeeded in "dispelling some of the preconceptions the reporting officer had formed about the new President on the basis of published and unpublished reports." Tuch also felt that Kreibich was not one-sided in his approach to the woes besetting the Free University. "He also appeared to have a sense of balance as when he talked about his opposition from the right but went on by saying, 'I must also tell you about the problems I have on the left.' He did not appear as one who was overwhelmed by his job nor as one who took his responsibilities lightly. He seemed to have thought deeply about his work and to have the confidence in himself without the appearance of cockiness or superiority."[34]

Despite this initial good impression, the new chief officer faced a daunting situation at the troubled university. There was precious little middle ground, and Tuch was anything but optimistic about the outcome of Kreibich's term in office.

> President Kreibich may easily fail in his presidency, and when he does it may be the result of a squeeze play from both the "right" and the "left." It is understandable that the faculty, among whom are many liberal and respected professors, would feel completely frustrated and opposed to Kreibich, who, after all, was voted in largely on the basis of support from the left.... On the other hand, the real danger for the university comes from the extreme and radical left who do not want to reform it but to destroy it. It seems to us therefore that at least for the moment Kreibich, who was elected democratically on the basis of a new if imperfect law, must be given a chance to succeed. This view, incidentally, is shared by the Governing Mayor who told the Allied Commandants last week that he feels Kreibich deserves this chance.

Only time would tell what would happen next, even to a well-meaning and idealistic individual. The American officials in Berlin warned their counterparts in Washington that "there is still no assurance that a 'good man' can succeed in this difficult and precarious job."[35] Indeed, the testing of the new president would continue. In fact, it seemed never to cease.

After a few months in office, Kreibich seemed to be presiding over a calmer university than had been the case before passage of the new law and his elevation to the presidency. In February 1970, U.S. Mission officials cabled further impressions about Kreibich and the Free University to their superiors at the State Department. "When viewed in perspective," they wrote, "it is possible to discern a degree of progress in the effort to return an air of normalcy to the campus. On the other hand,

many serious problems remain. It may not be correct to blame the existence of these problems on the 1969 University Law or on the new FU
President Kreibich, as many professors and much of the public are presently doing. To be sure both the law and the man have their shortcomings. After five months of the former and two of the latter, the Mission
—like the public—is still not in a position to make a definitive assessment as to the future of the FU."[36] For the moment the Americans
were willing to defer judgment.

AFTER-SCHOOL PROGRAM "RED FREEDOM"

Although Kreibich could not know it, another scandal was building during the first months of his presidency which would add more fuel to
the flames of discontent. On April 3, 1970, the CDU-oriented newspaper *Die Welt* made a sensational announcement. It revealed to the public that since July 1969, Psychology Professor Klaus Holzkamp and several students and assistants at the Free University's Psychology Institute
had been conducting an educational experiment with school children.
Journalist Hans Erich Bilges had obtained somehow the minutes of institute meetings about this project, which *Die Welt* also published. The article and accompanying document revealed that the project members had
been trying for the better part of a year to raise children to resist authoritarian behavior in the after-school program in Kreuzberg. More precisely,
they were being encouraged to be actively anti-authoritarian, and the
phrase "anti-authoritarian education" quickly entered the vocabulary of
the various political groups, who either applauded it or condemned it.
With such exposure, children, the critics said, were likely to view such
sinews of state power as the police with ambivalence at least and more
likely with open hostility.

Almost simultaneously the *Tagesspiegel* published an article on the
subject under the provocative title *Versuchskaninchen* ("Guinea Pigs")
and revealed that the entire project had been kept secret from the public. Furthermore, the project was not simply one of observation. Rather,
it was one of active experimentation with the children, who ranged in
age from eight to eighteen. The same newspaper carried an accompanying article which indicated that a move was now afoot to found a second psychology institute at the Free University, one which would avoid
the leftward political drift of the current institute.[37]

The political consequences were not long in materializing. President Kreibich issued an announcement strongly condemning the unau-
thorized publication of the minutes of institute meetings while they
were still in a raw, unedited state. Kreibich observed that whoever revealed the minutes had done so for political reasons, with the intent to
ruin the reputations of the Psychology Institute's director, Holzkamp,
and his co-workers. Almost immediately other prominent members of

the FU community began to sound off too. Otto von Simson, dean of the philosophy faculty and acknowledged NOFU spokesman, roundly condemned the entire project. Soon the State entered the fracas when Berlin's Senator for Family, Youth and Sport, Horst Korber, unceremoniously ordered the after-school program to close its doors forthwith. He also ordered the six student participants to have nothing further to do with the project. Korber justified his precipitate decision in no uncertain terms. The project did not fall under constitutional provisions for guaranteeing research, "because it has nothing to do with research," Korber announced. Besides, it was violating the rights of the children involved.[38]

Voluble debates on the subject took place in the Berlin House of Deputies, with angry and persistent questioning coming from CDU spokesmen such as the ever-watchful Ursula Besser. Aware that such a project could damage the credibility of the Free University in the eyes of the public, Senator Stein immediately called upon President Kreibich to investigate the after-school program controversy. He also warned the university's new leader not to allot any further funding for such projects from the FU budget. Stein followed through with a critical discussion about the "Red Freedom" project in the conservative newspaper Die Welt, hardly the normal channel through which the Social Democratic senator habitually communicated.[39]

Stein's concern was well founded. The affair continued to have political ramifications. The mass media picked up the cudgels and began to report on the project. Press reports and television programs spread word far and wide about the controversial experiment which had had such strong political overtones.[40] The Deutscher Kinderschutzbund (German League for the Protection of Children) issued a strong statement condemning the concept of an anti-authoritarian school. Its president, Walter Bäcker, saw it as an attempt to bolshevize children systematically and to encourage them to become sexual libertines.[41] The latter criticism was particularly telling with the general public. Especially disturbing for many had been the revelation that some of the co-workers had been encouraging the older children to experiment with sex, an issue that caused an emotional uproar. Obviously, the experiment had touched a raw nerve, and the repercussions were felt for years. The adult participants in the project, including the FU students, issued their viewpoint in a collectively authored work in which they made no concessions to their many critics. On the contrary, they lashed out at their critics, claiming that reactionary forces had instigated a campaign against them in the bourgeois press.[42] In defiance of their political foes, the author collective claimed to have learned much from the project which could be used in similar undertakings in the future. However, in June 1971, the German Psychological Society also criticized "Red Freedom" sharply as being carried out with doubtful scientific methods. They noted that there was no clear separation between observation of the children's behavior and efforts to alter that behavior. Moreover, the adult observers were for the most part not properly qualified to run the project.[43] In any case, the experiment proved to be a failure, with internal reports indicating a sharp drop in morale among the pupils and staff alike. Professor Rüthers, who sat on the board of trustees of the Free University, was incensed that the experiment, which had run with public funding, was a blatant effort to indoctrinate the children with Communist-revolutionary ideas. He even called for disciplinary proceedings against the student supervisors.[44] Eventually, Berlin's supreme court officially approved Senator Korber's 1970 order to close the after-school program.

NOFU AND THE BATTLE OF THE PRESS

Such revelations as the "Red Freedom" fiasco provided potent ammunition for the media-oriented NOFU, a coalition of conservatives and moderate Social Democrats. After a time, increasing numbers of academics and political figures alike began to speak of reform for the 1969 University Law. However, it was to be years before any significant amendment of the law took place. In essence, the complaints of NOFU about the tactics of the left were twofold. First, they maintained that the dissident groups were using virtually terrorist methods to gain their political ends, namely, the bolshevization of the universities. Second, the polarization, with commensurate increase in left influence in university affairs, was leading to a drastic drop in academic performance for the Free University and for the other West Berlin institutions of higher learning. Testing of students was being influenced by political factors and experiments in collective testing, and collective publication of research results was leading to a decline in the value of the degrees offered and in the research results. Moreover, the far left was using blatant partisan politics in selecting new university personnel, be they lowly student tutors, assistants, or even full professors. These were certainly grave charges for any university, and they were particularly damaging for the Free University, which had long been in the political limelight.

It is fair to say that the most critical period in the Free University's internal polarization occurred from 1969 to about 1973. Thereafter, despite occasional flare-ups, the general trend was toward a lessening of tensions and toward a tinkering with the 1969 University Law to produce a modified democratic system weighted more toward the traditional pillar of a university—the professors. In fact, not even the 1969 law produced a fully democratic decision-making system. That would have required the implementation of a one-person-one-vote arrangement and would have meant that the numerous committees at all levels would have been controlled by simple majority rule. With low voter turnouts especially by students in elections for the various committees and delibera-

tive bodies at the Free University—about twenty percent student participation became the norm—the far left would have come to dominate
university proceedings to a far greater degree than it actually did. Even
so, the new arrangement of the constitution, concentrated in triple parity, witnessed an unhealthy trend toward decision-making by blocs, the
blocs in turn determined by outright political considerations. The ivory
tower was shaken to its very foundations in those years of seemingly endless strife.

The NOFU group went about their task with bitter seriousness, as
did the radical left, each attacking the other unreservedly. The former,
as part of the larger BFW (League of Scholarly Freedom), began distribut-
ing publication after publication in 1970, drawing public attention to incidents and trends at the Free University. A rough index of the NOFU
group's activity can be seen in the fact that it issued twenty reports, including press conferences, in its first year of operation in 1970. A year
later, the pace doubled to forty. By 1972 it had reached sixty publications; in 1973 NOFU had seventy-four publications to its credit, and it
reached its high point with about a hundred bulletins, press conferences, and the like in 1974. Even more important, its distribution list
reached a circulation of approximately 11,000 at its high point. It
would be folly to underestimate the strategic intent of that distribution
list. It came to include all members of the Bundestag, all ten *Landtage*
in the Federal Republic, plus Berlin's House of Deputies. Similarly, the
ministries of the federal government and of the states received copies,
as did major employer associations and even some of the more conservative trade unions. The list was tantamount to a "Who's Who in German
Government and Employers." The major media received copies too.
Thus, such peccadilloes as the "Red Freedom" after-school program scandal took place in the full glare of publicity, a scandal that became well
known among influential centers of politics and economics.[45]

To understand the implications of this increasingly powerful group,
it is worthwhile to understand that NOFU began to publish lists of individuals at the Free University and elsewhere whom it identified as
being integral members of the various left-wing groups that formed the
leftward pole at the university. Members of the red cells, of the
K-groups, of the ADS factions, and many more became fair game for
NOFU information gatherers. Subsequently, alphabetical lists of dissidents, including the names, addresses, phone numbers, and political activities and affiliations of the mostly young radicals, went to all of the
above-mentioned centers of power.[46] In other words, both sides were playing political hardball. One of the left-wing preoccupations became the
identification of the increasingly dreaded NOFU members. It was in
some respects a heartless game, one that was played out in a climate of increasing fear and anxiety as the terrorist factions continued to operate
and to expand their operations in the Federal Republic and Berlin.

Such personal publicity seemed hardly to be a deterrent to left-wing dissidents, whose fury with and paranoia about right-wing conspiracies seemed if anything to increase. These blacklists, or perhaps grey lists, might on the surface seem more an irritant than anything else. However, the overall political developments in the Federal Republic in the early 1970s produced for a time a potentially unhealthy climate that threatened basic democratic premises. On the one hand, the emergence of terrorist groups such as the Baader-Meinhof gang gave plentiful ammunition to those who wished to attack the left. Waves of terror rose and ebbed in the 1970s. Even as late as the spring of 1975, a trend toward moderation seemed to have been cut short when the kidnapping by terrorists of Berlin's most prominent CDU political leader, Peter Lorenz, seemed to throw the city into the worst period of turmoil since the late 1960s. Such incidents were the backdrop behind a growing public urge to combat potentially dangerous trends, and they led to a fateful decision on the part of the government of SPD Chancellor Willy Brandt in early 1972.

If there was concern at the local level at the Free University that radicalized students were trying to take over the university or at least to make it conform to their political tenets, this was merely a microcosm in a national concern about the "generation of 1968" and its future impact upon society. In the four to five years since the growth of the student movement, the founders of the so-called APO (extraparliamentary opposition) had begun to emerge from the universities and to enter upon the careers for which their studies had prepared them. In a certain sense they became in 1972 victims of their own propaganda. Rudi Dutschke had proclaimed with no little bombast in 1968 that the dissidents were beginning their "long march through the institutions," that is, they were beginning through their individual careers a slow process of change that would ultimately dispense with a capitalist, pluralistic, in their eyes authoritarian state and society. By 1971 or 1972, the yellow press was already referring to the prominent student leaders of 1968, such as Sigrid Fronius, Rudi Dutschke, and others, as the *APO-opas* or APO-grannies. In other words, some of them were beginning to exceed those arbitrary age limits of thirty or thirty-five after which they were no longer formally members of the youthful generation. Indeed, for many the rhetoric was still there, and naturally press attention centered upon those who had not moderated their behavior or their radical goals, especially those who had joined the tiny terrorist bands.

This was the climate in which Chancellor Brandt convened the various ministers president of the *Länder* in January 1972 and declared an *Extremistenbeschluss*, an exclusion order from the civil service professions for those deemed to espouse radical politics such that they would endanger or undermine the constitution of the Federal Republic. This solidified into an agreement by the federal government and the Land governments to bar anybody from entering a public service position who had participated in unconstitutional activities. It was left to the authorities and later to the courts to decide the unconstitutionality for such actions as participation in a demonstration, the signing of various protest statements or petitions, or membership in certain organizations. The problem with this policy lay in the "preventive" powers of state authorities and in the fact that participation in legal activities could be construed as unconstitutional. The whole phenomenon can and has led into legal quagmires. For example, the West German Communist Party, the DKP, is an officially registered party and takes part in almost all federal and state elections; yet DKP members generally are not accepted in public service positions. This policy has been known popularly ever since as *Berufsverbot*, and its implications were wide-reaching, since a large number of positions in society are considered to be civil service positions. Unlike in the United States, German teachers and university faculty are also civil servants, and an exclusion order could potentially affect the careers of hundreds of thousands of individuals.

The story of *Berufsverbot* in the Federal Republic has received much attention from the many political groupings and from social scientists, and it would be repetitious to enumerate the many difficulties West German society has faced because of it. Suffice it to say here that *Berufsverbot* was from the first a highly controversial law that still excites political passions to this day. In this context, the publication of NOFU's lists of radicals and their political activities was much more than an embarrassment or minor irritant to left-wing dissidents. It had the potential to prevent them from entering a career at all. Nor was it confined strictly to the public sector. If the various employers' associations were receiving similar "black or grey" lists, it was conceivable that those seeking to establish careers with private firms would be similarly banned. The political right and the political left lost no time in engaging in charges and countercharges of unfair practices. This at least was the general political atmosphere in which developments at the Free University unfolded. Therefore, if it appeared that the rhetoric and the actions of various groups were characterized by excessive emotion and unreasonable suspicion, it was because of the lingering feud between the "'68ers" and their sworn enemies who ranged from moderate socialists to conservatives. On the one hand, many of those who had embraced the various left-wing splinter groups seemed unable to renounce their adherence to a given ideology. Public confessions of error on the left were a rarity. On the other hand, forbidding them access to careers which had any kind of official capacity, especially in an age when unemployment among university graduates was rising to an alarming degree, was also harsh. In a certain sense such young people were receiving the same treatment they would have liked to impose upon former National Socialists. The Americans in 1945 had initially looked upon former National Socialists as incorrigible and incapable of redemption, a policy that, in essence, held reeducation to be impossible. Later, especially in German hands, denazification came to be seen as a policy of rehabilitation. In a certain sense *Berufsverbot*, in attempting to eliminate alien or extreme ideologies from society one generation later, was committing the same mistakes as the conquerors of 1945. "I joined a Communist youth group because it was a lot of fun," commented one former member. "It was only later when I served with the *Bundeswehr* and was denied entry into certain fields that I realized that there could be negative consequences from such a membership."[47]

FAHNENFLUCHT (DESERTING THE FLAG)

For some, the perpetual crisis atmosphere had simply been too much. Starting in the late 1960s, a number of well-known academicians began leaving the Free University, and were replaced usually by younger academics who were in the earlier stages of their careers. Some but by no means all of those who left made public statements that usually condemned the university administration and conditions at the Free University generally. Perhaps one of the more famous personalities to depart with a rhetorical flourish was a historian and SPD member, Thomas Nipperdey. He felt that the 1969 University Law was a turning point in the affairs of the Free University, and not one for the better. Nipperdey was not at all happy about the role of city officials in the reform process. "The expressed intention of the legislator was to attain the modernization of the University through so-called 'democratization,' i.e., the participation of all groups in decision-making, and thereby to calm down the students, or—as was not always openly expressed—by a kind of appeasement policy to remove the radicals from the streets of the city and from opposition to the government back to the campus and its problems."[48]

There were those who sharply opposed the assertions of Nipperdey, most especially the university's vice president in charge of negotiating contracts for prospective professors, Uwe Wesel. "German professors do not like to lose," Wesel commented later in explaining the resentments felt by full professors who were outvoted under the triple or quadruple parity schemes after 1969. To be sure, Wesel, too, was surprised at the vehemence with which the radicals protested at the Free University after passage of the new law. "The worst confrontations at the FU did not occur in the period 1967-1968. Rather, the worst confrontations at the FU came in the period 1969-1972," he commented later. "The focus shifted to Dahlem."[49] Thus, the first years under the new law witnessed the most difficult conditions under which a professor could teach and research.

Even given those unfavorable conditions, Wesel felt that a myth had grown up around the "exodus" of professors away from the Free University in the late 1960s and early 1970s. He liked to compare the record of his administration under Kreibich to that of his predecessor in the same function, Fritz von Bergmann. Wesel's claim was that given the better financial situation at the university in the period under consideration—the Berlin Senate was generous in its funding of the Free University at that time—he actually compiled a better success rate in retaining capable faculty than had been the case before 1969. Claims by NOFU and other critics that there was too large a number of in-house appointments were only partially correct. In reality, in-house appointments had always been a common phenomenon at the Free University and were no more numerous in the years under consideration than they had been before. Wesel felt that claims from the right that radical student politics were the deciding factor for such departures ignored other, more pertinent factors. Wesel felt that Berlin, once the *Endstation* or place where a professor had truly "arrived," no longer had that enviable attractiveness. Formerly the capital of a united Germany, Berlin had offered cultural, geographic, and urban advantages unrivaled in the German-speaking world. Obviously that changed after 1945, so that other locations such as Munich now offered those advantages once associated with Berlin. Located well inside the GDR, West Berlin had to endure rigid geographical restrictions plus the political uncertainties and isolation of an island in a foreign ideological sea. Even if a prospective professor was interested in taking an appointment to the Free University, Wesel and other recruiting officials noted that frequently the spouse of the potential appointee was not so enthusiastic. Since the conclusion of the 1971 Quadripartite Agreement on Berlin, the problem of access greatly diminished, but it did not disappear. Geographical location continues to be a negative rather than a positive factor in attracting academics as well as citizens from any other walk of life to West Berlin.[50] The life of an FU recruiter was not enviable.

What Wesel did not address were the tensions that arose over the dramatic expansion of professorships at the Free University to include the C-2 and C-3 designations in addition to the C-4s, formerly the *Ordinarien*. Further tensions had arisen over the dramatic expansion of the *Mittelbau*, i.e., the *Assistenzprofessoren* and the *wissenschaftliche Assistenten*, who formed the bulk of the recently formed Mittelbau. Two Free University professors, Jürgen Domes and Armin Paul Frank, composed statistics on the shifting composition of faculty and found some striking results. In five areas—law, philosophy and sociology, political science, modern languages and literature, and mathematics—the number of full professors actually fell slightly from 59 to 58 during a two-year period. Among the junior untenured ranks the numbers of those teaching without a doctoral degree rose from 138 to 329 in the same period. "The vast majority of the junior teachers were brought very close to the level of the students in their academic qualifications," the two authors wrote. "In fact, most of the former are still postgraduate students, but as a rule they teach independent courses of their own planning. This is one of the reasons why students and junior faculty members frequently join forces on university boards."[51] To be sure, many of the senior professors were not pleased at the sudden diminution of their power at the Free University or at the other German universities where similar reforms and restructurings began to take place. This resentment served as at least one background reason for the departure of many of the more prominent full professors.

Perhaps one of the bitterest disputes within the Free University arose over the restructuring of the medical school. Because its main specialties were divided into *Fachbereiche* or departments like the rest of the university, critics immediately voiced concern that they were being artificially separated. Moreover, clinic directors complained that while they were still saddled with tremendous responsibilities, they no longer exercised the power to carry out those responsibilities because of democratization through triple-parity decision-making. For the senior medical professors at least, it was an intolerable situation, and the giant clinic at Steglitz, for which so many hopes had been raised as a pioneering effort at integration of medical specialties, went through no fewer than five directors in three years. There had even been mumblings among the senior staff, including the by now aged former rector, Hans von Kress, to split away from the Free University and create a separate medical university. That radical move came to nothing, but the dissatisfaction of the senior medical experts at the university was palpable. One manifestation of this deep dissatisfaction was the sudden resignation in March 1973 from the Free University of a respected internist and current director of the clinic at Westend, Günter Neuhaus.

A student of von Kress, for seventeen years a member of the Free University, and at age fifty-one one of its most successful medical scientists, Neuhaus chose a particularly dramatic way to demonstrate his dissatisfaction. Other professors had gone elsewhere, but Neuhaus decided not only to resign from the university, but to abandon his professorship entirely. He chose to work in a private clinic instead. While such options were more readily open to medical scientists than, for example, to social scientists, it was most unusual for someone in Neuhaus's senior position in the prestigious German academic world to take such a drastic step. It also meant giving up his status as a civil servant, another prized feature of a German professorship. It is fair to say that Neuhaus, in making such a gesture, was trying to make a statement. He sent a strongly worded letter to Governing Mayor Klaus Schütz outlining the reasons for his actions, and he repeated the same message over West Berlin's second major radio network, *Sender Freies Berlin* (SFB). "The reasons for my departure are intimately connected to developments in the clinical realm at the University, which have resulted directly from the [1969] University Law.''[52] It was Neuhaus's contention that the democratically intended reforms stemming from that law had come at the expense of the patient. "Activities in those committees ordained by law, which in the end consumed over half of my working day, are no substitute for patient care, research, and teaching," Neuhaus maintained. He contended that besides the usual human weaknesses exhibited during committee feuding, he was particularly galled at the constant harping about medicine serving the needs of society to the point that that platitude had become, he said, "an ideological fetish," one which did not, in fact, serve the patient. Instead, the atmosphere of political contentiousness and the constant struggle to shepherd a clinic's means, personnel, and facilities through the endless chains of committees finally produced the opposite of professional collegiality. Rather, widespread mistrust and finally resignation resulted. Neuhaus ponted out that he, along with other colleagues, had presented reform proposals in the field of clinical medicine only to be ignored by the authorities at the university and in the Berlin Senate. He, for one, was retreating to private medical practice in order to continue with the vital work in his field. NOFU duly distributed Neuhaus's open letter to its comprehensive list of governmental officials and agencies and added its own stinging commentary about further desertions from the Free University by other qualified medical personnel. Neuhaus's reputation scarcely suffered from his resignation and the wide exposure it received. The German Society for Internal Medicine promptly elected him to be its next chairman, and he continued his medical career outside the academic world.[53]

Two critical observers at the Free University, Professors Domes and Frank, also commented on the situation: "Most recently [1975], a number of head nurses and other persons have given notice of intention to resign, citing the deteriorating medical service as the reason for their resignation. It is beyond doubt that both in the medical school and in the rest of the FU, the number of truly renowned scholars who do come to Berlin is smaller than it used to be."[54]

OPINION SURVEY

Despite the truth to Wesel's assertions that some professors remained unmoved by the tensions and either remained in Berlin or were not deterred from arriving there, it was also an undeniable fact that the general mood of the professors in the first half year after passage of the 1969 University Law showed unmistakable signs of discontent. Not only individual professors like Nipperdey told the story. In January 1970, a national polling group, the Allensbach Institute of Lake Constance (much like the Gallup Poll), interviewed 58 full professors, 48 associate professors and lecturers (termed *ausserplanmässige Professoren und Dozenten* according to the old system of classification), 49 assistants, and 266 students. The results showed some distinctive differences in general political attitudes and opinions on specific FU-related issues among the groups listed above. First, none of the professors and only 2 percent of the middle-level faculty and assistants claimed to hold "far left" political views. Yet, 20 percent of the students made that claim. If asked if they held "moderate left" views, no less than 37 percent of the full professors answered yes, and mid-level tenured faculty gave 36 percent. However, fully 65 percent of the assistants claimed to have moderate left convictions, followed by 46 percent for the students. Those who responded with "middle" to the same question of political loyalty included 43 percent for the full professors, 33 for the mid-level tenured professors, 15 for the assistants, and 20 percent for the students. The numbers of respondents who described themselves as moderate conservatives fell sharply in each category (e.g., 15 percent for professors, and 11 percent for students), and virtually no one staked out a "strongly conservative" position. Thus, the FU community—if it could still be labeled as such—was largely grouped in the moderate left and middle categories.[55] Significant was the fact that fully a fifth of the students rated themselves as having "far left" political views, and nearly two-thirds of the untenured assistants were "moderate left," almost double the proportion of the full professors. However, the academic community as a whole was anything but conservative in its political views, a fact that is even more striking since the general political spectrum among West Germans was to the left of its American counterpart.

Nevertheless, some salient facts emerged from the survey. First, the professors were much better informed on the details of the 1969 law than the students (91 percent as opposed to 25 percent). When asked whether they viewed the new law positively, 42 percent of the professors answered yes and 48 percent answered no. For the tenured mid-level professors and untenured assistants the reply was 63 and 70 percent positive but only 27 and 22 percent negative. Surprisingly, 40 percent of the students opposed the new law. Other divergences could be seen. Half of the professors opposed the idea of an assistant being president—an obvious reference to Kreibich. Yet, 94 percent of the students and 88 percent of the self-same assistants responded positively. After two months of a Kreibich presidency nearly half of the professors disagreed with his policies (only 14 percent were in agreement), whereas only 7 percent of students disagreed. Half of the professors felt that the proportion of students in decision-making bodies was too high, and, not surprisingly the students, or nearly half of them, felt that the proportion was too small.[56]

Pertinent to the matter of faculty satisfaction or dissatisfaction were the results of two questions. The respondents were asked: "Is your teach-

ing at the FU adversely affected or not affected by the tense relationships at the FU?" The professors responded with 31 percent claiming
either to be strongly or moderately affected, but 69 percent said they
were not adversely affected. This statistic was a striking reminder that
the disruptions, sit-ins, teach-ins, and the like affected only certain faculties or departments or certain professors. They were not a blanket phenomenon. Nevertheless, the generally tense atmosphere had other negative consequences. When asked the same question but with respect to
their research as opposed to their teaching, 52 percent of the professors
agreed that the tense atmosphere had had a negative effect. Perhaps
most telling of all was the professors' reply to the following question:
"Would you leave the FU if that were possible?" Fully 48 percent said
they would leave the university. Furthermore, 47 percent listed the
tense atmosphere as the reason for leaving; only 1 percent cited other reasons. That was a sobering statistic and demonstrated that professors
like Nipperdey were not major exceptions.[57] He had had the option to
leave, and he had voted with his feet. So for a time did others. The
Allensbach survey, conducted in January 1970, was not entirely representative of the Kreibich years since it was conducted so early in his
time in office. However, the height of the radical wave had not been
reached yet. It reached its apex by around June 1971 with the Meinecke-
Institute takeover and with physical attacks upon Professor Alexander
Schwan, an episode described below. Thus, the statistics were unlikely
to have shown an improvement in professorial assessment of conditions at the Free University in the succeeding one or two years. Moreover, the survey showed consistent differences in attitudes between the
professors and the assistants or *Mittelbau*. The latter, whose untenured
status left them more vulnerable, were understandably more enthusiastic about the new constitution and the Kreibich administration. After
all, they and the students were largely responsible for electing him in
the first place.

MORE TESTIMONIALS

There were ample testimonials to this time of the professors' discontent. Some broadcast their opinions about conditions at the Free University far and wide. Thus, Werner Philipp at the Institute of Eastern European Studies wrote to a colleague at the Ford Foundation in New York,
David Bell, with whom he had just had a discussion while the latter
was visiting the Free University. Philipp hastened to assure Bell that
"the friendly picture of a mediating president between the 'progressive-
radical students' and the 'reactionary professors' is unfortunately a false
one." He, like Nipperdey, saw some student groups as aiming "at the disintegration of parliamentary democracy while pursuing either utopian-
perfectionist conceptions or picking up notions of the socialist move-

ment of the nineteenth or early twentieth centuries." Even when it was a leftist vision, this turning to the past was, Philipp decided, fundamentally conservative. "Furthermore," he continued, "it is abstract and emotional and in this respect conforms only to bad German thought patterns." Philipp claimed that the great majority of professors had not wanted to revive the old-fashioned form of German university. The Free University, from its beginnings a reform university, had pioneered in employing student representation at all levels. Yet, the mood in 1970 was utterly different. "My colleagues and I are deeply concerned about the improper politicization of the University," he told Bell. "Within the framework of a scientific search for truth, political decision-making has no part," he complained. The validity of a joint research project or an individual initiative could not be decided by a political majority but only by objective discussion on a case by case basis. "Our greatest concern, however," the embittered Philipp stated, "is that among the students there is one and only one truth, namely the Marxist-Leninist one. This is axiomatic, and so from the first it precludes the search for other verities. I for one do not want the German university to lose its openness and to degenerate into a confessional school."[58]

Philipp's assessment of Kreibich represented one body of opinion among the senior professors, many of whom were members of NOFU. Yet, for the time being there was little he and others could do about it. "At the Free University," reported Ford Foundation representative William B. Bader in November 1971, "while the electors 'elect' and the senior faculty despair, brood, or take to drink in their tents, President Kreibich seems to have drawn all power to himself and to his team."[59] Kreibich hardly felt so omnipotent. He recalled later that during an official visit to the United States on behalf of the Free University, he became painfully aware of his NOFU critics' success in explaining their position and of calling into doubt the reputation of the Free University. Moreover, he was eventually compelled by events to take on other vice presidents with differing political views, thus creating an internal system of checks and balances which reduced his influence considerably, he felt.[60]

Other critics of the new system agreed heartily with Philipp's assessment. Nipperdey, while admitting that Kreibich was no violent revolutionary, nevertheless felt he was dependent upon his left-wing constituents and so reacted to violence on campus "with a policy of appeasement, wherein he strives to implement the nucleus of radical demands, the so-called 'rational nucleus.'" Like Bader, Nipperdey saw the position of the president as much stronger than that of the former rector. "Endowed by the law with strong powers," Nipperdey continued, "he has set up a uniformly leftist administration, interprets his competence quite widely and as widely applies the law in favour of the New Left. He exercises massive pressure on other bodies, e.g., in the senate where he has no clear majority he can determine its course because he is chairman and sets up the agenda, and furthermore because he has the exclusive right of nominating members of commissions." Nipperdey's indignation grew. "With various tricks he tries to block decisions not corresponding to his wishes. Since he has agents or followers in every body and collaborates with the Jacobins of the campus and their mass meetings, his power position is enormous." The efforts of the lawmakers to create a new constitution with the usual checks and balances had come to nothing. The position of the president was, according to Nipperdey's assessment, nearly unassailable.[61]

In essence, Nipperdey's strongest objection to the new president was that he was not effective in bringing a halt to left-wing efforts to subvert the Free University from within. "The Jacobins among the students," he wrote, "once anarchy had run its course, became communists." They did not proclaim adherence to communism as practiced in the Soviet Union, the GDR, or any other communist-run state, dismissing them as examples of "vulgar Marxism." For them, the Free University was a means to an end: "All of the leftist groups have as their principal goal not the change of the university, but the change of society in the socialist sense." Once again, the socialist ideal was not directed at an existing society but rather toward an ideal instead. "There is a lot of talk about the responsibility of the university toward society," Nipperdey continued, "but this never refers to society as it exists, but to the ideal, usually neo-Marxist society postulated by the leftists, to which empirical society is expected graciously to accommodate itself." Nipperdey was convinced that this attempted transformation of the university by the left was unrealistic. "In place of the conservative idea of the ivory tower, we have the idea of a red ivory tower, in which the self-appointed elite decides what is beneficial for society."[62] Perhaps his strongest criticism arose with respect to those who now embraced the radical movement. "When I came to Berlin in 1967," Nipperdey wrote, "the majority of the radical students were intelligent and knowledgeable. Despite their ideological narrowmindedness, discussion with them was still possible. This is no longer so at all." The radical students of the early 1970s were a breed apart. Nipperdey continued: "Since the movement has become fashionable, there is a high percentage of rather stupid students among the radicals. The ideology of revolutionary action has led to an extraordinary decline of knowledge and intellectual interest." What he found in discussions was that while Marxism might be in vogue, that did not necessarily mean that the participants were well read. Many had gained their Marxism third-hand. "I simply cannot bear it when leftists are stupid," stated Nipperdey's avowedly left-leaning assistant. He replied: "I am afraid you will have to get used to that here."[63]

The emotional effect of the New Left's seeming success at the Free University upon some of the full professors was certainly profound.

Ford Foundation representative William Bader was struck by the vehemence expressed by otherwise deliberate and rational professors during a visit to the university at the end of 1971. "I still have in my mind a clear picture of Ric Löwenthal," he reported, "one of the most articulate and thoughtful commentators on the international political scene, all but reduced to a stuttering incomprehensible attack on the 'roten Kaderschmiede.' No doubt Löwenthal has been profoundly shaken by his experience with the radicals in the classroom and with the Wesels in the new power structure," Bader added. "But I was simply not prepared for the contempt, loathing and fear which Löwenthal and his colleagues displayed. . . . They were 'out' and seeking an air raid shelter as Löwenthal put it."[64]

Other observers were nearly as adamant about the need to modify the recent university reforms. Ursula Brumm, a historian and professor of American literature who had remained at the John F. Kennedy Institute despite numerous offers of professorships abroad, relayed her feelings to members of the Ford Foundation at almost the same time. One of them recorded her sentiments: "She says there is growing sentiment in Berlin that the law which created the present situation must be changed, but she said even if the change were to come soon, it would be three to five years before the 'desperate situation' could be reversed. She emphasized that in her view the conflict was not between progress and reform on one side and the status quo and conservatism on the other. She says the present situation is just anarchic and is destructive of all features of the intellectual life of the Institute."[65] Brumm had a point. There were times when the politicization process reached intolerable levels, as the following example indicates.

A QUESTION OF BASIC LIBERTIES

This incident was representative of the disruptions and confrontations that became a feature of life at the Free University during the all-but-unknown academic "war" of the early 1970s. Scores of cases that unfolded during those troubled times on the Dahlem campus could also serve to illustrate the problem of academic freedom versus radical confrontation. However, in this instance the event brought into bold relief the basic issue confronting a democracy: the right of members of a society to express themselves freely. That it affected some of the most left-oriented faculty at the Free University lent a special poignancy to the dispute.

In January 1972, the Free University's Department of Political Sciences hosted a three-day international conference on "crisis research." Political scientists from various Western nations gathered in West Berlin to discuss practical and theoretical possibilities for the research of crises. On the first day the participants were to gather at the Henry Ford Bau for an opening session. However, members of the KSV (League of Communist Students) had gotten wind of the crisis conference, and as one observer noted, they used it "to stage a crisis of their own making." As the crisis experts approached the main building, "about one hundred KSV members linked arms to prevent about twice that number of conference participants from entering the auditorium. When it was decided to move the conference to a smaller auditorium in the same building, some of the burlier communist students rushed to barricade the entrance to the new location." One of the professors tried to shove his way through and a melee developed at that point. After more confusion and milling about, the organizers decided to hold their meeting at West Berlin's famed Congress Hall (dubbed the "Pregnant Oyster" by the irreverent Berliners because of its bulbous shape), across town and well away from the Free University. After some delay, about a hundred professors, assistants, and students showed up, and many of them objected to the police protection that had been provided in an effort to prevent a repetition of the morning's event.[66]

The KSV protesters were objecting to the presence of "specialists of international counterrevolution" at the conference, and their ire settled especially upon the American participants such as political scientist Ted Gurr, from Northwestern University, whom they claimed was a CIA agent. They also claimed that the U.S. Department of Defense was funding other crisis research projects, and they included President Kreibich in their condemnations for having allowed the conference to take place at the Free University.

This was not to say that the conference participants were all ideological foes of the KSV. A strong Marxist faction among the university's political scientists had helped plan the conference, and they found themselves confronted with a dilemma at the Congress Hall, having been ousted from the university by physical force. Their justification for inviting the American experts in addition to the others was "that an intellectual confrontation with the 'agents of the Pentagon' was preferable to denying the Americans and the other conference participants the right to speak at the University." That afternoon, the attendees voted to return to the university despite rough handling by the KSV demonstrators.

Thereupon the participants trooped back to the Free University. "With their assistance," an American chronicler noted, "passage was opened to the University auditorium, where subsequent sessions were filled with the rhetoric of competing leftist groups." The second day saw a wearisome repetition of the first day's events. The KSV forces blocked passage to the conference rooms once again, "while leftist groups pushed and grabbed for control of the bullhorn and launched end-

less harangues against each other and against all things American."
Once again the crisis-plagued crisis experts retreated back to the distant
Congress Hall.

Sadder and wiser, the conference organizers announced that henceforth all remaining conference sessions would take place at the Congress
Hall. No sooner had they announced the decision than the first speaker
that day, Norwegian social scientist Johann Galtung, stated that he
would deliver his paper at the Free University or else he would not
deliver it at all. What to do? Heads conferred, and the crisis experts
trekked the by-now familiar route back to Dahlem. This time, however,
they instituted a tactical diversion. While the KSV were patrolling
the ramparts of the Auditorium Maximum, the participants swarmed
into the nearby Otto Suhr Institute, where they resumed their work.
"The KSV was caught off guard," U.S. Mission officials recounted,
"but about fifty of their group entered the back of the hall and interrupted
the speaker with a bullhorn. There followed a spirited debate in which
the pro-conference leftists, led by Professor Galtung and FU Professor
Altvater, succeeded in exposing the simplistic anti-intellectualism of
the KSV and arguing its spokesmen into a sullen silence." The legitimate
speakers were able to resume their activities and the conference ended
with a reaffirmation of the right to free speech at the Free University.[67]

The much buffeted conference on crisis research brought into bold relief the limits of protest in a democratic society. It should be remembered that the German student movement had made its start in 1965
over the issue of free speech, and its early leaders had consciously
adopted the principle of the Berkeley Free Speech movement, demanding free discussion on all topics at any place and at any time. Seven
years later a distant offshoot of that reform movement, the KSV, was engaged in massive and palpable violations of the fundamental principle
of free speech, so much so that it forced other left-wing groups finally
to take a stand. "Previous neutrality, or benign acceptance of radical behavior was replaced by strong, public condemnation of the anarchist-
communist denial of free speech," commented a U.S. Mission official.
"The office of the President of the Free University reminded the students that one basis for the reform of the University, with which the President is identified, was to give all political philosophies, including Marxism, absolute freedom of expression. It was pointed out that this
principle must apply to all groups or it would end up applying to none."[68]

One result of the events surrounding the crisis conference of January 1972 was that it began to give some students pause about supporting the truly radical organizations such as the KSV. It also caused the
Kreibich administration to consider doing what it claimed it would
never do, namely, call in the police to restore order. An American
official heard that the confrontation had caused intense debate in the
university president's staff as to how to meet this latest crisis. "An

inside observer reported that the president's office was at one point ready to call police onto the campus to break the blockade. This reflected a certain feeling of desperation among the University's reform socialists, the moderates from which Kreibich draws much of his support." Yet, in the end, the final decision was to refrain from taking such drastic action. The American observer added that "most University leaders recognize that the presence of police on campus would be the one catalyst which could unite the splintered left in serious demonstrations." He felt that the militants within the KSV may have overplayed their hand and may have caused some to desert that cause since even they felt that discussion was preferable to mere obstructionism. "General student sentiment," he added, "much of it receptive to the standard Marxist shibboleths about U.S. imperialism, etc., was hostile to the KSV imposition of their minority will on the majority." The discrediting of the far left in the eyes of the moderate majority was no bad thing for the Americans, but they also were worried about another phenomenon associated with the tactics of violence. It directed attention toward the perpetrators. The Mission observer concluded that "the publicity received by the KSV has established it as an organization which is not afraid to challenge authority. This kind of reputation can be very attractive to new university entrants, many of whom are imbued with a Gymnasium-bred contempt for all authority."[69]

As it turned out, the militant core of the KSV apparently had learned nothing and forgotten nothing from the unsettling confrontation. Within a matter of months it renewed its disruptive actions. President Kreibich had continued to receive severe criticism for not reacting strongly enough to the violence or the threat of violence that hung like a cloud over the Free University campus. Now public attention had been drawn to the unsavory actions of the KSV, thus forcing his hand. Several political leaders had begun calling for legislation to ban the KSV as an illegal terrorist organization. It is perhaps just as well that this ill-conceived initiative fizzled out, since the KSV's members could have changed their name more quickly than the clumsy political apparatus could issue bans. Nevertheless, a showdown of some kind was coming. To understand it, it is instructive to follow the career of one of the original architects of university reform in Berlin.

UNIVERSITY REFORM RECONSIDERED: THE METAMORPHOSIS OF ALEXANDER SCHWAN

Alexander Schwan, a political scientist, was one of the early faculty advocates of constitutional reform at the Free University. It would be an exaggeration to name him as the principal architect of the 1969 University Law, because that legislation resulted from the efforts of many individuals and groups. However, Schwan was certainly a central figure in the evo-

lution of that law and, just as important, in the creation in 1968 of a
new constitution for the Otto Suhr Institute. The latter had been made
possible in turn by the *Vorschaltgesetz* (enabling law) passed by the Berlin House of Deputies. Schwan's initial support of the reform process,
his disillusionment following its implementation, and his efforts to sal-
vage the most workable parts of it afterward offer a worthwhile description of the rise and fall in the fortunes of that controversial legislation.

In 1966, Schwan arrived at the Free University from Freiburg im
Breisgau, already a reputed political scientist, and at age thirty-five one
of the younger full professors in German higher education. A member
of the mainstream SPD and simultaneously a practicing Catholic, the
youthful Schwan was not easily categorized, but he was hardly a supporter of conservative causes either. He looked with considerable sympathy upon the dissidents' early calls for free speech, their demands for a revival of student participation in deciding the affairs of the university,
and their concern about general social and political issues of the day.
Schwan was one of those who felt that the university administration's
early responses to student criticisms had been unimaginative and unac-
ceptably inflexible. He was appalled at the almost continuous police
presence at the FU campus in the late 1960s. "In the summer of
1968, we experienced repeated occupations of the OSI which we could
not prevent even with the use of the police," he recalled. "Given
these circumstances, the uppermost concern for my colleagues and
me was how we could resolve a highly dangerous situation."[70] Because
the confrontations and tensions hit the OSI with particular severity,
there was no way that he and his colleagues in the institute could
ignore the sit-ins, teach-ins, "go-ins," and other actions of the dissident
groups. Schwan was convinced that the solution to the woes facing
the Free University in general and the OSI in particular was not to
be found in placing ever greater reliance upon the power apparatus
of the State, namely, the police. The continuous confrontations should
cease and the political scientists, strategically located within a mul-
tidisciplinary institute, the OSI, should take the lead in attempting
a new structural form that was capable somehow of accommodating
both full professors and the increasingly radicalized students. It was
Schwan's hope that such a reform would help mobilize the moderate
students and bring them back into the political life of the institute
where they would act as a counterbalance to the radicals.

Schwan maintained that it would be best to fashion a new university constitution in which the various factions shared power and engaged in a constructive dialogue with each other. The practical realities
of the situation would force the extremist groups to modify their demands. Students and especially the many social and political scientists
at the OSI would obtain practical as well as abstract exposure to their discipline as they learned to carry on the affairs of the university. Schwan
was acting director at the OSI in 1967 and 1968, and therefore in a key po-

sition to further the reform process. Schwan and other reform-minded professors, such as Werner Skuhr, hoped to rescue the concept of a community of teachers and learners at the Free University. Given these motives and the fact that the university's existing constitution was thoroughly discredited, Schwan joined various professors, assistants, students, and political leaders in fashioning a new constitution at the OSI in 1968. They did so under the widespread impression that the *Ordinarienuniversität*, the university run by full professors, was dead.[71] Schwan was, as mentioned, a prominent coauthor of the 1969 University Law as well.

The structure that emerged for the OSI was not, strictly speaking, *Drittelparität*. The professors by no means held a majority, but they were still the single most influential group. Moreover, their assumption was that the representatives from the *Mittelbau* and qualified, older students would participate positively in the decision-making process, a process which would act to moderate extremist tendencies. In any case, they reasoned, the old structure no longer sufficed. The philosophy faculty had grown over the years to the point that it seemed ungovernable, and there was a general feeling that the old system could not and should not be revised.[72] Besides, the new regulations were seen as frankly experimental and were to remain in effect for only a year before being reviewed.

Then, in 1970, Schwan took a half-year sabbatical to England before returning to his duties at the Free University. What he saw upon his return convinced him that the 1969 University Law had gone wrong, terribly wrong. The various factions instead of working together were farther apart than ever, and blatant partisan politics were everywhere to be seen. Being an academician of conviction and aware that he bore the responsibility for much of what had happened, he determined to try to correct the abuses and weaknesses in the new law which he felt were undermining the character and reputation of the Free University. Thus motivated, Schwan proceeded to write a series of articles in newspapers and journals, critical of the new university law and the way it was being implemented at the Free University.[73]

Schwan noted that the end of the 1960s had seen many observers of the German universities expressing pessimism and sharp criticism of the way the universities had developed. Foremost among them was Helmut Schelsky, a famed sociologist at the universities in Bielefeld and Münster. Such critics of German higher education spread the blame liberally among students, assistants, professors, educational administrators, and even the public at large. Schwan explained that he had not succumbed to any such universal despair. In 1968 he had believed instead that it would be possible to create new forms of governance for select parts of the university which could then serve to guide the rest to a new kind of working relationship.

In 1971, a sobered Schwan had come to different conclusions. "I confess that I cannot maintain any such conviction today," he wrote in a widely circulated journal, Die Neue Rundschau. "Not only the old but also the new university appears to have become the stage of a major failure. . . ."[74] Schwan's biggest disappointment was that the new university law, instead of lessening the polarization process, had actually increased it to an alarming degree. The restructured or newly constituted committees at the Free University had come to be seen by the radical students, preaching their firebrand forms of Marxism, as springboards for the advancement of their own ideology. Now they posed fully as much of a threat against a freely functioning institution of higher learning as had the radical mobs of the late 1960s whose actions in essence had destroyed the old form of university. Worse still, this latest threat from the newest of the New Left was largely unknown to the general public. They remained ignorant of the secret war being waged in the corridors and seminars at the universities.

Although disappointed with the results of the reform legislation to date, Schwan had by no means turned into a blind opponent of reform. "On the contrary," he wrote, "I maintain that we should redouble our efforts with respect to university politics to save the substance of that reform. I am convinced more than ever of the need for a reform of higher education."[75]

Schwan had expected that the new democratic university structure would win over enough of the left-wing splinter groups and give them practical experience in decision-making, so that it would take the wind out of the sails of the most disruptive groups and return the dissidents to more moderate positions. "This hope was not fulfilled for various reasons," Schwan conceded. "For one, within the ranks of the liberal students, assistants, and professors, too few were willing to become active and to mobilize themselves despite the new opportunity to take an active part in the affairs of the university and to provide a counterbalance to extreme, radical, and revolutionary tendencies." He also observed later, like many others, that with the passage of time, the majority of students became bored with constant appeals to support one cause or another, and thus disengaged from voting in student elections. In effect, this left the field open to a relatively small minority of committed students who usually espoused one radical doctrine or another. This led to a sometimes gross overrepresentation of splinter groups on university committees, groups which were well outside the political mainstream. Schwan also blamed the ranks of conservative professors who all too frequently had withdrawn from the fray and whose absence had eliminated another counterweight to the radical elements. Finally, the reformers who in the period from 1967 to 1969 had worked on reform legislation could not have predicted that the various splinter groups that became successors to the SDS would evolve into dogmatic Marxists or blind followers of other ideologues and would display, said Schwan, "an unscrupulousness and decisiveness in their agitation and propaganda and also in their actions which hitherto had been unknown." Indeed, the various splinter groups displayed the most varied tactical and strategic goals and were constantly feuding with each other. However, they had this much in common: They were bent upon building authoritarian cadres, the "avant-garde of the proletariat," which would engage in a radical class struggle against capitalism and its "bourgeois handservants." This meant that they condemned bourgeois democracy, seeking instead to establish the dictatorship of the proletariat. "With this struggle in mind they intend in good Leninist fashion to make use of a wide spectrum of political power groups depending upon the constellation. In a minority situation it is the popular front strategy, ruthless exploitation of committees where a majority exists, also disruptions and boycotts of . . . 'bourgeois' classes, and finally actions of physical violence and even flirting with the methods of urban guerillas."[76]

Such groups tended to bend all discussions and debates concerning society, politics, and economics into simplistic arguments about capital and wages. Political groupings were arrayed into "friend versus enemy" relationships. This had an especially notable effect upon those who were just entering university studies, Schwan wrote, so that such "dogmatic training nips in the bud all critical work, and the ability to ask critical questions." As a consequence, socialist or Marxist studies were being demanded in various disciplines, "which would guarantee that from beginning to end students would be concerned only with Marxist ideology in previously decided learning materials and class work. They would use only Marxist theories and methods and would confront 'bourgeois' scholarship exclusively through Marxist interpretations and during Marxist lectures. This may sound absurd, but if it succeeds—and they are well on their way—then a Marxist party school at the university will be established, financed by means of state budgets." Initially, the intent was to institute such blatantly ideological curricula alongside the others and then to use that secure base to eliminate bourgeois scholarship and bourgeois science. Thus, the intention of these determined groups was to pervert the university reforms which originally had sought to make the universities function more democratically. "If we look at developments in the last six years since 1965, then we see that the German university is moving on its way from an *Ordinarienuniversität* [a university run by full professors] not to a democratic one with the free association of all groups as was intended. Rather it is leading to its being overpowered by dogmatic leftist ideologues and revolutionaries."

Schwan's concern was that the universities would not be able to free themselves through their own efforts from this insidious politicization process, and he did not attempt to make light of what he felt was a sinister development. "Democracy combined with those who have contempt for democracy, tolerance toward those who are intolerant, jobs and civil-service status for . . . revolutionaries—those are in the long run deadly inconsistencies. They could lead to a situation where 'Bonn' turns into another Weimar in the realm of the universities." Schwan urged instead that state authorities and the members of the academic community devote greater attention to their universities, that they examine more closely the curricula, the testing procedures, and the appointment especially of younger faculty. Schwan referred to the splitting up of the Free University's Psychology Institute as a positive development since the one, he claimed, had become an openly Marxist-Leninist institute which needed a pluralistic one to counterbalance it. He was even willing to see that state authorities intervene directly in the affairs of specific departments which had fallen into an ideological trap. "Where the refunctioning of institutes and departments into party schools is advanced and scholarly/scientific work is materially threatened, then the appropriate state authorities should not hesitate in future to close such institutes or departments temporarily until the conditions for free, cooperative work on the basis of tolerance have been created again."[77] With the issuance of that statement an irony became complete. Berlin's Free University had come into existence in 1948 through a coalition of democratically motivated students, professors, and others who were protesting against state interference in the internal affairs of the old university. Now, almost exactly a generation later, Schwan and the rapidly growing movement he represented were demanding openly that the State exercise its authority comprehensively within the Free University. Indeed, the goal was to restore democratic procedures and pluralistic learning in the Western sense. Nevertheless, the irony remained.

Schwan announced that he was now disavowing the reform experiment featuring triple parity that had begun in modified fashion and with high hopes at the Otto Suhr Insitute. "This principle came ten years too late or too early, and it is possible that its chances of realization have been destroyed for all time," he commented. However, he also targeted the leading office of the university for criticism. "For a truly democratically functioning decision-making body at the university, it is of greatest importance to place limits upon the powers of the new university presidents, including their staffs, who were chosen in a decidely partisan way." This was a thinly veiled reference to President Kreibich and to kindred spirits like Wesel or the university's first chancellor under the new law, Detlef Borrmann. If it was once claimed that the old rectors were too partisan and too much the representatives of the full professors, now the successor presidents were proving to be even more partisan, he felt, and too much the representatives of the left-leaning groups. Schwan hoped for a rationalization of the various new committees and representative bodies at the universities, stating that their sheer increase in numbers and complexity simply strengthened the power of the central executive instead. He was not calling for a halt to reform, but he was declaring that the reform as presently executed was leading to a disastrous decline in the reputation of the German university.[78]

In a kind of one-man crusade, Schwan repeated his harsh condemnation in broad-circulation newspapers and personally before various groups of academics.[79]

The one-time reformer's continuing criticisms brought forth strong reactions at all levels. Foremost among them, FU Vice President Uwe Wesel sought to refute Schwan's arguments in a similarly lengthy rebuttal in the same journal in which Schwan had launched his campaign. Wesel remained a wholehearted advocate of the reforms which had been enacted in 1969, and he did not shrink from calling the critics, including Schwan, advocates of a "counterreformation" in university affairs. For Wesel, the SDS proposals of 1961, a key provision of which was triple parity, had been unusually prescient and deserved to be perpetuated. Wesel pointed out that the new law had streamlined university administration, creating a unified, stronger presidency to replace the superannuated dual-track rector-curator system that had signally failed to surmount the crises of the 1960s. Now, he professed to see through the efforts of backsliders like Schwan and conservative elements in NOFU among others, an unwarranted rise in state interference in the affairs of the university, a sin which the great Humboldt had attempted to prevent in 1810. "It is beginning again in Berlin," Wesel warned, referring to Stein's interference in FU affairs. "Senator Stein is forbidding three seminars in German Studies, which are allegedly Communist."[80] Wesel argued forcefully that Schwan, too, had become a supreme advocate of state interference in university affairs, motivated by his personal disappointment with reform as he had experienced it at the OSI. Wesel was at pains to point out that among the approximately 500 professors at the Free University, perhaps one was a Marxist, as he saw it. There were 400 assistants and assistant professors of whom perhaps 30 to 40 were Marxists, and perhaps as many as 50 of what he called "leftists." Of the 1,300 part-timers, tutors, and work-study students, only 10 percent could be put into the left-wing camp, according to his reckoning. This hardly amounted to the kind of subversion, Wesel stated, that Schwan was claiming had occurred at the Free University. Wesel spoke of subterfuges and machinations on both sides, but he was especially incensed, he said, at the tactics of one NOFU-oriented professor who appeared to be seeking a physical confrontation with students so that the shocking event would appear in the newspapers.[81]

There was much more in Wesel's rebuttal, but he ended his statement with the claim that Schwan had misunderstood the nature of university reform. It was not, first of all, democratization and the improvement of efficiency at the universities; rather, it was the reform of studies, i.e., curricular reform, that was the desired goal. Wesel called for a new interpretation of *Wissenschaft* (science or scholarship), and claimed that Schwan had failed to address himself to this new orientation. "Alexander Schwan is one of those reformers," Wesel said, "who saw changes in higher education as formal institutional reform." Wesel interpreted Schwan's reform expectations as basically conservative. "In essence, everything was to remain the same," the Vice President said of Schwan's intentions. "He had not thought about changes in *Wissenschaft*. Now he notices suddenly what consequences occur from the reform of institutions, and he draws back." However, Wesel was prepared to continue with the reform process: "We must attempt," he concluded, "to come to a well-ordered coexistence of bourgeois *Wissenschaft* and scientific socialism." He claimed that the older professors could not comprehend the problem, and so he placed his faith instead on the younger ranks of professors, assistants, and students. He asked that the reader understand that the Marxists as a minority would always appear dogmatic, a feature which all minority groups shared in common. Changes in laws were not the solution, Wesel stated. "Ten years ago this reform must have appeared utopian. Two years ago it went into effect. It stood to reason that difficulties would arise, and it was also to be expected that some reformers could not go the distance. One of these is Alexander Schwan. Pity."[82] Obviously, Schwan's journalistic attack had struck a raw nerve in the university's second most influential administrative official.

However, events conspired to strengthen the position of Schwan and correspondingly to weaken that of Wesel. On June 24, 1971, a few days after Schwan had called yet again in the press for an open debate about university reform, approximately sixty students, none of whom were connected with the Otto Suhr Institute, stormed into the OSI and trapped Schwan in his seminar session. What followed came uncomfortably close to actions seen forty years earlier in another Germany. Hurling eggs and other objects at Schwan and his students, the largely Maoist KSV radicals cursed him as an anticommunist agitator. Then, someone shouted "Let's throw him out the window!" Thereupon, several of the radicals grabbed Schwan by his arms and legs and began carting their struggling captive to a nearby window. Fortunately, moderate students at the OSI, including Schwan's wife, rallied and, mounting a charge, were able to prevent this latter-day "defenestration of Berlin" in the nick of time.[83] A fight ensued, and in the confusion Schwan escaped to his office. Shortly after, President Kreibich, alerted by the commotion, appeared at the OSI with several of his staff and began trying to calm tempers in hopes of putting a peaceful end to the ugly episode. They were too late. The damage had already been done, and even some of the presidential staff were subjected to physical abuse. It was an event that put the worst possible light upon the radicals and provided potent ammunition for those who were saying that the reforms were not working properly and that freedom at the university was endangered. Even among those more disciplined leftist groups such as the ADS (*Aktionsbündnis Demokraten und Sozialisten*) there was anguish and sharp criticism of the openly illegal actions of the KSV. To be sure, their criticisms were couched not in moral terms but rather as a condemnation of the latter's errant tactics. The press and media quickly spread word throughout the entire country, and it brought further discredit upon the Free University and upon the 1969 University Law. The secret war at the Free University was rapidly becoming less secret.[84]

The full repercussions from this disturbing incident were by no means clear at first. Because the perpetrators had come from other departments—some may have not have been students at all—and because positive identifications were difficult in such mob-like actions, no arrests or dismissals occurred. The seeming helplessness of the university's administration to stop physical violence led to charges of blatant appeasement by more conservative elements at the university. Nor had the nasty episode appeared to have had a sobering effect on some of the radicals. Other instructors at the OSI, such as political scientist Werner Skuhr, were worried by the increasing appearance of radical graffiti and leaflets calling upon students to "Destroy bourgeois science and scholarship!" Others openly called for the destruction of the very institutions Wesel was hoping still to reform. "Don't Transform. Destroy!" became another watchword of the far-left extremists, appearing on walls and flyers throughout the university.[85]

At about this time, shortly after the creation of the Quadripartite Agreement for Berlin, President Kreibich received a distinguished guest, Sir Roger Jackling, the British Ambassador to Germany. He informed the Ambassador about the state of the Free University, and Jackling recorded Kreibich's views about the university situation in light of the lessening international tensions in the divided city. "He thought this was a step in the right direction," Jackling recorded, "which will be of practical importance to him insofar as it served to reduce the tensions in the University itself." Kreibich felt this applied particularly to the Otto Suhr Insitute, whose many students of political science had been particularly inclined to engage in political confrontations. "Now that a first step had been taken towards reducing tensions within Berlin itself, there was a good chance that this would be reflected within the University."[86] It proved to be a rash prediction.

By April 1972, the differences and disputes at the OSI had grown so heated that its moderates began seriously proposing the creation of a separate institute, one which would remain pluralistic, whereas the rump they left behind would be free to develop into an openly Marxist institute. Schwan had already commented favorably on such a split among the psychologists, and now he saw it as a solution for the political scientists. The summer semester for 1972 had begun rockily enough with a student protest strike against Senator Stein's refusal to appoint a leftist professor, Hans Heinz Holz, to the ranks of the university's political scientists. Aware of the OSI's role in 1968 in spearheading university reform, U.S. Minister David Klein began taking a special interest in developments at the troubled institute. He and his staff chronicled what happened. The OSI, they observed, was "confronted by the . . . question of whether an academic community founded on the principle of intellectual pluralism can function effectively when a significant group in its midst professes a 'true faith' and employs intransigence or even forceful disruption to further that faith." The American officials, like so many of their German contemporaries, were struck by the fact that the erstwhile reformers at the OSI, who had pioneered in the creation of a new university law, were now disillusioned. "After two years of strenuous efforts to make the university-reform model work in the face of growing Marxist influence, the majority of moderate professors at the . . . OSI have concluded that the answer to the question is no."[87]

That conclusion was hardly the exclusive opinion of Alexander Schwan. Five moderate professors at the OSI, part of a group known as the Reform Socialists, were now calling for a split. Soon, they merged with other moderate groups, which in the autumn of 1971 came to be called "Liberal Action." The U.S. Mission officials noted the irony in the situation, stating that "this desperate measure was proposed by men who were originally strong proponents of the university-reform measures which opened the way for the rapid growth of Marxist influence in the OSI and elsewhere in the FU. . . ." As far as the Mission staff could tell, the central figure in this episode remained Schwan, "who had struggled long and hard to make the reform model work." They pointed out to their superiors that Schwan was continuing to put his views forthrightly before the press. They explained further that, "after the non-Marxists had applied the principle of pluralism by naming some Marxists to teaching positions, the Marxists used their growing strength to admit only more Marxists." This in turn had brought an influx of other Marxist students, "who sought Marxist indoctrination rather than a balanced education and simultaneously scared off non-Marxist students and teachers." The Marxist faction had opposed any limits on student admissions to the OSI, with the result that the institute's enrollments now exceeded 3,000 students. The reform of curricula and learning did not appear to be the radicals' goal. The moderates claimed that examining procedures, for example, had tended to test "true belief" in Marxist tenets, and Klein's staff recounted that "leftist student extremists" disrupted the classes of "bourgeois professors." Schwan, they reported, was now willing to concede that only conflict and chaos had resulted from efforts to work with such groups.[88]

In consequence, Schwan and the Reform Socialists proposed setting up a new institute with other non-Marxists, forming a department of history and political science with closer ties to existing institutes, such as the Friedrich Meinecke Institute, the John F. Kennedy Institute for North American Studies, or the Central Institute for Social Science Research. The Marxists could, according to this scheme, gravitate toward the department of philosophy and social science. However, Schwan's proposal by no means had the backing of everyone at the OSI. Another moderate, Hans Hartwich, the current chairman at the OSI, along with four other non-Marxists, claimed, according to the American observers, "that such a move would not solve the ideological clash but would destroy the study of political science at the FU." The OSI might join other departments, such as the historians, Hartwich counseled, but should do so as an intact unit.

The Marxists were not eager for a split either. The red cell which had emerged at the OSI among the assistants and was currently known as the *Sozialistische Assistenten Zelle* (SAZ), or Socialist Assistants Cell, accounted for 35 assistants, a Mission official reported, "as well as two avowed Marxist professors Altvater and Agnoli [who] voted separately to resist the splitting of the OSI and announced that its members would accompany the non-Marxists into whatever other department they might choose to move." The reason for the Marxists' reluctance to go along with the split suggested by Schwan was not hard to discern. The Mission official continued: "A consideration in the back of everyone's mind was that if any department at the FU were to become formally identified as Marxist, there would arise great political pressure on the [Berlin] House of Representatives and the Senate to withhold public funds for its support." Some of the less perceptive elements might not have comprehended that fundamental fact of life in West Berlin, but more discerning groups did. "This was no doubt well understood by the more 'moderate' or disciplined Marxists at the FU," the Mission spokesman wrote, "whose program of gradual increase in influence was endangered by the excesses of the leftist extremist students. The ADS (Action Group for Democrats and Socialists, closely connected with the official communist parties of West Berlin and East Germany) expressed concern that extreme strike action would provide the conservatives with an excuse to close or restructure the FU."[89]

Seen in its broader context, this seemingly minor conflict in one institute of the Free University proved to be a lever which soon set larger political forces in motion. For one, it unleashed a call for the university's leadership to examine the entire structure of its many *Fachbereiche*. President Kreibich and Senator Stein announced jointly, in April 1972, a project to investigate departmental organization at the Free University. This in turn led to demands in the press and among various pressure groups to look into the entire issue of higher educational reform in Berlin since 1969. Berlin's Senator for Science and Art, Werner Stein, had had more modest intentions at first, the American officials maintained. "But within a few days," they reported, "Stein was speaking of a review of the entire University Law, to be completed by fall taking into account the developing Federal *Hochschulrahmengesetz* (University Framework Law) as well as events at the FU during the summer semester." This was precisely what the leftists feared and more moderate elements desired. "Formal reconsideration of the University Law is likely to lead to proposals for its amendment, which," they added, "in the current political atmosphere, will certainly be of a conservative nature, asserting greater government control over the universities. That President Kreibich would associate himself with a project leading toward that possible result is an indication of his movement away from his vanishing left-center support and toward his only feasible alternative in the face of increasing polarization—the SPD-controlled Senate."

Minister Klein's staff, at least, were not sanguine about immediate prospects for an improvement in the political climate at the Free University. They felt the university might be entering another crisis. "In sum," they concluded to their superiors in Washington, "the developing crisis at the Free University at the beginning of the summer semester presented a picture of a weak and harassed moderate majority being forced increasingly to take sides in an ideological faceoff, thus intensifying the polarization of the university and raising the likelihood of political intervention to stabilize the situation."[90]

The reasons for predicting future problems were clear. Radical elements seemed to increase their violent rhetoric, especially toward the moderates. In their report about the precarious situation at the OSI, Klein's staff had noticed this continuing hard line. "Meanwhile an extremist student group calling itself the *Grundsemesterorganisation* [First Semester Organization] issued leaflets calling for the 'exemplary punishment,' to include disruption of classes, of all those favoring a division of the OSI. As a result, President Kreibich announced the cancellation of a seminar which was to be taught jointly by several of the moderates." However, one Mission official added, "Prof. Schwann [sic] refused to move his classes from the OSI to another, police-guarded building."[91] Despite a history of rough treatment at the hands of radicals, Schwan gave every evidence of continuing his offensive, and now a gathering public reaction to the excesses of the far left was clearly discernible.

Thus, by a complicated series of circumstances, the call for a split of the OSI in 1972, spearheaded by an erstwhile reformer, Alexander Schwan, had set in motion a growing public demand for reexamination of those very same university reforms which had seemed irresistible just two years earlier. Skillful rejoinders from left-oriented spokesman Uwe Wesel notwithstanding, the momentum for change was mounting rapidly from the other side of the political spectrum.[92]

This was not to say that chaos reigned at all times and everywhere at the Free University. This bears emphasis if the complex institution that was the Free University is to be understood in those crisis-ridden years. In some disciplines, such as physics, for example, the transition from the old university structure to the new was conducted in an orderly and peaceful manner. Other fields such as law and chemistry remained relatively calm, and even in some specialized areas of medicine, especially in medical research, the political storm appeared to fly over without inflicting the damage seen in the other disciplines. Early in Kreibich's presidency, the staff of U.S. Minister Brewster Morris had also kept their superiors in Washington informed on developments at the Free University, and had hastened to caution them to put events in perspective. "In view of the concern expressed in various quarters about the continued orderly functioning of the Free University," they wrote in February 1970, "one should state at the outset that, at present, no faculties are closed; and most classes are being conducted with only minor and sporadic disruptions." Nevertheless, there were cases where radicalism was a major concern. "There are notable exceptions," Morris's staff continued, ". . . in the case of the Mathematics Institutes, the Germanistics and Romanistics Seminars and the Economics and Social Faculty." At least, the Americans stated in consolation, matters had not fallen to the level of disruption in the winter semester of 1968/69 when entire faculties seemed to be shut down.[93]

Obviously, that improving trend did not last. Not only had Schwan nearly experienced a "defenestration," but other violent actions had occurred at virtually the same time in June 1971. The historians of the Free University, organized into the Friedrich Meinecke Institute, had been pioneers in establishing the university's tutorial system in the 1950s. Generally, their faculty had enjoyed a harmonious relationship with the students. However, such innovations and past reputations counted for little now. On the basis of a dispute over requirements and grading in a seminar on medieval history, other radicals decided to occupy the Meinecke Institute, and a dangerous confrontation ensued. President Kreibich and his most successful spokesman with the far left, Vice President Wesel, received word of the event and hastened over to the institute. It appeared to be as bad as rumors had indicated. Wesel discovered several professors barricaded in a room on one level. Student occupiers were threatening to set fire to the library upstairs. The police were hovering outside preparing to storm the building at the word from the president. It was a tense moment. Nevertheless, Kreibich and Wesel began talking to both sides in hopes of working out a compromise solution. Wesel knew one of the radical students and enlisted her aid in getting the occupiers to give up their protest action and to leave the building peacefully. "We did not really administer," Wesel said of those turbulent years. "Kreibich and I were crisis managers."[94] That was literally the truth in this instance. However, it hardly stilled the criticisms being leveled at Kreibich and his staff. This violent action and the seemingly feeble response brought in its wake stormy debates in the Berlin House of Deputies and the establishment of an FU investigative committee to examine the incident. On balance, the critics had the upper hand, claiming that the president had compromised too readily with the radicals. The far left seemed to be going out of their way to test the tolerance of the university's administration.[95]

However, patience with such methods could not last indefinitely. By June 1972, with the change in political mood clearly visible, President Kreibich was faced with a challenge to his authority which he could no longer afford to ignore. In this instance, tempers had flared at the German Studies Department over the fact that one of the left-leaning professors had been denied the right to administer state (i.e., final) examinations. This was one means of curbing the influence of the left, and, as far as officials such as Senators Stein and Löffler were concerned, of preventing a further decline in testing standards. Not surprisingly, it caused resentments in the ranks of left-oriented students. Accordingly, KSV adherents, the same group that had attacked Schwan the previous year, called for a strike meeting for June 5. Sensing trouble, Kreibich sought to avoid yet another clash and ordered the German Studies Department closed for two days.

Ignoring that cautionary gesture, the KSV members broke into the building and occupied it from top to bottom. This time, however, the results were different. After three years of such actions even Kreibich had had enough. He called in the very police he had sworn not to use upon assuming office in 1969. They surrounded the building and then, in a new tactical move, cut off all utilities to it. Kreibich, at least, had recognized the swing of the political pendulum even if the radicals had not. Discouraged, they left the building later that evening, angry at being outmaneuvered, and called instead for a mass protest meeting at the Auditorium Maximum the following day. Approximately 1,500 students assembled there and hotly discussed the previous day's events with Kreibich's trusted conduit to the left, Vice President Wesel. They reproached him and the president for using police force, claiming that the university's administration had broken its promise to the students. Thereupon it fell to the administration's closest link to the radicals, Wesel, to tell his accusers that they were the ones who had broken the pact first. With his skill in discussion with the radical elements still intact, Wesel avoided an open break, but the implications from the event and subsequent mass meeting were clear. There were limits on the kind of behavior the university administration was willing to accept from the protesters. It was a telling moment in the fortunes of the dissident movement at the Free University.[96]

Other observers noted the shifting mood too. At this time Klein's staff perceived a change in attitude on the part of the FU leadership and reported it to their superiors. They pointed out that Kreibich had maintained distinctly cool relations with American authorities shortly after assuming office, "leaving invitations from senior Mission officers unanswered, and refusing to receive the Berlin PAO [Public Affairs Officer] for 1-1/2 years."[97] Now, for the first time, Kreibich was showing stiffening resistance to the dissidents' demands, and the American officials claimed that the balance of power within the Free University's first presidency was shifting. "With dissension among the ranks of his close advisers, the loss of support among leftist radical groupings within the University, increased pressure for more moderate behavior from Berlin's political leaders, and some decline in the University's academic standards, Kreibich is looking for friends."[98] At about the same time, other observers noted a difference between Kreibich's leftist reputation and his private views. Britain's Ambassador to Bonn, Sir Roger Jackling, had spoken to Kreibich about the Free University some months earlier and was surprised at the results. "On no subject throughout the meeting," he told his government, "did he express views that were markedly left-wing. He did say, however, that he thought that there was room at any university for a handful of Marxist professors but that such a situation as that which existed at some French universities, where many professors had Marxist tendencies, would be too much for him."[99] Now, in June 1972, he had had to match deeds with words in responding to violence at the Free University.

A turning point had been reached, and the FU administration, in concert with the new mood in Berlin, began plotting a different course. Although it was not immediately apparent, the worst years of protest were coming to an end, and a healing process, erratic to be sure, had finally set in.

THE CHANGING OF THE LAW

From the first, the 1969 University Law in Berlin had been controversial and had been passed by the SPD despite bitter opposition of the CDU. With the passage of time a mounting public outcry became obvious to all over such revelations as the "Red Freedom" after-school program and repeated claims that academic standards were falling and that quality faculty were abandoning the Free University in favor of quieter academic pastures. There was also little doubt that this process was furthered by the increasingly militant methods of the various radical groups whose very shrillness seemed to increase in reverse proportion to their declining numbers. Thus, the demand for yet another university reform became irresistible. As the authors of an amendment in 1974 remarked: "The changes in the university law . . . go back to a declaration of the Governing Mayor in April, 1971, in which he announced that the

Senate of Berlin viewed developments at the institutions of higher learning with concern and wished to examine the new structure resulting from the [1969] University Law."[100]

The first concrete breach in the reform euphoria came in 1974 in a court case involving Otto von Simson, an art historian at the Free University and last dean of the old philosophy faculty, and Detleff Borrmann, a chancellor under President Kreibich. Von Simson, it should be recalled, was a founding member of and prominent spokesman for the NOFU group which had organized in opposition to the leftward political trend at the Free University after 1969. On January 24, 1974, in an angry article in Berlin's evening newspaper, Der Abend, von Simson reported that matters had reached the point that only candidates with left-wing affiliations had a chance to be appointed within his Department of Art History. What was even worse, he noted, was that the president's office was supporting this unhealthy trend.[101] Specifically, von Simson accused Borrmann of misusing his office in appointing a part-time assistant in the Department of Art History. This produced an equally angry response from Chancellor Borrmann, who sued von Simson in the courts. The normally cumbersome wheels of justice began now to turn at an unusually rapid rate. In April 1974, Berlin's Landgericht (appellate court) supported Borrmann's contention that he had behaved correctly in appointing the part-time assistant in question. It also concluded that von Simson's charge of general political bias in university appointments could not be levelled at Borrmann as an individual. As a result, the university administration, in its turn, sued von Simson.

The decision of the appellate court was memorable. It not only rejected the university's suit against von Simson; it went much further and supported his claim that only persons of left-wing political persuasion had a chance to be hired at the Free University. In essence, the judge, a member of the SPD, confirmed that personnel appointments at the Free University were being decided on the basis of outright political considerations, and the practice must stop forthwith. The decision was nothing short of sensational. The consequences from this case were manifold and far-reaching. First, it was a more than gentle slap on the wrist to Kreibich and to the members of his left-oriented administration. Second, it was a warning to the SPD leadership in Berlin and even in Bonn from one of their own number, albeit in the judiciary branch rather than in the executive or legislative, that the reform impulse was having undesirable effects at the universities and that the limits of reform had been exceeded. One of the notable local effects was that the court decision encouraged more conservative elements at the Free University to redouble their efforts to counter the leftward political drift and to amend the 1969 University Law, which they saw as the root of so much trouble.[102]

This impulse for a modification of university laws on the order of the 1969 University Law was hardly confined to Berlin. For example, already in May 1973, in a case brought against a similar university law in Lower Saxony, the Federal Republic's Constitutional Court ruled that *Hochschullehrer* (university professors) must be accorded the decisive vote on university committees that dealt with teaching, research, and faculty appointments. The court went so far as to say that nonacademic personnel (epitomized by the cleaning ladies once again) could not participate in decisions in those three areas. However, the guidelines of the Federal Constitutional Court were not automatically binding on Berlin, because of its special status. Thus, the Berlin Senate, following usual practice, submitted a special bill to the Berlin House of Deputies to make the Berlin University Law conform to the federal guideline. However, the Berlin Senate, which had already been at work amending the 1969 law even before the higher court reviewed the Lower Saxon law, hastened to provide a kind of compromise measure in 1973. With the creation of new categories of tenured associate professors, the C-2s and C-3s mentioned earlier, the Senate concluded that such mid-level professors also fell within the definition of *Hochschullehrer* even though earlier—before passage of the *Fachhochschulgesetz* of 1971—they had usually been arrayed in the *Mittelbau* as *Assistenten* and *akademische Räte*.

The U.S. Mission's political adviser in Berlin, C. Arthur Borg, described what happened next. "This Senate proposal . . . ," he reported, "aroused heated opposition on the part of certain professorial groups and conservative politicians, who termed it a 'labelling trick' and charged that it made a mockery of the Constitutional Court's definition of a *Hochschullehrer*."[103] Taken aback by the vociferous criticism, Stein withdrew the bill for further reworking. The SPD caucus with the FDP as allies began to evolve a compromise scheme whereby the nonacademic employees at the university would act only in an advisory capacity in decisions affecting teaching, research and appointments. In the event of tie votes, the issue would be decided by the majority of *Hochschullehrer*. However, the compromise solution also left it to the Senator for Science and Art, in this instance Werner Stein, to decide which university issues affected those crucial areas, thus, in effect deciding how much power the nonacademic employees would retain. This amended version met with almost as hostile a response from the conservatives. "The Berlin CDU charged that it did not assure the *Hochschullehrer* as a group the predominant influence in decision-making required by the Constitutional Court, and the Berliner *Hochschulverband* [Association of University Professors] and the *Notgemeinschaft* [NOFU] threatened lawsuits should the measure be enacted."[104]

It had become obvious that Stein and others in his party who were concerned with university affairs were increasingly concerned with the way the Free University and West Berlin's other higher educational institutions were handling their affairs. Their effort in the new legislation which became law in November 1974 was, as Borg related to his superiors, "to arrest through an infusion of greater government control, the present efforts of the radical left to seize control of the universities from within, and thereby to preserve—or restore as the case may be— academic pluralism and high scholarly standards on the Berlin campuses."[105] Needless to say, this was precisely the kind of change which reformers like Schwan and critics of the current FU administration like von Simson were hoping to obtain. The means for accomplishing this feat was, according to the lawmakers, to enhance the powers of the Kuratorium (Board of Trustees). This took the form of allowing the board, or a committee which it might designate, to play a strong role in faculty appointments. Moreover, the new law transferred away from the president to the board the right to appoint a university disciplinary committee.[106] This was indirectly a slap at FU President Kreibich, who had seen to it that such disciplinary committees, while not formally dissolved, had nevertheless become a dead letter, a move much heralded by student groups but heavily criticized among the more conservative circles of professors. In sum, the Board of Trustees, which hitherto had handled budgetary issues for the university, could now intervene in a wide range of administrative matters. Since the board included city officials and other non-university members, the move demonstrated a clear increase in state intervention into the internal affairs of the Free University.

A measure of the concern with which some political leaders had viewed the power of the far left could be seen in their efforts during the debates on the new university law to impose certain conditions if the elections showed poor participation. "As indicated most recently in connection with the January-February [1974] elections to the Free University Konzil," wrote Borg to his superiors, ". . . the radical left is substantially over-represented on most university governing bodies inasmuch as the more conservative 'silent majority' generally fails to participate in elections." If, for example, one of the recognized groups in the parity system achieved less than 50 percent participation in an election, its representation on the given university body would be reduced by a quarter. A 30 percent participation would reduce representation by half. Since it was obvious that students had consistently shown a poor turn-out in recent elections, there was little doubt which group would have been affected the most. However, the provision never saw the light of day, and the sliding scale system was never adopted. Nevertheless, the proposal demonstrated the acute concern with which state authorities viewed the activities of the left radicals.

The first reading of the reform bill in the Berlin House of Deputies proved to be relatively quiet and without the heated controversy that had attended the debates on the 1969 University Law. Senator Stein was a central figure in the debates, claiming that the inability or refusal of university personnel to put their own affairs in order had inevitably led to growing state interference in internal university affairs. "Stein defended the proposed augmentation of state control as the only means to guarantee academic pluralism, and assured his listeners that a balance of power would be preserved between the state and the university authorities," Borg informed U.S. State Department officials.[107] By that time, after approximately five years of political uproar at the Free University and at the other institutions of higher learning in West Berlin, there seemed to be few who disagreed. Even Ursula Besser, the CDU's Argus-eyed expert on university affairs, expressed support for Stein's bill despite obvious differences between her party and the Social Democrats over university issues. Outwardly, the 1969 University Law still stood. However, the amendments which became law in November 1974 created, in effect, a new law.

Yet, outward forms had to be preserved. In the preface to the new legislation, Stein assured its readers that the "reform law of 1969 has proved itself and will continue to be useful to the universities." In reality, the amending legislation of 1974 was an important first step in correcting the abuses which had so obviously disrupted the work of too many institutes and departments at the Free University and elsewhere. Stein, in justifying further tinkering with reform, hastily added a corollary to his first statement: "The changes became necessary," he explained in the law's preface, "as a result of experiences . . . with the [1969] University Law."[108] That was a masterful understatement.

However, the new law was hardly the end of the matter. The 1969 law had set in motion a complex legislative undertaking which is by no means settled even today. At the federal level the lawmakers were also busy, and their *Hochschulrahmengesetz* (University Framework Law) finally went into effect in January 1976, based upon the various drafts that had been under consideration in Bonn at least since 1973. The result was that the Berlin University Law of 1974 was itself succeeded by another Berlin law in December 1978. Among its salient features was the following: "In all committees the professors must have at least one more vote than the rest of the members of the committee combined on issues concerning research, artistic development, teaching, and professorial appointments."[109] Accordingly, at the various committee levels at the Free University, such as in the *Fachbereiche* (departments) or in the Academic Senate, the professors regained a majority, albeit a slim one. The Academic Senate's powers were more fully prescribed, and the law made it clear that the *Konzil* dealt with only specific issues, such as the election of the president. This law engaged in further fine-tuning of the regulations, such as the transfer of responsibility for forming disciplinary committees from the hard-pressed *Kuratorium* to the Academic Senate. Trust in the presidency had risen to the point that appointees to these disciplinary committees once again required the approval of the chief executive.

Another indication of a return to more normal conditions was the revival of student government. The new law specifically called for the creation of an AStA and student parliament after that body had been
nearly ten years in abeyance. The Konvent was no longer known by its traditional title. Instead, it was officially renamed the *Studentenparla-
ment*. Given their penchant for acronyms, the students soon applied to
it the less than elegant appellation of *Stupa*, which it retains to this
day. The stated objectives of this new student government were concerned exclusively with student affairs. The law stated specifically that
one of its chief objectives was "to make decisions concerning the fundamental affairs of the student body."[110] In other words, the lawmakers
had no intention of permitting the student government to exercise a general political mandate, the source of so much difficulty ten years earlier. Another significant change was a set of provisions concerning student examinations. The new law stated bluntly that such examinations
"serve to determine whether or not a student through his individual efforts has attained the objectives for a segment of studies [*Zwischenprü-
fung*] or for the completion of studies [*Abschlußprüfung*]."[111] Previous legislation had contained no such clauses because the notion of collective
examinations or departures from traditional testing procedures had simply not been an issue before the late 1960s. Given the public controversy surrounding the collective awarding of grades and degrees at the
Technical University as well as the Free University at the beginning of
the 1970s, the lawmakers were determined to make explicit the individual examining of students in the new law. This was a necessity if such institutions of higher learning were to regain their reputations for academic excellence.

Striking though the changes in higher educational law were in the
late 1970s, they were by no means the last word. The federal legislators
leapfrogged the Berlin legislation with their second piece of guideline legislation in this matter: the University Framework Law of 1985, which
was an amendment of the first framework law passed in 1976. Acting in
concert with those shifting federal guidelines, the Berlin House of Deputies then approved its latest act in the ongoing process of reform: the Berlin University Law of 1986. In essence, this set of federal and local legislation continued the process of restoring power to those traditional
elements of a university community. Crudely put, this was seen, by leftist critics at least, as returning the Free University to the status of an *Ordinarienuniversität*, a university dominated by the full professors. The political basis for these major changes was, of course, the electoral victory
of the CDU with FDP help over the SPD in Berlin in 1981. Therefore,
the Berlin Senate was dominated by the CDU, especially after 1983
when a full-blown CDU-FDP coalition came into existence. For those
who preferred a more traditional university structure, the CDU-FDP-
inspired legislation was naturally a healthy development, but those ar-

rayed on the left end of the political spectrum were filled with foreboding.

West Berlin was hardly unique in passing successive university acts over a lengthy period of time. All *Länder* of the Federal Republic displayed similar records of ongoing university legislation during the same decade and a half following passage of the original Berlin University Law of 1969. The issues dealt with by this complex set of legislation concerned not only the political structure of universities in general; it also attempted to cope with other pressing problems. In essence, the lawmakers were trying to regulate the affairs of all of West Germany's and West Berlin's institutions of higher learning in light of such factors as fluctuating student enrollments, financing of higher education, experimentation with *Gesamthochschulen* (comprehensive universities which brought several types of advanced technical, vocational, scientific, and scholarly education under one university roof), plus other social and educational needs. For example, the future employment of university graduates was one of the lawmakers' major concerns. The fact that the Social Democrats were the majority party during most of the time under consideration, that is, until 1981 in Berlin and until 1982 at the federal level, gave room for greater social experimentation than would have been the case under the CDU. That West German society in general underwent striking social and political changes undoubtedly played a crucial role in inspiring the experimentation which took place. In essence, the Germans were tinkering with their universities in an attempt to make them conform to society's needs. Yet those perceived needs changed from year to year, so that reforms which had appeared urgent in 1969, seemed irrelevant in the mid-1980s. One aspect of university reform demonstrates this shifting perception: the furor over creating the *Gesamthochschulen*. In 1970 it seemed to be the wave of the future and the model for all subsequent university development. By the end of the decade enthusiasm for this new form of university structure had largely withered away. Through these rounds of lawmaking, a recurring, fundamental theme preoccupied the legislators: the need to determine who would make the basic decisions at the university.

Throughout this long, wearying legislative process, it can be said that perceptions of what was the proper formula for power relationships and decision-making at the universities depended in part upon the broad political trends that affected society. In 1969 the political pendulum in West Germany and West Berlin had swung about as far left as it was going to go. At the Free University and at many other institutions of higher learning, the wave of protest crested and a new constitution emerged under what can only be described as riotous conditions. Reform was, therefore, inevitably of a political nature, and the adjustment in the decision-making process, epitomized by *Drittelparität*, reflected that leveling or democratic trend in society. It was, after all, the beginning of a lengthy Social Democratic term in national office, and Social Democrats like Berlin's Governing Mayor Klaus Schütz scarcely concealed their desire to use the universities as a lightening rod for protest. Demonstrators on the Kurfürstendamm would, like the squeaking rats of Hamelin, follow their leaders into some dark and secret place—in this instance the corridors of the Free University—where they would no longer be a visible bother to the burghers of the town.

Needless to say, the shifting of the scene of protest was hardly a solution to the basic problem. At the university level, at least, a period of disillusionment soon set in, and discussions began almost immediately among the public and at the universities as to whether or not the new reforms were having their desired effect. Obviously, disillusionment was great among a number of the original reformers, such as Alexander Schwan and Werner Skuhr. Scandals rocked the Free University seemingly without pause in those years, and its young first president presided over an institution in which the polarization worsened, if anything, under the impact of the reforms. The skill with which opponents of the reforms such as the NOFU membership put their case before the public soon forced the political leadership to reopen discussions on the nature of reform. The dissident movement itself had become splintered and fractious in the meantime and had failed to produce any articulate spokesmen to counter the criticisms from the right. Gradually, the public became more aware of the abnormal conditions at the Free University and elsewhere. The many occupations of institutes, disruptions of classes, the radicals' flirtation with terrorism, and attempts by some of them to impose an alien ideology on curricula and units within the Free University caused a mounting public anger which the politicians could no longer ignore. The resulting legislation mirrored that concern, so that by the mid-1980s, university laws at the federal level and at the local level openly decreed that all university committees that dealt with matters of teaching, research, and faculty appointments must contain an outright majority of professors. However, this did not imply a return to the Ordinarienuniversität as left-wing critics claimed. By this time the title "professor" at the Free University referred to a spectrum of middle and upper-level academicians of whom the Ordinarien or full professors were merely one modest segment. Thus, while it did not by any means imply a wholesale reaction, the amending legislation of the 1980s spelled the end of an unusual experiment in German higher education. The underlying premise of advocates of Drittelparität and Viertelparität had been that responsible citizens would decide issues responsibly and rationally. For a short time the Free University operated under a system so democratic as to excite the astonishment of any Communist-bloc nation or institution. Yet, in the end the experiment did not work, primarily because the polarization process that had taken place at the Free University starting in 1965 had reached the stage that rational decision-making usually did not materialize. If it did succeed for a time in some fields, such as physics, certain areas of medical research, and other hard sciences, to name a few, there were striking examples at other parts of the campus, such as at the Otto Suhr Institute or the Kennedy Institute, where parity or bloc voting based on blatant ideological considerations produced a striking failure. Seventeen years after reformers such as Alexander Schwan had shifted the focus of power to the left, he and other erstwhile reformers, sadder and wiser, shifted it back to the right again.

The blunt fact was that no amount of tinkering with laws and constitutions could restore a precious item that had once made the Free University a unique institution for nearly a generation. When the community of teachers and learners at the university broke apart in 1965 in the midst of student protests which had had some justification, a mighty social and political change began to take place that greatly transformed the Free University along with the society in which it functioned. However, even as the laws governing universities demonstrated a long evolution, the problems facing individual departments and institutes at the Free University lingered on for years, seemingly without solution.

THE JOHN F. KENNEDY INSTITUTE: A STUDY IN POLARIZATION

It may be an exaggeration to describe the John F. Kennedy Institute for North American Studies (JFKI) as the problem child of the Free University. It would also be a mistake to exaggerate its importance, since it was one of the smaller institutes at the Free University, with a projected strength of eight professors and relatively modest enrollments of a few hundred students or so. Nevertheless, the JFKI displayed significant problems over a lengthy period of time, and was hurt by the polarization process as much as any unit within the university. It is therefore representative of the problems and pressures which most of the departments and institutes faced in the late 1960s and early 1970s.

Plans to create an interdisciplinary institute offering American studies, including literature and language, political science, history, geography, and economics and sociology, date back to the 1950s. The obvious model was the Free University's highly successful institute for Eastern European Studies, the Osteuropa Institut. The central figure in the founding of the JFKI was Ernst Fraenkel, who became its first director in 1963. With the help of the Ford Foundation, the institute created an excellent library, with over 150,000 volumes, second only to the American Library in Paris for holdings in American literature on the Continent. The institute moved into a generously appointed former school in Dahlem, with offices and classrooms adjoining the library. Moreover, the library permitted open-stack privileges, typical of American libraries but, along with the American Memorial Library, a unique feature in Berlin.

Obviously, the organizers of the institute hoped to create a major center for American Studies in Central Europe, but from the beginning it was clear that the project would be accompanied by certain difficulties. First, student enrollments, although not expected to be large, lagged even more than was expected. A degree in that field did not specifically prepare a student for a future profession in Germany. The core of students who came to the insitute were those who expected to become highschool teachers, plus a modest number of students interested in specializing in American history and politics. Moreover, the programs at the JFKI were dependent upon the requirements set by the various departments of the Free University, and relations between the new JFKI and those departments were not always smooth. "This is especially true of the English Department," stated several of the institute's professors in a memorandum of May 1972, "although American literature has, for a long time, been an integral part of the course offerings at English departments elsewhere in Germany and ought to be regarded as an integral part of the equipment of academic training in English literature."[112] Finally, it proved difficult to recruit specialists in most of the fields in American Studies among German professors. And, like some other departments and institutes, the JFKI was affected by the departure of several of its key staff with subsequent difficulties in obtaining replacements. Even under ideal conditions, the JFKI faced certain obstacles to its development. The conditions in the early 1970s were hardly ideal.

In April 1972, five of the institute's six professors sent an open letter to Senator Stein, claiming that the JFKI's structure had to change or else they would no longer accept responsibility for its continued operation. The letter was published in the *Tagesspiegel* and was obviously a criticism of President Kreibich and his administration. The American cultural affairs officer for the U.S. Mission in Berlin, Herman Zivetz, read the article and hurried over to see the institute's director, Armin Paul Frank. The latter immediately enlightened him on the ongoing problems there. Two professorships had been vacant for years, Zivetz learned, "and one of these positions in economics has been the center of a year-long dispute between five professors on one side, and the majority assistant-student coalition in the Council [*Institutsrat*] on the other." The sixth professor, according to Frank, "owes his recently acquired professorship to the new rules under the reform legislation and to the support from leftist elements."[113] In other words, profound political differences were causing evident disharmony at the ailing institute.

The five professors who wrote to Senator Stein had many complaints, including the excessive number of committee assignments they had had to fill in order that the JFKI satisfy the requirements of the 1969 University Law. For example, four professors were entitled to sit on the all-important Institute Council, and given the vacancies and the usual comings and goings of academic personnel on leave of absence, it was difficult to keep the professors' representation up to its required level. "Absence from any of these meetings would turn over complete control to the opposition by default," commented Zivetz to his superiors. Thus, even professors who were on leaves of absence felt honor-bound to serve on the council anyway.[114]

Probably their most serious grievance was the effect of parity voting. "In all important academic matters and decisions concerning personnel," the five dissenting professors wrote, "the professors are constantly outvoted by a coalition of assistants, students, and non-academic staff in the Institute Council, the decision-making board of the Institute." They claimed that no one in the coalition that had consistently outvoted them for two years even had a doctorate. Yet the coalition had made many decisions, thus incurring the wrath of the full professors. "Applicants up to the level of assistant professor and full guest professor were rejected by this coalition on political grounds," the five protesters claimed, "and a vacant professorship was redefined by this majority along fashionable ideological lines." Ultimately, after a long struggle, the university's Academic Senate and its Kuratorium turned down the redefinition of the position, but in the long interim it had not been possible to fill the slot.[115]

This was the heart of the matter. The professors found that parity voting was robbing them of an effective voice in crucial issues. "We feel that assistants and students should have a say in academic matters," the petitioners wrote. "But the current Berlin Model, which makes it a standard practice that the group most qualified for questions of research and teaching can be outvoted in the decision-making boards, has led to the chaotic situation here described. In this University, as it has been modelled along political lines," they continued, "the professors, who are supposed to be responsible for academic matters, are permanently reduced by law to the position of a minority government—a situation which, in a parliamentary democracy, even the most seasoned prime minister would hesitate to accept."[116]

The institute now offered an alternative curriculum to the standard one, and the five professors were critical of it. "All curriculum changes made at the Institute in the last two years have tended to reduce the level of competence," they claimed, referring to a general relaxation of standards and what later came to be called grade inflation.[117] Difficult though they found the situation, the full professors were not claiming that violence was endemic at the institute. The American officials received word from the then director, Frank, "that only a very few of the extreme radicals were involved in the problems of the Kennedy School [sic!]. His major concern was with the watering down of academic achievement resulting from politicization of decision-making, the inordinate time spent on administrative-political work, the power of policy-making, and teaching that now resides in the hands of unqualified assistants, tutors and students."[118] The professors in their joint report claimed a more sinister reason for the outward calm that seemed to prevail at the JFKI as opposed to the violent outbursts at the Otto Suhr Institute. Referring to the destabilization of the Kennedy Institute they claimed that "most of those who have an interest in disorganizing the University have come to realize that violence attracts pubic attention, and that their aim can be better achieved by other means." Thus, they observed, ". . . the desolate situation at JFKI is masked by a quiet facade."[119]

The reporting officer for the Americans, Herman Zivetz, while not discounting the earnestness of the protest, saw the professors' anger as "more a reflection of the frustration of the minority professors than a response to a new or developing threat to the Institute's survival." He feared it might even have negative consequences. Zivetz continued: "However, this gambit on the part of the professors may well hasten the demise of the Kennedy Institute. . . . If this demand for confrontation results in an absorption of the Kennedy Institute into the English Seminar, or conversion into a research institute, as the professors desire, U.S. interests, in both cases will be the loser."[120]

Other American observers showed greater concern about the general political drift since 1969. Another American official, C. Arthur Borg, a political adviser to Minister Klein, recorded a few weeks later that

> the Institute professors found themselves in a running battle with the coalition of students and assistants who could, and did, outvote them in those Institute committees charged with determining personnel policies, academic requirements, and materials procurement. Furthermore, student interest in the offerings of the professors dropped as they found that they could get what they wanted from those teaching assistants who were hip on the class struggle and Vietnam. According to the professors, the JFKI was never the target of violent student demonstrations because the leftist students and assistants were successful from the start in "marching through" this particular institution.[121]

In May 1972, at a time when the polarization process seemed to be deepening, and voices were being raised to split the larger OSI into separate Marxist and non-Marxist institutes, the chronic woes at the Kennedy Institute took on added significance. President Kreibich, accompanied by Vice President Wesel and Foreign Affairs Director Hartwich, met with Terrence Catherman, the Public Affairs Officer at the U.S. Mission. They discussed a wide variety of topics—tensions were running high again, with strike actions imminent at the Free University—and the JFKI received special attention. Kreibich and Wesel reiterated a plan to incorporate part of the institute into an English-language teachers' preparation center with a portion of the new curriculum to be devoted to American Studies. The Americans remained cautious, saying only that such a program would normally employ Americans as experts in the field along with German experts. Yet, the JFKI had no Americans whatsoever as part of the permanent faculty. "Kreibich readily agreed that Americanistics could best be taught by Americans," Catherman recorded, "and said he would look into the problem immediately."[122] However, soon after, further troubles arose for the Americanists. At this time the university's *Ständige Kommission für Forschung und wissenschaftliche Nachwuchs* (Central Commission for Research) recommended a ban on the hiring of any further faculty or staff at the institute until it could prove that it was capable of serious research or, more ominously, capable of reorganizing the institute. The immediate effect on the hiring freeze was that three full-professor slots, seven mid-level positions, and several library staff positions would not be filled, a serious blow to the diminutive institute.

Several years earlier, in 1968, JFKI had acquired a coveted "special research status" from the prestigious *Deutsche Forschungs-Gemeinschaft* (DFG), or German Research Council. Yet, when several JFKI professors submitted a grant a year later, it was denied for various technical reasons, including the fact that the enterprise was simply too small. According to the institute's senior professor for American literature and a cultural historian, Ursula Brumm, the DFG was accustomed instead to funding much larger projects, such as in the natural and medical sciences. Moreover, with the Kennedy Institute's strong teaching function, it was difficult for the applicants to devote most of their time to the research project as the DFG expected. Thereafter, several succeeding proposals were defeated, including one submitted mostly by assistants and students in 1971. The latter had a decidedly Marxist approach, bearing such subtitles as "Property as an Element of Social Conflict in the United States of America" or "Capital and Labor; a Study Concerning the Relationship among the Movement of Capital, Worker Organizations, and Worker Consciousness."[123] None of these proposals secured approval from the DFG. Instead of cooperating on common themes, the professorial ranks and the junior members appeared to want to try their luck separately. One of the protesting professors, Arnulf Baring, mentioned the problem to Jan Zehner, director of the Amerika Haus in Berlin: "Currently research projects proposed by the professors are vetoed by the assistants, and research projects proposed by assistants are disapproved by the authorities because they lack the professors' support." The mistrust obviously ran deep. "The professors," according to Political Adviser Borg, "want to continue stressing individual research in the traditional American Studies fields, while a student-assistant coalition is, according to the professors, hell-bent on giving everything a Marxist twist."[124]

Baring, so mentioned Zehner, regarded the Kennedy Institute as "much more important as a symbol of the American presence in Berlin and German-American cooperation than an objective assessment of its pure academic value would indicate." Some, like Baring, even hoped that the Americans would begin to put pressure upon the leadership of the Free University to bring order back to the troubled institute. "At one point," Zehner continued, "he suggested we might go so far as to tell the University that we didn't feel the institution should continue to carry the Kennedy name unless its future and importance were more assured." Zehner was not impressed with such tactics: "When I suggested to him that some circles in the University would be delighted with such a proposal, he backed off, saying that such a step should be considered the last resort."[125]

The proposed reorganization of the Kennedy Institute, whereby political science, economics, history, and geography were shifted to a new central institute for secondary school teachers, while literature would join a separate unit, met with a cool reception among the professors. If American literature were joined with other area studies, or what was called *Landeskunde*, it might suffer the same fate as German Studies, which renamed the subject as "Socialist Studies," using GDR history texts to interpret recent German history. "The professors are also worried that the fine graduate-level research facilities offered by the JFKI's library would go begging for customers and eventually atrophy if undergraduate teacher-prep students were pumped in and out, with little or no need or desire to do real research." The professors were not alone in their argument. "Senator Stein, stressing that he was also speaking for the Governing Mayor," related Political Adviser Borg, "has indicated to us that the *Senat* has no intention of allowing the *JFKI* to disintegrate; quite the contrary, new life should be pumped into the ailing body, and its existence in Berlin made purposeful." That was a worthy goal, but not so easily solved. Borg added: "The question is—how?"[126] Later, in a conversation with one of Senator Stein's staff, Senatsdirektor Gerhard Heimann, Terence Catherman, who by this time had been watching developments at the Kennedy Institute with more than passing concern, indicated his disappointment over the present state of affairs despite Heimann's promise of written assurances. "Mr. Catherman," the minutes of the meeting revealed, "said that we were not so much interested in letters as actions. Speaking personally, he could not help comparing the flourishing East-West Institute [sic, Osteuropa Institut] with the moribund John F. Kennedy Institute, which fact hurt him, as an American deeply interested in Berlin's future. Prof. Heimann agreed that it was in Berlin's interest to have a healthy JFKI. . . ."[127] The American officials in Berlin asked their colleagues in Bonn and Washington if they could come up with any ideas to restore the JFKI's sagging fortunes.

Even after other departments and institutes at the Free University had begun to quiet down from 1973 onward, differences at the JFKI remained unresolved.

In February 1975, Shepard Stone, long a supporter of the Free University, wrote to McGeorge Bundy, then president of the Ford Foundation, to say that "the University has been relatively quiet, but divisive problems remain. The John F. Kennedy Institute . . . is a shambles, and the question remains if it can be saved."[128] Other observers were also distressed. Moselle Kimbler, a Ford Foundation representative, visited the Kennedy Institute later that year and reported no improvement. "The early promise and hopes for the Institute are now tattered," she reported, joining the chorus of those who felt that it had fallen victim to extremist politics and internal divisions. With a possible amendment to the 1969 University Law in the offing, she felt that it was not yet time to offer a final assessment. "As of today," she concluded, "the Foundation would be compelled, unfortunately, to consider the Kennedy Institute as a failure."[129] By 1975, however, the situation at last appeared to change for the better. Another Ford representative, Peter Ruof, had submitted highly critical reports on the JFKI as recently as April 1975. He had even gone so far as to urge the Ford Foundation to threaten the removal of its library holdings, a drastic proposal that would undoubtedly have failed had it been attempted. Fortunately, cooler heads at the Ford Foundation refused to consider such a move in any case.[130] Yet by the autumn of the same year, the once militant Ruof suddenly began to hold out new hope. "There seems to be a decrease in the radicalization of the student body at German universities, particularly in Berlin," he reported in October 1975. An impending election for a new FU president seemed to indicate a new mood of being less tolerant with the disruptive methods of the radicals. Finally, he noted, the "new student body at the J. F. Kennedy Institute is less politicized, harder working, and again more interested in the United States and American Studies than the students who turned anti-American during the Vietnam War years."[131]

The sheer passage of time and the eclipse of the radical movement thus began to heal the open wounds of the recent past.

CURRICULAR REFORM: THE TEACHING OF ENGLISH

The Kennedy Institute's chronic woes spilled over into other departments and sections of the Free University. Within the general context of the teaching of the English language at the university these frictions pointed up some problems which help explain at least one source of student dissatisfaction: the issue of creating an appropriate curriculum of studies which related to the student's future professional needs. One official American source referred to the fact that "bad blood seems to have developed between the JFKI and the other University departments, which must approve the courses taught in their special areas of competence at the JFKI. In some cases, the competent University departments refused to accept credits earned by students enrolled in JFKI courses, e.g., the University's English Department, which still evidently has trouble swallowing the idea of an American literature course as such."[132]

By the 1960s and 1970s, the teaching of English in European countries in general had had to confront the diversities of pronunciation, grammar, linguistics, literature, and culture in the English-speaking world, especially between the British and the Americans. In a certain sense it became an issue, crudely speaking, of updating the curriculum offerings to recognize that fact. Traditionally, British English and the emphasis on literature from Great Britain had formed the core of such curricular offerings to generations of German students, especially to aspiring secondary-school teachers, who immersed themselves in everything from William Shakespeare to Christopher Isherwood to the peculiarities of the unwritten British constitution and English eccentricities in general. American Studies, including its literature, pronunciation, society, and culture, had really come into its own in Continental university curricula after 1945, and even then only fitfully and unevenly. The numbers of students, teachers, professors, and other academics whose first exposure to English had been in Great Britain was considerably higher than those who had traveled to the more distant United States—at least until the postwar period.

Then, gradually, but with growing frequency, the cultural exchange patterns began to change. Official government and privately sponsored exchanges brought thousands of young Germans of leadership potential to America in the late 1940s and 1950s for varying periods of time to acquaint them with the practicalities of life there. As the Federal Republic prospered, many thousands more traveled under official or private auspices to North America for the same reason. Many participated in yearlong high school exchange programs, frequently prolonging their gymnasium education to gain linguistic and cultural experience of life outside Europe. Yet, these same young people who chose to major in English at a university discovered that the curricular offerings had remained largely if not completely unchanged. Strong emphasis continued to be placed on such subjects as Old English, Chaucerian or Middle English, Elizabethan English of course, and the greats of English literature through succeeding centuries. To be sure, serious American students of English learned those same subjects as well as their own literature and Americana in general, and those young Germans who were exchange high school or especially college students also benefited from this two-pronged approach during their stays in the United States. Yet, what awaited them upon their return to Germany as they enrolled at a university? Their professors and senior instructors sought with varying degrees of success to speak English with an Oxford accent, a source of frequent confusion to young ears attuned to American slang, American music, American film, and that sometimes-damned, sometimes-praised "American Way of Life."

At the Free University in particular, the contrast in this field between student experiences and expectations was great, and it was precisely at the Free University that the students had demonstrated little hesitation in making their grievances known. As a consequence, the hapless English Seminar proved in its own way to be nearly as riven as the Kennedy Institute or the Otto Suhr Institute. However, this time the heart of the matter was *Studienreform* (curricular reform).

With the passage of the 1969 University Law, the English Seminar became known officially as the Institute for English Philology, within the even less glamorously named "Department 17" (Philology of Modern Foreign Languages). It had already experienced its share of disruptions, sit-ins, "go-ins," and teach-ins during the initial phase of the student protest movement of the late 1960s. However, in the period thereafter to approximately 1974, a wearisome series of protest actions caused considerable tension and unpleasantness to a department that had up to the late 1960s led a relatively untroubled existence.[133] The problem was in good part due to the extreme polarization that affected so many departments and institutes at the Free University in those troubled years. The institute found itself confronted with a red cell too: *Rote Zelle Anglistik* (*Rotzang*). The English Seminar also had only four full professors in 1969 to direct the studies of literally hundreds of students, most of whom aspired to become secondary-level English teachers. To be sure, the *Rotzang* hard core was capable of considerable mischief, and they would, in all probability, have tried the patience of even the most kindly-disposed professor. Moreover, their antics showed at times a lamentable irresponsibility and an astonishing naiveté. In 1970, for example, a group of about fifteen *Anglisten*, as they were called, decided to travel to Ireland. In the past, university groups had traveled periodically to the British Isles with good results. Such field trips were a recognized and attractive feature of studying English at the Free University. This time, however, the group, under the direction of an assistant, announced to all and sundry that they intended to contact the Irish Republican Army in order to understand better the aspirations of the IRA and presumably to offer whatever sympathy, moral support, and perhaps financial support were within their modest means. To their astonishment, the advance group of three were promptly taken into custody by British authorities in London, and after being dispossessed of their support funds, propaganda leaflets, and illusions, spent 20 hours under strict confinement before being bundled off ignominiously onto a return flight to Germany. Her Majesty's Britannic Government were not inclined to cast so forgiving an eye upon the group as the FU authorities had done. In retrospect, the affair suggests that an air of astonishing unreality surrounded the perspectives of such students as were attracted to the *Rotzang*.

And yet, the voice of dissidence at the English Seminar was sufficiently powerful and persistent as to suggest that other problems underlay the tensions that were so visibly present. The enlisting of hundreds of young adults in various protest actions was not due above all to magical propagandistic abilities by a handful of dedicated Marxists, Leninists, Trotskyists, Maoists, Stalinists, or whatever other ideological persuasion they were proclaiming at the moment. The phenomenon of protest was better understood in the context of dissatisfied groups of students at a burgeoning mass university who were also trying to address themselves to issues of curricular reform. It was unfortunate, to say the least, that they chose a disastrous way in which to raise their concerns, and they proved extraordinarily exasperating even to those who might have offered a sympathetic ear.

The Free University had not had an easy time in building up its *Anglistisches Seminar*. While it attracted specialists in Old English and Middle English, the university seemed to have chronic bad luck in filling a professorship in Modern English. An apparent success in 1961 turned out to be illusory, as the prospective candidate chose otherwise following the construction of the Wall. Thereafter, a succession of temporary guest professors provided course offerings in the field but never consistently enough to supply demand and to produce a balanced curriculum. Although the negative effects of the Wall were considerably dampened by the Quadripartite Agreement in 1971, the Free University's English Department still had only four professors by then and a total staff numbering thirty-three. Even with the rapid transformation of several *akademischer Rat* positions into tenured C-2 and C-3 professor positions, the curricular offerings continued to be weighted toward earlier developments in the language.

All English majors were obliged to take history of the English language, and once again the early evolution of the language took decided preference in that crucial prerequisite course. Moreover, they were required to pass a written midsemester examination, hardly an unusual requirement in American universities but atypical at a German university at that time. Students of all political persuasions were less than happy about it. An English sociologist and guest lecturer at the Free University, Stewart Anderson, compiled a sociological survey of students of English in the early 1970s. The resulting study revealed strong student discontent on a wide range of issues, including teaching practices, curricula, orientation efforts, and advising by the staff. Anderson also asked in-coming freshman students about the obligatory coursework in Old English. "I have nothing against Old English," responded one student. "Language is a great joy to me, but I must ask myself: Why bother if we are not going to use it?" Another less articulate respondent com mented forcefully: "Old English is rubbish, Middle English too."[134] Anderson's queries about student reactions to courses in the same field elicited negative reactions among most students, most of whom described the course content of Old English as being "poor" and the teaching of the subject "moderate to poor." Most students, he found, preferred to take courses in the English language as opposed to its history, and they generally rendered a much higher estimation of content and teaching in that field.[135]

The student critics had a point, and they were not making it in utter isolation. A general trend had emerged in German higher education from the mid-1960s onward to pay greater attention to updating academic programs and curricular offerings with the intent of tailoring them more closely to the future professional demands of students. Thus influential circles in the German academic world were calling for *praxisbezogene Ausbildung*, profession-oriented higher education. The German Federal Republic's *Wissenschaftsrat* (Science Council) began issuing position papers and publications on the subject, and it became a broad theme of discussions at all higher education institutions in Berlin and the Federal Republic.[136] This later found practical expression in the Berlin University Law of 1978: "Institutions of higher learning in cooperation with the appropriate state authorities have a continuing obligation to examine and to develop further the contents and structure of studies with consideration given to developments in science, scholarship, and art. [They must consider] the needs of professional practices and the needs for change in the professional world."[137] The general goal seemed unexceptional. However, the issue was hardly susceptible to a straightforward solution, since in most fields there was no common consensus as to what was the ideal way to achieve a professionally oriented program or curriculum. That required a minimum of trust among those seeking to establish standards, and trust was notably lacking in those troubled times.

Anderson's investigation disclosed, for example, that the reasoning of many students in offering their preferences for curricular change was not only the relevance of the coursework to their careers and interests. Many respondees often cited the desire for Marxist interpretations of literature and society. It should not be forgotten that the "Marx Renaissance" was in full bloom in Dahlem in those years. Thus, in the spring of 1971, Manfred Scheler, recently promoted to a mid-level professorship in the English Department, asked for police protection of his courses since he had become the bête noire of the radicals' *Rotzang*. The latter were demanding that coursework in English Studies concentrate on such subjects as class conflict in Ireland and British imperialism in Ghana. Such themes might be appropriate to political science and international affairs but departed radically from the department's intentions—namely, the instilling of language skills for students, the majority of whom still hoped to become teachers of English. The students might complain about the irrelevance of Old and Middle English; the professors could with equal legitimacy complain about blatant efforts to transform departmental offerings into indoctrination courses.

Finally, in May 1971, after a lengthy boycott action by a majority of students, followed by a week-long closing of the department by the professors over the issue of obligatory Old and Middle English and continuing student disruptions, Vice President Wesel made an appearance at the English Department. In essence he found fault with both sides. Wesel called for an end to the much-hated history of English with its emphasis on the early development of the language. Wesel had had to intercede following a scuffle between Professor Bitterling and some red-cell adherents. He castigated *Rotzang* for its disruptive practices, which at times approached the level of terrorism. Sometimes the violence erupted among the students themselves, as when at a meeting of all students of English some red-cell members grabbed a moderate student's written account of a red-cell meeting. The young woman resisted in vain, and as a result twelve professors and staff wrote a protest letter to Senator Stein condemning such methods. The respected conservative (liberal by American standards) newspaper *Frankurter Allgemeine Zeitung* castigated the incident as an example of growing political intolerance at the Free University. However, at about the same time the smaller but well-informed *Weser Kurier* observed that the unruly actions at the English Department were not serving merely political goals. Rather, they were intended to institute concrete reforms in the curricula and in testing procedures.[138]

The tensions and disagreements that plagued the English Department of the Free University in the years of dissidence were in some ways characteristic of many departments and institutes of the time. The phenomenon of student protest was fed not merely by youthful cussedness or evidenced by superb feats of agitation by a radical hard core. As the student population mushroomed, overwhelming the fragile infrastructure designed to orient and to support the growing mass of aspirant graduates, disillusionment and alienation became an undeniable trend among sizable groups of young people. This was hardly peculiar to the Free University, but because protest actions at the Free University continued to attract widespread media attention, public knowledge of the university's internal squabblings was commensurately higher. Thus, the "silent majority" of students, in this case the English majors, while not formally joining the ranks of the radicals, nevertheless remained passive for the most part. They were prepared to tolerate the antics of colorful dissidents not because they believed in the confused ideology of the chaotic *Rotzang*, but rather because they were amused at the discomfort if not horror which a modest band of dissidents could inspire among the full professors with their preference for *Beowulf* and *The Canterbury Tales*.

Thus, the Free University limped along, plagued by boycotts and strikes, actions and counteractions. Sometimes even the brigades of cleaning ladies joined in, and it appeared that disruptions had become the normal pattern of existence in Dahlem. It transpired that the largely female janitorial staff at the OSI had finally tired of cleaning up the "slop," as they called it, caused by the endless demonstrations and protest actions in the confined building. The disgruntled women issued a flyer of their own to the dissidents stating that they had had enough of cleaning up rotten eggs and removing the endless graffiti smeared over walls, doors, and windows in the decrepit building. They reasoned that "this is greater exploitation than what we would expect from the capitalists. . . . Instead of a university we have here a kindergarten." The delighted *FAZ* commented on the unusual protest by saying that at at last somebody was demonstrating for a clean university.[139]

WOLFGANG WIPPERMANN AND UMFUNKIONIEREN: THE LIMITS OF PROTEST

There was no magical date when the turmoil at the Free University ended and tranquility reigned. Indeed, throughout its forty-year history the Free University has never been truly tranquil and probably never will attain that laudable if dull state. As the decade of the 1970s wore on and it became apparent that the steadily increasing stream of incoming students could not expect automatically at the end of their studies to find secure positions and the beginning of a career, the general trend was to concentrate on completing their higher education expeditiously in order to start as early as possible. At least this was the case with the more perceptive students. Others, who for various reasons continued to be active in the dissident movement, either did not or could not understand the trend and seemed to adopt protest and demonstration as a new form of life. One convincing piece of evidence for this phenomenon was the fact that the merging, shifting welter of protest groups, such as the red cells, the KSV, and its successor the *Kommunistische Hochschulgruppe* (KHG), or Communist University Group, produced no able or well-known figures like Knut Nevermann, Sigrid Fronius, or Rudi Dutschke. Rather, they remained for the most part anonymous, and since many of them were constantly engaged in illegal or semilegal actions, they preferred to keep their identities unknown. Moreover, they had in a certain sense reached the stage described in 1971 by Thomas Nipperdey where they were dismissing thoughtful analysis and criticism in favor of ideological rigidity—or purity, as they might have described it. What this meant in effect was that the best minds went elsewhere, back to their studies with the intention of building careers in the existing society.

Yet, this was not a process that took place overnight. The trend was toward greater calm from approximately 1973 onward, but it was by no means a transition that was smooth or trouble-free. Periodically strikes and boycotts, attempts at *Umfuntionieren*, the transforming of courses to the tastes of the radical left, took place for years after the high point in tensions of 1971-1972. However, the calming trend was unmistakable, and is exemplified in the experiences of one young instructor at the Free University in the mid-1970s.

Wolfgang Wippermann was a junior history instructor at the Friedrich Meinecke Institute. With an interest in modern history, he worked as an assistant under Professor Ernst Nolte, simultaneously preparing his habilitation and teaching courses to FU students. Wippermann was especially interested in the origins and workings of fascism but taught a variety of subjects, and so he decided to offer a course on "Marx and Engels's Theory of History," a trendy subject which he hoped would attract sufficient numbers of students to make the course succeed. Wippermann was also an SPD loyalist and therefore a bit to the left in the German political spectrum. The topic he chose proved to be popular. Several dozen students were in attendance during the first meeting of the seminar. So far so good.

However, it transpired that the course had attracted the attention of the KHG, and about a dozen of its members were in attendance. They were not impressed with Wippermann's approach to the subject or with his reading list, and they let their displeasure be known. Whereas other junior instructors might have allowed some compromises, Wippermann disagreed with the self-styled experts, indicating that he, the instructor, was entitled to choose the subject, prepare the reading lists, and lead the discussions. What followed was a long running feud between the instructor and the KHG adherents who were determined to make good their claim as reigning experts in the field.

The seminar sessions proved to be stormy, as Wippermann and the KHG group refused any compromise. At least twice the disagreements and the disruptions became so vituperative that he called off the seminar meeting for that day. In two other instances the students declared a boycott. As a result, by the middle of the semester the seminar had covered considerably less than half the material originally planned. Wippermann announced that he wanted to complete the seminar in the scant time remaining. He was prepared to devote his Saturday afternoons during the remaining month in addition to regularly scheduled class time to complete the seminar. However, he had also decided to impose certain conditions. He expected the students to attend faithfully. The students would have to complete a written assignment individually, with their own signatures affixed. In other words, there would be no collective assignment as the KHG members were demanding. He also expected them to confine the discussions to the topic and content planned for the course. He demanded, too, that the students not use the seminar as an "operations center" for planning further strike actions or for discussing any and all current social and political topics as they had tried to do to date. "In short," Wippermann informed his immediate superior, Ernst Nolte, "for legal reasons a transformation of this seminar into a political indoctrination course or into a strike action is unacceptable."[140] Finally, Wippermann expected the students to sign an attendance sheet to demonstrate their regular participation in class. The conditions met with an angry response from the students, who categorically refused to accept them. A shouting match ensued, and Wippermann finally canceled yet another class, stating that any further discussion with interested students could take place in his office. The sole result was that the confrontation simply shifted to another part of the giant *Rostlaube*, the university's huge building complex containing numerous departments and institutes. When the noise had reached the point where Meinecke Institute Chairman Nolte felt compelled to intervene, the latter backed Wippermann, who, he said, was within his rights to set the conditions for the seminar. Thereupon several of the excited students retorted that they, not Wippermann, would impose the conditions.[141] The stage was set for a fateful confrontation.

The KHG group was sufficiently well organized and financed to publish its own small news sheet, which it rather grandly called the *Kommunistische Hochschulzeitung*, the Communist University Paper. Under the headline "Falsifier," its members began a press campaign against Wippermann, attacking him as a "specialist for Bonapartism and fascism ... defeated by the student movement, revealed as sloppy, as a falsifier and as an idiot."[142] By that time Wippermann had already made his decision. He canceled the seminar. There would be no credit given for it. The Meinecke Institute authorities accepted the decision without demur.

That was hardly the end to the affair. On the afternoon of February 1, 1977, twelve students entered an office in the *Rostlaube* used by faculty for advising students, and, in effect, sealed off the door and windows while a very surprised Wippermann looked on. The angry group of students had a new demand of their own. They wanted credit for the seminar Wippermann had canceled, and they expected him to sign the necessary forms then and there. Wippermann adamantly refused, and the same deadlock that had plagued the seminar for the entire semester ensued. After an hour of fruitless exchanges, Wippermann announced that he was leaving the office, picked up his belongings, and started for the door. The students acted as one and shoved him back from the exit. A large, burly man, thirtyish and in his prime, Wippermann was also a former dueling-fraternity member and was not known to be shy or retiring. Indeed, his strong self-assurance and determination to lead the seminar may have contributed as much to the confrontation with the KHG students as any haggling over Marxist theory. An old-fashioned fistfight ensued, an unusual event even at the Free University and one in which nearly half of the participants were young women! Amidst overturned chairs and files, Wippermann remained in the office, bruised but unbowed. It was a standoff.

The commotion finally attracted the attention of passersby and eventually word of the incident reached the FU president's office. By this time Eberhard Lämmert, a left-oriented German Studies expert of professorial rank, had replaced Kreibich, and it was unsure how the new chief official would respond to this minor crisis. Only the president could order police onto the campus, and within an hour a staff member, Kurt Zegenhagen, arrived with seven city policemen. Finding the door still locked, four of them crossed an inner courtyard to enter the office by a window. The three remaining policemen and Zegenhagen manned the doorway. As the first unit began climbing through windows, the twelve students hurled open the door, galloped past the "blocking force," and immediately submerged themselves among the hundred-odd students who had gathered to view the dramatic action. Although the worst years of police-student confrontations were already past, the presence of city police on campus was still far from popular. Zegenhagen and the officers on the spot apparently decided that discretion was the better part of valor. Afterward Wippermann was angry that no one had apprehended his would-be captors.

This unfortunate episode had a lengthy and unpleasant end. The university authorities under President Lämmert were not convinced that Wippermann had the right to impose so many special conditions on the students and cited a precedent in an earlier course where the instructor had had to back down from some of his demands.[143] However, Wippermann was now more concerned with the indisputably illegal acts of February 1, and, having recognized a number of the students who had seized him and threatened him and his family, he initiated legal proceedings against them.[144] Dismayed at the lack of support from the president's office, he consulted Otto von Simson about his plight, and the latter, an avowed NOFU member, advised him to use a tried and true method: He should bring his case before the public. Shortly afterward, a reporter and photographer from the sensationalist but widely read *Berliner Zeitung* appeared and took down his account of what happened. The following day Wippermann's story, photo and all, appeared in the *BZ*—juxtaposed to the paper's usual daily shot of a smiling semi-naked young woman—and his fame was made.[145]

In retrospect, the Wippermann Affair proved to be another milestone in the political development of the Free University. The ensuing publicity forced events to a head. The university authorities, under President Lämmert, suspended those three or four students whom Wippermann and other eyewitnesses could positively identify. The legal proceedings proved to be lengthy and involved, but with bulldog tenacity

Wipperman pursued his erstwhile pursuers through the courts. He even identified another of his antagonists in a police lineup. The resulting convictions of half a dozen students led to legal fines. Pertinent to the university's development was the fact that they were also dismissed for a time from the university. The KHG continued periodically to denounce Wippermann, and even as late as April 1978 a few of the expelled students appeared in one of his seminar meetings to challenge him. It was then that the change in mood at the Free University became apparent. Instead of joining the dissidents or tacitly endorsing their methods, other students finally lost patience and denounced the disrupters instead. They demanded that the seminar get on with the business of learning.[146] A new era was at hand.

The Wippermann Affair was a marked defeat for the dissident KHG in several ways. Unlike student dissidents of the 1960s, who regularly had held press conferences and brought their grievances before the public, the shifting groups of radicals in the early to mid-1970s had virtually abandoned that field to the moderates and to the conservatives. Their extremist political views would hardly have found an echo among the public in any case, but they compounded the problem with their conspiratorial methods and illegal actions, which then forced them to submerge their identities. By flirting with terrorist methods, they finally alienated the majority of students, most of whom by this time were channeling their energies in other directions toward careers and personal advancement. Had they shown greater articulateness and skill, the KHG adherents might even have mounted an effective protest against Wippermann's list of conditions by claiming to be defenders of freedom of expression. But by employing strong-arm tactics instead, methods which no society based upon law could condone, and by addressing their side of the story solely to the KHG faithful, they succeeded only in discrediting themselves before their fellow students. Besides, it had become painfully obvious that these would-be practitioners of *Umfunktionieren* were neither pursuers of truth, defenders of justice, nor friends of liberty.

THE DAY OF THE MAMMOTH

In 1960, the Free University had had 12,000 students in attendance. In 1970, enrollments had been held to about 15,000, the result of a strong *numerus clausus* in many fields. In 1980, the Free University counted no fewer than 43,000 students in its midst! The dam had burst. Critics in the 1960s had already begun to complain that expansion of the student body had been a contributing factor in producing a feeling of alienation among students. Social services such as the tutorial system threatened to be overwhelmed. The dramatic expansion of the Free University in the 1970s made it one of the two largest universities in the German-speaking world. That simple fact goes far in explaining why the Free University took on a different institutional character after 1969. It was hardly alone. German higher education in general expanded tremendously. In 1950, for example, there had been 172,000 students enrolled in German universities. In 1983 that figure had risen to 1,273,000, with most of the increase coming in the period after 1969. Not only did the college-age population expand rapidly; the percentage of those young people deciding to study, or to abandon other careers for studies instead, rose dramatically. In the postwar period four or five percent of the youthful population had attended German universities. By the late 1970s that figure had quadrupled to twenty percent or more. In short, a demographic revolution had struck German higher education, and the Free University felt its impact as keenly as any university in the nation.[147]

President Kreibich and members of his planning commission, headed by Traugott Klose, had hoped in the first years of his presidency to hold enrollments to a maximum of 21,000 students, and it was the pride of his administration that the Free University for the first time was engaged, he claimed, in long-range planning for the future.[148] However, enrollments were hardly the exclusive preserve of higher educational planners in those years when the German baby-boom was coming of age. The political leadership was acutely aware of the rising demand for expanded universities to meet the flood of *Abitur* recipients seeking a place to study. Thus, the Berlin Senate was not inclined to accept at face value the modest limits set by the FU planners. By 1973, the Senate raised the ceiling to 30,000 enrollments, and that, too, soon went out of date as the remorseless demand for higher education continued to press upon the institutions. Even planning experts like Traugott Klose felt helpless in such a situation.[149] Senator Stein readily conceded that the SPD political leadership had foreseen the negative political ramifications for them if the universities could not cater to the high demand. Wanting to survive politically, the Berlin Senate acted accordingly. Stein bent every effort to support the Free University financially, and in those years of expansion its budget rose by almost a third from year to year.[150] It was this dramatic increase in public largess which allowed the Kreibich administration to create hundreds of new professorships in less than two years, a record expansion of faculty in German higher education which holds to this day.

In 1972, Kreibich explained the university's difficulties caused by population expansion to the British Ambassador to Germany, Sir Roger Jackling. Concerned by the university's continuing rapid growth, Kreibich predicted that the Free University would exceed 25,000 students within three years. That seemed to be a rash prediction, and Kreibich ultimately was proved wrong in making it. By 1975, the Free University had over 31,000 students instead! According to Jackling, the

FU president had resigned himself to the fact that the university would have to change its expectations about students' abilities and goals at the emerging mass university. "It had to be accepted," Jackling informed his government, "that all of this vast number could not be given adequate possibilities for studying for the really top academic openings available; only perhaps 500 or 1000 students could be given the really intensive attention required. The remainder would have to be trained in a much less academic manner in order to equip them more realistically for a practical career. This was a departure," Jackling recounted, "from the classical Humboldt pattern of encouraging 'creativity.'" The negative effects of so rapid an expansion were well known to the Free University's first president. The problem was that without the imposition of a severe and inevitably unpopular *numerus clausus* there was little he felt he could do to stop such growth. Kreibich realized that its very expansion was altering the nature of the Free University.[151]

Kreibich's successor, Eberhard Lämmert, considered the large, sustained increase in enrollments as exacerbating social and political problems at the Free University, but he was equally helpless when confronted with the unyielding demographic trends.[152] To be sure, such startling growth had resulted partly from changes brought about in higher educational policy by the dominant political party of the time, the Social Democrats. They were determined to raise the percentage of the youthful population who could attend a university, and in this they were partly successful. The immediate effect of such vast increases was to strain virtually all of the facilities and programs at the Free University and elsewhere. There had already been tensions aplenty prior to the decade of growth. Yet, to understand the Free University in its hour of discontent, it is necessary to realize that the former community of teachers and learners had been transformed seemingly overnight by impersonal social forces into an amorphous corporate structure. Its numbers were so vast that no building, including the dependable old Auditorium Maximum, sufficed anymore to bring them together. The university's twenty-four streamlined departments (later reduced to twenty-one) and six central institutes had less to do with each other than the admittedly unwieldy five *Fakultäten* had allowed earlier, a source of regret to many faculty. By 1972, on the basis of much painful experience, a consolidation process began with the dissolution of four of the departments and two central institutes. Nevertheless, the pattern established under the 1969 law still held sway. Once again, this was a typical feature of German universities in the aftermath of so many reforms. Nevertheless, it struck friends and observers of the Free University with a particular poignancy because they could ask: When had the Free University ever been a typical university? It had begun to emerge from the era of protest and polarization better intact then its many doomsayers had predicted. It was now in the process of becoming a different institution.

PRESIDENTIAL POLITICS

It was no secret that President Kreibich had begun his seven-year term of office in 1969 largely with the support of the *Mittelbau*, students, and various left-oriented political groups at the Free University. They had perceived him to be a kindred spirit, and his first three years in office had appeared to confirm that assessment. However, as it became apparent that the extreme polarization was continuing to take place and that the 1969 University Law far from ameliorating the situation was magnifying it instead, Kreibich had been forced to modify his political views to some extent. He might be able to ignore or dismiss for a time criticisms levelled at him by such groups as NOFU because of its highly partisan viewpoint. However, by 1972, signs of a stiffening political reaction to internal developments at the Free University were too many and too serious to ignore.

The evidence came from all sides. For example, in a meeting between Kreibich and his staff with an official of the U.S. Mission in Berlin, Public Affairs Officer Terrence Catherman, the worried president revealed that he had just received word from the University of Texas at Austin "cancelling a bi-lateral exchange program due to reports Texas had received about declining academic standards at the FU." Kreibich fumed about the development, ascribing it to "anti–Free University activities on the part of 'immigrant professors' from Berlin in the United States. . . ." Catherman reported that Kreibich and Wesel heatedly denied the allegations of a decline in standards. However, Horst Hartwich, one of Kreibich's senior staff members, privately contradicted the brave face which the president had put on for his American guest. Hartwich was, in effect, Kreibich's link to the Americans and was acknowledged as such by the FU president. He could afford to be and, with Kreibich's blessing, was more open. At one point Hartwich took Catherman aside and told him "that Kreibich was 'very depressed' at the present time due to some indications of just such an academic decline observable in some university departments."[153]

At first, the Texans had minced their words. Some months earlier, their German Exchange Committee chairman, Martin Kermacy, had written to the FU leadership saying the Americans' shaky finances were one consideration for the termination. "A second factor," he added, "in all candor, is the unsettled academic environment in Berlin. Under prevailing conditions we do not believe that our students can benefit as much from a year at the Free University as they have in the past, or presumably will in the future."[154] The Berliners were stung, and Hartwich asked for a more detailed explanation. This time the Texans were more forthcoming: "Interviews with our returning students indicated that the German universities exhibit the same restive spirit which characterizes the American university today," Kermacy replied. "Only at the Free University, however, did our students find that unrest interfered with the educative process and made normal progress in formal studies impossible."[155] Little wonder that Kreibich was distraught. In this instance, no one could shrug off such charges as being NOFU-inspired. It was students returning from Berlin who had registered their complaints directly about the situation at the Free University. For several years, at least, the exchange link with Texas was severed. (It was restored in 1981 when it became obvious that a new spirit was afoot at the Free University.)

Other evidence of alarm in foreign lands about the Free University continued to mount. Articles in Swiss, Belgian, American, Canadian, and other foreign publications demonstrated a genuine wave of concern among outside observers about the affairs of the Free University. Those were distress signals which few, least of all the university's president, could ignore.[156] The Texans, however, had jolted the FU leadership with a concrete action.

Nevertheless, the timing of the Texans' decision was ironic because the summer semester of 1972 was roughly the point when political passions had begun slowly to ebb. Nor was it a false dawn. The signs of a change in political climate in Berlin and at the Free University continued to mount as the decade waned. Earlier, the election first of Rolf Kreibich as president in 1969 and then of Uwe Wesel as first vice president at the Free University a few months later had been an indicator of a leftward trend in the senior administration. Later, in 1974, Wesel departed from that office and was replaced by more moderate officials. These included Hartmut Jäckel and Hajo Riese, moderates from the FU political faction known as the Reformsozialisten, the Reform Socialists, plus Jorge Cervos-Navarro and Siegfried Baske, from the slightly more conservative Liberale Aktion. In essence, their election produced a kind of counterweight to President Kreibich in the last two years of his presidency. The senior vice president among the four new officials was political scientist Hartmut Jäckel, like Kreibich an SPD member, but nevertheless considerably to the right of him politically. Jäckel had made no secret of his opposition to Kreibich's policies at the Free University, and his election was a strong indication that a shift in political mood among sizable portions of the university was under way. An American public affairs officer, Gunther Rosinus, recorded Jäckel's views on the state of the Free University in the summer of 1974. "In general," the official stated, "Dr. Jäckel felt that the FU was over the hill with its time of troubles, had weathered the storm—albeit with considerable damage— and could look toward increasing shifts from radical to more moderate elements in its governing councils and ultimately in its teaching circles." To be sure, there were still trouble spots with many festering wounds. Jäckel pointed out that radicalism and polarization were still acute at the Kennedy Institute and at the Fachbereich 11 (Department of Philosophy and Social Sciences). He expected no speedy recovery there. In general, however, the new vice president prophesied "improvements in governance and faculty coming slowly and only after some hard battles, especially in the 'personal-politik' area."[157]

Jäckel felt that the FU president also comprehended the changes in direction. "As to President Kreibich's own current views," Rosinus recounted, "Dr. Jäckel said that Kreibich had 'recognized realities' and was no longer insistent on giving radical elements a voice in all matters." It could hardly be otherwise. The shift in mood was taking place not merely at the top but throughout the various parts of the university. "Current shifts toward moderation he noted particularly among students and the non-teaching faculty members of the university, although faculty members, too, he felt, were leaving the ideological barricades in increasing numbers." Jäckel, the American official recorded, "felt that the presidential and university council elections in '76 would climax the shift and confirm his prediction."[158]

The new political realities were brought home even more forcefully in West Berlin political circles. Alexander Schwan recalled that the young president had had to accept his more moderate vice presidents "because of the changed realities in the Konzil but also because of political pressure from the [Berlin] Senate following a dramatic discussion at the guesthouse of the Berlin Senate to which Governing Mayor Klaus Schütz had invited him. Besides Kreibich, Senator Gerd Löffler and several Social Democratic professors including Helmut Coper and Alexander Schwan participated in order to signal the same message." Schwan, too, felt it was a significant turning point. "This new constellation [lasting to the end of Kreibich's time in office in 1976] was a consolidation phase for the F.U."[159]

Kreibich understood some of the major implications of shifting political mood quickly, as when Hanna Reuter, widow of the much revered Ernst Reuter, threatened to bring a lawsuit against the university if its authorities did not remove a radical KSV poster which proclaimed the Free University on the occasion of its twenty-fifth anniversary to be an "imperialist university" and included a photograph of the former governing mayor. Faced with this sharp protest from Frau Reuter, Kreibich wasted no time. He personally began the removal of the offensive—and patently untrue—placards from the FU property.[160] It was just one of thousands of examples of posters, brochures, flyers, and broadsides that literally cloaked the campus environment in the years of protest. Walls, doors, windows, sometimes even ceilings, and seemingly every other surface were bedecked with graphic material, not unlike a frantic advertising blitz or the high point of a confetti-strewn political campaign. It was simply not to be avoided. Students ate their meals in the commons amidst stacks of flyers and other political sheets that bewildered the uninitiated and the veteran alike. Every day it was the same thing, and anyone who studied at the Free University in those years grew used to being confronted by images crowded one upon another. Each piece of propaganda proclaimed the path toward the true political solution, toward moral surety, social responsibility, and, somewhat later, ecological responsibility.

Despite the radicalism attached to his name, Kreibich witnessed in his last two years in office a general relaxation of the tensions that had caused so much alarm in the late 1960s and early 1970s. Given his angry denunciations of American policy in Southeast Asia in 1970, following the Kent State Affair, the American officials in Berlin simply accepted as fact his deliberate distancing of himself and his staff from official contacts with them for a time. Later, in 1975, they cautiously sounded him out about a government-sponsored trip to the United States and were pleasantly surprised when he immediately accepted the offer. Knowing his concern about social and political issues, the organizers urged officials at home to follow Kreibich's advice and avoid pure protocol visits. Instead, they stated, "we would suggest that Mr. Kreibich be exposed to social and political problems in the U.S., their complexity, and the various programs and proposals being discussed and implemented for their alleviation." Their reasoning for this approach was based in part upon recent historical developments at the Free University: "In the context of the difficulties of Berlin's Free University, we feel it highly important that he be exposed to the ways in which Americans attempt to find solutions to their problems, with particular emphasis on non-ideological, pragmatic approaches."[161] Kreibich made the official journey in the spring of 1975, along with his more conservative staff members, such as Jäckel and Hartwich, another indication of a normalization in the affairs of the Free University.

However, the 1976 elections for the university's second president did not turn out quite as Jäckel had expected. The polarization at the Free University might have been ebbing, but it had by no means fully ebbed. There were still some surprises in store.

THE PRESIDENCY OF EBERHARD LÄMMERT

Controversy had seemed constantly to surround Rolf Kreibich, although his last two years in office were considerably quieter than the first five. In the end, he declared himself satisfied that the Free University was now a restructured reformed university. He also felt that the University Framework Law of 1976 was restricting the powers of the university president, and so in May 1976 Kreibich announced that he would not attempt to run for the office again. He was fully aware that his time in office had been controversial and that his reelection was unlikely.[162] His successor, Eberhard Lämmert, aroused considerably less sensation on one level if only because his academic qualifications to be president

were considerably more orthodox than those of his predecessor. However, although not formally a member of any party, he was judged by
more conservatively inclined FU professors such as Alexander Schwan
and the *Liberale Aktion* to be somewhat to the left of the SPD and therefore suspect. The same critics felt that his vice presidents, given the success of the left-oriented groups at the university in the spring of 1976
in forming a majority coalition, were also uniformly left of center.[163]
Therefore, political conservatives like Schwan viewed the election of
Lämmert as a throwback to the early Kreibich years rather than as a continuation of a consolidation process.

Lämmert was a professor of German Studies and comparative literature and enjoyed high standing in his field. He was not, formally speaking, an in-house choice for FU president, because he had held a professorship at Heidelberg University at the time of his nomination and
election in June 1976. However, Lämmert was hardly a stranger to the
Free University. He had been a longtime FU faculty member until 1970,
when he accepted an appointment at Heidelberg. Unlike the professors
who had left the Free University in those difficult years with a flourish
of angry rhetoric, Lämmert had departed on good terms with the FU administration and with the SPD leadership in Berlin. He had burned no
bridges. It was indicative of his good standing with Berlin's SPD leadership that Governing Mayor Klaus Schütz and Ministers Stein and
Löffler had sought to convince Lämmert to be a presidential candidate
in 1969, a nomination he turned down because of his intent to achieve
greater standing in his field before entering a demanding administrative
post.[164]

Lämmert had also maintained steady ties to the Free University in
his six years away from Berlin. He estimated that on average he had returned to the city fortnightly during the entire period he was at Heidelberg in order to examine graduate students and complete other tasks he
felt he still owed the Free University. Thus, Lämmert had hardly lapsed
into obscurity when the selection of presidential candidates began. He
discussed his candidacy with Kreibich, whom he met by chance in the
spring of 1976 while in Berlin, and the latter urged him to seek a nomination. About the same time, individual representatives within the Free
University's German Studies and English Studies departments also visited Lämmert at Heidelberg to suggest the same thing. Besides, the German Studies Department especially needed his return in order to restore its depleted ranks of distinguished scholars. They still felt the loss
of one of their most promising experts, Peter Szondi, who had taken his
own life in October 1971. Many of the Germanists at the Free University had long had a good academic reputation despite the fact that it
was a *Fachbereich* frequently rent by political tensions. Nevertheless,
the long-term prospects for the German Studies Department appeared attractive to Lämmert, who was looking beyond the presidency to the

time when he would resume his normal academic duties. Then, when the university's senior vice president and political moderate, Hartmut Jäckel, approached him too, Lämmert realized that he was a serious contender to be the next leader of the Free University.[165]

Unlike the 1969 race, the 1976 contest was anticlimactic. Lämmert allowed his name to be entered, but he did not actively campaign. An ad hoc *Linke Fraktion* composed of left-leaning political groupings of professors and of the *Mittelbau* at the Free University, including the left-oriented *Aktionsgruppe Hochschullehrer*, supported him strongly. Lämmert recalled that they were the university's liberal-to-left professors, including a large contingent of the *Mittelbau* from the medical school. Another moderate left group, the *Reformsozialisten*, also supported him for the most part. The more conservative *Liberale Aktion* and especially the full professors in it were generally opposed. Lämmert spoke just once to the *Konzil*, which met with numerous journalists and as many of the university community as could jam themselves into the huge Auditorium Maximum. An articulate spokesman for the left-oriented factions, he fielded questions well and demonstrated that he had broad appeal to the left spectrum even though some of the conservative circles were dismayed by his candidacy. The largest of the political factions, the *Liberale Aktion*, which encompassed the great majority of the full professors, was anything but pleased at the prospect of a Lämmert victory. "We stood in opposition to Lämmert during his entire presidency," stated one of their number, Alexander Schwan. "However, this was not so much the case with Kreibich at least with respect to his last two years in office."[166] Lämmert was, in a sense, entering a role similar to that of the liberal rector of the mid-1960s, Hans-Joachim Lieber, and had to reckon with suspicion and opposition of middle-to-right groups and especially NOFU. Yet he was undeniably popular with other influential groups at the university. "The frequently heavy applause in the Auditorium demonstrated that Lämmert's manner of speaking, his humor, and his quick-wittedness hit the mark with most of the audience," commented one observer.[167] He won easily over his more conservative rival, Siegfried Baske. However, the proceedings were made into a complete FU event only when two representatives from the tiny but well-organized *Kommunistische Hochschulgruppe* (KHG) announced with long-winded solemnity to all assembled that they could not support either candidate. To be sure, the gesture meant little. It was becoming apparent that the radicals' influence among the students was rapidly waning away. The NOFU membership was showing definite signs of relaxing its publicity campaign as well. The polarization that had plagued the Free University for a decade was showing unmistakable signs of drawing to a close.

Or was it? Like Kreibich before him, Lämmert immediately experienced bitter attacks from both left and right. For their own tactical reasons, the ADS group, which maintained close ties to the tiny West Berlin Communist party, the SEW, had decided to support Lämmert. This excited the easily aroused suspicions of some in the NOFU circle, and they promptly labeled him the second *Volksfront* president after Kreibich, i.e., a kind of popular-front president who, the label hinted, was working in league with Communists and other radicals. *Volksfront* in German political parlance usually meant a coalition of the *Arbeiterparteien*, i.e., the socialists, the Social Democrats, and the Communists. It is often misused to identify a left coalition under Communist domination with some social democratic *nützliche Idioten* (fellow travelers), and was seen as the last step before a Communist takeover as happened in Prague in 1948. In politically charged West Berlin such labels and suspicions were by this time the norm. Kreibich, too, had faced similar if even bitterer attacks when he entered upon the presidency. Even Werner Stein noted afterward with some amusement that he, a biophysicist who had been appalled at the scientific perversions of Lysenko at the time of Stalin and who had left Humboldt University for ideological reasons to become one of the Free University's first assistants in 1949, was dubbed "the Red Senator" by conservatives in the heyday of the student protest movement.[168] Name calling and political labeling were simply a fact of life at the Free University during its decade of discontent.

Lämmert was therefore an immediate target for the more conservative elements. Schwan, from the *Liberale Aktion*, did not hesitate to claim bias on the part of the new president. "His tendency from the outset was to build an exclusively leftist team of vice presidents, which he was able to achieve only temporarily and even then only incompletely."[169] Lämmert had to reckon with strong opposition from the right.

However, the Free University's second president had to face troubles and threats from the left too. Lämmert began his presidency in the midst of yet another student boycott, or strike-action as they preferred to call it. For their part, the student organizers were protesting against numerous issues. They wished to indicate their disapproval of a requirement that faculty members register their loyalty to the West German political and social system. This issue was, in essence, a kind of aftershock of the long-march-through-the-institutions contra *Berufsverbot* that had been troubling the political waters in West Germany and West Berlin since 1972. However, Lämmert recognized that there were more immediate issues which were bothering the students. They were reacting to a general tightening of study conditions at all the universities as the SPD authorities, stung by public criticisms of heavy educational expenditures without commensurate results, were demanding ever greater efficiency. The students should finish their studies with greater dispatch, the authorities claimed. Ceilings on the number of semesters to finish a set of studies were expected momentarily. There were other factors, but Lämmert saw that larger issues overhung them all: ". . . growing uncertainty over future professional progress, [and] the limitations of securing an academic career for those caught in the baby boom." Perhaps the most unsettling prospect for many was, according to the new president, "the political examination of all candidates for the civil service." While Lämmert could show some sympathy for the boycotters—or strikers—his basic message to the activists was that no one outside the university community was paying much attention to them anymore. As he noted in the headline of his first article to the FU community: "The strike steals power from the University alone." In other words, such actions had become so passé that few could take them seriously now.[170] What was new about the boycott action at the end of 1976 was that it bore the marks of spontaneity. The protesters were not being herded or manipulated by the K-groups. In fact, the opposite was true. Those tiny groups were unceremoniously shouldered aside by hitherto unknown students who wanted to address issues without resort to ideological cant and the artificial language of revolution.[171]

Fortunately, the new president took on the responsibilities of office at a time when the polarization process was in marked decline. The student boycott of December 1976, although voluble, proved to be short-lived. It was definitely not a harbinger of things to come in the sense of rekindling the dissident movement. A crude but reliable indicator of the temper of the times could be seen in the number of publications which the self-appointed watchdogs in NOFU felt compelled to issue concerning the Free University. In 1975, for example, they had published no fewer than 112 reports of various kinds. In 1976, the figure had dropped to 64, and in 1977, to 41. Starting in 1980, NOFU was issuing on average only about ten publications per year.[172] In other words, the level of perceived stress from the more conservative elements at the university had dropped sharply even if it had not disappeared. Obviously, the passions of the decade between 1965 and 1975 were becoming ever more remote. This did not mean that the Free University returned immediately to a state or condition like that existing before 1965. Too much had happened for that to occur. Tensions still remained high in some institutes and departments, as Jäckel had already observed. After all, the Kennedy Institute was a good example of how the estrangements and polarization could continue for years after other academic units had long since overcome or at least come to terms with their internal woes.

Lämmert, too, was painfully aware that not all was normal. The various political factions were still busily publicizing their respective positions, an action which could not help but leave negative impressions among the public. Lämmert felt that one of his goals was to work toward lessening this form of self-inflicted damage. Originally, he had considered stepping down from the long seven-year presidency as early as

1979 to return to his academic pursuits. He was engaged in several hot disputes with NOFU by then, however, and felt he could not abandon his post in the midst of ongoing controversy. He chose instead to stay on in his post for the full length of his term, leaving the presidency only in 1983.[173]

Gerd Löffler, who had taken over the post of Senator for Science and Art from an ailing Werner Stein in 1975 but who had played a central role in developing university legislation ever since 1968, also saw the period after 1976 as much calmer at West Berlin's institutions of higher learning. Löffler felt that no outstanding differences arose between him and the university's second president. This was in marked contrast to the troubled years when Kreibich had held that office.

Löffler's personal experiences with respect to the decrease in tensions at the Free University was suggestive. At some point, shortly after Lämmert had assumed office, Löffler and several of his staff went to the Auditorium Maximum to discuss outstanding issues with students. The police were worried for Löffler's safety, he recalled, and wanted to accompany him, but Löffler absolutely refused to appear at the gathering with a police escort. As a compromise, he reluctantly agreed to carry a miniature beeper in his clothing which he could activate if violence broke out. Feeling rather foolish, he kept his appointment with the students, which, although marked by a spirited debate, went off smoothly. The police heard no beeps on that day.[174] To be sure, many of the students present were unhappy with Löffler, claiming that he epitomized the State's determination to impose Berufsverbot upon them, but he was able to address them in debate without the usual battle of the microphone or the disruptive chants, jeers, and rhythmical clapping that had marred so many other gatherings in the past.

In the years that followed Lämmert's election, the issues that confronted the Free University merged into the larger problems associated with higher education in Germany in general. As the student population in Germany exceeded a million and the percentage of young people engaging in studies soared above twenty percent for their age group, the inevitable expansion of the universities to meet the demands of the baby boom caused undoubted problems for all concerned. Thus, when Lämmert issued his first major report on the Free University in February 1978, he concentrated first of all on the effects of overcrowding at the university and the growing problem of future employment for the thousands of young people engaged in studies. They were being pressed by the State to finish their studies more promptly with the issuance of a Regelstudienzeit, a requirement limiting the number of semesters a student was allowed to complete his or her studies. Yet, the prospects for employment in a given profession were dwindling. Future secondary-school teachers were already in the midst of an unemployment crisis, and the prospects were that other professions such as law and even medicine were following suit. Lämmert noted that morale among those widening circles of students affected by these broad social and economic trends had tended to drop. Resignation and despair, punctuated by aggressiveness, were common among those who began to realize that future careers in their chosen field were becoming less likely. This undoubtedly affected their performance. Whereas in 1972, 28 percent of all students were in their eleventh semester of studies—an overly long scholarly career for most professions—the number had risen to 42 percent in 1978, an alarming trend.[175] The president outlined various ideas and plans to ameliorate the situation, including a call for better counseling, better orientation of beginning students, and the development of new curricula to match newly emerging fields of work and research. However, those were palliatives, and Lämmert, like most of those connected with German higher education, be they university officials or higher education administration officials at the Land or the federal level, seemed powerless to overcome the distress caused by these alarming demographic trends.

In other respects, the picture looked considerably brighter for the Free University after a year under its new president. Funding from Drittmittel, from third-party or private-sector sources, rose by 30 percent in one year alone. Of thirty-three new faculty appointment attempts in that same period, the Free University was successful in twenty-one cases, he said. Other universities had made offers to fourteen FU professors, but eight of them had decided to remain in Berlin. To be sure, there were still occasional angry outbursts from disgruntled individuals, but Lämmert was correct in pointing out that the overall trend was a healthy one.[176] The mending of the university's academic reputation was under way.

One development in the 1970s upon which many knowledgeable observers felt it necessary to comment was the growth within the Free University of outright political factions which then gave rise to a political spectrum that mirrored the political groupings of society at large. The process had started with the creation of the left and right wings of that spectrum. This was represented by NOFU and the anticommunist Bund Freiheit der Wissenschaft on the right. Unable to hinder the election of Kreibich as the Free University's president, they found themselves outvoted by a kind of middle-left coalition which for convenience' sake was referred to as the "Kreibich Faction." However, the latter was hardly monolithic and, within a short time, various splits occurred on the left, helping to create the other end of the spectrum. A small group of left-oriented university professors had been willing to support Kreibich from the start. At first they had called themselves the Aktionsgruppe Hochschullehrer (AH), the Faculty Action Group. By 1971, the AH had split into two left-wing factions, an Aktionsbündnis Demokraten und Sozialisten (ADS), an Action Coalition of Democrats and Socialists, and a milder body, the *Reformsozialisten*, or reform socialists. At the far-left end of the spectrum were the red cells, composed almost entirely of students but with an occasional faculty member, such as Professor Bauer, a Germanist, or Professor Holzkamp in the Psychology Institute. These department-related red cells tended to concentrate within a few years into the larger so-called K-groups such as the KSV and the KHG that had caused so much mischief in 1971 and 1972. Thus, the Free University had the odd experience of seeing its political body build up first from its outer wings, leaving a kind of gap in the middle. This phenomenon was understandable, given the extreme polarization that had taken place.

As the extremes established their positions and a revulsion against continual confrontation gradually set in, a development of groupings away from the poles and toward the center occurred. Distancing themselves somewhat from the admittedly confrontational tactics of NOFU, some of the faculty formed up a moderate-right *Liberale Aktion* group which had analogous factions among the *Mittelbau*, students, and service personnel. When it became apparent that the ADS group was moving uncomfortably close to the miniscule SEW, the West Berlin Communist party, a parallel breakaway movement occurred on the left. Dissenting faculty formed up a, for Berlin conditions at least, moderate left group known as the *Dienstagskreis*, or Tuesday Circle. It, too, had its comparable factions among the junior faculty, students, and support personnel.

What evolved from this political process was a set of three *Fraktionen* around which the various groupings clustered. The *Fraktionen* were roughly equivalent to political caucuses in American political assemblies, although in German usage the *Fraktion* encompassed all members of the grouping rather than just the assembly delegates who formally represented their group's interests. In this case, the Free University's Academic Senate and to a certain extent the *Konzil* became the political forum for the three *Fraktionen*. In its own modest way, this political system functioned much like the SPD, the CDU, and the FDP in the Berlin House of Deputies. From 1969 to approximately the end of 1973, Kreibich had held a majority in the Academic Senate with the support of the left-wing and moderate set of two of the larger groupings, leaving the "conservative" *Liberale Aktion* to fill the role of the somewhat less than loyal opposition. By the time elections for four vice presidents took place in May 1974, a shift in political mood had occurred, with the result that two vice presidents from the moderate left *Reformsozialisten* and two from the moderate right *Liberale Aktion* were elected. Foremost among those new officers was Hartmut Jäckel, who had commented so forthrightly to the Americans after his election about the shift in political mood at the Free University. Thus, the FU president was neatly ringed by political opposition among the elected officials at the secondary level. Obviously, this circumscribed the president's powers and erected a system of checks and balances, which is a hallmark of a Western democracy. This is not to say that the shift toward political moderation marked a "Thermidor" or sharp turn to the right. The elections of May 1974 were extremely close in the Konzil, with just a vote or two separating winners from losers. Nevertheless, the trend was significant, given the extreme polarization that had existed just a short time earlier.

It was not as if this political constellation had come into existence as an ad hoc solution to the crisis of the Kreibich years. It proved to be a long-lasting feature. "The existence of firmly established 'Fraktionen' . . . with previously decided voting positions," wrote Traugott Klose, one of Kreibich's close staffers, "is the hallmark of FU university politics, a most problematical development for a scholarly/scientific institution."[177] Klose was correct in that the system became an institutional feature of the Free University. Thereafter, the phenomenon became known as a Gruppenuniversität, a university in which the formally organized political caucuses contended with each other for power. It contrasted strikingly with the less formal circles and groupings that once had proved so influential in running the affairs of the university before 1965. After all, the Fraktionen produced a far more highly developed system than the unofficial groups of professors which habitually had met up to the mid-1960s to discuss university affairs and to put forward, in essence, the future rectors of the still modest Free University. It was inevitable that the older, informal, and, one might almost say, amateurish system could not endure the strains of the protest years and the equally pronounced strains that resulted from the creation of the mammoth university after 1970. The Fraktion system, somewhat modified and less rigid, endures to this day, necessarily an impersonal system but one which faithfully reflects the huge social organization that has become the Free University.

Lämmert's presidency coincided with a growing movement in West Germany to create greater efficiency in German higher education after the dizzying growth years of the 1970s. In fact, "efficiency" became one of the major preoccupations of the framers of amendments to the University Framework Law and other university-related legislation in the early-to-mid-1980s. The purpose of such tinkering, the lawmakers wrote, was "to increase the efficiency of the institutions of higher learning." Finance ministers in the various Länder began drawing up lists of measures for cultural ministers to increase efficiency. This is in distinct contrast to the primacy of reform which attended so much of the complex higher educational legislation in West Berlin and the Federal Republic in the 1970s. Shrinking budgets at all levels, which paralleled a general economic slowdown, obviously had a profound effect on how the public and governments perceived higher education.[178] An example of the suddenness with which the priorities changed was that at the same time some observers were beginning to discuss greater efficiencies and consolidation in higher education others were discussing seriously the creation of a third university in West Berlin. The obvious primary cause was the rapid expansion of the existing universities, especially the Free University. However, sheer economics brought an end to the proposed new university before any concrete planning or financing ever began. So sudden was the shift in priorities in German higher education.

Within West Berlin itself, the shifting mood of the electorate was borne out by a striking political change in local government. For thirty years, the Social Democrats had held a nearly unshakeable grip upon the reins of government, and at times many must have wondered if the city would not always remain an SPD stronghold. However, no political system is fully secure, and the West Berlin elections of 1981 amply bore that generalization out. Political observers had noted for some time a slackening of energy and inspiration in the SPD. Willy Brandt's departure for Bonn in 1966 to enter the Great Coalition before taking the chancellorship in his own right in 1969 had seen the departure of West Berlin's last truly notable mayor of national stature in the tradition of Ernst Reuter. Successive mayors, such as Heinrich Albertz, Klaus Schütz, and Dietrich Stobbe, had failed to attain the prominence of their predecessors. This would not necessarily have proved fatal. However, a major financial scandal rocked the city as the new decade began, and although Governing Mayor Stobbe was not involved, a number of SPD senators were. Sensing trouble, the Social Democrats brought in one of their prime performers, Hans Jochen Vogel, to take control of affairs and prevent the unthinkable: a Social Democrat defeat in West Berlin.

The SPD mobilization came too late. Smelling victory, the CDU mounted an energetic campaign of its own, and produced an equally stellar candidate in the person of Richard von Weizäcker. The latter forced an election in May 1981, and while not able to win an absolute majority, the CDU succeeded in becoming the largest party in the city. Simultaneously, the Social Democrats' share of the vote dropped below 40 percent for the first time in postwar Berlin. Thereupon, several liberal FDP representatives, recognizing the inevitable, shifted their allegiance to the Christian Democrats and gave them an outright majority. It was only the second time since 1945 that a CDU member had become the Governing Mayor of Berlin. This electoral upset in West Berlin proved to be the harbinger of a major political shift on the national level when, in September 1982, the internally divided Social Democrats also lost control of the Bonn government.

West Berlin also demonstrated another pacesetting trend in the 1981 elections. The city's Alternative List (AL), a close affiliate to the newly formed ecological Green Party, gained 7.2 percent of the vote, a respectable showing for its first effort and an indication that among the young, especially, there was disillusionment with the major political parties. Hitherto, West Berliners had shunned the marginal single-issue protest parties, but starting in 1981 the AL consolidated itself and became a permanent fixture on the West Berlin political scene. Many of those who had formally been associated with the APO movement, plus succeeding generations of splinter groups and disillusioned youth, found refuge in the AL, a trend which continues today.

Developments at the Free University neatly paralleled the rightward political trend that had developed in city politics. Despite accusations about alleged left-wing biases on the part of President Lämmert and his administration, the university's leadership was devoting most of its energies to settling normal higher educational issues, rather than trying to manage constant political crises as the unhappy Kreibich administration had had to do. A hint of the abnormal conditions that had once prevailed but which prevailed no longer can be gleaned from the experiences of two visiting professors, Sterling Fishman and Jurgen Herbst, from the University of Wisconsin, who in the summer of 1977 were attending an FU panel discussion on employment trends among university graduates. Before the proceedings could even begin, an altogether familiar incident occurred. An unannounced speaker suddenly grabbed the microphone and began haranguing the listeners about the general social and political issues of the day. He spoke angrily and with great conviction about his cause, and the two visiting professors were appalled at the partisanship of the audience, who alternately praised or denounced the unscheduled speaker. After several minutes of this unexpected development, President Lämmert walked over to the radical. In one of the quickest battles of the microphone ever to be seen at the Free University, he managed with a flick of his wrist and a swivel of his hips to emerge with the microphone in hand while the erstwhile disrupter was deftly propelled to the side. Amazingly, the young protester did not return to the fray, preferring instead to submerge back into the crowd. Lämmert calmly picked up with the main theme, announcing to the audience that the proceedings would now begin. The discussants entered upon their affairs as if nothing untoward had occurred. Later, at a reception, Lämmert spoke with his American guests and waxed enthusiastic. It was a great day for the Free University, Lämmert maintained. For the first time in years they had been able to hold a forum without its being terminated or badly interrupted. For Free University conditions, at least, that was correct. It was too minor an affair to have excited any oral comment among the listeners, much less to attract newspaper space.[179] The university community had developed strong nerves and thick skins over the preceding decade. In a certain sense the incident was a fitting testimony to the fact that a university is an enduring institution. Rash predictions about the demise of the Free University had proved to be premature, to say the least.

A NEW DECADE

The members of the Free University seem to thrive on scandals and controversies, and they uncover them frequently enough to keep this unusual institution of higher education in the headlines.

A vivid demonstration of this fact and a reminder that old political wounds were still not entirely healed occurred two years after the death of FU historian, Friedrich Zipfel. Zipfel had died of a heart attack at age fifty-seven in February 1978, seemingly a personal tragedy and an unlikely event to cause subsequent controversy. However, the matter was hardly as simple as that. Zipfel had experienced considerable tension with some dissident students in the winter semester of 1976/77, and isolated protest actions had continued thereafter. Protesters occupied his office on occasion and found other ways to demonstrate their discontent. In some ways it paralleled the experiences of Wolfgang Wippermann, and it took place in the same Meinecke Institute. In this case, the outcome was different.

Immediately, suspicions surfaced that the protesters' actions had caused such stress that it had contributed to Zipfel's untimely death, and a court action began against one of the dissenting students, Hannelore Schmidt. The wheels of justice began slowly to grind, and despite two lower court decisions which relieved her of guilt, a third appeal reversed those decisions and fined her a modest sum plus court costs. The matter hardly ended there.

One of the university's more famous personalities, historian and fascism expert Ernst Nolte, had been a friend of Zipfel, and following the court decision, he commented angrily on the situation both within the Free University and to the press. Once out in the open, the matter attracted widespread attention, with articles appearing in the *FAZ* and the *Bayernkurier*, the official newspaper of CSU party leader Franz Josef Strauss, which, not surprisingly, were critical of the dissidents and their methods. Now the big guns began to shoot. In December 1979, at an emotional meeting of the Academic Senate, Nolte repeated his charges and criticisms concerning the unfortunate Zipfel, which prompted Lämmert to threaten to cut off his right to speak to the Senate. Tempers were obviously running high. It must be said that there was no attempt to hush the matter. The university's official weekly news bulletin, the *FU Info*, gamely recorded the whole unfortunate affair, allowing space for all of the main protagonists to state their opinion.[180] Each accused the other of hurting the reputation of the Free University before the public, and even Ursula Besser, the CDU's university expert, commented as well. The matter enlivened the newspapers and media for a time and then was forgotten. In retrospect it was seen as a kind of aftershock stemming from the unrest of the age of protest and dissent. Fortunately for the Free University, such incidents were becoming rarer with the passage of time.

Other, more immediate concerns crowded in upon the FU community. The highly controversial *Fachbereich 11* (Department for Philosophy and Social Sciences), reputedly a hotbed of radical politics, was split up, an indication that the political winds inside the university were blowing to the right.[181] The Free University found itself forced into a kind of shotgun wedding with West Berlin's *Pädagogische Hochschule* (PH), the teachers college which had been located in the southern part of West Berlin in Lankwitz. The Technical University and the Fine Arts Academy also had to absorb parts of the PH, and although no one was enthusiastic about it, the change took place nonetheless. The election of four new vice presidents in June 1981, confirmed the rightward drift, and the Free University began to tighten its belt as economy measures set in even before the Social Democrats left office. The SPD/FDP coalition in Bonn had begun the process of retrenchment by abruptly cutting back 20 percent of its matching share of capital grants for Federal-Land building programs in higher education. That proved to be a foreshadowing of other stringencies that were a notable feature of the 1980s. The early 1980s saw a decline at all German universities of 20 percent of *Sachmittel*, or grants for building and equipment. The Free University was no exception.[182]

In June 1983, the Free University elected its third president, to a new four-year term of office, and this time the choice fell upon a lawyer, Dieter Heckelmann. He was a political conservative—the university community looked carefully at the politics of its presidents and other high officials. With Heckelmann's election, a turning point had indeed come to the Free University. Some on the left grumbled that the Free University was returning to the status of an *Ordinarienuniversität*, but that assessment did not bear scrutiny. The *Ordinarien* now carried the more humble "C-4" designation, and they were still just one part of the professoriate, with its various gradations of associate professors. What was notable about the Free University by this time was that it had become a university whose identity had merged to a significant degree with the other West German universities. This process had been developing since 1969 at least.

Peter Glotz, the SPD's Senator for Science and Art during most of the Lämmert years, wrote approvingly of the outgoing second FU president's activities in office. "Because in the intervening time," he stated, "the dogmatic socialist siege of the Free University had long since been broken off." Lämmert had helped to produce a healing trend at the Free University which Glotz found admirable. "Because his policy of maintaining a dialogue, his unflagging willingness to represent the University before the scientific community on the one hand and to settle or at least lessen its internal conflicts on the other, produced decisive results." Glotz praised Lämmert's willingness to return to the Free University in 1976 to take over the presidency. "When Lämmert became president, the atmosphere at the Free University was controversial and at times filled with hate," he admitted. A soothing and consolidating process had set in which, he claimed, was restoring the reputation of the Free University.[183] Glotz had admitted that the departing president's left-liberal views had aroused suspicion and controversy among the more conservative members of the university. It was also true that even Glotz and Lämmert had had their differences, most notably over the breaking up of the controversial *Fachbereich 11*. Now, in 1983, the election of a conservative successor more nearly matched the temper of the times. Thus, in a sense, the departure of Lämmert marked the end of an era of conflict at the Free University. Now the stage was set for his successor, Heckelmann, to continue the same consolidation process. A new era was at hand.

CONCLUSION

It was apparent by the end of the 1960s that a university reform was needed at the Free University and elsewhere. Research and teaching needed to adapt to new social conditions. The university had to streamline and improve its administration. It had to expand considerably and reform the composition of its teaching staff. Finally, advocates of reform felt the Free University had to bring its curricula more into line with the needs of the various disciplines and professions for which it was preparing its students. There was considerable urgency attached to these reforms because of the chaotic situation that had emerged in the late 1960s, and virtually all observers agreed that the old Berlin Model, dating from the 1940s, was in abeyance. What followed during nearly a decade and a half of tinkering with reform was the creation of a prolonged atmosphere of crisis, polarization, and disillusionment among reformers and critics of reform.

The original architects of Berlin's 1969 University Law had claimed that university reform would be an ongoing process. In that prediction they were entirely correct. The restructuring of university committees through such schemes as *Drittelparität* in order to create democratic decision-making bodies boomeranged. The advent of responsibility did not bring a corresponding moderation in political goals or activities by student dissidents, and erstwhile reformers soon began to back away from the reforms they had helped to initiate in 1968 and 1969. The splintering of the student dissident movement into many bickering factions, some of which became militant ideologues and others of which turned anarchic, did much to prevent sober and reasoned student representation in administering the affairs of the Free University. Those fringe groups took advantage of low student turnout in university elections to achieve influence far out of proportion to their numbers. The sudden growth of the Free University and the increasing alienation felt by newly arrived students at what had become a mass university meant that at times student radicals could at least count on the passive support of students who did not necessarily share the radicals' political views.

Other pillars of stability had crumbled too. With the dilution of power in the newly constituted professorial ranks, and the increased strength of the *Mittelbau* and of the students, the power position of the full professors had diminished sharply. Some despaired of any improvement and left. Others retreated to their own sheltered scholarly world and left the field of conflict altogether. Still others stood and fought the chaos and the declining academic standards that seemed to be damaging the once worthy reputation of the Free University. A few helped to close at least partially the Pandora's box which they had helped to pry open in the late 1960s. And some professors carried on with their research and teaching, seemingly unaffected by the political maelstrom that had swept over the Free University. It should always be remembered that while some departments and institutes were immobilized and damaged by extremists, many others were not.

With the polarization that took place at the Free University, strong opposition groups materialized either to continue the reform process or to condemn it. In any case, the university conducted its reform efforts and its confrontations in the full glare of publicity. Both the right and the left—with the major exception of the semiconspiratorial far-left militant groups—appealed their case before the public, and the Free University, among others, became the object of considerable attention by the political parties. Charges of outright political bias became common with respect to such crucial activities as the appointing of faculty, and political scandals followed one upon another. In essence, the 1969 University Law saw an increase of state interest in and interference in the affairs of the Free University. Senators Stein and Löffler, among others, took a prominent role in participating in the affairs of the Free University, and this process continued through much of the 1970s as the original university law and federal framework laws were steadily amended so as to restore more order to the university. In essence, the sometimes chaotic situations that arose from reform efforts brought on a growing sense of disillusionment by the political leaders, and they began to retreat from taking so prominent a role in managing the affairs of the Free University. Subsequently, the responsible Berlin Senators began to exercise considerably more caution when mixing into the affairs of the university. This process began to take shape following the election of a more orthodox candidate to the FU presidency, Eberhard Lämmert, but it became much more pronounced under his successor, Dieter Heckelmann. Although the current considerably modified university law still allows significant state interference in the Free University's internal affairs, in practice the members of the university community have retrieved the initiative in settling their own affairs. On the whole, that is a healthy development. The Free University was certainly traumatized by the polarization that had taken place during that undeclared academic war of the 1970s, but reports of its death proved to be premature. It emerged from those difficult times largely intact and entered upon a second consolidation stage, one which continues to this day.

SIX

Retrenchment and Consolidation

The election of Dieter Heckelmann to a shortened, four-year presidency of the Free University in the autumn of 1983 confirmed a growing conservative mood which many observers had professed to see since the mid-1970s. Thus, the electoral victory of the CDU over the long-dominant SPD in the Berlin elections of 1981 was a harbinger of the CDU's return to power in Bonn in late 1982 and its national victory in early 1983. At the more local, academic level, Heckelmann's victory presented a parallel development in that the Free University moved steadily away from the polarization and era of protest that had been so noticeable just a few years earlier.

There were several developments at the Free University after 1983 which reflected this trend. First, the university experienced a painful financial retrenchment as the CDU leadership continued a trend started by the Social Democrats in 1981. Gone were the budgets that had increased by as much as a third from year to year in the early 1970s. Instead, an era of frozen budgets was at hand and a period of painful retrenchment ensued. It continues today. Certain personnel decisions made in the late 1960s and early 1970s aggravated an already difficult situation. Having expanded its student population three-fold between 1970 and 1980, and having appointed literally hundreds of C-2 tenured assistant professors at that time, the university was forced later to institute blanket hiring freezes on personnel for long periods of time. This in turn meant that new programs and services either had to be deferred or were developed more slowly than would otherwise have been the case.

Perhaps the most dramatic example of budgetary retrenchment was the decision to close the Free University medical clinic Westend in Charlottenburg and to transfer its services to the Rudolf Virchow Hospital in the north of the city. The justification for this drastic move was straightforward: West Berlin simply had too many hospital beds, and with closings inevitable, the aging and cramped facilities at Westend made it the logical choice for the budget cutter's axe. Despite protest demonstrations by hospital personnel whose jobs were threatened, the closing took place.

One compensating factor for the belt-tightening in the public sector was the ability of Free University faculty to attract ever increasing support from *Drittmittel*, i.e., outside funding or third-party resources.

Whereas in 1978 such sources contributed just under 30 million Deutschmarks to FU programs, by 1985 the figure had nearly doubled to DM 56 million.[1] Such aid, combined with the still sizable public budgets, enabled the Free University to maintain uninterrupted its extraordinary international programs. Its Office of International Affairs continued to build exchange programs, guest professorships, and other institutional connections which tied the Free University to virtually every part of the globe. This commitment of the West Berliners and their Free University to maintaining comprehensive outside relations despite the Wall is one of of the enduring features of the university throughout its forty-year history.

Despite hiring freezes at several levels, the Free University was able to compete well in attracting full professors to Berlin and in retaining senior personnel. Heckelmann noted that the university had made thirty-six new appointments of C-4 (full) professors and retained ten of them in the period 1984 to 1986. Of significance was the fact that many of these senior academicians had held senior appointments elsewhere. In the German academic world the number of Berufungen or "calls" to a university which a professor had to his credit is of great significance. A university that can retain professors and attract new ones in their third and fourth appointments is a promising sign. "This is a clear indication," Heckelmann observed, "that the academic reputation . . . of the Free University has markedly improved in recent years."[2] In addition, the Free University under Heckelmann created eight Stiftungsprofessuren or endowed chairs during the same two-year period with generous funding from private and public sources. For example, Schering, the giant pharmaceutical firm, began to endow professorships. Other private foundations and agencies such as the Volkswagen Foundation provided similar support, as did various governmental agencies in Bonn. The sums involved were considerable, running to several million Deutschmarks yearly over and above other forms of Drittmittel. Such developments were a promising sign of renewed trust in the Free University's performance by the industrial, financial, and political world. It is safe to say that such confidence had sagged at the end of the 1960s and in the 1970s. Outside largess of this magnitude was a welcome sign of a return in the 1980s to a more normal relationship between the university and the public and private sectors.

It is a characteristic of German institutional planning to prepare for any manner of eventualities over a long period. Sometimes this can prove awkward if the planning is caught by unpredictable variables. However, the desire to prepare for, to anticipate potential difficulties and to pose solutions or at least ameliorations is a mild vice if it is one at all. "The furthering of new generations of scholars and scientists is one of the most important duties of a university," Heckelmann stated, echoing an ancient truth. "Lapses in this regard will have been shown to produce an irretrievable loss in the university's ability to compete, if sizable numbers of a scholarly generation are lost to it." Consequently, he outlined various plans to produce emergency solutions and to keep the best and brightest young scholars in the system long enough that the opening of new positions would see them establish stable careers in academia.[3] Fiebinger professorships, federally inspired professorships at various German universities, including the Free University, would provide positions for a limited number of gifted academicians until regular academic chairs came open. These professorships were dependent upon local funding, and West Berlin, along with a few other *Länder* of the Federal Republic, was willing to provide such support. Heckelmann's commitment and the concern of the FU leadership for its future scholars proved to be a constant theme as the ninth decade drew to an end. In December 1987, at the conferring of prizes by the Ernst Reuter Gesellschaft on five outstanding Ph.D. recipients at the Free University, Heckelmann reiterated his concerns. Referring to the chronic lack of openings for qualified young academic personnel, he uttered the following sentiment: "The coming generation of scholars are irreplaceable for a creative, enquiring university and for the process of discovery. They bring with them that critical mass of openness and dynamism, curiosity and a desire to experiment without which the scholarly process would atrophy." For him, the provision of healthy succeeding generations of scholars was not merely beneficial to the well-being of a university. Rather, the up-and-coming academics were a precondition "that the universities will execute their responsibility to society. For me," he added, "a core consideration of the affairs of institutions of higher learning is that the universities are of central importance for the state. Our living standard, our ability to compete on the international stage, and our very prosperity are dependent upon our continued furthering of the sciences."[4]

Heckelmann raised an important point on the same occasion. The surplus of qualified candidates for academic positions was not a mere fluke. It had its historic reasons. "Unfortunately, university policy has been characterized during the last two decades by excessive expansion and contraction. Simultaneously the institutions of higher learning were not permitted to maintain the necessary continuity in size and growth." In the late 1960s and in the 1970s the political parties outdid each other in offering the universities financial support; hence, a wave of rapid expansion and wild growth. Now, in recent years, the opposite course was to be seen, and it was introduced too abruptly and too harshly. It was true, Heckelmann observed, that the universities would have to share the burden of harder times, but such drastic cuts were inflicting major injuries upon the universities. "The enormous expansion of personnel since the 1960s is having its effect now," Heckelmann stated.[5]

Other senior officials at the Free University voiced similar concerns. The university's senior vice president, Michael Erbe, examined in detail the financial problems facing the Free University. The institution was forced to save millions of dollars in important areas of university operations simply to pay vast sums for the salaries of its much increased faculty and staff. "The basic problem facing us," Erbe wrote in November 1986, "is the sheer size of personnel costs. Civil servant status and protection against dismissals for those in public service make it impossible to remove anyone even in individual cases where the will to work and competence in no way measure up to the salary offered." Erbe was in no doubt as to how this had come about. "During the euphoria of the early 1970s when reform notions received uncritical support from full public treasuries . . . when the transformation of *Akademische Oberräte* and *Oberassistenten* to university professors was permitted and when the administration unthinkingly advanced its officials in grade, it was at this time that the entire misery of today began."[6] Erbe pointed out that a large bulge of relatively young people in their late twenties and in their thirties began to move through the institution in the early 1970s, receiving automatic pay increases biennially as they increased in seniority. The normal pattern for them was to marry and to have two children, and given Germany's generous social welfare system, they received handsome benefits, much of which came out of the university's budget. In consequence, positions that came open because of retirements or moves usually were eliminated to save on the limited budget. This did not bode well, because, Erbe noted, "the way open into the University for younger academicians has largely been blocked ever since."[7]

Heckelmann judged that the plight of qualified academicians seeking positions at the Free University would not change until the mid-1990s, when the older generation of scholars begins retiring. "Between 1993 and 2005 over 300 professorships will come open at the FU," the President predicted. "The annual rate of turnover which is normally under five percent will have reached nearly eight percent in 2003. That is a demand which, I believe, we can scarcely meet with qualified successors. . . ." On-going programs such as the Fiebinger professorships were much needed, but they were no solution. They were instead mere palliatives. "Today, we experience time and again how much in the passing years the estimation of universities by those in positions of political responsibility have changed." Nowadays, the blunt fact was that none of the major parties had much of anything to say about the universities. Obviously they were no longer a matter of particular concern to the politicians.[8]

The ebbing of political interest in the universities could certainly have tragic consequences in some ways, especially for those who deserved job security but were without it. However, there was a plus side to this phenomenon. If the universities had come to reflect the political trends and tensions of society as a whole in the 1970s, then the lower profile displayed by politics in the society of the 1980s was matched by a healthy lessening of tensions in internal university affairs. It should be recalled that a transformation of university politics had taken place from amorphous groups of professors, *Mittelbau*, students, and support personnel into formally established *Fraktionen* or caucuses in the early 1970s. This trend had reflected faithfully the political polarization that had taken place on campus. Starting in the early 1980s, this sharply defined political edifice began to soften and to melt. "The tendency toward a loosening up of caucus fronts in favor of individual opinion with corresponding voting behavior is unmistakable," Heckelmann reported to the entire FU community at the end of 1986.[9] Be it in the major committees such as the *Kuratorium* (Board of Trustees) or the Academic Senate, or in the smaller committees, it was a healthy sign of a normalization in the internal affairs of the Free University.

However, if it was true that the Lämmert administration had had its ups and downs, confrontations and crises which engendered hard feelings among some factions, the same held true for the Heckelmann administration. A scandal of sorts began to emerge in the summer of 1987 when it was ascertained that Heckelmann had proofread an article written anonymously by a press official on the president's staff just before the 1983 FU presidential elections. It had appeared in the *Deutsche Universitäts-Zeitung* and was critical of the FU president. Because it contained insider information, Lämmert was immediately suspicious of his press chief, Johannes Schlootz, and suspended him from office (with pay) until an investigation settled the matter. Lämmert left the investigation in Heckelmann's hands while he was away from Berlin on university business, and the latter announced that the investigation had produced no results and closed the books on the affair. Years later word surfaced about the article's authorship and about Heckelmann's involvement. Outrage erupted immediately, especially since Heckelmann was now the president, and following a by now tried and true FU tradition, the various political factions appealed to the bleachers. This otherwise minor affair promptly received a thorough and prolonged laundering in the press and other mass media. The various aggrieved parties gnashed their teeth. The left, especially, which had felt itself in decline and hardpressed since 1983 at least, bristled with indignation over such goings-on in the conservative (by German standards at least) Heckelmann administration. The latter admitted his sins and offered apologies for the incident, but this manly gesture was lost in the uproar of invective and vituperation that continued into the autumn of 1987.

Yet, the matter settled down after a few months. The latest elections for FU president were held at the end of November, and the slate of serious contenders consisted entirely of "conservative" candidates from the *Liberale Aktion*. Heckelmann and his chief rival, Professor Walter Schunack, finished in almost a dead heat in the first round. However, a week later, when it became obvious that the balance was swinging slightly toward Heckelmann, the leftist factions, who had sworn not to support their bête noire, Heckelmann, decided to cast invalid ballots.

Other more moderate and conservative groupings, recognizing that he had provided conscientious and able administrative leadership for the preceding four years, rallied behind Heckelmann again. Thus, for the first time, the Free University reelected its president, and the university went back to the business of rendering higher education.

The brief affair demonstrated that political tensions were still by no means dead at the Free University. Moreover, it demonstrated anew that the game of politics at the Free University would forever be carried out in the white glare of the public gaze.[10] The university community seems destined forever to savor a scandal, and given the political motives ascribed to almost any activity in Dahlem, scandals will surely occur again.

WHAT'S IN A NAME?

The Free University never freed itself—from political tensions at least. But what's in a name? It became a major institution of higher learning, after all, and it demonstrated that it could serve the academic needs of its society and its citizens. It serves them still. Moreover, it demonstrated over time its ability to transform itself to meet the changing concerns of its society. This does not mean that the transitions that took place at the Free University occurred gracefully or in timely fashion. There were times when the Free University was in advance of its society and its sister universities, as when it put itself in the vanguard of those institutions that restored German respectability in the social sciences. Its early emphasis on extensive international contacts, its pioneering efforts to create extension programs, such as evening divisions and university-of-the-air innovations, as well as tutorial programs for its regular students were all decades in advance of other institutions of higher learning.

Thus, the Free University was and remains a maverick in many ways. Its Berlin Model, which above all encouraged strong student involvement in the management of its affairs, proved to be fully a generation in advance of such thinking elsewhere. In fact, it was so much in advance that the self-same Berlin Model had had time to atrophy almost completely by the mid-1960s. The Free University had transformed itself in many ways to match the conservative trends that had always dominated the West German universities, and it did so at the very moment it was overtaken by the central event of the 1960s: the greening of a new generation of students. These students, conveniently called the Generation of 1968, had little knowledge of and scant use for the concerns and values of the generation of students that preceded them. The Western world as a whole was transformed in circa 1968 from a postwar world to a less-than-brave new world with fewer certainties, more complex and less easily solved social and economic problems, and a greater ambivalence about progress, especially technological progress, than had been the case earlier.

It was perfectly true that the leadership of the Free University, including its chief administrators and the senior professors, realized too late the dimensions of student discontent and unrest in the mid-1960s, and they lost the initiative in transforming their university to meet the changing times. The result was that the initiative passed to political circles, largely in the SPD. Public concern about universities and university policies increased sharply in the late 1960s and in the 1970s as more and more students entered the hard-pressed institutions. Many experienced unprecedented expansion, and the Free University was probably the most dramatic example of that demographic trend. Not only did the Free University feel the strains of political polarization. It experienced a period of such forceful growth that the very nature of the institution changed in the 1970s. Perhaps political confrontations grabbed headlines, but the unheralded but nevertheless drastic increase in student numbers and in the numbers of faculty to cope with them transformed the Free University. The brave little enterprise with 2,000 students in 1948 was still recognizable in the Free University of 14,000 students of 1968. That was no longer the case a decade later, and now, as it enters its fortieth year, the mammoth that is the Free University, with at least 56,000 students, is the largest institution of higher learning in the German-speaking world.

In most respects the Free University has become a normal German university. Its once special American connection is no longer markedly different than the relationships other German universities have with various institutions of the United States. It is still true that the Free University has an active and highly developed international affairs program, an indication that West Berlin is still a divided city, existing as an island in the same ideological sea that emerged in 1945. Other institutional peculiarities also exist. The present university still shows some of the traumatizing effects of its turbulent past. The flap that occurred in 1987 with President Heckelmann seems disproportionately passionate to an outsider like this author. However, it was a kind of afterglow from the time when it seemed that every political faction in the rainbow was seeking solely its own advantage. Fortunately, such episodes are now a rarity. The Free University continues to be a leading institution of higher learning in adopting new and innovative programs. In 1980, for example, it created a *Zentraleinrichtung zur Förderung von Frauenstudien und Frauenforschung*, a Center for Women's Studies and Research. It encourages the advancement of women in academic careers, and although the Free University by American standards has a modest number of women professors and other senior ranks, it has an excellent record in that respect in the German academic world. In 1985, in collaboration with the Volkswagen Foundation and the German Marshall Fund, the Free University created "Berlin Program for Advanced German and European Studies" to assist doctoral candidates and junior postdoctoral scholars to conduct historical and social science research in contemporary German and European affairs.

A more positive legacy from the not so distant past is the fact that pluralistic learning really does exist at the Free University now. Gone is the rigid, unreasoning anticommunism of the 1940s and 1950s. Gone too are the red cells, the *K-Gruppen*, and the extreme ideologues and true believers who had sworn to destroy pluralistic learning and the bourgeois society that advanced such beliefs. No longer does one hear the call: "Let's *umfunktionieren* so-and-so's course." Instead, the various departments and institutes have their collections of professors, assistants, and students who proclaim themselves to be conservatives, liberals, Marxists, non-Marxists, or any number of other political callings. They dispute openly and intensely with each other, as should happen at a *universitas litterarum*. Now, however, as distinct from the early 1970s, they talk to each other and communicate with one another. The shouting has died away. The quest for truth and understanding has resumed.

At one tense stage in this study, the author received an urgent request from the FU administration to serve on a faculty examining committee to select FU students for direct exchange programs with American universities. Despite grumblings about the needs of the present project, the author obliged. That was a fortunate decision. Eighty or more applicants presented themselves from a wide variety of disciplines, and it became apparent that the FU students were showing once again the qualities that had bestowed a fine reputation upon the Free University up until the mid-1960s. They proved to be articulate. They held definite opinions on current social and political problems and they were knowledgeable in their own fields. The selection process was painful, if only because there were too many qualified candidates for too few positions. Those veterans who had served on the same selection committee in years past gave assurances that so fortunate a circumstance was not always the case. Time was, they claimed, when the dwindling number of qualified candidates had filled them with foreboding. Thus, an outsider could agree with the insiders that the healing process at the Free University was well advanced.

In a sense, the Free University has finally earned its title. No longer a small, idealistic institution reacting to an alien ideology and operating on a shoestring, it is instead a large, inevitably somewhat impersonal center of higher learning where the individual has the freedom to choose from seemingly the entire spectrum of truths and ideas. It is hardly a utopia—the members of its community would be the first to attest to that fact. However, it is again serving the needs of its city and its society. There are certain limitations placed upon it because of its location. Yet the last word has hardly been uttered about the Metropolis on the Spree. The same holds true for the Free University, which, at the tender age of forty, has experienced its full share of trials and tribulations but which is yet to show signs of middle-age.

Notes

ONE: THE ORIGINS OF THE FREE UNIVERSITY, 1944 TO 1948

1. For a good, brief summary of the Friedrich Wilhelms University see Georg Kotowski, "Der Kampf um Berlins Universität," in *Veritas, Justitia, Libertas*, Berlin, 1954, pp. 10–15, hereafter cited as Kotowski.

2. Sir Charles Webster and Noble Frankland, *The Strategic Air Offensive against Germany*, London, 1961, II, iv, p. 190.

3. Ibid., p. 264.

4. See Daniel J. Nelson, *Wartime Origins of the Berlin Dilemma*, Tuscaloosa, Ala., 1978; William M. Franklin, "Zonal Boundaries and Access to Berlin," *World Politics*, XVI, 1 (October 1963), pp. 1–33.

5. See also George F. Kennan, *Memoirs, 1925–1950*, Boston, 1967, I, ch. 7.

6. Kennan, *Memoirs*, I, p. 166.

7. Robert Murphy, *Diplomat among Warriors*, New York, 1964, pp. 284–287.

8. See Franklin, "Zonal Boundaries. . . ," pp. 30–31.

9. On the inability of Berlin to maintain a defense see Earl F. Ziemke, *Stalingrad to Berlin: The German Defeat in the East*, Washington, 1968, pp. 488–490.

10. For an admittedly hostile account of Wandel's wartime activities see Wolfgang Leonhard, *Die Revolution entlässt ihre Kinder*, Cologne and Berlin, 1955. The author is grateful to Paul Wandel for granting two lengthy interviews, on 15 July and 5 December 1986, in which he explained in detail the kinds of reforms which he and the SED were attempting to execute in the postwar years in Berlin and the Soviet Zone.

11. For the agreement see *Berlin: Quellen und Dokumente 1945–1951*, Berlin, 1964, I, pp. 131–132; see also Frank Howley, *Berlin Command*, New York, 1950, pp. 52–56, 61–62.

12. For American postwar planning see John L. Gaddis, *The United States and the Origins of the Cold War, 1941–1947*, New York, 1972, ch. 4; Paul Y. Hammond, "Directives for the Occupation of Germany: The Washington Controversy," in Harold Stein, ed., *American Civil-Military Decisions*, Birmingham, Ala., 1963.

13. U.S. State Department, Berlin Mission Reference Library, Appendix to Book II, Historical Report, OMGBD, V, Education and Religious Affairs Branch, memorandum, "MG, ED, No. 100," n.d. (Spring 1946), activities of OMGBD education section, pp. 1, 3, 6; hereafter cited as *Shafer Report*.

14. John Maginnis, *Military Government Journal*, Amherst, Mass., 1971, pp. 304–305, hereafter cited as Maginnis.

15. *Shafer Report*, p. 2.

16. Maginnis, p. 301.

17. Eduard Spranger, *Gesammelte Schriften*, X, p. 276.

18. U.S. National Archives, Record Group (RG) 260, Office of Military Government (U.S.) for Germany (OMGUS) (hereafter cited as OMGUS with file classification), 5/297-3, report by Eduard Spranger, "Private Darstellung meiner Tätigkeit als kommissarischer Rektor. . . ," 7 September 1945, p. 2; hereafter cited as *Spranger Report*.

19. Ibid.

20. Ullrich Schneider, "Berlin, der Kalte Krieg und die Gründung der Freien

Universität, 1945–1949," in *Jahrbuch für die Geschichte Mittel- und Ost-deutschlands*, vol. 34 (1985), p. 44, hereafter cited as Schneider.

21. Interview, author with Paul Wandel, 15 July 1986. Wandel was pleased to discover that some full professors cooperated with his administration and were willing to try new structures, admissions criteria, and social priorities. Among those he listed in this category were Theodor Brugsch, a physician, Johannes Stroux, a philologist, Hermann Dersch, a law professor, Robert Rompe, a physicist, and Eilhardt Mitscherlich, an agricultural expert. The Soviet authorities placed academic leaders in the same food rationing category as heavy workers, cared for their physical needs and generally emphasized their importance in society. This was in striking contrast to their treatment in the western sectors of Berlin.

22. *Spranger Report*, p. 5.

23. Bundesarchiv Koblenz (hereafter BA), Spranger Papers, box 38, memo, Spranger to Winzer, 9 July 1945. Spranger pointed out that the main buildings of the old university were destroyed. "Unfortunately, the Luftgaukommando in Dahlem, which we examined first, had proved to be unacceptable, since larger lecture halls can be had only through extensive renovation," he told Winzer.

24. Original in BA, reprinted in Spranger, *Gesammelte Schriften*, X, p. 306.

25. Interview, author with H. J. Lieber, 20 January 1986; in a letter to the author, 1 August 1986, Lieber reiterated his claim that Diem had overestimated his influence with the British.

26. *Spranger Report*, p. 5.

27. OMGUS, 5/297-3, report, Shafer to Director of Berlin Detachment, 8 December 1945.

28. Spranger, *Gesammelte Schriften*, X, p. 298.

29. Theodor Brugsch, *Arzt seit fünf Jahrzehnten*, Berlin, 1957, pp. 344–345. Brugsch seems to have undergone a major social and political transformation following defeat in 1945. He became a deputy to Wandel in the *Zentralverwaltung für Volksbildung* and finished his career in the GDR. British Military Government observers admitted that they knew little about the newly constructed education administration in the Soviet Zone under Paul Wandel, but they had decided opinions about Brugsch: "He is inspired almost entirely by personal ambitions and has taken very adequate steps to get in favour with the Russians. His behaviour towards his university colleagues has been dishonest and unpleasant." Public Record Office, London, Files of the Foreign Office, (FO) 1004/1617, British Troops Berlin (BAOR), Monthly Report no. 1 (October 1945), p. 3; hereafter cited as FO with appropriate file designation.

30. Spranger, *Gesammelte Schriften*, X, p. 301.

31. E. Y. Hartshorne Diary, entry for 5 September 1945, copy in author's possession.

32. Spranger, *Gesammelte Schriften*, X, pp. 302–303.

33. See Spranger, *Gesammelte Schriften*, X, pp. 303–304 ff., 462–463. In a letter from John W. Taylor to the author on this subject, dated 31 July 1986, Taylor recalled having tried to contact Spranger but cannot recall Spranger's return visit. After reading Spranger's account of the meeting, Taylor commented that Spranger's seemingly memorable details of the frosty meeting were new to him. Whereas the former claimed that Taylor appeared "with a pipe in his mouth," the American noted the sarcastic allegation and emphasized that he had never smoked a pipe in his life.

34. British Military Government observers noted the change, stating that it was their opinion that Stroux "will be more complaisant to the wishes of his new masters." See FO, 1005/1617 (BAOR), Monthly Report no. 1 (October 1945), p. 1.

35. BA, Spranger Papers, file 253, letter, Rörig to Spranger, 16 October 1945.

36. BA, Spranger Papers, file 194, letter, Paul Hofmann to Spranger, 12 October 1945.

37. *Spranger Report*, p. 6.

38. OMGUS, 4/16-1, box 145, minutes of AKEC meeting, 3 September 1945.

39. Ibid.

40. OMGUS, 4/16-1, box 145, minutes of AKEC meeting, 6 September 1945. The capital letters are in the original document.

41. OMGUS, 4/10-3, box 122, f. 10, memo, Paul Shafer, "History of the Control of the University of Berlin," 26 March 1946, p. 5.

42. Maginnis, p. 315.

43. See Kotowski, pp. 16–17.

44. Henny Maskolat, "Die Wiedereröffnung der Berliner Universität im Januar 1946," in *Forschen und Wirken: Festschrift zur 150-Jahr-Feier der Humboldt Universität zu Berlin*, 1960, p. 612.

45. For an examination of the legal issue see Schneider, pp. 45–46; see also Kotowski, pp. 16–17. Interviews, author with Dr. Paul Wandel, 15 July and 5 December 1986. Wandel pointed out that his *Zentralverwaltung*, with nearly 200 employees, had only one lawyer on the staff in the early postwar period. Soviet decisions, be they the creation of new school laws or the regulation of higher education, often came at short notice and required extraordinary efforts by his administration in order to create the necessary legislation.

46. Interview, author with Wandel, 15 July 1986.

47. A number of the younger founding students at the Free University, such as Helmut Coper and Horst Hartwich, received their school-leaving certificates from this school; interviews, author with Horst Hartwich, 30 August 1985, and with Helmut Coper, 4 September 1985.

48. Interview, author with Otto Hess, 24 September 1985.

49. See Michael Engel, *Geschichte Dahlems*, Berlin, 1984, p. 266. Havemann was appointed by the Magistrat on 6 July 1945.

50. See *Deutsche Volkszeitung*, 9 October 1945; also *National Zeitung*, 9 October 1945.

51. *Tagesspiegel*, 9 October 1945.

52. OMGUS, 4/10-2, f. 5, Dr. Glum, "Report about the University of Berlin," 18 October 1945.

53. OMGUS, 5/297-3, report, Paul Shafer to Director, OMG Berlin Detachment, 8 December 1945.

54. *Humboldt Universität zu Berlin, Dokumente, 1810–1985*, ed. Helmut Klein, p. 73.

55. For a description of the goals of the *Studentische Arbeitsgemeinschaft* see OMGUS, 5/297-3, memo by Rudi Böhm entitled, "Arbeitsgemeinschaft demokratischer Studenten," 22 May 1946.

56. OMGUS, 5/297-3, memo, Shafer to Director, OMGBD, 7 November 1945.

57. OMGUS, 5/297-3, confidential memo prepared by R. G. Riedl, 22 January 1946.

58. Interview, author with Wandel, 15 July 1986. The latter noted that on average the authorities in the Soviet Zone had dismissed 72 percent of all teachers, due in large part because of Nazi efforts earlier to bind that profession to its cause. In Thuringia, over 90 percent dismissals occurred. Unless they had been involved in criminal acts, those dismissed were put into common-labor jobs.

59. OMGUS, 5/307-2, minutes, E&RA staff meeting, 6 September 1945; 5/308-1, report from G-5 Headquarters, Berlin District, 4 August 1945; Hartshorne Diary, entry for 5 September 1945, copy in author's possession.

60. For statistical information see Henny Maskolat, "Arbeiterbewegung und

Berliner Universität in der Periode der Wiedereröffnung, 1945–46," in *Wissenschaftliche Zeitschrift der Humboldt-Universität zu Berlin*, XV (1966), 4, p. 537; see also Schneider, pp. 46–47.

61. OMGUS 4/16-1, box 145, Minutes of the AKEC, 28 January 1946, p. 2.

62. See *Tägliche Rundschau*, 30 January 1946.

63. Theodor Brugsch, *Arzt seit fünf Jarhzehnten*, Berlin, 1957, pp. 346–347.

64. OMGUS, 4/10-2, memo, "Who is allowed to study?" Concerning admittance for students," n.d.

65. Ibid.; for the official admissions criteria see *Berlin: Quellen und Dokumente, 1945–1951*, pp. 556–558.

66. See *Berlin: Quellen und Dokumente, 1945–1951*, pp. 556–558.

67. Hochschularchiv, FU Berlin (hereafter cited as HSA FUB), Rector's Office/Immatrikulationsbüro, Matrikelakte-Nr. 20193, *Lebenslauf* (vita) of Georg Wrazidlo, written 11 November 1956.

68. Interview, author with Joachim Schwarz, 14 January 1987.

69. Interview, author with Stanislaw Kubicki, 17 January 1986.

70. Interviews, author with Otto Hess, 24 September 1985, and with Helmut Coper, 4 September 1985.

71. Interview, author with Horst Hartwich, 30 August 1985.

72. Interview, author with Eva Furth, née Heilmann, 15 January 1986.

73. Interview, author with Horst Rögner-Francke, 25 February 1986.

74. Interview, author with Peter Lorenz, 7 January 1986.

75. Reprinted in *Tagesspiegel*, 9 May 1946.

76. OMGUS, 5/297-3, memo by Otto Hess, 9 December 1946, "Über die Aufgabe und Ziel der Studentischen Arbeitsgemeinschaft." Hess also gave a detailed account of the volunteer organization in his "Berliner Studentenpolitik," in *Der Student*, Marburg University vol. 1, no. 1 (1947). In an interview with the author, 24 September 1985, Hess recalled that SED student Friedrich Wolf was popular with the other students and earned their respect. However, the majority feeling was that following Wrazidlo's removal, the students should elect their own leader in democratic fashion.

77. See Rudi Böhm, "Berlin: Gesicht einer Universität," in *Forum*, 1, 1, 1947, pp. 15–17. Most other sources put the first semester enrollment lower, at about 2,800 students.

78. OMGUS, 5/297-3, unsigned memo in German, September 1946, concerning university admissions, p. 1.

79. OMGUS, 5/297-3, abstract of a letter, Manfred Klein to Franz Steber, 23 August 1946, by U.S. Civil Censorship Division, USFET.

80. OMGUS, 5/297-3, abstract of a letter, Robert Wien to Eugenie Wien, 29 September 1946.

81. Rudi Böhm, "Berlin: Gesicht. . . ," in *Forum*, 1, 1, January 1947, p. 15.

82. OMGUS, 5/297-3, report by Else Knake, "Material über die Zulassung der Studenten zum Wintersemester 46–47 an der Universität Berlin," 22 October 1946, pp. 5–6, hereafter cited as Knake Report.

83. Ibid., p. 6.

84. Ibid., p. 13.

85. Ibid., p. 17.

86. Ibid., pp. 16–17.

87. OMGUS, 5/297-3, letter, Otto Stolz to Fritz Karsen, 21 September 1946.

88. Interview, author with Otto Hess, 24 September 1985.

89. See *Tagesspiegel*, 17 October 1946.

90. Interview, author with Paul Wandel, 15 July 1986. Wandel observed that German exile groups in the Soviet Union, captured German officers in the Soviet-

supported National Committee for a Free Germany, and even German Communists and other socialists who had been incarcerated in concentration camps had been active in preparing reform plans for the postwar society. One goal which emerged from those diverse groups was the opening up of higher education to all classes in society. For his party, the SED, that meant the strong promotion of children of worker and peasant origins, and his opinion was that the other parties were not as committed to this course. On the other hand, representatives of the other parties complained loudly that the SED was identifying student applicants as being compatible with this goal only if they were members of the SED or its auxiliary organizations, such as the FDJ and the FDGB. The whole issue was made the more emotional by the fact that there was so little space at the universities and such a huge backlog of student applicants.

91. See *Tagesspiegel*, 25 October 1946, for a lengthy article highly critical of Stroux. For statistical information on student admissions during this controversial period see Schneider, pp. 46–49.

92. Interview, author with Paul Wandel, 15 July 1986.

93. See *Tagesspiegel*, 25 and 31 October 1946; *Kurier*, 31 October 1947.

94. Statistics quoted in Schneider, p. 48.

95. OMGUS, 5/297-3, handwritten copy of [SPD, CDU, and LPD leaders'] letter to Wandel, 10 October 1946.

96. See *Tagesspiegel*, 18 October 1946.

97. *Tagesspiegel*, 18 October 1946.

98. For an account of Karsen's career see Gerd Radde, *Fritz Karsen: Ein Berliner Schulreformer der Weimarer Zeit*, Berlin, 1973.

99. OMGUS, 5/297-3, letter, Stolz to Karsen, 21 September 1946; Hess informed the author that the atmosphere at the Marburg meeting was outstandingly democratic and helped give rise eventually to a national student organization, the *Verband deutscher Studentenschaften* (VDS), interview, author with Hess, 28 April 1986.

100. See OMGUS, 5/297-3, letter from Hess to Karsen, 9 December 1946, transmitting information concerning the *Studentische Arbeitsgemeinschaft*, and requesting a meeting.

101. OMGUS, 5/297-3, letter, Martin Meyer to OMGUS-Berlin, Education Section, 2 November 1946.

102. *Tagesspiegel*, 3 November 1946.

103. *Telegraf*, 3 November 1946.

104. *Horizont*, 24 November 1946.

105. Interview, author with Otto Hess, 24 September 1985. Hess was convinced that the SED authorities learned of the students' intention to found a journal and prepared *Forum* in response.

106. Interviews, author with Otto Hess, 24 September 1985, and with Joachim Schwarz, 14 January 1987.

107. Ibid.

108. Hess's early works included "Jugend und Sozialismus . . . ," in *Telegraf*, 18 May 1946, "Grosse Politik in einer kleinen Stadt," in *Kurier*, 4 October 1946, Peter Pitz (pseud.), "Krise der Universität . . . ," in *Der Sozialdemokrat*, 3 February 1947, "Sozialistische Universität," in *Das Sozialistische Jahrhundert*, 1, 9/10, March 1947, pp. 146–147.

109. Among Schwarz's writings in the *Tagesspiegel* were an article on the *Studentische Arbeitsgemeinschaft*, 30 May 1946, reports on Palestine and Turkey, 5 and 19 July 1946 respectively, reports on India and Vietnam, 19 and 28 July 1946 respectively, and an extensive report on the future of Egypt, 12 September 1946. In an interview with the author, 14 January 1987, Schwartz stated that journalism

was not merely an avocation for him. It was also a livelihood which allowed him to maintain a precarious existence during those lean years. Schwarz recalled that Bleistein's initial reaction to the proposed student journal was frosty, but he soon warmed to the project.

110. For an account of Stolz's career see Klaus Peter Schulz, "Porträt eines Unbequemen," in *Monat*, no. 166, July 1962, pp. 82–84; interviews with Otto Hess, 24 September 1985, and Horst Rögner-Francke, 22 February 1986, confirm Stolz's journalistic zeal and his sometimes extreme willingness to confront the SED authorities.

111. See OMGUS, 5/297-3, Hess memo, 9 December 1946; see also Hess's article in *Der Student*, Marburg, 1 (1947).

112. Hess memo, 9 December 1946, pp. 2–3, and article in *Der Student*, Marburg, 1 (1947); interviews, author with former members of the *Studentische Arbeitsgemeinschaft*: Hess, Rögner-Francke, Heilmann, Hartwich, Besser, Kubicki, and Coper, among others, autumn 1985 through spring 1986.

113. Hess memo, p. 3.

114. OMGUS, 5/297-3, "Protokoll über die Besprechung zwischen der SMA Karlshorst, Prof. Solotuchin und den Leitern der Studentischen Arbeitsgemeinschaft . . . ," 11 December 1946. The main points of this meeting between students and Solotuchin also came to the attention of the British authorities in Berlin, who noted in addition that the Soviet official had "emphasized the need for a higher percentage of farmers and labourers amongst the student body and regretted that there was so little contact between Russian officers and the students." See FO, 1005/1728, Berlin Political Intelligence Report (PIR), no. 49 (fortnightly ending 15 December 1946), p. 3.

115. OMGUS, 5/297-3, announcement by Paul Wandel, "An den Wahlausschuss der Universität Berlin," 27 January 1947; reprinted in *Telegraf*, 30 January 1947.

116. *Telegraf*, 30 January 1947.

117. *Tagesspiegel*, 4 February 1947.

118. Eighty percent according to *Forum*, 1, 2, February 1947, p. 1.

119. See *Personal- und Vorlesungsverzeichnis der Universität Berlin*, Sommersemester 1947, p. 14.

120. FO, 1105/1729, Berlin PIR no. 53 (weekly ending 8 February 1947), p. 2.

121. See *Tagesspiegel*, 6 February and 15 February 1947.

122. Interview, author with Helmut Coper, 4 September 1985.

123. BA, Spranger Papers, no. 250, letter, Redslob to Spranger, 31 January 1947.

124. *Telegraf*, 15 February 1947.

125. See *Sozialdemokrat*, 10 February 1947.

126. *Tagesspiegel*, 18 March 1947.

127. See Kotowski, pp. 18–19.

128. Interview, author with Stanislaw Kubicki, 17 January 1986.

129. Interview, author with Eva Furth, née Heilmann, 15 January 1986.

130. Interview, author with Horst Rögner-Franke, 25 February 1986.

131. Kotowski, p. 19.

132. *Forum*, 1, 2, February 1947, p. 29.

133. Letter, Stanislaw Kubicki to author, 7 June 1986.

134. *Tagesspiegel*, 7 March 1947.

135. Today the Cafe Kranzler is prominently located on West Berlin's famous Kurfürstendamm.

136. *Telegraf*, 23 March 1947.

137. National Archives, RG 59, Lot 55D 374, records of the Central European Division, G 801.4, Berlin II (Excerpts from paper on "Developments in the Soviet

Zone of Germany, 1945–1948"), p. 2. In an interview, author with Gerda Rösch, 23 January 1987, Rösch observed that most of those arrested were also from pious Catholic families and may have been identified erroneously by SED authorities as part of a conservative circle. She recalled that during her lengthy interrogation by a Soviet officer, the more the American and British authorities attempted to secure her release and that of the other students, the more convinced the Soviets became that those whom they had arrested had been engaged in espionage. Rösch denies any such activity to this day.

138. Student acquaintances of Wrazidlo recalled that he had become friendly with one or more American soldiers in Berlin—the Americans had liberated him from Buchenwald—and he had been observed in an American jeep being driven by a young army captain along Unter den Linden. Most students felt that was not a wise gesture given the increased East-West tensions in 1947. Interviews, author with Horst Rögner-Francke, 25 February 1986, with Otto Hess, 28 April 1986, with Gerhard Petermann, 27 October 1986, and with Gerda Rösch, 23 January 1987. The latter recalled that during her interrogation the Soviet officer, a lieutenant, had informed her that the Soviet authorities were convinced that there was a conspiracy by dissident students afoot and that they were determined to end such resistance before it infected the entire university. The British authorities were aware of the students' bold move in confronting the Soviet authorities about student arrests and noted afterward that the delegation "was told in round terms that it was not the business of the Studentenrat to interfere with the actions of the Soviet authorities." See FO, 1005/1729, Berlin PIR no. 56 (weekly ending 3 April 1947), p. 12.

139. For an account of the experiences of one of those students who was arrested in March 1947, see Manfred Klein, Jugend zwischen den Diktaturen, 1945–1956, Mainz, 1968, pp. 78–91.

140. Interview, author with Helmut Coper, 4 September 1985.

141. Howley, Berlin Command, pp. 110–112.

142. Tagesspiegel, 24 April 1947.

143. Maginnis, p. 269.

144. OMGUS, 5/297-3, minutes of the thirty-sixth meeting of the Allied Control Authority Coordinating Committee, 7 February 1947.

145. Interview, author with Ursula Besser, 29 January 1986.

146. OMGUS, 4/16-1, box 145, minutes of AKEC, 6 January 1947, pp. 8–10.

147. Tagesspiegel, 7 January 1948.

148. OMGUS, 5/297-3, memo, Karsen to Alexander, 13 January 1948.

149. OMGUS, 4/10-3, memo, Louis Glaser to Chief, Education Branch, 19 January 1948.

150. For a good description of the research facilities see Michael Engel, Geschichte Dahlems, Berlin, 1984.

151. Maginnis, p. 315.

152. OMGUS, 5/305-1, box 21, f. 19, memo to Murphy, 19 October 1945.

153. OMGUS, 4/10-2, box 121, f. 5, memo, Monuments and Fine Arts to Winzer, 21 December 1945, plus numerous other correspondence dealing with the Botanical Garden; 5/297-3, memo, Zucker to Stroux, 16 May 1946.

154. OMGUS, 5/297-3, memo, Shulits to Taylor, 11 April 1946.

155. 5/305-1, box 29, f. 20, petition by pharmacy students to U.S. Military Government, 4 July 1946.

156. OMGUS, 5/305-1, box 29, f. 20, memo, Major R. Duder, Assistant Controller, Education Branch (British) to Rector, Technical University, 25 July 1946.

157. BA, Spranger Papers, file 238, Noack to Spranger, 19 September 1946.

158. OMGUS, 5/305-1, box 29, Text of a radio interview . . . , 18 December 1946.

159. Interview, author with Paul Wandel, 15 July 1986.

160. Interviews, author with Eva Furth, née Heilmann, 15 January 1986; with Horst Hartwich, 27 November 1985; with Horst Rögner-Francke, 20 March 1986. Rögner-Francke claimed that the student gatherings at the Epsteins were such a well-known phenomenon among the students that many of them made their visits furtively so as not to arouse unwanted attention from the Soviet authorities. Memories of Georg Wrazidlo and his too friendly contacts with Americans were still fresh.

161. BA, Epstein Papers, file 9, letter, Epstein to Fisher, 19 December 1947.

162. OMGUS, 5/302-2, Minutes of Meeting of E&RA Branch Chiefs, Berlin, 4–5 February 1948, pp. 4–5.

163. OMGUS, 5/297-3, f. 22, memo, John R. Sala to E&CR Division, Education Branch, 22 March 1948, with attachments.

164. Interviews, author with Otto Hess, 24 September 1985, and with Dietrich Spangenberg, 6 January 1986.

165. Colloquium, 1, 1, May 1947, p. 2.

166. Neue Zeitung, 26 April 1947; Tagesspiegel, 25 April, 1 and 8 May 1947.

167. Neue Zeitung, 26 September 1947.

168. Colloquium, 1, 5, September 1947, pp. 14–15. In this instance, Wandel had the stronger argument. Hoffmann may have encountered difficulties with one or more National Socialist organizations in 1935, but evidence in the Berlin Document Center (BDC) clearly indicates that she had continued to belong to the Hitler Jugend (HJ, the Hitler Youth) since 1934 and had carried on as a part-time physician for the Bund deutscher Mädel (BDM, the League of German Maidens) until 1944 at least. Moreover, she had been a member of another small auxiliary organization, the N.S. Studentenkampfhilfe, an offshoot of the Nazis' Studentenbund or Student League, since 1937. This hardly made her a member of the party. However, the assertion in Colloquium that she had been dismissed from all Nazi youth organizations in 1935 was based on inadequate information. The Berlin Document Center contains her entry card into the N.S. Studentenkampfhilfe for 1 September 1937 with membership number 265, plus a card file indicating her activities, including that of BDM physician and director of a seminar at the Hochschule für Leibesübung as of 6 March 1944.

169. Gerhard Petermann Papers, letter, Heubner to medical faculty involved in admissions, 1947/48, 17 November 1947. Copy in author's possession.

170. Interview, author with Claus Reuber, 10 July 1987.

171. Colloquium, 1, 8, December 1947, p. 13.

172. Colloquium, 2, 1, January 1948, pp. 13–15.

173. Colloquium, 2, 1, January 1948, p. 24.

174. Ibid., p. 26. Interviews, author with Paul Wandel, 15 July and 5 December 1986. Wandel rated such cartoons and glosses as mere pinpricks. He even produced another cartoon for the author from the youth magazine Horizont which depicted a statuesque individual looking decidedly like Humboldt scurrying away from his university, while another, triumphant figure bearing an uncanny resemblance to Wandel regally assumed his place. See Horizont, 3, 9 (7 May 1948), cover page. Wandel's wrath centered, he said, on the political commentaries in Colloquium instead. He cited one article, "War Again?" in which an emotional student editorialist claimed that the present war-like situation that was no war was for him worse than the recent world conflict. For long-time exiles like Wandel, who had experienced Nazi persecution at first hand, such assertions were infuriating. See Colloquium, 2, 8, September 1948, cover page. To be sure, by September 1948 matters had already come to a head, and a split was inevitable.

175. *Colloquium*, 2, 2, February 1948, p. 25.

176. *Colloquium*, 1, 8, December 1947, p. 19.

177. *Colloquium*, 2, 3, March 1948, p. 25.

178. FO 371/70706, memo, Birley to Dean, 15 March 1948.

179. Lucius D. Clay, *Decision in Germany*, New York, 1950, p. 354.

180. *Berlin: Quellen und Dokumente*, Vol. I, 574–575.

181. See accounts of the meeting in *Colloquium*, special issue, April 1948, p. 26; interviews, author with Horst Hartwich, 30 August 1985, with Horst Rögner-Francke, 25 February 1986, with Ernst Benda, 28 May 1986, and with Gerhard Löwenthal, 11 February 1987.

182. OMGUS, 2/266-3, unsigned, undated memo in English, re. student expulsions, from approximately 19 April 1948.

183. *Sozialdemokrat*, 22 April 1948.

184. Resolution reprinted in *Colloquium*, special issue, April 1948, pp. 12–13. Interview, author with Gerhard Löwenthal, 11 February 1987. The latter recalled that the meeting was sufficiently tense and his live coverage sufficiently provocative that a quick exit was in order once he could no longer broadcast the proceedings. Hauling the crippled but equally defiant Otto Stolz onto his back, Löwenthal dashed to a RIAS vehicle just outside the university and sped away as two Soviet vehicles pulled up to the gates. Löwenthal has since become widely known as the Federal Republic's most prominent conservative television commentarist.

185. See *Colloquium*, special issue, April 1948, pp. 12–13.

186. Announcement in *Kurier*, 21 April 1948.

187. See *Berliner Zeitung*, 22 April 1948.

188. See, for example: "Die Folge," in *Berliner Zeitung*, 20 April 1948; "Studentenrat gegen den Streik," in ibid., 22 April 1948; "Die Berliner Universität braucht keine Saboteure," in *Neues Deutschland*, 23 April 1948; "Warum sie gehen mussten," in *Vorwärts*, 23 April 1948.

TWO: THE FOUNDING OF THE FREE UNIVERSITY, 1948

1. Detailed plans for an expansion of the Technical University appeared in an SPD memorandum in the spring of 1948, signed by SPD functionaries Kurt Mattick and Friedrich Weigelt. See OMGUS, 4/10-2, box 121, folder 2, memo, Begründung des Verschlages der SPD . . . für den Ausbau der Technischen Universität zu einer Voll-universität," n.d.

2. For initial reports among the Americans concerning a new university in the west sectors see OMGUS, 5/266-3, memo on Berlin University, n.d. (probably 21 April 1948); National Archives RG 84, records of the Political Adviser's Office (hereafter cited as POLAD), decimal file 842, education, box 805 (1948), memo, John A. Calhoun to Robert Murphy, 4 May 1948; for evidence of Foss's early interest in the students of Berlin see his article "A New Freedom—For Education," *New York Post*, 24 February 1947. Gerhard Löwenthal was part of the group of students that first approached Ernst Reuter for support. They were surprised, he recalled, by the soon-to-be governing mayor's first reaction to the proposed founding. An exasperated Reuter informed the students that he had more immediate concerns than such lofty enterprises as a new university to worry about. At the moment, for example, he was trying to find sources of milk for Berlin's hungry infants. Despite this unpromising start, Reuter soon became an ardent supporter of the enterprise. Interview, author with Gerhard Löwenthal, 11 February 1987.

3. Letter, Wells to Tent, 28 December 1977, in author's possession.

4. OMGUS, 5/301-2, memo, by Clay, "Displaced Persons, University Students," 24 June 1947.

5. Wells to Tent, 28 December 1977.

6. Ibid.

7. Herman B Wells, *Being Lucky: Reminiscences and Reflections*, Blooming-ton, Indiana, 1980, p. 310.

8. Interview, author with Herman B Wells, 25 July 1985.

9. OMGUS, Adjutant General (hereafter cited as AG) Files, box 1948, decimal file 128, memo, Wells to Clay, 28 April 1948; hereafter cited as Wells memo, 28 April 1948. Interview, author with General Frank Howley, 17 September 1986. "The students wanted education not propaganda," Howley recalled of his first meeting with them in the spring of 1948. "The students told me about fellow students who had been arrested or who had disappeared, and I remember that the students had had to be secretive in meeting with me. They said that if I could help them, they would leave Berlin University."

10. Wells memo, 28 April 1948.

11. Ibid.

12. OMGUS, AG Files, box 1948, decimal file 128, report on university in American Sector, n.d., attached to Wells memo to Clay of 28 April 1948.

13. POLAD, decimal file 842 education, box 805, letter classified secret, Calhoun to Murphy, 4 May 1948.

14. Ibid.

15. OMGUS, 5/301-2, memo, Karsen to Alexander, 6 May 1948.

16. FO 371/70706 memo, Birley to Patrick Dean, 15 March 1948.

17. FO 371/70493; also cited in Schneider, p. 70.

18. Ibid.

19. FO 371/70706, memo, Birley to Dean, 15 March 1948.

20. *Colloquium*, 2, 5 (May 1948), p. 8.

21. See FO 371/70617, "German Weekly Background Notes," no. 122, January 1948, for reports of new arrests in Berlin; Summaries of Foreign Office Research Department (F.O.R.D.), 28 February to 24 May 1948, describe a new wave of arrests at Rostock University. Robert Murphy's Political Adviser's Office received information that student dissatisfaction at Jena had risen to the point that as many as two hundred faculty and students were planning a mass migration to the west. See POLAD, box 805 (1948), decimal file 842, secret memo and attached report, Dana B. Durand to Murphy, "Planned Student Flight from the University of Jena," 16 March 1948.

22. Interview, author with Dietrich Spangenberg, 6 January 1986. However, Claus Reuber, the last chairman of the *Studentenrat* at the University Unter den Linden before the split and a student of physics, opted for the Technical University. Although on the outs with the SED authorities and unable to continue his studies there any longer, Reuber viewed the Technical University as his logical refuge since the proposed Free University would not be able to construct a natural sciences faculty so quickly. Nevertheless, Reuber viewed a new university as inevitable by that time. He felt that tensions over higher education in the Soviet Sector had become unbearable in the spring of 1948. During a tense meeting at Karlshorst, a Soviet officer had issued a thinly veiled threat to him in his capacity as *Studentenrat* chairman: "You are not only endangering yourself. You are endangering other students!" Interview, author with Claus Reuber, 10 July 1987.

23. See chapter one, p. 74 (also footnote 156).

24. OMGUS, 4/10-3, box 122, folder 10, letter, Johnston to J. Patricia Morrison, 10 December 1948.

25. OMGUS, 5/301-2, memo, Karsen to Alexander, 11 May 1948.

26. Ibid.

27. OMGUS, 5/304-3, folder 23, memo, Karsen to Alexander, "Trip into the Zone . . . ," 7 June 1948.

28. OMGUS, 5/301-2, memo, Karsen to Alexander, 26 May 1948.

29. OMGUS, AG Files, box 1948, decimal 128, memo, Foss to Clay, "Feasibility of Establishing a German University . . . ," 21 May 1948, hereafter cited as Foss Report.

30. Ibid., p. 2.

31. Ibid.

32. Ibid., pp. 4–5.

33. German Original: Warburg to Clay, 6 May 1948, HSA FUB, Rector's Office, Akte Schriftwechsel im Zusammenhang mit der Gründung der FUB; English translation: OMGUS, 4/10-3, box 122, f. 10, letter, Warburg to Clay, 6 May 1948.

34. Foss Report, pp. 6–7.

35. Ibid., p. 8.

36. OMGUS, AG Files, box 1948, decimal file 128, report, R. T. Alexander and Sterling W. Brown to Clay, 29 May 1948, hereafter cited as 29 May Report.

37. 29 May Report, p. 3.

38. Ibid., p. 5.

39. OMGUS, 5/301-2, memo, Karsen to Alexander, 7 May 1948.

40. Herman B Wells, Being Lucky, p. 305.

41. Ibid.

42. For Alexander's views about the Germans see author's Mission on the Rhine: Reeducation and Denazification in American-Occupied Germany, Chicago, 1982, p. 299; Karsen described in some detail the enormous task that would befall his successor in a farewell letter to the leaders of E&CR. See OMGUS, 5/291-3, folder 21, letter and report, Karsen to Alonzo Grace, 25 August 1948. The education files of Military Government contained numerous reports of Karsen's reform hopes and activities. See author's Mission on the Rhine, p. 276.

43. OMGUS, AG Files, box 1948, decimal file 128, memo, Friedrich to Clay, 19 June 1948.

44. Ibid.

45. BA, James Pollock Papers, file 3, diary notes, 21 May 1948.

46. Berliner Zeitung, 24 April 1948.

47. Neues Deutschland, 27 April 1948.

48. Tagesspiegel, 27 April 1948.

49. See Neue Zeitung, 27 April 1948.

50. Ibid.

51. Interview, author with Hans Ulrich Bach, 7 July 1986.

52. Minutes Stadtverordnetenversammlung. Reprinted in Tagesspiegel, 29 April 1948. The SPD faction, led by Franz Neumann, had composed the resolution on April 24, only one day following the Hotel Esplanade meeting, an indication of how explosive the situation had become.

53. See Die Welt, 30 April 1948, Tagesspiegel, 30 April 1948, and, for the SED perspective, Vorwärts, 30 April 1948.

54. Interview, author with Claus Reuber, 10 July 1987.

55. See Der Abend, 4 May 1948; Tagesspiegel, 4 May 1948.

56. Tagesspiegel, 4 May 1948.

57. See Telegraf, 5 May 1948.

58. See Kurier, 5 May 1948.

59. Forum, 2, 5, May 1948, p. 21.

60. Tagesspiegel, 5 May 1948.

61. Kurier, 7 May 1948.

62. *Tagesspiegel*, 8 May 1948.

63. Ibid.

64. See *Tagesspiegel*, 25 May 1948.

65. *Telegraf*, 8 May 1948.

66. Letter reprinted in *Kurier*, 12 May 1948.

67. Reprinted in *Kurier*, 12 May 1948.

68. See *Der Tag*, 20 May 1948.

69. Interviews, author with Otto Hess, 28 April 1986, and with Hans Ulrich Bach, 7 July 1986.

70. National Archives, RG 59, U.S. Department of State, decimal file 862-4212/5-1348, memorandum, Richard W. Sterling, "Movement to establish a free university . . . ," 13 May 1948, enclosure to despatch no. 779, Chase to Secretary of State, 13 May 1948, hereafter cited as *Sterling Report*.

71. Ibid., p. 2.

72. Ibid.

73. Ibid.

74. See Schwarz Papers, letter, Schwarz to Disciplinary Committee, 24 May 1948. Schwarz wrote to the disciplinary committee on the day of the hearing explaining his absence: "because on the basis of my own experience I have every reason to believe that my personal safety will be strongly endangered." Copy in the author's possession.

75. *Die Welt*, 5 May 1948.

76. Interview, author with Otto Hess, 24 September 1985; see contemporary account of the hearing in *Neue Zeitung*, 25 May 1948.

77. HSA FUB, Rector's Office, AStA, Akte ohne Nummer, Juristische Fakultät . . . bis 11.11.1951, copy of a letter, Hess to AStA, 6 January 1950.

78. Ibid. See also Papers of Gerhard Petermann, minority report by students Petermann and Bornemann, 25 May 1948, copy in author's possession.

79. *Forum*, 2, 5, May 1948, p. 21.

80. FO 371/70506, letter, Garran to Bevin, 29 May 1948; letter, Steel to Bevin, 4 August 1948.

81. See *Kurier*, 24 May 1948; *Neue Zeitung*, 25 May 1948.

82. *Sterling Report*, p. 3.

83. BA, Spranger Papers, no. 253, letter, Fritz Rörig to Eduard Spranger, 20 August 1948.

84. BA, Spranger Papers, no. 253, confidential declaration by Rörig for his lecture of 8 June 1948.

85. *Berliner Zeitung*, 10 June 1948.

86. See *Neues Deutschland*, 10 June 1948; reprinted in *Forum*, 2, 6, June 1948, p. 17.

87. See *Der Tag*, 15 June 1948.

88. See *Tagesspiegel*, 10 June 1948; *Der Abend*, 10 June 1948. Interview, author with Frank Howley, 17 September 1986. The latter admitted that he and Clay had had their differences during their time in Berlin. However, they were both of one mind about supporting the Free University. As the senior officer in the American Sector, Howley felt he was allowed considerable discretion, and he was prepared to offer plant and facilities to the students in Dahlem, where many Military Government functions were ceasing operations or transferring elsewhere.

89. *Der Abend*, 10 June 1948, *Tagesspiegel*, 10 June 1948.

90. Interview, author with Hans Ulrich Bach, 7 July 1986. To be sure, Bach and fellow Technical University student-government officers expected that the dissident groups arriving from the old university would be absorbed into an expanded

Technical University. He felt that there was room for more buildings and that the British education officers were supportive of this scheme.

91. *Vorwärts*, 12 June 1948.

92. *Tagesspiegel*, 12 June 1948; *Kurier*, 12 June 1948. Even fellow dissidents like Horst Rögner-Francke blanched sometimes at Stolz's provocative acts, and there was general agreement in their ranks that Stolz seemed always to be in the lead in the confrontations that occurred with the Soviet and SED authorities; interview, author with Horst Rögner-Francke, 25 February 1986.

93. *Der Tag*, 16 June 1948; *Tagesspiegel*, 16 June 1948. The officials at the University Unter den Linden were as good as their word. Reuber was nearing the end of his studies but could not reach an agreement with physics Professors Rompe and Möglich to take the final examinations. He was exmatriculated from the old university in January 1949 and entered the Technical University shortly after. See Reuber Papers, memo, Rector Dersch to Reuber, 11 January 1949, removing Reuber's right to study at the university; see also Reuber's *Exmatrikelschein* or deregistration notice, dated 22 December 1948, in which Reuber explained his deregistration on the grounds that "Professors Rompe and Möglich refuse to examine me." Copies in author's possession.

94. Newspaper accounts varied in their estimate of the *Studentenrat* membership from 27 to 30.

95. List supplied by Horst Rögner-Francke with copy in author's possession.

96. *Telegraf*, 13 June 1948.

97. HSA FUB, Kurator, persönliche Akte ohne Nummer, Gründungsvorgänge; Vorbereitender Ausschuss der FUB, Sitzungsprotokolle, 1948; cited in Siegward Lönnendonker and Tilman Fichter, eds., *FU Dokumentation*, I, no. 36, pp. 38–39. Hereafter cited as *FU Dokumentation* I, with document number.

98. OMGUS, AG Files, 1948, box 128, Foss to Clay, 21 June 1948.

99. Protokoll der Sitzung im Haus der "Freunde der Natur- und Geistenwissenschaften," in Wannsee, am 19. Juni 1948, 4 Uhr nachmittags. HSA FUB: Kurator, persönliche Akte ohne Nummer, Gründungsvorgänge, cited in *FU Dokumentation* I, no. 37, pp. 39–40.

100. *FU Dokumentation* I, no. 37.

101. HSA FUB, Rektor, persönliche Akte ohne Nummer, Gründung, Sitzungen des Vorbereitenden Ausschusses, Fakultäten, reprinted in *FU Dokumentation* I, no. 38.

102. HSA FUB, Rektorat, AStA, Akte ohne Nummer, Juristische Fakultät . . . bis 11.11.1951, letter, Hess to AStA, 13 January 1950. In an interview between the author and Professor Wilhelm Wengler on 5 March 1987, the latter observed that he was disturbed by the lack of academic credentials of some of the key organizers. Specifically, he noted that Edwin Redslob was the former *Reichskunstwart*, the leading fine arts official in the time of the Weimar Republic, and not a university professor. Similarly, Fritz von Bergmann had not built an academic career. Thus, Wengler was in doubt about the seriousness of the enterprise on June 19. Later, as the political situation at Humboldt University intensified and Law Professor Lange departed for the Free University, Wengler, too, opted for the new enterprise.

103. *FU Dokumentation* I, no. 37.

104. OMGUS, AG Files, box 1948, decimal file 128, memo, Foss to Clay, 21 June 1948.

105. Ibid.

106. See Willy Brandt and Richard Löwenthal, *Ernst Reuter: Ein Leben für die Freiheit*, Berlin, 1957, p. 465.

107. OMGUS, AG Files, box 1948, decimal file 128, memo, Wells to Clay, 28 April 1948.

108. HSA FUB, Kurator, persönliche Akte ohne Nummer, Gründungsvorgänge: Vorbereitender Ausschuss . . . Sitzungsprotokolle, 22 June 1948, hereafter cited as Preparatory Committee Minutes.

109. Preparatory Committee Minutes, 22 June 1948.

110. Robert Birley, "British Policy in Retrospect," in Arthur Hearndon, ed., The British in Germany, London, 1978, pp. 60–61. The appearance of CDU member Peters, a bitter critic of the Free University, at Birley's gathering with SPD leaders appears on the surface unlikely. However, Birley, too, had held serious reservations about the founding.

111. Tagesspiegel, 23 June 1948.

112. Tagesspiegel, 18 July 1948.

113. HSA FUB, Rektor, persönliche Akte ohne Nummer, Gründung, Sitzungen des Vorbereitenden Ausschusses, Fakultäten, Knake to Reuter, 20 July 1948, reprinted in FU Dokumentation I, no. 40.

114. Interview, author with Otto Hess, 24 September 1985.

115. OMGUS, AG Files, box 1948, decimal file 128, memo, Foss to Clay, 4 November 1948, p. 3.

116. HSA FUB, Rektor, persönliche Akte ohne Nummer, Gründung, Sitzungen des Verbereitenden Ausschusses, Fakultäten. "Aufruf zur Gründung einer freien Universität Berlin," 23 July 1948.

117. OMGUS, AG Files, box 1948, decimal file 128, Clay to Reuter, 30 August 1948.

118. Colonel Frank Howley was as good as his word, and within the considerable limits of his office provided physical facilities to the new project. It was indicative of the high priority he set for the Free University that he, not R. T. Alexander at the OMGUS Education and Cultural Relations Division, appointed Howard W. Johnston to the post of university officer for the Free University in the spring of 1948. Interviews, author with Frank Howley, 17 September 1986, and with Howard W. Johnston, 2 June 1987. The latter described his activities in a paper entitled "My Role in the Founding of the Free University of Berlin," held at the Free University, Fachbereich Erziehungswissenschaften, 3 June 1987; copy in author's possession.

119. OMGUS, 4/10-3, box 122, folder 10. "Bemerkungen zum Aufbau der neuen Universität in Berlin" with English translation: "Notes on the erection of a new university in Berlin," by August Wilhelm Fehling, n.d.

120. Ibid.

121. Ibid., p. 2.

122. Ibid.

123. BA, Fehling Papers, file no. 5, letter, Frau Fehling to Dr. Ruml, 27 August 1948.

124. OMGUS, 4/10-3, box 122, folder 10, memo, Sala to Howley, 7 August 1948.

125. Ibid., p. 3.

126. BA, Spranger Papers, file 250, letter, Redslob to Spranger, 26 July 1948.

127. For a contemporary account of the highly improvised start-up work for the Free University with the Preparatory Committee, the Committee of 25, admissions committees, and the like see Horizont, 3, 16 (22 August 1948).

128. Colloquium, 2, 7 (July/August 1948), pp. 13–14.

129. Ibid.

130. Neue Zeitung, 27 July 1948.

131. Interview, author with Stanislaw Kubicki, 17 January 1986. Contemporary news accounts frequently mentioned the brevity of the application.

132. Helmut Coper, "Boltzmannstrasse 4," *Colloquium*, 2, 8 (August 1948), p. 12.

133. Statistics from FU Berlin, *Gründungsfeier der Freien Universität Berlin*, Berlin, 1949, p. 64.

134. Interviews, author with Horst Hartwich, 30 August 1985, and with Stanislaw Kubicki, 17 January 1986.

135. Coper, "Boltzmannstrasse 4," *Colloquium*, 2, 8 (August 1948), p. 12.

136. Ibid.

137. Interview, author with Horst Hartwich, 11 June 1986; letter, Otto Hess to author, 25 July 1986.

138. OMGUS, AG Files, box 1948, decimal file 128, memo, Foss to Clay, 4 November 1948; for German accounts of the improvisational nature of the first weeks see *Tagesspiegel*, 4 August 1948, *Neue Zeitung*, 14 September 1948, and Helmut Coper, "Boltzmannstrasse 4," in *Colloquium*," 2, 8 (p. 12), 9 (p. 12), and 10 (p. 13), August, September, and October 1948, respectively.

139. *Vorwärts*, 10 August 1948; the SED-connected *Berliner Zeitung* entitled an announcement of student applications with the provocative headline: "Nazi Universität West." See *Berliner Zeitung*, 12 August 1948.

140. *Neues Deutschland*, 7 August 1948.

141. Richard W. Sterling, personal notes from Berlin, 16 July 1948, copy in author's possession.

142. Frank Howley admitted that the Blockade and Airlift were a trying time for him and that the founding of the Free University was hardly as immediate a problem as providing for a population of over two million people. The food supply at the outset of the Blockade would last the population for only six weeks, he recalled. Howley's special nightmare was that the eastern authorities would interdict the water supply to the western sectors, thus putting them into a hopeless situation. Interview, author with Frank Howley, 17 September 1986.

143. Robert Murphy, *Diplomat among Warriors*, New York, 1964, p. 381.

144. Lucius D. Clay, *Decision in Germany*, New York, 1950, p. 364.

145. Richard W. Sterling, personal notes from Berlin, 16 July 1948, copy in author's possession.

146. OMGUS, 4/10-3, box 122, folder 10, letter, Ringmann to Johnston, 22 September 1948.

147. OMGUS, 4/10-2, unsigned letter in German from two students to Johnston, 6 August 1948.

148. BA, Epstein Papers, File no. 4, letter, Sterling to Epstein, August 1948.

149. Personal notes, Richard W. Sterling, 13 July 1948, copy in author's possession.

150. Richard W. Sterling, notes from Berlin, 16 July 1948, copy in author's possession.

151. See W. Phillips Davidson, *The Berlin Blockade*, Princeton, 1958, p. 321.

152. FO 371/70506, office memos, Rolleston, and Thackeray, dated 11 August and 16 August respectively.

153. FO 371/70506, letter, Christopher Steel to Ernest Bevin, 4 August 1948.

154. FO 371/70506, letter, Bevin to Robertson, 31 August 1948.

155. See HSA FUB, Rector's Office, Akte Schriftwechsel im Zusammenhang mit der Gründung der FUB, minutes of philosophy committee meeting, 31 August 1948, hereafter cited as Philosophy Faculty Minutes.

156. OMGUS, AG Files, box 1948, decimal file 128, Clay to Reuter, 30 August 1948.

157. *Proceedings of the Stadtverordneten-Versammlung von Gross Berlin* (City Assembly of Great Berlin), Drucksache Nr. 130, 79. Ordentliche Sitzung (79th ses-

sion) vom 29. Juli 1948, Nummer 957 "Mitteilung . . . über Hochschulen . . . ,"
dated 31 July 1948.

158. See reprint of May report of 13 September 1948 to Magistrat in *FU Dokumentation* I, document no. 53, pp. 46–47.

159. *FU Dokumentation* I, document no. 54, p. 47.

160. OMGUS, AG Files, box 1948, decimal file 128, memo, Foss to Clay, 4 November 1948.

161. Edwin Redslob, *Von Weimar nach Europa: Erlebtes und Durchdachtes*, Berlin, 1972, pp. 320–321.

162. OMGUS, 4/10-3, box 122, folder 10, letter, Warburg to Clay, 6 May 1948.

163. OMGUS, 4/10-3 box 122, folder 10, report in German: "Bericht über den augenblicklichen Stand der Vorarbeiten für die Freie Universität," also in English translation ("Report on the present status of the preliminary work for the Free University"), dated 20 August 1948, hereafter cited as *Recruitment Report*; see also Philosophy Faculty Minutes, 13 September 1948. A confidential American report of the time included such names as Fischer-Baling (history), Braune (Oriental Studies), Kluke (history), Nestriepke (theater), D. Heinrich Vogel (theology), Redslob (art history), and Menzel (musicology), among others. OMGUS, AG Files, box 1948, decimal file 128, "List of Prospective Faculty members" (marked confidential), n.d. but probably August 1948, hereafter cited as *AG Prospective Faculty List*.

164. See FU Berlin, *Vorlesungsverzeichnis, Winter Semester, 1948/1949*, pp. 17–20.

165. Redslob, *Von Weimar nach Europa*, p. 323. Interview, author with Gerhard Petermann, 27 October 1986. Petermann never joined the Free University although he served on the Preparatory Committee. Instead, he completed his medical examinations at Humboldt University, unhindered by the authorities, and made his medical career in the west.

166. See *Recruitment Report*.

167. See FU Berlin, *Vorlesungsverzeichnis, Winter Semester 1948/1949*, pp. 13–15; see also *Recruitment Report*, 20 August 1948, and *AG Prospective Faculty List*.

168. See *Recruitment Report*.

169. *AG Prospective Faculty List*.

170. See FU Berlin, *Vorlesungsverzeichnis, Winter Semester, 1948/1949*, pp. 15–17; see also *Recruitment Report*, and *AG Prospective Faculty List*.

171. Statement by Georg Kotowski at an Aspen Institute Symposium, "American Higher Educational . . . Policy in Germany, 1945–1952," in Berlin, 5 July 1984, proceedings, p. 43, copy in author's possession.

172. HSA FUB, Rektor's Office, Akte Schriftwechsel im Zusammenhang mit der Gründung der FUB (Philosophy Faculty Minutes), 31 August 1948.

173. BA, Spranger Papers, folder 250, letter Redslob to Spranger, 26 July 1948.

174. See Redslob, *Von Weimar nach Europa*, p. 323.

175. Letter, Hans-Joachim Lieber to author, 1 August 1986; interview, author with Hans-Joachim Lieber, 20 January 1986.

176. Interview, author with Otto Hess, 28 April 1986; for Reuter's initiative in seeking Meinecke for the rectorship see Willy Brandt and Richard Löwenthal, *Ernst Reuter, Ein Leben für die Freiheit*, Berlin, 1957, p. 466.

177. Interview, author with Dr. Ingeborg Sengpiel, 31 October 1985.

178. Nordwestdeutscher Hochschultag [predecessor of the Westdeutschen Rektoren-Konferenz], "Protokoll der Rektorenbesprechung in Braunschweig," 27 July 1948, p. 10, hereafter cited as WRK Minutes with appropriate date and location.

179. Ibid.

180. OMGUS, 4/10-2, folder 11, two memos, Johnston to Dunlap, 8 September 1948, and Dunlap to Johnston, 11 September 1948.

181. OMGUS, 4/10-2, memo for record concerning conference between Johnston and Freygang, 14 September 1948.

182. OMGUS, 4/10-2, folder 11, memo, Johnston to Thompson, 20 September 1948.

183. OMGUS, 2/10-2, folder 11, memo, Johnston to Garnett, 2 December 1948.

184. Statements by Hans-Joachim Lieber and Georg Kotowski at Aspen Institute Symposium, "American Higher Educational Policy . . . in Germany, 1945–1952," 5 July 1984, minutes, p. 59, copies in author's possession.

185. See author's *Mission on the Rhine: Reeducation and Denazification in American-Occupied Germany,* Chicago, 1982, p. 296.

186. OMGUS, 4/10-2, folder 11, memo, Johnston to Sander, 11 December 1948.

187. "Satzung der Freien Universität Berlin," 2 November 1948, reprinted in *FU Dokumentation* I, no. 61.

188. Eva Heilmann, "The Students' Role in the Free University," *The American-German Review,* 18, 2 (December 1951), p. 12.

189. Interview, author with Wolfgang Kalischer, 30 October 1985.

190. National Archives, RG 59, files of the U.S. Department of State, decimal file 862.4212/11-2048, (post files, reeducation in Germany with date), dispatch, Murphy to State, 20 November 1948.

191. Ibid.

192. Numerous eyewitnesses attested to Kruspi's strong resistance to the organizational structure of the Free University. Interviews, author with Otto Hess, 28 April 1985, Carl Hubert Schwennicke, 7 February 1986, Ingeborg Sengpiel, 31 October 1985, Dietrich Spangenberg, 6 January 1986; see also critical article about Kruspi in *Tagesspiegel,* 28 October 1948.

193. Preparatory Committee Minutes, 27 August, 4, 7, and 25 September 4, 7, 9, and 26 October, 9 and 13 November 1948. The Social Democrats enthusiastically endorsed students on the University Senate. See *Sozialdemokrat,* 6 November 1948. The initial appointments of leading officers and professors were all dispatched under Ernst Reuter's signature on the same day, 15 November, including the reference to the secret nomination of the two unnamed professors, i.e., Leisegang (Jena) and Lübtow (Rostock). Reprinted in *FU Dokumentation* I, nos. 66 and 67.

194. See *Tagesspiegel,* 27 and 28 October 1948, and *Der Tag,* 27 October 1948.

195. *Der Abend,* 16 November 1948.

196. Ibid.

197. *Der Tag,* 16 November 1948.

198. POLAD, decimal file 842 (education), box 805, memo, Johnston to Political Affairs Office, OMGUS, 18 November 1948.

199. Quoted in David Phillips, ed., *German Universities after the Surrender: British Occupation Policy and the Control of Higher Education,* Oxford, 1983, p. 90.

200. FU Berlin, *Gründungsfeier der Freien Universität Berlin,* Berlin, 1949, pp. 9–18.

201. Ibid., pp. 19–22.

202. Ibid., pp. 31–32.

203. Ibid., p. 36.

204. Ibid., pp. 38–39.

205. Ibid., p. 51.

206. Archives of the University of Keele, Scotland, reference, L 221, letter, Lind-

say to Lowe, 27 November 1948.

207. BA, Epstein Papers, box 12, letter, Marcuse to Epstein, 2 December 1948.

208. FO 371/70528, confidential despatch, Garran to Bevin, 14 December 1948.

209. *Neues Deutschland*, 4 December 1948. The reference to Meinecke fulfilling the role of a Hindenburg was a particularly nasty allusion: the latter, after all, had been responsible for appointing Hitler as chancellor in 1933. It is also noteworthy that Schmitt, despite any claims by the Communists to the contrary, never obtained an academic affiliation of any kind with the Free University.

210. FO 371/70528, confidential despatch, Garran to Bevin, 14 December 1948.

211. FO 371/70528, Foreign Office comments to Garran despatch, 20 December 1948 (Giles), 4 January 1949 (Worsfold).

212. OMGUS, AG Files, box 1948, decimal file 128, memo, Foss to Clay, 4 November 1948.

213. OMGUS, AG Files, box 1948, decimal file 128, letter, Meinecke and Redslob to Clay, 17 November 1948.

214. WRK Minutes, Würzburg, 6–7 November 1948, pp. 49–52.

215. See *Berliner Morgenpost*, 6 December 1973. The *Morgenpost* erroneously attributed this hostile interpretation concerning the university's founding to Fichter himself. The latter's views on the founding of the Free University are to be seen in the first volume of the FU documentation series, especially in its chronology. See *FU Dokumentation* I, preface and pp. 1–16.

THREE: THE CONSOLIDATION OF THE FREE UNIVERSITY, 1949 TO 1961

1. For a brief description of West Berlin's early economic plight see Hubert G. Schmidt, *Economic Assistance to West Berlin*, HICOG publication, Bonn, 1952, 135 pp.

2. HSA FUB, Kurator, persönliche Akte ohne Nummer, Gründungsvorgänge, report, Behrmann to von Bergmann, 18 February 1949.

3. See *Tagesspiegel*, 26 January 1949.

4. See HSA FUB, Kuratorialverwaltung, Akte Nr. 1/1000, Gründung, Verfassung, Stiftungen/Allgemeines, letter, Redslob to Reuter, 26 January 1949.

5. See HSA FUB, numerous memoranda in the files of Kurator von Bergmann and of his administration, the Kuratorialverwaltung: Kurator, persönliche Akte ohne Nummer, Gründungsvorgänge, memo of 17 March 1949 from Howard W. Johnston permitting Bergmann to inspect Dahlem institutes still financed by Humboldt University and the Deutsche Wirtschaftskommission; confidential list of institutes compiled by Bergmann, dated 7 March 1949; authorization of transfer, Howley to Reuter, 25 April 1949; decision of Magistrat No. 259, dated 27 April 1949, ordering the transfer and signed by Reuter and May. The matter also received a public airing on radio in an interview between Gerhard Löwenthal of RIAS and Walter May, 31 May 1949. Transcript in HSA FUB, Kuratorialverwaltung, Akte Nr. 1/1000 (allgemeines).

6. See HSA FUB, Rector's Office, Akte ohne Nummer, Spenden HICOG, "Progress Report . . . April 1st to June 30th, 1951."

7. *FU Dokumentation* II, pp. 137–141, memorial by the Law Faculty, 8 June 1951.

8. See HSA FUB, Rektor, persönliche Akte ohne Nummer, Gründung, Sitzungen des vorbereitenden Ausschusses, Fakultäten, memo, "Work of the Admittance Department," 16 February 1949; for enrollment figures see Georg Kotowski, ed., *Die Freie Universität Berlin*, Berlin, 1965, p. 18.

9. OMGUS, 4/11-2, box 126, folder 2, memo, Johnston to Intelligence Officer, OMGBS, 16 November 1948, p. 2.

10. HSA FUB, Rektor, persönliche Akte ohne Nummer, Gründung, Sitzungen des vorbereitenden Ausschusses Fakultäten, "The Work of the Social Department."

11. Ibid.

12. OMGUS, 4/10-3, box 122, folder 10, letter, Morrison to Johnston, 30 November 1948, and Johnston's reply, 10 December 1948.

13. HSA FUB, Rector's Office, Akte ohne Nummer, Spenden HICOG, memo, Johnston to Redslob, 27 January 1949.

14. OMGUS, 4/11, box 126, folder 2, letter Robert Von Pagenhardt, Stanford University, to J. C. Thompson, OMGBS, 1 March 1949, and reply, 19 March 1949.

15. See "Marlowe Society in Berlin . . . ," in The Times, Educational Supplement, 18 September 1948.

16. HSA FUB, Rektor, persönliche Akte ohne Nummer, Gründung, Sitzungen des vorbereitenden Ausschusses, Fakultäten, memo, "The Work of the Outside Relations Department," 31 March 1949.

17. See Horst Hartwich, "Bilanz der Aussenbeziehungen," in FU-Info, 3 (20 March 1987), p. 15.

18. OMGUS, 4/14-2, box 139, memo, Thompson to U.S. Command, Berlin, 9 September 1949; for the book budget see OMGUS, 4/11-2, memo, C. B. Garnett Jr. to J. C. Thompson, 14 September 1949.

19. Ibid., Thompson to U.S. Commandant, Berlin, 9 September 1949.

20. National Archives, RG 466. McCloy Papers, D (49), 188a, memo, Taylor to McCloy, 15 September 1949, and McCloy to Morgan, 19 September 1949, hereafter cited as McCloy Papers.

21. McCloy Papers, D (49), 265, minutes of HICOG Staff Conference, 11 October 1949.

22. National Archives, RG 59, Department of State, 862.51/10-1749, telegram, McCloy to Acheson, 17 October 1949, Acheson's reply, 20 October, and McCloy's follow-up telegram, 862.42/10-2949, 29 October 1949.

23. OMGUS, 5/301-1, box 76, memos, Thompson to Maxwell Taylor, 24 October 1949 and 31 October 1949.

24. OMGUS, 5/301-1, box 76, memo, Thompson to Maxwell Taylor, 4 November 1949.

25. Interview, author with Ingeborg Sengpiel, 9 February 1987.

26. HSA FUB, Rektor, persönliche Akte ohne Nummer, Der Regierende Bürgermeister . . . , 1948-1957, letter, Redslob to Reuter, 23 May 1950.

27. HSA FUB, Rector's Office, Akte ohne Nummer, Spenden HICOG, copy of letter, Maxwell Taylor to Reuter, 21 October 1949.

28. National Archives, RG 84, State Department Post Files, HICOG, lot 59A 543, box 2175, memo, Maynard to Conant, 17 December 1953.

29. National Archives, RG 59, Department of State, decimal file 811.42762/11-749, memo, Michael Weyl to Helen Wessels, 7 November 1949.

30. OMGUS, 4/14-2, box 139, memo, Thompson to H. S. Stearns, Intelligence Branch, OMGBS, 30 July 1949.

31. Ibid.

32. National Archives, RG 59, Department of State, decimal file 862.4212/3-849, airgram, Riddleberger to Kellermann, 9 March 1949.

33. Ibid., 862.4212/3-849, telegram, Riddleberger to Kellerman, 9 March 1949; 862.4212/11-749, letter, Franz L. Neumann to Henry Kellermann, 7 November 1949, and Kellermann's reply, 25 November 1949. (Franz L. Neumann of Columbia University is not to be confused with Franz Neumann of the SPD in Berlin.)

34. National Archives, RG 59, Department of State, decimal file 811.71562/12-1649, letter, Friedrich to Perry Laukhuff, 16 December 1949.

35. See OMGUS, 4/11-2, box 126, folder 2 for correspondence between Howley and the Ford and Rockefeller Foundations and the Carnegie Corporation for the period 29 December 1948 to 2 June 1949.

36. Edwin Redslob, Von Weimar nach Europa, Berlin, 1972, p. 353; see also HSA FUB, minutes, meeting of the FU Aussenkommission, 13 February 1950, describing Redslob's mission to the United States.

37. OMGUS, 5/300-1, box 69, folder 4, Franz L. Neumann, "Preliminary Report on My Trip to Berlin," 10 February 1950, p. 5.

38. Neumann's assessment of May is at odds with that of the leading American education officer in Berlin, John C. Thompson. The latter felt that May led the fight against the merger. See OMGUS, 5/301-1, box 76, memo, Thompson to Taylor, 4 November 1949.

39. OMGUS, 5/300-1, box 69, folder 4, Neumann, "Preliminary Report . . . ," 10 February 1960, pp. 1–5.

40. Colloquium, 3, 4 (Summer 1949), p. 1.

41. HSA FUB, I. Konvent, Sitzungsprotokolle, 1950, decision of 20 April 1950; reprinted in FU Dokumentation II, no. 117.

42. OMGUS, 5/299-3, box 68, memo, Wann to rectors, 5 January 1948.

43. For the arguments of both sides see the FU Dokumentation II, especially documents 95, 96, and 97 cited above. See further documents 117, 130, 139, 149, 151, 155–157, 169–172, and Zeitgenössische Kommentare, pp. 141–147.

44. OMGUS, 5/291-3, box 12, folder 3, monthly report, November, 5 December 1949.

45. Interview, author with Horst Rögner-Francke, 25 February 1986.

46. Interviews, author with Eva Furth, née Heilmann, 15 January 1986, and with Otto Hess, 28 April 1986.

47. OMGUS, 5/300-1, box 69, folder 4, Neumann Report, 10 February 1950, pp. 4, 8.

48. See Eberhard Diepgen, "Korporationen und Freie Universität," in Fünfzehn Jahre Freie Universität, 1948–1963, Berlin, 1963, p. 36.

49. Interviews, author with Horst Hartwich, 30 August 1985, with Helmut Coper, 4 September 1985, and with Dietrich Spangenberg, 6 January 1986.

50. Dietrich Schmidt-Hackenberg, "Freie Universität und Korporationen" in Fünfzehn Jahre Freie Universität, 1948–1963, Berlin, 1963, pp. 32–34.

51. Interview, author with Hans-Joachim Lieber, 20 January 1986; see also Brigitte Berendt, "Studenten helfen Studenten: Elf Jahre Tutorenarbeit an der Freien Universität," in Fünfzehn Jahre Freie Universität Berlin, 1948–1963, Berlin, 1963, pp. 40–41; The Friedrich Meinecke Institute described its early efforts in building up the tutorial system in Das Friedrich-Meinecke-Institut der Freien Universität Berlin, 1948–1959, Berlin, 1959, pp. 16–17; see also C. Schulz-Popitz, "Tutoren," in Deutsche-Universitäts-Zeitung, 12, 15, (August 1957), pp. 3 ff.

52. HSA FUB, Rector's Office, Akademisches Aussenamt, Akte, Ford Foundation . . . , ca. 1952–1966, George N. Shuster, "Report on the Free University of Berlin," p. 20, with cover letter to Andreas Paulsen, 11 April 1956.

53. McCloy Papers, D (51) 1566, memo, Koopman to Stone, 8 October 1951.

54. BA, Epstein Papers, box 57, letter by Epstein, 22 August 1950.

55. See Eva Heilmann, "The Students' Role in the Free University," in American-German Review, 18, 2 (December 1951), p. 12.

56. Ibid.

57. Interview, author with Wolfgang Kalischer, 30 October 1985.

58. HSA FUB, Philosophy Faculty, Dean's Office, Akte Assistenten (vor

1959), memo, Asmuss, Schmidt, and Lieber to Redslob, 7 January 1949.

59. HSA FUB, Philosophy Faculty, Dean's Office, Akte Assistenten (vor 1959), memo, Margass and Freygang to Goethert, 27 January 1949.

60. Ibid.

61. HSA FUB, Philosophy Faculty, Dean's Office, Akte Assistenten (vor 1959), report by Leisegang, 30 May 1949.

62. See *Mitteilungen für Dozenten und Studenten*, FU Berlin, no. 2 (15 March 1951).

63. HSA FUB, Philosophy Faculty, Dean's Office, Akte Allgemeine Assistenten-Angelegenheiten, report, "Zur Situation der wissenschaftlichen Assistenten an der Freien Universität Berlin," n.d. but probably 1957, 11 pp.

64. HSA FUB, Rector's Office, Akte ohne Nummer, Spenden HICOG, notes for a meeting on 10 June 1950 with General Taylor, by Edwin Redslob.

65. BA, Epstein Papers, box 57, letter, Epstein to Riedl, 22 August 1950.

66. HSA FUB, Rector's Office, Akte ohne Nummer, Spenden HICOG, memo and cover letter by von Bergmann on the finances of the Free University, 14 June 1950; copy of FU announcement confirming Johnston as its honorary citizen, 16 June 1950; note of appreciation, Redslob to Johnston, 11 October 1950.

67. HSA FUB, Rector's Office, Akte ohne Nummer, Spenden HICOG, memos, von Bergmann to rector, 27 September 1950, and von Bergmann's report of 6 April 1951, listing American financial contributions.

68. HSA FUB, Kurator, persönliche Handakte, Tätigkeitsberichte für die HICOG . . . , 1950–1954, memo, "Tätigkeitsbericht der FU . . . vom 1.1 bis 31.3.1951."

69. HSA FUB, Rector's Office, Akte ohne Nummer, Spenden HICOG, letter, Redslob to Anthon, 25 October 1950; von Bergmann, notes of a conference with Anthon, 9 December 1950.

70. Cited in Richard Magat, *The Ford Foundation at Work: Philanthropic Choices, Methods, and Styles*, New York, 1979, pp. 18–19. For a recent account of Ford Foundation activities by a knowledgeable insider see Francis X. Sutton, "The Ford Foundation: The Early Years," *Daedalus: Journal of the American Academy of Arts and Sciences*, 116, 1 (Winter 1987), pp. 41–91.

71. Ford Foundation Archives (hereafter cited as FFA), roll 89, PA 51-41, letter, McCloy to Hoffman, 15 January 1951.

72. Ibid., memo, Stone to McCloy, n.d. (probably late 1950).

73. Ibid., letter McDaniel to McCloy, 22 January 1951.

74. Ibid., letters Kellermann to Hoffman, 26 April 1951, and Mathewson to Hoffman, 19 April 1951.

75. HSA FUB, Philosophy Faculty, Dean's Office, Akte Raumverteilung, Bauvorhaben . . . , copy of letter, von Kress to Hoffman, 29 March 1951, plus attached memorandum.

76. HSA FUB, Kurator, pers. Handakte, Tätigkeitsberichte für die HICOG . . . , 1950–1954, report for period 1 April to 30 June 1951, pp. 3–4; see also *Tagesspiegel*, 10 June 1951.

77. National Archives, RG 59, Department of State, decimal file 862.43/8-951, despatch, W. J. Convery Egan to State, 9 August 1951.

78. Ibid., p. 4.

79. FFA, roll 489, PA 51-41, letter, Stone to W. H. Ferry, 31 August 1951.

80. *FU Dokumentation* II, pp. 137–141, memorial by the Law Faculty, 8 June 1951.

81. HSA FUB, AStA, Akte ohne Nummer, Juristische Fakultät . . . bis 11.11.1951, letter, Brandt to Studentenrat, 27 April 1948.

82. HSA FUB, AStA, Akte ohne Nummer Juristissche Fakultät . . . bis 11.11.1951, resolution of the eighth meeting of the Konvent (parliament), 23–24 February 1950, plus accompanying declaration of same date; see in same series a resolution of SPD Hochschulgruppe der Freien Universität, 28 February 1950.

83. Interview, author with Wilhelm Wengler, 5 March 1987.

84. FFA, roll 489, PA 51-41, report by Neumann, 19 September 1952, hereafter cited as *Neumann Report, 1952.*

85. Information on Forstmann derives from the Berlin Document Center (hereafter cited as BDC), which has his party book, his letters to relatives written during his imprisonment, plus numerous Gestapo reports on his incarceration. See also HSA FUB, Wirtschafts- und Sozialwissenschaftliche Fakultät (Economics and Social Sciences Faculty), Dekanat, Personalakten, Ordinarien, Buchst. A-K, "Prof. Dr. Forstmann," report dated 15 September 1950. His works included *Der Kampf um den Internationalen Handel,* Berlin, 1935, and *Volkswirtschaftliche Theorie des Geldes,* Berlin, 1943.

86. The BDC has voluminous reports on Möglich, including the charges against him, his justifications of his actions, his private correspondence, and his appeals for reinstatement into the NSDAP.

87. For a detailed treatment of denazification see Lutz Niethammer, *Entnazifizierung in Bayern: Säuberung und Rehabilitierung unter amerikanischer Besatzung,* Frankfurt am Main, 1972; see also the author's *Mission on the Rhine: Reeducation and Denazification in American-Occupied Germany,* Chicago, 1982, ch. 3.

88. National Archives, RG 59, U.S. Department of State, decimal file 740.00119, control (Germany)/10-2949, memo, Wendelin to Babcock and Taylor, 29 October 1949.

89. See, for example, Rolf Seeliger, ed., *Braune Universität: Deutsche Hochschullehrer Gestern und Heute,* vol. 4: *Westberlin* (Munich, 1966), pp. 27–84. This comprises a collection of documents authored by a number of Berlin professors under the Nazis, including five from the Free University: Karl Thalheim, Andreas Paulsen (formerly an FU rector from 1955 to 1957), Hans Knudsen, Emil Dovifat, and Richard Beitl. Each had an opportunity to respond to the materials selected for presentation to the public by the editor. The reader can judge the individual cases for himself. See also the FU student magazine, *FU Spiegel,* 14 (November/December 1968), p. 13 for its "revelations" about Rector Ewald Harndt. It should be noted that Harndt initially made his postwar dental career at Berlin University, where SED loyalist Theodor Brugsch had approved his appointment to the medical faculty. He did not join the Free University until 1956.

90. OMGUS, 5/300-1, box 69, folder 4, report, Sigmund Neumann, "Status and Progress of Social Sciences in German Universities," 22 August 1949.

91. Ibid.

92. OMGUS, 5/300-1, box 69, folder 4, Franz L. Neumann, memo, "Preliminary Report on My Trip to Berlin," 10 February 1950.

93. HSA FUB, Rector's Office, Akte ohne Nummer, "Spenden HICOG," Redslob's notes for a conference with General Taylor, 13 June 1950.

94. Otto Stammer, "Institut für politische Wissenschaft . . . ," in Georg Kotowski, ed., *Die Freie Universität Berlin,* Berlin, 1965, pp. 70–71.

95. *Neumann Report, 1952,* p. 8.

96. For a detailed treatment of the establishment of the Osteuropa Institut see Klaus-Dieter Seemann, "Die Slavistik an der Freien Universität Berlin," in Herbert Bräuer et al., eds., *Materialien zur Geschichte der Slavistik in Deutschland,* Berlin, 1982, p. 19–44.

97. See HSA FUB, Kurator, persönliche Akte, Ford Foundation, ca. 1951–1952, memo, von Bergmann to Senator for Finances, Lange, 6 June 1952.

98. HSA FUB, Rector's Office, Akte ohne Nummer, Spenden HICOG, memo, Conant to FU, "Grant-in-Aid Award," 29 June 1953, hereafter cited as Conant Memo, 29 June 1953.

99. Neumann Report, 1952, p. 8.

100. Conant Memo, 29 June 1953.

101. BA, Epstein Papers, folder 57, letter, Epstein to Riedl, 22 August 1950.

102. Neumann Report, 1952, p. 11.

103. Ibid.

104. HSA FUB, Kurator, persönliche Akte, Ford Foundation, ca. 1951–1952, Memorandum des Rektors von Kress, 29 March 1951: see also Georg Kotowski, ed., Die Freie Universität Berlin, pp. 66–69.

105. HSA FUB, Rector's Office, Akademisches Aussenamt, Akte Ford Foundation . . . , ca. 1952–1966, George N. Shuster, Report on the Free University of Berlin, 11 April 1956, pp. 27–28, hereafter cited as Shuster Report.

106. Neumann Report, 1952, p. 15.

107. Ibid.

108. Neumann Report, 1952, pp. 15–17; see also National Archives, RG 84, Foreign Service Despatches (hereafter cited as FSD), 862A 43/6-1052, memo by M. E. Allen, 10 June 1952; 862A 43/9-2253, memo by J. C. Polarek, 22 September 1953; and 862A 43/3-1154, memo by T. J. Garolan, 11 March 1954.

109. FFA, roll 2419, PA 58-260, reports Hartwich to Ford Foundation (hereafter cited as FF), 18 January 1960, Burckhardt to FF, 6 August 1962.

110. HSA FUB, Kurator, persönliche Akte, Ford Foundation, ca. 1951–1952, Memorandum des Rektors von Kress, 29 March 1951, p. 3.

111. Cited in FSD 862A 43/6-1052, memo, M. E. Allen, 10 June 1952.

112. FSD, 862A 43/3-1153, memo, T. J. Garolan, 11 March 1954.

113. Neumann Report, 1952, p. 20.

114. FFA, roll 2419, PA 58-260, "Progress Report . . . Meinecke Institute . . . 1960–1963," p. 1.

115. OMGUS, 4/10-2, box 121, f. 2, memo, Funk-Universität, by Thomas Eckert, August 1948.

116. HSA FUB, Kurator, persönliche Akte, Ford Foundation, ca. 1951–1952, Memorandum des Rektors von Kress, 29 March 1951.

117. HSA FUB, Kurator, persönliche Akte, Ford Foundation, ca. 1951–1952, report, Eduard May to Chairman, Evening University Committee, 24 June 1952.

118. Quoted in FSD, 862A 43/6-1052, memo, M. E. Allen, 10 June 1952.

119. Neumann Report, 1952, pp. 19–20.

120. National Archives, RG 84, Berlin Post Files, lot 59 A 543, box 2173, memo, 20 August 1952; interview, author with Horst Hartwich, 14 November 1985.

121. HSA FUB, Rector's Office, Akte 2/2200/1, Veterinär-Medizinische Fakultät, Dekanat, 1950–1957 (hereafter cited as VMF), report, "Übersicht über die politische Entwicklung an der veterinär-medizinischen Fakultät der Humboldt Universität Berlin, prepared by members of that faculty and forwarded by Redslob to Reuter, 8 May 1950.

122. HSA FUB, Rector's Office, Akte 2/2200/1, VMF, memo by Redslob, 22 April 1950, plus letter, Redslob to Kaiser, 26 April 1950.

123. HSA FUB, Rector's Office, Akte 2/2200/1, VMF, memo by Redslob, 22 April 1950.

124. HSA FUB, Rector's Office, Akte 2/2200/1, VMF, Aktenvermerk (internal memorandum) by Rögner-Francke, n.d. (May 1950).

125. HSA FUB, Rector's Office, Akte 2/2200/1, *VMF*, letter, Emergency Committee member Siegert to Bevollmächtigter der Bundesrepublik Heinrich Vockel, 18 November 1950.

126. HSA FUB, Rector's Office, Akte 2/2200/1, *VMF*, letter, Mathewson to Reuter, 14 June 1951.

127. National Archives, RG 59, Department of State, decimal file 862A.43/1-1253, memo, Polarek to State, 12 January 1953.

128. National Archives, RG 59, Department of State, decimal file, 862A.431/1-854, memo, Polarek to USIA Washington, 8 January 1954.

129. Ibid., p. 4

130. HSA FUB, Rector's Office, Akte 2/2007/2, "Feier der Rektoratsübergabe . . . 1950–1955," report, "Bericht des scheidenden Rektors . . . Hirsch . . . ," 14 October 1955. Professor Hirsch fell ill at the end of his duties and left Berlin for medical treatment immediately. To his embarrassment, his report never found its way into the hands of his successors until April 1984, when he forwarded it to the Free University just months before his death.

131. BA, Epstein Papers, folder 57, letter, Epstein to Riedl, 22 August 1950.

132. Interview, author with Werner Skuhr, 23 July 1987.

133. Interview, author with Hermann and Irene Oberländer, 30 June 1987.

134. Interview, author with Hannelore and Christian Horn, 8 July 1987.

135. Interview, author with Ingrid Vietig, née Friedmann, 16 March 1987.

136. Interviews, author with the Oberländers, 30 June 1987, and with the Horns, 8 July 1987.

137. Interview, author with Skuhr, 23 July 1987.

138. Interview, author with Vietig, 16 March 1987.

139. FFA, roll 2419, PA 58-260, letter, Doris Esch to FF, 30 July 1959.

140. Ibid.

141. Ibid.

142. *Shuster Report*, pp. 4–5.

143. Ibid., p. 6.

144. Ibid., p. 11.

145. Ibid., p. 10.

146. Ibid., p. 9.

147. Ibid., p. 48.

148. Ibid., p. 39.

149. Ibid., p. 26.

150. Ibid., p. 25.

151. Ibid., p. 48.

152. Ibid., p. 49.

153. Ibid., p. 49.

154. Ibid., p. 17.

155. Ibid., p. 20.

156. See *FU Dokumentation* II, no. 210.

157. See *FU Dokumentation* III, report, von Bergmann, "Die Hilfe der USA für die Freie Universität Berlin," p. 189.

158. FU Aussenamt, Akte Ford Foundation Spende, vol. 2, report, John H. Stibbs, Tulane University, to Ralph Brown, American Mission, re. Studentendorf, 7 July 1964.

159. See *FU Dokumentation* II, document, nos. 178, 198.

160. FSD, 862A.43/3-1154, despatch, Thomas J. Garolan to State, 11 March 1954.

161. See *FU Dokumentation* II, no. 187.

162. *FU Dokumentation* III, no. 217.

163. See *FU Dokumentation* III, nos. 253–263.

FOUR: THE FREE UNIVERSITY IN CRISIS, 1961 TO 1968

1. For an overview on recent trends in Berlin and with statistical informa-tion see Richard L. and Anna J. Merritt, *Living with the Wall, West Berlin, 1961–1985*, Raleigh, North Carolina, 1985.

2. FFA, document no. 009112, discussion paper, "International Affairs, Ber-lin," n.d. (Spring 1962).

3. FFA, roll 2419, PA 58-260, report, Sigmund Neumann to FF international affairs program, attached to a cover letter, Neumann to Stone, 4 July 1962, p. 2, hereafter cited as Neumann Report 1962.

4. FFA, roll 2419, PA 58-260, letter, Sigmund Neumann to Joseph Slater, 15 May 1960.

5. FFA, roll 2419, PA 58-260, memo, Joseph Slater to Shepard Stone, 7 April 1958.

6. Ibid.

7. Neumann Report 1962, p. 2.

8. Ibid.

9. FFA, roll 1292, PA 63-348, letter, Shepard Stone to James R. Killian, 10 June 1965.

10. See David Phillips, *Zur Universitätsreform in der britischen Besatzungs-zone, 1945–1948*, Cologne and Vienna, 1983. For a useful collection of essays on British observations of German universities after the war by British partici-pants see David Phillips, ed., *German Universities after the Surrender: British Occupation Policy and the Control of Higher Education*, Oxford, 1983.

11. FFA, roll 1292, PA 63-348, Hans Simons, "Berlin Report," 20 January 1967, p. 4.

12. See Uwe Schlicht, "Von der skeptischen Generation bis zur Protestjugend," in Uwe Schlicht, ed., *Trotz und Träume: Jugend Lehnt Sich Auf*, Berlin, 1980, pp. 190–209.

13. The SED in West Berlin was renamed SED-W (Sozialistische Einheitspartei Deutschlands—Westberlin). Some years later, the party adopted the name SEW (Sozialistische Einheitspartei Westberlins).

14. *Süddeutsche Zeitung*, 26 November 1949; *Colloquium*, 3, 6 (1949), p. 3.

15. *FU Dokumentation* III, no. 226 for 12 June 1958, p. 77.

16. Interview, author with Wolfgang Lefèvre, 5 February 1987.

17. HSA FUB, AStA, Akte ohne Nummer Erich Kuby, leaflet, "Restauration oder Neubeginn . . . ," Flugblatt Nr. 2, n.d.

18. Interview, author with Horst Hartwich, 8 December 1986. Hartwich main-tained that he and several other senior FU officials urged Lüers to accede to the students' wish, thus defusing the Kuby issue. However, Lüers, following his own conscience and the advice of more militant advisers, such as Hoppe and Völz, re-fused to budge.

19. See *Süddeutsche Zeitung*, 10 May 1965.

20. Interview, author with Ekkehart Krippendorff, 21 January 1987.

21. Quoted in *Die Welt*, 21 May 1965.

22. *Berliner Zeitung (B.Z.)*, 19 May 1965. (This is a Springer-owned West Berlin newspaper.)

23. See *Neues Deutschland*, 14 May 1965, in which the GDR paper noted that several professors had declared themselves in sympathy with the students. See also the *Berliner Zeitung* of East Berlin, 19 and 20 May 1965, in which the eastern press pointedly referred to the irony contained in the word "free" in the title of its

long-standing competitor.

24. See the *Frankfurter Allgemeine Zeitung* from 19 and 28 May 1965.

25. See *Die Welt*, 24 and 27 May 1965, and the *Berliner Morgenpost*, 16 and 21 May 1965.

26. Interview, author with Wolfgang Lefèvre, 5 February 1987. See also *Der Abend*, 1 June 1965, and *Kurier*, 29 May 1986.

27. Interview, author with Wolfgang Lefèvre, 5 February 1987. For contemporary accounts see *Der Abend*, 1 June 1965, *Kurier*, 1 June 1965, *Tagesspiegel*, 1 June 1965; the rest of the Berlin press joined in, some reporting the stormy meeting as a victory for moderates, others claiming it a moral victory for Lefèvre.

28. *Der Abend*, 5 June 1965.

29. Ibid., report and interviews assembled by Ulrich Eggenstein for *Der Abend*.

30. *Tagesspiegel*, 16 June 1965.

31. See *Süddeutsche Zeitung*, 11 July 1965.

32. Ibid.

33. *Die Welt*, 28 July 1965.

34. This was also the opinion of Berlin's education minister, Senator Werner Stein. See his report of 15 October 1967, concerning "The Development and Causes of Tensions at the Free University of Berlin," p. 7, hereafter cited as Stein Report, 15 October 1967.

35. Quoted in Uwe Schlicht, *Vom Burschenschafter bis zum Sponti: Studentische Opposition Gestern und Heute*, Berlin, 1980, p. 56. See also Tilman Fichter and Siegward Lönnendonker, *Kleine Geschichte des SDS*, Berlin, 1977, pp. 88–89, hereafter cited as *Kleine Geschichte*.

36. HSA FUB, Akademischer Senat, Sitzungsprotokolle nebst Vorlagen und Anglagen (hereafter cited as Files of the Academic Senate), 1965, letter by six former *Senatssprecher* to Lüers, 14 June 1965.

37. Interview, author with Ekkehart Krippendorff, 21 January 1987.

38. *Spandauer Volksblatt*, 14 May 1965.

39. *Spandauer Volksblatt*, 19 May 1965.

40. *FU Dokumentation IV*, Die Krise, p. 206.

41. Reprinted in *Christ und Welt*, 30 July 1965.

42. Interview, author with Ekkehart Krippendorff, 21 January 1987.

43. *Kurier*, 14 July 1965.

44. *Tagesspiegel*, 23 July 1965.

45. HSA FUB, Akademischer Senat, Sitzungsprotokolle nebst Vorlagen und Anglagen (hereafter cited as Files of the Academic Senate), 1965, letter, Lüers to Sontheimer, 18 March 1965; reprinted in *Tagesspiegel*, 28 July 1965.

46. Interview, author with Knut Nevermann, 2 March 1987.

47. Interview, author with Ekkehart Krippendorff, 21 January 1987.

48. *Die Zeit*, 6 August 1965, p. 9.

49. *Die Zeit*, 24 September 1965.

50. *Tagesspiegel*, 17 July 1965.

51. *Tagesspiegel*, 22 July 1965.

52. *Telegraf*, 23 July 1965.

53. *Tagesspiegel*, 23 July 1965.

54. *Die Welt*, 28 July 1965.

55. *Tagesspiegel*, 28 July 1965.

56. Interview, author with Werner Stein, 30 March 1987.

57. Cited in Hartmut Häussermann, Niels Kadritzke, and Knut Nevermann, *Die Rebellen von Berlin*, Cologne, 1967, p. 71; hereafter cited as *Rebellen*.

58. See Wolfgang Juche, "Studentenvertretung an der Freien Universität Ber-

lin," in Georg Kotowski, ed., *Die Freie Universität Berlin*, 1965, pp. 81–82.

59. Ibid., p. 83. The FU Senate was not pleased with Juche's contribution, but it appeared in the official publication anyway. See HSA FUB, Files of the Academic Senate, 1965, minutes of meeting for 28 July 1965, p. 10.

60. *Tagesspiegel*, 1 August 1965.

61. *New York Times*, 8 August 1965.

62. Report by the Senator for Science and Art of 15 October 1967 to Berlin House of Deputies, " . . . Concerning the Development and Causes of Tensions at the Free University of Berlin," p. 9, in the Gerd Löffler Papers, copy in author's possession; hereafter cited as Stein Report of 15 October 1967.

63. Interview, author with Hans-Joachim Lieber, 13 February 1987.

64. Interview, author with Wolfgang Lefèvre, 5 February 1987.

65. Hans-Joachim Lieber, *Blick Zurück: Biographisches zur Hochschulpolitik in Deutschland, 1945–1982*, Cologne, 1982, p. 18.

66. See *Rebellen*, p. 73; interview, author with Hans-Joachim Lieber, 13 February 1987.

67. *Kleine Geschichte*, p. 90.

68. Ibid.

69. See Stein Report of 15 October 1967, p. 13.

70. See *FU Spiegel*, no. 50 (February 1966), pp. 15–18.

71. FFA, roll 1292, PA 63-348, memo, "Student Unrest at the Free University Berlin" with accompanying letter, Richard Löwenthal to Shepard Stone, 28 March 1967.

72. See *FU Dokumentation IV*, no. 547, Resolution of the Konvent, Meeting of 10 June 1966.

73. See *FU Spiegel*, no. 52 (June 1966), p. 5.

74. See *Tagesspiegel*, 19 June 1966.

75. Interview, author with Hans-Joachim Lieber, 13 February 1987; letter, Günter Neuhaus to author, 27 January 1987, in author's possession, copy in HSA FUB. Professor Neuhaus, too, was a member of the group, which met regularly in the homes of the various participants. The group had existed since the first years of the Free University's existence, and the membership of this inner circle changed only slowly. It discussed among other matters the selection of possible future rectors. It was unofficial but hardly conspiratorial and provided occasion for informal discussion of outstanding issues.

76. See Stein Report, 15 October 1967, p. 16.

77. See Ludwig von Friedeburg et al., *Freie Universität und politisches Potential der Studenten: Über die Entwicklung des Berliner Models und über den Anfang der Studentenbewegung in Deutschland*, Neuwied and Berlin, 1968, p. 324.

78. See Stein Report, 15 October 1967, p. 18.

79. See *Kleine Geschichte*, p. 100.

80. Interview, author with Knut Nevermann, 2 March 1987.

81. See *Kleine Geschichte*, p. 103.

82. As early as 1961, members of the SDS, which was considerably less radical then than in the late 1960s, proposed a triple parity scheme for university governance. It later became the core of the 1969 University Law at the Free University. See Sozialistischer Deutscher Studentenbund, *Hochschule in der Demokratie*, Berlin, 1961. For evidence of its influence on later reformers see Uwe Wesel, "Zur gegenwärtigen Situation der Hochschulreform," in *Neue Rundschau*, 83, 1 (1972), p. 87.

83. FFA, roll 1292, PA 63-348, memo, Löwenthal to Stone, 28 March 1967.

84. *FU Spiegel*, 55 (January 1967), p. 8.

85. See Stein Report, 15 October 1967, p. 25; interview, author with Hans-

Joachim Lieber, 13 February 1987.

86. Interview, author with Gerd Löffler, 4 March 1987. Ohnesorg's death became the subject of intense investigation by various authorities and student groups. The students discounted the rock-throwing incidents, and the police as stoutly defended the claim. There was little doubt that police crowd-control measures were not skillfully applied on that evening. On the other hand, individual students were beginning to cross a significant threshold in the spring of 1967, when they began to hurl objects at police during the increasingly violent demonstrations. Ohnesorg's tragic death had one beneficial result at least. It pointed out unmistakably that the police needed to improve their methods of controlling demonstrations. To be sure, more violence was to follow in the years ahead. However, the events of 2 June 1967 were not repeated. For a report with official bias on the events leading to Ohnesorg's death see Berlin Interior Senator Wolfgang Büsch, ed., "Die Protestbewegung unter den Studenten der Freien Universität Berlin," Berlin, July 1967 (mimeographed), pp. 2–21. For a viewpoint more sympathetic to the students see Knut Nevermann, ed., *Der 2. Juni 1967: Studenten zwischen Notstand und Demokratie. Dokumente zu den Ereignissen anlässlich des Schah-Besuches*, Cologne, 1967. The event still retains popular interest twenty years later. See Michael Sontheimer, "Ein Schuss in viele Köpfe," *Die Zeit*, 29 May 1987, pp. 13–17.

87. The Great Coalition of Christian Democrats and Social Democrats in the Bundestag accounted for 90 percent of the vote. Thus there was no effective opposition from 1966 until 1969 when the Social Democrats won at the polls and entered a smaller coalition with the Free Democrats. Leftist student suspicion of the Great Coalition prompted the use of the term "APO."

88. FFA, roll 1292, PA 63-348, internal memo by Stone, 14 June 1967,

89. Interview, author with Gerd löffler, 4 March 1987.

90. Interview, author with Otto von Simson, 11 March 1987.

91. Interviews, author with Wolfgang Lefèvre, 5 February 1987, with Knut Nevermann, 2 March 1987, and with Werner Stein, 30 March 1987.

92. Interview, author with Werner Stein, 30 March 1987.

93. The founders of the "KU" looked at it as a major new institutional founding and as a counterbalance to the Free University. See *Kleine Geschichte*, pp. 112–114. The FU AStA, discontented with official accounts of the student movement at the Free University, published its own version in a volume with a characteristic title, *Von der Freien Universität zur Kritischen Universität: Geschichte der Krise an der Freien Universität Berlin*, Berlin, 1967.

94. Quoted in Cyril Levitt, *Children of Privilege: Student Revolt in the 1960s*, Toronto, 1984, p. 125.

95. Quoted in *Kleine Geschichte*, p. 102.

96. Interview, author with Knut Nevermann, 2 March 1987.

97. See Gretchen Dutschke-Klotz, Helmut Gollwitzer, and Jürgen Miermeister, eds., *Rudi Dutschke, Mein Langer Marsch*, Hamburg, 1980, p. 128.

98. *Der Spiegel*, 28, 18 (29 April 1968), pp. 8, 20. Those who knew Dutschke personally were struck by his charm and his engaging personality. Richard Löwenthal, no friend of the student radicals, found him to be a worthwhile student and a brilliant disputant. Interview, author with Richard Löwenthal, 24 March 1987. Dutschke even corresponded with young Bachmann in prison and, ever the proselytizer, tried to educate him politically. He was saddened when Bachmann took his life. See *Rudi Dutschke, Mein Langer Marsch*, pp. 130–137.

99. Quoted in *Rudi Dutschke, Mein Langer Marsch*, p. 129.

100. See Harold Hurwitz, "Germany's 'New Jews,'" *Transition*, 7, 37 (9 October 1968), 32–34; Hurwitz repeated the theme in "Germany's New Left Revolt," *The New Leader*, 45, 12 (6 May 1968), 9–12.

101. Joint Berlin AStA proclamation reprinted in *Tagesspiegel*, 17 April 1968.

102. HSA FUB, Kuratorialverwaltung, Akte, Nr. 1/1000 (Allgemeines), memo, Bergmann (n.d.), "20 Jahre Freie Universität Berlin . . . ."

103. Interview, author with Knut Nevermann, 2 March 1987.

104. FFA, roll 1292, PA 63-348, Hans Simons, "Berlin Report," 20 January 1967, p. 4.

105. Interview, author with Knut Nevermann, 2 March 1987.

106. FFA, roll 1292, PA 63-348, Hans Simons, "Berlin Report," 20 January 1967, p. 5.

107. For an excellent contemporary examination of the dissident movement by an informed eyewitness to the events at the Free University, see Richard L. Merritt, "The Student Protest Movement in West Berlin," in *Comparative Politics*, 1, 1 (1968–1969), pp. 516–533.

108. See *Tagesspiegel*, 10 October 1968, p. 8.

109. For sources on the planning of the Klinikum Steglitz see HSA FUB, Kuratorialverwaltung, Akte 6/6235, Universitätsklinikum Steglitz. Planning began in 1958. Planning for the JFK Institute began in 1962. See FFA, roll 1292, PA 63-348, for various reports on its progress from 1962 to 1975.

110. Files of the FU Aussenamt, "Leningrad Austausch Vertrag," minutes of meeting of 20 January 1966, recorded by Dr. Horst Hartwich, p. 1.

111. Files of the FU Aussenamt, "Leningrad Austausch Vertrag," letter, Horst Hartwich to Jürgen Mayer, 27 May 1970.

112. Files of the FU Aussenamt, "Leningrad Austausch Vertrag," letter, Ewald Harndt to Julius Speer, DFG, 1 September 1969.

113. Interview, author with Horst Hartwich, 13 May 1987; for Gerhard Löwenthal's commentary see Jochen Staadt, Annemarie Kleinert, and Peter Jahn, eds., *FU Dokumentation VI*, entry for 4 December 1969. Although the Free University and Leningrad University had concluded an exchange, this had no effect upon relations betwen the two sister universities in Berlin. Relations between the Free University and Humboldt University remained as frosty as ever. (N.B. Volume VI of this series has new editors who were appointed by President Heckleman to replace the previous editors of volumes I-V.)

114. Interview, author with Ewald Harndt, 16 March 1987.

115. BDC retains Harndt's records indicating he joined the NSDAP on 1 May 1937. The Center contains no evidence of any further activity although student editors in one of the last unofficial editions of the *FU Spiegel* claimed Harndt had also been a member of various National Socialist auxiliary organizations. See *FU Spiegel*, 14 (November/December 1968), p. 1.

116. HSA FUB, AStA, Akte Nr. 117, *FU Spiegel*, Schriftwechsel, 1967–1968, press announcement by rector, 15 February 1968.

117. See *FU Spiegel*, 63 (February 1968), p. 30. The apology notice appeared in the *FU Spiegel*, 67 (November/December 1968), p. 1; for individual reactions by the Free University faculty to the appearance of the letter see HSA FUB, AStA, Akte Nr. 345, 346. *FU Spiegel*, Leserbriefe . . . , 1964–1968, letter, Ernst Fraenkel to editors of the *FU Spiegel*, 4 March 1968; the editor, Reinhard Mayer, wrote a prompt apology to Mayor Schütz on 14 February 1968. The young editors received numerous reader complaints about their poor judgment in publishing the letter. However, there was also little doubt that controversy also stirred interest. Various magazines, journals, student governments, news-clipping services, and individuals began ordering subscriptions to the *FU Spiegel*.

118. See *FU Spiegel*, 65 (June/July 1968), p. 28. Fronius commented in bitter fashion upon university reform and social/political themes in the same issue, pp. 3–4.

119. See *Frankfurter Allgemeine Zeitung*, 29 June 1968.

120. For a catalogue of the confrontations that took place under Harndt's rectorship see the minutely detailed collection of documents in *FU Dokumentation* V, *Gewalt und Gegengewalt, 1967–1969*, Berlin, 1983.

121. FFA, roll 1292, PA 63-348, memo, Simons to Swearer, 12 March 1970.

FIVE: THE FREE UNIVERSITY AND REFORM, 1968 TO 1983

1. For some positive prognostications about Berlin as a center of high technology in the late 1980s see Julian C. Hollick, "West Berlin: Forty Years After," in *World View*, 28, 6 (June 1985), pp. 7–10. See also Richard L. Merritt and Anna J. Merritt, *Living with the Wall: West Berlin, 1961–1965*, Raleigh, North Carolina, 1985.

2. FFA, roll 1292, PA 63-348, memo, Hans Simons to Howard Swearer, 12 March 1970.

3. See *FU Dokumentation* V, *Gewalt und Gegengewalt, 1967–1969*, Berlin, 1983, p. 412; it is worth comparing to Senator Stein's original bill of 19 June 1967, which is reprinted, along with SPD, CDU, and FDP proposals, in Wilhelm Wengler and Josef Titel, eds., *Berliner Entwürfe zu einem Universitätsgesetz sowie das Hochschulgesetz vom 21.1.1963*, Berlin, 1968.

4. *FU Dokumentation* V, pp. 412–413.

5. Interview, author with Horst Hartwich, 24 November 1985.

6. Interview, author with Werner Stein, 30 March 1987.

7. Files of the U.S. Information Service (hereafter cited as USIS) in Berlin, File Educ FU 9, memo, Brewster Morris to State Department, 11 February 1970.

8. Cited in *FU Dokumentation* V, p. 412.

9. Interview, author with Eberhard Lämmert, 27 July 1987.

10. Interview, author with Rolf Kreibich, 26 January 1987.

11. Interview, author with Gerd Löffler, 4 March 1987.

12. Interviews, author with Werner Stein, 30 March 1987, with Ingeborg Sengpiel, 9 February 1987, with Gerd Löffler, 4 March 1987, and with Rolf Kreibich, 26 January 1987.

13. Interview, author with Rolf Kreibich, 26 January 1987.

14. FFA, roll 1292, PA 63-348, memo, William B. Bader to Francis X. Sutton, 19 November 1971.

15. Files of the USIS in Berlin, File Educ FU 9, memo, Morris to State, 11 February 1970.

16. Interview, author with Rolf Kreibich, 26 January 1987.

17. FFA, roll 1292, PA 63-348, memo, William B. Bader to Francis X. Sutton, 19 November 1971.

18. *New York Times*, 25 November 1969.

19. Interview, author with Werner Stein, 30 November 1986.

20. See *FU Dokumentation* VI, entry for 10 November 1969.

21. See *FU Dokumentation* VI, entry for 19 November 1969.

22. See *FU Dokumentation* VI, entry for 15 December 1969.

23. Interview, author with Uwe Wesel, 22 October 1986. A jovial personality with a quick wit which was to stand him in good stead during the many tense confrontations to come, Wesel played in some respects the role of a "Danton" at the Free University in its days of incipient revolution.

24. Files of the USIS in Berlin, File Educ FU 9, memo by Hans N. Tuch to Brewster Morris for dispatch to U.S. State Department and Department of Health, Education, and Welfare, 22 December 1969, copy on file with HSA FUB; hereafter cited as USIS Report with appropriate date. Tuch followed events closely at the Free University during the years of crisis. His positive initial impression of

Kreibich rapidly evaporated. Interview, author with Hans N. Tuch, 28 December 1987. Although Morris as Minister sent the memoranda to the State Department under his signature, they represented the efforts of U.S. Mission officials like Tuch.

25. USIS Report, 22 December 1969.

26. Ibid.

27. Ibid., p. 2.

28. See *FU Dokumentation* VI, entries for 3 December and 26 December 1969.

29. For an overview of Besser's activities as the Berlin CDU's expert on universities see *FU Dokumentation* VI, "Zeitgenössischer Kommentar," interview, Annemarie Kleinert with Ursula Besser, 11 March 1987.

30. See *FU Dokumentation* VI, entry for 8 December 1969.

31. Interview, author with Richard Löwenthal, 24 March 1987.

32. Ibid.

33. USIS Report, 22 December 1969, p. 2.

34. Ibid., p. 3.

35. Ibid. U.S. Mission officials met with Kreibich and with the university's long-serving director of foreign affairs Horst Hartwich during the lengthy interview. The Americans greatly respected Hartwich, "who vis-a-vis some previous rectors had occupied the position of an 'eminence grise,'" stated the American officials in their internal report. Hartwich, whose well-known political conservatism was at odds with Kreibich's politics, nevertheless had positive words on that occasion to say privately to the Americans about the young president, declaring him to be "honest" and "positively motivated . . ." although he had reservations about the new president's largely unknown staff. It spoke well for Kreibich's acumen that despite the sentiment of other staffers to transfer Hartwich to an administrative position at Klinikum Steglitz, he retained his older official as the university's director of foreign affairs, a key administrative position that demanded experience and expertise. The choice reflected the university's continuing commitment to international programs and ties that were unique among universities in the German-speaking world. Hartwich, with Kreibich's full knowledge and blessing, remained the FU president's contact to the American officials in Berlin.

36. Files of the USIS in Berlin, File Educ FU 9, memo, Morris to State, 11 February 1970.

37. See *Tagesspiegel*, 3 April 1970.

38. See *FU Dokumentation* VI, entry for 8 April 1970.

39. See *Die Welt*, 13 April 1970.

40. See TV magazine *Panorama* for 29 May 1970.

41. See *FU Dokumentation* VI, entry for 13 April 1970.

42. See Author Collective of the Psychological Institute of the Free University, *Sozialistische Projektarbeit im Berliner Schülerladen Rote Freiheit*, Frankfurt, 1971. "The authors of this report," so read the preface, " . . . are not specified because this project represents a collective assignment, and its ideas were formulated by the author collective." See preface, p. 2.

43. See *FU Dokumentation* VI, entry for 2 June 1971.

44. See *FU Dokumentation* VI, entry for 19 October 1970.

45. For an overview of NOFU activities see H. J. Geisler, R. Hentschke, I. Pommerening, eds., *Fünfzehn Jahre Notgemeinschaft, 1970 bis 1985*, Berlin, 1986. See also reprint of a speech by Uwe Wesel in Das Argument, ed., *Die NOFU: Rechskräfte an der Uni*, Studienheft Series, no. 22, Berlin, 1979, pp. 17–26.

46. In 1980, for example, NOFU published a list of no less than 1,700 names of radicals. See *FU Info*, 16/80 (31 October 1980), p. 7, and 18/80 (28 November 1980), p. 9.

47. Interview, author with Wolfgang Dumke, 1 July 1986.

48. FFA, roll 1292, PA 63-348, report by Nipperdey, "Decline and Fall of the Free University of Berlin," n.d. (1971), p. 6; hereafter cited as Nipperdey Report.

49. Interview, author with Uwe Wesel, 22 October 1986.

50. Ibid.

51. Jürgen Domes and Armin Paul Frank, "The Tribulations of the Free University of Berlin," *Minerva*, 13, 2 (Summer 1975), p. 188.

52. Speech reprinted in NOFU publication, "2. Medizinerbrief," n.d. (March or April 1973).

53. Ibid., pp. 2–3; interview, author with Günter Neuhaus, 23 March 1987.

54. Domes and Frank, "Tribulations . . . ," in *Minerva*, 13, 2, p. 195.

55. See Allensbach Institut für Demoskopie, *Universitäts-Report Berlin*, Lake Constance, February 1970, p. 2.

56. Ibid., pp. 3–5.

57. Ibid., pp. 7–9.

58. FFA, roll 1292, PA 63-348, letter, Philipp to Bell, 3 August 1970, original in German with English translation.

59. FFA, roll 1292, PA 63-348, memo, William B. Bader to Francis X. Sutton, 19 November 1971, p. 3.

60. Interview, author with Rolf Kreibich, 26 January 1987.

61. Nipperdey Report, p. 9.

62. Ibid., pp. 9–10.

63. Ibid., p. 13.

64. FFA, roll 1292, PA 63-348, memo, Bader to Sutton, 19 November 1971. Löwenthal's emotional response was not without some reason. He had incurred the special wrath of the far left at the OSI, who hanged him in effigy at least once and were fond of referring to him as the *Oberschwein*, or chief pig.

65. FFA, roll 1292, PA 63-348; Craufurd D. Goodwin to Francis X. Sutton, 6 December 1971.

66. Files of the USIS in Berlin, File Educ FU 9, memo, David Klein to State, 26 January 1972.

67. Ibid., p. 3.

68. Ibid.

69. Ibid., pp. 3–4.

70. See *FU Dokumentation VI*, "Zeitgenössischer Kommentar," interview, Annemarie Kleinert with Alexander Schwan, 12 March 1987; hereafter cited as Schwan-Kleinert Interview.

71. Interview, author with Werner Skuhr, 23 July 1987. Skuhr recalls that following a tense confrontation between police and students who had occupied the OSI in 1968, the police decided at the last moment not to remove the demonstrators. However, the strain had been such that a number of OSI professors gathered in a nearby residence to discuss matters. It was then, Skuhr recalls, that Prof. Ziebura announced the death of the *Ordinarienuniversität*, and there was general agreement among all of the OSI professors from each part of the political spectrum. Skuhr recalls that even future critics of the reforms cooperated at first. Arnulf Baring, for example, wrote the preamble to the OSI constitution. Richard Löwenthal, despite his reservations about its practicality, loyally supported it before the Academic Senate.

72. Schwan-Kleinert Interview, p. 2.

73. Interview, author with Alexander Schwan, 23 February 1987.

74. Alexander Schwan, "Die Hochschulreform in der Krise," Neue Rundschau, 82, 4 (1971), p. 693.

75. Ibid., p. 694.

76. Ibid., p. 702; see also Schwan-Kleinert Interview, p. 3.

77. Schwan, "Hochschulreform . . . " Neue Rundschau, pp. 706–707.

78. Ibid., pp. 709–710.

79. See Berliner Stimme, 27 May 1971.

80. Uwe Wesel, "Zur gegenwärtigen Situation der Hochschulreform," Neue Rundschau, 83, 1 (1972), p. 94.

81. Ibid., p. 100.

82. Ibid., p. 105. In referring to the coexistence of bourgeois Wissenschaft and wissenschaftliche or scientific socialism, Wesel was making use of a play on words. However, he did not elaborate on what he meant by that form of socialism. Marx referred to his form of socialism as "scientific" as compared to what he disparagingly called utopian socialist schemes among his predecessors. Presumably, Wesel, too, was using the same terminology, and, in essence, openly endorsing Marxism. To be sure, this did little to endear him to the more conservative elements at the Free University.

83. There were certain compensating factors that made this "defenestration" less grave than the launching of two imperial representatives from the top of Prague's Hradschin Castle into a pile of dung in 1618. Fortunately for Schwan his seminar room was on the ground floor, although a second attempt to launch him from his second-floor office was potentially more serious. In any case there was no cushioning mound of manure to be found anywhere near the OSI.

84. Interview, author with Alexander and Gesine Schwan, February 1987; see also FU Dokumentation VI, entry for 24 June 1971, for summaries of news coverage of the event. Virtually all the major newspapers reported on the violent episode.

85. Interview, author with Werner Skuhr, 23 July 1987. The slogans read in German: Zerschlagt die bürgerliche Wissenschaft! and Nicht Umfunktionieren, Sondern Vernichten!

86. Files of the USIS in Berlin, File Educ FU 9, minute sheet, 14 January 1972, meeting, Jackling with Kreibich, attached to memo, Klein to Department of State, 15 February 1972; hereafter cited as Jackling Report.

87. Files of the USIS in Berlin, File Educ FU 9, memo, Klein to State, 28 April 1972, p. 2.

88. Ibid., pp. 2–3.

89. Ibid., pp. 3–4.

90. Ibid., p. 6

91. Ibid., p. 4.

92. In his lengthy rebuttal to Schwan's article in the Neue Rundschau, Wesel had noted in passing the former's rough treatment at the hands of students, but he also stated that Schwan had provoked the encounter with strong language in one of Berlin's mass-circulation dailies, Der Abend. See Wesel Report, p. 102. Eventually, Wesel's differing political views led to a parting of the ways from his old party, the SPD. Schwan, too, underwent a major shift in his political allegiance. Like Wesel, he left the SPD, but unlike Wesel, Schwan moved steadily to the right, ending up in the CDU instead.

93. Files of the USIS in Berlin, File Educ FU 9, memo, Morris to State, 11 February 1970.

94. Interview, author with Uwe Wesel, 22 October 1986.

95. See FU Dokumentation VI, entry for 14 June 1971.

96. See *FU Dokumentation* VI, entry for 5 June 1972.

97. Files of the USIS in Berlin, File Educ FU 9, memo, Klein to Department of State, 2 June 1972. Kreibich, Klein noted, had engaged in a public anti-Vietnam demonstration. Although he did not mention the specific incident, it may refer to Kreibich's public declaration of protest along with American university presidents after the deaths of four students at Kent State University in 1970. See *FU Dokumentation* VI, entry for 8 May 1970.

98. Files of the USIS in Berlin, File Educ FU 9, memo, Klein to Department of State, 2 June 1972.

99. Jackling Report, p. 2.

100. Senator for Science and Art, ed., *Berliner Hochschulgesetze,* Berlin, 1974, p. 5; hereafter cited as 1974 Berlin University Law.

101. See *Der Abend,* 24 January 1974.

102. For a follow-up report on the legal maneuvering and the political implications surrounding this affair, see Jürgen Engert, "Nachholbedarf der Linken," in *Christ und Welt,* 6 September 1974.

103. Files of the USIS in Berlin, File a-81, memo, Borg to Department of State, 27 March 1974, p. 2; hereafter cited as Borg memo with date.

104. Ibid., p. 3.

105. Ibid., p. 4.

106. 1974 University Law, p. 4.

107. Borg memo, 27 March 1974, p. 5.

108. 1974 University Law, p. 3.

109. The Senator for Science and Research, ed., *Gesetz über die Hochschulen im Land Berlin (Berliner Hochschulgesetz-BerlHG),* Berlin, 1979, p. 32 (¶62).

110. Ibid., p. 21 (¶23).

111. Ibid., p. 27 (¶37).

112. FFA, roll 1292, PA 63-348, memo by Professors Baring, Brumm, Frank, Lenz, and Peper, "based on a letter of May 2, 1972, to Senator Stein"; hereafter cited as JFKI letter of May 2, 1972.

113. Files of the USIS in Berlin, file cultural-general, memo, Zivetz to Catherman, 24 April 1972, pp. 2–3, hereafter cited as the Zivetz Report.

114. Ibid.

115. JFKI letter of May 2, 1972, p. 4.

116. Ibid., pp. 4–5.

117. Ibid., p. 5.

118. Zivetz Report, p. 2.

119. JFKI letter of May 2, 1972, p. 6.

120. Zivetz Report, p. 3.

121. Files of the USIS in Berlin, File Educ FU 9, memo, Borg to Department of State, 7 August 1972, p. 4; hereafter cited as Borg Report.

122. Files of the USIS in Berlin, File Educ FU 9, memo, David Klein to Department of State, 2 June 1972, attachment, "memo of Conversation," 25 May 1972.

123. FFA, roll 1292, PA 63-348, "Report on the John F. Kennedy Institute," by Ursula Brumm, attached to memo by Moselle Kimbler, 1 December 1973.

124. Borg Report, p. 2.

125. Files of the USIS in Berlin, File Educ FU 9, memo of conversation, Jan Zehner with Arnulf Baring, 27 February 1973, p. 2; hereafter cited as Zehner Report.

126. Borg Report, p. 3.

127. Files of the USIS in Berlin, File Educ FU 9, memo, Klein to Department of State, 10 November 1972, enclosure, memo of conversation, Lee and Catherman with Heimann, 31 October 1972, p. 2.

128. FFA, roll 1292, PA 63-348, letter, Shepard Stone to McGeorge Bundy, 18 February 1975.

129. FFA, roll 1292, PA 63-348, memo, Moselle Kimbler to Craufurd D. Goodwin, 1 December 1973.

130. FFA, roll 1292 PA 63-348, memo with office slip from Peter Ruof to McGeorge Bundy and Francis X. Sutton dated 14 April 1975. Another Ford Foundation official, senior to Ruof, poured cold water on making threats about removing the library. It was "not clear to me that we help Kreibich to do the right thing by pressing him on the JFK Library . . . ," quoted in a memo, Sutton to Ruof, 14 April 1975.

131. FFA, roll 1292, PA 63-348, memo, Peter Ruof to Craufurd D. Goodwin, 23 October 1975.

132. Borg Report, p. 4.

133. For a charming if somewhat idealized description of English Studies at the Free University in the early and mid-1960s see Uwe Schipper, "Erinnerungen an das Englische Seminar der Freien Universität Berlin in den frühen 60er Jahren," in Manfred Scheler, ed., Berliner Anglistik in Vergangenheit und Gegenwart, 1810–1985, Berlin, 1987, pp. 197–200; hereafter cited as Scheler.

134. Stewart Anderson, Zur Sozialstruktur des Englischen Seminars der Freien Universität Berlin: Interim Findings from a Research Project into the Social Structure of a University Department, Berlin, 1971, p. 36. To be sure, Anderson's study aroused considerable anger among some members of the English Department's staff who claimed he was being uniformly critical of all operations in the department. One of his many critics, Hubert Gburek, dismissed Anderson's criticisms as so many sour grapes, claiming that the visiting lecturer was disappointed at not acquiring a permanent teaching position at the Free University in modern languages (see Hubert Gburek, "Erinnerungen an das Englische Seminar der Freien Universität Berlin in den späten 60er und frühen 70er Jahren," in Scheler, p. 203). Anderson's work later appeared as a sociology dissertation, The Social Pathology of a University Department, University of Surrey, 1974. Thus, it was unlikely, to say the least, that frustrated career plans at the Free University induced him to undertake his sociological survey. It is, in fact, a useful survey with valuable firsthand student accounts concerning the workings of a troubled department in a troubled time.

135. Ibid., p. 62.

136. See Wissenschaftsrat, Empfehlungen zur Neuordnung des Studiums an den wissenschaftlichen Hochschulen, Berlin, 1966, pp. 5–36. See also Ulrich Teichler, "Higher Education Reforms and Changing Employment Prospects of Graduates," in Günter Kloss, ed., Education Policy in the Federal Republic of Germany, 1969–1984, Manchester, England, 1985, pp. 57–77.

137. See Senator für Wissenschaft und Kunst, Gesetz über die Hochschulen im Land Berlin (Berliner Hochschulgesetz—BerlHG), Berlin, 1979, p. 16 (¶ 10).

138. See FU Dokumentation VI, entries for 20 April, 5 May, and 9 June 1971. See also Weser Kurier, 5 July 1971. See also Frankfurter Allgemeine Zeitung, 20 May 1971.

139. See FU Dokumentation VI, entry for 30 June 1971.

140. Private papers of Wolfgang Wippermann (hereafter cited as Wippermann Papers), Wippermann report, " . . . Session . . . of 14 December 1976," pp. 1–2; copy in author's possession.

141. Ibid., pp. 5–6.

142. Kommunistische Hochschulzeitung (hereafter cited as KHZ), 11 January 1977.

143. Wippermann Papers, copy of a Decision of II Chamber of the Berlin Court

of 29 May 1974, Christian Raseneck versus the Free University of Berlin. The Court found that the instructor's self-imposed conditions were too restrictive of the principle of freedom of expression. This undoubtedly contributed to the reluctance of President Lämmert and his staff to support Wippermann at first.

144. Both sides gave their detailed version of the story. See Wippermann Papers, letter, Wippermann to Vorsitzender des Fachbereichrates Nolte, 3 February 1977, with attached report. See also article in KHZ from 3 February 1977, "Wippermann festgenommen! Bedingungslose Scheinvergabe!" The KHG members declared openly their actions of February 1 and continued to demand that Wippermann give them passing grades in the seminar. Thus, they provided more evidence, if any were needed, of their illegal actions. The article proved to be highly damaging to themselves and was striking evidence that the KHG members were living in a world of their own ideological fantasy.

145. See Berliner Zeitung (B.Z.), 11 October 1977. In typical B.Z. fashion the layout of the article was sensational and could have been interpreted by the reader in such a way that the scantily clad model was one of those female students who had attacked Wippermann. It undoubtedly drew many smiles; it also drew attention to Wippermann's case.

146. Wippermann Papers, letter, Wippermann to Nolte, 11 April 1978. See also the KHG's flyer, "Wippermann Wandzeitung Nr. 1" of 30 January 1978, and the KHZ, 10 April 1978, p. 3.

147. For a general treatment of these trends in German higher education, see the Bundesminister für Bildung und Wissenschaft, ed., Grund- und Strukturdaten 1984/85, Bonn, 1984, pp. 108–183.

148. Interview, author with Rolf Kreibich, 26 January 1987.

149. Interview, author with Traugott Klose, 9 January 1987.

150. Interview, author with Werner Stein, 30 March 1987.

151. Files of the USIS in Berlin, File Educ FU 9, minute sheet, 14 January 1972, meeting between Jackling and Kreibich, attached to memo, Klein to Department of State, 15 February 1972.

152. Interview, author with Ernst Lämmert, 27 July 1987.

153. Files of the USIS in Berlin, File Educ 9, memorandum of conversation, 25 May 1972, Catherman with Kreibich, Hartwich, and Wesel, attached to memo, Klein to Department of State, 2 June 1972.

154. Files of the FU Aussenamt, letter, Martin Kermacy to Horst Hartwich, 3 November 1971.

155. Files of the FU Aussenamt, letter, Kermacy to Hartwich, 26 July 1972. However, the episode ultimately had a happy ending. In 1981, after a productive guest professorship by one of their faculty at the Free University, Bärbel Becker-Cantarino, the Texans reinstated the exchange program, which continues to this day. See Files of the FU Aussenamt, letter, Bärbel Becker-Cantarino to Horst Hartwich, 27 May 1981, confirming the resumption of the exchange program. Fortunately for the Free University's somewhat battered reputation at the time, news of the discontinuation did not spread far. Hartwich had been especially worried that forceful critics of the university's administration such as NOFU might have given the incident wide publicity in order to gain immediate political advantage. Such action might have led to other cancellations and to a further decline in the university's reputation.

156. See, for example, "Battle of Berlin," Time Magazine, 3 July 1972, p. 31; editorial, "Free University in Danger," New York Times, 9 March 1972; editorial, "The Death of a University," The Ottowa Journal, 30 March 1972, among others.

157. Files of the USIS in Berlin, File Educ FU 9, memorandum of conversation, Gunther Rosinus with Hartmut Jäckel, 29 August 1974.

158. Ibid., p. 2.

159. Interview, author with Alexander Schwan, 27 August 1987.

160. HSA FUB, Poster Collection, Special Category: University Politics, poster entitled "25 Jahre FU: Universität im Dienst des Imperialismus," dated 4 December 1973.

161. Files of the USIS in Berlin, File Educ FU 9, International Visitors Program file for Rolf Kreibich, p. 3, attached to airgram, Hillenbrand to State, 31 July 1974.

162. See interview with Kreibich in FU Info, 9/76 (9 June 1976), p. 12.

163. Interview, author with Alexander Schwan, 27 August 1987.

164. Interview, author with Eberhard Lämmert, 27 July 1987.

165. Ibid.

166. Interview, author with Alexander Schwan, 27 August 1987.

167. See FU Info, 10/76 (23 June 1976), p. 10.

168. Interview, author with Werner Stein, 30 March 1987.

169. Interview, author with Alexander Schwan, 27 August 1987.

170. See FU Info, 18/76 (8 December 1976), p. 8.

171. See Uwe Schlicht, Vom Burschenschafter bis zum Sponti: Studentische Opposition Gestern und Heute, Berlin, 1980, p. 130.

172. See Hans Joachim Geisler, Richard Hentschke, and Ingo Pommerening, eds., 15 jahre Notgemeinschaft, 1970 bis 1985, Berlin, 1986, pp. 82–93.

173. Interview, author with Eberhard Lämmert, 27 July 1987.

174. Interview, author with Gerd Löffler, 4 March 1987; see also Schlicht, Vom Burschenschafter . . . , p. 134.

175. See Eberhard Lämmert, Rechenschaftsbericht des Präsidenten der Freien Universität, 14. Februar 1978, Berlin, 1978, p. 4. For a fuller treatment of the trend toward the mass university as well as the malaise affecting students in the late 1970s see also Uwe Schlicht, Vom Burschenschafter . . . ," pp. 109–153.

176. See Lämmert, Rechenschaftsbericht . . . , p. 5.

177. Quoted in FU Info, 17/76 (18 November 1976), p. 10.

178. See Günther Kloss, "The Academic Restructuring of British and German Universities and Greater Efficiency: a Comparative Perspective," in Oxford Review of Education, 11, 3 (1985), pp. 271–282.

179. Interview, author with Jurgen Herbst, 29 August 1987.

180. See FU Info, 1/80 (18 January 1980), pp. 17–18, and 3/80 (15 February 1980), pp. 13–16.

181. For a brief description of the political maneuvering that led to the reorganization of the Fachbereich 11, see FU Info, 4/80 (14 March 1980), pp. 9–10.

182. See H. G. Altenmüller, "Der Rückgang ist dramatisch," in Deutsche Universitäts-Zeitung, 5/1984, p. 12. See also Ulrich Teichler, "Higher Education Reforms and Changing Employment Prospects of Graduates," in Günther Kloss, ed., Education Policy in the Federal Republic, 1969–1984, Manchester, 1984, pp. 64–65. The Free University's own weekly journal began to devote much attention to the tightening budget. See Wolf-Peter Rousselet, "Die fetten Jahre sind vorbei," in FU Info, 13/82 (22 October 1982), pp. 8–9.

183. Peter Glotz, "FU an geachtetem Platz," in FU Info, 14/83 (25 November 1983), pp. 7–8.

Six: Retrenchment and Consolidation

1. See Dieter Heckelmann, Rechenschaftsbericht . . . 25 November 1984 to 24 November 1986, p. 8; hereafter cited as 1986 Rechenschaftsbericht.

2. Ibid., pp. 4, 6–7.

3. Ibid., pp. 14–18.

4. FU President's Office, address by Dieter Heckelmann on the occasion of the conferring of Ernst Reuter Prizes, 11 December 1987; hereafter cited as Heckelmann Address. The Ernst Reuter Foundation was established in 1953 by former friends and admirers of the recently deceased Governing Mayor. Its membership included founding students like Otto Hess and Horst Hartwich plus leaders in Berlin's financial, commercial, and industrial circles. Since the early 1980s it has provided generous financial awards annually to five top Ph.D. recipients at the Free University for the award winners to defray the costs of publishing their dissertations.

5. Heckelmann Address.

6. Michael Erbe, *FU Info*, 10/86 (17 October 1986), p. 19.

7. Ibid.

8. Heckelmann Address, p. 2.

9. *1986 Rechenschaftsbericht*, p. 2. See also Uwe Schlicht, "Das Ende des hochschulpolitischen Bürgerkriegs," in *Tagesspiegel*, 5 September 1985.

10. The affair began modestly with an article written by "Reinhard Wagner" [a pseudonym generally ascribed to Johannes Schlootz], "Wende mit Haken und Ösen," which appeared in the *Deutsche Universitäts-Zeitung*, 7 April 1983. It then heated up in the summer and autumn of 1987 as the German press, faced with a generally quiet political scene, had a field day with the affair. See *Tagesspiegel*, 30 June 1987, 3 July 1987, and 7 November 1987, and *FAZ*, 27 June 1987, among others. See also Dorothea Hügenberg, "Ein Kandidat mit Haken und Ösen," in *Die Zeit*, 27 November 1987.

Sources

I. PRIMARY SOURCES

A. Archival Material

Archives of the University of Keele, Scotland
Lindsay Papers

Berlin Document Center
Personnel Files for thirty-six university professors

Bundesarchiv Koblenz
Fritz Epstein Papers
August Wilhelm Fehling Papers
James Pollock Papers
Eduard Spranger Papers

Ford Foundation Archives, New York
roll 489, Project PA 51-41
roll 2419, Project PA 58-260
roll 1292, Project PA 63-348

Free University of Berlin
Files of the Freie Universität Aussenamt
Files of the Hochschularchiv der Freien Universität Berlin (HSA FUB)
Academic Senate files
Allgemeiner Studenten-Ausschuss (AStA) files
Aussenkommission files
Erich Kuby file
Kurator (Chancellor) files
Kuratorialverwaltung (Chancellor's Office) files
Kuratorium (Board of Trustees) files
Law Faculty files
Philosophy Faculty files
Rector's Office files
Student Parliament files
Veterinary Medicine Faculty files
Georg Wrazidlo files

Public Record Office, Kew, London, Foreign Office Files
FO 371/70493
FO 371/70506
FO 371/70528
FO 371/70617
FO 371/70706
FO 1005/617
FO 1005/1729

U.S. Department of State, Berlin Mission
Reference Library, Historical Report, Office of Military Government, Berlin District, vol. V (1945–1946)

U.S. Information Service (USIS), Berlin
Education File FU 9

U.S. National Archives and Records Administration, Washington, DC
R.G. 59, U.S. Department of State, Lot 55D 374, Central European Division, G
    801.4, Berlin II
R.G. 59, U.S. Department of State, Central Decimal Files
    740.00119 Control, Germany
    811.42762 Cultural Relations, United States and Germany
    811.71562 International Parcel Post Arrangements
    862.42 Education, Germany
    862.4212 Higher Education, Germany
    862A.43 Education, West Germany
R.G. 84, Records of Foreign Service Posts of the Department of State
Records of the Office of the Political Adviser (POLAD), File 842, Education
R.G. 260, Records of the United States Occupation Headquarters, World War II
Records of the Office of Military Government (U.S.) for Germany (OMGUS)
R.G. 466, Records of the United States High Commission for Germany (HICOG)

Westdeutsche Rektorenkonferenz (WRK), Bad Godesberg
Proceedings of Rectors Meeting in Braunschweig, 27 July 1948
Proceedings of Rectors Meeting in Würzburg, 6–7 November 1948

Privately Owned Archival Material (copies in author's possession)
Aspen Institute Berlin, Symposium, 1–7 July 1984, unpublished proceedings
Edward Y. Hartshorne Papers, Silver Lake, New Hampshire
Gerd Löffler Papers, Berlin
Gerhard Petermann Papers, Munich
Claus Reuber Papers, Berlin
Horst Rögner-Francke Papers, Berlin
Joachim Schwarz Papers, Berlin
Richard W. Sterling Papers, Norwich, Vermont
Wolfgang Wippermann Papers, Berlin

B. Interviews conducted by James F. Tent (T)
and Peter Th. Walther (W)

Hans Ulrich Bach, Mühlheim am Rhein, 7 July 1986 (T)
Ursula Besser, Berlin, 29 January 1986 (T/W)
Helmut Coper, Berlin, 30 August and 4 September 1985 (T)
Wolfgang Dumke, Berlin, 1 July 1986 (T)
Eva Furth, née Heilmann, Berlin, 15 January 1986 (T/W)
Ewald Harndt, Berlin, 16 March 1987 (T/W)
Horst Hartwich, Berlin, 30 August, 4 September, 14, 24, and 27 November 1985,
11 June, 8 December 1986, and 13 May 1987 (T)
Jurgen Herbst, Berlin, 29 August 1987 (T)
Otto Hess, Berlin, 24 September 1985 and 28 April 1986 (T/W)
Christian and Hannelore Horn, Berlin, 8 July 1987 (T)
Frank Howley, New York, 17 September 1986 (T)
Howard W. Johnston, Berlin, 2 June 1987 (T)

Traugott Klose, Berlin, 9 January 1987 (T/W)
Rolf Kreibich, Berlin, 26 January 1987 (T/W)
Ekkehart Krippendorff, Berlin, 21 January 1987 (T/W)
Stanislaw Kubicki, Berlin, 17 January 1986 (T/W)
Eberhard Lämmert, Berlin, 27 July 1987 (T/W)
Wolfgang Lefèvre, Berlin, 5 February 1987 (T)
Hans Joachim Lieber, Cologne, 20 January 1986 (T/W) and 13 February 1987 (T)
Gerd Löffler, Berlin, 4 March 1987 (T/W)
Gerhard Löwenthal, Mainz, 11 February 1987 (T)
Richard Löwenthal, Berlin, 24 March 1987 (T/W)
Peter Lorenz, Berlin, 7 January 1986 (T/W)
Günter Neuhaus, Berlin, 23 March 1987 (T)
Knut Nevermann, Berlin, 2 March 1987 (T/W)
Hermann and Irene Oberländer, Berlin, 30 June 1987 (T)
Gerhard Petermann, Berlin, 27 October 1986 (T/W)
Claus Reuber, Berlin, 10 July 1987 (T/W)
Horst Rögner-Francke, Berlin, 25 February (T/W) and 20 March 1986 (T)
Gerda Rösch, Berlin, 23 January 1987 (T)
Alexander and Gesine Schwan, 23 January 1987 (T/W)
Alexander Schwan, Berlin, 27 August 1987 (T)
Joachim Schwarz, Berlin, 14 January 1987 (T)
Carl Hubert Schwennicke, Berlin, 7 February 1986 (T/W)
Ingeborg Sengpiel, Bonn, 31 October 1985 and 9 February 1987 (T)
Otto von Simson, Berlin, 11 March 1987 (T/W)
Werner Skuhr, Berlin, 23 July 1987 (T/W)
Dietrich Spangenberg, Berlin, 6 January 1986 (T/W)
Werner Stein, Berlin, 30 March 1987 (T)
Hans N. Tuch, Washington, D.C., 28 December 1987 (T)
Ingrid Vietig, née Friedmann, Berlin, 16 March 1987 (T)
Paul Wandel, Berlin, 15 July and 5 December 1986 (T)
Herman B Wells, Bloomington, Indiana, 25 July 1985 (T)
Wilhelm Wengler, Berlin, 5 March 1987 (T/W)
Uwe Wesel, Berlin, 22 October 1986 (T/W)

C. CORRESPONDENCE

Otto Hess to author, 25 July 1986
Stanislaw Kubicki to author, 7 June 1986
Hans Joachim Lieber to author, 7 June 1986
Günter Neuhaus to author, 27 January 1987
Herman B Wells to author, 28 December 1977

II. SECONDARY SOURCES

A. BOOKS

Anderson, Stewart. *The Social Pathology of a University Department.* Ph.D. diss. University of Surrey, 1974.
Anderson, Stewart. *Zur Sozialstruktur des Englischen Seminars der Freien Universität Berlin: Interim Findings from a Research Project into the Social Structure of a University Department.* Berlin, 1971.
AStA (Allgemeiner Studenten-Ausschuss) der Freien Universität Berlin, ed. *Von der Freien Universität zur Kritischen Universität: Geschichte der Krise an der Freien Universität.* Berlin, 1967.

Autorenkollektiv des Psychologischen Instituts der Freien Universität Berlin, ed. *Sozialistische Projektarbeit im Berliner Schülerladen Rote Freiheit*. Frankfurt am Main, 1971.

Berlin: Quellen und Dokumente 1945–1951. Berlin, 1964.

Bräuer, Herbert, et al., eds. *Materialien zur Geschichte der Slavistik in Deutschland*. Berlin, 1982.

Brandt, Willy, and Richard Löwenthal. *Ernst Reuter: Ein Leben für die Freiheit*. Berlin, 1967.

Brugsch, Theodor. *Arzt seit fünf Jahrzehnten*. Berlin, 1957.

Bundesminister für Bildung und Wissenschaft, ed. *Grund- und Strukturdaten 1984/85*. Bonn, 1984.

Clay, Lucius D. *Decision in Germany*. New York, 1950.

Davidson, W. Phillips. *The Berlin Blockade*. Princeton, 1958.

Dutschke-Klotz, Gretchen, Helmut Gollwitzer, and Jürgen Miermeister, eds. *Rudi Dutschke: Mein Langer Marsch*. Hamburg, 1980.

Engel, Michael. *Geschichte Dahlems*. Berlin, 1984.

Fichter, Tilman, and Siegward Lönnendonker, eds. *Freie Universität Dokumentation*, Vols. I-V. Berlin, 1973–1983.

Fichter, Tilman, and Siegward Lönnendonker. *Kleine Geschichte des SDS*. Berlin, 1977.

Freie Universität Berlin, ed. *Fünfzehn Jahre Freie Universität Berlin, 1948–1963*. Berlin, 1963.

Freie Universität Berlin, ed. *Gründungsfeier der Freien Universität Berlin*. Berlin, 1949.

Freie Universität: Vorlesungsverzeichnis. Wintersemester 1948/49. Berlin, 1949.

von Friedeburg, Ludwig, et al., eds. *Freie Universität und politisches Potential der Studenten: Über die Entwicklung des Berliner Models und über den Anfang der Studentenbewegung in Deutschland*. Neuwied and Berlin, 1968.

Friedrich Meinecke Institute, ed. *Das Friedrich-Meinecke-Institut der Freien Universität Berlin 1948–1959*. Berlin, 1959.

Gaddis, John L. *The United States and the Origins of the Cold War, 1941–1947*. New York, 1972.

Geisler, Hans-Joachim, Richard Hentschke, and Ingo Pommerning, eds. *Fünfzehn Jahre Notgemeinschaft, 1970 bis 1985*. Berlin, 1986.

Häussermann, Hartmut, Niels Kadritzke, and Knut Nevermann. *Die Rebellen von Berlin*. Cologne, 1967.

Hearndon, Arthur, ed. *The British in Germany: Educational Reconstruction after 1945*. London, 1978.

Howley, Frank. *Berlin Command*. New York, 1950.

Jahn, Peter, Annemarie Kleinert, and Jochen Staadt, eds. *Freie Universität Dokumentation*, Vol. VI. Berlin (forthcoming).

Kennan, George F. *Memoirs, 1925–1950*. Boston, 1967.

Klein, Helmut, ed. *Humboldt-Universität zu Berlin, Dokumente, 1810–1985*. Berlin, 1985.

Klein, Manfred. *Jugend zwischen den Diktaturen, 1945–1956*. Mainz, 1968.

Kotowski, Georg, ed. *Die Freie Universität*. Berlin, 1965.

Krieger, Wolfgang. *General Lucius D. Clay und die amerikanische Deutschlandpolitik 1945–1949*. Stuttgart, 1987.

Leonhard, Wolfgang. *Die Revolution entlässt ihre Kinder*. Cologne and Berlin, 1955.

Levitt, Cyril. *Children of Privilege: Student Revolt in the 1960s*. Toronto, 1984.

Magat, Richard. *The Ford Foundation at Work: Philanthropic Choices, Methods, and Styles*. New York, 1979.

Maginnis, John. *Military Government Journal*. Amherst, Massachusetts, 1971.

Merritt, Richard L., and Anna J. Merritt. *Living with the Wall: West Berlin, 1961–1985*. Raleigh, North Carolina, 1985.

Murphy, Robert. *Diplomat among Warriors*. New York, 1964.

Nelson, Daniel J. *Wartime Origins of the Berlin Dilemma*. Tuscaloosa, Alabama, 1978.

Nevermann, Knut, ed. *Der 2. Juni 1967: Studenten zwischen Notstand und Demokratie: Dokumente zu den Ereignissen anlässlich des Schahbesuches*. Cologne, 1967.

Niethammer, Lutz. *Entnazifizierung in Bayern: Säuberung und Rehabilitierung unter amerikanischer Besatzung*. Frankfurt am Main, 1972.

Phillips, David, ed. *German Universities after the Surrender: British Occupation Policy and the Control of Higher Education*. Oxford, 1983.

Phillips, David, ed. *Zur Universitätsreform in der britischen Besatzungszone, 1945–1948*. Cologne and Vienna, 1983.

Der Präsident der Freien Universität Berlin. *Rechenschaftsberichte*. Berlin, 1971–1986.

Radde, Gerd. *Fritz Karsen: Ein Berliner Schulreformer der Weimarer Zeit*. Berlin, 1973.

Redslob, Edwin. *Von Weimar nach Europa: Erlebtes und Durchdachtes*. Berlin, 1972.

Scheler, Manfred, ed. *Berliner Anglistik in Vergangenheit und Gegenwart, 1810–1985*. Berlin, 1987.

Schlicht, Uwe, ed. *Trotz und Träume: Jugend Lehnt Sich Auf*. Berlin, 1980.

Schlicht, Uwe. *Vom Burschenschafter bis zum Sponti: Studentische Opposition Gestern und Heute*. Berlin, 1980.

Schmidt, Hubert G. *Economic Assistance to West Berlin*. Bonn, 1952.

Seelinger, Rolf, ed. *Braune Universität: Deutsche Hochschullehrer Gestern und Heute*, Vol. 4: Westberlin. Munich, 1966.

Der Senator für Wissenschaft und Forschung [Peter Glotz]. *Gesetz über die Hochschulen im Land Berlin (Berlin Hochschulgesetz—BerlHG)*. Berlin, 1979.

Spranger, Eduard. *Gesammelte Schriften*, Vol. 10: *Hochschule und Gesellschaft*, ed. by Walter Sachs. Heidelberg, 1973.

Stadtverordneten-Versammlung von Gross-Berlin. *Veröffentlichungen*, No. 130, 79th Session. Berlin, 1948.

Tent, James F. *Mission on the Rhine: Reeducation and Denazification in American-Occupied Germany*. Chicago and London, 1982.

Universität Berlin: Vorlesungsverzeichnis. Sommersemester 1947. Berlin, 1947.

Universität Berlin: Vorlesungsverzeichnis. Sommersemester 1948. Berlin, 1948.

Veritas, Justitia, Libertas: Festschrift zur 200-Jahrfeier der Columbia University New York überreicht von der Freien Universität Berlin und der Deutschen Hochschule für Politik Berlin. Berlin, 1954.

Webster, Sir Charles, and Noble Frankland. *The Strategic Air Offensive against Germany*. Vol. 2. London, 1961.

Wells, Herman B. *Being Lucky: Reminiscences and Reflections*. Bloomington, Indiana, 1980.

Wengler, Wilhelm, and Josef Tittel, eds. *Berliner Entwürfe zu einem Universitätsgesetz sowie das Hochschulgesetz vom 21.1.1963*. Berlin, 1968.

Wissenschaftsrat. *Empfehlungen zur Neuordnung des Studiums an den wissenschaftlichen Hochschulen*. Berlin, 1966.

Ziemke, Earl F. *Stalingrad to Berlin: The German Defeat in the East*. Washington, D.C., 1968.

B. ARTICLES AND PAPERS

Allensbach Institut für Demoskopie. "Universitäts-Report Berlin," *Allensbacher Berichte*, Lake Constance, February 1970.

Altenmüller, H. G. "Der Rückgang ist dramatisch." *Deutsche Universitäts-Zeitung*, May 1984.

Berendt, Brigitte. "Studenten helfen Studenten: Elf Jahre Tutorenarbeit an der Freien Universität." *Fünfzehn Jahre Freie Universität 1948–1963*: 40–41.

Birley, Robert. "British Policy in Retrospect." In Arthur Hearndon, ed., *The British in Germany*. London, 1978: 60–61.

Böhm, Rudi. "Berlin: Gesicht einer Universität." *Forum*, 1, no. 1 (January 1947):15–17.

Diepgen, Eberhard. "Korporationen und Freie Universität." *Fünfzehn Jahre Freie Universität, 1948–1963*. Berlin, 1963: 35–36.

Domes, Jürgen, and Arnim Paul Frank. "The Tribulations of the Free University of Berlin." *Minerva*, 13, no. 2 (Summer 1975).

Engert, Jürgen. "Nachholbedarf der Linken." *Christ und Welt*, 6 September 1974.

Erbe, Michael. "Hochschulplanung unter dem Rotstift?" *FU Info*, 10/86 (17 October 1986): 17–21.

Foss, Kendall. "A New Freedom for Education." *New York Post*, 24 February 1947.

Franklin, William M. "Zonal Boundaries and Access to Berlin." *World Politics*, XVI, no. 1 (October 1963): 1–33.

Gburek, Hubert. "Erinnerungen an das Englische Seminar der Freien Universität in den späten 60er und frühen 70er Jahren." In Manfred Scheler, ed., *Berliner Anglistik in Vergangenheit und Gegenwart, 1810–1985*. Berlin, 1987: 201–204.

Glotz, Peter. "FU am geachteten Platz." *FU Info*, 14/83 (25 November 1983): 7–8.

Hammond, Paul Y. "Directives for the Occupation of Germany: The Washington Controversy." In Harold Stein, ed., *American Civil-Military Decisions*. Birmingham, Alabama, 1963.

Hartwich, Horst. "Bilanz der Aussenbeziehungen." *FU Info*, 3/87 (8 March 1987):15.

Heilmann, Eva. "The Student's Role in the Free University." *The American-German Review*, 18, no. 2 (December 1951):12.

Hess, Otto, and Joachim Schwarz. "Zum Geleit." *Colloquium. Zeitschrift für junge Akademiker*, 1, no. 1 (May 1947): 1–2.

Hollick, Julian C. "West Berlin: Forty Years After." *World View*, 28, no. 6 (June 1985): 7–10.

[Horizont]. Editorial to "Die Berliner Studenten haben das Wort." *Horizont. Halbmonatsschrift für junge Menschen*, 1, no. 26 (24 November 1946): 10.

Hügenberg, Dorothea. "Ein Kandidat mit Haken und Ösen." *Die Zeit*, 27 November 1987.

Hurwitz, Harold. "Germany's 'New Jews'." *Transition*, 7, no. 37 (9 October 1968): 32–34.

Hurwitz, Harold. "Germany's New Left Revolt." *The New Leader*, 45, no. 12 (6 May 1968): 9–12.

Johnston, Howard W. "My Role in the Founding of the Free University of Berlin," paper given at the Freie Universität Berlin, Fachbereich Erziehungswissenschaften, 3 June 1987.

Juche, Wolfgang. "Studentenvertretung an der Freien Universität Berlin." In Georg

Kotowski, ed., *Die Freie Universität Berlin*. Berlin, 1965: 81–82.

Kloss, Günther. "The Academic Restructuring of British and German Universities and Greater Efficiency: A Comparative Perspective." *Oxford Review of Education*, 11 (1985): 271–282.

Kotowski, Georg. "Der Kampf um Berlins Universität." In *Veritas, Justitia, Libertas*. Berlin, 1954: 7–31.

"L.G., Law Student," "Studentenwahlen in Berlin." *Forum*, 1, no. 2 (February 1947): 29.

Maskolat, Henny. "Arbeiterbewegung und Berliner Universität in der Wiedereröffnung, 1945-1946." *Wissenschaftliche Zeitschrift der Humboldt-Universität zu Berlin*, XV, 1966.

Maskolat, Henny. "Die Wiedereröffnung der Berliner Universität im Januar 1946." In *Forschen und Wirken: Festschrift zur 150-Jahr-Feier der Humboldt Universität zu Berlin*. Berlin, 1960: 605–627.

Merritt, Richard L. "The Student Protest Movement in West Berlin." *Comparative Politics*, 1, no. 1 (1968–1969): 516–533.

Rousselet, Wolf-Peter. "Die fetten Jahre sind vorbei." *FU Info*, 13/82 (22 October 1982): 8–9.

Schipper, Uwe. "Erinnerungen an das Englische Seminar der Freien Universität Berlin in den frühen 60er Jahren." In Manfred Scheler, ed., *Berliner Anglistik in Vergangenheit und Gegenwart, 1810–1985*. Berlin, 1987: 197–200.

Schlicht, Uwe. "Von der skeptischen Generation bis zur Protestjugend." In Uwe Schlicht, ed., *Trotz und Träume: Jugend Lehnt Sich Auf*. Berlin, 1980: 190–209.

Schmidt-Hackenberg, Dietrich. "Freie Universität und Korporationen." In *Fünfzehn Jahre Freie Universität, 1948–1963*. Berlin, 1963:32–34.

Schneider, Ullrich. "Berlin, der Kalte Krieg und die Gründung der Freien Universität, 1945–1949." *Jahrbuch für die Geschichte Mittel- und Ostdeutschlands*, 34 (1985): 37–95.

Schulz, Klaus Peter. "Porträt eines Unbequemen." *Der Monat*, 166 (July 1962): 82–84.

Schwan, Alexander. "Die Hochschulreform in der Krise." *Neue Rundschau*, 82, no. 4 (1971): 693–710.

Seemann, Klaus-Dieter. "Die Slavistik an der Freien Universität Berlin." In Herbert Bräuer et al., eds., *Materialien zur Geschichte der Slavistik in Deutschland*. Berlin, 1982: 19–44.

Der Senator für Inneres [Wolfgang Büsch]. "Die Protestbewegung unter den Studenten der Freien Universität Berlin," (mimeographed). Berlin, 1967.

Sontheimer, Michael. "Ein Schuss in viele Köpfe." *Die Zeit*, 29 May 1987: 13–17.

Sutton, Francis X. "The Ford Foundation: The Early Years." *Daedalus: Journal of the American Academy of Arts and Sciences*, 116, no. 1 (Winter 1987): 41–91.

Teichler, Ulrich. "Higher Education Reforms and Changing Employment Prospects for Graduates." In Günther Kloss, ed. *Education Policy in the Federal Republic of Germany, 1969–1984*. Manchester, England, 1985: 57–77.

Wagner, Reinhard [pseudonym]. "Wende mit Haken und Ösen." *Deutsche-Universitäts-Zeitung*, 7 April 1983: 11–12.

Wesel, Uwe. "Die NOFU." In *Das Argument*, ed., *Die NOFU: Rechtskräfte an der Uni*. Studienheft no. 22. Berlin, 1979: 17–26.

Wesel, Uwe. "Zur gegenwärtigen Situation der Hochschulreform." *Neue Rundschau*, 83, no. 1 (1972): 87–105.

C. NEWSPAPERS AND JOURNALS

Der Abend
Bayern Kurier
Berliner Morgenpost
Berliner Stimme
Berliner Zeitung (B.Z.)
Berliner Zeitung (East Berlin)
Christ und Welt
Colloquium
Comparative Politics
Deutsche Universitäts-Zeitung
Deutsche Volkszeitung
Forum
Frankfurter Allgemeine Zeitung
Frankfurter Rundschau
FU Info
FU Spiegel
Horizont
Kommunistische Hochschulzeitung (West Berlin)
Kurier
Mitteilungen für Dozenten und Studenten (Free University)
National Zeitung
Neue Rundschau
Neues Deutschland
Die Neue Zeitung
New York Post
New York Times
Ottowa Journal
Panorama (television magazine)
Der Sozialdemokrat
Spandauer Volksblatt
Der Spiegel
Der Student (Marburg)
Süddeutsche Zeitung
Tägliche Rundschau
Der Tag
Der Tagesspiegel
Telegraf
Time Magazine
Times (London)
Die Welt
Weser Kurier
World Politics
World View
Die Zeit

Index